BY
THE
PEOPLE

BY THE PEOPLE

DEBATING AMERICAN GOVERNMENT

Brief Edition

JAMES A. MORONE
Brown University

ROGAN KERSH
Wake Forest University

NEW YORK OXFORD
OXFORD UNIVERSITY PRESS

Oxford University Press is a department of the University of Oxford.
It furthers the University's objective of excellence in research,
scholarship, and education by publishing worldwide.

Oxford New York

Auckland   Cape Town   Dar es Salaam   Hong Kong   Karachi
Kuala Lumpur   Madrid   Melbourne   Mexico City   Nairobi
New Delhi   Shanghai   Taipei   Toronto

With offices in

Argentina   Austria   Brazil   Chile   Czech Republic   France   Greece
Guatemala   Hungary   Italy   Japan   Poland   Portugal   Singapore
South Korea   Switzerland   Thailand   Turkey   Ukraine   Vietnam

For titles covered by Section 112 of the US Higher Education
Opportunity Act, please visit www.oup.com/us/he for the latest
information about pricing and alternate formats.

Published by Oxford University Press
198 Madison Avenue, New York, New York 10016
http://www.oup.com

ISBN: 978-0-19-538332-4

Printing number: 9 8 7 6 5 4 3 2

Printed in the United States of America
on acid-free paper

Many teachers and colleagues inspired us. We dedicate this book to four who changed our lives. Their passion for learning and teaching set the standard we aim for every day—and on every page that follows.

Richard O'Donnell
Murray Dry
Jim Barefield
Rogers Smith

This book's title comes from the Gettysburg Address. Standing on the battlefield at Gettysburg, President Abraham Lincoln delivered what may be the most beautiful presidential address in American history—defining American government as a government "of the people, by the people, for the people." Here is the full address.

Four score and seven years ago our fathers brought forth on this continent, a new nation, conceived in Liberty, and dedicated to the proposition that all men are created equal.

Now we are engaged in a great civil war, testing whether that nation, or any nation so conceived and so dedicated, can long endure. We are met on a great battle-field of that war. We have come to dedicate a portion of that field, as a final resting place for those who here gave their lives that that nation might live. It is altogether fitting and proper that we should do this.

But, in a larger sense, we can not dedicate—we can not consecrate—we can not hallow—this ground. The brave men, living and dead, who struggled here, have consecrated it, far above our poor power to add or detract. The world will little note, nor long remember what we say here, but it can never forget what they did here. It is for us the living, rather, to be dedicated here to the unfinished work which they who fought here have thus far so nobly advanced. It is rather for us to be here dedicated to the great task remaining before us—that from these honored dead we take increased devotion to that cause for which they gave the last full measure of devotion—that we here highly resolve that these dead shall not have died in vain—that this nation, under God, shall have a new birth of freedom—and that government of the people, by the people, for the people, shall not perish from the earth.

Brief Contents

Contents

About the Authors

JAMES MORONE (BA, Middlebury College, and MA and PhD, University of Chicago) is the John Hazen White Professor of Political Science and Public Policy at Brown University and five-time winner of the Hazeltine Citation for outstanding teacher of the year. Dr. Morone, an award-winning author, has published nine books, including *The Heart of Power* (2009, a "New York Times Notable Book"), *Hellfire Nation* (2003, nominated for a Pulitzer Prize), and *The Democratic Wish* (1990, winner of the American Political Science Association's Kammerer Award for the best book on American politics). Dr. Morone served as president of the politics and history section of the American Political Science Association and the New England Political Science Association. He has been on the board of editors for eight scholarly journals, has written over 150 articles and essays, and comments on politics in the *New York Times*, the *London Review of Books*, and the *American Prospect*.

ROGAN KERSH (BA, Wake Forest University, and MA and PhD, Yale) is Provost and Professor of Political Science at Wake Forest University. A leading scholar in American political science, Dr. Kersh is best known for his work on health reform, obesity politics, and interest groups/lobbying. As a political science faculty member at Syracuse from 1996–2006, he won three different teaching awards; from 2006–2012, as Associate Dean of NYU's Wagner School of Public Service, he won both Wagner and NYU-wide teaching awards, as well as the Martin Luther King Jr. Award for scholarship, teaching, and university service. Dr. Kersh has published two books and more than fifty academic articles, and has provided commentary on US politics for dozens of different media outlets including CNN, *Newsweek*, and the *New York Times*. He was president of the American Political Science Association's organized section on health politics and policy in 2011–2012 and is an elected fellow of the National Academy of Public Administration.

Preface

The film crew set up in the middle of a bustling city park. As soon as they saw the camera, people crowded around. "What are you doing?" they asked. Rogan—one of the authors of this book—explained that we were filming some publicity for our new textbook. We had taken the title from Abraham Lincoln's Gettysburg Address, he said, and we wanted people to recite bits of the speech, revolving around the most famous line: "Government of the people, by the people, and for the people . . ."

Help or Clash?

Everyone offered to help out. OK, part of it was getting on camera. But it was more. People—strangers—were ready to pitch in and lend a hand. Rogan gave them their lines and they cheerfully repeated them for the camera. Repeated them again if they didn't come out quite right. They mostly turned down the little Starbucks gift cards we offered them. They were happy to help. They milled around and talked about the book, about politics, about their own stories.

  That's America in a nutshell. People pitch in. This is a nation of joiners and helpers and activists. It always has been. Visitors in the nineteenth century were astonished by the nation's civic spirit. To this day Americans form book groups, organize car washes to raise money for good causes, stack

see for yourself

Go online to see the "street reading" of the Gettysburg Address.

sandbags during floods, send checks to the Red Cross, wave flags at Olympic games, support the military, and sometimes insist that the government help those who need help.

But that's only one side of the story. Flip on your television and what do you see? Fights! A few years ago, one of us (Jim) was about to go on a news show to discuss the fallout after singer Janet Jackson inadvertently (and very briefly) went X-rated during the Super Bowl halftime show. Jim was scheduled alongside another commentator who was very agitated about Jackson's behavior and believed that it signaled the decline of America. Jim told the producer that, after exploring our different views, it would be great if we could find some common ground. No way, retorted the producer, who explained her ideal closing shot: You'll be shouting over each other on a split screen while the host coolly ends the segment by saying, "We'll have to leave it there for now, but feelings run high and we'll be hearing a lot more on this topic." Unfortunately, searching for common ground does not draw an audience like people screaming on a split screen.

The producer was demonstrating another side of America: rugged individualists push their own views and self-interests. Individualism is also an all-American story. Its origins lie in a frontier culture that expected everyone to watch out for themselves. This is the America that resents anyone—especially the government—telling people what to do.

Which is the real America? They both are. Sometimes it's a land of cooperation, sometimes a nation of competition. American politics, as you'll see, reflects both.

By the People?

This brief edition of *By the People* was created for those who want a shorter, streamlined, and less expensive version of the more comprehensive edition. While we have condensed the longer book's story of American government—there is less history and policy here—we think we have preserved the book's essential features, engagement, insights, and tone.

We picked the book's title—*By the People*—because we think Lincoln's phrase raises the deepest question in American politics: Who has the power? Or to put it more pointedly, do the people rule in this day and age? Democracy is a constant struggle; it is an aspiration, a wish, a quest. In every chapter we'll ask how well Americans are living up to Lincoln's ideal. Does the new media (Chapter 7) or the contemporary Congress (Chapter 10) or the bureaucracy (Chapter 12) or state government (Chapter 3) support or subvert government by the people? We'll present the details—and let you decide where you stand, and whether we should press for reform or leave things alone.

We'll be straight with you: we won't pretend there was a golden age in some imaginary past. After all, the United States has been home to political machines that enthusiastically stole votes, maintains an Electoral College designed to distort the people's vote for president, and governs through an elaborate system of checks and balances that blunts the popular will. (Again, you'll soon see two sides to each of these features of American government.) At the same time, you'll read about bold popular movements and unexpected electoral surges that changed the face of the nation. In many ways, these are the most exciting moments in American history. They spring up at unexpected times, inspiring ordinary Americans to achieve great things.

Who Are We?

Here's Jim's very first political memory: My parents were watching TV, and as soon as I walked into the room I could see that my mother was trying hard not to cry. "What's going on?" I asked my parents nervously. My dad—a proud Republican who had fought in World War II—said, "Well, the US had a racial problem, but that man there, he's going to get us past it." "That man there" was Martin Luther King Jr., giving one of the most famous speeches in American history: "I have a dream," said King, that "my four little children will one day live in a country where they will not be judged by the color of their skin but by the content of their character." My mother had been born in Poland and her near tears were tears of pride in her new nation—and the beautiful aspirations of that August day.

Both of us authors grew up thinking about the dream—and about the nation that dreams it. America is constantly changing, constantly new. In every chapter we'll ask the same question: *Who are we?* We'll explore a lot of different answers.

Four themes are going to be especially important in this book. **Race** touches everything in the United States, from the Constitution (Chapter 2) to the political parties (Chapter 9). The nation rose up out of both freedom and slavery; race quickly became one of the great crucibles of American liberty. Similarly, **immigration** includes some of history's saddest passages involving the mistreatment of recent arrivals. And yet we are a nation of immigrants that continues to welcome the world's "huddled masses yearning to breathe free"—the famous words long associated with the Statue of Liberty. More than a fifth of all the emigrants around the globe are coming to the United States every year. Race and immigration are tied up in another powerful topic: **gender and sexuality**. From women in Congress to same-sex marriage, from teen pregnancy to abortion, we'll show how negotiating an answer to "Who are we?" always puts an emphasis on questions of gender and sexuality. Finally, we're especially interested in **American generations**, and more specifically the attitudes and contributions of today's young people, the millennial generation. If you're one of them, the future belongs to you. This book is an owner's manual for the government that you're going to inherit. We'll have much to say about you as we go along.

The most important thing about all these categories is not their history, or the ways they've influenced voting behavior, or the way the courts treat them—although we'll cover all those topics. Rather, what matters most about American politics are the opportunities for getting involved. As you'll see, groups and individuals can and do make a difference in a nation that is always evolving. We hope our book inspires you to actively participate in making the American future.

How Government Works

We won't oversell the role of individuals. That role is always framed by the way the government is organized and operates. From the very start, this book emphasizes the unusual structure of American government.

Begin with a Constitution full of checks and balances, add a multilayered federalism, develop a chaotic public administration (President Franklin Roosevelt cheerfully called the uproar a three-ring circus), spin off functions to the private sector (especially during wars), complexify Congress (thirty-one different committees and subcommittees tried to claim jurisdiction over just one national health insurance proposal), and inject state and federal courts into every cranny of the system. Then throw the entire apparatus open to any interest group that shows up. The twenty-first century adds a 24/7 news cycle with commentary all the time and from every angle.

Turn to foreign policy, where high principles contend with tough-minded realism in a fractious world. When the most formidable military in human history is mustered into action, watch presidential power expand so rapidly that it sets off international debates about whether the great republic is morphing into an empire.

In Short

As you read this book, you'll be engaging four questions:

- Who governs? This is the question of democracy and power—or, as we put it above: Is this government by the people? And if and where it falls short, how might we refresh our democracy?

- How does American politics work? Our job is to make you think like a political scientist. What does that involve? You'll learn in the next chapter—and throughout the book.

- What does government do? You can't answer the first two questions if you don't know what the courts or the White House or Congress or interest groups actually do—and how they do it.

- Who are we? Americans endlessly debate America's identity. We are students, businesspeople, Hispanics, seniors, Texans, environmentalists, gays, Republicans, Democrats, Christians, Muslims, military families—and the list goes on. Sometimes it adds up to one united people; at other times we're left to wonder how to get along. Either way, American politics rises up from—and shapes—a cacophony of identities and interests.

Getting Involved

By the People is a new text for the course in American government. It takes on US government in all its glory, messiness, and power. Like every textbook, this one informs our readers. But, as we hope you can already see, we don't describe government—or ideas about government—as inert and fixed. What's exciting about American politics—and America itself—is how fast it changes. And the arguments—the constant, endless arguments—about what it is and what it should be next. Our aim is to get you engaged—whether you already love politics or are a complete newcomer to politics or, indeed, whether you are a newcomer to the United States itself. In the pages that follow, we'll bring American government to life. Get ready to start a great debate—about your future.

One final word: We've been working out the story line for this book throughout our teaching careers. We've taught everything from very large lectures to small seminars. Like all teachers, we've learned through trial and error. We've worked hard to pack this book with the stories, questions, and features that our own students have found effective. That spirit—the lessons we've learned in the classroom—animates everything that follows.

A GUIDED TOUR OF *BY THE PEOPLE*

Brief Edition

Chapter Introductions

Each chapter of *By the People* begins with a story that illustrates the theme of the chapter. A set of objectives clearly highlights the learning goals for the student.

By the Numbers

Fun facts introduce each chapter and help frame the surprising contours of American politics and government.

A Balanced Debate Supported by Innovative Scholarship

More than a textbook full of facts and figures, *By the People* provides a ringside seat to American politics, noting the fights, ideas, institutions, and unforgettable characters through which we govern.

By the People is informed by the most current scholarship available. The textbook offers a balanced, though critical, viewpoint that broadens the student's understanding of America's government and the way it works.

2

The Constitution

BY THIS CHAPTER, YOU WILL

Discover the roots of the Constitution in colonial and revolutionary America. — See why Americans declared independence from England and learn about the first constitution, the Articles of Confederation. — Follow the arguments that shaped the Constitution and get an overview of the final document. — Read about the great national debate over whether to adopt it. — Learn how Americans have changed the Constitution—and how the Constitution has changed America.

THE R. R. MOTON HIGH SCHOOL, in Farmville, Virginia, was a mess. The roof leaked, the heat worked poorly, the classrooms were overcrowded, and the school bus kept breaking down. When it rained, students sat under umbrellas and shivered in their coats. Moton was a black school; across town, the white students were warm and dry. On April 23, 1951, a junior named Barbara Johns decided to take action. She fooled the principal into leaving the school for the day and forged notes to the teachers calling an assembly. When the students had all filed into the auditorium, the sixteen-year-old stood on stage, called for a strike, and led a student march to the Prince Edward County Courthouse to protest the shabby state of the school.

The students and their families called a leading civil rights group, the National Association for the Advancement of Colored People (NAACP), which dispatched a team of lawyers. The lawyers explained that local governments run American schools, and there was not much the NAACP could do about the conditions at Moton High School. However, continued the lawyer, they could challenge the entire policy of racial segregation. If the black students went to the same school as the white students, they would probably have a nicer schoolhouse. The NAACP sued the school district, arguing that forcing African Americans into a separate school violated the United States Constitution. The Supreme Court took the case, *Davis v. School Board of Prince Edward County*, bundled it together with two similar cases, and three years after the student strike, delivered one of the most famous court decisions in American history, a ruling known as *Brown v. Board of Education*.

A sixteen-year-old took a bold risk, the Supreme Court unanimously ruled that she was right, and hundreds of laws across many states were struck down for violating the Constitution. The Court ruled that segregated education facilities are inherently unequal and violates the Fourteenth Amendment of the United States Constitution, which declares: "No state shall . . . deny to any person . . . the equal protection of the laws."

Stop and think about the power Americans invest in this document written more than 225 years ago. The Constitution is the owner's manual and rule book for American government. It specifies how the government operates. It

● *The student activists at Moton High School, led by Barbara Johns. They had an enormous impact: few would imagine lawyers found a way to place their grievance in the context of the US Constitution toward. Moton strikes famous three words, "We the people."*

Civil Liberties | **CHAPTER 4** | 125

BY THE NUMBERS *Civil Liberties*

Number of rights listed in the Bill of Rights: 31
Number of rights protecting freedom of religion: 2
Number of rights protecting people accused of crimes: 19

Number of times that the Supreme Court has permitted the government to block publication of sensitive material: 0
Number of years after the Bill of Rights was ratified before the Supreme Court ruled that state governments could not interfere with freedom of speech: 134
Number of years before it ruled that states could not interfere with the right to bear arms: 219

Number of new rights secured by constitutional amendment in the past forty years: 1 (the 26th Amendment extended the right to vote to 18- to 20-year-olds)

Percentage of Americans who favor a constitutional amendment to ban flag burning (according to a Gallup poll in 2006): 56
Percentage who would be "upset" if Congress failed to ban flag burning: 40
Number of votes by which a flag-burning amendment failed to clear Congress: 1

Rank of the United States among all nations for number (and percentage) of citizens in jail: 1
Ranks of Russia, Rwanda, Iran, and England: 2, 3, 40, 83

Percentage of Americans who supported the death penalty in 1990 and today: 78, 62

Percentage support for the death penalty:
Among white evangelicals: 74
Among the nonreligious: 51
Among Hispanic Catholics: 43
Among black Protestants: 37

Number of states that have not executed anyone since 1976: 16
Total number executed in Texas, Virginia, Oklahoma, and Florida since 1976: 724
Total number executed by the federal government in that period: 3

outlawed segregated restaurants. That legal action freed blacks and Latinos to eat where they wished but limited the liberty of racist restaurant owners to serve whomever they wanted to serve.

In practice, the two concepts are not opposites. The long battle for civil rights led to more robust civil liberties for everyone. The fight against slavery eventually led to the Fourteenth Amendment, which—as we'll soon see—is the cornerstone of modern civil liberties. Without the long American

---

204 | By the People

BY THE NUMBERS *Public Opinion*

Year that "public opinion" was first mentioned by a public official (in France): 1588
Year the French Revolution began: 1789
Percentage of the American public unable to name their House member, 1960, 2010: 97, 59

Percentage of US college students expressing trust in US government, 1981: 74
Percentage of US college students expressing trust in US government, 1991: 44
Percentage of US college students expressing trust in US government, 2011: 28

Highest approval rating recorded by Gallup for any president throughout term (John F. Kennedy): 70.1
Lowest average approval rating (Harry Truman): 45.4
Average approval rating for Ronald Reagan and George H. W. Bush, respectively: 52.8, 60.9

Japanese prime minister Kan approval rating, February 2012: 20
Russian president Putin approval rating, February 2012: 73

President Obama approval rating during first month in office (Gallup, February 2009): 71
President Obama approval rating, February 2011, 2012, 2013: 52, 51

Percentage turnout of voting-age population, US presidential election, 1840: 80
Percentage turnout of voting-age population, US presidential election, 1940: 53
Percentage turnout of voting-age population, US presidential election, 2008: 58
Proportion of eligible black residents registered to vote, Lowndes County, Alabama, 1965: 0
Proportion of eligible black residents registered to vote, Lowndes County, Alabama, 2008: 81

system. So, who we are rests, to a large extent, on who is willing to join in, express their views, and become part of our political debate.

● Measuring Public Opinion

Professional polling firms like Gallup, major media organizations, partisan outfits, and academic research centers all jostle to provide the most up-to-date polls. Candidates for office commission private polls to tell them how

---

● Party Competition . . . and Partisanship

Parties began to lose their influence over politics and government in the mid-1960s. Interest groups muscled in on party territory, mobilized voters, and shaped issue positions. Americans began to identify with movements and organizations—civil rights, environmentalism, right to life, libertarians. The parties floundered. By the 1970s and 1980s, political observers were publishing books like *The Party's Over* and *The Decline of American Political Parties*.[16] The central role of parties in organizing elections also slipped, with the rise of the "candidate-centered election" that we met in the preceding chapter.

Parties Rise Again

Just as political science analysts declared the death of parties, however, their revival began. During the 1980s, changing congressional rules shifted power from committee chairs back to party leadership, strengthening the party-in-government. A huge influx of money into politics further revitalized party organizations, buoyed by the widespread adoption of political action committees (PACs) in the 1980s, "527" committees in the 2000s, and super PACs in the 2010s. The DNC and RNC, along with the congressional campaign organizations, became the chief recipients of campaign funds—and directed them in turn to candidates, who became more dependent on the parties as a result.

The parties also became ideologically purer. Conservative southern Democrats switched to the GOP. Liberal Republicans moved—or were pushed—to the Democrats. Each party was now organized around a clear set of ideas and principles. Each side could concentrate on defeating its foes—rather than on negotiating the differences within its own ranks.

Competition Intensifies

Today the two parties are thriving, contesting very close national elections. The three presidential elections between 1996 and 2004 featured the clos-

…government activity… …vital… …planned, wide-ra…… are an essential part of any successful lobbying strategy. But other ingredients matter as well.

THE BOTTOM LINE
- Lobbyists working in specific areas sometimes still form "iron triangles" with congressional staff and executive-branch officials.
- More fluid "issue networks," featuring lobbyists as central players, increasingly characterize today's complex policy-making environment.
- Lawmakers also lobby: they seek to persuade other public officials (intergovernmental lobbying) or secure assistance from interest groups (reverse lobbying).
- Interest groups also lobby the judicial branch, through funding confirmation battles, filing amicus curiae briefs, and financing litigation.

Political Parties and US Government

Two main political parties ha… …dominated Am……… and gov… …Democra…

The Bottom Line

A brief recap concludes each chapter section, underscoring the most important aspects of the discussion.

LEARNING FEATURES

Photos, Tables, Infographics

A compelling visual program brings essential themes to life.

What Do You Think?

These critical-thinking activities reflect our belief that students will have the last word in the ongoing debate. We ask you to take a stand on important issues found in each chapter.

> **What Do You Think?**
>
> ### Does the Media Enhance Democracy?
>
> Return to the question that opened this chapter. When you think about the American media, what do you see for the future of democracy and politics? Are you with the optimists or the pessimists?
>
> **Agree.** A booming media enhances American democracy. Media offers new ways to process news, build networks, and interact with leaders. Clicktivism works as a robust new form of political action.
>
> **Disagree.** Media harms democracy. The Babel of voices hastens national decline by chasing sensation and fomenting conflict. New media in particular erodes our news-producing capacity, increases inequalities, and offers dark corners that incubate malice.
>
> **Unsure.** Of course, the answer may lie somewhere in the middle, but keep the range of possibilities in mind as you monitor the media in the years ahead.

attention. As in every other aspect of politics, the new media raise the prospect of great changes in campaigning. Facebook and Twitter give candidates a targeted way to circumvent the mass media and speak directly to supporters. Online messaging creates a sense of movement, of belonging. It offers a way

See for Yourself

Mobile links using QR (Quick Response) codes supplement the reading by connecting students to selected historical and contemporary audio and video content.

...porters go easy on segregation... or liars... seem irresp...

Watergate was especially significant in fostering skepticism. Reporters investigated a burglary of Democratic Party headquarters that led directly to the White House. President Nixon had secretly taped conversations in the Oval Office and, pursuing the case of the botched burglary, the Supreme Court forced the release of the tapes. Their content stunned Americans. Nixon had always seemed a bit sanctimonious. Now the public could hear him order aides to "stonewall" the Watergate investigations. Even more shocking, the presidential tapes bristled with ethnic slurs, anti-Semitism, and foul language. (The newspaper transcripts were full of the notation, "expletive deleted.")

Reporters redefined their roles. Rather than acting as chummy insiders, they became skeptics, aiming to pierce through official propaganda and find the hidden truth. Relations between press and politician turned adversarial. Each time the members of the press felt misled by an administration, their skepticism grew. For example, Bill Clinton claimed he did not have sex with an intern. (He did.) George W. Bush insisted that Iraq owned dangerous weapons that threatened the United States. (It did not.) The reporter's gold standard became uncovering lies or bad behavior. When reporters find some dirt, the whole media races after the scandal in a breathless pack.

Watergate scandal: A failed effort by Republican operatives to break into Democratic Party headquarters in the Watergate office complex in Washington, DC; tapes revealed that President Nixon attempted to cover up the event—costing him the presidency.

see for yourself 7.5

President Clinton claims he did not have sex with "that woman."

The Fairness Bias

The effort to be fair introduces an unexpected bias. Reporters energetically try to present both sides of each issue. However, when issues do not have two equal sides, the effort creates the impress... debate that does n... t...

Key Terms in Chapter Margins

A running glossary of key terms appears in chapter context. A complete glossary in the back of the book collects all key terms in one location.

Legislative hold: An informal way for a senator to object to a bill or other measure reaching the Senate floor. The action effectively halts Senate proceedings on that issue, sometimes for weeks or longer.

Filibuster: Rule unique to the US Senate that allows any senator to hold the floor indefinitely and thereby delay a vote on a bill to which they object. Ended

senator a little king"; the old quip still resonates today.[4] Each woman and man in the Senate possesses a remarkable degree of autonomy, especially compared to the average House member. Any senator—even the most junior—is able to halt the entire body's consideration of a bill merely by placing a **legislative hold** on it.

Let's consider a typical example. Before the US military can promote an officer, the Senate must vote its approval. Normally this is a routine formality. In 2003, however, Senator Larry Craig (R-ID) quietly put a hold on all Air Force promotions. No Air Force officer could advance to the rank of major, colonel, lieutenant general, or anything else. The Senate tabled—put aside—every proposed promotion. What had upset Senator Craig? The Air Force had promised to station some planes in Idaho, and Craig charged that they had reneged on their promise. So he did what any senator is permitted to do—bring action on an issue to a halt with a one-man veto.[5]

Popular American culture, in films such as M... th Goes to Washing...

Chapter-Ending Summary and Study Questions

Each chapter concludes with a summary of key points, list of key terms, and several thought-provoking study questions that reach beyond the facts and figures.

roles in Washington, or fighting back when the police raided a gay bar in New York City. It was collective action that helped shape the meaning of the legislation and court decisions. Through their passion and their activism, the people are constantly pushing the United States to live up to its founding ideals.

CHAPTER SUMMARY

✪ The battle for civil rights generally includes seven stages. The group seeking rights must define itself, challenge society, and change the cultural story. The contest for rights spills across federalism: the executive branch can break the ice; Congress is the key to deep social change; the courts are the final arbiters of civil rights.

✪ The Fourteenth Amendment contains the crucial legal rule for civil rights: "No state shall . . . deprive any person of . . . the equal protection of the laws."

✪ A great mass movement rose up in which ordinary men, women, and children turned the legal promise of the *Brown v. Board of Education* decision into a practical reality. Protests eventually led to the Civil Rights Act of 1964 and the Voting Rights Act of 1965. The black civil rights movement set the model for future civil rights campaigns by many other groups.

✪ In order to make up for past discrimination, legislatures and courts turned to affirmative action in the 1960s and 1970s. The courts, and the public, have become increasingly skeptical of these programs.

✪ Women first won voting rights in the states—across the West—before finally securing the Nineteenth Amendment, guaranteeing the right to vote regardless of gender.

✪ The Civil Rights Act of 1964 bars gender discrimination. The women's movement organized

to take advantage of the legal changes. The results transformed American gender roles in political and professional life.

✪ Following *Roe v. Wade* (in 1973) and (in the mid-1970s), gender politics became especially controversial.

✪ Latinos are the largest immigrant group and one of the fastest-growing populations in the United States today. Latinos are a diverse people with many different national identities, histories, cultures, and concerns. The great political question is whether they will mobilize around shared interests and concerns. If they do, they will become a formidable political force.

✪ Asian Americans are the third-largest minority group in the United States and now comprise 5 percent of the population. They are also a tremendously diverse group.

✪ Native Americans lost their way of life in the face of disease, armies, and settlers. The Supreme Court gave them a special status: a separate people without rights. Though they retain the special status, they became US citizens in 1924.

✪ People with disabilities leveraged an obscure bureaucratic rule, used it to mobilize, and eventually won the sweeping rights of the Americans with Disabilities Act.

✪ The gay (and lesbian) movements were born in a burst of pride and anger in 1969. Gays were the

first to confront AIDS—a harrowing plague (in its early years) that pushed them into politics, health provision, and community building.

✪ Gay, lesbian, bisexual, and transgender communities have moved from taboo to mainstream.

NeverUnless, the conflict over marriage and child-rearing remains a flash point of contemporary culture wars.

KEY TERMS

1963 March on Washington, 174	Equal Employment Opportunity Commission (EEOC), 182	National Organization for Women (NOW), 182
Abolition, 164	Equal protection of the laws, 167	*Plessy v. Ferguson*, 168
Affirmative action, 184	Equal Rights Amendment, 183	Quasi-suspect category, 182
Brown v. Board of Education, 173	Freedom Rides, 179	Reconstruction, 168
Civil rights, 160	Free rider problem, 174	Reframe the issue, 165
Civil Rights Act of 1964, 174	Great Migration, 170	Section 504, 196
Chinolinism, 186	Jim Crow, 168	Seneca Falls Convention, 181
Class action, 184	Laws of coverture, 180	Strict scrutiny, 182
Compromise of 1850, 163	Literacy test, 168	United Farm Workers, 186
De facto discrimination, 170	Missouri Compromise, 168	
De jure discrimination, 170	National Association for the Advancement of Colored People (NAACP), 171	
Domestic dependent nation, 194		
Dred Scott v. Sandford, 163		
Emancipation Proclamation, 166		

STUDY QUESTIONS

1. Name the seven steps involved in civil rights campaigns. Give examples of these, drawing on historical material in this chapter.
2. Describe the Civil War Amendments. Why was the Fourteenth Amendment important?
3. What was Jim Crow legislation?
4. Describe the sit-ins and Freedom Rides of the civil rights movement. What was the point?
5. Describe three effects of the Civil Rights Act of 1964.
6. What is affirmative action?

For further reflection: Write your own Supreme Court decision on affirmative action

in higher education. Would you accept affirmative action in your school? Why or why not?

7. What are undocumented aliens?

For further reflection: What should the United States do about undocumented aliens?

8. What is the Lilly Ledbetter Law?

For further reflection: Why do you think President Obama chose that as the first law to sign as president?

Ensuring Student Success

Oxford University Press offers instructors and students a comprehensive an-
cillary package for qualified adopters of *By the People*.

- **Companion Website at www.oup.com/us/morone**
  - For instructors, this site includes the teaching tools described below,
    available for immediate download. Contact your local OUP sales
    representative for access.
  - For students, the companion website includes a number of study
    tools, including learning objectives, key-concept summaries, quizzes
    and essay questions, web activities, and web links.
- **Nationally Hosted Learning Management System**—Online homework made easy! Tired of learning management systems that promise
  the world but are too difficult to use? *Oxford* offers you a simple, nationally hosted, online learning course—including study, review, interactive, and assessment materials—in an easy-to-use system requiring less
  than fifteen minutes to master. Assignment and assessment results flow
  into a straightforward gradebook allowing you a clear view into your
  student's progress. And the system works on every major platform and
  device, including mobile devices! Free with the price of a new book, or
  available for sale stand-alone. Contact your local OUP representative for
  ordering information.
- **Instructor's Resource Manual with Test Item File**
  - The Instructor's Resource Manual includes chapter objectives, a
    detailed chapter outline, lecture suggestions and activities, discus-
    sion questions, video resources, and web resources. Available on the
    Instructor's Resource CD or as a download from the web at www.
    oup.com/us/morone.
  - The Test Item File includes multiple-choice, short-answer, and es-
    say questions. Questions are identified as factual, conceptual, or
    applied, and correct answers are keyed to the text pages where the
    concepts are presented.
- **Computerized Test Bank**—Using the test authoring and management
  tool Diploma, the computerized test bank that accompanies this text is
  designed for both novice and advanced users. Diploma enables instructors to create and edit questions, create randomized quizzes and tests
  with an easy-to-use drag-and-drop tool, publish quizzes and tests to
  online courses, and print quizzes and tests for paper-based assessments.
  Available on the Instructor's Resource CD.
- **PowerPoint-Based Slides**—Each chapter's slide deck includes a succinct chapter outline on key concepts and incorporates relevant chapter
  graphics. Also available are clicker questions to be used in conjunction

with any classroom response system. Available on the Instructor's Resource CD or as a download from the web.

- **Instructor's Resource CD**—This resource puts all of your teaching tools in one place. The CD includes the Instructor's Resource Manual with Tests, the Computerized Test Bank, the PowerPoint-based slides, and the graphics from the text.

- *Now Playing: Learning American Government Through Film* **Video Guide**—Through documentaries, feature films, and YouTube videos, *Now Playing: Learning American Government Through Film* provides video examples of course concepts to demonstrate real-world relevance. Each video is accompanied by a brief summary and discussion questions.

- **CNN Videos**—Offering recent clips on timely topics, this DVD provides 15 films tied to the chapter topics in the text. Each clip is approximately 5–10 minutes in length, offering a great way to launch your lectures. Contact your local OUP sales representative for details.

- **E-Book**—Available through CourseSmart.

- **Course Cartridges**

To order the Instructor's Resource CD or course cartridges, please contact your Oxford University Press sales representative at (800) 280-0208.

Packaging Options

Adopters of *By the People* can package **ANY** Oxford University Press book with the text for a 20 percent savings off the total package price. See our many trade and scholarly offerings at **www.oup.com**, then contact your local OUP sales representative to request a package ISBN. In addition, the following items can be packaged with the text for free:

Oxford Pocket World Atlas, **Sixth Edition:** This full-color atlas is a handy reference for international relations/global politics students.

Very Short Introduction Series: These very brief texts offer succinct introductions to a variety of topics. Titles include *Terrorism* by Townshend, *Globalization*, Second Edition, by Steger, and *Global Warming* by Maslin, among others.

Acknowledgments

When he was signing us up to write this book, publisher John Challice looked us each in the eye and said, "You know, this is going to be so much work—you're going to be married to us." He was right. Yes, it was lot of work. And yes, the Oxford team was like a family that carried us through the process.

There would be no book without Jen Carpenter, our extraordinary editor. She guided us through the process with enormous skill. Along the way, Jen earned the highest praise authors can give their editor: she cared about the book as much as we did. Our development editor, John Haber, proved to be the book's most ardent supporter; he delivered thoughtful ideas at lightning speed. Development manager Thom Holmes arrived in the middle of the process and gracefully turned our messy manuscript into a tight narrative bursting with special features. Assistant editor Maegan Sherlock guided the art program and tracked down every picture in the following pages. Barbara Conover gave the book a stunning coat of polish. Managing editor Lisa Grzan and production editor Shelby Peak coordinated an amazing production process; we broke the publishing record for the number of times two authors wrote, "Good point!" in the margins of an edited manuscript. Teresa Nemeth did a very special copyedit on an impossible schedule. Art director Michele Laseau did the beautiful design. And Teri Spina designed a marvelous website. We are especially grateful to Erin Brown and Tierra Morgan for getting this book into your hands. To all of you in our immediate Oxford family: Thank you! Thank you!

We had an even more important team at our side—our families and our friends. Over the course of this book's initial conception and subsequent writing, Rogan moved from Syracuse University's Maxwell School to New York University's Wagner School, with a sabbatical leave at Yale along the way—and then, just as we were finishing the manuscript, to Wake Forest University. Colleagues in all four places were unfailingly generous with ideas and comments; thanks especially to Suzanne Mettler, Jeff Stonecash, David Mayhew, Ellen Schall, Shanna Rose, and Shankar Prasad. Because we strive throughout to get both the political science and the practical politics right, a group of experienced and reflective inside-the-Beltway friends cheerfully and patiently provided insight into their world: Bill Antholis, Matt Bennett, Laura Schiller, Erik Fatemi, Tom Dobbins, Dan Maffei, Bob Shrum, Marylouise Oates, and Don and Darrel Jodrey. Grateful thanks to them as well as a wonderful set of current and former students, many now working in government and politics.

By the People's long journey to completion grew infinitely more enjoyable once Sara Pesek joined me for the trip—through this book and everywhere else, from Australia to Ze Café in midtown NYC. Sara's insights into public policy made for the liveliest newlyweds' conversations (if you're a politics junkie) imaginable; my biggest bouquet of thanks to her for that rarest of gifts: loving, fully joined partnership.

Jim offers warm thanks to my colleagues at Brown who form a wonderful community of scholars and teachers—always ready for coffee, lunch, or wine and a conversation about political science. And my wonderful students sampled every idea in this book. They are my constant teachers.

My brothers, Joe and Peter Morone—and their families—are lifelong companions always ready with a cheerful take on the state of politics and the world. Special thanks to Lindsay, Ann, Joe, James (now a rising political scientist at Penn), Noreen, and Maegan Morone. My mother, Stasia, kept reminding me to enjoy the journey—and that there might be more to life than *By the People*. And the memory of my dad visited me all the time as I read, and thought, and wrote.

I have the incredible privilege of living with the author I most admire, Deborah Stone. We relish one another's intellectual adventures and everything I write is better thanks to her. Deborah also understands other kinds of adventures, and between chapters we grew an amazing garden (featuring New England's spiciest peppers) and explored the world—specializing in Paris, Beaujolais, and Aarhus.

Manuscript Reviewers

We have greatly benefited from the perceptive comments and suggestions of the many talented scholars and instructors who reviewed the manuscript of *By the People*. They went far beyond the call of duty in sharing thoughts and making corrections. Their insight and suggestions contributed immensely to the work.

Patrick R. Miller
University of Cincinnati

Michael K. Moore
University of Texas at Arlington

Roger Morton
California State University, Long Beach

Yamini Munipalli
Florida State College at Jacksonville

Gary Mucciaroni
Temple University

Jason Mycoff
University of Delaware

Steven Nawara
Valdosta State University

Anthony Neal
Buffalo State College

Mark Nicol
Saginaw Valley State University

Stephen A. Nuño
Northern Arizona University

Michael Parkin
Oberlin College

Richard Pious
Barnard College

Elizabeth A. Prough
Eastern Michigan University

Wesley B. Renfro
St. John Fisher College

John F. Roche, III
Palomar College

Amanda M. Rosen
Webster University

Anjali Sahay
Gannon University

Joanna Vecchiarelli Scott
Eastern Michigan University

Samuel Shelton
Troy University

Majid Shirali
University of Nevada, Las Vegas

Joyce Stickney Smith
Hillsborough Community College, Ybor Campus

Mitchel A. Sollenberger
University of Michigan–Dearborn

Chris Soper
Pepperdine University

Barry L. Tadlock
Ohio University

Edwin A. Taylor III
Missouri Western State University

Delaina Toothman
Texas State University

Jan P. Vermeer
Nebraska Wesleyan University

Jennifer E. Walsh
Azusa Pacific University

Donn Worgs
Towson University

Larry L. Wright
Florida A&M University

Shoua Yang
St. Cloud State University

Mike Yawn
Sam Houston State University

Melanie C. Young
University of Nevada, Las Vegas

Khodr M. Zaarour
Shaw University

Academic Reviewers and Testers

Oxford University Press would also like to acknowledge the contribution of additional scholars and instructors who class tested and provided their assessment of the completed manuscript, using this work with hundreds of students in classrooms across the nation.

Gayle Alberda
Owens Community College

Herrick Arnold
Orange Coast College

Alex L. Avila
Mesa Community College

John Barnes
University of Southern California

Charles Barrilleaux
Florida State University

Ronald Bee
Cuyamaca College

Michael Berkman
Pennsylvania State University

Angelina M. Cavallo
San Jacinto College

Paul M. Collins
University of North Texas

Adam Chamberlain
Coastal Carolina University

Matt Childers
University of Georgia

Benjamin Christ
Harrisburg Area Community College

Diana Cohen
Central Connecticut State University

William Corbett
New Mexico State University

Mark Ellickson
Missouri State University

Deborah Ferrell-Lynn
University of Central Oklahoma

Paul Foote
Eastern Kentucky University

Peter L. Francia
East Carolina University

Rodd Freitag
University of Wisconsin–Eau Claire

Fred Gordon
Columbus State University

John I. Hanley
Syracuse University

Jeff Hilmer
Northern Arizona University

Jeneen Hobby
Cleveland State University

Ronald J. Hrebenar
University of Utah

Mark Jendrysik
University of North Dakota

Aubrey Jewett
University of Central Florida

Gary Johnson
Weber State University

Michelle Keck
The University of Texas at Brownsville

William Kelly
Auburn University

John Klemanski
Oakland University

Richard Krupa
Harper College

Christine Lipsmeyer
Texas A&M University

Brent Lucas
North Carolina State University

Margaret MacKenzie
San Jacinto College

Jason McDaniel
San Francisco State University

John Mercurio
San Diego State University

Melissa Merry
University of Louisville

Roger Morton
California State University, Long Beach

Gary Mucciaroni
Temple University

Adam J. Newmark
Appalachian State University

Randall Newnham
Pennsylvania State University

Roger Nichols
Southwestern College

Anthony J. Nownes
University of Tennessee, Knoxville

Anthony O'Regan
Los Angeles Valley College

Kenneth O'Reilly
Milwaukee Area Technical College

Sunday P. Obazuaye
Cerritos College

Amanda M. Olejarski
Shippensburg University

Kevin Parsneau
Minnesota State University

Michelle Pautz
University of Dayton

Martin J. Plax
Cleveland State University

Sherri Replogle
Illinois State University

Kim Rice
Western Illinois University

Ray Sandoval
Dallas County Community College District

Laura Schneider
Grand Valley State University

Scot Schraufnagel
Northern Illinois University

Ronnee Schreiber
San Diego State University

Ronald Schurin
University of Connecticut

Jeffrey M. Stonecash
Syracuse University

Katrina Taylor
Northern Arizona University

Ryan Lee Teten
University of Louisiana

John P. Todsen
Drake University

Delaina Toothman
University of Maine

Dan Urman
Northeastern University

Ronald W. Vardy
University of Houston

Adam L. Warber
Clemson University

Gerald Watkins
Kentucky Community & Technical College System

Patrick Wohlfarth
University of Maryland, College Park

Wayne L. Wolf
South Suburban College

Jeff Worsham
West Virginia University

Finally, thanks to you for picking up this book. We hope you enjoy reading it as much as we did writing.

Jim Morone and Rogan Kersh

BY
THE
PEOPLE

1

Ideas That Shape American Politics

ARMY CAPTAIN RUSSELL BURGOS hunkered down in his bunker as mortars ripped through the night. A year ago he had been a political science professor; now he was fighting in Iraq. Burgos's unit was operating in the Sunni Triangle, where the fighting was fiercest. "A mortar attack in the middle of the night," he mused, "is an odd place to reconsider a course syllabus." But that is exactly what he found himself doing. Experiencing war made him see politics and societies in new ways.

As shells fell on the American base, Burgos thought about something that his classes had been missing: the study of ideas. The United States entered the war because of what key decision makers believed. American leaders spent enormous energy insisting that the United States was in Iraq as a liberator rather than as a conqueror or occupier; explaining American ideas seemed crucial to both civilian and military leaders. In the war zone, Burgos saw the same thing. All around him, men and women were fighting and dying over ideas—ideas like freedom, democracy, equality, power, and faith in God.

Strangely enough, Burgos wrote later, ideas—and especially how ideas affect politics—had barely come up in his own political science classes. Yet ideas helped explain why the United States launched the war, how it fought the war, and why everyone up and down the chain of command acted as they did. Burgos ended up rethinking his approach to politics.[1]

Who are we? Our ideas tell us—and they tell the world. The United States is a nation built on ideas. You will see ideas at work in every chapter of this book, for they touch every feature of government and politics. They affect the way Americans define their national ideals, their political goals, and their nation itself. But how exactly do ideas work in politics? In this chapter we first introduce a framework for understanding American government and then explore the most important American ideas and how they impact politics.

● The Spirit of American Politics

Throughout this book we make sense of American politics by exploring four questions: Who governs? How does American politics work? What does

● Army Captain Russell Burgos hands out supplies to Iraqi children in 2004.

BY THE NUMBERS *American Ideas*

The Declaration of Independence talks about protecting *life, liberty, and the pursuit of happiness.* Rank order of American citizens in self-reported happiness compared to citizens of other nations, according to three recent studies: **15, 19, 23**

Number of times the words "right" or "rights" appear in the Declaration of Independence: **10**
Number of times the word "right" appears in the original Constitution: **0**
Number of times the word "right" appears in amendments to the Constitution: **15**

Percentage increase in inequality in the United States since 1970: **30**
Percentage increase in inequality in Canada since 1970: **5**
Percentage *decrease* in inequality in Germany since 1970: **10**

Percentage of Americans who say it is "more important to be free to pursue my own goals rather than making sure that no one is in need": **58**
Percentage of Spaniards and French, respectively, who say this: **30, 36**

Percentage of Italians, Poles, and Americans, respectively, who agree that "it is the role of the government to take care of people who cannot care for themselves": **66, 56, 23**

Percentage of Americans who belong to a church or religious organization: **57**
Percentage of British, Swedes, and French who belong to a church: **22, 9, 4**

Percentage of Americans who agree that "everyone who works hard will get ahead," 2005: **86**
Percentage agreeing in 2011: **61**

Percentage of young people who say it is very important for them to achieve the American dream: **55**
Percentage of baby boomers (age 50s–late 60s) who say this: **33**

government do? And who are we? By the time you finish reading, you will understand the debates each question has generated—and be ready to participate knowledgeably yourself.

Republic: A system of government that rests ultimate governing power in its people, who may rule directly or via representatives.

Who Governs?

As Benjamin Franklin left the Constitutional Convention in 1787, a woman stopped him. "What kind of government have you given us?" she asked. According to legend, the wise old Franklin responded, "A **republic**, madam—if you can keep it." The United States organized itself around a ringing declaration of popular rule: governments derive "their just power from the consent of the governed." In a republic, the people are in charge. Franklin knew, however, that popular governments are extremely difficult to "keep." All previous republics—like Athens, Rome, and Florence—had collapsed. His point was that the people have to be vigilant and active if they are to maintain control.

Who governs? Do the people rule? Some of us would answer "yes—and today more than ever." Others are not so sure. What if the people are not in charge—then who is?

Over the years, political scientists have developed three theories to answer the question of where power really lies in American politics. *Pluralism* suggests that people can influence government through the many interest groups that spring up to champion everything from fighting global warming to banning abortions. *Elite theory* counters that power actually rests in the hands of a small number of wealthy and powerful people—corporate executives or top government officials, for example. *Social movement theory* answers that mass popular uprisings have the potential to introduce great changes regardless of who is in control of ordinary, day-to-day politics.

We will return to this question in every chapter. Who rules? How well have we, the people, kept the republic? It is one of the most important questions in America today.

How Does American Politics Work?

Consider a classic definition of politics: who gets what, when, and how.[2] Every society has scarce things like money, prestige, and power. Politics helps determine how those resources are distributed—to which people, in what amounts, under which rules. A second definition is even simpler: politics is how a society makes its collective decisions. Every nation has its own way of deciding. This book explains how collective decisions are made in the United States. The key to understanding our political decision-making lies in four "I's": ideas, interests, individuals, and institutions such as Congress, the Supreme Court, and the media.

Ideas.   Powerful ideas shape American politics. As you'll see later in this chapter, we stress seven essential ideas: liberty, democracy (or self-rule), individualism, limited government, the American dream, equality, and faith in God. At first glance, they may all look simple; as you will quickly learn, however, each has at least two very different sides. Each idea provokes long, loud controversies about what values and policies Americans should pursue.

Institutions.   When most people talk about politics, they think about individuals: presidential candidates like Barack Obama and Mitt Romney, commentators such as Jon Stewart or Rush Limbaugh. Political scientists, on the other hand, stress **institutions**—*the organizations, norms, and rules that structure political action*. Congress, the president, the Supreme Court, the Senate's filibuster rule, and the Department of Homeland Security are all institutions.

Institutions: The organizations, norms, and rules that structure government and public actions.

● *The US Capitol, Washington, DC. Tourists see an impressive monument to democracy. Political scientists see an institution with complicated rules that advantage some individuals and groups in the nation's political debates.*

Think about how institutions influence your own behavior. Students may compete in a classroom by making arguments. If the debate gets heated and they shove someone, however, they are in trouble. But on the basketball court, after class, things are quite the opposite. There, a little shoving is fine, but no one wants to play hoops with someone who is always arguing. Different institutions—the classroom, the gym—have different rules, and most people adopt them without a second thought. Notice how the different institutional rules give some people advantages over others. Smart students who think quickly have an advantage in one institution (the classroom), while athletic students who move fast have an advantage in another (the gym). Political institutions work in the same way. The Supreme Court, the House of Representatives, the city council in Chicago, the Texas legislature, the state courts in Georgia, and governor's office in Wisconsin, the Marine Corps, the Department of Homeland Security, and thousands of others all have their own rules and procedures. Each institution organizes behavior. Each gives an advantage to some interests over others. By the time you finish this book, you will know to ask the same question every time you encounter a political issue. Which institutions are involved, and how do they influence politics?

Rational-choice theory: An approach to political behavior that views individuals as rational, decisive actors who know their political interests and seek to act on them.

Interests.   For many social scientists, interests are the center of the story. Political action often springs from individuals, groups, and nations pursuing their own self-interest. In the chapters that follow, we explore three types of interests: we examine whether rational self-interest motivates people's political actions and opinions (known as **rational choice theory**); we trace the political influence of interests and groups; and we consider the ideal of a public interest shared by everyone in society.

Individuals. Finally, individuals make politics. This book puts special emphasis on how ordinary people change their world. Our hope is simple: we want to inspire you, the reader, to get involved. Civic engagement in any community and at any level can be profoundly rewarding. It can change the world—as you will see, again and again.

What Does Government Do?

There are three sectors of society. *Private life*, of course, involves individuals and their families, acting on their own. *Civil society* refers to people joining with others to achieve some goal. Examples might include a bowling club, a business association, a student government, a Bible study circle, or a group of recycling volunteers. Finally, *government* involves formal organizations that make decisions for the whole society.

Americans have a very active civil society. In the abstract, at least, they prefer voluntary groups to government action. Polls consistently reflect public disapproval for all aspects of government: bureaucrats, the mainstream media, lobbyists, and Congress. Today, only about 10 percent of Americans trust the national government "to do the right thing most of the time."[3]

You can get a good idea of the federal government's priorities by looking at its major budget categories. Figure 1.1 shows you how the federal government spends its $3.5 trillion annual budget. Many people are surprised when they see the federal budget for the first time. More than 65 percent of all federal government spending goes to just four programs: the military, Social Security (which provides a steady income for people over sixty-five, as well as for people with disabilities and other groups), Medicare (which provides health care for people over sixty-five), and Medicaid (which provides health care for some poor people; about half of Medicaid spending also goes to people over sixty-five). These "big four" total over $2.3 trillion—that's "Big Government," regardless of anything else the government does. Notice that America's national government devotes most of its resources to the military and to seniors.

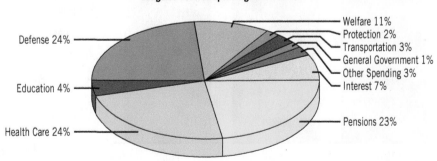

Budgeted Federal Spending for FY 2013

- Defense 24%
- Education 4%
- Health Care 24%
- Welfare 11%
- Protection 2%
- Transportation 3%
- General Government 1%
- Other Spending 3%
- Interest 7%
- Pensions 23%

● **Figure 1.1** *The US federal budget. (Christopher Chantrill, usgovernmentspending.com)*

All four of these big-ticket items are very popular programs. Although every politician is for smaller government, very few have the courage to take on any of these four programs—no matter how much they cost. In short, Americans dislike government in the abstract. However, by and large they support many of the things that government actually does.

By the time you finish this book, you will have the tools to make informed judgments about what public officials actually do, and whether government is a problem, a solution, or perhaps a bit of both.

Who Are We?

In a rapidly changing, diverse, immigrant nation, this is the deepest question of all. If the people aspire to rule, we have to understand who the people are. The United States is a nation of immigrants, a country where individuals come to reinvent themselves. The nation is always changing as well: Figure 1.2 displays our shifting demographics. American politics constantly addresses the most fundamental question about a people: Who are we?

We begin every chapter of this book by showing how its major topics help explain who we are. All the features of American politics—enduring ideas, the Constitution, presidents, justices, media personalities, bureaucrats,

● **Figure 1.2** *Race and ethnicity in America—yesterday, today, and tomorrow. (US Census)*

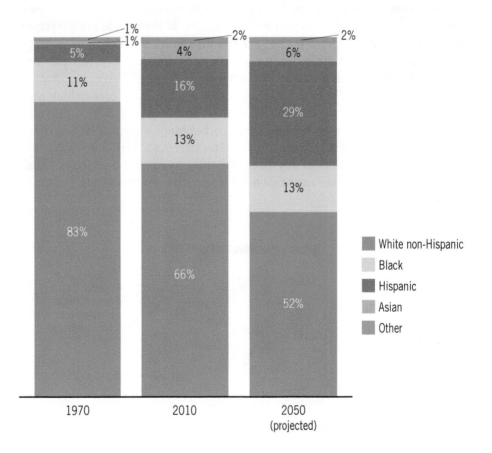

interest groups, and more—are part of the struggle to define and redefine the nation.

Who are we? The most important answer to that question is you. As part of the next generation, you are the future of American politics. To us, that is a comforting thought. Studies of the millennial generation show that you are, on average, more responsible, harder working, and more law-abiding than the generations that came before (including ours). You tend to volunteer more, donate a higher share of your income to charity, and start more entrepreneurial organizations with social impact. You might just be the generation that finally redeems the endless American quest for racial harmony and gender equality. You are also a generation at home in a rapidly changing and diverse world.

We have one worry, however. Will this generation take up the challenge of American politics and government? Compared to previous generations, millennials show less interest in government service, trust national leaders less, and follow political news at a lower rate. If a whole generation is reluctant to get involved, American democracy will suffer.

THE BOTTOM LINE

- We explore American government by asking four questions: who governs? How does American politics work? What does government do? And who are we?
- In a republic, power rests with the people. However, this is a difficult form of government to maintain.
- American political decisions are shaped by four "I" factors: ideas, institutions, interests, and individuals.
- Americans tend to dislike their national government—but like the benefits that government programs provide.
- Because the nation is so diverse—and so rapidly changing—the answer to the question of who we are is constantly being rewritten.
- Every feature of American politics influences this constant debate over defining the nation and its people.

A Nation of Ideas

As the colonies broke away from England, on July 4, 1776, American leaders issued a Declaration of Independence explaining their revolutionary actions. Its second paragraph describes the idea that animated them:

> *We hold these truths to be self-evident, that all men are created equal, that they are endowed by their Creator with certain unalienable rights, that among these are life, liberty and the pursuit of happiness.*

JOHN HANCOCK'S DEFIANCE.

● *Ideas have consequences. John Hancock of Massachusetts defiantly signs the Declaration. According to legend, he signed it in big, bold letters so King George could read Hancock's name without his spectacles—and "double the reward for my head."*

American exceptionalism: The view that the United States is unique, marked by a distinct set of ideas such as equality, self-rule, and limited government.

Most people have heard that line so often that it has lost its force, but it is one of the most powerful ideas in history. It explains the role of government—securing each individual's rights to life, liberty, and the pursuit of happiness. Every American generation argues about how it can best achieve the Declaration's shimmering ideal and "secure" the rights of every citizen.

Political scientists often describe the United States as a unique nation, different from every other. That view is known as **American exceptionalism**. Of course, every nation is distinctive in some way. The United States is exceptional, in large part, because of seven key ideas that guide our politics. Most of them can be traced back to the Declaration of Independence.

What are the seven big ideas? Liberty, self-rule (which is often called democracy), individualism, limited government, the American dream, equality, and faith in God. These ideas touch almost everything we do as a nation. They are the foundation of US national government and lie at the core of what makes America unique.

There is an unusual twist to these ideas. Americans rarely agree on what they mean. Instead, we constantly argue about them. The Declaration of Independence declares that all men are created equal, but many of the men who signed it owned slaves. Our stamps and coins say "In God We Trust," but Americans passionately disagree about whether the Constitution permits prayer in schools or menorahs in public parks. All our foundational ideas have (at least) two sides and spark ardent disputes. To reveal the real truth about American politics, we should post signs at all the airports that say: *"Welcome to the great argument that is the USA."*

Now let's consider the first key idea.

Liberty

As the Revolutionary War broke out, the royal governor of Virginia promised freedom to any slave who joined the British. Eighty thousand slaves ran for the British lines. Some of them fought in black units, with their motto—"liberty for the slaves"—sewn onto their uniforms.[4]

The slave men and women who fought for the British saw their hopes vanish when their side surrendered at the Battle of Yorktown in 1781—effectively the end of the Revolutionary War. After the battle the Redcoats, as the English soldiers were known, began to withdraw, rowing out to the warships bobbing in the harbor for their long retreat. One desperate group of slaves dashed past the sentries on the wharf, dove into the sea, and swam toward the long rowboats that were ferrying the defeated British troops out to the naval vessels.

As the desperate black men tried to clamber aboard the small boats, British troops pushed them away. Fearful that the swimmers would swamp the craft, the troops pulled out axes and hacked off the slaves' hands and fingers. And *still* they kept coming, trying to surge aboard, thrashing after their fading dream of liberty. The image is unforgettable: these men were so desperate for freedom that, even as the Redcoats swung their bloody hatchets, they kept clutching for the boats that might carry them to freedom.

"The Land of the Free"

No idea comes up more often in American history than freedom or liberty (we use the words interchangeably in this book). The national anthem declares America "the land of the free." During the civil rights movement of the 1950s and 1960s, young high school students spilled out of Baptist churches and marched toward dogs and high-pressure fire hoses, singing "everyone shout freedom, freedom, freedom!" The Statue of Liberty is inscribed "Give me your huddled masses . . . yearning to breathe free." Americans have tried to spread their faith in freedom to countries across the globe; as President George W. Bush put it, "The best hope for peace in our world is the expansion of freedom in all the world."

What is **freedom**? *It means that the government will protect your life, your liberty, and your property from the coercion of others (including government) in order to permit you to pursue the goals you define for yourself.*

Freedom: The ability to pursue one's own desires without interference from others.

The Two Sides of Liberty

Everyone agrees that freedom is a basic American value. But, in practice, Americans disagree about what it means—and what governments should do to ensure it. There are two different views: negative liberty and positive liberty.[5]

The more familiar view is **negative liberty:** *freedom is the absence of constraints.* Society's responsibility, from this perspective, is to make sure that others (especially government officials) do not interfere with individuals pursuing their own goals. The government protects your right to believe what you wish, to say what you like, to profess any faith, and to go into whatever business you care to. Negative freedom is the right to act as you want.

Negative liberty: Freedom from constraints or the interference of others.

The alternative is **positive liberty:** *the freedom to pursue one's goals.* From this perspective, individuals cannot really be free—they cannot pursue their desires—if they lack the basic necessities of life. Protecting liberty means ensuring that every citizen has education, food, shelter, and health care. After all, how can people truly be free if they are hungry or homeless? This view justifies government action as a way to give all people an honest chance to achieve their desires.

President Franklin D. Roosevelt forcefully expressed this view in 1941. As the United States prepared for World War II, he proclaimed that the nation

Positive liberty: The freedom and ability to pursue one's goals.

COUNTERTHINK

FREEDOM OF SPEECH   FREEDOM OF RELIGION   "FREEDOM" OF HEALTH   SUBMIT TO CHEMOTHERAPY!

ART - DAN BERGER   CONCEPT - MIKE ADAMS   WWW.NATURALNEWS.COM

● *A conservative cartoonist celebrates negative freedom (no one interferes with freedom of speech or religion) but mocks positive freedom (the idea that society should provide everyone with basic needs like health care). Beginning with Franklin Roosevelt in 1933, liberals disagreed with this cartoon's perspective and embraced "freedom from want."*

see for yourself 1.1

Go online to hear President Roosevelt deliver this speech.

Libertarians: People who believe in minimal government: public officials' only role should be defending borders, prosecuting crime, and protecting private property.

was fighting for four freedoms: freedom of speech, freedom of worship, freedom from want, and freedom from fear. The first two—freedom of speech and religion—were traditional negative liberties: no one could infringe on these individual rights. However, "freedom from want" was something new, a positive update of the original American idea of freedom. Freedom from want means helping needy people who have fallen on hard times. Roosevelt was suggesting that social welfare policies like unemployment insurance and Social Security were part of the all-American idea of freedom. Contemporary ideas of positive freedom include efforts to ensure that all people are well educated or to stop them from smoking. The theory: a lack of education, or addiction or disease, will make it difficult for them to pursue their goals.

Which side is correct? That depends on your values. Beneath these two visions of liberty lie different approaches to the good society. The negative view emphasizes personal autonomy. Strong proponents of negative liberty are known as **libertarians** and oppose most forms of government action. The positive view follows Roosevelt: membership in a free society means sharing enough wealth so that everyone enjoys freedom from want. The two perspectives reflect different values, different visions of society, and different definitions of liberty.

The Idea of Freedom Is Always Changing

Once upon a time, Americans permitted slavery. And racial segregation. Women lost all their legal rights the day they were married; their possessions—even their very bodies—passed into the custody of their husbands. Chinese immigrants were denied any hope of becoming Americans no matter how long they lived in the country. And gay couples could be prosecuted as sexual criminals. The ideal of freedom moved Americans to reverse each of these prejudices.

Scholars disagree about how to interpret the results. Some see American history as a steady march toward greater liberty. Yes, they admit, American history is full of oppression. However, our faith in freedom leads oppressed groups to fight for their rights.

Other political thinkers, like Rogers Smith, warn against seeing anything like a steady rise of freedom. The outcome in the fight is never inevitable. Instead, freedom is won and lost . . . and won and lost again. Americans fought their bloody civil war to end slavery—only to watch new forms of racial segregation and oppression take hold and last almost for another century. Native Americans have never fully been restored to their place on the land or in society. Gay rights, immigrant rights, the rights of people with disabilities, and many others are still part of an ongoing battle for freedom; no one can say how those conflicts will end. Nor should we ever take liberty for granted.[6]

THE BOTTOM LINE

- Liberty—or the freedom to pursue your goals—is perhaps the greatest American value.
- There are two different views of what liberty means. *Negative liberty* emphasizes a lack of constraints on individuals, even if those constraints are to help others. *Positive liberty* requires the community to help everyone satisfy their basic needs.
- Liberty has grown with time. Some scholars see it as an inevitable growth that reflects the American ideal; others, as a constant battle that can always go either way.

Self-Rule

As the American Revolution began, mobs gathered in the towns and cities and insisted that they were now the legitimate political power. The People, they declared, would seize authority from royal governors (appointed by the tyrannical king) and exercise power themselves. "The mob has begun to think for itself," complained one wealthy New Yorker. "Poor reptiles, before noon they will bite" (meaning *revolt*).[7]

Patriotic crowds ignored the critics and skeptics. At mass meetings, the people voted for laws, enforced decrees, and even issued wedding licenses. They dispatched boisterous pro-American toughs, who used sticks and stones to discourage individuals from acknowledging British institutions. Here is a powerful image of democracy: American people bypassing government officials and running the country themselves from the town commons. The people ruled.

•.. Negative Versus Positive Liberty

Americans often disagree about the meaning of "freedom." Is freedom the absence of constraints (negative liberty) or the freedom to pursue one's goals with equal opportunity (positive liberty)?	**Do you believe in negative liberty?** Government should not interfere with individuals. Freedom means leaving every person alone to do what he or she wishes—without interference.	**Or do you believe in positive liberty?** Freedom simply is not a meaningful concept if you or your family are chronically hungry. A decent society has to lift everyone to a basic minimum. That's what living in a democracy should be about.	**Do your beliefs fall somewhere in between?** The truth is that very few people would build a society around a pure form of negative or positive liberty. Think about how you might combine these two concepts. You might find it easier to answer this question after reading about the other major ideas. If you are not ready to choose, read on—and then return to this question.

That principle sounds simple. The United States is the world's longest-running democracy—of course, the people rule. But from the very beginning, a great debate arose about how to achieve **self-rule**. The Constitution was meant to settle the issue—but we are still arguing about it 225 years later.

Self-rule: The idea that legitimate government flows from the people.

How do we achieve self-rule? Americans have long vacillated between two very different paths—a *democracy* and a *republic*.

One Side of Self-Rule: Democracy

Democracy: A government in which citizens rule directly and make government decisions for themselves.

Democracy means that citizens participate directly in making government decisions. (*Demos* is the Greek word for "the people.") In early New England, citizens governed directly in town meetings—without relying on elected officials. To this day, some towns are still run this way: How high should taxes be? How much should the town pay its schoolteachers? Is this the year to rebuild the town hall? Eligible voters (originally, white men) all have their say before voting to decide the matter.

Many states still reach for this democratic ideal—let the public make decisions without relying on elected officials. California, for example, puts most important questions (and many unimportant ones) directly to the voters. In 2012, voters across the country weighed in on such issues as legalizing marijuana (yes, in Colorado and Washington), same-sex marriage (approved in

Maine and Maryland), affirmative action (rejected in Oklahoma), and a ban on the death penalty (rejected in California). In the 2010 election, California voters weighed in on fourteen items ranging from legalizing marijuana (voted down) to increasing car license registration by eighteen dollars to fund state parks (also voted down). People vote directly on an issue through a **referendum**, allowed by twenty-seven states and the District of Columbia. **Initiatives** permit the public to circulate a petition that proposes a new law or amendment to the Constitution. And almost every city and state has **sunshine laws** that open government meetings to the public.

Referendum: An election in which citizens vote directly on an issue.

Thomas Jefferson, who drafted the Declaration of Independence and served as the third US president, was the most vocal proponent of maximizing democracy. "The will of the majority," wrote Jefferson, is a "sacred principle" and "the only sure guardian of the rights of man." If the people cannot govern themselves, asked Jefferson, how can they possibly be trusted with the government of others?[8]

Initiative: A process in which citizens propose new laws or amendments to the state constitution.

The result is a rich American legacy of taking to the streets to demonstrate, rally, and protest. Examples from the past fifty years include the massive Latino demonstrations against immigration restrictions in 2006; the March on Washington for jobs and freedom, which was electrified by Martin Luther King's "I Have a Dream" speech in 1963; student protests against the war in Vietnam; Americans rallying for and against abortion rights; the Nation of Islam's Million Man March on Washington (1995); the "million pound marches" held around the country, protesting fat discrimination; Tea Party protests against taxes and big government that sprang up in 2009 and soon became a major force in the Republican party; the Occupy movement that began in New York in 2011 to protest inequality and spread across the nation—and the world; and women's "CodePink" rallies in Chicago and elsewhere to protest the continuing war in Afghanistan (in 2012).

Sunshine laws: Laws that permit the public to watch policy makers in action or to access the records of government proceedings.

Thomas Jefferson's dream of direct democracy lives on. Idealists through American history return to the democrat's first principle: the people should exercise power as much as possible.

Another Side of Self-Rule: A Republic

Most of the men who drafted the Constitution did not agree with Jefferson about democracy. The states had tried to create direct democracy right after the American Revolution. George Washington thought the result was chaos. "We have probably had too good an opinion of human nature," he grumbled. James Madison put it most famously: "Democracies have [always] been spectacles of turbulence and contention, . . . as short in their lives as violent in their deaths." The problem, said Madison, was that in direct democracy the majority often gets carried away. They race after their self-interest without paying attention to the rights of the minority. Direct democracy, he concluded, offers no barrier to lynch mobs crying for blood.[9]

National Rally for Equal Rights

● *Another form of democracy in action? Americans take to the streets to express their views. Here they demonstrate in support of the Equal Rights Amendment (ERA), which was meant to guarantee rights for women. There were also demonstrations against the amendment. (And for and against almost every cause in every era.)*

Republic: A government in which citizens rule indirectly and make government decisions through their elected representatives.

The alternative is a **republic**. In this form of government, the people rule indirectly through their elected representatives. The constitutional framers made an important contribution to the theory of self-rule: classical democratic theory was wrong in expecting that popular government would only work if the people were virtuous; the people are often not virtuous at all. "If men were angels," wrote Madison, "no government would be necessary." The great challenge, he argued, was to devise government institutions that would protect individual rights even if a majority of the people were selfish and corrupt.

As a result, American government is organized to check the majority. House members are elected every two years, presidents every four, and senators every six years; Supreme Court justices are selected by the president (and approved by the Senate) for lifelong terms. The House, the Senate, the president, and the Court all put the brakes on one another. And all of them face fifty different state governments, each with its own politics, powers, and programs.

A Mixed System

Which view of self-rule holds in the United States? Both do. We can say that the United States is a democratic republic because it includes elements of a democracy *and* a republic. There are plenty of opportunities for direct participation. At the same time, American government operates through elected and unelected officials who answer (sometimes indirectly) to the public.

The sheer number of elected officials—five hundred thousand—reveals our hybrid form of government. That's one elected government official for every six hundred people in the country. Few other nations come close to this ratio. We elect representatives, reflecting our origins as a republic; but the enormous number of opportunities to serve in elective office move us closer to a democracy.

You may have noticed that these two principles—the democratic and the republican—are also the names of the two major political parties. However, to complicate matters, the party labels don't really correspond to the principles. Many Republican Party members are committed democrats, and vice versa. We always spell the parties with capital letters—Democrats and Republicans—so as not to confuse them with the two pathways to self-rule.

THE BOTTOM LINE

- Self-rule is a powerful and enduring idea guiding American government. Lincoln put it best: "government of the people, by the people, for the people."
- There are two great pathways to government by the people: a *democracy* and a *republic*. Americans have always balanced these two ideals.

● Limited Government

Back in 1691, while America was still part of Britain, the king appointed Benjamin Fletcher to be governor of New York and gave him control over the New England colonies (which had been independent until then). The Connecticut legislature did not want to cede its power to Governor Fletcher and immediately selected a new commander for the local militia—a direct challenge to the new governor's authority. Fletcher could not ignore this intransigence, so on a beautiful October day he sailed to Hartford, the capital of Connecticut, with a small detachment of troops. He assembled the Connecticut militia and had an officer read the royal proclamation declaring his authority over the state—and its militia.

As the officer read aloud, the Connecticut militiamen began to beat their drums in defiance. Fletcher tried to restore order by commanding his soldiers to fire their muskets in the air; in the ensuing quiet he threatened to punish the militia members for their insolence. In response, the commander of the Connecticut militia stepped forward, put his hand on the hilt of his sword, and issued his own warning: "If my drummers are again interrupted, I'll make sunlight shine through you. We deny and defy your authority." Outnumbered and in no mood for bloodshed, Fletcher beat a quick retreat to his vessel and sailed ignominiously back to New York City. Since the king and his ministers were more than three thousand miles away, they never even heard about this little rebellion against their authority.[10]

The Origins of Limited Government

The tale of Governor Fletcher illustrates an enduring idea: Americans distrust their national government and have consistently sought to limit its power.

Even eighty years before the revolution, Connecticut had grown used to electing its own leaders and going its own way. The people saw the king as a distant figure with no right to interfere in their affairs. That image runs through American history: central government as a remote, unfeeling, untrustworthy authority that threatens our freedoms.

Why did Americans develop this distrust? The answer lies in how the people secured their rights in the first place. In most nations, the central government—made up of kings or aristocrats, or both—grudgingly granted the people rights like the vote or jury trials. Sometimes the people rebelled (as in France), sometimes they negotiated with kings (England), and sometimes monarchs expanded rights to modernize their nations (Thailand). All these countries share a common experience: kings or the central governments that replaced them were the source of rights and liberties. No wonder people in these nations instinctively look to the government for help in solving their problems.

The United States was dramatically different. Americans enjoyed political rights like voting long before they even had a central government. As Governor Fletcher's humiliation illustrates, for most of colonial history the king was too far away to meddle in colonial affairs. Experience taught Americans to see the central government, not as a potential source of rights, but as a threat to their life, liberty, and happiness.

Perhaps this is why Americans are slow to trust their national government. When new programs are proposed, they often hit resistance.

The United States has a low tax rate compared to most nations. Yes, you read that right. Americans complain bitterly about government taxes (our deep dislike of government again), even while US tax rates are among the lowest in the industrial world. Take a look at Figure 1.3. The American tax rate ranks twenty-seventh out of the thirty nations listed.

And Yet . . . The United States Has a Big Government

Here is the paradox lying at the heart of the limited-government idea. People across the political spectrum demand government action. Many **conservatives** seek to use federal authority to crack down on drugs, root out obscenity, limit marriage to heterosexual couples, get tougher on crime, or enhance homeland security.

Most **liberals** reject the idea that public officials should interfere in people's private lives. But they are all for active government when it comes to economic policy or corporate regulation. They call for government-subsidized transportation, tighter regulations on banks, national health insurance, and school lunch programs (there's the freedom from want, again).

A substantial band of libertarians breaks with both liberals and conservatives and challenges America to live up to ideals of limited government. Government, say the libertarians, should protect public safety, private property, and national borders—and do little else. No great army or navy, no

Conservatives: Americans who believe in reduced government spending, personal responsibility, traditional moral values, and a strong national defense. Also known as *Right* or *right-wing*.

Liberals: Americans who value cultural diversity, government programs for the needy, public intervention in the economy, and individuals' right to a lifestyle based on their own social and moral positions. Also known as *Left* or *left-wing*.

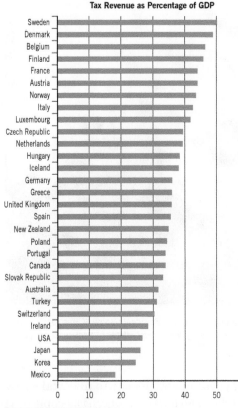

Tax Revenue as Percentage of GDP

Sweden
Denmark
Belgium
Finland
France
Austria
Norway
Italy
Luxembourg
Czech Republic
Netherlands
Hungary
Iceland
Germany
Greece
United Kingdom
Spain
New Zealand
Poland
Portugal
Canada
Slovak Republic
Australia
Turkey
Switzerland
Ireland
USA
Japan
Korea
Mexico

0   10   20   30   40   50   60

Data includes federal, state, and local taxes.

● **Figure 1.3** *Citizens in the United States pay less in taxes than in many other countries. In the countries near the top of the chart, roughly half the economy goes into the government's coffers. In the United States, the figure is closer to one-quarter of all economic activity. Is this too little? Or still too much? These questions get right back to the size of the government and what the government should do. (OECD)*

public schools, no regulating banks, no telling people they can't use drugs, no helping people who are hungry, or homeless, or need health care, no laws against discrimination. This perspective has never gained much traction, however; every crisis—from a food poisoning outbreak to a bank failure to a terrorist attack—inspires widespread demands for government action. However, libertarians reflect a deep American suspicion of government that goes back to colonial times.

Limits on Government Action

In short, Americans often say they do not like government and then demand government action for causes they care about. Their calls for action generally face two hurdles: the desire to limit government, and the Constitution.

When the framers designed our political system, they organized suspicion of government right into the system. The federal Constitution includes an intricate system of **checks and balances** on power, which we will explore in the next chapter. The Constitution carefully limits what Congress may do—although Americans vigorously debate exactly where those boundaries actually are.

Checks and balances: The principle that each branch of government has the authority to block the other branches, making it more difficult for anyone to exercise too much power. It makes passing legislation far more difficult in the United States than in most other democracies.

● **Incompetent government?** *Residents of New Orleans wait for assistance 10 days after Hurricane Katrina struck. The slow government response infuriated residents—and shocked many Americans.*

● **Inspiring Leader.** *President George W. Bush at Ground Zero following the terrorist attacks of September 11, 2001.*

Finally, although it is difficult for government officials to undertake new tasks, the barriers are not insurmountable. During times of crisis, people turn to the government and demand action. Skilled leadership can also negotiate sweeping changes. And once programs go into effect, they often prove popular.

Ironically, the limits on change that make it hard to introduce new programs also make it difficult to repeal them once they are up and running. For example, Social Security was passed in 1935 during the economic crisis of the Great Depression; Medicare passed in part because of a great electoral landslide (in 1964) and in part because of the adroit maneuvering of President Lyndon Johnson. Both are now extremely popular policies; in fact, they are so popular that they are known in Washington as "the third rails" of American politics—touch them and risk electoral "death."

When Ideas Clash: Self-Rule and Limited Government

When Barack Obama ran for re-election in 2012, a key campaign position was raising taxes on wealthy people—those making $250,000 or more. His Republican opponent, Mitt Romney, denounced this idea, and instead claimed that reducing taxes for everyone would boost economic performance.

Democrats and Republicans offered very different economic policies. And in the 2012 election, the people made a clear choice: Obama over Romney. Did this mean that the winning Democrats could swiftly act on this signature issue? No! There were too many barriers in Congress. Even after his big re-election victory, Obama had to compromise with the Republicans who controlled the House of Representatives.

Note the clash between two ideas that we have discussed: self-rule and limited government. Self-rule says: Since the Democrats won the election, they should put their policies into place. Jefferson expressed this point plainly: "The will of the majority" is a "sacred principle" and "the only sure guardian of the rights of man." So President Obama should be able to do what he promised. Most democratic nations more faithfully follow this path to government by the people.

But another value, limited government, says: Not so fast. We don't like government doing lots of things, so we make it very difficult for elected officials to follow through on their promises and actually get things done. Even a president who wins a national election by a large margin must still convince the majority in the House of Representatives and 60 percent of the Senate to vote his way—or, in this case, a substantial tax hike on everyone making $250,000 or more. (Why 60% of the Senate? You'll see in Chapter 10.) Ultimately the main Democratic plan to boost the economy wound up as a compromise hammered out between President Obama, Vice President Joe Biden, and Senate leaders of both parties—with the Republican-led House reluctantly going along. Even

What Do You Think?

Self-Rule Versus Limited Government

Many observers think we no longer have government by the people because it is too difficult for elected officials to get things done. These reformers seek an easier path to government action. However, that prospect raises fears of a more active government. Which should we emphasize, self-rule or limited government? It's time to make your own choice.

I'm with Thomas Jefferson. It should be easier for elected officials to enact the programs they promised. If they cannot do so, elections become less meaningful. When the people vote for something and their representatives fail to deliver, it fosters cynicism about the entire political process. Self-rule requires us to follow the people's mandate. If the majority does not like the results, it can express its displeasure in the next election.

I'm with James Madison. The checks and balances that make large-scale reforms difficult protect the United States from overbearing government and from sudden changes— whether rapidly expanding or cutting programs. The barriers to government action *should* be high. If the public really wants something, it will probably happen over time. Limited government is more important. Don't change the process.

Not sure? This is a formidable question. You may very well change your mind—maybe more than once—as you continue to read this book.

see for yourself 1.2

Go online to see what happened to a popular public policy to reduce greenhouse gases, "cap and trade" (NPR report).

when Congress does pass a law—never easy—the program may still face challenges in the courts for violating constitutional limits on government power.

The result is an important question for political scientists—and for all Americans: How should we balance self-rule and limits on government? Erecting too many boundaries means that we undermine self-rule. But if voters get everything the winning candidates promise them, the result could be a host of new programs and policies. Ironically, the barriers to government action also make it difficult to cut programs and reduce the size of government—as the conservative Republicans rediscover to their chagrin each time they win an election.

THE BOTTOM LINE

- Americans *distrust their government* far more than the people in most other democracies. The Constitution builds that distrust into our governing rules by providing for *limited government*. The result is a very durable status quo.
- In other countries, when politicians are elected promising a program, they can usually deliver. In the United States, winners confront multiple barriers to fulfilling the promises they made on the campaign trail. That's the antigovernmental strain in American thinking.
- However, once programs do go into effect, they often prove popular and difficult to change.

Individualism

Political scientist John Kingdon was visiting his niece in Norway. She was expecting a baby and Professor Kingdon asked what she would do about her job. Casually, she replied that she would receive a full year's leave at 80 percent of her normal pay, and that her company was required to give her job back after the leave. "Who pays for all this?" asked Professor Kingdon. "The government, of course," his niece replied. She was surprised the question had even come up. "Is it any different in the United States?" she asked innocently.[11]

As Kingdon explained, it is completely different in the United States: advocates fought for years to win the Family and Medical Leave Act (1993), which requires employers with more than fifty workers to allow up to twelve weeks of *unpaid* leave for pregnancy, adoption, illness, or military service. In 2012, the Supreme Court struck down part of the law by ruling that a state government employee who had been denied leave could not sue the state for cash.

Norwegians, through their government, take care of new parents. In fact, they take pretty good care of all their citizens. To pay for an array of public services, tax rates are much higher than ours. Almost half of a Norwegian's income goes to taxes.

Americans generally value **individualism**: *the idea that individuals, not the society or the community or the government, are responsible for their own well-being.* We, as a society, do not pay for maternity leave. Instead, we expect private individuals and families to handle birth, or adoption, or caregiving.

Community Versus Individualism

The idea of individualism is a source of controversy in every nation. There are two ways to see any society: as a single *community*, or as a collection of *individuals*. Clearly every nation is both, but government policies can be designed to emphasize the community or to focus on individuals. Let's take a closer look at the two principles.

Countries that emphasize the community are called **social democracies**. Social democrats believe that members of a society are responsible for one another. They use government as a source of mutual assistance. The public interest is best

● *Solidarity in Columbus, Ohio: Students from Central State University give the black power salute during a 1960s-era meeting on the steps of the statehouse. About 500 students from the university staged demonstrations to press demands for more state financial support for the school.*

served, from this perspective, if everyone has a decent life. The government provides citizens with the basics: good health insurance, retirement benefits, generous unemployment packages, and—as we saw in the Norwegian case— maternity benefits.

In exchange, people pay high taxes. The effect of high taxation is to make it difficult for most citizens to get very rich. At the same time, the extensive welfare state makes it far less likely that people will live in poverty. Communal societies are far more equal—not in opportunity, but in outcome. Most western European nations are social democracies.

Social democracies are based on *solidarity*, the idea that people have a tight bond and are responsible for one another. Some societies exhibit a very strong sense of solidarity; in general, this tendency increases during wars, economic depressions, or other crises that get everyone to pull together. Scholars have found that more homogeneous societies—where people look alike, share the same values, and practice the same religion—exhibit higher rates of solidarity than very diverse societies. They point out that even long-established social democracies in Europe (populated primarily by Christians) have seen their sense of solidarity falter with the arrival of Muslim immigrants. Growing diversity challenged national solidarity.

American politics includes a streak of solidarity. Martin Luther King put it eloquently: "We are inevitably our brother's keeper because we are our brother's brother." However, the commitment to solidarity rises and falls in the United States.

Social democracy: A government whose citizens are responsible for one another's well-being and use government policy to assure that all are comfortably cared for.

Some groups in the United States are more likely to express high levels of solidarity within their group. Immigrants often feel this way. From Irish in the nineteenth century to Latinos today, historians have chronicled a sense of shared fate among first- and second-generation Americans. African Americans, too, have traditionally displayed very high levels of solidarity. Political scientist Michael Dawson found that the legacy of slavery and discrimination created a lingering sense of linked fate among African Americans. Drawing on an old blues song, he called it the legacy of standing "behind the mule."[12]

Now let us turn to individualism. In this view, people and their families are responsible for their own welfare. The economist Milton Friedman famously wrote that "the world runs on individuals pursuing their separate interests." Leave people free to choose their interests, Friedman continued, and the public interest of the whole society will emerge.[13] Rather than taxing people and using funds to aid the less well-off, this perspective opts for low taxes. People who work hard will get ahead, and society will grow and prosper.

Individualists value the chance to get ahead (and get rich!) more than they value a society where everyone is equal. In social democracies, government regulations aim to protect workers. In contrast, individualists oppose government controls and believe that private companies should be able to expand or contract their workforce as they see fit (as long as they hire and fire without discriminating). American business leaders often express disdain for social democracies, which regulate every aspect of business—from requiring maternity leaves to restricting layoffs. Individualism points toward limited government, faith in economic markets, and a strong emphasis on *negative liberty*.

Opinion polls confirm what political theorists have long suspected: Americans tend to lean more to individualism than to social democracy—much more so than most other nations. In one prominent cross-national study, for example, people in many nations were asked whether "it is the responsibility of the government to take care of very poor people who cannot take care of themselves." Over 60 percent of the public strongly agreed in England, France, and Italy; 70 percent agreed in Spain. In contrast, only 23 percent of Americans agreed. In another survey, people were asked which is more important: being free to pursue life's goals (individualism), or making sure that nobody in society is in need (community). Once again the American majority (58 percent) chose freedom, whereas in nations like Germany and Spain most people chose taking care of those in need. Western European nations prefer community-oriented social democracies by roughly two to one; Americans lean more heavily toward individualism by the same margin, two to one.

The Roots of American Individualism: Opportunity and Discord

Americans lean toward individualism and away from social democracy. Why? Two leading explanations look to the past. One finds the answer in golden opportunities. A second emphasizes social and racial discord.

Golden Opportunity. For centuries, most Europeans and Asians lived as serfs or peasants working small plots of land. Powerful rulers kept them firmly in their place—there was no chance for individuals to get ahead by working hard. Peasants, all in the same dismal situation, would have to revolt as a group. Their shared conditions fostered a sense of solidarity. In early America, by contrast, there appeared to be endless land. With hard work and a little luck, anyone (at least any white male) could gain a decent living and perhaps even a fortune. Stories about early settlers clearing their own land were later reinforced by images of rugged individuals on the western frontier. Hard workers relied on themselves—not the government.

There is a lot of myth in these stories. Frontier life was less about brave individualism and more about people helping one another out. Settlers couldn't build a barn, a church, or a meetinghouse without their neighbors' help. But the image of hardy individuals on the frontier remains a powerful ideal in American politics. And there was an important truth at its core: few societies have ever offered so many individuals as much opportunity to rise and prosper as early America did.[14]

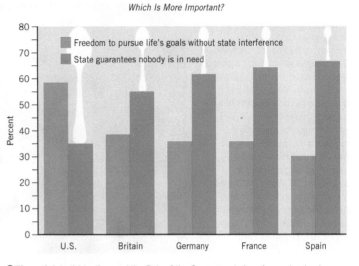

Which Is More Important?

● **Figure 1.4** *Individualism and the Role of the Government. Americans stand out from other nations: they worry about the poor less and about individual freedom more. Source: Pew Global Attitudes, November 17, 2011.*

Social Conflict. An entirely different explanation for American individualism emphasizes the enormous differences within the society: the country is too big and the population too diverse to develop a sense of solidarity. What, after all, did Calvinist Yankees in New England have in common with Roman Catholics in Baltimore or Anglican planters in Virginia—much less Spanish speakers in Florida or Texas? Moreover, a nation that included four million black slaves by 1860 had a terrible divide running through its heart. Amid the misery and guilt over slavery, it was difficult for black and white people to feel solidarity with one another.

By the 1830s there was still another source of division. Immigrants were arriving by the tens (and later hundreds) of thousands—people with different languages and what seemed like strange customs. Each generation of immigrants added to the American cacophony. For example, Irish Catholics (who arrived in the 1830s and 1840s) seemed strange and threatening to the English Protestants who had immigrated a century earlier. Could Catholics, with their allegiance to a foreign pope, really understand or uphold American values? All these divisions made solidarity far more difficult to feel than in more stable, homogeneous populations.

● *Individualism in historical memory: At high noon on April 22, 1889, bugles sounded and a great mob—lined up impatiently outside the Oklahoma territory—surged across the border and snatched up as much land as they could stake out. Although the government sponsored the land giveaway, the image that sticks is of the people grabbing their land for themselves. Oklahoma still honors the scalawags that snuck in early (or sooner) and grabbed the good land ahead of time—that's where the motto "The Sooner State" comes from.*

Both explanations are on target. Unprecedented economic opportunity and vast social divisions each make the United States different from other nations. Together they can limit feelings of solidarity and lead to a philosophy of individualism.

Who We Are: Individualism and Solidarity?

It is not correct to conclude that Americans are individualists alone. Rather, the two themes always compete in American politics. Individualism is more robust and more often in evidence. But a sense of solidarity also unites the American population. We often pull together as a nation. We often take care of our neighbors and pass government programs to improve the lives of people we do not know. The United States may have deep divisions, but it is remarkable how quickly they can disappear. A substantial majority of Americans today are children, grandchildren, or great-grandchildren of immigrants— many of whom were once regarded as strange and different.

All this raises another question to ponder: Where would you draw the line between solidarity and individualism? The answer directly relates to one of this book's central questions: *Who are we?* Take the test in the "What Do You Think" on page 28 to learn where you stand on the continuum between rugged individualism and strong solidarity.

THE BOTTOM LINE

- American politics includes both individualism and solidarity.
- Different leaders, parties, groups, and individuals weigh the two values in different ways. However, compared to other nations, the United States is very much at the individualist end of the spectrum.

The American Dream

Benjamin Franklin perfected a classic American literary form—tips for getting rich. Anyone, he assured his readers, could be successful by following a formula: be frugal ("A penny saved is a penny earned"), hardworking ("No gains without pains"), steady ("Little strokes fell great oaks"), bold ("God helps those who help themselves"), and—most important—morally upright ("Leave your vices, though ever so dear").[15]

Franklin was summarizing what later became known as the American dream: *if you are talented and work hard, you can achieve financial success.* A popular historian, James Truslow Adams, was the first to actually call it an American dream: "a land in which life should be better and richer and fuller for everyone, with opportunity for each according to ability or achievement."[16] The idea scarcely changes across generations. "The American dream that we were all raised on is a simple but powerful one," averred President Bill Clinton, more than two centuries after Ben Franklin. "If you work hard and play by the rules, you should be given a chance to go as far as your God-given abilities will take you." President Ronald Reagan put it even more plainly: "What I want to see above all is that this country remains a country where someone can always get rich."[17]

Spreading the Dream

The legacy of the Revolutionary War, according to historian Gordon Wood, was the spread of the American dream to all classes. What did the common people care about? "Making money and getting ahead," writes Wood. Yes, it was vulgar, material, crass, and even anti-intellectual. But the revolution made the common people the basis of government and gave them an unprecedented chance to make their fortunes. That had never happened on such a scale before.[18]

By the nineteenth century, the race to get ahead had turned fast and reckless. "Go ahead is our maxim and our password," wrote New York politician Philip Hone in 1837. "We go ahead with a vengeance, regardless of consequences." A young French aristocrat, Alexis de Tocqueville, who visited the United States and later wrote the classic study *Democracy in America*, agreed. "The great mass of citizens do not want to talk about anything but private business . . . through and through." Tocqueville concluded that "The love of money [and] even base greed" was "the characteristic trait which now distinguishes the Americans . . . from all other nations."[19]

Enabling the dream of success remains an important part of any policy debate. Will a proposal help small business? Will it create jobs? Will it stifle entrepreneurs? Immigrants come in large numbers—far more than to any other country—partially to pursue the dreams of success. Politicians from both parties eagerly try to spread the idea to other nations (which are not always enthusiastic about receiving it, for it can threaten the solidarity principle).

Individualism Versus Solidarity

Please score yourself on the following ten statements:

0 = Disagree strongly
1 = Disagree
2 = Agree
3 = Agree strongly

1. It is the responsibility of the government to take care of poor people who cannot take care of themselves. **0 1 2 3**

2. Everyone should have health insurance in case they become ill. **0 1 2 3**

3. In fact, everyone should have the *same* health insurance. It doesn't make sense for some people to get better care than others just because they can afford it. **0 1 2 3**

4. I'd be willing to pay *a little more* in taxes so no person in America goes hungry or homeless. **0 1 2 3**

5. I'd be willing to pay *a lot more* in taxes so that everyone in America has a pretty decent life. **0 1 2 3**

6. I agree that "the betterment of the poor enriches the rich . . . whatever affects one directly affects all indirectly" (Dr. Martin Luther King). **0 1 2 3**

7. I don't believe big companies should be permitted to fire people without providing two months' salary and some retraining. **0 1 2 3**

8. Most Americans want the same things out of life. **0 1 2 3**

9. We should think about others as much as we think about ourselves. **0 1 2 3**

10. It is wrong to step over others to get ahead in life. **0 1 2 3**

Scoring

0–5 You are truly a rugged individualist!
5–14 You are largely an individualist.
15–20 You are a moderate who sees both sides of the issue.
20–24 You are a social democrat.
25–30 You are a true-blue believer in solidarity!

Now, speak with someone who scored very differently from you. Try to explain how and why you came to hold your views.

Challenging the Dream

Like every important idea, the American dream generates conflict. Critics raise two questions: Has the system become rigged to favor some (usually the wealthy) over others? And is the pursuit of wealth an undesirable value or one that crowds out other important values?

Is the System Tilted Toward the Wealthy?   Some critics question whether the dream is still open to everyone or whether it has grown biased toward the rich and powerful.

In the years after World War II, middle-class incomes rose faster than incomes at the top. Then, starting around 1979, this trend changed. Money began to flow to the wealthiest more than to the other classes. Figures 1.5 and 1.6 compare the two periods.

Today, the top 1 percent of Americans own more than the bottom 90 percent. Three million people enjoy more wealth than 270 million others. Sixty million Americans at the bottom of the charts own almost nothing—one-tenth of one percent of the national wealth. Many social scientists now argue that the chance of moving up—from poverty to wealth—is fading in the United States. Studies suggest that someone in the bottom fifth of the income distribution is twice as likely to move up at least one category (or quintile) in

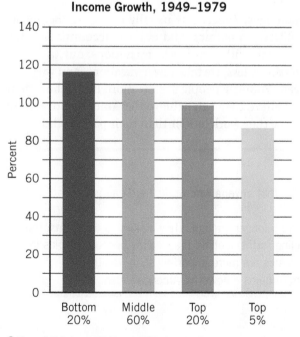

● **Figure 1.5** *Between 1949 and 1979, those on the bottom saw their earnings grow faster than those on the top. (Robert Frank, Falling Behind)*

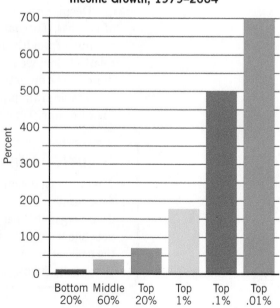

● **Figure 1.6** *. . . but look how that changed after 1979. Now those on the bottom have very little income growth while the wealthy have very rapid growth. Is this a bad thing? Americans disagree. (Sawhill and Morton, Economic Mobility)*

Canada, Denmark, or France than in the United States. Critics—both liberal and conservative—increasingly challenge the system for not offering real equality of opportunity.[20]

Does the American Dream Promote the Wrong Values?   A second critique questions the chase for wealth as a human value. Environmentalists criticize the damage caused by big houses, sprawling suburbs, gas-guzzling cars, and opulent lifestyles. Others cite the harm to old-fashioned communal ideals. "These dark days will be worth all they cost us," said President Franklin Roosevelt during the depths of the Great Depression, "if they teach us that our true destiny is . . . to minister . . . to our fellow man." Repeatedly, he urged Americans to rethink their basic values before an upturn in the stock market "dulled their moral sense."

President Lyndon Johnson put civil rights in the same larger context. "Should we double our wealth and conquer the stars, and still not be equal to this issue [race], then we will have failed as a people and as a nation. For with a whole country as with a person, 'What is a man profited, if he should gain the whole world, and lose his own soul?'" Voices like these have questioned the pursuit of economic success to the exclusion of community and social justice.[21]

The capitalists who celebrate wealth often have to wrestle with economic populists who would rather share it. During difficult economic times—like those accompanying the "great recession," which began in the fall of 2008—faith in the American dream lags.

Despite critics and challenges, Americans usually celebrate the gospel of success. The nation's politics, economics, and culture accommodate the dreams of wealth. In comparison with other wealthy nations, our taxes are relatively low, we regulate business less, we take fewer vacations, and we place more stress on getting ahead. Younger people are far more likely than their parents or grandparents to believe they can achieve the American dream in their lifetime. They also believe they work harder than their parents did.

THE BOTTOM LINE

- The American dream is a belief that anyone who works hard can get ahead and grow wealthy.
- Critics argue that hard work is no longer enough. They make two criticisms: the poor and middle class are falling farther behind the wealthy because of bias in the political economy; other values are more important than wealth.
- Despite the critics, the dream remains a powerful American idea.

Equality

When Tocqueville arrived in the United States, he was amazed by the equality. In one of his first letters home, he reported watching servers in a tavern sit down at the next table to eat and drink alongside the guests. People who declared bankruptcy were not shunned, as they would have been in France, but were treated the same as any other businessperson who had suffered a temporary setback. Here was a society where people from all ranks shook hands, discussed politics, and chased money. Everyone seemed to be equals.

Tocqueville distilled this thought into the first sentence of his great book *Democracy in America*: "No novelty in the United States struck me more vividly . . . than the equality of condition." In a world that was still full of aristocrats and inherited privilege, American society itself embodied the great idea at the heart of the Declaration of Independence: "All men [and women] are created equal."[22]

Equality means that *every citizen enjoys the same privileges, status, and rights before the laws*. There are three different kinds of equality to consider when analyzing the concept: *social*, *political*, and *economic*.

Three Kinds of Equality

Social equality means that all individuals enjoy the same status in society. There are no American barons or archdukes who inherit a special place when they are born. Except for slavery, there have never been fixed social classes. Few American politicians boast of noble origins or good family lineage. On the contrary, for the past 150 years candidates have flaunted (or invented) their working-class roots. Even very wealthy politicians often claim to have risen up from humble origins (for many years, they boasted about the log cabins they supposedly grew up in). An old cliché in American politics—one with a lot of truth to it—is the saying that any little boy or girl could grow up to be the president—or a millionaire. You don't have to be born into the "right" family.

Political equality means that every citizen has the same political rights and opportunities. Americans enjoyed universal white, male *suffrage*—or the right to vote—much earlier than did most nations. Over time the opportunity to vote spread. Today there are lively debates about whether we still ensure everyone an equal opportunity to affect the political process.

Some reformers suggest, for example, that if everyone is to have the same chance to influence the political process, we should remove money from elections. Otherwise, the wealthy will have more influence than everyone else. Others counter that individuals who are excited by candidates should be allowed to contribute to them. The Supreme Court intervened in 2010 by ruling that campaign donations are a form of free speech—which the government cannot usually restrict.

The quest for political equality raises a range of other issues: Does everyone enjoy an equal right to a fair trial—or have the costs of going to court

Equality: All citizens enjoy the same privileges, status, and rights before the laws.

Social equality: All individuals enjoy the same status in society.

Political equality: Every person has the same political rights and opportunities.

elevated this basic right beyond the reach of many people? Does the voting system make it too difficult for some people to register and cast their ballots? Should states forbid convicted criminals from voting even after they have served their sentence? All these questions reflect the fundamental issue of political equality: Does every citizen have an *equal opportunity* to influence the political process and are they all treated the same way before the law?

Economic equality: A situation where there are only small differences in wealth between citizens.

Economic equality focuses on differences in wealth. When President Washington toured the states in the 1790s, he noticed that in some regions there was little wealth and no poverty. At the time, the United States was truly exceptional in its economic equality.

Today the United States has changed dramatically—toward inequality. In 1970, the level of economic inequality in the United States was similar to most other wealthy democracies. On one measure of economic inequality, known as the Gini coefficient, the United States ranked between France and Japan on the equality tables. Today, in contrast, American society has become far less equal than nations like Japan, Sweden, or Germany. We are now closer to the inequality levels of less-developed nations, like Argentina or South Africa, than to the wealthier but more egalitarian nations of the world. Should we adopt public policies to limit inequality? That is one of the great political debates today—as we'll see in the next section.

How Much Economic Inequality Is Too Much?

Another illustration of national differences in economic inequality arises from the "salary gap." In 1965, the **median** (or typical) American chief executive officer (CEO) made 26 times more than a typical worker in his or her company. In Japan today the figure is roughly the same. But in contemporary United States, the CEO makes (depending on the study) between 300 and 500 times the average employee. Is this a problem for the idea that "all men are created equal"?

Median: A statistical term for the value in the middle of a series when the items are arranged in numerical order.

People in many countries would answer yes. Too much inequality, they say, divides society. In Japan, cultural norms encourage individuals to avoid attracting attention through great wealth or ostentation. In western Europe, high taxes make it more difficult to grow very wealthy (or very poor). These are policies pursued by societies that want to achieve what once impressed foreign visitors about America—the absence of great extremes of wealth or poverty. In fact, Tocqueville warned Americans that they might be vulnerable to economic inequality: "The friends of democracy should keep their eyes anxiously fixed in [the] direction [of] . . . the manufacturing aristocracy we see rising up."[23]

But, as we have seen in our discussion of the American dream, our public policies (and public opinion) often endorse the race to wealth. Great riches are the glittering prize of the American dream. Why not let the winners—basketball stars, successful musicians, bank CEOs, and breakthrough entrepreneurs—enjoy fabulous success? The debate continues today. Some activists charge that the richest one percent take advantage of everyone else; critics on the other side dismiss such activists as un-American agents of "class warfare." In fact, this is an old debate stretching back through time.

Opportunity or Outcome?

Many Americans accept high levels of economic inequality, contending that these are not fatal to our hopes for an egalitarian society. That's because of an important distinction between *equal opportunity* and *equal outcome*.

Equal opportunity is the idea that every American has an equal chance. In politics, this means each person gets one vote and the process is transparent and open to all. In economics, it means that every individual gets a fair shot at achieving the American dream. Whether you're white or black, Anglo or Latina, male or female, rich or poor, you have a similar opportunity to influence the political process and to win economic success.

Equal outcome, in contrast, is the idea that a society guarantees not just an opportunity but also the results. Some nations reserve a minimum number of seats in the national legislature (whether it be a parliament or Congress) for women or members of specific ethnic groups. And, as we have already seen, others keep their taxes high and offer extensive social benefits, knowing that this arrangement will keep successful people from getting too far ahead of everyone else.

Equal opportunity: The idea that every American has an equal chance to win economic success.

Equal outcome: The idea that citizens should have roughly equal economic circumstances.

● **Should we worry about economic inequality?** *LeBron James makes $44.5 million a year for playing basketball. Is that too much for a superstar—even one as good as James? Should we change the rules so that the wealthy get less and poor people more? Today these are hotly debated political questions. Where you stand depends on different ideas about equality.*

Today, the United States emphasizes equal opportunity. The winners fly private jets; the losers may end up with nothing. Still, there are questions—and hard political choices—about equal opportunity. How do we give people an honest chance to affect the governing process? How much education is enough to give someone a fair chance at making it in the marketplace? Do we need to provide early childhood reading programs? Offer English-language programs for everyone who is not fluent? Guarantee basic nutrition? Remove lead paint that might leave children mentally impaired? And what should we do about past injustice? Does the long legacy of slavery, segregation, and repressive policies toward toward blacks or Chinese immigrants or American Indians require our society to offer special forms of compensation to groups that suffered generation after generation of mistreatment?

These questions return us to the same policy debates we introduced during the discussion of positive and negative liberty. Should we ensure the basics—or simply protect individual rights and let every person run the great race alone? As you can see, debates about equality lead back to debates about freedom (positive or negative) and individualism.

● **Figure 1.7** *The gap between rich and poor in 2005 (Growing Unequal? OECD, 2008)*

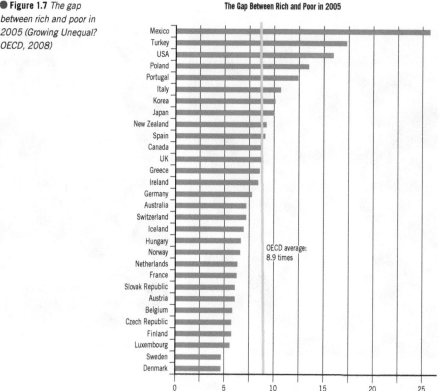

The Gap Between Rich and Poor in 2005

The average incomes of the richest 10% as a multiple of the average income of the poorest 10%. In the US, the richest 10% make sixteen times more than the poorest.

The economic side of the debate raises a powerful challenge for contemporary America: Might the gap between rich and poor grow so large that it undermines equality of opportunity? As the gap continues to widen, liberals warn that growing disparities are creating a land of billionaires and hungry children with grim future prospects. Conservatives respond that the effort to redistribute wealth from rich to poor violates the American gospel of success. Robbing the rich to help the poor, they insist, will not help either group. The have-nots, they conclude, should work harder and develop better habits.

Over time, the United States has gone from the most equal society in the world to one that is considerably less equal than other wealthy nations (see Figure 1.7). The past thirty-five years, in particular, have seen a very sharp spike in inequality. American politics has come to emphasize other ideas—negative liberty, individualism, the American dream of getting ahead—over equality.

THE BOTTOM LINE

- Equality means that every citizen enjoys the same privileges, status, and rights before the law.
- Equality applies to social status, political rights, and economic conditions.
- Today, America generally aims for *equal opportunity* rather than *equal outcome*.
- A great debate now rages over what government must provide to ensure equal opportunity.

Religion

In the 1630s, a large contingent of Puritans sailed to New England with an ambitious aim: to establish a biblical commonwealth that would serve as a Christian model for the rest of the world. Governor John Winthrop called their settlement "a city upon a hill" and expected "the eyes of all people on us." How did they fare? If anyone was really watching, they soon saw unexpected complications.

For example, Quakers from Pennsylvania—whom the New England Puritans despised for lacking discipline—began sailing north to convert the New Englanders. If the Quakers succeeded, they would subvert the whole idea of a model Puritan society. New England's women, the ministers worried, might be especially vulnerable to Quaker heresies. The authorities banned the Quakers under threat of having an ear cut off (one each for the first and second offense), their tongues pierced by hot pokers (third offense), and finally death. Quaker martyrs piously and joyfully challenged the Puritan authorities. Four were hung before English authorities ordered an end to the punishment.

The story reflects enduring American themes: the importance of religion, the intense competition between sects, and a missionary fervor about saving the world. Even today, politicians of every stripe repeat the idea of a "city on a hill" (although few realize that it is a quotation from the Sermon on the Mount in the New Testament).

Remaining Religious

Religion plays an enduring role in American politics and society. The centrality of religion may not surprise you. But it is a powerful example of American exceptionalism, helping inspire a sense that this nation is unlike any other. As most nations grow wealthier, their religious fervor wanes. Citizens in advanced countries, from Britain and France to Japan and South Korea, tell pollsters that God is not very important in their lives. In contrast, Americans maintain high (and by some measures, rising) levels of religiosity. Some 95 percent of Americans say they believe in God, almost 60 percent belong to a church, and nearly 40 percent attend church regularly (see Figures 1.8 and 1.9). To find higher levels you have to go to poorer nations such as India, Egypt, and Indonesia.[24]

So Many Religions

Americans have a lot of religions to choose from. One recent survey found sixteen different Christian denominations with more than a million members

● **Figure 1.8** *Look how American religiosity stands out. As nations grow wealthy, religion nearly always loses its importance. The United States is the great exception. (Pew Center for Religion)*

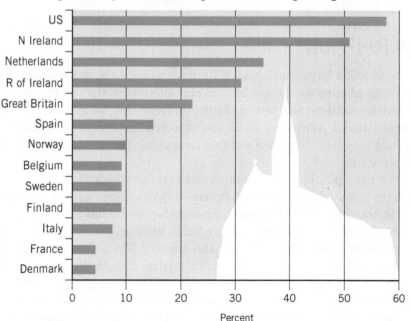

Percentage of the Population that Belongs to Church or Religious Organization

What Do You Consider Yourself First?

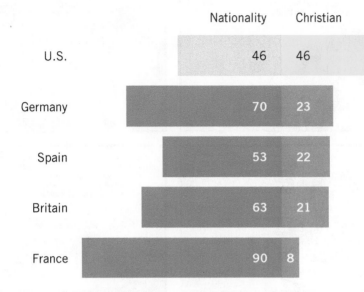

	Nationality	Christian
U.S.	46	46
Germany	70	23
Spain	53	22
Britain	63	21
France	90	8

● **Figure 1.9** *For many Americans, religion is as important as national identity. This chart shows that American Christians take their faith as seriously as being American—in contrast to European Christians, who emphasize their country over their religion. (Pew Research)*

each. That is just the beginning. Jews number some 6.6 million, Muslims nearly 3 million, and seven other non-Christian groups have over 100,000 adherents each (two of the fastest growing are Wiccans and Pagans).[25] In contrast, many other nations have a single major faith, often supported by the government through tax dollars.

Why so many religions? By forbidding the federal government from boosting any official faith, the Constitution kept the field open for any new preacher with a religious idea that might attract a following. Since none can win official recognition, each religious institution is only as strong as the congregation it can muster.

This open market explains why new religions spring up all the time. It does not explain why Americans respond. One of the great mysteries of our political culture is why Americans continue to worship, while citizens in other wealthy nations show a declining interest in religion.

Religious observance is not the same throughout the United States. Texas and Georgia (proud members of the "Bible Belt") have very high religiosity, Florida and Missouri are in the middle, Colorado and Wisconsin are not especially religious, and Maine is the least religious state of all 50. Generational change is also at work: while Americans under 30 continue to report high rates of religious faith, an unusual number do not affiliate with any denomination. Most believe in God but not organized religions.[26]

The Politics of Religion

How is religion relevant to politics? The First Amendment declares, "Congress shall make no law respecting an establishment of religion or prohibiting the

● What constitutes religious teaching?

free exercise thereof." Thomas Jefferson described "a wall of separation between church and state." And yet America's energetic religious life—marked through our history by great evangelical revivals—injects three different kinds of political issues into American politics.

First, there is the question of what exactly the Constitution forbids. May teachers lead prayers in public school? May students in the bleachers organize prayers before football games? May judges post the Ten Commandments in a courthouse? May cities put up a menorah in a public park to celebrate Chanukah? Questions like these (explored in Chapter 4) spark intense debates about just where to draw the line between church and state.

Second, religious faith often inspires people to throw themselves into political issues. A religious revival sparked the abolitionist fight against slavery, beginning in the 1830s; abolitionists condemned slavery as a sin. More than a century later, the civil rights movement spilled out from Baptist and Methodist churches across the South with religious rhetoric, religious symbols, and religious zeal. The opponents of racial equality—arguing for slavery and segregation—also framed their response in religious terms. In American politics, both sides often invoke God. The controversies swirling around the politics of peace, abortion, the environment, gay marriage, and many other issues have all, to varying extents, made the same leap from pulpit to politics. Today, conservatives are more likely to take their faith into the political arena, but this has not always been true. Over time religion has inspired people all across the political spectrum.

Third, religious fervor sometimes fosters a missionary sense in American politics. As the nation expanded westward, Americans declared their "manifest destiny"—God had given an entire continent to his chosen people. Many foreign policies also express a special American mission in the world. During the Cold War, American leaders constantly invoked God as a way of contrasting the United States with Communism. Congress added "under God" to the Pledge of Allegiance (in 1954) and "In God We Trust" to paper money (1955). A half-century later, President George W. Bush invoked "God's gift of freedom" to explain America's mission in Iraq. John Winthrop's idea—a model for the world—echoes from one generation to the next. (We discuss the missionary theme in American foreign policy in Chapter 14).

Political scientists often write about liberty, democracy, and equality. Religion usually slips below the radar screen, but it is a constant element in American politics. Ignoring religion means regularly being surprised as intense religious feelings sweep past the separation between church and state. We will keep an eye on this distinctive and important feature in the chapters that follow.

THE BOTTOM LINE

- Religion plays an enduring role in American politics and society. This is unusual—almost unique—among wealthy countries.
- Americans have an unusually large number of faiths to choose from, although younger people are less likely to affiliate with an organized religion.
- Religious politics raise questions about the role—and the extent—of religion in politics. They inspire political participation on a host of issues—from civil rights to abortion. And they foster a missionary sense in American foreign policy.

How Do Ideas Affect Politics?

Most political scientists agree that the seven ideas of this chapter are central to US society. But how do these ideas influence our politics? There are two familiar answers. Ideas influence our culture, or they operate through our institutions. There is still another possibility to bear in mind, however: perhaps they have a life all their own.

Ideas in American Culture

Political culture: The orientation of citizens of a society toward politics.

Tea party: A national social movement, primarily attracting fiscal and social conservatives, that seeks to limit government spending and cut taxes.

Occupy Wall Street: A social movement, originating in New York City, that protests the inequality of wealth and power, targeting the "top 1 percent."

Each nation has a unique **political culture**, constructed over the years by a people and its leaders. Anthropologist Clifford Geertz described culture as the stories a group tells about itself. Ideas such as liberty, the fear of government, individualism, and the American dream add up to a portrait of American political culture. They are the stories we tell about ourselves.

A culture shapes the way people think about politics and government. When **Tea Party** activists rallied against President Obama's health plan, they drew on a shared set of traditions, references, and values (like direct democracy, negative liberty, and the American dream) that would make no sense to people in, say, Denmark or Mexico. **Occupy Wall Street** seized on overlapping parts of the American legacy—direct democracy, equality, and positive liberty—to promote a very different set of political aims.

Culture develops slowly over time, shaped by history and experience. "There is no country," wrote Tocqueville, "where the law can foresee everything or where institutions should take the place of mores." What he meant by *mores*, he explained, was "the sum of ideas that shape the habits of the mind [and] . . . the habits of the heart."[27] From this perspective, an already existing culture—colonial Americans' shared beliefs, stories, and mental habits—inspired the founding generation to develop a Constitution that limits the power of government.

Why did the framers add a Bill of Rights to the Constitution? Their abiding faith in individualism. Why are there so many checks and balances in our national government? The old American fear of too much government. Why do we regulate and tax less than other nations? The American dream's gospel of success. This shared culture leads men and women to fight for policies that reflect freedom or democracy; policies that reflect social-democratic solidarity are more difficult to win because they resonate more softly through American culture. American hopes and fears often seem peculiar to people in other nations—just as their hopes and fears may not make sense to us.

We can see these cultural differences in every corner of our politics, past and present. In many European nations, Socialist and Communist parties sprang up in the twentieth century. Today, the president of France is a member of the Socialist Party who quietly drew on members of the Communist Party to win the 2012 election. In the United States the Socialist movement has had comparatively little traction. After all, how would it fit into the culture that reveres Benjamin Franklin's dream of getting ahead?

Cultures change slowly. To be sure, the American dream has expanded to include African Americans, Asians, Latinos, and women—all excluded from basic rights a century ago. But they pursue a vision of success that looks quite similar to the one that a much smaller circle of Americans found alluring a century or two ago.

The Ideas in Political Institutions

A different perspective suggests that political institutions, more than political culture, drive events. According to this view, the Constitution's drafters were guided less by cultural values; rather, they were looking for organizational arrangements that would regulate political behavior.

James Madison explained the *institutional perspective*. Past political theory expected republican citizens to virtuously seek the public interest. But, Madison continued sardonically in the Federalist Papers, "enlightened statesmen will not always be at the helm."[28] The Constitution would not ask people to be virtuous; instead, it developed a government that would operate smoothly even if citizens were greedy and their leaders corrupt. The institutions—the rules and organizations built into the government—would shape popular behavior.

Many political scientists follow Madison's argument. It is our governing institutions, starting with the Constitution, that shape American political behavior. Institutions, they say, even influence our values. Government organizations and programs create their own self-reinforcing political dynamics. Each new organization and public policy readjusts the political world.

From an institutional perspective, the barriers to winning new programs emerge not from a dislike of government but from the way the government is organized in the first place. A look at Congress reveals checks, balances, fragmented power, and multiple barriers to getting anything done. Similar

● Through the years, ideas move politics. Malcolm X converted to Islam and preached a rousing black nationalism.

● Occupy Wall Street protesters, 2012.

limits affect government in the states and cities. US government is slow to act, according to this view, because we have *designed* it to be slow to act. When Americans criticize their policy makers for inaction, perhaps they miss the point: gridlock is a consequence of the institutions we have inherited.

Culture or Institutions?

While historians and sociologists tend to emphasize political culture, many political scientists are skeptical about its explanatory power. How, they ask, can something as static as national culture explain the fluid, fast-changing American political scene?

For example, the cultural perspective suggests that the United States has never passed national health insurance, supplied and paid by the federal government, because Americans don't trust government. The institutional perspective counters that it is less a matter of popular belief and more the way we've designed the government. After all, they continue, Harry Truman won the election of 1948 in part by promising national health insurance. No deep-seated fear of government reared its head while Americans were voting. If we had been operating with a Canadian or English legislature, we would have had the program when Truman won the election. But Congress—using the checks and balances central to our national government's institutions—buried the proposal.

In fact, continue institutionalists, when government actually manages to create universal programs—such as Social Security or Medicare—they generally turn out to be extremely popular. If Americans are habitually suspicious of government, why are programs like Social Security so cherished?[29] The way to understand our politics, conclude institutionalists, is to study the laws and organizations that make policy.

Students of culture respond that cultural values are not meant to explain every possible political action. Events, leaders, movements, and government agencies all introduce change. But culture forms the boundary of those changes. It limits the possibilities, shapes our perceptions, and influences our reactions. When terrorists launch an attack, for example, the American response—and the debate about that response—is deeply influenced by the values and ideas we share.

THE BOTTOM LINE

- How do the foundational ideas influence politics? Political scientists point to three different ways.
- First, ideas shape American culture, which in turn affects our politics.
- Second—and most popular among political scientists—ideas operate through political institutions. We have to study those institutions to appreciate how ideas shape politics and policies.
- Third, the ideas may have their own independent power.

● Conclusion: Culture and Institutions, Together

Do the ideas described in this chapter add up to a political culture that shapes the attitudes of American men and women? That cultural argument seems intuitive to many people. On balance, however, most political scientists underscore the importance of institutions.

As a political science student, you can decide for yourself on the relative power of culture and institutions as you read this book. But you don't have to choose one or the other. We believe that culture and institutions together play a role in American politics. They reinforce each other. Yes, national institutions make it difficult to pass national health insurance; and, yes again, opponents invoke powerful cultural norms—like individualism and liberty—to persuade Americans that the legislation threatens their values. For us, the most interesting question is how ideas, culture, and institutions (along with interests and individuals—the four "I's" introduced early in this chapter) all interact to shape American politics.

Finally, ideas have a power of their own—above and beyond the culture and institutions they have helped to shape. Ideas of liberty, democracy, or the American dream can move people to act. That's exactly what Captain (and Professor) Russell Burgos was thinking as the mortars came flying into his post in northern Iraq.

As you read through this book, you will constantly encounter the seven ideas we have described in this chapter. Think about which seem most important and most powerful to you. And pay attention to how they appear to operate—through the culture, through institutions, with a life of their own, or (as we believe) in all these ways at different times and in different circumstances.

CHAPTER SUMMARY

● This book examines four key questions: Who governs, how does American politics work, what does government do, and who are we?

● Seven important ideas influence American politics. Each idea has at least two different sides—differences that spur intense political debates.

● *Freedom* means that the government will protect your life, liberty, and property from the coercion of others (including government) so that you can pursue the goals you define for yourself. In one view, freedom requires *positive government* action to make sure that everyone has the basics to permit them to pursue their goals. In another view, the government guarantees only *negative freedom*—the freedom to pursue your goals. You are free to succeed or to fail on your own, but there are no guarantees about food, or homes, or health care.

● *Self-rule* means that people govern themselves through clearly defined procedures like elections. In a democracy, citizens participate directly in making government decisions. In a republic, the people rule indirectly through their elected representatives. The American system is a combination of the two, a democratic republic.

● Americans value *limited government*: they distrust government and place limits on the authority it can exercise.

● *Individualism* means that individuals—not society or the community or government—are responsible for their own well-being. For those who favor community or social democracy, the public interest is best served when members of a society use government to take care of one another. Americans take both an individual and a communal view, but in contrast to many other nations, the individualistic view is more powerful.

● The *American dream* holds that if you are talented and work hard, you will succeed and grow wealthy. Critics argue that the system is rigged or that the dream promotes the wrong values. However, the dream remains a powerful force in American politics.

● *Equality* allows each citizen to enjoy the same privileges, status, and rights before the law. Some define equality as a matter of *opportunity*—the idea that every American has an equal chance. Others promote equal *outcome*—a guarantee of results. There are three kinds of equality to consider: Social equality means that all individuals enjoy the same status in society. Political equality guarantees every citizen the same rights and opportunities to participate in politics. Economic equality minimizes the gap between citizens' wealth and earnings.

● *Religion* plays an enduring role in American politics and society. The great question is how we limit government interference without limiting religion itself.

● These seven ideas mark Americans' beliefs as a people. They can shape politics through national culture, through political institutions, and through their own influence on Americans.

KEY TERMS

American exceptionalism, 10
Checks and balances, 19
Conservatives, 18
Democracy, 14
Economic equality, 32
Equal opportunity, 33
Equal outcome 34
Equality, 31
Freedom, 11
Individualism, 23

Initiative, 15
Institutions, 5
Liberals, 18
Libertarians, 12
Median, 32
Negative liberty, 11
Occupy Wall Street, 40
Political culture, 40
Political equality, 31
Positive liberty, 11

Rational-choice theory, 6
Referendum, 15
Republic, 4
Self-rule, 14
Social democracy, 23
Social equality, 31
Sunshine laws, 15
Tea Party, 40

STUDY QUESTIONS

1. The second paragraph of the Declaration of Independence boldly explains exactly why "governments are instituted among men." Why? Why are governments formed? Do you agree with that assertion about government's most basic function?

2. Liberty is often described as the most important American idea. Define it. Describe the two different views of liberty. Which do you think is more accurate?

3. Review the seven principal "American ideas" we have identified in this chapter. Are *new* foundational ideas bubbling up in American politics today? If so, what are they?

4. The Declaration of Independence asserts that all men are endowed by their creator with the inalienable rights to life, liberty, and the pursuit of happiness. Over time, Americans have extended that idea to more and more people, such as former slaves and women. Are there groups in our society who are *not* getting the full benefits of this ideal?

5. What is the difference between a democracy and a republic? Which principle does contemporary American government reflect, or does it reflect both? If you were a Founder, which of these principles would you emphasize?

6. Think of the various groups that you belong to. How would you describe each group? And in what ways is each group part of larger American society?

7. There are three forms of equality—social, political, and economic. Define each.

8. There are two approaches to economic equality: opportunity and outcome. Describe each.

9. When it comes to religion, the United States is different from most wealthy societies. How? How do young people differ in their approach to religion than previous generations?

10. Ideas operate through both culture and institutions. Explain.

Bonus: You've studied seven key ideas. Choose and describe another that you would add to the list of important American ideas.

2

The Constitution

IN THIS CHAPTER, YOU WILL:

Discover the roots of the Constitution in colonial and revolutionary America. See why Americans declared independence from England and learn about the first constitution, the Articles of Confederation. Follow the arguments that shaped the Constitution and get an overview of the final document. Read about the great national debate over whether to adopt it. Learn how Americans have changed the Constitution—and how the Constitution has changed America.

THE R. R. MOTON HIGH SCHOOL, in Farmville, Virginia,

was a mess. The roof leaked, the heat worked poorly, the classrooms were over-crowded, and the school bus kept breaking down. When it rained, students sat under umbrellas and shivered in their coats. Moton was a black school; across town, the white students were warm and dry. On April 23, 1951, a junior named Barbara Johns decided to take action. She fooled the principal into leaving the school for the day and forged notes to the teachers calling an assembly. When the students had all filed into the auditorium, the sixteen-year-old stood on stage, called for a strike, and led a student march to the Prince Edward County Courthouse to protest the shabby state of the school.

The students and their families called a leading civil rights group, the National Association for the Advancement of Colored People (NAACP), which dispatched a team of lawyers. The lawyers explained that local governments run American schools, and there was not much the NAACP could do about the conditions at Moton High School. However, continued the lawyers, they could challenge the entire policy of racial segregation. If the black students went to the same school as the white students, they would probably have a nicer schoolhouse. The NAACP sued the school district, arguing that forcing African Americans into a separate school violated the United States Constitution. The Supreme Court took the case, *Davis v. School Board of Prince Edward County*, bundled it together with two similar cases, and three years after the student strike, delivered one of the most famous court decisions in American history, a ruling known as *Brown v. Board of Education*.

A sixteen-year-old took a bold risk, the Supreme Court unanimously ruled that she was right, and hundreds of laws across many states were struck down for violating the Constitution. The Court ruled that segregated education facilities are inherently unequal and violate the Fourteenth Amendment of the United States Constitution, which declares: "No state shall . . . deny to any person . . . the equal protection of the laws."[1]

Stop and think about the power Americans invest in this document written more than 225 years ago. The Constitution is the owner's manual and rule book for American government. It specifies how the government operates; it

● **The student strikers at Moton High School, led by Barbara Johns.** *They had an enormous impact because civil rights lawyers found a way to place their grievance in the context of the US Constitution (insert). Notice those famous three words, "We the people."*

tells us what the government may do and how it should do it. If you want to learn about any feature of American politics, always check the Constitution first.

Who are we? The answer to that question is always changing, but the Constitution provides the ground rules for those changes. It organizes our political life. The Declaration of Independence declares the ideas behind America. The Constitution takes those ideas and turns them into laws. It creates an institution that can put the ideas into effect. It *institutionalizes* American ideas.

This sounds simple: the Constitution guides the government. But there is a wrinkle. It is often unclear how the Constitution applies to modern questions. After all, it is just 4,400 words written on four pages of parchment over 225 years ago. Many provisions can be read two (or more) different ways; and the document is silent on many topics. As a result, we always have to *interpret* how the Constitution applies to a case today.

Segregation is a prime example. The Constitution did not say anything about racial segregation. Back in 1896, the Supreme Court ruled that segregation did not violate the "equal protection" clause. In 1954, the Court ruled that it did. Different justices in different eras read the same words differently. We constantly debate exactly how to read the words in the Constitution and how to apply them to the questions we face.

The Colonial Roots of the Constitution

No nation in the eighteenth century had anything like the American Constitution. Most nations wrote their governing documents much later; some countries, like England and Israel, never wrote one at all. However, the American Constitution did not spring up from nowhere. Many features of colonial politics propelled the new nation toward its constitution.

- First, the colonies were three thousand miles away from the king and his armies. The authorities back in England debated policies and issued orders; the American colonists frequently ignored them and did what they wished. No one back in London paid much attention. The English policy of ignoring colonies was known as *salutary neglect*; it permitted the colonies to develop their own political institutions. When England started interfering in colonial affairs, the Americans revolted.

BY THE NUMBERS *The Constitution*

Number of articles (or sections) in the US Constitution: **7**

Number of articles in the constitution of India (1950) and the constitution of South Africa (1996), respectively: **395; 244**

Number of times the word *power* or *powers* appears in the US Constitution: **16**

Number of times the word *liberty* appears in the Constitution: **1**

Number of times the word *equality* appears in the Constitution: **0**

Years after the Constitution was written that the 14th Amendment added the idea of equality to the document: **81**

Number of *proposed* amendments to the US Constitution since 1791: **over 10,000**

Number of *successful* amendments since 1791: **17**

Number of amendments to the California State Constitution (as of 2010): **512**

Percentage of the US population that can block a constitutional amendment: **3**

Number of the 13 states that ratified (voted for) the Constitution within six months: **6**

Number of states that initially voted down the Constitution: **2**

Number of delegates in New York, Virginia, and Massachusetts who could have defeated the entire Constitution by switching their votes: **18 (3%)**

Number of words that the Constitution uses to describe and empower Congress: **2,243**

Number of words that the Constitution uses to describe and empower the president: **1,015**

Number of words that the Constitution uses to describe and empower the courts: **364**

- Second, beginning with the Virginia House of Burgesses in 1620, every colony elected its own legislature. As a result, the colonists had a great deal of experience with representation. New settlements demanded seats in the assemblies. New immigrants wanted the right to vote (for example, Polish men went on strike in Virginia over the issue). In some places, like New Jersey, women with property voted. America grew up arguing about representation—and that prepared them for the debate over the Constitution.

- Third, plentiful land created opportunity for ordinary people. It was not an equal society by any means: there were aristocratic families and slaves, prosperous merchants and **indentured servants**. However, by the standards of the time, the New World was a land of extraordinary social mobility. When North Carolina tried to set up titles and social classes, the effort collapsed as ordinary people made their fortunes and soon were wealthier than the would-be lords and dukes. Economic conditions helped foster a republic.

- Fourth, some colonies began with mutual agreements between the settlers, known as **compacts** or **covenants**. The Pilgrims, who landed in Massachusetts in 1620, introduced the idea; before they went ashore all forty-one adult males signed a mutual agreement known as the Mayflower Compact (named after their vessel, the *Mayflower*). In most nations, the right to rule stretched back through history and was based on tradition and military force. In contrast, the individuals on the *Mayflower* deliberately formed a new society, based on their mutual agreement and consent. Many New England communities would begin with such compacts or covenants—rough, often religiously inspired forerunners of a constitution. In fact, the preamble to the US Constitution would take the same form as the New England covenants.

● *The Mayflower Compact. The settlers agree among themselves to enter into a "civic body politic"—a government. The authority of their government rose from their own agreement—signed only by men.*

- Fifth, many colonists came to the New World in order to practice their religion in peace. Across the colonies, different religions flourished: Calvinists in Boston, Quakers in Philadelphia, Catholics in Baltimore, Anglicans in Virginia, and an unusually rich religious diversity in Savannah, Georgia, which was home to Anglicans, Lutherans, and Jews, among others. All these different faiths did not always live in harmony; the Massachusetts Puritans hung Quaker missionaries who had sailed there from Philadelphia—and never mind what they thought of Catholics. But, beginning in Rhode Island in 1636, a revolutionary idea began to emerge: the individual's freedom to practice religion without government interference. In some colonies, it was followed by other rights, like freedom of speech and freedom of the press. The rights of citizens would become the single greatest issue in the debate over whether to accept (to ratify) the new constitution.

- Sixth, border areas were violent and insecure. Brutal wars with the Native Americans marked many of the colonies. The French claimed land to the north and west, the Spanish to the south and west. Colonists also constantly fought one another over their own boundaries. After the break with England, insecure borders helped inspire the colonists to adopt a strong central government.

Each colony governed itself in its own way. However, the six features described here—distance from English authority, representation, social mobility, covenants, individual rights, and violent borders—all propelled Americans toward the Constitution of 1787.

Why the Colonists Revolted

The roots of the American Revolution lie in a great English victory. Centuries of rivalry between England and France burst into war in 1754. Known as the French and Indian War, the conflict spread through the colonies from Virginia all the way to Canada. Colonial American militias fought side by side with the British army and defeated the French in 1763. Thirteen years later the colonists declared independence and turned their muskets on the English.

Why did the Americans suddenly revolt? Because the victory over France introduced two fateful changes. First, ten thousand English troops remained in the colonies to protect the newly won land. The existence of those "Redcoats" meant that England could now enforce its policies: the days of salutary neglect were over. Second, the English had run up a crushing debt during the ten years of war and decided that their colonists should help pay it. Americans' reaction was explosive.

The Colonial Complaint: Representation

It was not just Britain's demand for money that provoked the colonists. Americans had grown used to making their own decisions through their elected assemblies. When the English imposed new taxes, without the approval of the colonial assemblies in the thirteen colonies, they violated the colonial idea of self-rule. This was an unusual revolution. Most revolutionaries rise up against regimes that have long repressed them. In contrast, the Americans fought to preserve rights that they had been exercising during the many years of happy neglect.

Beneath the conflict lay a deep philosophical difference about representative democracy. The colonists considered their assemblies the legitimate voice of the people; if taxes had to be raised, they were the ones to do it. Colonial assemblies were very responsive to the voters and their daily concerns—they worried about things like building roads and surveying new lands. Political theorists call the colonial view **delegate representation**.

Delegate representation: When representatives follow expressed wishes of the voters.

The British never understood this view of representation, because they operated with an entirely different one. Unlike the colonists, the English did not change their election districts every time the population shifted. The election districts in England had not been changed in more than a century. Bustling new cities like Birmingham and Manchester had no representatives, while sleepy country villages had more than one. However, this arrangement did not pose a problem for the English because their elected officials were expected to pursue the good of the whole nation. Your representative is not an "agent" or an "advocate," argued English statesman Edmund Burke, but a Member of Parliament who must be guided by "the general good."[2] This English view of representation is known as **trustee representation**.

Trustee representation: Representatives do what they regard as the best interest of the voters—regardless of what the voters might wish for.

The Conflict Begins with Blood on the Frontier

After the French and Indian War, settlers poured westward (Figures 2.1 and 2.2). Native Americans fought back; they rallied around Chief Pontiac and overran colonial settlements and English forts in Virginia, Maryland, and Pennsylvania. To end the fighting, England closed the border and prohibited settlers from going westward, past the crests of the lengthy Appalachian Mountain chain. The colonists were stunned. The arbitrary boundary, announced in the Proclamation of 1763, had been drawn amid lobbying by land speculators, who could make or lose fortunes depending on whether their own land was open to settlement. The proclamation threatened the westward thrust that spelled opportunity to the restless colonists. American settlers did not care about Native American rights to the land. As they saw it, a corrupt English monarchy was blocking American pioneers from settling the wide-open spaces that they had helped win from France.

The colonists responded in their traditional way—they ignored regulations that did not suit them. But now there was a British army in America, enabling the

● **Figures 2.1 and 2.2** *The colonies before (left) and after (right) the French and Indian War. Spain lost Florida but gained the land west of the Mississippi in compensation for having supported France. Napoleon would grab it back from Spain and then, in 1803, sell it to the United States. Note the line formed by the Proclamation of 1763 on the map on the right. England tried to forbid settlers from crossing that line.*

English to enforce their policies. The Proclamation of 1763 was followed by the Quartering Act (1765), which required colonial assemblies to house British troops in empty barns and warehouses. Suddenly, the Redcoats began to feel like an occupying army.

Britain also began to enforce its **mercantile** trade policies, which meant American ships had to bypass their traditional (and lucrative) partners and do business only with English colonies at worse prices. Colonists who ignored the decree were charged with smuggling; wealthy merchants suddenly faced imprisonment or large fines for trading with French colonies. To make matters even worse, the English introduced taxes to help support their army of redcoats. These widely reviled duties culminated in the Stamp Tax of 1765.

Mercantilism: An economic theory in which government controls foreign trade in order to maintain prosperity and security.

The Stamp Tax and the First Hints of Independence

Stamp taxes were a common way to raise money in England, but the effort to impose one on the colonies set off a firestorm. Parliament ignored the colonial assemblies (violating colonial ideas of representation) and simply declared the tax. Colonists responded with a Stamp Act Congress that met in October 1765. Delegates from nine colonies sent a protest to the king and to Parliament. The English policies were pushing the colonists into working together. In fact, the name *Stamp Act Congress* may have been more alarming to the English authorities than the petition the body drafted. In the eighteenth century, the word *congress* meant a diplomatic assembly of representatives from independent nations. The very name of this meeting intimated independence.

Protests against the stamp tax spread through the colonies. Mobs hung, burned, and beheaded tax collectors in effigy. They attacked tax collectors' offices and homes. Across the sea, the English authorities were incredulous about the violence. All they could see were ungrateful colonists who refused to pay for their own protection.[3]

The Townshend Acts Worsen the Conflict

After an alarmed Parliament reluctantly lifted the stamp taxes, colonists celebrated the repeal and tensions eased—until Parliament followed up with a set of Townshend Acts in 1767. These acts instituted another round of new taxes; revenues were earmarked to pay a new colonial authority, the American Board of Customs, which would collect taxes independently of the colonial assemblies. Now an imperial bureaucracy was explicitly pushing aside the colonial assemblies. The Townshend Acts suspended the New York State Assembly for refusing to house and supply British troops.

Once again, American colonists responded with meetings, petitions, and mobs. Bostonians seethed with anger over having their legislature closed. Mobs harassed the customs officials, who found it impossible to carry out their duties and called for help. A British warship arrived and officials seized a vessel owned by John Hancock, one of the resistance leaders, and charged him with smuggling. That move set off riots, bringing British troops into the city to restore order. Before long, there were almost four thousand Redcoats in a city of fifteen thousand people. The mobs harassed the soldiers with taunts, rocks, and snowballs until, on March 5, 1770, one detachment of Redcoats panicked and fired point-blank on the crowd.

The Boston Massacre, as it quickly became known, left five civilians dead. The first to fall was a sailor named Crispus Attucks, the son of an African slave and a Natick Indian. Attucks himself is thought to have escaped slavery some twenty years earlier. Ironically, the son of two groups who would not be liberated by the revolution—an African slave and an American Indian—was the first to bleed for the cause. Paul Revere memorialized the massacre with an engraving that transformed the panicky soldiers threatened by a mob into a line of killers firing into a heroic cluster of civilians. Historian Gordon Wood has called the engraving "perhaps the most famous piece of anti-military propaganda in American history."[4]

English policy was in shambles; colonists' anger at a fever pitch. At the start of the crisis, six years

● An engraving of the Boston Massacre done by Paul Revere. This version of the event makes the British look like cold-blooded killers—not historically accurate but powerful propaganda for independence.

earlier, colonial leaders were respectfully petitioning the king to rescind imperial policies. Now, blood had been shed and the colonists began to talk about rebellion.

The Boston Tea Party

British repealed all the Townshend duties except a tariff on tea. Tea was a global industry in 1773; think of it as the must-have Apple product of the eighteenth century. But the East India Tea company, which had a monopoly in England, was on the verge of bankruptcy. In 1773, Parliament tried to rescue the company by granting it a monopoly on tea in the New World. Many colonial shippers would be shut out by this rival trading network.

When ships with East India tea arrived, mobs in Philadelphia and New York forced them to sail away without unloading their cargo. In Boston, however, Governor Thomas Hutchinson would not permit such nonsense. He insisted that the three ships in Boston Harbor would not leave until their tea was safely delivered. On a dark December night, about fifty men blackened their faces, some "dressed in the Indian manner," and boarded one of the ships. They hefted 342 chests of tea onto the deck, bashed them open with hatchets, and dumped the contents—worth a fortune of about £90,000 (between $1 million and $3 million today)—into Boston Harbor.[5]

Revolution!

British leaders were furious. Past insubordination paled next to this direct economic hit on a struggling British company. They first demanded compensation; when a Boston town meeting voted that down, the English introduced what colonists dubbed the Intolerable Acts. The laws closed Boston Harbor until the tea was paid for, abolished town meetings, authorized the quartering of troops in any home in Massachusetts, and essentially put the state under military control. King George himself put it bluntly: "The colonists must either triumph or submit."

Americans were not going to submit. Instead, twelve colonies sent representatives to the **First Continental Congress** in September 1774. The Congress petitioned for an end to the Intolerable Acts, called for a boycott on British goods, and asserted colonial rights to "life, liberty, and property." They agreed to meet again in May 1775.

Before the Continental Congress reconvened, fighting had begun. In April 1775, the British commander in Boston, General Thomas Gage, sent one thousand troops out from Boston to seize guns and ammunition stored at Concord, Massachusetts. Armed colonists who called themselves "minutemen" blocked the way and took British fire at Lexington and Concord. Eight were shot dead. The British found and destroyed the weapons, but their march back to Boston was horrific. Minutemen hid behind rocks and trees and sniped at them all along the way. By the time the English army limped back into the city, they had lost three hundred men.

First Continental Congress: A convention of delegates, from twelve of the thirteen colonies, that met in 1774.

THE BOTTOM LINE

- For over a century, royal governors negotiated with American colonists through their elected assemblies. After the French and Indian War, the English bypassed the colonial legislatures and imposed new rules and taxes.
- These actions violated traditional colonial rights and exposed two different ideas of representation—*delegate representation* in America (representatives respond to their constituents' desires) and *trustee representation* in England (representatives do what they consider best for all, regardless of constituent demands).
- English action also harmed colonial economic interests. The conflict very quickly escalated.
- Americans fought an unusual revolution: rather than demanding new rights, they were trying to preserve rights and economic interests they had long been exercising.

The Declaration of Independence

Second Continental Congress: A convention of delegates from thirteen colonies, which became the acting national government for the duration of the Revolutionary War.

The **Second Continental Congress**, which met in May 1775, faced the job of declaring independence, mobilizing an army, organizing a government, and rallying thirteen very different colonies around a single cause. A year later, on July 4, 1776, the Congress voted to adopt a Declaration of Independence as a statement to the world of America's purpose. The document has two parts: a statement of principles and a list of grievances. (The full document is reprinted in Appendix 1.)

The Principle: "We Hold These Truths . . ."

In one elegant paragraph the Declaration of Independence distills America's political philosophy into five towering ideals:

- All people are equal.
- They are endowed with rights that cannot be taken away.
- These rights include life, liberty, and the pursuit of happiness.
- People form governments to protect those rights.
- Governments derive their just powers from the consent of the governed.

These ideas were not new. Political philosophers, especially the English thinker John Locke, had used very similar language. In his *Two Treatises on Government*, published more than a century earlier, Locke had argued that in a natural state, there are no rules. Life is ruled by force and violence. To secure a measure of safety and freedom, people contract with one another, enter into civil society, and form a government that can protect one another's life, liberty, and property.

As a statement of governing ideals, the Declaration of Independence was—and to this day, still is—breathtaking. In 1776, it was also a far cry from reality. Thomas Jefferson, who drafted much of the document, was a slaveowner. The Declaration essentially invites future cruelty when it refers to "merciless Indian savages." Its authors did not live up to their noble sentiments. We do not fully live up to them today. Even so, it stands as the great statement of American idealism—something every generation can fight for.

Grievances

The second part of the Declaration lists twenty-seven grievances against King George III. These tell us what the American colonists cared about as they began the revolution. Three complaints dominate the list:

- *Violations of the right of representation.* This complaint comes up in ten of the twenty-seven charges against England. It is by far the most intensely felt grievance described in the Declaration.

- *Maintenance of a standing army not under civilian control.* In particular, British soldiers acted in peacetime without consent of American legislatures. Five complaints are about the British military.

- *Loss of an independent court.* This violation of traditional justice comes up six times.

Today the Revolution is often boiled down to the colonists' slogan "No taxation without representation." The Declaration emphasized *representation* much more than taxation; taxes did not show up until way down the list, as grievance number 17 ("Imposing taxes on us without our consent").

THE BOTTOM LINE

- The Declaration of Independence asserted philosophical ideals as the basis of the new American government.
- The first part of the Declaration features five ideals that sum up the nation's political principles.
- The second part of the Declaration lists twenty-seven grievances that led to the break.

● The First American Government: The Articles of Confederation

When the United States declared its independence, it linked the thirteen former colonies—now states—into a **confederation**, or *alliance of independent states.* Although this first American government lasted only a little more than a decade, it taught the new nation valuable lessons about effective government.

Confederation: A group of independent states of nations that yield some of their powers to a national government, although each state retains a degree of sovereign authority.

Table 2.1 The Declaration of Independence and America's Enduring Ideas

HOW DOES THE DECLARATION OF INDEPENDENCE REFLECT THE KEY AMERICAN IDEAS DISCUSSED IN CHAPTER 1?
Liberty. The Declaration asserts that liberty is an "unalienable right" (meaning that no one can take it away), endowed to all people by their Creator.
Self-rule. The right of representation is one of the Declaration's central themes: it contends that governments derive "their just powers from the consent of the governed." Ten of the twenty-seven grievances charged against the king directly address the issue of self-rule.
Limited government. The idea of limited government got more space than any other in both the Declaration and the Constitution. Most of the Declaration recites the ways King George III overstepped his "just powers." Eleven years later, the Constitution would carefully limit the powers given to the federal government.
Individualism. "Governments are instituted among men . . . to secure [the] rights" with which the Creator has endowed each individual. These include "life, liberty and the pursuit of happiness." Here is the cornerstone of American individualism. At the same time, the Declaration also talks about "one people" and "the people"—collective ideas that have to be balanced with individualism. Recall the great American debate: How do we balance individualism and communalism? The Declaration emphasizes both.
The American dream. The Declaration of Independence promises the pursuit of happiness. What does this mean? The line is borrowed from John Locke, who wrote that governments are instituted to protect "life, liberty, and *property.*" Jefferson, in his first draft of the Declaration, changed "property" to "happiness." But right from the start, "the pursuit of happiness"—what we now call the American dream—has often been cast as the pursuit of wealth. The emphasis on property is one of the things that make the United States distinctive.
Equality. This idea seems clear enough: since "all men are created equal," they all have the same rights to life, liberty, and the pursuit of happiness. But how much equality ensures "the pursuit of happiness"? Do we as a society need to feed the hungry and clothe the poor to ensure that everyone has an equal shot at the pursuit of happiness? This remains a controversial matter.
Faith in God. The words "the Creator" appear right at the start of the Declaration. But religion soon became controversial. Thomas Jefferson, who drafted the Declaration, was not a religious man. (As a Deist, he thought that God did not interfere in human affairs.) Jefferson later ignited a controversy during his presidency, when he refused to call national days of prayer as George Washington had. Instead, Jefferson argued that there must be "a wall of separation between church and state." But Jefferson's wall raises as many questions as it resolves, as debates and court cases have attested for generations.

The National Government

The Continental Congress approved its first constitution, called the Articles of Confederation, in November 1777. The document, which reflected Americans' recent experience with England, kept the national government weak and dependent on the states. The Articles named the new nation the United States of America and described the central government as "a league of friendship" among states: "each . . . retains its sovereignty, freedom and independence, and every power, jurisdiction and right." In a sign of what was to come, Congress had to wait more than three years to get approval from all thirteen states for the Articles of Confederation.

Central government power was placed in a Congress whose members were selected and paid for by the states. There was no chief executive (the states would implement the laws), no central authority to tax (all revenues would come from state governments), and no central power to muster an army (the states supplied the troops). Each state had a single vote in Congress. Important matters required the vote of nine states. Any changes to the Articles of Confederation required the agreement of all thirteen states. Today, we call such extra-large majorities **supermajorities**. It was a very weak central government.

Some Success . . .

Americans had good reason to be proud of their new government. Power remained close to the people. The new government overcame incredible odds and, by April 1783, had defeated the most powerful military force in the world. The population grew rapidly in the 1780s—the fastest rise of any decade in American history. After a brief postwar recession, the economy also expanded. Americans were democratic and prosperous.

The Continental Congress also won a major policy success when it stopped the squabbling among states claiming western land. Instead, the Northwest Ordinance of 1787 established a process through which individuals could buy western lands: when an area attracted a minimum number of settlers, it could apply to be a state with all the same powers and privileges as the existing states. With this act, the United States established its mechanism for western expansion and political development.

. . . And Some Problems

But four major problems plagued the new American government.

First, Congress could not raise taxes and had no money of its own. The states were reluctant to provide funds. The Confederation Congress had trouble supplying (much less paying) the army throughout the Revolutionary War.

Second, requiring unanimity made it impossible to amend the Articles. When Congress tried to fix its financial problems by levying a 5 percent tax on imported goods, twelve of the states agreed. However, Rhode Island's legislature denounced the proposal as "the yoke of tyranny fixed on all the states."[6] When loans from France and Holland came due, there was no way to pay them. Again, many leaders drew a lesson: *a vigorous national government needed a stable source of revenue.*

Supermajority: An amount higher than a simple (50% plus one) majority—three-fifths or two-thirds are typical requirements in order for a proposal to be adopted.

● *A series of legends have grown up around Molly Pitcher, whose real name was Mary Ludwig Hays McCauley. The most famous has her stepping in to take the place of her fallen husband at the cannon during the Battle of Monmouth. The stories are most likely a composite of descriptions of many women who fought with the American army.*

● *Captain Daniel Shays led a rebellion in protest of farm foreclosures in 1786. This engraving depicts a scuffle between one of Shays's men and an official of the courthouse in Springfield, Massachusetts—one of six courthouses that the rebels captured.*

Third, state governments were dominated by their legislatures without any checks and balances. The result was too often bias and even chaos. Legislatures wrote (and repealed) laws to benefit individuals. Leaders eventually drew an important lesson: *different sources of government power should balance one another; governors should balance legislatures, the central government should balance the states.*

Fourth, the weak national government had a difficult time standing up to foreign powers. Americans drew an obvious conclusion: *a weak central government left the nation vulnerable.*

One event, Shays's Rebellion, dramatized the problems of government under the Articles. Captain Daniel Shays, a veteran of the Revolutionary War, led a rebellion that broke out in western Massachusetts in August 1786 and spread across the state. Thousands of farmers, protesting high taxes and interest rates, took up their muskets and shut down courthouses to stop foreclosures on their farms. When Governor James Bowden summoned the local militia to defend the Worcester courthouse, members refused; some joined the rebellion. Finally, Bowden hired an army and broke the rebellion. Shays's sympathizers shifted strategy: they won several seats in the legislature the following year and legislated the debt relief that the farmers had been fighting for.[7]

Winner and Losers

For many national leaders, Shays's Rebellion was the last straw. Under the Articles of Confederation, neither the national government nor an individual state was strong enough to protect public property (like courthouses) or private property (the repayment of loans). They set out to build a stronger government.

Others defended state governments under the Articles. Problems like Shays's Rebellion, they argued, were simply the growing pains of a more democratic government. The Articles of Confederation reflected the people and their desires. They set out to build a stronger government.

America faced a choice. Would it have a weak but democratic alliance under the Articles of Confederation? Or would it adopt a new, more powerful central government, more distant from the people, and capable of projecting power across the continent—and beyond? Shays's Rebellion pushed the most influential men in the colonies to write a new constitution.

The First Step: Annapolis Convention

Alarmed by spreading chaos, the Continental Congress called for a national meeting in Annapolis to impose order on commerce among the states. Only twelve delegates from five states showed up—not enough to do official business. With Shays's Rebellion raging, the delegates requested each state to appoint representatives to meet in Philadelphia the following May, in 1787, to devise such "provisions as should appear to them necessary to render the constitution of the federal government adequate to the exigencies of the union." That may not sound earthshaking, but the twelve delegates in Annapolis had quietly authorized a convention that would write an entirely new constitution.

● *George Washington posed for this portrait in Philadelphia during the convention. Washington presided over the convention and brought his enormous prestige to the effort. In the background is William Lee, a slave who served as Washington's personal attendant throughout the Revolutionary War and after. When former military officers visited Washington, they often stopped in to see this old comrade as well.*

Secrecy

Spring 1787 arrived cold and blustery, delaying many of the delegates on their way to Philadelphia. On the first day, the delegates unanimously elected George Washington to chair the convention. Then they agreed on a controversial rule: the deliberations would be completely secret. Guards were placed at the doors. Windows were shut and remained closed, even after the Philadelphia summer turned stifling. George Washington made only three comments during the convention—and one was to rebuke an unknown delegate who had carelessly dropped a copy of proposed resolutions. Most of what we know about the convention comes from James Madison himself, who took a seat at the front of the room and kept meticulous notes.

Was it a good idea to impose secrecy? The young republic had only recently opened up its political process to the people. Thomas Jefferson called

Your Advice Is Needed

If you could go back and offer advice to American leaders in 1787, what would you tell them?

Yes, stick with the Articles of Confederation and give the current system more time. It is weak and at times chaotic. But this balanced arrangement is also very democratic and reflects popular wishes for self-government. It does not rely on a distant national government to make and impose policies. America is best off with small, local, democratic governments. That means it will not be a world power—but preserving democracy makes this a good trade-off.

No, build a new central government. Leaders will be less responsive to the public on day-to-day matters. However, the nation will be more stable, more powerful, and more secure. The government, while less democratic, will be more efficient.

I am divided about this. Of course, at the time, the colonists voted no—but it was a close call, as you will see. Since Americans were quite evenly divided, it is useful to think about where you would have stood. It helps clarify the political values you care about most.

the decision to close the convention "an abominable precedent." In a republic, he argued, the people should always know what their leaders are doing.[8]

However, the delegates wanted to speak their minds freely without worrying about how their words would appear in the newspapers. Many also believed that powerful politicians in their home states would withdraw their delegation as soon as they heard that the convention was debating an entirely new constitution. Without secrecy, they might have to abandon their bold plan and simply amend the Articles of Confederation—which was, after all, what they had been asked to do.

THE BOTTOM LINE
- Under the Articles of Confederation, thirteen independent states bound themselves into a confederation with a weak central government that had to rely on the states to implement its decisions.
- Though feeble, this first United States government was, by the standards of the time, a very democratic one.
- Delegates to the Constitutional Convention convened to fix the problems with the Articles of Confederation but chose to go much further and propose a new American government.

The Constitutional Convention

As they thought about reorganizing their new government, American leaders balanced the two political dangers they had recently encountered.

- British officials' behavior warned them that a powerful central government could strip the people of their rights.

- Experience with the Articles of Confederation warned them that a weak government could fail to protect their rights.

The delegates debated from May into September. They touched on almost every aspect of government, ranging from how to elect the legislature to what to do about slavery. Throughout the discussions, six major themes dominated their attention.

1. How Much Power to the People?

The delegates faced a dilemma. They wanted their government to answer to the public; that was why they had fought the revolution. Recent experience, however, also made them fear a system that responded too readily to the people (or, more precisely, white men with property). The delegates wished to represent the public through better-educated, wealthier, and more experienced leaders—men like themselves.

Over the course of the convention, the delegates developed a view of representation that Madison called *filtration*, or *indirect elections*: the public would vote for men (and later women) who would, in turn, vote for public officials. Delegate speeches during the Convention's first days are a bit shocking to the contemporary reader. The delegates were making the public *less* involved in government than they had been in the eleven years since the United States declared its independence. The new Constitution would permit the public to vote for only one federal office—members of the House of Representatives.

What Do You Think?

Was Delegate Secrecy Warranted?

How would you have voted on the question of secrecy if you were in Philadelphia?

Yes! Without secrecy the delegates could never have spoken their minds, fearing negative press reports. And many delegations would have been recalled—killing the entire constitutional project before it got off the ground.

No! I am with Jefferson. Secrecy was an elitist, undemocratic principle. In the long run, decisions are better when the public can see and comment.

● *Over time, common men began voting in American elections. This painting by George Caleb Bingham, ironically titled* The Verdict of the People, *shows the raucous results.*

The debate about public involvement did not end with the Constitution. Over time, Americans would get a more active role in their governance. Citizens would win more control over electing presidents (beginning in the 1820s with voting reforms on the state level); they started voting directly for senators (with the Seventeenth Amendment in 1913). The "public" would also expand to include all women (with the Nineteenth Amendment in 1920) and African Americans (who won the legal right to vote with the Fifteenth Amendment, ratified in 1870 and finally guaranteed by the Voting Rights Act in 1965). Younger Americans (eighteen- to twenty-year-olds) won the right to vote in 1971.

The debate that began at the Constitutional Convention continues to this day. It animates one of the key ideas we discussed in Chapter 1: self-rule, balanced between direct democracy and indirect representation. At a still more fundamental level, the debate speaks to one of the great questions of American politics: *Who governs?* Public involvement in government has grown dramatically over the centuries, but Madison's principle of filtration still keeps the people at arm's length from their government in many areas.

2. National Government Versus State Government

The Articles of Confederation left most power with the states. Madison's plan for the new government took that power and vested it in a strong national government. The very first motion that the delegates debated called for "a national government . . . consisting of a *supreme* legislature, executive, and judiciary."[9]

Many delegates disagreed with this dramatic change. They believed that state and local governments were closer to the people and could more accurately reflect public sentiments—precisely what Madison was trying to avoid. Some pro-states' rights delegates walked out of the convention, and others refused to sign the final document. Two of the three delegates from New York left; once they were gone, New York lost its quorum and could not vote for the rest of the convention. Since Rhode Island had refused to participate, the convention was now down to just eleven of the thirteen states.

In the end, the delegates compromised on a system that included both national and state power. The federal government took over many functions— but far fewer than Madison had originally proposed. The states kept many duties—but far fewer than the state advocates would have liked. This mixed system, with a stronger national government that nevertheless leaves considerable power with the state governments, is called **federalism** (and we'll discuss it in Chapter 3).

The debate about how to balance national government power and state power began on May 30, 1787, and continues to the present day. At the convention, that debate got tangled up with another issue: dividing power among more and less populous states.

Federalism: Power divided between national and state government. Each has its own independent authority and its own duties.

3. Big States Versus Small States

Another intense dispute at the Constitutional Convention revolved around a division we rarely think about today: the large states (led by Virginia and Pennsylvania) versus the small states (led by New Jersey and Delaware). Debate turned on how to apportion power in the national government. Large states argued that representation should be based on population; small states wanted each state to have an equal voice. That debate led to two different plans, one put forward by Virginia (a big state) and the other by New Jersey (on behalf of the small states).

The Virginia Plan   Large and small states squared off early in the convention, when Governor Edmund Randolph of Virginia presented Madison's original plan for the Constitution. A powerful speaker, Randolph addressed the delegates for four hours. The plan, which became known as the **Virginia Plan**, had five key points.

The Virginia Plan: Madison's plan, embraced by Constitutional Convention delegates from larger states; strengthened the national government relative to state governments.

1. Congress would have two chambers, a form known as a **bicameral** legislature, with representation in both chambers based on state population.
2. Citizens would vote for members of the House of Representatives. The House of Representatives would, in turn, vote for senators from a list of candidates provided by the state legislatures. This limited the states' role and is an example of filtration, or indirect elections.
3. Congress would elect the president. Here the Virginia Plan suddenly turned vague and did not specify whether the president would be one

Bicameral: Having two legislative houses or chambers—like the House and the Senate.

man or a committee; nor did it say how long the executive would serve. Madison told George Washington that he had not made up his mind.

4. A national judiciary with one or more supreme courts would be established and the judges would have life tenure.

5. Congress would have broad powers to legislate in all cases where the states were "incompetent." A "council of revision" made up of the president and the Supreme Court would have the authority to review and nullify any state law.

Delegates who had not already been briefed by Madison were stunned. Randolph was urging them to build a robust national government. The Virginia Plan empowered Congress to "call forth the force of the union" against any state "failing to fulfill its duties" under the new constitution. The federal government could strike down state laws.

Delegates from less-populated states. Smaller states like New Jersey lamented that they would soon "be swallowed up." Each state had "its peculiar habits, usages, and manners," small-state advocates insisted, and these must be protected. Under Madison's plan, three states (Virginia, Pennsylvania, and Massachusetts) would have enough members in Congress to form a majority all by themselves. Representatives from the smaller states repeatedly threatened to walk out of the convention.[10]

Big-state representatives (and those who favored a strong national union) insisted that the government should reflect the people, who would vote for the House which, in turn, would choose Senators. What kind of representation would allow 128,000 people in Rhode Island and Delaware to outvote the 747,000 residents of Virginia?

The New Jersey Plan.   The small states eventually pushed back with their own plan, introduced by William Paterson of New Jersey and known as the **New Jersey Plan**. Rather than construct a new national government, this plan focused on strengthening the Articles of Confederation. It had four key points:

1. Congress would have only one chamber, a form known as a **unicameral** legislature. Each state would have one vote in Congress, regardless of its size—exactly the same as in the Articles. However, congressional acts would be the supreme law of the land, making the new constitution stronger than the Articles of Confederation.

2. Congress would elect a committee to serve as federal executive for one term only.

3. The executive committee would select a supreme court, which would be responsible for foreign policy, economic policy, and impeachment of federal officials.

The New Jersey Plan: Put forward at the convention by the small states, it left most government authority with the state governments.

Unicameral: Having a single legislative house or chamber.

● *The last day of the Constitutional Convention. In this romanticized image, George Washington presents the Constitution to the delegates.*

4. The national government could tax the states and would have the exclusive right to tax imports.

The New Jersey Plan left the states at the center of American government but took a step toward union by building a stronger national government that could raise its own taxes and exercise more authority over interstate commerce. When the vote was called, only three states supported the New Jersey Plan.

The Connecticut Compromise. Convention delegates decisively approved the Virginia Plan's bicameral Congress with a House and a Senate. They voted for a House of Representatives based on population. Then debate turned to the Senate. If the delegates voted with the Virginia Plan—that is, the House of Representatives would vote for senators—the big states would essentially win the debate. Tempers grew short. "I do not, Gentlemen, trust you," declared Gunning Bedford of Maryland. He hinted darkly that the small states would look for foreign allies if they lost this vote. William Paterson announced that he would rather "submit to a monarch, a despot," than accept the Virginia Plan.[11]

Big states seemed to have the votes to win the Virginia Plan's version of Senate elections. In fact, it looked as though they would win seven states. But when the roll was called, on July 2, one big-state supporter from Maryland and two from Georgia slipped out of the convention hall. With their exits, both states shifted and the vote came out a tie: five states for the Virginia Plan, five against, and one evenly split.

To break the deadlock, the delegates formed a committee, tilted toward small states. It came up with a compromise, brokered by Roger Sherman of

Connecticut and therefore known as the Connecticut Compromise. The House would be based on population; the Senate would have two representatives for each state, chosen by the state legislature. (Americans did not vote directly for their senators in all states until 1913.) Since legislation had to pass through both houses, the public and the states would each have a say. Because the delegates wanted power over taxes and spending to be in the people's hands, they required that all finance-related bills had to be introduced first in the House.

The compromise squeaked through—five states voted "yes," four "no," and one split. The big states won the House of Representatives; the small states got their way in the Senate. The compromise continues to confer on rural states a great deal of clout in the Senate—and, since all legislation requires approval from both houses, in Congress.

More immediately, the Constitution had its legislature. Two difficult issues, however, remained—the power of the president and the agonizing question of slavery.

4. The President

Delegates, including the master planner James Madison, arrived at the convention without a clear design for the presidency—also known as the *executive authority* since it *executes* (or puts into effect) the laws. The delegates even wavered about whether executive authority should be placed in one individual or a committee.

Committee or Individual?   Many delegates worried that a single executive would grow too powerful. Madison and his allies, however, feared that the Connecticut Compromise opened the Senate door to the same petty state politics that had wrecked the Articles of Confederation. They therefore decided that the president should be one individual, independent of Congress, who could represent the public. After much back-and-forth, they settled on a four-year term and permitted reelections.

Arguments about the presidency never got very heated. Why? Because every delegate in the room knew exactly who the first president was going to be. There sat George Washington, calmly presiding over the convention. Knowing that Washington would almost certainly be thrust into the role of president cooled the temperatures in the room.

The Electoral College.   How would the United States choose the president? The Constitution's framers saw a problem with every option. They did not think the people had enough information or wisdom. They did not trust state legislators to put aside their own narrow concerns and think about the national interest. Delegates from the big states no longer wanted to give Congress the job, now that state legislators were picking the senators. What could they do? In response, they came up with the most complicated rigmarole in the Constitution: the **Electoral College**. Each state would select individuals

Electoral College: The system established by the Constitution to elect the president; each state has a number of electors (equal to the size of its congressional delegation in House and Senate); the public in each state votes for electors who then vote for the president.

Electoral College Map

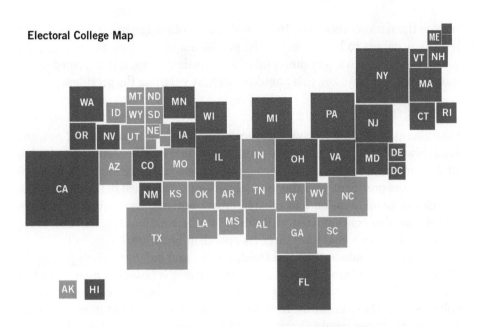

● **Figure 2.3** *Electoral College map for the 2012 presidential election. The size of each state is distorted to emphasize its share of electoral votes.*

known as *electors*—the delegates hoped that the electors would be well-known individuals with sound judgment; the electors would then choose a president.

How many electors per state? Another compromise: each state would have the same number of electors as it had members of Congress. That meant a state's population would matter (given proportional representation in the House) but also that every state was assured of two more votes (as in the Senate). If no individual received a majority of electoral votes—which last happened in 1824—the House of Representatives would choose from among the five candidates with the most votes. They would vote by state, and each state would get just one vote—again, a concession to small states.

Who would elect the electors? The convention simply left this question to the states. At first, the state legislatures got the job of voting for the electors. But by the late 1820s the states ceded this right to the people (again, white men, although now they did not need to own any property). The people voted state by state for their electors—as we still do.

Today, all the electors in a state generally cast their votes for the candidate who won the state (although only 26 states require them to do so) (Figure 2.3). The system has elected four men who lost the popular vote—but won in the Electoral College.

The President: Too Strong or Too Weak? All these details can obscure a crucial fact about the Constitution and the presidency. The delegates arrived less certain about this office than any other. Some feared putting too much power in one person's hands. The abuses of King George were fresh in their minds. Others recognized the need for a firm national leader who could energetically pursue the nation's interests. In the end, they built a general framework and left many details to be defined by the presidents themselves. Sometimes, the presidency has been a very powerful office. At other times, it has seemed perilously weak. We'll explore this paradox when we examine the presidency.

5. Separation of Powers

One idea that evolved during the convention was the separation of powers. Each branch of government—the president, Congress, the Court—has its job to do: the delegates vested "all legislative powers" in Congress, the executive power in the president, and the judicial power (to try cases) in the courts. The Articles of Confederation had created only a national legislature; in Britain power was also concentrated in Parliament, their national legislature. Now, the United States would have three independent branches.

The framers added a crucial twist: checks and balances. *Each power the Constitution grants to Congress or the presidency is balanced by a "countervailing" or checking power assigned to the other branch.* Each branch is involved in the others' business. In this way, as Madison later put it, one branch's ambition for power would always check the other branches' ambitions.

For example, Congress passes legislation but needs the president to sign a bill into law. The president can veto (reject) the bill (checking Congress); Congress can override the veto by a two-thirds vote of both chambers (balancing the president).

The president is commander in chief, but the Constitution gives Congress the power to declare war and set the military's budget. The president negotiates treaties, but the Senate must ratify them by two-thirds vote. The president appoints ministers and Supreme Court justices, but Congress must approve (or confirm). Congress holds the ultimate power over all federal officers. The House can impeach (or formally accuse) the president or any other officer in the executive or judicial branch of "Treason, Bribery or other high Crimes and Misdemeanors"; the Senate looks into the accusation and decides whether to actually remove the person from office. What is a "high crime and misdemeanor"? Well, as they have never been fully defined, Congress must use its judgment.

These checks and balances are one of the most distinctive features of the American Constitution. The French political philosopher Montesquieu wrote an influential treatise, *The Spirit of the Laws* (published in 1748), which argued that to avoid tyranny, the executive, legislative, and judicial functions of government must be separated from one another—and never placed in a single individual or body. However, very few governments have ever developed this principle as fully as the United States Constitution did.

In fact, the feature grew more pronounced as the convention debates went on. Neither the Virginia nor the New Jersey Plan had anywhere near as many checks and balances as the final Constitution. Moreover, these limits on authority would continue to develop over time. One dramatic example occurred, in 1803, when the Supreme Court asserted one of the greatest checks of all: the authority to strike down acts of Congress or the president as unconstitutional.

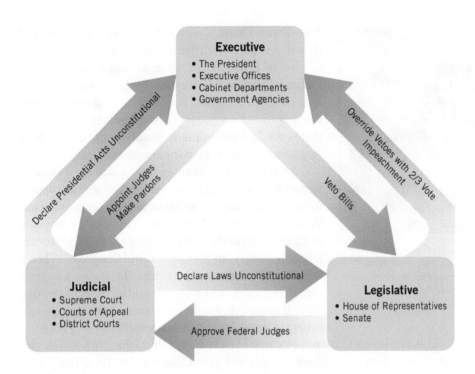

● **Figure 2.4** *Separation of powers—the checks on the federal level. Multiply them across all three levels and a vital question of American politics arises: Is this chaotic and fragmented state ready to govern effectively? We've been posing the question since 1787.*

The Constitution itself was silent on whether the Court had such authority. In Chapter 13, we will see how the Court shrewdly managed to claim authority despite the constitutional silence.

Checks and balances continue to spark disagreement in the present: Has the US government developed too many checks and balances to meet the challenges of the twenty-first century? Has the executive power slipped its constitutional leash, especially in controlling military and foreign policy? Or do the Constitution's checks and balances remain in good working order, controlling power and preserving self-rule—just as James Madison predicted they would?

6. "A Principle of Which We Were Ashamed"

The convention rethought almost every aspect of government—except slavery. Why? For some delegates, the answer came down to self-interest. Of the fifty-five delegates, twenty-five were slave owners. George Washington brought three slaves with him to Philadelphia. In three states—Georgia, South Carolina, and Virginia—slaves made up more than one-third of the population. And the men and women in bondage were a source of wealth and power. Each time the subject of slavery came up, delegates from South Carolina and Georgia offered the convention a stark choice—protect slavery or form a union without us.

In the end, the delegates wanted a strong union more than they hated slavery. The Constitution includes three major references to slavery. Each time, the slaveholding states pretty much got they wanted.

● *This painting records (and criticizes) a nineteenth-century slave auction. As the painting suggests, slavery would provoke a powerful national debate in the decades ahead. Fifty years after the Constitutional Convention, abolitionists rose up and denounced the Constitution as a "covenant with death and an agreement with hell" because of its slavery compromises.*

The Three-Fifths Compromise. Slavery was first thrust on the convention's agenda with the question of how to count slaves when allocating seats in the House of Representatives. As Table 2.2 shows, nearly four in ten of Virginia's residents were slaves. If slaves were counted as part of the population, southern states would have as many members in the House of Representatives as the northern states.

As soon as the issue came up, James Wilson of Pennsylvania sprang to his feet and offered a compromise. For the purpose of apportioning representation, Wilson proposed, let the total number of slaves count as three-fifths of the free people of a state. The strange fraction came from the Continental Congress. When it was trying to raise revenue from the states, Congress calculated each state's wealth on the basis of population. It then arbitrarily estimated that slaves would generate three-fifths as much wealth as free people. This crude calculation now came back to haunt the Constitution. The delegates immediately accepted the Three-Fifths Compromise. Its actual wording is as peculiar as the rule itself.

> *Representatives . . . shall be apportioned among the several states according to their respective numbers, which shall be determined by adding the whole number of free persons, including those bound to service for a term of years [indentured servants] and excluding Indians not taxed, three fifths of all other persons.*

The Constitution never says "slave," but simply "three fifths of all other persons." In fact, a reader who did not know that the passage refers to slavery would have a hard time understanding it. Why did the Constitution's framers—who were usually so precise—write such a convoluted sentence? They did not want the word *slavery* to appear in the Constitution. John Dickinson, a thoughtful delegate from Delaware, put it best: the awkward wording was, he said, "an endeavor to conceal a principle of which we were ashamed."

The Slave Trade. A second question involved the slave trade. Could the federal government regulate or abolish it? Many delegates were repulsed by the idea of stealing human beings from Africa, chaining them into the hulls of ships, dragging them to America, and selling the survivors to the highest bidder. George Mason from Virginia rose and gave the most prophetic speech of the convention: "Every master of slaves is born a petty tyrant. They bring the judgment of heaven on a country. As nations cannot be rewarded or punished in the next world they must be in this. Providence punishes national sins, by

Table 2.2 Population in 1790

STATE	TOTAL POP.	SLAVES	SLAVES, %
Connecticut	237,655	2,648	1.1
Delaware	59,096	8,887	15.0
Georgia	82,548	29,264	34.5
Maryland	319,728	103,036	32.2
Massachusetts	378,556	0	0.0
New Hampshire	141,899	157	0.1
New Jersey	184,139	11,423	6.2
New York	340,241	21,193	6.2
North Carolina	395,005	100,783	25.5
Pennsylvania	433,611	3,707	0.9
Rhode Island	69,112	958	1.4
South Carolina	249,073	107,094	43.0
Virginia	747,550	292,627	39.1

national calamities. I lament that our eastern brethren [Georgia and South Carolina] had from a lust of gain embarked on this nefarious traffic." It was a powerful speech. However, Mason himself owned more than three hundred slaves. Their worth would rise if the slave trade were abolished.

In the end, backers of a strong Constitution struck a bargain and permitted the slave trade for another twenty years, in exchange for more national power over interstate commerce and the authority to tax imports. Historian William Beeman calculates that permitting the slave trade for another 20 years condemned 200,000 Africans to slavery—almost equaling the total (250,000) from the preceding 170 years.[12]

Fugitive Slaves. Finally, in August, as the convention was winding down, delegates from the slave states proposed a fugitive slave clause—requiring the rest of the nation to assist in returning runaway slaves. This time there were no deals and barely any debate. The northern delegates simply accepted the proposal.

"The National Calamity." Many Americans revere the document that has guided the nation for 225 years. However, George Mason was right when he predicted a "national calamity." Seventy-two years later, Abraham Lincoln would echo Mason as he reflected on the carnage of the Civil War: "God . . . gives to both North and South this terrible war as the woe due to those by whom the offense [of slavery] came."

The slavery passages—like the Civil War that led to their repeal—remind us that the Constitutional Convention was the beginning of an American journey. Each generation has to face up to the same challenge that confronted the Founders. Who are we? Can we try to make the United States more just, more democratic, and more inclusive? The Declaration of Independence gives America its ideals: all people are created equal. The Constitution, in turn, provides the rules. Americans have struggled over the meaning of the ideals and the implementation of the rules ever since these documents were written.

THE BOTTOM LINE

- The constitutional framers balanced two dangers: government that was too strong (the king of England) versus government that was too weak (the Articles of Confederation).
- The debates focused on five great issues:

    (1) Should the people be directly involved in government? Most delegates believed in filtration, or indirect elections.

    (2) National versus state power, which came down to a standoff between larger and smaller states. Led by Madison, the big states introduced the Virginia Plan. Small states countered with the New Jersey Plan. The Connecticut Compromise offered a solution: House members were elected on the basis of population, but every state had two Senate seats.

    (3) The nature of the presidency.

    (4) A separation of powers and a system of checks and balances, both of which got more pronounced as the debate went on. For the most part, these limits on concentrated authority would continue to develop long after ratification of the Constitutional Convention.

    (5) Slavery. Pragmatic compromise in the name of union overcame moral qualms. Delegates took care to not use the word *slavery*, but several clauses enabling the institution to grow and expand would lead to the greatest conflict in the nation's future.

An Overview of the Constitution

By September 17, after four months of deliberation, the Constitutional Convention had done its work. Thirty-nine of the original fifty-five delegates lined up to sign the document. Benjamin Franklin, pointing to a sunburst painted on the back of the president's chair, reflected on how he had gazed at that sun throughout the convention "without being able to tell if it was rising or setting. But now, at length I have the happiness to know that it is a rising and not a setting sun."[13] A more pessimistic observer might have pointed out that sixteen delegates—almost a third—had either left the convention or refused to sign: a portent of the battles ahead.

Franklin was proven right: the American government that operates today rose in that Philadelphia chamber in the summer of 1787. There are only seven articles in the Constitution, each broken down into multiple sections. (Their full text appears in Appendix II.) These passages remain the institutional foundation of the American political system.

Preamble

The Constitution begins with a preamble, the most elegant sentence in the document:

> *We the people of the United States, in order to form a more perfect union, establish justice, insure domestic tranquility, provide for the common defense, promote the general welfare, and secure the blessings of liberty to ourselves and our posterity, do ordain and establish this Constitution for the United States of America.*

The Constitution's authority rests, not on the states, but on "we the people." As we have seen, the Constitutional Convention produced a weak ideal of the people—one that permitted slavery, excluded women, and permitted "we the people" to vote for exactly one branch of Congress. The next phrase—"in order to form a more perfect union"—addresses these limitations. Americans always struggle toward that more perfect union.

The preamble also offers six goals for a successful government. Ask yourself how you would rate the United States government on each of them today.

Article 1: Congress

Article 1, the longest in the Constitution, describes the new Congress. Section 2 of the article establishes a House of Representatives whose members are elected every two years to represent a district of 30,000 voters. (Today, average district size has grown to more than 710,000 voters.) Representatives must be twenty-five years old and have been a citizen for seven years. Section 3 establishes a Senate with two members from every state, elected every six years; they must be at least thirty and have been a citizen for nine years.

Section 8 is the most important passage in article 1—and perhaps the entire Constitution. Its seventeen short paragraphs tell Congress what it may do, including the "power to lay and collect taxes," declare war, regulate interstate commerce, coin money, and raise an army.

Think about the reach of congressional authority. The largest and most expensive program that Congress oversees is Social Security, which pays monthly pensions to retired people over sixty-five. If you read all of section 8, you may be puzzled—nothing in it remotely justifies paying for retirement

Have We Achieved the Constitution's Goals Today?

Think about the goals listed in the preamble. Then give the grades: an "A" if you think the United States has lived up to its goals, and a . . . well, we're sure you know all about grades!

Goal:	Grade Today:
Form a strong union	_____
Establish equal justice for all	_____
Insure domestic tranquility (or, peace at home)	_____
Provide for the common defense (today, we might say Homeland Security)	_____
Promote the general welfare	_____
Secure liberty for ourselves and posterity	_____

pensions. How, then, could Congress pass and run the Social Security program? Because the very last paragraph of section 8 empowers Congress

> to make all laws which shall be necessary and proper for carrying into execution the foregoing powers, and all other powers vested by this Constitution in the government of the United States.

That phrase, known as the *necessary and proper clause*, gives Congress—and the government—a great deal of creative leeway. What are the limits of the power granted to Congress by this clause? This is another place where the delegates in Philadelphia disagreed. Not surprisingly, scholars argue still about how far the necessary and proper clause stretches congressional authority.

Section 9 of article 1 lists the things Congress may *not* do. Its second prohibition is especially important today: "the privilege of the writ of Habeas Corpus shall not be suspended unless when in cases of rebellion or invasion the public safety may require it." *Habeas corpus* means that government cannot hold prisoners without accusing them of a specific crime. The US government may not simply throw someone in jail without a charge. What about terrorist suspects held without charges? Again, experts disagree. Advocates of the Obama administration's policy argue that "public safety" requires indefinite detention—as clearly stipulated in section 9 (and besides, say some, terrorist attacks constitute "an invasion"). Critics argue that government officials have been too quick to claim threats to "public safety"; doing so, they argue, undermines liberty, one of the basic rights that the Constitution was established to protect.

Article 2: The President

The Constitution's second article shifts focus from the legislature to the executive branch. The president, article 2 specifies, must be a natural-born

What Do You Think?

⠐ Detention of Terrorism Suspects

Should the United States indefinitely detain terrorism suspects without formally charging them with a crime?	**No.** The Constitution goes out of its way to specifically guarantee the right of *habeas corpus*. The framers considered this a foundation of liberty. While they made exceptions for war and public safety, these must be urgent—and rare. By making a broad and indefinite exception to one of the most fundamental rights in the Constitution, we undermine American liberty.	**Yes.** The Constitution makes a clear exception to the right of *habeas corpus* when the public safety requires it. The framers were very sensibly signaling that government's first duty is to protect its citizens from the kind of harm posed by terrorism. The Constitution's rights extend to ordinary criminals, not to members of an international movement committed to death and destruction.	**Unsure.** We will return to this very important question in other chapters. Keep the question in mind as you study American politics.

American at least thirty-five years old, and is chosen by electors for a four-year term. As we saw, each state originally decided who elects the electors—today the people make the choice in every state.

Whereas article 1 lists congressional dos and don'ts in detail, article 2 says very little about presidential powers and duties. The president is commander in chief of the army and the navy. Presidents make treaties if two-thirds of the Senate approve; they appoint ambassadors, Supreme Court justices, and all other officials—again with the advice and consent of the Senate. Although that seems like a limited set of powers, the Constitution includes another clause that has permitted an enormous expansion of presidential powers: "The executive power shall be vested in a President of the United States." What that "executive power" is, and how far it can stretch, has been debated throughout American history.

Section 4 allows for removing a president "on impeachment for, and conviction of, treason, bribery, or other high crimes and misdemeanors." What constitutes a high crime or misdemeanor? Again, the Constitution does not say, which makes any impeachment effort highly charged on all sides. Three presidents have faced formal impeachment proceedings, although only one, Richard Nixon, was forced to resign his office.[14]

Article 3: The Courts

Article 3 creates the Supreme Court and authorizes Congress to organize additional courts. Alexander Hamilton later called the Supreme Court "the least dangerous" branch of government, and the Constitution describes it only briefly—article 3 is only one-sixth as long as article 1. The justices are selected by the president, approved by the Senate, and have tenure for life—still another buffer from democratic politics. Article 3 grants Supreme Court power over all cases "arising under this Constitution, the laws of the United States and treaties made."

The Constitution is silent on the Court's most formidable power: May it overrule an act of Congress? Sixteen years after the Constitutional Convention, Chief Justice John Marshall, in deciding a case called *Marbury v. Madison*, ruled that the Court could strike down an act of Congress. In other words, since the Court has authority over all cases "arising under this Constitution," it has a responsibility to review the constitutionality of legislation. The delegates debated this power but, in the end, sidestepped the controversy and left the language vague. Once again you can see how Americans are constantly challenged to read and interpret precisely what the Constitution requires.

Article 4: Relations Between the States

Article 4 defines the relationship between the states that had so plagued the Articles of Confederation. A state may not discriminate against citizens of other states, and each must give "full faith and credit" to the official acts of other states. Article 4 also describes the process for adding new states and requires the United States to guarantee every state a republican form of government.

The "full faith and credit" clause raises some controversial questions today. When gay couples marry in states like Massachusetts, does the "full faith and credit" clause bind other states to recognize those marriages? Many states have refused, adopting rules that define marriage as a heterosexual union. The Supreme Court has not yet ruled on the matter. Stay tuned.

Article 5: Amendments

Article 5 authorizes amendments to the Constitution. Creating an amendment is an extremely difficult process. Two-thirds of both House and Senate must approve. Then three-fourths of the states must ratify—either through the state legislature or through state conventions. (The only amendment to be ratified the second way was the Twenty-First, which repealed the prohibition on alcohol in 1933, fourteen years after the Eighteenth Amendment prohibited its "manufacture, transportation or sale.") Over one hundred thousand amendments have been proposed since 1791 (when the first ten amendments, or Bill of Rights, went through); only seventeen have passed. When citizens or organizations disagree with a Supreme Court ruling, occasionally they try for a constitutional amendment. As you can see from the numbers, it is a very difficult thing to actually win.

The Constitution forbids amendments on two matters: no amendment could stop the slave trade before 1808, and no state can be denied equal suffrage in the Senate (two seats) without its approval. In this way, the two fiercest debates at the convention were placed beyond the reach of future generations.

Article 6: The Law of the Land

Article 6 makes the Constitution the supreme law of the land. It also specifies that there must be no religious test for holding any federal office. Some states, however, had religious tests for holding office and even voting until the 1830s.

Article 7: Ratification

Article 7 announced that the Constitution would go into effect after nine states had ratified—a controversial move because the United States was still operating under the Articles of Confederation, which could be amended only by all thirteen states.

The Missing Articles

Soon after ratification in 1789, many Americans thought that the original Constitution was missing something important. Only a handful of individual rights were mentioned in the document. It said nothing about free speech, free press, freedom of religion, jury trials, or the right to bear arms. The debate over ratifying the Constitution would quickly expose this weakness. As we will see, ratification required an important addition: the ten amendments known as the Bill of Rights.

Ratification

The new Constitution now went to the states, where ratifying conventions would vote it up or down. Most states were closely divided over whether to ratify, but the Constitution had two big advantages. First, it offered a clear plan in a time of trouble; opponents could only say "no" and force the nation to start all over again. Second, the convention had attracted many of the most prestigious men in America, beginning with Washington and Franklin, who were the most widely admired figures in two of the largest states. Supporters of the Constitution were known as *Federalists*—making their opponents the *Anti-Federalists*.

The Anti-Federalists

The Anti-Federalists rooted their argument against ratification in **classical republicanism**. Popular government, in this view, ought to model itself on ancient republics like Athens and Rome. Republics should be small and local, permitting maximum popular participation in public affairs. When we discussed the idea of self-rule in Chapter 1, we introduced the idea of direct

Classical republicanism: A democratic ideal, rooted in ancient Greece and Rome, that requires citizens to participate directly in public affairs, seek the public interest, shun private gains, and defer to natural leaders.

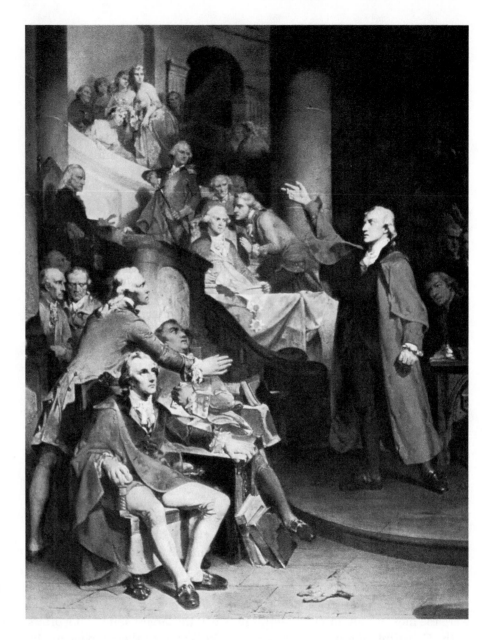

● *The ratification of the Constitution was a close call. Patrick Henry, a powerful orator, led the opponents (known as Anti-Federalists) in Virginia. Virginia was one of seven states where the vote was close.*

democracy (celebrated by Thomas Jefferson); classical republicanism is the original version of that idea.

The Anti-Federalists were not interested in a muscular nation-state like the European empires. They had four major criticisms of the new Constitution:

• First, it stripped political control away from citizens and placed it in a powerful national government where the people would not have much influence.

- Second, the president looked too much like a king.

- Third, standing armies and navies were a threat to peace and liberty. Republics relied on citizen militias—which could be mustered during wartime—to protect the people.

- Fourth, and most important, the Anti-Federalists hammered away at the Constitution's missing piece, a Bill of Rights.

Politics also played a role in the Anti-Federalist argument. Many of the men who opposed the Constitution were powerful political figures in their own states. A national government would diminish their influence.[15]

Aspects of the Anti-Federalist (and civic republican) argument remain alive and well in the United States. Americans often criticize the federal government and cheer the idea of restoring power to state and local officials, who are closer to the people. This localist view is much stronger in the United States than it is in other advanced democracies, from Japan to Britain to Brazil. The Anti-Federalists may have lost the debate in 1788, but their fear of federal power and their yearning to return authority to the people endures—and shapes one answer to our great question, *Who are we?*

The Federalists

The arguments in favor of the new Constitution were summarized by an editorial dream team. James Madison and Alexander Hamilton (with a little help from John Jay, who would become the first chief justice of the United States) wrote eighty-five short essays that appeared in newspapers to explain and defend the Constitution to the voters of New York. Known as the Federalist Papers, they achieve three very different purposes. First, they are pro-Constitution editorials, even propaganda; the authors were fighting to get New York to approve the new Constitution and they did not pretend to be neutral. Second, they are the single best guide to the thinking that guided the Constitution. However, we have to read carefully, always weighing the Papers as persuasive rhetoric on the one hand and explanations of constitutional logic on the other. Finally, the Federalist Papers are outstanding theoretical essays about politics and government.

The two most famous Federalist Papers, no. 10 and no. 51, are reprinted in an appendix to this book. The eighteenth-century language may sound strange to our ears, but the argument is brilliant. Federalist no. 10 argues, surprisingly, that a large national government can protect liberty more effectively than small local governments. Madison begins by introducing the "mortal disease" that always destroys popular government. You might think that he was referring to tyrants like George III. Instead, he points to *factions*—groups that pursue their self-interest at the expense of others.

How can we control the effects of factions? Not through local governments, argued Madison. In each local area, one economic interest is likely to predominate—farmers, merchants, big manufacturers, or even poor people eager to tax the rich. Since the same local group will always be in the majority, it is difficult to stop that group from taking advantage of the minority.

Madison's realistic assessment was a breakthrough in political theory. The classical view assumed that for popular government to survive, the people—that is, the voters—had to be virtuous and respect one another. Madison introduced a more modern view: expect people to pursue their own self-interest. As he wrote in Federalist no. 51, "if men were angels, no government would be necessary." If popular government is to survive, it must be organized to protect minorities from majorities who are going to pursue their own self-interest.

How can we do this? Move the debate to the national level, said Madison. A larger political sphere—a bigger government—will always have a great many diverse interests, arising from all the states. With so many different factions, no one interest will be able to dominate. Each faction will form a small minority of the whole and will therefore need to form alliances. As the issues change, so will the groups that are in the majority and the minority. As a result, no one faction will be able to impose its will on the minority for very long.

Two Strong Arguments

To this day, both sides—Anti-Federalist and Federalist—sound persuasive. The Anti-Federalists tapped into a deep American yearning for local governments that respond directly to popular concerns. The Federalists argued that only a national government could really protect the people's rights and turn the new nation into a great power.

A Very Close Vote

The small states, having gotten their way at the Constitutional Convention, ratified quickly and unanimously—Delaware, New Jersey, and Georgia all signed by January 2, 1788. In Pennsylvania, some members of the assembly hid to slow down the process. Enthusiastic mobs found the reluctant members and marched them to the very hall where the Constitutional Convention was written. This time there was no secrecy. The public crammed into the hall and gathered outside the building. After a month, Pennsylvania ratified the Constitution 46–23, and Benjamin Franklin led a cheering throng through the streets and, eventually, to Epple's Tavern for celebratory toasts. (See Table 2.3 for a summary of the voting.)

In Massachusetts, Governor John Hancock, who had been the first delegate to sign the Declaration of Independence, dramatically switched to the Federalist side—on a crucial condition. He asked that amendments protecting individual rights be introduced to the new Constitution. It was the first prominent insistence on a Bill of Rights. Even with the switch, the Constitution won narrowly, 187 to 168. Once the votes were counted, the Anti-Federalists announced that they would "support the Constitution as cheerfully and as heartily as though [they] had voted on the other side."

Table 2.3 The Final Vote for the Constitution

STATE	DATE OF RATIFICATION	VOTE IN STATE CONVENTION
1. DE	December 7, 1787	Unanimous [30–0]
2. PA	December 12	46–23
3. NJ	December 18	Unanimous [38–0]
4. GA	January 2, 1788	Unanimous [26–0]
5. CT	January 9	128–40
6. MA	February 7	187–168
7. MD	April 28	63–11
8. SC	May 23	149–73
9. NH	June 21	57–47; required two meetings
10. VA	June 26	89–79
11. NY	July 26	30–27
12. NC	July 21, 1789 [after election of Washington]	194–77
13. RI	May 29, 1790 [first Congress in session]	34–32

Key: Easy Ratification   Tough Fight   Originally refused

Other states followed the two Massachusetts precedents: request a Bill of Rights and unite after the debate.

After Maryland and South Carolina voted for the Constitution, the action moved to Virginia—the largest state and the most intense contest to date. Anti-Federalist opposition was led by Patrick Henry, known as "the son of thunder" for his rhetorical power; at one point, he spoke for seven straight hours. Governor William Randolph, who had presented the Virginia Plan at the convention, and George Mason, who had scorched the slave trade, both refused to sign the Constitution and joined Henry on the Anti-Federalist side. After twenty-two days, Virginia voted for the Constitution 89 to 79.

New York was even more contentious than Virginia. New York City supported the Constitution, but the rest of the state opposed. The New York debate inspired both the Federalist Papers and an Anti-Federalist rejoinder, *The Federal Farmer*. In the end, the new Constitution squeaked through by 30 to 27.

Not every state voted in favor. Rhode Island town meetings rejected even holding a convention to debate the Constitution. Rhode Island would reluctantly join the union after George Washington had been president for two months. North Carolina initially rejected the Constitution by a lopsided vote of 184 to 83. In New Hampshire a convention met, refused to ratify, and adjourned; four months later the delegates reconvened, voted yes, and on June 21, 1788, New Hampshire became the ninth state to ratify. The Constitution would now be the law of the land.

This was a very close contest. If a total of just 3 percent of the delegates across Virginia, Massachusetts, and New York had changed their vote, the Constitution would have gone down to defeat. Americans came within a whisker of rejecting the Constitution that now defines the nation and its government.

A Popular Surge Propels People into Politics

The Federalists won the debate and created a strong central government far removed from the people. At first it seemed as if Roger Sherman's comment at the convention had won the day—"the people . . . should have . . . little to do . . . [with] government." But something unexpected happened. The revolution set off a democratic surge that liberated popular energies. Not everyone was included—not women, not black people, not Native Americans. But the idea that ordinary citizens should be kept at arm's length was soon swamped by a great tide of participation that many of the founders neither imagined nor desired.[16] People raced to participate in both economic and political life. However, American history is not a simple story of ever-expanding participation. Rather, the battle for a more perfect union has been long and unpredictable. Over more than two centuries, rights, liberties, and democracy have been gained and lost and gained again.

THE BOTTOM LINE

- The debate over ratifying the Constitution featured two visions of American government.
- The *Federalists* argued that only an energetic national government could protect the nation and secure liberty. The *Anti-Federalists* called instead for a modest government that left power in state and local hands.
- The state-by-state voting on ratification was very close, and took well over a year before the Constitution was approved.
- More than 225 years later, Americans are still debating the same question—how strong should the federal government be?

● Changing the Constitution

Although most Anti-Federalist leaders eventually rallied to the new Constitution, they insisted on and won a crucial promise: a Bill of Rights would be added to the Constitution.

The Bill of Rights

Today, the first ten amendments to the Constitution, known as the **Bill of Rights**, form a crucial feature of the Constitution and of American government. *These set out the rights—the protections from government—that every citizen is owed.* Freedom of speech, freedom of the press, freedom of religion, the right to bear arms, and the long list of additional rights are an essential part of America's identity. Table 2.4 summarizes the amendments that make up the Bill of Rights.

   Originally, the Bill of Rights applied only to the federal government. The First Amendment reads, *"Congress shall make no law . . .* abridging the freedom of speech." At the time, states that wanted to limit speech or set up an official religion were free to do so. The Fourteenth Amendment, ratified after the Civil War to protect the former slaves (in 1868), commands that no *state* may deny "any person . . . the equal protection of the laws." In theory, this

The Bill of Rights: The first ten amendments to the Constitution, listing the rights guaranteed to every citizen.

Table 2.4 Summarizing the Bill of Rights

1. Congress may not establish a religion or prohibit the free exercise of religion; it may not abridge freedom of speech or of the press or of the people's right to assemble and to petition government.
2. Citizens have the right to bear arms.
3. No soldier may be quartered in any house without the consent of the owner.
4. There must be no unreasonable search or seizures. Government authorities may not break into your house without a search warrant.
5. No one may be forced to testify against themselves (declining to do so is now known as "taking the Fifth"); no one may be deprived of life, liberty, or property without due process of law. The government may not take private property (if, for example, it wants to build a highway) without just compensation.
6. Certain rights are guaranteed in criminal trials.
7. Accused persons are guaranteed the right to trial by jury.
8. The government may not force citizens to pay excessive bails or impose cruel and unusual punishments.
9. Enumerating these rights does not diminish the other rights retained by the people.
10. Any powers not given to the federal government are reserved for the states and the people.

Incorporation: The process by which the Supreme Court declares that a right in the Bill of Rights also applies to state governments.

amendment extended the Bill of Rights to the states—meaning state governments must honor the right as well as the national government. However, the Fourteenth Amendment only began a long process, known as **incorporation**, of applying the Bill of Rights to the state governments, one right at a time. That process continues down to the present day: the Supreme Court "incorporated" the right to bear arms in 2010. Ratifying the Constitution and the Bill of Rights was just the start of a long debate.

The Seventeen Amendments

After the Bill of Rights, constitutional amendments became rare events. Only four more were ratified in the next 115 years. Every year, hundreds are proposed, but only seventeen have passed since 1791. The successful amendments all do one of four things: They extend rights—for example, guaranteeing the right to vote to eighteen-year-olds (seven amendments extend rights). They adjust election rules—for example, limiting the president to two terms (eleven amendments focus on elections). They change the operations of government—for example, switching Inauguration Day from March to January (four amendments focus on government rules). Or they adjust governmental powers over individuals—for example, prohibiting alcohol and then (fourteen years later) permitting alcohol again. Table 2.5 summarizes the seventeen amendments that have been ratified since 1791.

Apart from formal amendments, American government—and how we interpret the Constitution—changes over time. We constantly debate how to apply the Constitution and its amendments to current issues. May Congress limit the money corporations give political candidates? May the CIA waterboard suspected terrorists? May students pray before a football game? May the City of Chicago stop people from carrying guns? The wording of the Constitution permits different interpretations. These questions—and many more—require Americans to read the Constitution and reflect on what it tells us, more than 225 years after it was ratified.

● *What does the Constitution say about praying in schools? Americans disagree. In 2012, Florida governor Rick Scott signed legislation permitting prayers in public schools, over vociferous objections that the legislation was unconstitutional. The courts will eventually have to decide which side is correct.*

Table 2.5 Amendments to the US Constitution

AMENDMENT	DESCRIPTION	YEAR RATIFIED	RESULT
11	Required state consent for individuals suing a state in federal court	1795	Modified government operations
12	Separated votes for president and vice president within Electoral College	1804	Shifted election rules
13	Prohibited slavery	1865	Expanded individual rights
14	Provided citizenship to former slaves; states could not deny civil rights, civil liberties, or the equal protection of the laws	1868	Expanded individual rights
15	Granted voting rights to all races	1870	Expanded individual rights
16	Permitted national income tax	1913	Expanded government powers over individuals
17	Provided direct election of senators	1913	Shifted election rules
18	Prohibited alcohol	1919	Expanded government powers over individuals
19	Extended the vote to women	1920	Expanded individual rights
20	Changed Inauguration Day from March to January	1933	Modified government operations
21	Repealed Prohibition	1933	Adjusted government powers over individuals
22	Limited president to two terms	1951	Shifted election rules
23	Extended the vote for president to citizens in Washington, DC	1961	Expanded individual rights
24	Prohibited a poll tax [one way to keep black people from voting]	1964	Expanded individual rights
25	Established succession plan in case of president's death or disability	1967	Modified government operations
26	Extended the vote to 18- to 20-year-olds	1971	Expanded individual rights
27	Established that congressional pay raise couldn't go into effect until the next election	1992	Modified government operations

Seventeen amendments in 215 years, ten of which are about elections and individual rights:
   Expanded individual rights
   Shifted election rules
   Modified government operations
   Expanded or adjusted government powers over individuals

The Constitution Today

The political life of the American colonies prepared the way for something no nation had done before: the United States organized a new government around a Constitution, written in the people's name, and voted on by the people's representatives in every state. The document still guides American politics. Who are we? Reading the US Constitution is one important way to find out.

But there is a catch. Americans disagree about how to read the Constitution. One view, called **originalism**, or *strict construction*, insists that *Americans are bound to the literal meaning of the Constitution and its amendments, as the people who wrote and ratified understood them.* From this perspective, the Constitution's meaning does not change with the times.

Another view was first articulated by Thomas Jefferson, who warned Americans not to view the Constitution with "sanctimonious reverence," as if it were "too sacred to be touched." The nation's founders were not superhuman in their wisdom, he insisted. He knew their limits, he said, because he was one of them. "I know also," concluded Jefferson, "that laws and institutions must go hand in hand with the progress of the human mind." Many scholars and politicians have followed Jefferson's advice. They see a living, breathing, changing Constitution—one that speaks to each generation a little differently. This view of an evolving Constitution is known as **pragmatism**. *We cannot help bringing our own background, ideas, and judgments to bear as we think about the meaning of the document.*

Originalism: A principle of legal interpretation that relies on the original meaning of those who wrote the Constitution.

Pragmatism: A principle of legal interpretation based on the idea that the Constitution evolves and that it must be put in the context of contemporary realities.

What Do You Think?

How Strictly Should We Interpret the Constitution?

After considering the two approaches to interpreting the Constitution known as originalism and pragmatism, choose a position.

I am an originalist. Contemporary justices should not try to substitute their judgment for that of the Constitution's framers. We cannot avoid the arbitrary use of power if we permit everyone to read the Constitution as they like. Before long, the Constitution will not mean anything at all.

I'm a pragmatist. Times change and conditions evolve. The modern world imposes challenges that the framers could not have imagined. Failing to permit the text to evolve would turn the document into an eighteenth-century straitjacket.

I'm in the middle. I believe the difference between these positions is far less stark than it appears at first glance. Even if we try very hard to get back to the original meaning, we always read the Constitution in the light of the present. Every effort to interpret the Constitution will be guided by our own ideas and our own times.

As we will see throughout this book, it is often very difficult to tell exactly how the Constitution applies to our times. Different people reading the document come to very different conclusions. In the end, the difference between originalism and pragmatism may not be as large as its proponents think.

see for yourself 2.1

Go online to view *The 10-Minute Guide to the Constitution* from Cornell University.

Conclusion: Does the Constitution Still Work?

Every chapter that follows will focus on a different feature of the Constitution as it operates today—federalism, civil liberties, civil rights, Congress, the presidency, the courts, and so on. As you explore these institutions, keep a major question in mind: Does the world's oldest Constitution still work? Almost all politicians—and most Americans—would surely say that it does. That's why it has lasted so long. But some disagree. Robert Dahl, a leading political scientist, argues that the Constitution is not democratic enough.[17] It does not include modern rights. The checks and balances are sometimes too cumbersome, making it difficult to pass needed laws. Congress no longer checks the president when it comes to war.

The debate takes us back to the very first question we asked in Chapter 1. Who governs? Do "we the people" still rule? Or has real power slipped away to the rich and powerful? These are questions that, directly or indirectly, every chapter will address.

Regardless of whether you're an *originalist*, a *pragmatist*, or somewhere in between, you should check to see what the Constitution says every time you study another feature of American politics. Start with the Constitution and you'll know the system's basic rules of American politics.

THE BOTTOM LINE

- The Bill of Rights comprises the first ten amendments to the Constitution, which define the rights of American citizens.
- Seventeen more amendments (of more than 100,000 proposals) followed in the next 215 years.
- American politics is always changing, but the Constitution still stands as the American political rule book. However, the Constitution must be interpreted, for it is often unclear what the document means and how it applies to contemporary cases.

CHAPTER SUMMARY

● The Constitution provides the ground rules for American politics. However, it is often unclear exactly how the Constitution applies to contemporary issues. We have to interpret its meaning.

● The colonial experience prepared America for thinking about a constitution. The English practice of *salutary neglect* permitted the colonies to develop their own political institutions, centered on their legislatures. Americans got used to *delegated representation* (reflecting voter sentiment), which contrasted with the British view of *trustee representation* (representing the whole nation regardless of public opinion).

● The Declaration of Independence has two parts. First, it states the American ideal: all people "are created equal" and "endowed by their creator with certain unalienable rights" including "life, liberty, and the pursuit of happiness." Second, it lists colonial grievances, emphasizing the rights of free people to elect their legislatures.

● The first American government, under the Articles of Confederation, was an alliance of independent states that maximized popular participation. This government had some great successes, but many leaders felt that it was too weak and left the United States vulnerable to foreign powers.

● The Constitutional Convention, convened to fix the problems with the first American government, focused on six broad issues: popular involvement; national versus state power; big versus small states; checks and balances; the presidency; and slavery.

● Ratification of the Constitution involved an extremely close battle between Anti- Federalists, who opposed the Constitution, and Federalists, who supported it. The first ten amendments, known as the Bill of Rights, came out of the ratification debates and were approved by the First Congress. Seventeen more amendments followed in the next 215 years. American politics has changed enormously, but the Constitution continues to stand as the American political rule book.

KEY TERMS

Bicameral, 65
Bill of Rights, 85
Classical republicanism, 79
Compact, 50
Confederation, 57
Covenant, 50
Delegate representation, 52

Electoral College, 68
Federalism, 65
First Continental Congress, 55
Incorporation, 86
Indentured servant, 50
Mercantilism, 53
New Jersey Plan, 66

Originalism, 88
Pragmatism, 88
Second Continental Congress, 56
Supermajority, 59
Trustee representation, 52
Unicameral, 66
Virginia Plan, 65

STUDY QUESTIONS

1. Describe five ways that the colonial experience prepared the United States for a constitution.
2. Winning the French and Indian War drove two wedges between England and the colonies. What were they?

3. What is the difference between delegate or actual representation and trustee or virtual representation? How did the difference lead to the American Revolution?

4. What are the five overarching ideas introduced by the Declaration of Independence? In your opinion, how close are we to achieving those ideals today?

5. Describe the first government that Americans organized after they broke away from England. Where was most of the power located? What problems arose under this government? What was successful about it?

6. When it came to writing the Constitution, the delegates had to balance two fears. One emerged from the battle with England, the other from American experience under the Articles of Confederation. Describe these two fears.

7. What did Madison mean by "filtration of representatives"? List two examples of filtration in the original Constitution.

What do you think? Would you support filtration or the direct election of representatives?

8. Describe the differences between the Virginia Plan and the New Jersey Plan. If you had to choose between them, which would you choose and why?

9. Describe what the Constitution says about the following:

How the House of Representatives is elected
How the president is elected
How the Supreme Court is chosen
How amendments can be added to the Constitution

10. Describe the differences between the Federalists and the Anti-Federalists. Which side would you be on? Why?

Optional assignment: Choose one of the thirteen original states. Now, write a speech before its ratifying convention arguing for or against the new constitution.

3

Federalism and Nationalism

BETWEEN 2005 AND 2012, Arizona passed more than seventy-five laws restricting immigration. Today, undocumented immigrants in Arizona have no access to state-funded services, employers are subject to heavy fines if they hire someone with false or missing papers, and police officers are empowered to halt and question anyone they suspect of being an illegal alien. Police are required to check the immigration status of those they stop for any reason, even minor traffic violations, if there is reason to suspect they are undocumented.

Immigration enforcement is a *national* responsibility. However, Arizona officials claim that the federal government has failed to enforce immigration restrictions, permitting a wave of illegal residents—mostly Latino—to enter the state. Arizona officials insist that undocumented aliens strain state services, increase drug trafficking, and drive down wages for working-class Arizonans (including legal immigrants). Tensions were further heightened by the economic downturn that began in 2008, which hit the state especially hard.

National protests erupted in the wake of Arizona's restrictive policies. Latino advocacy groups and their allies led marches calling for fair treatment toward all immigrants. They launched an economic boycott that alarmed Arizona business owners. Democrats in Congress sponsored immigration reform legislation in 2010 and again in 2012, but their bills went nowhere. The Obama administration denounced Arizona's crackdown on immigration—and took the state to court, charging that the state had violated the national government's authority over immigration policy. Foreign leaders including Mexico's president, Felipe Calderón, criticized Arizona's policy as a denial of human rights.

Among many conservatives, however, Governor Jan Brewer—who signed the recent Arizona laws—became a hero. Her poll numbers surged, topping 70 percent in some surveys, and she handily won reelection. "We are all Arizonans now," declared the former GOP vice-presidential candidate Sarah Palin in 2010.[1] Other states—Alabama, Georgia, and South Carolina—passed similar legislation. The Supreme Court weighed in during summer 2012,

● *The contentious relationship between state and federal government, personified when Arizona governor Jan Brewer publicly scolded President Barack Obama over immigration control.*

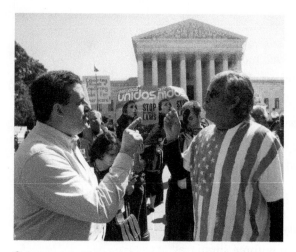

An opponent of the Arizona law (left) confronts a supporter (wearing red, white, and blue) in front of the Supreme Court building as the justices deliberate.

striking down much of Arizona's law for infringing on federal authority; however, it unanimously permitted the mandatory immigration check (known as "show me your papers")—at least for the time being (more suits are expected).

In many other states—North Carolina and Maryland, for example—the issue is less politically controversial, even though immigration (legal and illegal) is now rising more quickly than in Arizona. These states have passed less-stringent immigration laws without setting off any reaction: no protests, no counterprotests, no high-stakes legislation, no dispute with the federal government, and no lawsuits between state and national branches. How best to explain the difference?

Looking at immigration policies across the different states reveals the latest chapter in a long history of American clashes over federalism. The term denotes our separate levels of government, sharing and sometimes squabbling over power. This complex interplay between state, local, and national governments stretches all the way back to the debates between Federalists (who wanted a strong national government) and Anti-Federalists (who sought more power for the states) that we described in the last chapter. The controversy led to an elaborate division of power between national and state governments. The result is an overlapping, sometimes chaotic, often clashing division of political authority in America. At their core, conflicts between state, local, and national levels reflect deeper questions about protecting values like democracy, fairness, and effective government. The dispute between Governor Brewer and President Obama is part of the long tradition of American federalism.

Who are we? A nation of divided loyalties and governments. The results facilitate innovation, protect liberty, and create confusion. A hurricane in Louisiana, an oil spill off the Alaskan coast, or bombs exploding at the Boston Marathon bring out a response from local authorities, state officials, and national agencies, all scrambling to get on the same wavelength. Despite the messy lines of authority, federalism is permanently ingrained in our Constitution, our institutions, and our national culture. Amid waves of change in communications technology, economic and demographic trends, and political beliefs, the United States has managed to sustain its distinctive federalist system. This

BY THE NUMBERS *Federalism*

Estimated total number of governments in the United States: **87,576**
Percentage of these that are national (1): **0.0011**
Percentage of these that are state (50): **0.057**
Percentage of these that are county or parish (3,034): **3.46**
Percentage of these that are town or city (84,451): **96.4**

Number of counties in Texas, each with its own government: **254**
Number of counties in Hawaii, each with its own government: **4**
Number of US states whose capital is located in the state's largest city: **19**
Number of nonmilitary personnel who work for the federal government: **2.7 million**
Number who work for state governments: **4.4 million**
Number who work for local governments: **12.2 million**

Percentage of people who say the national government has a "positive" effect on their daily lives: **38**
Percentage who said this in October 1997: **50**
Percentage of people who have a great deal or fair amount of trust in state government: **53**
Percentage of people who have a great deal or fair amount of trust in local government: **68**

Rank of the United States among world's "most patriotic countries" in 2012: **1**
Rank in 1982: **1**

Percentage of Americans who are "extremely" or "very" proud to be American: **83**
Percentage of whites who express this sentiment: **86**
Percentage of African Americans: **81**
Percentage of 50- to 64-year-olds: **90**
Percentage of 18- to 29-year-olds: **71**
Percentage of Americans who expressed this sentiment in January 2001: **87**
Percentage of Americans who say they regularly display or fly the US flag: **59**
Percentage of Democrats who do this: **51**
Percentage of Republicans who do this: **72**
Percentage of Latvians who are "extremely" or "very" proud to be Latvian: **38**
Percentage of Americans expressing optimism about the US future: **61**
Percentage who did so in May 1999: **70**

chapter looks at federalism's remarkable persistence—as well as the sometimes surprising ways we have adapted to changing times. One key, as we shall see, is a long tradition of nationalism, American-style.

🔵 Why Federalism?

Ask a US citizen where he or she is from and you'll probably get a multiple-part answer. We are Americans *and* Coloradans *and* residents of Boulder; Americans *and* Texans *and* Houstonians. Even though Americans move frequently (on average, adults relocate six times during their lifetimes), more than two-thirds express strong positive feelings about their country, state, *and* city or town.[2]

Choosing Federalism

Unitary government: A national polity governed as a single unit, with the central government exercising all or most political authority.

Most nations in the 1780s had **unitary governments**. The national government—the king and Parliament in England, for example—made policy for the nation. Local governments simply carried out their decrees. To this day, almost all nations are organized this way. Local government is an administrative extension of national government. Unitary government was exactly what the United States had rebelled against. Early Americans were certainly not going to reintroduce the same system all over again: that, they agreed, would pose a threat to their liberties.

Confederation: A group of independent states or nations that yield some of their powers to a national government, although each state retains a degree of sovereign authority.

A second, less-used traditional form was the **confederation**, which leaves most power in member states or countries, while establishing a weak central authority to provide common defense or economic benefits. Today, the European Union is struggling to make a confederation work. Americans tried this system under the Articles of Confederation. As we saw in the previous chapter, it proved too weak and was replaced.

At the Constitutional Convention, the delegates devised an innovative hybrid: a *federal system* in which power is divided and shared between national and state governments. The Constitution reserves some decisions for the national government (declaring war, coining money), others reside in the states (establishing schools), and some powers go to both levels (taxing, spending, establishing courts, regulating business). Since each level is independent and their powers overlap, conflict is essentially built into the system—as we can see in the clash between President Obama and Governor Brewer of Arizona.

To complicate matters, the United States also has independent local governments, at the town, city, and county level. These add another layer of elected officials, government employees, services to provide, and taxes to be paid. However, local governments are *not* sovereign units of the federal system. Rather, they are, in legal terms, "creatures of the state." All local powers come from the state government. Some states grant local governments broad powers, known as *home rule*; others jealously hold onto authority and approve or reject every major action a local government wishes to take. When the mayor of Detroit wanted to take responsibility for the school system from an independent board, or the mayor of New York City wanted to introduce a fee on cars commuting into the city to cut traffic congestion, each had to ask the state to approve the plan. (In both cases, their states originally said no.) Local governments play an important role in American federalism, but they are subordinate to the states. Authority is balanced between state and national governments, while local leaders retain considerable responsibility to provide services like education and police protection.

The conflict between states and nation is so often intense because it taps something far more profound than a simple division of labor. From the United States' beginnings, the debate was about balancing liberty, which led Anti-Federalists to resist national government; and effective governance, for which Federalists demanded a stronger center. That battle goes on to this day.

On the surface, the states might seem to have a built-in advantage. As Figure 3.1 shows, the more local the government, the more the people trust it. But American national identity is distinctive. As we'll see, that unusual character directly affects our politics and government.

Like any system, federalism has advantages and disadvantages.

Federalism's Advantages

Why have two dozen countries followed the United States and chosen the federalist style? Advocates of federalism claim five advantages: protection of individual rights; protection against dangerous leaders; multiple sources of innovation; responsiveness to local needs; and the ability to choose between different kinds of communities.[3]

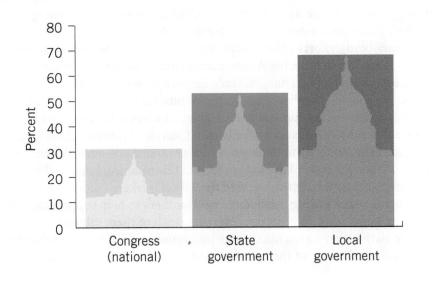

● **Figure 3.1** *Trust in government gets stronger as government gets closer to the public. (Gallup)*

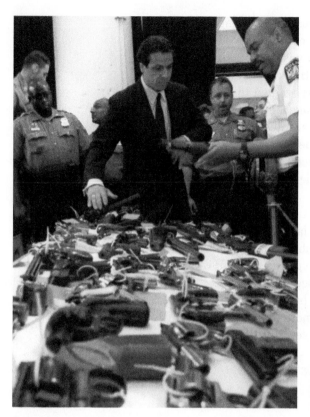

● *Sometimes government tries to limit violence by buying back guns. A program like this makes less sense in rural areas, where officials are more likely to emphasize hunting safety.*

Gridlock: A critical term applied to government's inability to advance policy solutions because of clashes among different branches or between national and state officials.

Diffusion: The spreading of policy ideas from one city or state to others; a process typical of US federalism.

First, proponents argue that federalism offers more *protection for individual rights*. If state officials won't respond to your complaints about pollution or gun laws, you can appeal to your member of Congress. Or you can seek a hearing in court—at the state or national level. When states denied African Americans the right to vote, the NAACP and other supporters of racial equality appealed to the national government. When the national government refused to let women vote, advocates focused on the states and first won voting rights there.

Second, federalist regimes provide *protection against dangerous leaders*. The constitutional framers termed these "demagogues" or "tyrants"—of course, they had King George III in mind. History offers many examples of charismatic leaders who gained power and then used it to repress or tyrannize their people. Checked by multiple officials at different government levels, it is extremely difficult for presidents, governors, Supreme Court justices, or anyone else to centralize control in their hands. Americans often take this feature for granted, or grumble about the **gridlock** caused by all the checks and balances, but their system protects liberty. Other countries recognize the advantage. After the horrors of Hitler and Nazism, for example, Germany restored a federalist system styled on the American model.

Third, federalism fosters *political innovation*. The Supreme Court justice Louis Brandeis called states "laboratories of democracy"—allowing states to test policies and see what works best. California's alternative energy policies have introduced new ways to reduce dependence on foreign oil. New York City's antiobesity efforts (like calorie counts on restaurant menus) represent novel approaches to reducing American waistlines. Individual states and cities have pioneered policy changes. Once they are judged successful, those policies can be adopted in other cities, states, or into national law.

This process of testing and spreading good ideas is termed **diffusion** by political scientists. Diffusion works best in federalist systems, where local officials have the authority to implement pilot programs and advertise their success or failure. US states have long exhibited this practice; back in the 1880s, for example, Massachusetts pioneered the idea of workers' compensation laws, and Illinois began paying pensions to new mothers to help support child nutrition and education. Within three decades, each of these initiatives had diffused to all the other states. Many other innovations bubbled up from the states before being taken up on the national level; examples include environmental protection, worker safety rules, women's suffrage, direct election of senators, business regulations, social security, and even alcohol prohibition.[4]

Fourth, proponents argue that federalism is *more responsive* to citizen needs and desires. The United States is a vast nation spanning states with very different problems and attitudes. Maine and Minnesota, with abundant freshwater sources, do not need to regulate water in the same way as do desert states like Arizona and Nevada. Large cities try to curb gang violence with curfews and gun buy-back programs that would not make much sense in rural areas. In short, state and local government can match policies to local conditions and values without a "one size fits all" national policy.

Finally, some advocates argue that federalism gives people more *choices*. Each state offers a different bundle of costs and services. People who want or need many government services can move to the Northeast; those who don't can move to the South or West. People who care about environmental or anti-smoking regulations can choose places with stringent rules like California or Oregon.[5]

The Disadvantages

Governing is more complicated in nations with multiple layers of independent officials. Critics point to four primary problems built into the complexities of federalism.

First, federalism introduces *problems of coordination* among federal, state, and local agencies. All respond to crises. All address chronic problems like poverty, pollution, and crime. Simply getting all the first responders onto

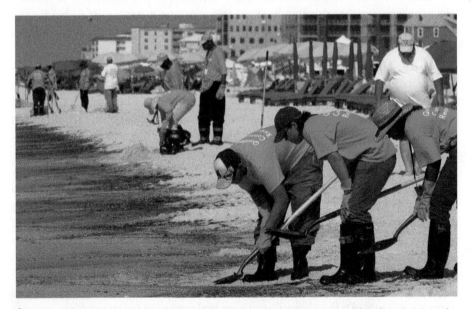

● *After a massive oil spill in the Gulf Coast in 2010, cleanup crews included personnel from federal, state, and local agencies as well as individuals hired by the oil company, and volunteers.*

Preserving Local Values or Continuing a Terrible Injustice?

Law-and-order issues are largely in the hands of local and state governments. One result: Texas and California have very high execution rates, yet many other states ban the death penalty altogether. Should we leave the question of executions to the states—with some minimal oversight by the Supreme Court to ensure that correct procedures are observed? What do you think?

Yes. Law enforcement ought to reflect local values. This is just the way it should be, because conditions such as crime rates vary from state to state.

No. Executions are too important a matter to leave up to such a patchwork of local laws regarding life and death. This should be a question we decide collectively as a nation, so that when it comes to the death penalty, punishment does not depend on the state you live in. We might decide as a nation to *abolish* the death penalty altogether, despite what some death-penalty supporters in individual states might desire. Or we might choose to permit executions, while seeking to ensure that no innocent person is executed, perhaps by mandating DNA testing of the accused.

the same communication frequency during crises has taken many years and millions of dollars.

Second, critics argue that diversity can lead to *poor policies.* A unitary government can standardize best practices across a nation. If policies vary across fifty different states, some will have good educational systems, others might have poor ones.

A third drawback, according to critics, is that federalism leads to *inequities* across layers of government, including vast differences in laws. A single mother working full time for eight dollars an hour can be treated for breast cancer in New York's Medicaid program but is not eligible for any treatment in Texas. Health advocates charge that this is unjust.

Fourth, critics fear that competition between states and localities leads to a *race to the bottom*—the idea that providing better social services for poor people will drive out businesses (which don't want to pay higher taxes) and attract poor people looking for enhanced benefits (this is called the "welfare magnet problem"). Leave social welfare policy to the states, argue defenders of national standards, and the result is a bidding war in which each state tries to cut programs (and taxes) more than neighboring states. Although the race to the bottom hypothesis is hard to measure, political scientists have found some evidence that states do follow one another as benefits are lowered (but not as benefits are raised); they have found very little support for the welfare magnet idea—lower-income people do not generally move to snap up better benefits.[6]

The Stakes

Why is this debate important? Because the ambiguity in federalism sets up a constant dispute about where to place specific decisions—which shape policies that potentially affect the lives of millions of people. Do we leave decisions with the states because they are "closer to the people"? Or do we place them on the national level to try to promote equality and high standards across the country, even if local people resent them? For many Americans, the preferable level shifts with the issue.

Most people conclude that national standards ought to override local control on some issues but not others. Should federal laws criminalizing marijuana possession trump state efforts to decriminalize? Liberals generally say no and support local choice. Should national clean-air standards override state pollution regulations, and national health care standards override state insurance regulations? Now most liberals would say yes, while conservatives say no. The debates are built right into our federal system.

One kind of issue, however, can never be left to local sentiment: *basic citizenship rights*. Our system is designed to protect rights, even if the majority does not want to honor them. The problem is deciding just what counts as an inalienable right. Do same-sex partners have a right to marry? In 2013 twelve states and the District of Columbia said yes—but the number fluctuates as the courts weigh in and voters overrule legislatures through referenda. Three additional states have recognized same-sex marriages performed in other states. Meanwhile, thirty states have constitutional amendments defining marriage as a relationship between a man and a woman. We discuss the details of rights and of same-sex marriage in the next two chapters. For now, here is the key point: *federalism gives advocates on both sides many different political venues in which to challenge policies and assert rights.*

THE BOTTOM LINE

- The United States rebelled against a *unitary* system and rejected a *federation* after trying one for a decade. The Constitutional Convention created a new form: a federal system of shared and overlapping powers.
- There are at least five rationales for federalism: allowing greater protection for individual rights; minimizing the possibility of a single individual or party gaining too much power; enabling political innovations in the "laboratories of democracy"; responding to local needs; and enhancing choice.
- There are four main shortcomings: chaos, poor policies in some places, inequities, and fears of a "race to the bottom" among states.
- The pros and cons of federalism are important as we decide whether to create national standards and programs or whether to leave judgment to local populations. This question is generally decided issue by issue and program by program.

How Federalism Works

Federalism offers endless opportunities for confusion and discord, as different layers of government clash over who has responsibility for what. For more than two centuries Americans have worked out successive sets of rules that enable our federalist system to function pretty well—most of the time. These rules, however, are not always clear and straightforward. Even the terminology can be elusive: Americans routinely call the national government the "federal government," a practice we also follow in this chapter, even though that term formally refers to the whole system of shared powers stretching across national, state, and local units.

The Constitution Sets the Ground Rules

The Constitution is alternately clear and vague about the division of national and state government responsibilities. Article 1, section 8, lists nineteen powers of the federal government: Congress has the power to pay debts, raise an army, punish pirates, establish a post office, handle US foreign policy, and so forth. Because they are laid out in black and white, scholars call them **granted powers**—also known as *express* or *enumerated powers* (you can read them in the Constitution in Appendix II). This section of the Constitution is crisp and clear about the limited list of national government powers.

The final clause of the section complicates interpretation by authorizing Congress to make all laws *necessary and proper* for carrying out the enumerated powers—*or any other power the Constitution vests in the national government*. As we saw in the last chapter, this **necessary and proper clause** is also known as the *elastic clause*, because it stretches national government authority to include anything implied in the Constitution's text. Over two centuries, the elastic clause has expanded national authority to include everything from creating banks to regulating airlines to overseeing zoos. These new areas of jurisdiction are **inherent powers**—powers that are implied by, but not specifically named in, the Constitution's text.

The **supremacy clause**, found near the end of the Constitution in article 6, buttresses these granted (or explicit) and inherent (or implicit) powers. The clause declares that the national government's laws and treaties are the "supreme law of the land" and are superior to state laws whenever the two clash. The supremacy clause formed the basis of the Obama administration's legal challenge to the Arizona immigration law, introduced at the start of this chapter.

States have their own authority guaranteed by the Tenth Amendment—the final amendment in the Bill of Rights. This "reserves" to the states all powers not expressly granted to the national branches in Washington. The Tenth Amendment is a favorite among small-government advocates. After the Republican Party won control of both chambers of Congress in 1994, its leaders distributed cards imprinted with the Tenth Amendment to House

Granted powers: National government powers set out explicitly in the Constitution.

Necessary and proper clause: Defines Congress's constitutional authority (in article 1, section 8) to exercise the "necessary and proper" powers to carry out its designated functions.

Inherent powers: National government powers implied by, but not specifically named in, the Constitution.

Supremacy clause: The constitutional declaration (in article 6, section 2) that the national government's authority prevails over any conflicting state or local government's claims.

and Senate Republican members, reminding them to limit federal government actions whenever possible. The states' **reserved powers** include public education, public health, commerce within the state, and organizing state elections. Police, prisons, and courts are also in each state's hands. State and local officials carry out most investigations, arrests, trials, and incarcerations—unless a federal law has been violated. State prisons and local jails hold 89 percent of the inmates in the United States.

It is a mistake to think of federalism simply as conflict between government levels. Many duties—termed **concurrent powers**—are shared by state and national authorities. Both national and state governments have the power to raise taxes, build roads, construct bridges, build railways, update telecommunications networks, borrow money, and regulate business. The next time you're stuck in traffic inching past a sign announcing new transportation construction, look it over carefully: you'll usually see a combination of national, state, and local funds listed as support.

Federalism also involves relations among the states. The Constitution directs each state to give **full faith and credit** to the actions of other states. This requirement becomes controversial, however, when states disagree with policies enacted by others. One fierce current debate swirls around the marriage of same-sex couples. Most states refuse to grant those marriages "full faith and credit"—as we'll explore in the next chapter. Another controversy concerns gun control laws, which vary widely from state to state. Washington, DC, restricts carrying guns in public. Virginia, which surrounds Washington's southern half, features a "concealed carry" law, allowing gun owners to bring legally registered weapons into restaurants and other public places. In 2012, the state went further, eliminating local Virginia communities' ability to fingerprint those applying for a concealed carry permit. Should DC officials grant "full faith and credit" to Virginia's generous policy? Constitutional law is unclear and must be sorted out case by case.

The Constitution also sets up some definite barriers. A state may not launch its own navy, conclude treaties with another country, or coin its own money. The Bill of Rights, which protects individual liberty (like freedom of religion) from government action, originally applied only to the federal government. But, as we'll see in Chapter 4, almost every individual right in the first ten amendments now applies to the states as well. For now, the important point is that the Constitution establishes an elaborate list of powers and limits for both the national and the state governments.

On balance, you can interpret the Constitution as emphasizing the power of either national or state government. An expansive national role is implied in the necessary and proper (or elastic) clause and the supremacy clause. On the other hand, the Tenth Amendment provides a more limited role for the national government. Again we return to a vital point: American government is a perpetual argument, a work in progress. The Constitution's ground rules for federalism are open to interpretation and reinterpretation. They have guided

Reserved powers: The constitutional guarantee (in the Tenth Amendment) that the states retain government authority not explicitly granted to the national government.

Concurrent powers: Governmental authority shared by national and state governments, such as the power to tax residents.

Full faith and credit clause: The constitutional requirement (in article 4, section 1) that each state recognize and uphold laws passed by any other state.

a long, often creative debate about which level of government should be doing what.

In different eras, Americans have organized the federal system in different ways. The next sections introduce the most important shifts.

Dual Federalism

Dual (or layer cake) federalism: Clear division of governing authority between national and state governments.

Across its first 150 years or so, the United States practiced a form of **dual federalism**, in which state and national governments had relatively clearly demarcated responsibilities. The state governments together wielded at least as much authority during this period as did national officials. American historians with an eye for metaphor describe this arrangement as "layer cake" federalism: the different levels of government—national, state, and local—fell more or less into separate layers. Each level of government was supreme within its own band of influence, connected to but operating largely separate from the others.

This division of labor left the national government in charge of three major areas. One was international relations—trade, war, diplomacy, and immigration. This was a significant role, as the United States deployed troops overseas 165 times in its first 150 years—and that count does not include a long and bloody series of conflicts with Native American tribes (we'll discuss military deployment in Chapter 14). Second, the national government was responsible for "internal improvements." These included developing transportation networks like roads, canals, and railroads; establishing a postal service that linked the growing nation; setting common standards like a single currency and a system of weights and measures; and acquiring new territory and setting the rules for distributing that land, as the nation spread across the continent. Finally, the federal government regulated relations and commerce between the states—a major question that could explode over issues like what to do about slaves running for their freedom.

States retained control over almost everything having to do with individual citizens—as well as corporations, which have been protected as "citizens" under the law since 1848. This arrangement remains substantially the same today. As political scientist Theodore Lowi notes, America has "no national property laws, no national corporate laws . . . no national marriage and divorce laws, no national compulsory education laws, no national contract laws for conveyance of property, no professions laws, not even any motor vehicle laws . . . and almost no national criminal laws except for crimes defined as interstate."[7]

The layer cake metaphor was never quite as accurate as it might seem. The national government gave away land in the unsettled territories. It wrestled endlessly with the slavery issue

● *Constructing canals, bridges, roads—and, later, railroads—was a major national-government responsibility in the nineteeth century. So was delivering the mail, briefly via the Pony Express. Both national responsibilities are pictured above.*

before the Civil War. It spent more than a decade trying to reconstruct racial relations in the South after the Civil War. It used control of interstate commerce to crack down on pornography, restrict contraception, and fight abortion (all in the 1870s); it crafted model morals legislation on these topics that every state copied and implemented (turning abortion, for example, from a common practice to an illegal one in the decades after the Civil War). In 1920, the Nineteenth Amendment forbade the transportation and sale of intoxicating liquors. State and national authorities had overlapping jurisdiction in enforcing the act.[8] Still, despite many exceptions, government activity remained, very roughly, separated into layers.

Cooperative Federalism

During the New Deal, the dual arrangement finally collapsed. President Franklin Roosevelt and large Democratic majorities in Congress responded vigorously to the Great Depression by passing a wide range of policies that decisively strengthened the national government's position. Roosevelt presided over a shift toward **cooperative federalism**, characterized by blurred lines of authority and a much more active national government (Table 3.1). A new bakery metaphor emerged: a *marble cake*, with its various ingredients—the different government functions—all swirled together. In one program after another, the responsibilities of federal, state, and local governments

Cooperative (or marble cake) federalism: Mingled governing authority, with functions overlapping across national and state governments.

Table 3.1 Comparing Dual and Cooperative Federalism

DUAL FEDERALISM	COOPERATIVE FEDERALISM
NATIONAL POWERS	
Enumerated: The national government may only utilize powers specifically listed in the Constitution.	**Elastic:** The national government may wield powers "necessary and proper" to support its function.
LOCATION OF SUPREME AUTHORITY	
Separate sovereignty: National and state governments each have authority within their own spheres.	**National supremacy:** States retain important powers but are subordinate to the national government except where the Constitution strictly forbids.
KEY PRINCIPLE	
States' rights: Each state is largely free to govern its own affairs.	**Power sharing:** National and state officials work together wherever possible—also with local officials, who became more prominent after the 1930s.
NATION-STATE RELATIONS	
Competitive: Relationship characterized by tension, not cooperation.	**Cooperative:** Relationship considered to be joint, not competitive.

American Federalism
Layer Cake or Marble Cake?

Layer Cake Federalism
has a clear division of governing authority between national and state governments.

Marble Cake Federalism
mingles governing authority with functions overlapping across national and state governments.

● **Figure 3.2** *Different federalist styles across US history.*

were increasingly mingled: funding, rules, administration, implementation, and execution cut across the different layers of federalism (Figure 3.2).

Officials in Washington provided federal funds through **grants-in-aid**—national funds accompanied by specific instructions to state and local officials about how the money could be spent. Governors and other state leaders, desperate for resources during the Depression, accepted these national grants for public works, health care, Social Security support for seniors, and so forth—along with accompanying Washington rules and oversight.

As the post–World War II era ushered in economic prosperity, some state and local officials expressed resentment at national meddling in their affairs. Federal funds continued to flow, however, with even the most ardent states' rights advocates unwilling to deny their constituents this national bounty.

The nationally slanted version of cooperative federalism, with Washington taking the lead in most policy areas, lasted from the New Deal through the 1970s. Senator Everett Dirksen (R-IL) quipped in 1964 that if the trend toward increasing national power continued, "the only people still interested in state boundaries would be Rand-McNally," the noted US mapmaker.[9]

New Federalism

Ronald Reagan's presidency (1981–1989) ushered in another significant change in American federalism, enthusiastically termed **New Federalism** by its advocates. Reagan and fellow conservatives tipped the pendulum of power away from national officials, promoting more decision-making authority by state and local officials. In place of grants-in-aid, with national officials carefully specifying the rules and regulations that accompanied the funds, the Reagan administration relied more heavily on **block grants**. Block grants still channel federal dollars to a specific policy area, like education or transportation or health, but leave the program's details to state and local bureaucrats. Block grants had developed and expanded through the 1970s under Presidents Richard Nixon

Grants-in-aid: National government funding provided to state and local governments, along with specific instructions about how the funds may be used.

New Federalism: A version of cooperative federalism, but with stronger emphasis on state and local government activity, vs. national government.

Block grants: National government funding provided to state and local governments, with relatively few restrictions or requirements on spending.

(1969–1974), Gerald Ford (1974–1977), and Jimmy Carter (1977–1981); Reagan used them to rethink federalism.

One feature of block grants has made them controversial. Grants-in-aid often provide unlimited funding for a specific purpose; for example, everyone who qualifies for Medicaid receives hospital coverage, and anyone eligible for food stamps gets food stamps. In contrast, block grants provide a fixed amount of funds for health care or nutrition. State and local officials face a tough trade-off: they get to do what they think best with the funds; however, block grants no longer automatically cover everyone who qualifies. They limit federal financial commitment and force state officials to make tough choices about how to allocate money that under earlier programs would have simply gone to everyone who qualified. As a result, every effort to shift an existing grant-in-aid program to a block grant creates controversy.

Notice that New Federalism does not restore the neat layers of dual federalism—if anything, the lines of authority are even more swirled together. Federal, state, and local authorities all compete for influence over programs. Perhaps you can think of it as a multi-flavored marble cake.

"In Two Words, Yes And No"

● Struggles over the extent of cooperative federalism, captured in 1949—and still an issue, more than 60 years later.

THE BOTTOM LINE

- The Constitution grants the national government both enumerated (or explicit) powers and inherent (or implicit) powers. You can read it to emphasize broad national powers (using the elastic clause) or state dominance (emphasizing the Tenth Amendment).
- There have been three important eras of federalism: dual federalism included clearly demarcated authority (the layer cake); cooperative federalism, arising with FDR's New Deal, introduced federal dominance and blurred lines of authority (the marble cake); President Reagan's New Federalism still relies on federal funds, but shifts more decision-making about spending those monies back to the states.

● Battles over Federalism Today

Across American history, the Tenth Amendment guarantee of states' reserved powers has raised conflicts with Congress's exercise of authority under the necessary and proper clause. The most difficult clash over states' rights, the tensions between North and South over the spread of slavery, eventually produced the Civil War. Today disagreements over federalism are fought with

Legislation + Litigation

States can enact laws that protect individual liberty and take the federal government to court to defend those laws.

Taxpayer Courts

Taxpayers can't sue the federal government for abuse of their tax dollars, but states can authorize taxpayers to bring lawsuits in state court to stop state and federal governments from using tax dollars in ways that violate the Constitution.

Expand Civil Rights Laws

Because state sovereignty is a protection the U.S. Constitution guarantees to all Americans, states can enact civil rights laws to protect that right and enable individuals to sue state and federal governments when they disregard state sovereignty.

Constitutional Defense Councils

States can create independent Constitutional Defense Councils that have the authority and funding to defend state sovereignty in court.

Coordination

Many federal agencies are governed by laws that contain "coordination" provisions. State and local governments can limit the impact of new federal regulations by requiring federal agencies to coordinate with existing local laws, regulations, plans, and policies.

Reinvigorate Reserved Powers

The Tenth Amendment says that powers not listed in the U.S. Constitution belong to the states. States can pass laws that invoke those reserved powers and force the feds to illegally commandeer state officials in order to enforce federal laws that upset the balance of power between the states and Washington.

Federalism

10 WAYS FOR STATES TO CHECK AND BALANCE WASHINGTON

Brought to you by **GoldwaterInstitute.org**

Empower the People

Sometimes we don't need new laws in order to protect individual rights. Sometimes we need to repeal laws that are already on the books. Many state laws actually invite the federal government to get involved in the minutia of local affairs. One way to stop that is to replace those laws with opportunities for citizens to protect their own rights.

Refuse Conditional Grants

States can limit or eliminate the power of state and local officials to accept federal grants that require the state or local government to give more control over local decision-making to Washington.

Amend the Constitution

State legislatures were given the same power as Congress to propose amendments to the U.S. Constitution. States can initiate the process by proposing amendments to the U.S. Constitution that would limit the size, scope, and intrusiveness of the federal government.

Interstate Compacts

Interstate compacts are contracts between two or more states. Compacts can be used to protect individual rights and state sovereignty, and they don't always need congressional approval. Interstate compacts could be used to prevent the federal government from enforcing key provisions of the federal health care bill, or from infringing on Second Amendment rights, for example.

● **Figure 3.3** *A poster published by a conservative organization offers strategies for empowering states and limiting the federal government. (Goldwater Institute)*

words and regulations rather than swords and cannonballs, but they remain heated.

One pillar of the New Federalism movement was **devolution**, or transferring responsibility for government programs from national to state and local authorities. Over the three decades since Reagan's presidency, devolutionists have remained fervent about reducing the influence and involvement of government at every level. One prominent conservative activist, Grover Norquist

Devolution: The transfer of authority from national to state or local government level.

Jr., vowed to reduce national government "down to the size where we can drown it in the bathtub."[10] Other advocates of devolution compile lists of ways in which states can block federal authority. (See Figure 3.3 for an example.)

Arguments over the proper extent of devolution are sure to continue. Even states' rights advocates sometimes find that devolving policies to the local level does not guarantee a less active government response. For example, conservatives in recent years have pushed hard to prevent national authorities from issuing regulations to manage wildlife, including protecting endangered species. Yet after the national government cut back Environmental Protection Agency and Forest Service supervision of wildlife management, invasive species like zebra mussels and milfoil (a plant native to Asia that has choked the life out of many American ponds and lakes) overwhelmed local wildlife agencies and caused billions of dollars in damage. Harmful plants and creatures are oblivious to local and state boundaries; a federal government response, coordinating eradication efforts across multiple jurisdictions, was needed.

Other voices in federalism debates accept that the national government has legitimate authority in some areas, but they argue that when responsibility is passed to state or local officials, there must be national resources to match. Otherwise, they claim, Washington will saddle their state or locality with an **unfunded mandate**—a law or regulation that imposes a duty that must be paid for primarily by state or local officials.

Officials at different levels of government often strongly disagree about what counts as an unfunded mandate. Congress acknowledged the problem in 1995, passing the Unfunded Mandates Act. This act set a $50 million threshold for national government mandates large enough to qualify as injuring a state. In the past few years, Washington has issued a stream of laws that exceed that threshold—requiring extensive state and local actions, without appropriating funds to pay for these. The total price tag of unfunded mandates, state and local officials estimate, is more than $150 billion annually—although this is a highly politicized number since officials often disagree about what exactly counts as an unfunded mandate.

Ultimately, trade-offs will always exist around federal funding and levels of control. Table 3.2 sets out the range of possibilities. The next time national officials pass a law in a policy area you care about, pay close attention to how much supervision from Washington is involved, and what proportion of required funding comes from national government.

Unfunded mandate: An obligation imposed on state or local government officials by federal legislation, without sufficient federal funding support to cover the costs.

Table 3.2 Trade-Offs: National Government Funds and Oversight

		Level of National Funding	
		High	Low
Degree of National Supervision	High	Cooperative Federalism (Grants-in-Aid)	Unfunded Mandates
	Low	New Federalism (Block Grants)	Dual Federalism

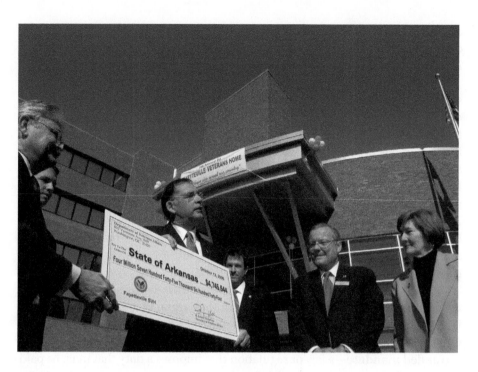

● A federal grant to an Arkansas Veterans Home allows officials from every level of government to claim credit. A Deputy Assistant Secretary in the Veterans Administration holds the big check with Representative John Boozman (R-AR) as State Senator Sue Madison (D-AR) looks on.

Federalism and the Parties

Dual, cooperative, and new: these successive versions of federalism point to ongoing negotiations about government power and accountability. Depending on the issue and on which officials are in charge, governing may be focused at the local, state, or national level. Party ideology provides some clues about how a policy will play out. Republicans continue to urge state and local control on most issues, while Democrats are more likely to seek Washington-based solutions.

This rule of thumb is often violated in practice. President George W. Bush, though a small-government conservative, strenuously promoted a national education policy. His administration's No Child Left Behind (NCLB) education program required strict (and frequent) student testing in order to evaluate schools. It led to widespread criticism from parents, teachers, and principals about "meddling Washington bureaucrats." Many of those critics also pointed out that NCLB programs also amounted to an unfunded mandate, since federal funds were rarely sufficient to cover the cost of preparing students and administering the tests.

Conversely, Bill Clinton's Democratic administration rewrote welfare policy to shift authority and discretion to state and local governments. Clinton took a program with roots in the Social Security Act of 1935, Aid to Families with Dependent Children (AFDC, often known simply as "welfare"), and turned it into a block grant program called Temporary Assistance for Needy Families (TANF). By the time Clinton was elected in 1992, AFDC was providing unlimited state funds (paying for roughly one in six American children) accompanied by strict regulations about eligibility for assistance and many other program details. TANF, in contrast, sends block grant funds and leaves most details up to the states. More recently Congress imposed new limits on how long a beneficiary could receive welfare and prohibited payments to all aliens, even if they have green cards and are in the country legally. The original TANF policy was, again, signed by a Democratic president.

Why would Democratic and Republican administrations stray so far from their parties' images? The context matters: abstract debates about national and state power run into policy reality as public officials struggle to make troubled programs more effective. Both the Bush and Clinton administrations also had an eye on politics, for each was trying to quiet criticism. Republicans wanted to show they cared about social policy; Democrats were trying to remove the stigma of being "pro-welfare."

The political art of **credit claiming** also influences federalism. If the national government authorizes significant block grant funding for a program, local or state officials cheerfully take the credit, because they designed the program specifics. In turn, members of Congress—who, after all, must win reelection in individual districts and states—crowd into the photo opportunities and point out that they provided the funds. That's why you'll often see a whole range

Credit claiming: The ability of political figures to generate a belief among their constituents or supporters that they are personally responsible for some government action or achievement.

What Do You Think?

Intergovernmental Lobbying, American Style

Although the title sounds deceptively plain, intergovernmental affairs (IGA) liaison offices keep the wheels of American federalism turning. No other country's chief executive has established a formal office to *lobby* (and be lobbied by) its own different levels of government: this is a hallmark of US federalism. Imagine that you join the president's IGA liaison team. You'll spend time smoothing the White House's relations with governors and mayors from all fifty states: sometimes a mayor seeks you out to secure a favor from the president, and other times you're tasked with winning a governor's backing for something the White House wants to achieve. If you were in this job, how would you characterize your role in government?

It would feel like a valuable public service. I would help build bridges across the different layers of federalist government.

I would just be another lobbyist. My role would rely on winning favors for my client—who happens, in this case, to be the president of the United States.

● *Children from public schools in the town of Chatfield, MN, seen with President Barack Obama in August 2011, as part of the Race to the Top program. Like other Obama administration initiatives, Race to the Top provides a pool of funds for which states or localities compete—a novel wrinkle in America's federalist varieties.*

of politicians—House and Senate members, the governor's top staff, state legislative and local leaders, even White House officials—line up for the cameras when a program is announced.

Today, the relationship among national, state, and local levels takes a dizzying array of forms—sometimes working in partnership, sometimes locked in combat. The one contemporary constant is *connection*: on almost no issue do different levels of government exert separate functions, as in the old dual federalist system. To keep all the tangled relationships clear, intergovernmental liaison officers work across national, state, city, and even town governments.

The Obama administration's stamp on federalism has been to emphasize *competition* among states or cities for federal funds. The administration seeks to nudge states toward desired policy goals without overbearing national regulations. The Education Department's Race to the Top program, for example, encourages states to compete for pools of national dollars by devising creative education policies. Winning proposals have included promoting charter schools, basing teacher pay on performance rather than the number of years served, and developing new measures to track student progress.

Like the administrations that preceded it, the Obama administration is not always consistent in its approach. Faced with the Bush administration testing requirements, the Obama administration permitted many states to waive national rules and design their own procedures. This was a step in the direction of reduced Washington regulations. On the issue of health reform, in contrast, the administration was far more eager to promulgate national requirements for insurance companies and health providers—despite protests from some states.

Federalism in the Courts

Most federalism disputes are about drawing the line where national power ends and states' authority begins—and how best to ensure that the division of power is honored in practice. US courts early on became a key source of allocating powers between state and nation. Judges have typically played a balancing role when it comes to federalism. Supreme Court decisions favored national prerogatives during the early republic, when many individual states had more power and prestige than the federal government in Washington. At the time it was not clear whether the national government could sustain its strength compared to the power enjoyed by long-established states. In a series of landmark decisions, the Supreme Court—led by Chief Justice John Marshall—protected national government powers from state incursions.

The first such case was *McCulloch v. Maryland*, decided in 1819.[11] A year before, Maryland's legislature sought to impose a tax on the Baltimore branch of the first US national bank. Invoking the necessary and proper clause, Marshall ruled that Congress could draw on "implied powers" required to operate a functional national government, and that states blocking such actions violated the Constitution. (See Chapter 13 for a description of this case.) In these and later decisions, Marshall and many other officials in the early republic were anxious to keep dual federalism in balance.

During Franklin Roosevelt's presidency, conversely, as power shifted to Washington, court decisions often upheld state and local (as well as individual corporations') authority. Have the courts—especially the Supreme Court—continued to support a balance between different levels of government today?

In recent years—beginning under Chief Justice Rehnquist in the mid-1990s, and gaining strength with a consistently conservative majority under Chief Justice Roberts since 2005—the Supreme Court has emphasized local and state power. A series of prominent cases has shifted power away from the national government toward states (see Table 3.3).

Table 3.3 Recent Supreme Court Decisions on Federalism

• *U.S. v. Lopez* (1995). Struck down a law prohibiting handguns near schools, claiming Congress had overreached its authority.
• *Seminole Tribe v. Florida* (1996). Reversed Congress's decision allowing Indian tribes to sue a state in federal court; limited individuals' right to sue a state for failing to uphold national laws.
• *Printz v. U.S.* (1997). Struck down portions of Congress-passed Brady bill requiring background checks before gun sales.
• *U.S. v. Morrison* (2000). Struck down portions of the Violence Against Women Act as "an unconstitutional exercise . . . of Congressional power."
• *Board of Trustees of the University of Alabama v. Garrett* (2001). One of a series of cases that upheld "state sovereign immunity" by expanding state rights under the Eleventh Amendment (which stipulates that states may not be sued in federal court by citizens of another state).
• *Gonzales v. Oregon* (2006). Ruled that national government power to regulate drugs was limited by states' right to exercise authority over drug laws within their jurisdiction.
• *Medellin v. Texas* (2008). Permitted states to file a type of legal petition repeatedly, overturning national government rules declaring otherwise.
• *Bond v. United States* (2011). Extended to individuals the right to challenge federal statutes on the grounds that they interfere with powers reserved to the states.
• *National Federation of Independent Business v. Sebelius* (2012). This decision on the Affordable Care Act, aka "Obamacare," struck down the national government's power to set standards for expanded Medicaid eligibility across the states.

Exceptions to the recent run of state-friendly decisions certainly exist. For example, the Supreme Court reversed a California law establishing reduced legal penalties for marijuana use. If history is a reliable guide, the current judicial trend will fade over time, as the pendulum of state and national power swings again.

THE BOTTOM LINE

- Devolution transfers responsibility back to state and local governments; unfunded mandates represent Congressional requirements that the states perform tasks without sufficient federal funding. Both strategies are controversial.
- Administrations trying to improve programs often take a pragmatic approach that belies the simple expectation that Democrats seek national programs while Republicans try to devolve power to state and local governments.
- The judicial system, especially the Supreme Court, has trended toward returning power to state and local government in recent years.

Nationalism, American Style

Federalism returns our focus to the Constitution (elastic clause versus the Tenth Amendment); on how institutions evolve (dual federalism versus cooperative federalism, layer cake versus marble cake); and on the clash between national versus state versus local ("drown it in the bathtub!"). However, something deeper holds the entire complicated apparatus in place. It is the vague, elusive, cultural feeling known as *nationalism*, or the US public's sense of identity as Americans.

Without a sense of nationalism, the entire federal experiment might have collapsed long ago. Tested by regional divides, Southern secession during the Civil War, economic strains in every era, and red-state-versus-blue-state partisan conflict today, it might seem a wonder the states remain united at all. More than one analyst has suggested that New England townships, the Bible Belt, and mostly liberal cities of the "Left Coast" belong in different countries. One secret to American nationhood lies in its unusual version of national identity. Nationalism helps maintain the federal balance by instilling loyalty to nation, state, and locality. In the next section we explore the development of American nationalism.

The Imagined Community

Time was running out on the US national soccer team at the 2010 World Cup. Stuck in a scoreless tie, with barely more than a minute left in the opening-round match, the US forward Landon Donovan knocked in a rebound off the Algerian goalkeeper. The result was an instant YouTube sensation: crowds of

see for yourself 3.1

Go online to hear the cheers of "U-S-A! U-S-A!" from this soccer match.

Americans, watching the match in city plazas, restaurants, and sports bars across the country (and around the world), exploded in delirium as the winning goal flew into the net. Wild cheers broke out: "U-S-A! U-S-A!"

Stop and ponder what these crowds were celebrating. The patriotic fervor was about something more than a goal scored by mostly unknown players in a sport that many Americans ignore. What did the nationwide burst of cheering represent? Put simply, the joy of fellow-feeling among members of the same country. That feeling, known as *nationalism*, can be difficult to explain. Yet it runs powerfully through most societies and even leads people to sacrifice their lives for their nation. One famous description comes from political scientist Benedict Anderson: nationalism is membership in an "imagined community," a sense of connectedness across millions of people who will, for the most part, never see or meet one another. A nation exists, Anderson concludes, because people believe that it does.[12]

Such a strong nationalist outlook presents a puzzle: The United States ranks very high—often first—in polls that ask about patriotism. Yet, as we have seen at various points in this book so far, Americans are also suspicious of "Big Government" in Washington, DC. In contrast to most other nations, the United States features a robust self-conscious national community (strong nationalism) and also a government split into multiple levels by federalism and then further divided on each level by multiple checks and balances. The juxtaposition—**strong nation**, weak national government—shapes American politics, governing practices, and policymaking.

Strong nation: Robust spirit of national identity shared by a people.

America's Weak National Government

The United States, virtually alone in modern national history, has long presented the unusual picture of a strong nation accompanied by a weak central government. Today, we measure the strength of central governments by examining three longstanding principles: size, authority, and independence.

Size. American national government was traditionally smaller than those in other nations. It grew, in leaps, during World War I, the Great Depression, World War II, the Cold War, and the Great Society of the 1960s. Each growth spurt brought protests and efforts to cut the government back to size. Opponents, fearful of the growing New Deal government, called President Franklin Roosevelt a Communist, a Socialist, and worse (in the 1930s). Recent critics blasted Presidents George W. Bush and Barack Obama for growing government still further. Despite all the fears—or perhaps because of them—the United States government is still smaller than those of most other wealthy nations.

What seems like big government to many Americans is relatively small in international context. The United States ranks near the bottom of industrialized nations in terms of total government spending as a share of the economy. The US government spends less—and leaves more to the private sector (see Figure 3.4).

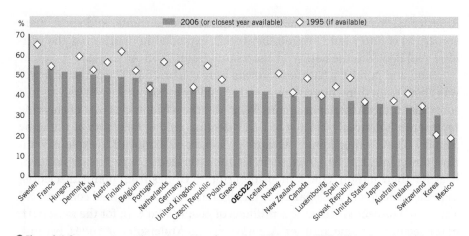

● **Figure 3.4** *Government spending as proportion of gross domestic product. While US levels are lower, they have held steady for the past decade while in much of Europe the amount fell. (OECD)*

Authority. By the mid-nineteenth century, most nations—from France to China and from Germany to the British colonies in India—had powerful, efficient, national bureaucracies, known as the civil service.

In sharp contrast, nineteenth-century American government engaged its citizens (that is, its white males) without a strong central administration or bureaucracy. Popular participation in the United States ranged from civic participation in communal projects to the spoils system which rewarded loyal party members with jobs in the local, state, and national government.

Civic voluntarism: Citizen participation in public life without government incentives or coercion (speaking at a town meeting, vs. paying taxes, for example).

American **civic voluntarism** presented a virtually unprecedented spectacle in the nineteenth and early twentieth centuries. The same spirit pervades American government today. Even the military—the most centralized and bureaucratic sector of American public life—emerged from a long tradition of citizen soldiers (or militias). For example, the National Guard continues the tradition of citizen soldiers drawn from local communities, commanded by local officers, and accountable to local public officials. The United States has always emphasized community participation over centralized administration. The same local spirit that helps define federalism limits the authority of national officials.

Independence. In a powerful centralized system, government officials can act forcefully—as long as their superiors approve. Strong national governments even limit the ways that lobbyists may approach decision makers. In contrast, Americans separate and divide governing power more extensively than any other modern country. Federalism operates along a vertical dimension, as power is shared among different levels of government—national, state, and local. At every level and within every branch and institution there are further internal checks. In short, checks and balances at every level multiply federalism's horizontal division of power. No public official can act independently. Each needs cooperation from others.

● *Civic voluntarism in action. European visitors like Tocqueville were amazed by the American participatory spirit—it was democratic, energetic, chaotic, and a key feature of nationalism American style.*

The Hidden Government

A weak national government has one unexpected attribute: it is hard to see. Scholars identify a "hidden" or "submerged" American central government,[13] hidden for two reasons.

First, many government programs work indirectly, hidden from public view. Programs often operate through private sources, as the issue of health care demonstrates. Europe's powerful central administrators simply created national health insurance programs. The American government, in contrast, developed a tax break for employers, who then offered health insurance to employees. The program was developed in the Eisenhower administration specifically to fend off more direct government health care programs. Today, the deduction amounts to a $130 billion federal program, making it one of the largest government-funded health care programs in the world. However, recipients do not see the government's hand. All they see is that their employer is providing health benefits.[14]

Second, note how health insurance is provided: through a tax deduction. The national government offers similar deductions that help people buy homes, save for retirement, pay for schooling, or receive support if their income is low. These are all massive programs. However, they don't *seem* like government programs because of the way they are funded. Most people do not think of a tax deduction as a government program at all (Figure 3.5). The tax credit is politically invisible (which makes it easier to pass). Add up all the invisible programs and you have a "submerged" central government.

The result is that Americans do not see the government programs they are benefitting from. In an important recent study, the political scientist Suzanne Mettler asked American citizens whether they receive federal benefits. Figure 3.5 shows the number of people who benefit from government programs but incorrectly answered no. Again we see that programs operating through the tax code (in blue) are much harder to track. More than half of the respondents

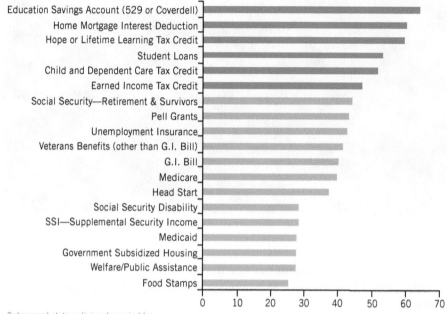

Percentage of program beneficiaries who report that they "Have Not Used a Government Social Program"

Figure 3.5 *Dislike of government meets the hidden state. Even beneficiaries of the biggest programs don't realize they are getting benefits from the government. The blue lines denote the percentage of people who didn't realize they were getting a tax benefit. Yellow lines denote the percentage of people who didn't realize they were getting a check or benefit. (Cornell Survey Research Institute)*

didn't stop to think that their retirement savings or their student loans were a government-provided benefit.

In short, a weaker central government does things indirectly. That makes people think that national officials are doing less for them (or nothing at all). And that, in turn, helps keep the government unpopular—and thus weak.

THE BOTTOM LINE

- Americans have long felt a strong sense of nationalism. This helps bind together a large and diverse nation with a fragmented government.
- "Strong nation, weak national government" is a great American paradox. A weak government means that American institutions (and officials) rank relatively low on three dimensions: size, authority, and independence.
- The political results of this paradox include an emphasis on citizen participation, the importance of building alliances, and a reliance on power and money.
- Another result is that the US national government is "submerged"—that is, Americans tend not to realize what benefits government officials actually provide.

● Conclusion: Who Are We?

Federalism seems, on the surface, like a simple matter of government engineering: How do we decide who does what on the federal, state, and local levels? In reality, federalism reflects an intense philosophical debate, carved into institutional stone.

The debate—about power and democracy, fairness and liberty—reappears across American history. Successive eras allocated power differently. Dual federalism (the layer cake) largely kept the spheres separate. The era of concurrent federalism saw the federal government expand its role and mix with state and local functions (the marble cake). Today, conservatives and courts promote a New Federalism that devolves more decisions to state and local governments. These efforts involve more layers of government and make more ambiguous than ever who is responsible for what.

Issue after issue returns us to this question of where to locate government authority: federal, state, or local. Who should decide whether to decriminalize marijuana? Oversee hydraulic fracturing, or fracking? Mete out the death penalty? Promote educational standards? Regulate insurance companies? Protect the homeland?

Federalism is the mark of a weak national government. However, the paradox of American politics is that weak government is balanced by a powerful nation with a robust, patriotic sense of national identity. That force helps bind together all the centrifugal institutions of a federal system shot through with checks and balances on every level of government.

Many critics suggest that the weak central government diminishes American capacity for the challenges of the twenty-first century. Others fear the opposite: an inexorably growing state marks the decline of American liberty. We'll revisit these fears throughout this book. For now, simply recognize that this debate echoes those that Federalists and Anti-Federalists were expressing in the 1780s. The conflict involves balancing the most important American values, never an easy task.

In summary, Chapter 1 examined seven enduring American ideas. Chapter 2 showed how those ideas were institutionalized in the American Constitution. Here, in Chapter 3, federalism tackles the question of how government institutions evolved, constantly balancing power and liberty, the fear of government, and the quest for equality. Federalism offers us the institutional framework—and philosophical arguments about the institutional framework—for everything that follows in this book. In the next two chapters, we will address the important role federalism plays in the great American quest for civil liberties and civil rights.

CHAPTER SUMMARY

● Americans are a people of multiple loyalties—to their nation, state, and home city or town. These divides are mirrored in our federalist politics. The United States separates power in multiple ways, both horizontally (across branches of government) and vertically (across national, state, and local levels).

● Only two dozen nations worldwide share America's federalist-style political organization; most have more centralized unitary governments. The American founders adopted a federalist system, in part to protect against concentrating too much power in one person or branch, but also to expand protections for individual rights, increase government's flexibility, and enable more political innovations to flourish. Federalism has drawbacks, but it has never seriously been questioned as the American governing style.

● Different versions of federalism are evident in US history, from dual federalism (states and nation performing largely separate functions) to cooperative and new versions that involve closer partnership across government levels. Issues like devolution and unfunded mandates mark ongoing negotiations over the terms of the elaborate arrangement of local, state, and national governing power.

● Given this divided authority, we might wonder what has held the United States together, especially given regional differences that culminated in civil war. An uncommonly strong sense of national identity is a large part of the answer. Born during the Revolution and powerfully evident after the Constitution's ratification, Americans' devotion to national unity was instrumental in building a robust nation—although nationalism has its ugly, xenophobic sides as well.

● Alongside the concept of a strong nation is an anomaly among most countries with a similarly robust national spirit: a relatively weak American national government. This less powerful set of government institutions is found across American history, in both of the limited size of our federal bureaucracy and Washington's constrained capacity to act.

KEY TERMS

Block grants, 106
Civic voluntarism, 116
Concurrent powers, 103
Confederation, 96
Cooperative (or marble cake)
    federalism, 105
Credit claiming, 111
Devolution, 108

Diffusion, 98
Dual (or layer cake)
    federalism, 104
Full faith and credit clause, 103
Granted powers, 102
Grants-in-aid, 106
Gridlock, 98
Inherent powers, 102

Necessary and proper clause, 102
New Federalism, 106
Reserved powers, 103
Strong nation, 115
Supremacy clause, 102
Unfunded mandate, 109
Unitary government, 96

STUDY QUESTIONS

1. Can you imagine the United States without federalism? Suppose that a central national authority ran the country, and governors and mayors—and other subnational officials—were entirely

subordinate to the national government. Describe some of the changes that would likely result. Would this unitary-state shift be an improvement, in your view? Why or why not?

2. The current Supreme Court tends to side with state and local governments in federalist clashes, limiting the national government's power in case after case. Why has the Court adopted this approach? Do you find it desirable?

3. Think about your own political loyalties. Are they most strongly felt for your hometown or home city? The state where you grew up (or where you live now)? Or the nation as a whole? What do you think accounts for your outlook? If you are not from the United States, reflect on your own sense of political identity: Is it primarily to a nation, a region, or a local place?

4. If you feel a strong sense of national pride, do you think it comes with any undesirable aspects? If you're not an especially avid American nationalist, why not? What would it be like if most citizens exhibited a skeptical outlook toward the country? If you are a citizen of another country, how would you describe the sense of patriotism in your national land? Does it differ from the nationalism and patriotism described in this chapter?

4

Civil Liberties

STORMS OF PROTEST greeted a proposed Islamic community center near the site of the 9/11 terrorist attacks in New York City. Sarah Palin, who had won an ardent following as a vice-presidential candidate, tweeted: "Doesn't it stab you in the heart as it does through the heartland? Peaceful Muslims pls. refudiate."[1] In Florida, Pastor Terry Jones announced plans to burn a Quran, the Muslim holy book. In New York, opponents lined up at a public hearing. "I do have a problem with having a mosque on top of the site where [terrorists] can gloat about what they did," said Al Santora, a fire department chief who had lost his son in the attack. Kathleen McFarland, a security analyst for Fox News, summarized the opposition: many New Yorkers consider the proposed center "an abomination" and "a recruiting station for terrorists."[2]

Imam Feisal Abdul Rauf, who had proposed the center, tried to win people over with a plea for tolerance—and for his rights. "We are Americans, we are Muslim Americans. . . . We have no higher aspirations than to bring up our children in peace and harmony in this country." The crowd blew up when he added, "Freedom of assembly is the right of all Americans." One woman shouted, "Not at the World Trade Center!" According to a CNN poll, 68 percent of New Yorkers and 61 percent of all Americans agreed: not at Ground Zero![3]

Was Imam Rauf correct? The First Amendment to the Constitution *does* protect "the right of the people peaceably to assemble," as well as their right to the "free exercise . . . of religion." This is bedrock of American liberty: protecting individuals when they want to speak out, practice their religion, or assemble in peace—even if what they say or believe is very unpopular.

However, every right has limits. Individual protections are always counterbalanced by community needs. As Supreme Court justice Oliver Wendell Holmes put it back in 1919, every action "depends upon the circumstances in which it is done. . . . The most stringent protection of free speech would not protect a man from falsely shouting fire in a crowded theater and causing a panic."[4]

Who are we? We are a nation always wrestling with a great trade-off—individual rights versus majority rule. On the one hand, we are the home of rugged individualism, which tilts us toward protecting individual rights. On the other

● *Imam Feisal Abdul Rauf (left) of the so-called Ground Zero Mosque answers questions from reporters amidst protesters.*

see for yourself 4.1

Go online to view the outcome of the Ground Zero Islamic Center.

hand, we believe in self-rule—which means the majority should get its way. The tension is exacerbated because we are (and always have been) a nation of minority groups—black, Latino, Hmong, Muslim, same-sex partners, and the list goes on. When the majority feels threatened or offended—as they did at Ground Zero—it sometimes moves to limit the minority's rights, making civil liberties all the *more* important.

What are **civil liberties**? They are the limits we put on governing bodies (and the majorities that elect them) so that individuals can exercise their rights and freedom. The Islamic center is a classic case. A minority claims its rights. The majority is offended, even angry. It calls on government to forbid the construction. The Constitution protects the minority's right to build the center unless it really is, or could become, "a recruiting station for terrorists." This brings us to the eternal complication of civil liberties—deciding who deserves which rights.

The Islamic center did open, fifteen months after the protests. The first exhibition in its gallery featured portraits of children from 160 countries taken by Danny Goldfield, a Jewish photographer. The new director of the center acknowledged that there would have been a better way to balance majority fears and minority rights. "We made an incredible mistake," he said, not to "include 9/11 families."[5]

The Rise of Civil Liberties

May a racist burn a cross as a symbol of white supremacy? May a skinhead stand on a street corner and urge people to attack Latinos, Sikhs, or Jews? Is pornography legal? The answer to all three questions is "sometimes." We always weigh the rights of individuals against the concerns and safety of the community. Who decides? Usually, the courts do. And there is often more than one reasonable answer when the courts take up a question.

Civil Rights and Civil Liberties

Civil rights: The freedom to participate in the full life of the community—to vote, use public facilities, and exercise equal economic opportunity.

Civil liberties: The limits on government so that people can freely exercise their rights.

Civil rights and **civil liberties** demand opposite things from government. Civil rights require government action to help secure individual rights; civil liberties restrict government action to protect individual rights. Until people have won their rights, the idea of protecting them is meaningless. When governments enforce civil rights for some people, they often limit the liberty of others. For example, as we will see in Chapter 5, the Civil Rights Act of 1964

BY THE NUMBERS *Civil Liberties*

Number of rights listed in the Bill of Rights: **31**
Number of rights protecting freedom of religion: **2**
Number of rights protecting people accused of crimes: **19**

Number of times that the Supreme Court has permitted the government to block publication of sensitive material: **0**
Number of years after the Bill of Rights was ratified before the Supreme Court ruled that state governments could not interfere with freedom of speech: **134**
Number of years before it ruled that states could not interfere with the right to bear arms: **219**

Number of new rights secured by constitutional amendment in the past forty years: **1** (the 26th Amendment extended the right to vote to 18- to 20-year-olds)

Percentage of Americans who favor a constitutional amendment to ban flag burning (according to a Gallup poll in 2006): **56**
Percentage who would be "upset" if Congress failed to ban flag burning: **40**
Number of votes by which a flag-burning amendment failed to clear Congress: **1**

Rank of the United States among all nations for number (and percentage) of citizens in jail: **1**
Ranks of Russia, Rwanda, Iran, and England: **2, 3, 40, 83**

Percentage of Americans who supported the death penalty in 1990 and today: **78, 62**

Percentage support for the death penalty:
    Among white evangelicals: **74**
    Among the nonreligious: **61**
    Among Hispanic Catholics: **43**
    Among black Protestants: **37**

Number of states that have not executed anyone since 1976: **16**
Total number executed in Texas, Virginia, Oklahoma, and Florida since 1976: **758**
Total number executed by the federal government in that period: **3**

outlawed segregated restaurants. That legal action freed blacks and Latinos to eat where they wished but limited the liberty of racist restaurant owners to serve whomever they wanted to serve.

In practice, the two concepts are not opposites. The long battle for civil rights led to more robust civil liberties for everyone. The fight against slavery eventually led to the Fourteenth Amendment, which—as we'll soon see—is the cornerstone of modern civil liberties. Without the long American

Legal? Sometimes!

struggle for civil rights, "we the people" would have many fewer civil liberties.

Both civil liberties and civil rights became increasingly important to American politics through the twentieth century. In this section we look first at why civil liberties matter. We then explain how they grew and spread. In 1943, the Supreme Court reversed a decision it had made just three years earlier and ruled that it was unconstitutional to require children to pledge allegiance if it violated their faith. In announcing its new position, the Court made a classic statement of civil liberties: *"The very purpose of a Bill of Rights was to withdraw certain subjects from the vicissitudes of political controversy, to place them beyond the reach of majorities and officials and to establish them as legal principles to be applied by the courts."*[6]

The Slow Rise of Rights

The Bill of Rights barely touched American life in the nineteenth century because it only applied to the federal government. The First Amendment begins, *"Congress* shall make no law" prohibiting the exercise of religion or restricting speech. Well, what about the states? Did the individual protections in the Bill of Rights also limit what they could do?

In 1833, John Barron found out. Barron owned a thriving wharf in Baltimore Harbor until the city diverted the water and left his wharf high and dry. Barron sued, arguing that the city had violated the Fifth Amendment by taking his property for public use "without just compensation." The Supreme Court ruled (in *Barron v. Baltimore*) that the amendment applied only to the federal government. The Anti-Federalists, reasoned the justices, had demanded the Bill of Rights to protect them from the national government. Washington could not strip Barron of his property rights—but Maryland or Baltimore could.[7]

The Bill of Rights eventually reached the states thanks to the quest for civil rights. After the Civil War, Congress passed the Fourteenth Amendment (ratified in 1868) to protect the newly freed slaves. Every discussion of civil liberties turns the spotlight on one passage in the Fourteenth Amendment:

> **No state** *shall . . . deprive any person of life, liberty, or property, without due process of law; nor deny any person within its jurisdiction the equal protection of the laws. [emphasis added]*

Look again at the first two words. Obviously, the amendment is addressed directly to the states. States may not deprive any person of life, liberty, or property, which are exactly what the Bill of Rights protects. The amendment *seems* to apply the Bill of Rights to the states. In 1873, the Supreme Court

Table 4.1 Incorporation of the Bill of Rights into the Fourteenth Amendment

THE BILL OF RIGHTS	YEAR	KEY CASE
I.* Free exercise of religion	1940	*Cantwell v. Connecticut*
No establishment of religion	1947	*Everson v. Board of Education*
Free press	1931	***Near v. Minnesota*** **
Free speech	1925	***Gitlow v. New York***
Right to peaceful assembly	1937	*De Jonge v. Oregon*
Right to petition government	1963	*NAACP v. Button*
II. Right to keep and bear arms	2010	***McDonald v. Chicago***
III. No quartering of soldiers		*Not incorporated*
IV. No unreasonable search and seizure	1949	*Wolf v. Colorado*
No search and seizure without warrant	1961	***Mapp v. Ohio***
V. Right to grand jury indictment		*Not incorporated*
No double jeopardy	1969	*Benton v. Maryland*
No forced confession	1964	*Escobedo v. Illinois*
Right to remain silent	1966	***Miranda v. Illinois***
No seizure of property without compensation	1887	*Chicago Burlington and Quincy RR v. Chicago*
VI. Right to public trial	1948	*In re Oliver*
Right to speedy trial	1967	*Klopfer v. North Carolina*
Right to trial by impartial jury	1966	*Parker v. Gladden*
Right to confront witnesses	1965	*Pointer v. Texas*
Right to compel supportive witnesses to appear	1967	*Washington v. Texas*
Right to counsel in capital punishment cases	1932	***Powell v. Alabama***
Right to counsel in felony cases	1963	***Gideon v. Wainright***
VII. Right of jury trial in civil cases		*Not incorporated*
VIII. No excessive bail		*Not incorporated*
No cruel and unusual punishment	1962	*Robinson v. California*
IX. Rights not limited to rights listed in the first eight amendments		*Not relevant to incorporation*
X. Powers not delegated to the national government are reserved to the states and the people		*Not relevant to incorporation*

Notice how the First Amendment rights were incorporated early in the process. Most protections for those accused of crimes were applied between 1962 and 1968.
** *Boldfaced cases are discussed in this chapter.*

disagreed: the Fourteenth Amendment applied only to freed slaves and to no one else.[8]

Over time, the Court changed its mind. In 1897 the Court returned to the issue in *Barron v. Baltimore* and ruled that state governments could not seize property without compensation. One phrase of the Fifth Amendment now applied to state and local government. The Supreme Court had incorporated the right into the Fourteenth Amendment. The Supreme Court decided, case by case, which rights applied to state governments—a process called **selective incorporation**.

The Court was very slow to force constitutional rights on the states. We have already seen this "hands off the states" approach: this was the era of the concurrent powers (the layer cake) for federalism (Chapter 3). And we will see it again: this was the period of **Jim Crow** segregation in Civil Rights (described in Chapter 5).

Slowly—very slowly—the Court incorporated more rights. In 1937, it formally declared its principle for deciding which rights to incorporate: Is the right in question essential to our idea of liberty? If so, the Fourteenth Amendment's due process clause—quoted above—required states to respect that right and the Court then incorporated, or applied, it to the states.[9] In time, the Court incorporated almost every phrase of the Bill of Rights, beginning with freedom of speech (in 1925), continuing with the practice of religion (1940), and moving recently to the right to own guns (in 2010). (Table 4.1 provides an overview of what rights the Court applied and when.)[10]

In the rest of the chapter, we examine the most important civil liberties and the issues they raise.

Selective incorporation: Extending protections from the Bill of Rights to the state governments, one right at a time.

Jim Crow: The system of racial segregation in the US South that lasted from 1890 to 1965.

THE BOTTOM LINE

- The Supreme Court neatly defined civil liberties in 1943: the Bill of Rights withdraws certain subjects from political controversy and places them beyond the reach of majorities and officials.
- The Bill of Rights did not apply to the states until the Fourteenth Amendment required that *no state* could deprive any citizen of life, liberty, or property.
- The Court applied the Bill of Rights to the states one right at a time between 1897 (no taking of property without compensation) and 2010 (the right to bear arms).

● Privacy

We begin with an especially controversial right that, unlike all the others we will examine, is never mentioned in the Constitution. Instead, a majority on the Supreme Court ruled that it is implied by the First, Third, Fourth, Fifth, and Ninth Amendments.

Penumbras and Emanations

In the mid-nineteenth century, contraceptives were widely available. Then, in the 1870s, every state, encouraged by the national government, banned them—partly because of fears that immigrants would have more children than native-born Americans. Almost a century later, the director of Planned Parenthood of Connecticut defied that state's ban and dispensed condoms at a birth control clinic in New Haven. The Supreme Court heard the case (*Griswold v. Connecticut*, 1965), struck down the law, and declared a dramatic new right: the right to privacy.

How could the Court protect privacy if the Constitution does not even mention it? Justice William O. Douglas explained: The rights that are specifically mentioned in the Bill of Rights "have penumbras . . . that give them life and substance." The *penumbras*—literally, the shadows—of the First Amendment create "zones of privacy" in which people have a right to make their own choices free from government interference. So do the "emanations" from other amendments, like the Third Amendment ban on quartering soldiers in private homes—which, he pointed out, was designed to protect privacy. In addition, the Ninth Amendment declares that other rights exist besides the ones mentioned in the Constitution and they are also "retained by the people." Privacy is one of those rights.

What Do You Think?

•.. Is There a Right to Privacy?

Are you ready to try your first case? How would you rule in *Griswold v. Connecticut*? Do you agree that there is "a right to privacy" in the Constitution that permitted the Court to strike down the Connecticut ban on contraceptives?	**Yes.** Although the Constitution does not specifically mention privacy, a modern reading of the document would conclude that privacy is a basic right that the courts ought to protect.	**No.** We have to stick to the simple language of the Constitution itself. We disrespect and even damage the document by reading things into it. Anyone who opposes Connecticut's ban on contraceptives can go to the legislature and lobby them to change it.	**What it means.** No matter how you voted, you're part of a long intellectual tradition. If you said yes, you agree with a school of thought (which we call *pragmatist*) that says the courts must be guided by the *general ideas* that underpin the Constitution to try and determine the best outcome in a particular case. From this perspective, the Constitution grows and changes with the times. If you voted no, you're voting with *originalism*, the school of thought that limits judges to considering the original intent as explicitly stated in the Constitution's text.

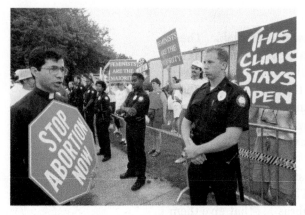

● *Pro-choice versus pro-life—one of the great conflicts in modern American politics.*

In 1787, when the Constitution was written, no one was thinking about condoms. But if you apply the logic of the Constitution to modern times, the right to privacy—and to contraceptives—emerges.

The *Griswold* case itself did not stir much controversy. After all, most people thought married couples had every right to use condoms. In 1973, however, the right to privacy led to one of the most controversial Court decisions ever.

Roe v. Wade

In *Roe v. Wade* (1973) the Supreme Court drew on the right to privacy and struck down a Texas law banning abortion. The Court ruled that the right to privacy is "broad enough to encompass a woman's decision whether or not to terminate her pregnancy."

Roe v. Wade changed American politics. People who support the decision—known as "pro-choice"—view the decision as essential to gender equality, for it enables women to control when (and whether) they have children. From this perspective, *Roe* opens the door to vocations and careers for women. It protects women's health by doing away with the dangerous "back alley" abortions that desperate women sought out before *Roe* made abortions safe and legal. Democrats, for the most part, are pro-choice.

Those who oppose the decision—known as "pro-life"—believe that life begins at conception and that abortion is murder. Many religious activists took *Roe v. Wade* as a call to enter politics. The grassroots campaign to overturn the decision became a powerful force in modern conservatism. Within a decade, the Republican Party had committed itself to overturning *Roe*.

The debate added new intensity to American politics, since activists on each side felt they were fighting for the soul of the nation: on the one side, equality for women; on the other side, the most basic rights of the unborn. The intensity helped politicize Supreme Court appointments. Each new nomination raised the same questions. What is the nominee's attitude toward abortion? Will he or she become a decisive vote and swing a closely divided Court?

Planned Parenthood v. Casey

Challenges to *Roe v. Wade* led to a string of Supreme Court decisions. In 1980, the Court accepted a congressional ban on federal funding for abortions. In 1989, it upheld a Missouri prohibition on abortions in public hospitals. In 1992, the Court took up a Pennsylvania law that seemed to directly challenge *Roe* by imposing regulations on women seeking abortions, even in the first trimester. Pennsylvania required a twenty-four-hour waiting period, parental notification for minors, and prior notification of spouses. Many observers, on both sides of the issue, predicted that the Court would overturn *Roe v. Wade* and permit states to outlaw abortions.

Instead, in *Planned Parenthood v. Casey* (1992), the Court voted (5–4) to take a middle ground. The court upheld a woman's right to terminate her pregnancy, as a "component of liberty." However, it rejected *Roe v. Wade's* trimester framework, which forbade any state limitations in the first trimester.

The original *Roe* decision had propounded a **judicial rule**. Rules set clear boundaries between what is lawful and what is not: the states may not interfere in the first trimester. Now, *Casey* replaced the rule with a **judicial standard**. A standard establishes a more general guiding principle rather than a hard-and-fast rule. What is an "undue burden"? That's a judgment call.

Abortions continue to be fiercely debated—on and off the Court. In 2000, the Court refused to ban a procedure known as partial-birth abortion. The Court argued (5–4) that the procedure might be necessary to protect the mother's health and that banning it imposed an "undue burden" on privacy. Seven years later, the Court reversed itself and upheld a ban (5–4).[11] What had changed? One member of the Court. Samuel Alito replaced Sandra Day O'Connor and voted the other way.

● *John Geddes Lawrence (left) and Tyron Garner (right). The police, investigating a gun disturbance complaint one September evening in 1998, broke into Lawrence's apartment—which had gay posters prominently displayed on the walls. When Lawrence began to argue, the police arrested both him and Garner for "deviate sexual intercourse." In* Lawrence v. Texas *(2003), the Supreme Court struck down the Texas antisodomy law for violating the Constitution's privacy protections.*

Sexuality Between Consenting Adults

Does the right to privacy extend to same-sex couples? In 1986, the Supreme Court ruled it did not, upholding Georgia's antisodomy law. In 2003, the Supreme Court reversed itself (in *Lawrence v. Texas*) and extended the right of privacy to same-sex couples. In striking down the Texas antisodomy law the majority echoed the original *Griswold* decision: "Liberty protects the person from unwarranted government intrusion into . . . private places."

The privacy cases reflect public opinion. By 1965, most Americans believed that couples should be permitted to use birth control. Although with *Roe v. Wade* the Court did not reflect popular views, later decisions have balanced a right to abortion with state restrictions—roughly in line with majority views. In the mid-1980s, gay rights too were controversial; by 2003 they were widely accepted.

It may seem a good idea that courts reflect majority opinion. But the Constitution and the Court are designed to stand up to the majority. They are supposed to protect the rights of unpopular minorities like gay Americans in the 1980s.

As we will see throughout this chapter, applying the Constitution is never simple. The story of civil liberties is the story of managing the collisions between the two great principles—the needs and desires of the community versus the rights of the individual.

Judicial rules: Hard-and-fast boundaries between what is lawful and what is not.

Judicial standards: Guiding principles that help governments make judgment calls.

> **THE BOTTOM LINE**
>
> - The Court discovered a right to privacy implicit in (or in the shadows of) the First, Third, Fourth, Fifth, and Ninth Amendments.
> - The Court applied the right to privacy to strike down laws banning abortion. In *Roe v. Wade*, the court issued a *rule* prohibiting states from interfering during the first trimester. In *Planned Parenthood v. Casey*, the Court replaced the rule with a *standard* forbidding laws that put "an undue burden" on the right to privacy.
> - The Court extended privacy rights to same-sex couples by striking down antisodomy laws in 2003.

● Freedom of Religion

The Bill of Rights begins with religion.

Congress shall make no law respecting an establishment of religion, or prohibiting the free exercise thereof.

The First Amendment gives two succinct commands regulating religion. The federal government may not establish an official religion—known as the **establishment clause**. And it may not interfere in religious practice—the **free exercise clause**.

The Establishment Clause

Establishment clause: In the First Amendment, the principle that government may not establish an official religion.

Free exercise clause: In the First Amendment, the principle that government may not interfere in religious practice.

By the time the Constitution was written, Americans already practiced many faiths: Puritans (or Congregationalists) in Massachusetts, Quakers in Philadelphia, Baptists in Rhode Island, Anglicans in Virginia, Catholics in Maryland, and Jews in Newport, Rhode Island. The First Amendment's establishment clause is designed to prohibit the federal government from imposing a national religion. But what exactly did it forbid the government from doing? The debate began immediately.

President George Washington (1789–1797) called for a national day of prayer each year. Was that encouraging religion? President Thomas Jefferson (1801–1809) thought so and rejected the practice. The First Amendment, wrote Jefferson, builds "a wall of separation between church and state."[12] When the Supreme Court extended the establishment clause to the state governments in 1947, Justice Hugo Black quoted Jefferson's "wall of separation."[13] Until recently, Jefferson's metaphor guided the court's efforts.

Jefferson's principle is a difficult guide because there has never been a true wall of separation. The cash in American pockets is inscribed "In God We Trust"; children pledge allegiance to "one nation, under God"; Moses, holding the Ten Commandments, is carved into the Supreme Court building. Congress opens each session with a prayer, and presidents end their speeches with "God bless America"—a sentiment that no president or prime minister would invoke in England, France, or Japan. Despite these and other interconnections, the courts have tried to separate church and state. The question is how?

The establishment clause is clearly designed to keep government officials from favoring one religion—or religion over nonreligion. In a blockbuster case, *Engel v. Vitale* (1962), the Court ruled that New York's practice of starting the school day with a prayer violated the establishment clause. The Court bluntly rejected any school prayer, even if it was optional and nondenominational.

A long string of controversial decisions followed. Each returns to the vexing question about exactly where to construct Jefferson's wall. May public schools introduce a minute of silent prayer or meditation? (No.) May graduation include a prayer? (No.) May students lead prayers at football games? (No.) May children recite "under God" during the Pledge of Allegiance? (No definitive ruling has yet taken place.) May a city put up a Christmas display? (Yes, if it includes secular as well as religious symbols—known sarcastically as the "two-reindeer" rule.)

● *Using the neutrality test, described on page 136, the courts struck down a Florida law for specifically targeting the Cuban Santeria religion when it forbade the use of animal sacrifices.*

In 1971, the Court established a test to guide decisions about separating church and state. In *Lemon v. Kurtzman* the Court ruled on a Pennsylvania law that paid teachers who taught nonreligious subjects in church-affiliated (mainly Catholic) schools. The Court forbade the practice and promulgated what became known as the *Lemon test* for judging what government actions are permissible. First, the law must have a *secular* purpose. Second, its principal effect must *neither advance nor inhibit religion*. Finally, it must not *excessively entangle* government in religion. Paying the teachers in religious schools was, the Court ruled, an "excessive entanglement," and Pennsylvania could not do it.

As the court became more conservative, establishment clause cases became unpredictable and even erratic. To illustrate the Court's current difficulty with the establishment clause, consider two decisions announced on the same day in 2005. The Court ruled that a display of the Ten Commandments on the grounds of the Texas state capitol did not violate the establishment clause but that the Ten Commandments in two Kentucky courthouses did. Both decisions were 5–4. What was the difference between the two cases? Justice Stephen Breyer, who accepted the Texas Ten Commandments and rejected Kentucky's, explained: the Texas Commandments had stood for forty years as part of a display about the development of the law, while the Kentucky tablets had been recently erected as a religious statement. Many court watchers—and all eight of the other justices—would have preferred a more consistent approach to the Ten Commandments.[14]

• May the Christian Youth Club Meet in School?

The Good News is a Christian youth club that wanted to meet in school after class hours. The school district said that this was religious worship and would amount to a public school's endorsement of Christianity. The case went to the Supreme Court. Justices Stevens (who argued against Good News) and Scalia (who supported Good News) each wrote opinions. Which opinion would you sign on to?

Justice Stevens:
"Evangelical meetings designed to convert children to a particular faith . . . may introduce divisiveness and tend to separate young children into cliques that undermine the school's educational mission." The school district is right to stop the practice.

Justice Scalia:
Religious expression cannot violate the establishment clause where it is (1) purely private and (2) open to all on equal terms. Milford [the school district] is discriminating against a religious group since it lets other groups meet.

Testing These Views.
As you consider whose side to take, it might help to consider the underlying theories. Justice Stevens sticks with strict separation of church and state. Justice Scalia, on the other hand, simply wants to insure that government does not give an advantage to any one religion or viewpoint. How did the court actually rule? The answer is in the endnotes.[15]

Free Exercise of Religion

The First Amendment also prohibits government from interfering with the "free exercise" of religion. Once again, the Court's view has evolved.

The first landmark case was decided in 1963. Adell Sherbert was a Seventh-Day Adventist who refused to work on Saturday because it violated her faith. She was fired. South Carolina rejected her claim for unemployment benefits because she refused other jobs that also required work on Saturday. Claiming that the state was infringing on her "free exercise" of religion, Sherbert sued the state for her unemployment benefits. In deciding the case, Justice Brennan introduced a two-part test, known as the *Sherbert* or *balancing test*. First, was the government imposing a "significant burden" on her ability to exercise her faith? Second, did the government have a "compelling interest" for imposing the burden? In this case, the Court ruled that there was a real burden on Adell Sherbert and no compelling state interest for denying her unemployment benefits.

The Sherbert test lasted until 1990, when the Court took a completely different approach. Two Oregon men participated in a Native American

What Do You Think?

David's Law

In April 2006, two men attacked David Rae Ritcheson, a Mexican American high school student. They beat him, burned him, sodomized him with a patio umbrella, poured bleach on his face, and left him for dead. One of the assailants, a self-proclaimed racist skinhead, screamed ethnic slurs during the torture. David spent months in the hospital, undergoing one operation after another. He struggled to regain a normal life, slid into depression, and committed suicide. Some members of Congress proposed what they called David's Law. This legislation would target **hate crimes** and **hate speech** by enhancing law enforcement and penalties. The sponsors' goal is to provide special protection for members of groups that sometimes face intense discrimination—African Americans, Latinos, gays, and others. These groups, proponents argued, need protection because too many people are ready to harm them. David's Law encountered fierce opposition. Of course, the two men must be punished for their crime. However, opponents argued, hate crime legislation would create taboo subjects. Anyone condemning or even criticizing immigrants or homosexuals could be prosecuted. Once again, we face the civil liberties balancing act. How would you vote?

Yes. Vote for David's Law.	We must protect Mexican Americans, gay people, African Americans, religious minorities, and other groups who face hatred and violence. Hate speech fractures communities and hurts people. It is frightening and painful to the targeted groups.
No. Vote against David's Law.	Everyone has the right to an opinion—even if it is a horrible opinion. We can punish criminal behavior. We should never punish people for simply expressing their views.
Not Sure?	In the next sections we'll examine freedom of speech and you'll learn how the Court has ruled on such cases.

ritual that included taking peyote—a hallucinogen. The men were fired from their jobs at a private drug rehab center and then were denied unemployment benefits for violating Oregon drug laws. The men sued, arguing that they should be exempted from the peyote ban because it was essential to their religious practice. Under the Sherbert test they might have won. However, the Supreme Court ruled (6–3) against the two men and, in the process, made it much more difficult to sue the government for interfering with religious expression. In *Employment Division v. Smith*, the Court asked simply if the Oregon drug law was a neutral law applied in a neutral way. Yes, the law was neutral. It was not aimed at Native American religious practice, because it forbids *everyone* from smoking peyote.

The *Employment Division* case replaced the Sherbert balancing test with a *neutrality test*. The new test does not ask whether a law interferes with religious practice or whether a compelling government interest is at stake (the two questions of the Sherbert test). It asks only whether the same law applies to everyone. So long as the law does not target a religious group, the Court will permit it. Obviously, this makes it much more difficult to sue on the basis of "free exercise" of religion.[16]

THE BOTTOM LINE

- The First Amendment has two religious clauses: the government may not establish a religion and it may not interfere with the free exercise of religion.
- The courts have ruled on establishment cases by trying to approximate Jefferson's wall separating church and state. The Court requires three things of government action: it must *have a secular purpose*, *neither advance nor inhibit religion*, and *not excessively entangle* government in religion. A more recent view (known as accommodation) simply requires that government not promote one religious view over another.
- In protecting the free practice of religion, the courts traditionally asked if the government had a compelling interest for imposing a burden. Today, they simply require that government action be neutral and apply to everyone. Congress and some state governments have tried to return to the original rule.

Freedom of Speech

Now we turn to the most fiercely protected civil liberty of all, freedom of speech. After its religious clauses, the First Amendment states:

> *Congress shall make no law . . . abridging the freedom of speech or of the press.*

A Preferred Position

Today, the Supreme Court gives the First Amendment a "preferred position" among all the amendments to the Constitution; free speech holds a "preferred position" among the rights in the First Amendment (free speech, religion, press, assembly, and petition government). Indeed, when freedom of speech conflicts with any other right, the Court generally will "prefer" or protect speech.[17]

Test Yourself: The Simpsons Versus the First Amendment—Which Do You Know Better?

Five rights are listed in the First Amendment, and there are five Simpsons.

Thirty-four percent of Americans can name four of the five Simpsons. Only 1 percent of Americans can name four of the five rights.

How about you? How many First Amendment rights can you name? How many Simpsons? (Answers below.)

Source: McCormick Tribune Freedom Museum (Chicago).

Answers:

The Simpsons from left to right: Homer, Bart, Lisa, Marge, and Maggie
First Amendment rights: Freedom of religion, speech, press, and assembly; and the right to petition government.

Why do contemporary courts put so much emphasis on the right to express opinions? Because democracy requires vigorous debate.

When the right to speak out clashes with other rights—like protecting minorities from abusive language—free speech usually wins. Immediately, we have one principle for judging **hate crimes** legislation, which curbs abusive **hate speech**. The courts will be skeptical of any effort to curb speech, however hurtful.

Of course, every right has limits. Much of the debate that surrounds the right to speech is about identifying the boundaries—the limits—of protected speech.

Hate crime: Crime stemming from prejudice based on someone's personal characteristics, such as race, ethnicity, religion, or sexual orientation.

Hate speech: Hostile statements based on someone's personal characteristics, such as race, ethnicity, religion, or sexual orientation.

Political Speech

The forceful defense of free speech took a long time to develop. In every generation, political leaders are tempted to stop subversive talk—or harsh criticism. Under the John Adams administration, just ten years after the Constitution was ratified, Congress drafted the Alien and Sedition Acts. Tensions with France were running high, and the acts made it illegal to "print, utter, or publish . . . any false, scandalous, and malicious writing" against the government. The meaning of the acts was brutally simple: criticize the government and face prosecution.

The first modern free speech cases arose during World War I. President Woodrow Wilson had signed the Espionage Act. Charles Schenck, general secretary of the Socialist Party of Philadelphia, was found guilty of violating the act by printing and distributing a document that urged men to resist military recruitment for a war designed, he claimed, to pour profits into greedy Wall Street. Was his freedom of speech abrogated? Under normal circumstances it might be, wrote Justice Oliver Wendell Holmes for a unanimous court, but this was wartime. Distributing these documents, he wrote, was like falsely shouting "fire" in a crowded theater. Holmes then formulated the most famous test for free speech: speech is not protected if it poses "***a clear and present danger*** that it will lead to 'substantive evils'" (*Schenck v. United States*, 1919).

Clear and present danger: Court doctrine that permits restrictions of free speech if officials believe that the speech will lead to prohibited action like violence or terrorism.

In the early 1920s, many Americans were anxious about foreigners, immigrants, Socialists, Communists, and anarchists. The Supreme Court hardened the "clear and present danger" test by ruling that judges did not have to "weigh each and every utterance." They could simply determine whether the "natural tendency and probable effect" of the speech was to "bring about something bad or evil"—even if that danger lay in the distant future.[18]

The clear and present danger test stood for decades. After fifty years, in 1969, the Court complained that "puny" threats, which no one took seriously except "nervous judges," were being declared a "clear and present danger." The issue arose when a Ku Klux Klan leader, Clarence Brandenburg, organized a rally where the Klan members burned crosses, waved guns, and called for "revengence" against Jews and African Americans. The Supreme Court struck down Brandenburg's conviction and rewrote the clear and present dangers test. The state may not interfere with speech unless the speech "incites imminent lawless action" *and* is likely to actually "produce such action."

The result makes it very difficult to curtail political speech for clear and present danger. The government may limit the speech only if the bad effects—the lynching, the overthrow of American government, or the terrorist attack—are likely to happen immediately. During this case, *Brandenburg v. Ohio* (1969), the Supreme Court formally declared the "preferred position" of free speech.[19]

An extreme example shows the force of contemporary free speech protections. Members of the Westboro Baptist Church protest homosexuality by picketing military funerals—because the military does not condemn it. While families bury their loved ones, the demonstrators wave signs that read "Fag sin = 9/11," "Thank God for dead soldiers," and "You're going to hell." Albert Snyder, the father of a marine killed in Iraq, sued the church when it picketed his son's funeral. Forty-eight states and

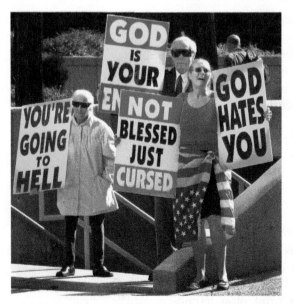

● *Members of the Westboro Baptist Church picket military funerals to protest homosexuality (and the military's refusal to condemn it). The Supreme Court acknowledged that the protests were hurtful but protected them as an exercise of free speech.*

a long list of veterans groups supported the suit. The Supreme Court did not. Chief Justice John Roberts acknowledged the pain that the demonstrations caused. However, writing for an 8–1 majority (notice that the Court was almost unanimous), he underscored the First Amendment's bottom line: "We do not stifle public debate."[20]

Symbolic Speech

When Clarence Brandenburg burned his cross, he engaged in a form of speech known as **symbolic expression**. He was demonstrating a point of view with an act rather than as a speech. The First Amendment protects symbolic speech—again, within limits.

In 2003, the Supreme Court identified those limits when it took two cross-burning cases on the same day. It began by acknowledging that the act itself was vicious. The Ku Klux Klan burned crosses to terrorize black neighbors. (In Klan lore, the original cross burnings, after the Civil War, signaled the murder of a former slave.) Then the Court drew a fine distinction. Individuals may burn crosses to express their views, but not to intimidate others.

Burning the American flag is another unpopular symbolic expression. Gregory Lee Johnson lit up a flag during the Republican National Convention in 1984 and was arrested for violating a Texas law against flag desecration. Forty-eight states and the federal government banned flag burning. The Supreme Court narrowly struck down the law (by a 5–4 vote). "If there is a bedrock principle underlying the First Amendment," argued Justice Brennan for the majority, "it is that government may not prohibit the expression of an idea simply because society finds the idea offensive or disagreeable."[21] The minority argued that the national flag deserved special protection. Congress responded by passing legislation defending the flag. The Court overturned that, too. Congress then debated an amendment to the Constitution protecting the flag. It passed in the House (286–130) but fell one vote short of the two-thirds vote required in the Senate.

Limits to Free Speech: Fighting Words

Is there any way to rein in cross burning, gay bashing, and other forms of hateful speech? Other democracies are much tougher on hurtful speech; so are many colleges and universities. The logic is simple: How can you build a good community if some members feel singled out and threatened?

One legal doctrine offers a limit to hate speech by restricting **fighting words**. The Supreme Court defined these as "personally abusive epithets which, when addressed to the ordinary citizen, are, as a matter of common knowledge, inherently likely to provoke violent reaction."[22] The Court states the principle but has been reluctant to apply it. If the words are political, they must be protected. If hate crime legislation singles out some fighting words (like racial epithets) but not others, the Court will reject it. However, even while the Court keeps striking down the efforts, it reaffirms that there *are*

Symbolic expression: An act, rather than actual speech, used to demonstrate a point of view.

Fighting words: Expression inherently likely to provoke violent reaction and not necessarily protected by the First Amendment.

"fighting words" not protected by the Constitution. The key test is that the language does not advance any specific political position. Reformers trying to create codes of decent language, like David's Law, generally rely on the logic of "fighting words."

Limited Protection: Student Speech

Student speech has sparked controversy and litigation. In the landmark *Tinker* decision, the Court announced that students "do not shed their constitutional right to freedom of speech or expression at the schoolhouse gate." That decision, however, has been qualified in a series of cases that balance student rights with the schools' educational mission.

In 1965, John (fifteen years old) and Mary Beth Tinker (thirteen) violated school rules by wearing a black armband to protest the Vietnam War. They were suspended and told to return when they were ready to abide by the rules. The Supreme Court overturned the suspension and established what became known as the Tinker rule: the students' right to free speech could be curtailed only if it "materially and substantially interferes with the requirements of appropriate discipline in the operation of the school."[23]

In subsequent cases, the Court found that teachers and school officials had an obligation to teach students proper conduct and could regulate speech that was vulgar, indecent, offensive (1986), or inconsistent with the educational mission of the school (1988).[24] The most celebrated recent case arose from an incident at Juneau-Douglas High School in Alaska. The school permitted students to leave class and watch the Olympic torch pass through town. One student, Joseph Frederick, unfurled a big banner reading "Bong Hits 4 Jesus," to the merriment of his schoolmates. The principal suspended Frederick for ten days. The Supreme Court upheld the suspension for advocating drugs in violation of the school's antidrug policy. Three justices dissented, arguing that Frederick had the right to his opinion. Not even

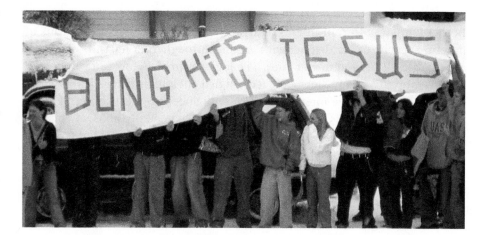

Joseph Frederick was suspended from school for five days for this banner and for five more days when he quoted Jefferson to the principal. The Supreme Court backed the suspension, 6–3.

"the dumbest student," they wrote, would change drug behavior because of a silly banner.[25]

In short, the First Amendment offers students less protection than adults. School officials may regulate speech as long as they do not do so arbitrarily. The reasons that the Court has accepted include disruption, violations of prevailing standards of good behavior, and behavior that contradicts the educational mission of the school. However, as the Frederick case shows, the justices disagree about how much latitude to grant high school students. What do you think? Should Frederick have been permitted his free speech? Or was he appropriately disciplined?

THE BOTTOM LINE

- Free speech is crucial to democracy, and the Court gives it a privileged position—even against angry public opposition to flag burning, cross burning, or homophobic displays at military funerals.
- Free speech can be curtailed if it poses a "clear and present danger." Today, the court requires the danger to be both imminent and likely to occur.
- There are limits to free speech, including fighting words and student speech. In the next section, we'll discuss additional limits on obscenity and libel.

Freedom of the Press

Freedom of the press follows most of the same rules as freedom of speech. The written word has always been essential to politics. The form changes—pamphlets during the revolutionary period, newspapers in the mid-twentieth century, and new media today. Written words share the "preferred position." Broadcast media are slightly different and subject to federal regulation (as we will explore in Chapter 7).

Prior Restraint

The effort to stop speech before it occurs is known as **prior restraint**. Although the Supreme Court has permitted government officials to punish people for what they have said or printed, it has never allowed federal government agents to gag citizens before they have had their say. In this view, prior restraint is nothing more than a technical term for *censorship*—the practice of dictators who close down newspapers or suppress stories they do not like. Some historians have argued that the real intent of the First Amendment was to forbid censorship.

The Supreme Court announced restrictions on prior restraint in 1931 after public officials in Minneapolis shut down a newspaper named the *Saturday*

Prior restraint: Legal effort to stop speech before it occurs—in effect, censorship.

● The courts have been reluctant to stop publication of information—a process known as prior restraint. New media and new sites like WikiLeaks make it very difficult for them to do so even when they try.

Press, published by an avowed racist who claimed that Jewish gangs were running the city. The Court ruled that the state could not suppress the paper, no matter how obnoxious, but it left the door open to prior restraint for national security reasons. The government would be justified for stopping someone from publishing information about "the number and location of troops in the field," it said, but not for publishing anti-Semitic harangues (*Near v. Minnesota*, 1931).

In the most famous case of prior restraint, a State Department official leaked a rich archive of classified material, the Pentagon Papers, that exposed the mistakes and deceptions that led the United States into the Vietnam War. The Richard Nixon administration, claiming a threat to national security, went to court to block the *New York Times* from publishing the papers. Within days, the Supreme Court heard the arguments and, by a 6–3 vote, lifted the ban and permitted publication. The majority opinion emphasized the "heavy presumption" against prior restraint.[26]

The shift from print media to the web has profoundly changed the logic of prior restraint. In 2008, WikiLeaks, a web-based venue for anonymous whistle-blowers, published internal documents from a Swiss bank that appeared to show tax evasion and money laundering at the bank's Cayman Islands branch. The bank went to court and won a restraining order against publication of the leaked documents. Stopping a newspaper from publishing is straightforward: the court enjoins the publisher. However, since WikiLeaks operates anonymously and globally, it is almost impossible for a court to suppress the information. In the WikiLeaks case the court tried to seal the site's American address. The documents simply appeared on mirror sites. Charges of censorship reverberated online—with links to the documents—and the print media picked up the controversy, sending still more traffic to the sites.

After two weeks, Judge Jerry White dissolved the injunction and acknowledged that the court's effort had only publicized the documents. There is "a definite disconnect," he commented, "between the evolution of our constitutional jurisprudence and modern technology."[27]

By flowing anonymously around national borders and court jurisdictions, new media poses dilemmas for every nation as it tries to regulate the written word. How will the courts respond?

Obscenity

The First Amendment does not protect obscenity. However, the courts always face the same problem: What is obscene? Justice Potter Stewart put it famously when he said simply, "I know it when I see it." Of course, different people see it in different things. The Court's emphasis on free speech leads it to reject aggressive regulation of obscenity.

In *Miller v. California* (1973), the Supreme Court created a three-part test for judging a work to be obscene. The Miller test holds that speech is not protected by the First Amendment if it has all three of these characteristics:

1. "The average person, applying contemporary community standards, would find that the work, taken as a whole, appeals to the prurient interest" (meaning that it is meant to be sexually stimulating).

2. It depicts sexual conduct in a "patently offensive way."

3. The work lacks "serious literary, artistic, political or scientific value."

The Miller test only created new questions. What does it mean to be patently offensive? Offensive to whom? How do we rely on community standards of decency when the Internet and the new media flow across borders?

In recent years, the Court has been hostile to most efforts at banning material. Feminist scholars like Catherine McKinnon have tried to change the framework. Pornography, they argue, is a form of hate speech. Pornography subordinates women the same way that hate speech demeans minorities. By promoting inequality, both undermine the whole point of free speech, which is to protect the democratic marketplace of ideas. Some nations, like Canada have essentially accepted this perspective. Although the courts have not taken this view, the feminist position on obscenity is an important voice in the contemporary debate.[28]

The Court flatly forbids child pornography, however. Abusing minors is criminal. In 2008, it upheld a law that forbade efforts to "provide or obtain child pornography." The case involved a man who boasted online, "Dad of toddler has 'good' pics of her and me for swap of your toddler pics, or live cam." He followed up with hard-core images of minors engaged in sexual behavior. Even in this case, two members of the Court disagreed. They argued that the posting violated the laws only if it could be proven that the pictures were really of minors. Simply having the defendant say so was not enough.

The First Amendment does not protect child pornography. However, the Court is so sensitive to free speech that even in a case like this one, some justices insisted on being cautious.

Libel

There are limits to the false things one can write or say about someone. (Written falsehoods are known as *libel*, spoken falsehoods are known as *slander*.) The courts have made it very difficult for public officials or celebrities to win a libel (or slander) judgment. To do so, they must prove not just that a state was false and that it caused them harm but that it was made with malice or a "a reckless disregard for the truth."

Today, the Court allows even outrageous claims, cartoons, spoofs, and criticism directed at public officials and celebrities. By contrast, English law is just the opposite and puts the burden of proof on the writers to prove the truth of what they have written.

THE BOTTOM LINE

- The rules for freedom of the press reflect those of free speech and strongly protect free expression.
- The courts are especially skeptical of any effort to impose prior restraint. The new media makes it especially difficult to even try.
- Obscenity is not protected by the First Amendment. The court has spent a long time wrestling with just what counts as obscenity and now uses the three-part Miller test.

● The Right to Bear Arms

The Second Amendment is a uniquely American right: no other national constitution includes it. The text in the Constitution is ambiguous:

> *A well regulated militia, being necessary to the security of a free state, the right of the people to keep and bear arms shall not be infringed.*

On one reading, it simply protects colonial-era militias. On the other, it guarantees the right to own weapons. Recently, the Supreme Court has rendered a decisive ruling—again by a 5–4 vote—guaranteeing the right to arms.

A Relic of the Revolution?

Skeptics question whether there is any right to bear arms at all. The Second Amendment, they say, protected state militias. Early Americans believed that only kings and tyrants kept permanent armies. In a republic, the citizens volunteered for service in local militias that defended their communities and their nation. The Second Amendment, in this reading, is a "relic of the American Revolution" and simply forbids the government from disarming the local militias that were so important in the eighteenth century. It does not involve a constitutional right to tote weapons.

Those who favor this view generally emphasize public safety and gun control. America's high homicide rate reflects the easy availability (and the rising caliber) of American weapons. Many cities and some states regulate or limit gun ownership.

Proponents of gun rights read the same constitutional sentence very differently. As Justice Scalia explained, the Second Amendment has two parts— a preface about militias and a clause that really matters, declaring that "the right . . . to . . . bear arms shall not be infringed." Many see the right to bear arms as the most important right of all. "When all else fails," declared Charlton Heston, actor and longtime honorary president of the National Rifle Association, "it is the one right that prevails. . . . It is the one right that allows rights to exist at all."[29]

There are roughly fifty gun shows a week in the United States. These are usually two-day events where people can browse, discuss and buy firearms— from rare antiques to newly released weapons systems.

The Supreme Court has been moving firmly to defend gun rights. In 2008, the Court struck down a District of Columbia rule that restricted guns in people's homes.[30] In 2010, the Court finally *incorporated* the Second Amendment. For the first time, the constitutional right to bear arms applied to state and local governments (*McDonald v. Chicago*). Both decisions were closely fought and decided by a single vote, 5–4. The *McDonald* decision is likely to make it far more difficult for cities and states to regulate weapons.

Few rights issues have split Americans like the Second Amendment. Conservative and rural Americans generally defend gun rights, which they view as deeply rooted in American culture and essential to personal protection. Where conservatives find safety, liberals fear carnage: domestic disputes turn deadly, children kill their friends, and urban neighborhoods become combat zones.

THE BOTTOM LINE

- Some critics see the Second Amendment as an outmoded defense of citizen militias.
- Others see it as an important individual right—perhaps even the most important right in the entire Constitution.
- In 2010, the Supreme Court incorporated the right to bear arms as an essential individual right.

Rights of the Accused

The Bill of Rights places special emphasis on protecting people accused of crimes. Four amendments (Four, Five, Six, and Eight) list thirty-one different rights for those who face criminal charges. No other issue gets as much attention. Protecting the accused involves another careful balancing act. On the one hand, the courts must restrain law enforcement and defend the constitutional freedoms that define America. On the other hand, too many curbs on law enforcement might lead to more crime. The challenge of civil liberties is finding the right balance between protecting the accused and keeping our society safe.

Americans Behind Bars

Recent court decisions offer stronger protection for free speech and gun rights. When it comes to the rights of the accused, however, the courts are moving away from individual protections and toward enhanced government powers. Again, this reflects a conservative trend. After vastly expanding the rights of the accused in the 1960s, the courts—in step with Congress, presidents of both parties, and most states—now tilt firmly toward law enforcement.

The results are dramatic. Today, 2.3 million Americans are behind bars—more than in any other nation. The United States incarcerates eight times as many people as European nations like Italy or Ireland and three times as many as relatively high-crime nations like Mexico (see Figures 4.1 and 4.2). The number of Americans in jail has risen about fivefold in the past forty years. Today, one in a hundred Americans are in prison (federal and state

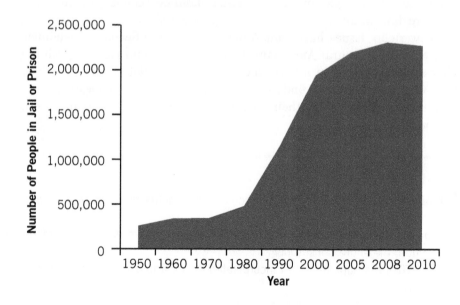

● **Figure 4.1** *Incarceration rates in the United States began to soar in the 1980s and now stand at five times their traditional levels. (Data from Justice Policy Institute and U.S. Bureau of Justice)*

Incarceration Rates in OECD Countries, (Most Recent Year, 2008–2009)

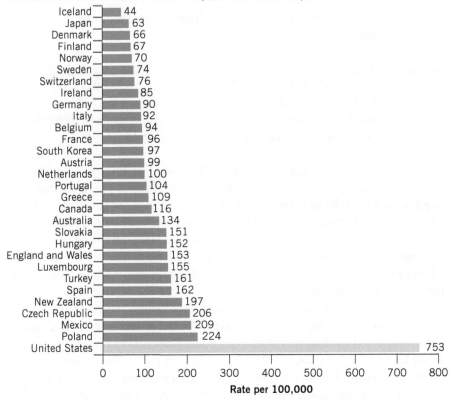

Country	Rate
Iceland	44
Japan	63
Denmark	66
Finland	67
Norway	70
Sweden	74
Switzerland	76
Ireland	85
Germany	90
Italy	92
Belgium	94
France	96
South Korea	97
Austria	99
Netherlands	100
Portugal	104
Greece	109
Canada	116
Australia	134
Slovakia	151
Hungary	152
England and Wales	153
Luxembourg	155
Turkey	161
Spain	162
New Zealand	197
Czech Republic	206
Mexico	209
Poland	224
United States	753

Rate per 100,000

● **Figure 4.2** *The United States stands out dramatically for the proportion of its population it incarcerates. This chart shows how many people are in jail for every 100,000 people in the population. (CEPR/ICPS)*

institutions) or jail (local); add in those on probation or parole, and the number rises to one in every thirty-two adults. Meanwhile, the level of violent crime has fallen in the United States to levels not seen in almost a century.

Do these numbers mean that we might have gone too far in dismantling the rights of the accused? Those who favor tough law enforcement respond by pointing to the low crime rates. Locking up criminals, they argue, has reduced crime. Skeptics, however, fear that American rights are eroding. Even many "crime hawks" (people who are tough on crime) worry that incarcerating too many people—especially for nonviolent crimes— might eventually make crime worse by destroying communities and leaving children without their parents. Many point as well to an alarming racial dimension, as blacks and Latinos are locked up at far higher rates than whites.

In this section, we examine the most important (and controversial) protections one at a time. As you read, think about the trade-offs between safe streets and civil liberties. As always, there are solid arguments on both sides of the issue.

The Fourth Amendment: Search and Seizure

The Fourth Amendment protects people from government officials bursting into their houses:

> *The right of the people to be secure in their persons, houses, papers, and effects, against unreasonable searches and seizures, shall not be violated, and no Warrants shall issue, but upon probable cause, supported by Oath or affirmation, and particularly describing the place to be searched, and the persons or things to be seized. . . .*

British officials in the 1770s ransacked people's homes, searching for weapons or smuggled goods. The Fourth Amendment prevents that from happening again. Justice Lewis Brandeis described it "as the right to be left alone—the . . . right most valued by civilized men."[31] The police may not enter a home unless they go before a judge and explain why they suspect that evidence of a crime can be found in a specific place. The judge determines whether there is "probable cause" to issue the warrant. It sounds simple, but there are large gray areas.

The landmark search and seizure case began in 1957 with a tip that Dollree (Dolly) Mapp was hiding a bombing suspect in her apartment. In addition, the police suspected she had illegal gambling paraphernalia in her apartment. The police knocked at her door, but she refused to let them in. They eventually broke the door down, and when she demanded to see a warrant they waved a piece of paper—not a warrant—in the air. The police searched the apartment and the basement. They never found the bombing suspect or the gambling material, but they did discover a suitcase of pornographic material—which was then illegal. Mapp was convicted on obscenity charges. The Supreme Court threw out the conviction and, in *Mapp v. Ohio* (1961, decided 6–3), devised the **exclusionary rule**: evidence obtained in an illegal search may not be introduced in a trial. Even evidence that clearly proves someone is guilty of a crime may not be used if it was improperly obtained.

Exclusionary rule:
The ruling that evidence obtained in an illegal search may not be introduced in a trial.

President Ronald Reagan (1981–1989) attacked the rule and urged both Congress and the courts to abolish it. John Roberts, the young Justice Department attorney who wrote the memos supporting Reagan's criticism, is now chief justice of the United States. During the Reagan years, the courts began making exceptions to the exclusionary rule. For example, in 1984 police arrested Alberto Leon when they discovered a large quantity of illegal drugs in his possession. Their warrant had expired but the Supreme Court made a "good faith" exception and permitted the drugs to be introduced as evidence.[32] By 2009, Justice Roberts wrote (in a 5–4 opinion) that there was no need to exclude evidence if the police violated a suspect's Fourth Amendment rights because of "isolated negligence."

A long list of cases explores when officers need a warrant. May they use wiretaps to eavesdrop without a warrant? (Yes, said the courts, in 1928; no, in 1967; sometimes, in 2001.)[33] May they search garbage put out on the curb, without a warrant? (Yes, 1988.) May they search students? (School officials may, but law enforcement officers need to show a cause.) May they search a dorm room? (Yes, 1982.) May they pat down suspicious people on the street? (Yes, 1968 and 1993.) May they search cars? (Yes, 1968.)

In 2011 the Supreme Court crossed an important threshold. It permitted officers to break into a house without a warrant. The officers in the case knocked, identified themselves, and heard movements that sounded like the destruction of evidence of drug use. Only one justice dissented. This ruling would, wrote Justice Ruth Bader Ginsburg, seriously curtail the use of warrants by police. Writing for the majority, Justice Samuel Alito took a hard line. Residents who "attempt to destroy evidence have only themselves to blame."[34]

The Fifth Amendment: Rights at Trials

The Fifth Amendment lists a long series of rights focused largely on criminal trials. Consider them one clause at a time.

> *No person shall be held to answer for a capital, or otherwise infamous crime, unless on a . . . indictment of a Grand Jury.*

Before the government can prosecute, it must persuade a jury. A **grand jury** does not decide on guilt or innocence but only on whether there is enough evidence for the case to go to trial. After the grand jury indicts, a petit (or small) jury of six to twelve individuals hears the case, weighs the evidence, and delivers a verdict.

Grand jury: A jury that does not decide on guilt or innocence but only on whether there is enough evidence for the case to go to trial.

> *. . . nor shall any person be subject for the same offense to be twice put in jeopardy of life or limb;*

An individual cannot face **double jeopardy**, or be tried twice for the same offense. ("Jeopardy of life and limb" refers to the old colonial practice of punishing people by lopping off an ear or damaging other limbs.) Without this provision, the government could simply keep trying people over and over.

Double jeopardy: The principle that an individual cannot be tried twice for the same offense.

Despite this prohibition, individuals sometimes face multiple trials. They can be tried on different charges, tried in federal court after being acquitted in state court, and—if they are acquitted on criminal charges—they can be sued for damages. Rodney King, a black motorist, was brutally beaten by four Los Angeles police officers. The officers were all acquitted in a state court (shocking observers and setting off riots). However, two of the officers were subsequently convicted on federal charges. In another famous case, former football star O. J. Simpson was acquitted of murdering his wife and her companion, only to lose a civil judgment for damages to the victims' families.

> *. . . nor shall be compelled in any criminal case to be a witness against himself.*

The Constitution aimed to protect citizens from torture and coerced confessions. The liberal Warren Court tried to put teeth into this right by requiring police officers to inform suspects that they have the right to remain silent, now known as the **Miranda warnings** (*Miranda v. Arizona*, 1966). The Court ruled that any evidence acquired before the warning could not be admissible in court. The ruling created an enormous outcry. Richard Nixon used *Miranda* in the 1968 presidential campaign as evidence that the United States had grown "soft on crime." Congress tried to pass a law to get around the ruling.

Miranda warnings: A set of rights that police officers are required to inform suspects of, including the right to remain silent.

Over the past forty years, the courts have limited the *Miranda* rights—permitting confessions made to a police officer posing as another inmate (1990), carving out an exception for public safety (1984), and limiting the rules when defendants take the stand in their own defense (1970).[35]

The controversy has long ago subsided, and the Miranda warnings have become "part of national culture," as Chief Justice William Rehnquist put it. Every TV cop show ends with the police nabbing the criminal while intoning, "You have the right to remain silent." In fact, some defense lawyers claim, half seriously, that the phrase is so familiar that what defendants actually hear is "We've caught you and you're in big trouble now."

This example raises an important point that applies to every aspect of the law. Constitutional rules constantly interact with popular culture. A controversial ruling filters through the media and sometimes becomes part of popular expectations. Today there are few calls for doing away with the Miranda warnings. The Constitution and the courts shape our popular culture. Popular culture, in turn, shapes the way we all read and think about the Constitution.

The Sixth Amendment: The Right to Counsel

The Sixth Amendment guarantees a speedy and public trial decided by an impartial jury. It includes another important provision, the right to counsel:

> *In all criminal prosecutions, the accused shall . . . have the assistance of counsel for his defense.*

The Supreme Court weighed in on the issue in an explosive case, known as the trial of the Scottsboro Boys. In 1931 nine young African American men, riding a freight train in Alabama, were accused of raping two white women. Despite evidence that the charges were false (one woman immediately recanted), angry mobs gathered, and eight of the young men were rushed through trials and condemned to death. In *Powell v. Alabama* (1932), the Court ruled that, at least in a capital case (a case that could end in death), the defendants are entitled to lawyers and that the lawyers must be given enough time to meet with their clients and prepare their case. This Scottsboro case was a civil rights breakthrough for another reason: none of the African Americans unfairly accused of raping a white woman was executed.

In 1963, the Court expanded the right to counsel to all felony cases. Clarence Gideon, a Florida drifter, was allegedly caught breaking into a poolroom where he had stolen beer, soft drinks, and the change out of the jukebox. When he came to trial, he demanded a lawyer, but the Florida court denied the request. Gideon was convicted and sentenced to five years, but from his jail cell, working with legal texts, he scrawled an appeal. "Something astonishing . . . happened," wrote Anthony Lewis in a book on the case. "This loser's plea made it all the way to the Supreme Court." In *Gideon v. Wainwright* (1963), the Supreme Court ruled that the Sixth Amendment supported his claim and that the state must provide a lawyer to defend those who cannot afford one. With a competent lawyer, Gideon was acquitted.[36] Attorney General Robert Kennedy commented, "An obscure Florida convict had . . . changed . . . the whole course of American legal history." A network of public defenders spread across the country.

● *The Scottsboro Boys, with their attorney Samuel Leibowitz, under guard by the state.*

In 2012, the Court dramatically increased the scope of the right to competent counsel by ruling that defendants have a constitutional right to effective attorneys during plea bargain negotiations (in a 5–4 ruling). Today, almost all federal cases (97 percent) involve a plea bargain, in which the defendant pleads guilty in exchange for a lighter sentence without actually going through a formal trial. The Court ruled that defendants can appeal if the negotiations were not competently handled.[37]

In practice, the right to counsel has grown increasingly difficult to maintain. The public is reluctant to spend tax revenues on lawyers who defend poor men and women accused of crimes. Public defenders face huge caseloads with small salaries—the average legal aid attorney in New York handles 592 cases a year and about 103 at any one time. Other cities and counties report similar ratios.[38] The attorneys' own clients often disparage them. Recent state fiscal problems have put even more pressure on an underfunded system. For all the problems, however, publicly funded criminal defense remains an essential part of civil liberty and American justice.

The Eighth Amendment: The Death Penalty

The Eighth Amendment introduces the question of capital punishment.

> *Cruel and unusual punishment . . . shall not be . . . inflicted.*

Is execution cruel and unusual punishment? Around the world, ninety-seven nations have abolished the death penalty—including all of western Europe, where it is considered a violation of human rights. In contrast, the United States executes between forty and fifty prisoners a year (with over 3,250 men and women sentenced to capital punishment and waiting on death row). Some 60 percent of the American public supports executions, although the number has been slipping over the past fifteen years (see Figure 4.3).

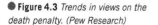

Figure 4.3 *Trends in views on the death penalty. (Pew Research)*

Proponents argue that some crimes are so terrible that justice demands capital punishment. It brings closure to grieving families. It may deter future murders (although there is no definitive evidence one way or the other). Moreover, some criminals are so dangerous they should be executed to protect other prisoners, prison officials, and the general public.

What Do You Think?

End the Death Penalty?

In a recent case, Justice Stevens called for ending the death penalty. Is capital punishment a form of "cruel and unusual punishment"?

No. Some crimes are so terrible they require this punishment. Justice demands it. It brings closure to the victims' families. American public opinion supports it. If there is a deterrent effect, executing criminals might save innocent lives. Some criminals are so hardened that they pose a safety threat to other prisoners, to prison officials, and to the public. Finally, multiple safeguards are in place to guarantee that innocent people are not executed.

Yes. It is time for the United States to join the other industrial democracies. Executions are unfair and fall almost entirely on poor and black defendants. No government should have this power. Killing is morally wrong, and two wrongs do not make a right. Furthermore, it is impossible to ensure that no innocent people will be killed. The deterrent effect is not proven. Even the American Medical Association refuses to let physicians participate.

Opponents respond that killing people is immoral and that no government should be given the power to "play God." Because social systems are imperfect, some—perhaps many—innocent people will be executed. The system is tilted against African Americans; blacks make up 12 percent of the population but, from year to year, between 25 and 50 percent of those executed.

In 1972, the Supreme Court halted all executions, arguing that state laws were so vague that similar cases produced different outcomes. "The death standards are cruel and unusual," wrote Justice Potter Stewart in *Furman v. Georgia*, "the same way that being struck by lightning is cruel and unusual"—meaning that death sentences seemed to be meted out randomly. Thirty-five states drafted new capital punishment laws using *Furman* as a guide. In 1976, the Court permitted executions to go forward where state statutes included clear criteria to guide judge and jury in weighing death sentences.

The Court has imposed some additional limits. It has ruled that it is "cruel and unusual" to execute people convicted of crimes other than murder, striking down five state laws that allowed execution for child rape (2008). It has forbidden the execution of mentally ill individuals (2002) and of juvenile offenders (2005). In a much-discussed case, however, the Court ruled that lethal injections did not constitute cruel and unusual punishment despite the claim that they caused "an intolerable risk of pain" (2007).[39]

Fighting Terrorism and Protecting Liberty

After the terrorist attacks on September 11, 2001, Congress passed the **USA Patriot Act**. In the fear and emotion of the terrible moment, few criticized the legislation, which passed in the Senate 98–1. The act tried to enhance security

USA Patriot Act: Legislation that sought to enhance national security, passed in the aftermath of the September 11, 2001, attacks.

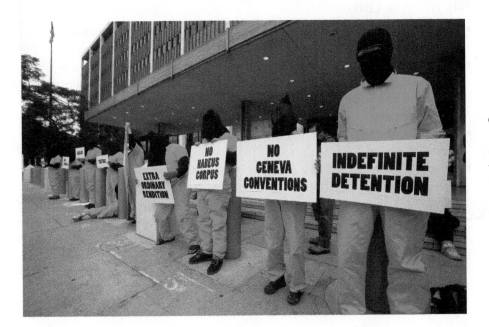

● *Ten years after Guantánamo Bay opened as a detention facility, protesters had made the orange jumpsuit a symbol of lost civil liberties—at home and abroad. The debate is so intense because it features two bedrock values: personal liberty and public safety.*

by removing restrictions on law enforcement. Removing restrictions, however, means limiting rights. The Patriot Act and the broader campaign against terrorism created a new debate about the balance between civil liberties and public safety.

Domestic surveillance requires a warrant. As part of the war on terror, the Bush administration issued a secret executive order permitting the National Security Agency (NSA) to conduct international surveillance without a search warrant. Although the order targeted foreign parties outside the United States, it applied to communications with American citizens in the United States. The agency apparently had access to fiber-optic cables transmitting information between major telecommunications systems. News of the program leaked and was published by the *New York Times* in 2005. (In order to sidestep government efforts to seek a prior restraint, once the editors decided to publish, the *Times* posted the story on its website.)

Congress approved the warrantless wiretap program in 2007 and the Obama administration continues to operate it. The program monitors phone calls, e-mails, and financial records. It may have led to over a million searches. Does wiretapping the international communications of American citizens without a warrant violate the Fourth Amendment prohibition against search and seizure? The case is working its way through the courts.

Critics of the Patriot Act charge that the United States is now so focused on fighting terrorists that it is trampling on the Constitution. Supporters argue that the United States faces peril and that the Constitution itself permits exceptions to basic rights when "public safety may require it" (article 1).

THE BOTTOM LINE

- The Bill of Rights places special emphasis on the rights of those accused of crimes. Even so, American incarceration rates are the highest in the world.
- The police may not search or seize without a warrant; they must inform suspects of their right to remain silent; the accused have a right to legal counsel. The courts have widened the legal right but it is often limited by underfunded public defenders.
- Under current interpretation, the death penalty is not considered "cruel and unusual punishment."
- Between 1962 and 1968, the Supreme Court vastly expanded the rights of the accused. Recent Court decisions have tilted the balance back toward law enforcement.

● Conclusion: The Dilemma of Civil Liberties

How should the government balance its duty to keep the public safe with its responsibility to protect private rights? It is the eternal dilemma of civil liberties and one of the most important issues facing American democracy. If we tilt too far toward combating terrorism, Americans lose the liberties that have defined the nation since 1776. If we tilt too far the other way, the nation may be vulnerable to attacks. Getting the balance right is a major challenge facing Americans today. The courts take the lead in protecting rights, but elected public officials define the policies that the courts are weighing. Ultimately, the balance between communal needs and individual rights is in the hands of the voters.

Isn't that exactly where it belongs? Not necessarily. Recall the Supreme Court's judgment in 1943: "The very purpose of a Bill of Rights was to withdraw certain subjects from the vicissitudes of political controversy, to place them beyond the reach of majorities and officials and to establish them as legal principles to be applied by the courts."[40]

The point of civil liberties is to protect the rights of individuals—even if it means stopping the majority of the country. We saw the birth of American liberty in Chapter 2 with the Declaration of Independence and the Constitution. In this chapter we have examined how American rights are interpreted and protected. In the next chapter, we'll see how they grew and spread.

CHAPTER SUMMARY

● Civil liberties are the limits we put on governing bodies (and the majorities that elect them) so that individuals can exercise their rights and freedom. Disputes are usually resolved by the courts and guided by the Bill of Rights.

● The Bill of Rights did not apply to the states until the Fourteenth Amendment required that *no state* could deprive any citizen of life, liberty, or property.

● The Supreme Court applied the Bill of Rights to the states one right at a time between 1897 (no taking property without compensation) and 2010 (the right to bear arms). The process is known as incorporation.

● The Court discovered a right to privacy implicit (in the shadows) in the First, Third, Fourth, Fifth, and Ninth Amendments. The Court applied the right to privacy to strike down laws banning abortion. In *Roe v. Wade* the Court issued a rule prohibiting states from interfering during the first trimester. In *Planned Parenthood v. Casey*, the Court replaced the rule with a standard forbidding laws that put "an undue burden" on the right to privacy. The Court extended privacy rights to same-sex couples by striking down antisodomy laws in 2003.

● The Constitution bans government from establishing religion. In one view, this means separating church and state. A three-part test, known as the Lemon test, guides judicial decisions. A more recent approach requires simply that government not promote one religious view over another. The Constitution also forbids government from interfering with religious practice. The courts traditionally asked if the government had a compelling interest for imposing a burden. Today, they require only that the government action be neutral and apply to everyone. Congress and some state governments have tried to return to the original rule.

● Free speech is crucial to democracy, and the Court gives it a privileged position—even against angry public opposition to flag burning, cross burning, or homophobic displays at military funerals. Free speech can be curtailed if it poses a "clear and present danger." Today, the Court requires the danger to be both imminent and likely to occur. There are limits to free speech involving fighting words, student speech, commercial speech, and obscenity.

● Some critics see the Second Amendment as an outmoded defense of citizen militias. Others see the right to bear arms as an important individual right—perhaps the most important right in the Constitution. In 2010, the Supreme Court ruled it an essential constitutional right.

● The Bill of Rights places special emphasis on the rights of those accused of crimes. Even so, American incarceration rates are the highest in the world. The police may not search or seize without a warrant, they must inform suspects of their right to remain silent, and the accused have a right to legal counsel. Under current interpretation, capital punishment is not considered "cruel and unusual punishment."

KEY TERMS

Civil liberties, 124
Civil rights, 124
Clear and present danger, 138
Double jeopardy, 149
Establishment clause, 132
Exclusionary rule, 148

Fighting words, 139
Free exercise clause, 132
Grand jury, 149
Hate crime, 137
Hate speech, 137
Jim Crow, 128

Miranda warnings, 150
Prior restraint, 141
Selective incorporation, 128
Symbolic expression, 139
USA Patriot Act, 153

STUDY QUESTIONS

1. What are civil liberties? How are they different from civil rights?

2. In *Barron v. Baltimore*, the Supreme Court ruled that the Fifth Amendment did not protect a landowner if the state took his property. Why?

3. Describe how the Bill of Rights was applied to the state governments.

First, describe the constitutional amendment that directly addressed the states.
Then, describe the process of incorporation by which the Supreme Court applied the Bill of Rights to the states.

4. Describe how the Supreme Court declared the right to privacy.

Discuss the case from a pragmatist's and an originalist's perspective.
Would you vote to maintain the right to privacy? Or to overrule the precedent? Explain your reasoning.

5. Describe the three-part Lemon test for determining whether a state action violates the establishment clause.

6. Sometimes the Court permits a racist to burn a cross. Sometimes it forbids it. Explain the reasoning in each case.

7. There are two interpretations of the Second Amendment right to bear arms. Describe each. Which do you support? Why?

8. The Supreme Court gives free speech a "preferred position" among the rights in the Bill of Rights.

   What does that mean?
   How does the Court justify that position?

9. How does the USA Patriot Act raise questions about the balance between public safety and civil liberties? How do you think about balancing civil liberties with protection against terrorism? If you had to emphasize one goal more than the other, which would you emphasize? Why?

5

The Struggle for Civil Rights

"WHAT DO YOU WANT TO BE when you grow up?" asked the eighth-grade teacher. Malcolm Little, the class president, responded. "I've been thinking I'd like to be a lawyer." "Malcolm," snapped the teacher, "you've got to be realistic about being a n——[he used a racial epithet]. A lawyer—that's no realistic goal for a n——." The student would later change his name to Malcolm X and redefine black nationalism. But when Malcolm was in eighth grade, black kids could not even dream of professional careers. The same year, novelist Richard Wright imagined a black teen in Chicago "playing white" by pretending to be an army general, a corporate executive, or an airline pilot. These professions were all out of reach for most African Americans—and for women.

When Congress unexpectedly outlawed sex discrimination in the Civil Rights Act of 1964 the *Wall Street Journal* quoted a flummoxed airline executive: "What are we going to do now when a gal walks into our office, demands a job as an airline pilot, and has the credentials to qualify?" The idea of a woman piloting a commercial airline was no more sensible than Malcolm becoming a lawyer or a black kid on the South Side of Chicago selling stocks. At least they all had an advantage over Chinese children, who were forbidden from becoming American citizens. Things we now take completely for granted—black professionals, women pilots, Chinese Americans—were either rare or illegal in the past.[1]

Who are we? We are a nation founded on the idea that all people are "created equal" and "endowed" with "unalienable rights" including "life, liberty and the pursuit of happiness." We are also a very diverse nation that often does not live up to its noble founding vision.

Civil rights are the freedom to participate in the life of the community—to vote in elections, to enjoy public facilities like parks, and to take full advantage of economic opportunities like good jobs. People face discrimination when they are denied rights and opportunities because of their race, gender, ethnicity, religion, disabilities, age, or other personal characteristics. Once citizens have won their rights, the attention shifts to protecting them. We covered that topic—known as civil liberties—in the last chapter.

Civil rights: The freedom to participate in the full life of the community—to vote, use public facilities, and exercise equal economic opportunity.

● *Authorities in Birmingham, Alabama, turned high-pressure fire hoses on young people during demonstrations against segregation in May 1963. "There was a certain kind of fire no water could put out," responded Martin Luther King.*

The long battle to win civil rights is the most powerful story in American history. It reveals the deepest truths about the United States and its values. It tells us who we are.

We can view the history of civil rights in two different ways. Some observers see a steady march toward a deeper and richer American equality. If you reread the opening paragraph of this chapter, it's hard not to see enormous progress. An African American lawyer? One has been elected to the Oval Office. Women pilots? Women began flying combat missions twenty years ago. Asian Americans? There are thirteen in Congress. The American promise marches relentlessly on.[2]

BY THE NUMBERS *Civil Rights*

Number of black mayors in 1965: **0**
Number of black mayors in 2012: **over 500**

Percentage of southern students who attended integrated schools 8 years after *Brown v. Board of Education* forbade segregated schools in 1954: **1**
Percentage of southern students who attended integrated schools 8 years after the passage of the Civil Rights Act of 1964: **91**

Poverty rate (percentage) of white and black Americans, respectively, in 1959: **18, 55**
Poverty rate of white Americans today: **8.6**
Poverty rate of Hispanic Americans: **21.5**
Poverty rate of black Americans: **24.7**
Poverty rate of Native Americans: **32.2**

Number of Hispanic members of Congress in 1990, 2000, 2012: 10, 18, 31
Number of women elected to full Senate terms between 1920 and 1970: **3**
Number of women serving in the Senate today: 20
Nations with more women serving in the national legislature than the US (2011–2012): 70

Year the Supreme Court struck down laws forbidding marriage between blacks and whites: **1968**
Percentages of whites, blacks, Hispanics, and Asians married to a member of a different race today: **9, 17, 26, 28**

Percentage of whites, Latinos, and blacks who report "a great deal" or "a fair amount" of confidence in the police: **78, 61, 53**

Other observers, however, believe that there is nothing inevitable about civil rights. Sometimes rights expand, sometimes they contract. Yes, Asians won full rights, but Native Americans did not. African Americans scaled the old barriers, but only three served in the Senate in the entire twentieth century. African Americans are almost three times as likely to be poor as the rest of the population. They have a life expectancy five years shorter than whites. There is nothing inevitable about American equality, say proponents of this perspective, and citizens should never take it for granted.[3]

As you read this chapter, ask which view seems most accurate to you: Has the United States marched toward greater civil rights for all? Or has the progress been unsteady?

Winning Rights: The Political Process

How does a group win political rights? Each effort has its own unique history. However, the efforts usually involve the following stages—not necessarily in order.

Seven Steps to Political Equality

1. *A group defines itself.* Discrimination usually stretches back through time and seems, to many people, the way things always were: whites ruled blacks, men took responsibility for "the weaker sex," Indians were "savages," society pitied the disabled, and psychiatrists defined homosexuality as an illness. In the first step toward civil rights, a group embraces its shared identity and redefines itself as a victim of discrimination.

2. *The group challenges society.* The next step involves entering the political arena and demanding rights. Civil rights campaigns often go beyond normal politics and include marches, demonstrations, creative protests (like kneel-ins before segregated churches), and even riots.

3. *The stories change.* Civil rights always involve a contest over the stories that a society tells about a group. Why does the United States discriminate against people in the first place? Because people see them as dangerous, inferior, or helpless. Winning rights requires changing the story.

4. *Federalism comes into play.* Civil rights politics splashes across local, state, and federal governments. Because many minority groups are concentrated in certain states and regions,

● *Lucretia Mott, who helped organize the Seneca Falls convention for women's rights, is attacked by a mob of angry men. Women who challenged their own subordination faced violence in the 19th century.*

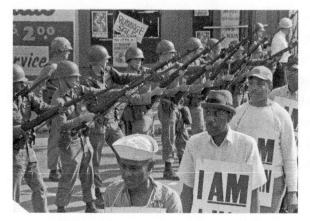

● *Groups redefine the story. Black sanitation workers demonstrate in August 1968 holding signs declaring, "I am a man." They would no longer be invisible or answer to a derogatory "boy."*

that discrimination often begins on the local level. Furthermore, state and local officials control many of the policies that define civil rights: education, law enforcement, and voting rules. In other cases (like women voting and gay rights), states and localities first introduce reforms.

5. *The executive branch often breaks the ice.* Presidents can issue executive orders (rules that have the force of law but do not require congressional approval); these can create opportunities and momentum for a civil rights campaign. Executive orders enabled Truman to desegregate the army in 1948, and Obama to enable young undocumented aliens to apply for work permits.

6. *Congress legislates a blockbuster.* Congress introduces the great changes, which finally secure civil rights and echo through history. The Fourteenth Amendment to the Constitution, ratified in 1868, still dominates every effort to win rights. The Civil Rights Act of 1964 profoundly changed civil rights in the United States.

7. *It all ends up in court.* The courts are the ultimate arbiters of civil rights. They rule on what the Constitution requires of Americans. They weigh laws, rules, regulations, and private actions for what is and is not permissible.

Notice how many moving parts there are in the reform process. We've already seen why this is so: American government is unusually fragmented, marked by overlapping actors and institutions all balancing one another. That makes it difficult to change deep social norms—like racial or gender discrimination. Reformers have to win over many different power centers—state legislatures, the US Congress, governors, the courts, the press, and the public.

How the Courts Review Cases

Since civil rights generally end up in court, the judicial framework is important. The courts use three categories for determining whether acts violate "the equal protection of the laws" guaranteed by the Fourteenth Amendment.

Strict scrutiny: The tendency to strike down as unconstitutional any legislation that singles out race or ethnicity, unless the government has a compelling interest in such legislation.

Suspect Categories. Any legislation involving *race, ethnicity,* or *legal aliens* faces **strict scrutiny**. The Supreme Court is primed to strike down any law that singles out a race or ethnicity unless there is a very strong reason for doing so. The Court will ask: Does the government have a *compelling government interest* in singling out a race or an ethnicity? In *Brown v. Board of Education,* for example, the Court decided that the state governments had no *compelling interest* in segregating schools.

Quasi-suspect category: A legal category that requires governments to have an important state purpose for any legislation that singles out sex or gender. This is not as strong as the *suspect category,* which requires strict scrutiny.

Quasi-suspect Categories. In 1976, women's advocates won a special category for gender cases. Any legislation—federal, state, or local—that introduces sex-based categories has to rest on an *important state purpose*. This is not as strong a test as a *compelling* interest. But it is still an important category that can touch many aspects of politics, economics, and society. For example, in 1996 the Court ruled that excluding women from the Virginia Military Institute did not serve an important state purpose. VMI had to open its doors to women cadets or forgo state funding.

Nonsuspect Categories.   Other categories do not face special scrutiny—at least not yet. Legislation based on age, sexual orientation, or physical handicaps simply has to have some rational connection between the legislation and a legitimate government purpose. This is a weaker test than those of the other two categories, but it can still bar discrimination. Using this test, for example, the Court struck down an Oregon law that banned Catholic schools from the state (in 1925) and a Colorado constitutional amendment that forbade all legislation designed to protect people based on their sexual orientation (1996). The Court ruled that there was no rational government interest in forbidding Catholic education or ruling out all protections of gay people.[4]

This threefold division is the framework for civil rights law. Like almost everything else in American government, politics produced these categories. Groups argued, lobbied, demonstrated, and sued to win stricter scrutiny.

THE BOTTOM LINE

- The battle for civil rights generally includes seven stages. The group seeking rights must define itself; it must challenge society and change the cultural story. The contest for rights spills across federalism; the executive branch can break the ice. Congress is the key to deep social change; the courts are the final arbiters of civil rights.
- Courts put charges of discrimination into three categories: suspect categories, quasi-suspect categories, and nonsuspect categories.

● Race and Civil Rights: Revolt Against Slavery

Few groups in American history have suffered worse treatment than African Americans. By now, the painful images are familiar: men and women chained in the holds of slave ships, sold at auction, raped at will, separated from families, and murdered for challenging their oppression. Even after liberation, black Americans faced another century of repression. In fighting back, African Americans developed the tactics that other groups would use in their battles for civil rights; black movements forged the laws, amendments, and judicial doctrine that opened the door to civil rights reforms across society. The black quest for freedom included two great crusades, one in the nineteenth century and one in the twentieth.

The Clash over Slavery

Slaves were permitted to have churches, and in the early nineteenth century, religion offered leadership, organization, and a powerful message. Black leaders drew on the Christian Bible to compare Africans to the Israelites, bound in slavery but waiting for deliverance to freedom. By the middle of the nineteenth century, the dream of freedom had become a kind of religious faith in the slave quarters.[5] Three additional forces mixed with black hope for freedom and precipitated a national crisis over slavery: a moral crusade for abolition, economic interests, and political calculations.

Abolition.   An **abolition** movement rose up, branded slavery sinful, and demanded its immediate end. The movement was small and radical, but its newspapers and pamphlets created a furious reaction. Many Americans—in the south and the north—feared the abolitionists would incite the slaves to rebellion. Most people preferred to ignore the issue.

Economics.   However, it was impossible to avoid the slavery question for a fundamental economic reason. As the United States spread west, every new settlement prompted the same question—would it be slave or free? Northerners opposed slavery on the frontier because it robbed them of the opportunity to claim their own land. Slave labor, they believed, drove out free labor. Southerners, however, believed that slavery needed to spread into

Abolition: A nineteenth-century movement demanding an immediate and unconditional end to slavery.

● *Branding slaves. This cruel practice was standard in slaveholding states up until the end of the Civil War.*

new states to survive. Because the federal government controlled territories until they became states, the question—slave or free?—constantly haunted Congress.

Politics. Every time a territory applied for statehood it raised the question of the political balance between slave states and free states in the Senate. Since every state has two senators, an equal number of free and slave states permitted the South to defend its peculiar institution.

The Senate managed to negotiate the tensions with a series of compromises. The **Missouri Compromise**, in 1820, drew a line through the Louisiana Territory (see Figure 5.1). All new states and territories north of the line except Missouri would be free; everything south of the line would be open to slavery. In 1845, as Americans moved west, Congress extended the line to include Texas. By 1850, the old compromise was collapsing. California wanted to enter the Union, but extending the old line to the coast would split the new state—half slave and half free. The solution was another compromise, the **Compromise of 1850**, which turned the decision over to the people in the territories.

Dred Scott v. Sandford

In 1857, the Supreme Court stepped in with a shattering decision that upset all the careful compromises. A slave named Dred Scott sued for freedom. He argued that he had been taken to live in a free territory before returning to Missouri, and that that experience meant he should be free. Chief Justice Roger Taney ruled that he was not free because neither the territories nor the federal government had the power to limit slavery or give a black man rights. As a "negro," wrote Taney, Dred Scott "could not be a citizen in the sense

Missouri Compromise: An agreement to open southern territories west of the Mississippi to slavery while closing northern territories to slavery.

Compromise of 1850: A complicated compromise over slavery that permitted territories to vote on whether they would be slave or free. It also included a fugitive slave law forcing northerners to return black men and women into bondage, and permitted California to enter the Union as a free state.

Dred Scott v. Sandford: A landmark Supreme Court decision holding that black men could not be citizens under the Constitution of the United States. It created a national uproar.

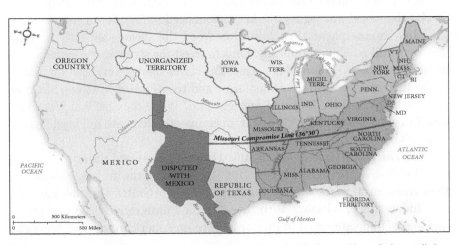

● **Figure 5.1** *The Missouri Compromise—all new American territory below the line would permit slavery, all above (except Missouri) would be free.*

● Dred Scott sued for freedom. Chief Justice Taney, from the slave state of Maryland, tried to settle the slavery issue once and for all.

in which the word is used in the Constitution of the United States." What about the Missouri Compromise? Unconstitutional, ruled Taney. Popular sovereignty? Also unconstitutional. The ***Dred Scott v. Sandford*** decision ruled that no territory could restrict slavery, much less elevate blacks to citizenship.

The Dred Scott decision created an uproar. The Republican Party rose to national prominence by explicitly rejecting it. Two years later, in 1860, Abraham Lincoln won the presidency on a platform that flatly opposed the extension of slavery into any territories. When Lincoln won, the southern states began withdrawing from the United States and the terrible Civil War began. In the four years from 1861 to 1865, more people lost their lives than in all the other American wars put together. However, from the blood and ashes arose a second American founding.

The Second American Founding: A New Birth of Freedom?

In his Gettysburg Address, President Lincoln announced "a new birth of freedom" and declared that the United States had been "conceived in liberty and dedicated to the proposition that all men are created equal." Lincoln lifted the principles of the Declaration of Independence back to the center of American government. Moreover, he expressed a view of self-government that the Declaration had not fully embraced and the Constitution had rejected: "government of the people, by the people, for the people."[6] With this simple declaration, Lincoln rewrote the American idea of freedom.

Emancipation Proclamation: An executive order issued by President Abraham Lincoln that declared the slaves in all rebel states free.

Lincoln's bold innovation was institutionalized in four documents. In 1863, Lincoln's **Emancipation Proclamation** freed the slaves—but only in areas that were still rebelling. Ironically, Lincoln freed the slaves in the states where he had no power to enforce his decree. The slaves themselves, however, bolted by the thousands toward the Union army and transformed it, as one historian wrote, into "a reluctant dragon of emancipation." When the Civil War was finally over, Congress wrote three "Civil War amendments" that gave full legal force to Lincoln's new birth of freedom.

The *Thirteenth Amendment* (ratified in 1865) abolished slavery.

The *Fourteenth Amendment* (1868) protected the former slaves and their freedom. It made anyone born in the United States an American citizen. Today, this provision is at the heart of the immigration debate; even the children of undocumented immigrants, born on American soil, are American citizens.

The crucial passage of the Fourteenth Amendment—and one of the most important in American law and politics—comes in the next sentence: *No state shall "deprive any person of life, liberty or property without due process of law; nor deny to any person . . . the equal protection of the laws."* By directing the language at the states—"no *state* shall deprive any person"— the Fourteenth Amendment applied the federal Constitution and the Bill of Rights to the states. (As we saw in Chapter 4, the application would proceed case by case, one right at a time.) The key phrase—the **equal protection of the laws**—would become the crucial legal weapon in the battle for civil rights. Remember that phrase. It might be the single most important addition to the Constitution in the last two hundred years. It forbids any law designed to harm a group.

The *Fifteenth Amendment* (ratified in 1870) guarantees the right to vote. "The right of citizens . . . to vote . . . shall not be denied . . . on account of race, color, or previous condition of servitude." Can you see what is not mentioned? Gender. Women had reasoned that since they were citizens, their right to vote should not be "denied or abridged," but the Supreme Court rejected this interpretation in 1875.

Like the original Constitution, all these amendments were inspired by political calculation. For example, the Republicans in the North, who controlled Congress, knew that the South would return to the Union with more seats in Congress than they had before the Civil War—the slave had counted for three-fifths of a vote; the freemen counted for a whole vote. Since the former slaves were very likely to vote for the party of Lincoln (and their former masters were not), the Republicans in Congress had a very good reason to protect their right to vote.

> **Equal protection of the laws:** The landmark phrase in the Fourteenth Amendment that requires equal treatment for all citizens.

Freedom Fails

What happened to the former slaves? The era after the civil war began with soaring hopes—and ended bitterly. Black families—torn apart during slavery—joyously reunited. African Americans formed communities, organized churches, voted, entered politics, and demanded respect from their former owners. Two African Americans were elected to the US Senate and twenty-one to the House of Representatives. However, black empowerment met fierce resistance. Many whites found it difficult to treat the former slaves as equals. Some were outraged when the freemen no longer stepped aside on the sidewalks; many whites faced economic hardship, even ruin, now that their labor force had disappeared.

Southern state and local governments reacted by passing *black codes*. These regulations tied blacks to the land, restricted their movements, established curfews, and stripped them of rights like owning property, voting, or owning guns. Legal restrictions were backed up by the violent Ku Klux Klan, which sprang up to intimidate the former slaves.

Reconstruction: The
failed effort, pursued
by Northerners and
Southerners, to rebuild the
South and establish racial
equality after the Civil War.

For a time, Congress supported the former slaves. In an effort known as **Reconstruction**, it tried to rebuild the South around a vision of racial justice. Congress organized a Freedmen's Bureau to assist the former slaves. The Civil Rights Act of 1866 guaranteed African Americans the same property rights as white Americans; the Civil Rights Act of 1875 limited private racial discrimination in hotels, restaurants, and theaters. African Americans participated in politics despite violence and intimidation.

However, dreams of racial equality began to slip away. The North, weary of the conflict, withdrew the army from the South in 1877. Congress repealed the laws that implemented (or put into effect) the Civil War amendments; no national mechanism was left to enforce "the equal protection of the laws." In the Civil Rights Cases of 1883, the Supreme Court struck down the Civil Rights Act of 1875, ruling that Congress did not have the authority to stop private discrimination. It would be eighty-nine years before Congress found a way around this barrier.[7]

By the 1890s, the state governments had found ways to gut the Fifteenth Amendment right to vote. The *grandfather clause* forbade people from voting if their grandfathers didn't vote; obviously, if your grandfather was a slave, he did not vote. Poll taxes required paying a fee that most black people could not afford. The heart of the effort lay in **literacy tests** that required voters to read and interpret any passage in the state constitution; wickedly difficult passages were introduced to make sure that no African Americans passed the test. The new rules did what violence and intimidation had failed to accomplish—they drove blacks out of politics. African Americans have been the only group in any democracy, commented political scientist Richard Valelly, to enter the electorate and then be thrust out all over again.[8]

Literacy test: A
requirement that voters be
literate; in reality, a way to
restrict black suffrage.

The white majority built a system of segregation known as **Jim Crow** (named after the minstrel shows in which white singers and dancers blackened their faces and pretended to be Africans). Jim Crow laws segregated—or held separate—the races. African Americans could not go to white schools, play in the park, visit the zoo (Thursday eventually became "black day" at the zoos), drink from the same fountain, eat at a white restaurant, stay in a white hotel, go to a white hospital, pray in a white church, or vote.

Jim Crow: The system of
racial segregation in the
US South that lasted from
1890 to 1965.

In 1896, the Supreme Court ruled in ***Plessy v. Ferguson*** that there was nothing inherently discriminatory in separating the races. "If one race be inferior to the other socially," wrote the majority, "the Constitution of the United States cannot put them upon the same plane."[9]

Plessy v. Ferguson: An
1896 Supreme Court
case that permitted racial
segregation.

The entire system of segregation was held in place by the raw brutality of lynching—ritualized murders of black men (and occasionally women) who had violated the codes. The murders—by hanging, mutilation, burning—were not crimes of mob passion but organized events with police directing traffic around the scene and white families posing for pictures by the victim's charred body. They served as a horrific way to enforce racial separation. The *Negro Year Book* recorded 1,799 blacks lynched between 1882 and 1920 alone.

The white majority directed extraordinary fury at men and women who fell in love across the racial divide, for they directly threatened the entire structure of segregation. Thirty states passed laws forbidding interracial marriage, and sixteen still had them in 1968 when the Supreme Court finally ruled that they violated "the equal protection of the laws" guaranteed by the Fourteenth Amendment.[10]

How could the majority accept such repression? Once again, the white majority told a false story about black men: they had not been ready for freedom after the Civil War. The heart of the matter, endlessly repeated, was the black men's supposed sexual lust for white women. Black men were dangerous. The state governments had stripped them of the vote because they were not ready to exercise it. The terrorism of the Ku Klux Klan (or KKK) was simply protecting innocent white women.

The story in its most blatant form provided the plot for one of the seminal works in cinematic history. *The Birth of a Nation* (1915) features lust-filled black men, backed by federal troops, menacing white women until the KKK saves the day. In one of the last triumphant scenes, the KKK disarms the skulking black men and stops them from voting. Woodrow Wilson screened the film in the White House and called it "like writing history with lightning." Protests by the NAACP fell on deaf ears.

By 1900, the dreams of equality had collapsed, and African Americans were, once again, denied almost all of their civil rights. Another generation—black and white together—would have to take up the fight again.

see for yourself 5.1

Go online to see clips from
The Birth of a Nation.

THE BOTTOM LINE

- The clash over slavery eventually led Lincoln to redefine the American idea of self-rule: "government of the people, by the people, for the people."

- *Institutional changes* marked the rise and the fall of civil rights. The president issued the Emancipation Proclamation, Congress passed the Civil Rights Acts, and the states ratified the Thirteenth, Fourteenth, and Fifteenth Amendments.

- The Fourteenth Amendment contains the crucial legal rule for civil rights: "No state shall . . . deprive any person of . . . the equal protection of the laws."

- Later, the courts struck down some civil rights legislation, Congress repealed the laws implementing the Civil War amendments, and the states introduced segregation, which the Supreme Court accepted.

- However, it was the *culture*—the terrible stories Americans told about their fellow citizens—that fixed the new legal chains in place by inducing the majority to ignore the violations of black rights.

● The Fight for Racial Equality

World War II revolutionized the race line by changing American attitudes. The United States fought a bitter war against a Nazi enemy with horrific theories of racial superiority; the memory made all ideas of racial superiority suspect. Over one hundred thousand black troops had fought in the war and returned home with new ideas of freedom and dignity.

The South had also changed. It was becoming more modern, industrial, and urban. Beginning in the 1920s, many African Americans left the South and moved to more lucrative factory jobs in the northern cities—a journey known as the **Great Migration**. By the 1950s, 40 percent of the black population lived in the North, where they faced a completely different kind of racial discrimination.

Great Migration: The vast movement of African Americans from the rural South to the urban North between 1920 and 1950.

De jure discrimination: Discrimination established by laws.

De facto discrimination: More subtle forms of discrimination that exist without a legal basis.

Two Kinds of Discrimination

There are two kinds of discrimination. Legal discrimination—known as **de jure discrimination**—involves laws that explicitly deny civil rights. By the time the civil rights movement came to an end, around 1970, Americans had ended de jure discrimination—an enormous achievement.

A second kind of discrimination—known as "in fact" or **de facto discrimination**—exists without explicit laws and is more subtly embedded in society. De facto discrimination is much harder to address. One of the thorniest questions to ponder is whether de facto discrimination still exists today—and, if so, to what extent.

● *"Separate but equal" for George McLaurin meant a desk in the hallway. McLaurin, who was pursuing his PhD at the University of Oklahoma, sued, and the Supreme Court ruled against segregated classes in graduate school.*

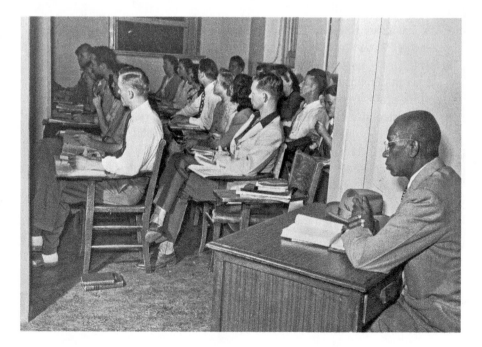

The Civil Rights Campaign Begins

In 1909, black leaders formed the **National Association for the Advancement of Colored People, or NAACP**, and began fighting segregation. In 1941 they finally won the first executive order on race since Reconstruction. President Franklin Roosevelt signed an order barring racial discrimination by defense contractors and created the Fair Employment Practices Committee to ensure compliance. What pushed Roosevelt to act? Black leaders, led by A. Philip Randolph, threatened a massive protest march on Washington just as the United States was gearing up to fight World War II. Seven years later, in 1948, Harry Truman desegregated the armed forces, making the military the first racially integrated institution in the United States.

World War II and the Cold War added an important twist to American politics. Segregation and racial unrest reflected badly on the United States, especially in Africa and Asia, where countries were throwing off colonialism and choosing between American democracy and Soviet Communism. Presidents from both parties worried about what racial segregation did to America's international image.

National Association for the Advancement of Colored People, or NAACP: A civil rights organization formed in 1909 and dedicated to racial equality.

The Courts

The NAACP also went to court and chipped away at Jim Crow laws enforcing segregation. In 1944 the Supreme Court struck down the all-white Democratic primary; the Court rejected the idea that the party could discriminate because it was like a private club.[11] The decision jolted observers because, just

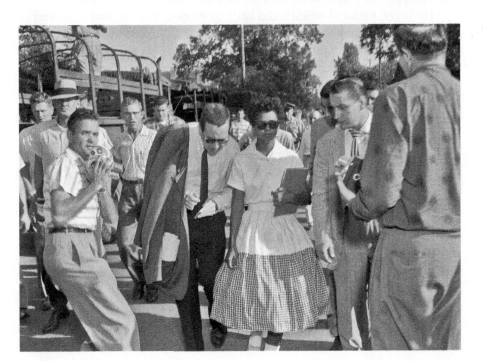

● *Elizabeth Eckford, one of nine black teens who integrated Little Rock High School in 1957, had to brave a gauntlet of jeering whites.*

● *The civil rights movement took courage. Here, protesters sitting at a whites-only lunch counter have been taunted and doused with ketchup.*

● *. . . and Freedom Riders escaped the burning bus, although some were beaten bloody.*

Brown v. Board of Education: The landmark Supreme Court case that struck down segregated schools as unconstitutional.

nine years earlier, the Court had unanimously upheld an all-white primary. Between the two decisions, President Franklin Roosevelt appointed eight new justices to the nine-person Supreme Court, changing the outlook of the Court toward race (and many other matters). The Court struck down various forms of segregation—on interstate buses, laws schools, graduate schools—and then took a monumental step.[12]

In May 1954, in ***Brown v. Board of Education***, the Court ruled that segregated schools violated the equal protection clause of the Fourteenth Amendment. In public education, ruled the court, "the doctrine of separate but equal has no place." Separate facilities were inherently unequal.

However, national officials did little to support *Brown*, and state and local leaders did much to oppose it. A decade after *Brown*, less than 1 percent of the schools in the South had been desegregated. Where desegregation did occur, the results could be explosive. The day before schools opened in 1957, Governor Orville Faubus of Arkansas announced that order could not be maintained if Little Rock's Central High School were to go forward with desegregation. The Arkansas National Guard turned away the nine high school students who tried to enter the school the next day.

The governor backed off in the face of a court order. When the students came back, two weeks later, the National Guard had been replaced by what the *New York Times* called "a mob of belligerent, shrieking hysterical demonstrators" shouting racial epithets at "two, three, a half dozen, scrubbed, starched, scared, and incredibly brave colored children." By noon, with the mob still screaming, nervous officials sneaked the children out a side door.

President Dwight Eisenhower, a Republican, reluctantly dispatched the 101st Airborne to enforce the court order and desegregate Central High. Elected officials throughout the South could not help but notice that Governor Faubus had became a local white hero and was returned to office for an unprecedented third term. Many white politicians reacted by staunchly supporting segregation. At the time, it was clear that, without political support, even a major court decision like *Brown v. Board of Education* would neither crack segregation nor integrate the schools.

The Civil Rights Movement

What defeated segregation was not the Supreme Court or the paratroopers from the 101st Airborne, but ordinary American people who rose up and seized the moment. There had been scattered protests throughout the country for years, but the organized movement began in Montgomery, Alabama, on a December afternoon in 1955.

Rosa Parks was riding the bus home. The white section filled up and, when a white man got on board, the driver called out that he needed another row. Everyone in the first black row was expected to get up and move—segregation meant that people from different races could not sit in the same row. Parks refused and was arrested. The local NAACP called a boycott of the Montgomery bus lines and put twenty-six-year-old Martin Luther King in charge.

It took a more than a year and direct intervention by the Supreme Court to desegregate the buses in Montgomery. The pattern was set: the Court had opened the legal door. Protesters braved arrest, scorn, and violence to win the change on the ground. The bravery of protesters under fire inspired others.

More and more people began to protest in more and more ways. In February 1960, four black college students from North Carolina A&T University sat at a white lunch counter and inspired a tactic that spread throughout the South. Within a year, seventy thousand people—black and white—had sat at segregated counters while onlookers gathered, jeered, and held cigarette lighters to the women's hair. From lunch counters the sit-ins spread to movie theaters, parks, pools, art galleries, libraries, and churches.

Freedom Riders: Black and white activists who rode buses together to protest segregation on interstate bus lines.

In 1961, activists came up with a new tactic. Groups of young people rented Greyhound buses as **Freedom Riders** to protest segregated interstate bus lines and terminals. The first bus was pursued by a "citizens' posse" and

---

What Do You Think?

•.. Would You Have Protested?

Look at the images on these pages—young people at a sit-in are humiliated, those on a Freedom Bus almost burned and then beaten. College students carried out the early sit-ins and Freedom Rides like those depicted here. The question for you to think about—one we often ask ourselves—is simple: *If you were in college between 1960 and 1962, would you have taken part?* It would have taken conviction, courage, and (for most students) a willingness to ignore parents horrified by the risks.

What would you have done? Explain why.

set ablaze. Angry men tried to hold the doors of the burning bus shut, and the students narrowly escaped—only to get a vicious beating with bats and pipes.

Despite the protests, segregation *still* did not yield. Schools did not integrate and southern politics did not change. The stalemate was finally broken by a civil rights campaign in Birmingham, Alabama. Marchers, including schoolchildren, tumbled out of church, which served as the protest headquarters, and marched singing and clapping into appalling police violence. Fire hoses sent marchers sprawling, police dogs snapped and bit. Television flashed the images around the world. The police overreaction illuminated the pain of segregation more effectively than anything that had come before. Americans who had mildly supported civil rights became incensed.

Protests now multiplied. The Kennedy administration had been urging caution. The Democratic Party was divided between northern liberals and southern segregationists, and the administration did not want to lose southern support. The images from Birmingham forced the issue, and the administration finally submitted strong civil rights legislation to Congress.

One problem for social activists is always the **free rider problem**. The civil rights protesters faced dog bites, criminal prosecution, and even death; those who stood on the sideline would reap all the same political benefits—civil rights—without any risks. In the early 1960s, hundreds of thousands of Americans ignored the cost-benefit calculations and joined protests and marches. Why did they put themselves in harm's way?

Congress and the Civil Rights Act

Even after the many protests, Congress blocked the Civil Rights legislation—as it had routinely done in the past. This time, however, events overran the usual political calculations. In May and June 1963, a great wave of protests followed Birmingham. Media stories about demonstrations, violence, and arrests fostered a sense of crisis. The **1963 March on Washington** marked the high point of the peaceful protest movement; the entire nation watched Martin Luther King put aside his prepared text and declare, "I have a dream." Hope filtered through the crisis and the result was enough to move the legislation in the House of Representatives.

In November 1963, President Kennedy was assassinated, and the Civil Rights Act became, as President Lyndon Johnson would put it, a martyr's cause.

The **Civil Rights Act of 1964** was powerful legislation. It forbade state and local governments from denying access to public facilities on the basis of race, color, or national origin. The law prohibited employers from discriminating on the basis of race, color, religion, sex, or national origin. It barred discrimination in private motels, hotels, theaters, and other public accommodations. There would be no more black Thursdays at city zoos. Congress slipped past the limits imposed by the 1883 Civil Rights Cases (Congress could

Free rider problem:
A barrier to group or collective action arising because people who do not participate still reap the benefits.

1963 March on Washington: A massive rally for civil rights highlighted by Martin Luther King's "I Have a Dream" speech.

see for yourself 5.2

Go online to see Martin Luther King's "I Have a Dream" speech.

Civil Rights Act of 1964: Landmark legislation that forbade discrimination on the basis of race, sex, religion, or national origin.

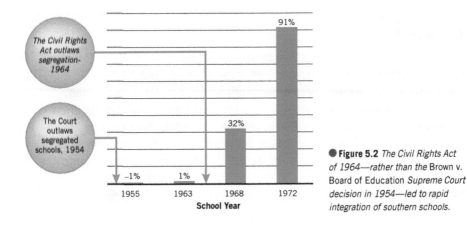

Figure 5.2 *The Civil Rights Act of 1964—rather than the* Brown v. Board of Education *Supreme Court decision in 1954—led to rapid integration of southern schools.*

not force private businesses to desegregate) by relying on its constitutional authority over interstate commerce.

The Civil Rights Act also empowered the federal government to withhold funds from segregated schools. In less than a decade the number of southern schoolchildren in integrated schools jumped from almost none to over 90 percent (see Figure 5.2). Today, almost every discussion of civil rights comes back to this blockbuster legislation.

The following year Congress passed the Voting Rights Act of 1965. This law protected the right to vote, struck down voter-suppression tactics like the literacy test, and empowered the attorney general and the US District Court of Washington, DC, to weigh any voting change in suspect areas for its potentially discriminatory effect. The legislation effectively secured the Fifteenth Amendment guaranteeing the right to vote. African Americans surged to the ballot boxes, and following behind black voters came black elected officials (see Table 5.1). As with most racial data, there is good news and bad news. The number of elected black officials has skyrocketed—increasing 129-fold in forty years. At the same time, African Americans, who comprise over 12 percent of the American population, still make up about only 2 percent of all elected officials.

Table 5.1 Total Number of Black Elected Officials

	1964	1970	1980	1990	2008
Mayors	0	81	x	314	641
Members of Congress	5	9	19	19	42
Total black elected officials in the United States	70	1,469	4,914	7,370	9,040

THE BOTTOM LINE

- The NAACP won a series of cases against segregation, culminating in *Brown v. Board of Education* in 1954; however, implementation proved difficult.
- In the early 1960s, a great mass movement rose up in which ordinary men, women, and children—black and white—turned the legal promise of the *Brown* decision into a practical reality. As the pictures and videos from marches became more violent and dramatic, public opinion surged in favor of action and pushed Congress to pass the Civil Rights Act of 1964 and the Voting Rights Act of 1965.
- Taken together, these institutional changes ended de jure segregation in the United States.
- The black movement set the model for future civil rights campaigns by many other groups.

● The End of the Civil Rights Era

After the successful challenge to de jure segregation, civil rights reformers faced the perplexing problems of subtle, de facto discrimination. Protesters can kneel in front of a segregated church, but how do they challenge poorer jobs and shabbier neighborhoods?

Years of frustration in northern cities burst into riots—also known as urban insurrections. Over the next four years, one northern city after another burst into violence, culminating in massive riots after Martin Luther King was murdered in April 1968.

Affirmative Action in the Workplace

In this difficult context, Americans faced a dilemma. Slavery and segregation had yielded three hundred years of poverty, political exclusion, and poor education.

The American ideal is often expressed as *equality of opportunity*: give every individual a fair chance at achieving success if they are talented and hardworking. What should the nation do to give African Americans a fair chance to achieve the American dream after all those years of slavery and segregation? Many of the remedies for past discrimination appeared to guarantee *equality of outcome*: reserving jobs or opportunities for individuals based on their race or gender. Is this necessary to right past wrongs? If so, for how long? And are these remedies—extended to minorities and women—unfair to white men?

In the 1960s and 1970s, a new approach emerged as a way to assist groups that had faced discrimination. **Affirmative action** means taking direct,

Affirmative action: Direct, positive steps to recruit members of previously underrepresented groups into schools, colleges, and jobs; sometimes involves setting aside positions (known as quotas).

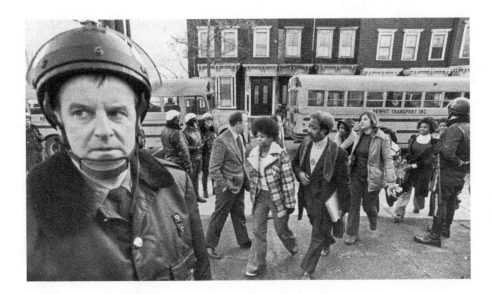

● *Civil rights move north. Busing in Boston, pictured here, created furious protests. In 1971 the Supreme Court unanimously ruled that busing schoolchildren was an acceptable way to overcome segregation. In 2007, the Supreme Court ended this practice.*

positive steps to increase the representation (especially in schools and work-places) of groups that have faced discrimination in the past.

Affirmative action eventually created a backlash from whites who failed to get jobs despite being qualified, and the Supreme Court began to narrow its use. In 1986, the Court warned that such programs could be used only in cases of "severe discrimination" and should not "trammel the interests of white employees."[13] By 1995, after almost twenty-five years of affirmative action programs, a more conservative Court rejected the idea of explicitly setting aside places for racial groups.

In 2009, the New Haven fire department offered a written exam for promotions. The top scorers on the test were all white. If the city accepted the test, black and Hispanic firefighters could sue—arguing that the test created "headwinds" unrelated to fighting fires. When New Haven threw out the test results, the white firefighters who had scored well on the test sued for the promotions that had been snatched away. The Court agreed, again 5–4, that New Haven should not have thrown out the results. The case is so difficult because both sides have a good argument: the New Haven fire department needs diverse leadership, but throwing out the test is seems unfair to individuals who did well.

Affirmative Action in Education

Schools, like companies, created affirmative action programs that, at first, reserved places for members of minority groups. Many schools sought to make up for past discrimination and, at the same time, create diversity among the students. These quotas, too, created a backlash.

One of the defining education cases focused on the medical school at the University of California at Davis, which held sixteen places in a medical school class of one hundred for members of minority or economically disadvantaged groups. Allan Bakke, a white man who had been rejected by the medical school, sued, arguing that his academic scores were higher than the scores of the minority applicants who had been accepted. In a 5–4 decision, *University of California v. Bakke* (1978), the Supreme Court ruled in favor of Bakke; setting a quota, as the university had done, violated the equal protection guarantee of the Fourteenth Amendment. Although the Court barred racial quotas, it accepted the use of race as a "plus" factor in the admissions process.[14] But how should the plus factor work?

The Court has painfully picked its way through the minefield of equal opportunity. The crucial questions are difficult ones: How does a nation make up for past discrimination? How long should the programs last? And what about people who feel they are losing out today because of efforts to address past injustice?

What Do You Think?

Higher Education and Affirmative Action

One of the most difficult problems in politics is how to make up for past injustice. What do we, as a society, owe to groups who have faced violence and discrimination for many generations? Consider the topic of higher education—the path to success in contemporary society. Which of the following positions would you support?

I favor affirmative action *for as long as it takes*. People who have faced many years of discrimination deserve affirmative action in education for as long as it takes them to catch up to the rest of society.

I favor affirmative action *with an end in sight*. People who have faced discrimination should get affirmative action in higher education for a fixed period. But, how long should that period run? *In Grutter v. Bollinger* (2003), the Supreme Court implied the correct period should last, roughly, three generations, or sixty years (1965–2025). Do you agree? If not, how much time you would allow?

I favor affirmative action only *if it doesn't set back others*. People who have faced discrimination should get special educational opportunities if and only if it does not harm other people's chances. (Can you think of some ways to do this?)

I am against affirmative action if discrimination has ended. People who have faced discrimination should not get any special treatment. Once the discrimination ends, they must compete like everyone else. But: How do you measure the end of discrimination? By the passage of a law or by practice in society?

Where Are We Now?

How close has the United States come to achieving racial equality? A few key indicators measure how the civil rights movement changed America—and how far we still have to go.

The progress is undeniable. African Americans once faced violence, segregation, poverty, and exclusion at every turn. Fifty years ago there were no black mayors anywhere in the United States. There were only five black members of Congress. Most professions were closed to blacks. It was an enormous cultural milestone when the Brooklyn Dodgers invited Jackie Robinson to play major league baseball (to the taunts and curses of both fans and players). Shops, parks, pools, restaurants, and hotels were all segregated. Many states forbade blacks and whites to marry. Today, these are all just painful memories from long ago. There are more than five hundred black mayors. A black man became president with a larger percentage of the vote than any Democratic candidate in forty-four years. The progress toward racial justice in America has been astonishing. In many ways, the United States has lived up to its founding principles.

Major issues remain, however. Health is the most basic indicator of social equality. In 1935, the difference between black and white life expectancy was enormous: whites lived 9.8 years, or 15 percent, longer than African Americans. The most recent numbers reduce the gap to 5 years, or 6 percent (see Table 5.2). What do you think? Is this enormous progress? Still a shocking disparity? Or perhaps both?

Income is another important metric of equality. In 1959, just before the sit-ins began, 55 percent of African Americans lived in poverty. By 1979, the black rate was 31 percent, and today it is 27.4 percent (see Figure 5.3). Few

Table 5.2 Amazing Progress or Shocking Disparity?

| YEAR | LIFE EXPECTANCY (YEARS) AT BIRTH, BY RACE | | | |
	TOTAL	WHITE	BLACK	DIFFERENCE
1935	61.7	62.9	53.1	9.8
1970	70.8	71.7	64.1	7.6
1980	73.7	74.4	68.1	6.3
1990	75.4	76.1	69.1	7
2000	76.8	77.3	71.8	5.5
2006	77.7	78.2	73.2	5

Source: US National Center for Health Statistics, National Vital Statistics Reports (NVSR), Deaths: Final Data for 2006, vol. 57, no. 14 (April 17, 2009), http://www.census.gov/compendia/statab/2010/tables/10s0102.pdf.

Percentage of Americans in Poverty, by Race

● **Figure 5.3** *Percentage of people in poverty, by race. (US Census)*

groups anywhere in history have experienced such a rapid rise out of poverty as African Americans did between 1959 and 1980. Yet, for the entire half-century, the black poverty rate has remained at three times the white poverty rate. Again, we can read the numbers as extraordinary progress or a need for greater action.

One final disparity raises alarms. African American men are seven times more likely to be in jail as white men. Is this truly the new Jim Crow, as some have argued? Americans disagree with one another. Some argue that all Americans benefit from rough enforcement. On the other hand, many believe that the United States has gone too far in sending people to jail—especially for minor offenses. As we discussed in Chapter 4, there are subtle forms of racial and ethnic discrimination at every stage in the criminal justice system.

> **THE BOTTOM LINE**
>
> - In order to make up for past discrimination, legislatures and courts turned to affirmative action in the 1960s and 1970s. Employers and schools that had previously excluded African Americans now set aside places for them.
> - The courts originally sponsored affirmative action programs but have become increasingly skeptical of any race-based categories, including those designed to ameliorate past injustice.
> - Did the nation do enough to give every member of society a genuine opportunity to succeed? By many measures, the United States has made extraordinary progress toward racial justice. By other measures, the United States still has a long way to go.

● Gender

Laws of coverture: An outmoded legal tradition holding that a woman's rights and duties all operate through her husband.

In the early nineteenth century, a woman had no political rights. She could not vote, serve on a jury, or enter into a contract after marriage. The **laws of coverture**, adopted from English common law, meant that her political rights and duties all operated through her husband. He controlled her property, her wages, and even her body. Husband and wife are one, mused Justice Hugo Black, and "that one is the husband."[15]

Suffrage

The struggle for gender rights in the United States goes back as far as the fight for racial equality, and the two battles have often been interconnected. The first convention for woman suffrage, the 1848 **Seneca Falls Convention**, grew directly from the abolition movement. After the Civil War, feminist leaders fought to have women included in the Fifteenth Amendment right to vote. Both Congress and the courts rejected the appeals.

In the 1870s, women began to organize into a movement. The Women's Christian Temperance Union enrolled almost two hundred thousand women, especially in small towns across America. The movement attacked alcohol as a cause of male violence against women. It championed voluntary motherhood (no more marital rape), suffrage for women, and decent wages. Two other groups focused on winning the vote. Led by Carrie Chapman Catt, the American Woman Suffrage Association focused on winning voting rights, state by state.

Success came first in the West, beginning with the Wyoming (1869) and Utah (1870) Territories. By 1916 an effective political campaign had won full suffrage in fifteen states, and partial suffrage in twenty-three others. Women voted in every state of the West and Midwest except New Mexico. The issue remained contentious, however. Four states in the North voted to reject suffrage during the 1916 presidential election, and the South remained strongly opposed for fear that women would oppose segregation (see Figure 5.4).

During World War I, women took on new roles while men went overseas. Led by Alice Paul and the National American Woman Suffrage Association (NAWSA), women stepped up political pressure for a national suffrage

Seneca Falls Convention: A convention dedicated to women's rights held in July 1848.

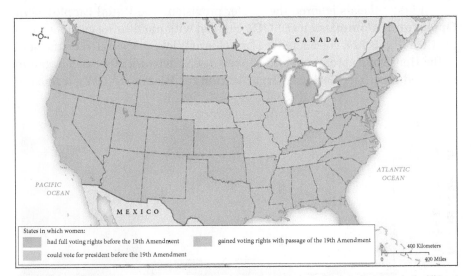

States in which women:
had full voting rights before the 19th Amendment
could vote for president before the 19th Amendment
gained voting rights with passage of the 19th Amendment

● **Figure 5.4** *Before the 19th Amendment, women had full voting rights in the West, limited rights in the Midwest, and none in the South and East. For women, winning the vote took a difficult political campaign that lasted more than 80 years.*

amendment. The group continued agitating during World War 1—Paul herself was jailed as a result—and eventually, President Woodrow Wilson put aside his condescension and supported suffrage as a "wartime measure." The Nineteenth Amendment cleared Congress, over stiff opposition in the Senate, in 1919 and was ratified by the states in 1920. Seventy-two years after the Seneca Falls Convention, women had won the right to vote.

Although they had secured suffrage, women were slow to win office, especially higher offices (see Figure 5.5). In the presidential election of 2008 both parties rallied around a female candidate. Hillary Clinton won seventeen million primary votes and almost became the first woman to win the presidential nomination of a major party; Sarah Palin won the Republican vice-presidential nomination and electrified the party base.

Despite the recent rise, the United States ranks seventieth (tied with Turkmenistan) in the percentage of women in Congress. The good news is that women who do run win just as often as men do.[16]

The Civil Rights Act of 1964

The breakthrough in the struggle for gender rights slipped into the Civil Rights Act of 1964. Opponents of the legislation originally introduced the provision hoping that it would make the act more controversial and lead to its defeat. At the time, no one predicted that the gender provision in the Civil Rights Act would have the same kind of far-reaching consequence for gender rights as *Brown v. Board of Education* had for African Americans—but it did. Like the Supreme Court decisions concerning race, the Civil Rights Act only opened the door to gender change. The women's movement had to seize the opportunity.

At first, officials ignored the gender provision. The **Equal Employment Opportunity Commission (EEOC)**, charged with monitoring compliance to the Civil Rights Act, considered it a "mischievous joke perpetrated on the floor of the House of Representatives." In response, a network of women began to meet and plan. The **National Organization for Women (NOW)**, formed in

Equal Employment Opportunity Commission (EEOC): Federal law enforcement agency charged with monitoring compliance to the Civil Rights Act.

National Organization for Women (NOW): An organization formed to take action for women's equality.

● Figure 5.5 Number of women in the US Senate.

1966, drew directly on the tactics of the civil rights campaign—demonstrations, rallies, lobbying, and litigation.

Congress and the EEOC began to pay attention. For example, in 1972, Congress passed Federal Education Amendments that denied federal funds for programs that discriminated against women (Title VI) and that required equal athletic opportunities for men and women (Title IX). When the EEOC vigorously enforced Title IX, it transformed college athletics. Sleepy, underfunded women's sports programs began getting the same treatment as the men's varsity. The number of girls playing high school sports rose tenfold. Properly funded, women's college basketball and soccer became popular spectator sports with national and even international followings.

The process continues, sometimes expanding and sometimes contracting civil rights protections. In 1984, the Supreme Court limited the Federal Education Amendments' reach into private institutions. However, by then the new programs had a powerful constituency, and Congress, overriding the Court's interpretation, responded by amending the legislation with the Civil Rights Restoration Act of 1988.

The Courts

The women's movement also copied the civil rights movement in targeting the courts. Led by Ruth Bader Ginsburg (now a Supreme Court justice), advocates challenged discriminatory state laws, case by case. Because gender was, at the time, a *nonsuspect category*, any state law was upheld as long as it had some "rational connection to a legitimate state purpose." In a series of cases, culminating in *Craig v. Boren* in 1976, the Court lifted gender into a new category of *heightened scrutiny*—not as rigorous a test as the scrutiny the courts give racial classifications, but more rigorous than that applied to other social groups. Ironically, the Court created the category—a major victory for women's rights—when men challenged an Oklahoma statute that set the drinking age for beer at eighteen for women and twenty-one for men.

The courts applied the prohibition on gender discrimination in the Civil Rights Act to sexual harassment. In 1998, the Supreme Court expanded the protection by ruling that the employee did not have prove a specific instance of sexual harassment if there was a hostile workplace environment—this might include sexual advances, lewd comments, or general attitudes. The Court ruled that even if employers were not aware of specific instances of harassment, they remained liable for the general culture of the workplace.

Women's advocates raised the issue of differential pay more than a century ago. Today, women

● These cheering fans don't realize how the Civil Rights Act changed their world. Today, women's basketball has become a major sport.

working full time earn, on average, three-fourths as much as men—although the exact amount of the disparity is hotly disputed and varies from 75 percent to 95 percent, depending on the methodology and assumptions. In a famous case, Lilly Ledbetter sued after a nineteen-year career as a supervisor with Goodyear Tire Company because she had been paid less than men in the same position. A jury found Goodyear guilty of pay discrimination, but the Supreme Court reversed the judgment by a 5–4 vote. The majority ruled that Ledbetter should have sued within 180 days after Goodyear set her pay—long before she knew about the salary differential. In 2009, President Obama signed equal-pay legislation that permits an employee to sue 180 days from her last paycheck (resetting the clock each time she gets a lower paycheck). It was the first act that Obama signed into law.[17]

Recent Supreme Court decisions, however, have made it more difficult to sue businesses for discrimination. In a major case, decided in 2011, the court turned down a **class action** suit brought against Wal-Mart. A class action is filed on behalf of everyone that falls into a class or group—in this case women working at Wal-Mart. The suit alleged that the company systematically discriminated against women by offering them less pay and fewer promotions. The Supreme Court ruled against the plaintiffs (the women who were suing)—again, 5–4. The Court argued that simply showing that women received less pay was not enough to prove discrimination. Rather, the plaintiffs needed to demonstrate a specific company-wide policy that set lower wages for all the women involved in the class action.

Class action: A lawsuit filed on behalf of an entire category of individuals, such as all people in public housing in a state, or all the female managers of a large company.

Progress—But How Much?

There had never been a woman Supreme Court justice until Ronald Reagan named Sandra Day O'Connor in 1981; today, four of the nine justices are women. There had never been a woman president of an Ivy League university before 1990; twenty years later, four of the eight schools had women at the helm. There had never been a woman CEO of a Fortune 500 company till 1972. In 2000 the number of women CEOs at Fortune 500 companies had inched to three; by 2012, it had risen to eighteen—the highest number of female CEOs in American history but a still not very inspiring 3.6 percent of America's largest companies (see Table 5.3). The conclusion: American society has witnessed extraordinary progress—but still has a long way to go to reach gender equality.

Reproductive Politics

Reproduction control may have introduced the greatest change in gender rights—and gender politics. When birth control pills went on the market in 1960, they seemed revolutionary. Controlling pregnancy made professional careers easier to manage.

Reproductive rights became far more controversial when the Supreme Court ruled, in *Roe v. Wade* (1973), that laws banning abortion violated a

Table 5.3 Women CEOs of Fortune 500 Companies: Steady Progress or a Long Way to Go?

Year	2000	2001	2002	2003	2004	2005	2006	2007	2008	2009	2010	2011	2012
Women CEOs	3	5	10	8	6	9	11	12	12	15	15	18	18

woman's right to privacy. The decision sparked intense political reaction on both sides. Some women organized to defend *Roe v. Wade*; others entered politics to fight it.

The fierce politics of abortion spilled into other areas of gender politics. Feminists had introduced an **Equal Rights Amendment (ERA)** in Congress every year between 1924 and 1972. The amendment was simple: "Equality of rights under the law shall not be denied . . . on account of sex." By 1972 it had become uncontroversial and Congress passed it by lopsided margins (354–23 in the House, 84–8 in the Senate). Five years later, the ERA was just three states short of ratification (thirty-eight states were needed to ratify an amendment). Then, a Republican activist from Florida named Phyllis Schlafly organized the STOP ERA movement. Schlafly argued that American women would lose their special rights and privileges—like the right to alimony and their exemption from the military draft. More important, she argued, the ERA threatened traditional family life. A conservative backlash stopped the Equal Rights Amendment in its tracks. What Schlafly did was to **reframe the issue.** She made people see it in a new way.

The divisions between liberal and conservative activists that first appeared around *Roe v. Wade* and the Equal Rights Amendment continue to this day.

Equal Rights Amendment: An amendment, originally drafted by Alice Paul in 1923, passed by Congress in 1972, and ratified by thirty-five states, that declared: "Equality of rights . . . shall not be denied or abridged . . . on account of sex."

Reframe the issue: To redefine the popular perception of an issue; to show it in a new light with a new set of costs or benefits.

THE BOTTOM LINE

- In nineteenth-century law, women's political rights operated through their husbands. When women organized to win rights, they met ridicule and violence.
- Women first won voting rights in the states—especially in the West and Midwest—before finally securing the Nineteenth Amendment guaranteeing the right to vote regardless of gender.
- The Civil Rights Act of 1964 bars gender discrimination. Like the civil rights movement of the 1950s and 1960s, the women's movement organized to take advantage of legal changes. The law transformed American gender roles in political and professional life.
- Following *Roe v. Wade* (in 1973) and the Equal Rights Amendment (in the mid-1970s), gender politics became especially controversial, spilling into many other issues.

A detail of Diego Rivera's magical mural, Pan-American Unity. Mexican gods, dancers, revolutionaries, and workers mix with George Washington, Abraham Lincoln, Henry Ford, and Charlie Chaplin in a vibrant celebration of an America without borders.

Hispanics

Hispanics, or Latinos (we will use the words interchangeably), play a powerful and growing role in American politics and culture. Latinos were already living in the Southwest—in Arizona, California, New Mexico, and parts of Colorado, Nevada, Utah, and Texas—before the United States took those lands from Mexico in 1848. The American borders expanded to include Latino lands. Today, Hispanics make up 16.5 percent of the American population. They constitute the largest minority group and one of the fastest-growing segments of the American population.

Challenging Discrimination

Latinos have long faced discrimination. They often found themselves pushed into segregated schools, excluded from jobs, and barred from housing in white neighborhoods. They also faced hostility and violence. For example, after sensational newspaper headlines reported that Mexicans had beaten up a sailor (during World War II), thousands of soldiers and sailors poured through Los Angeles attacking Mexican men. They stopped streetcars and ran through Mexican neighborhoods looking for victims. The police did not intervene.

Latinos took many of the tactics of the black civil rights movement and adapted them to their own needs. They organized the League of United Latin American Citizens (LULAC) in 1929. Like the NAACP, the organization fought segregation through lawsuits. In *Mendez v. Westminster*, decided in 1947, the court struck down Latino school segregation in Orange County, California; the case was an important precursor to *Brown v. Board of Education* and involved some of the same lawyers.

During the 1960s, young Latinos launched more active protests. In 1968, high school and college students called a massive student strike that reverberated through the Southwest. They pushed LULAC and other mainstream organizations to fight more aggressively against discrimination and they challenged the immigration policies that restricted movement across the Mexican border. "We are a people without borders," they chanted, claiming the rights of a people who inhabited the land before the United States had acquired it. Many young people took a slur against Mexicans, *Chicano*, and turned it into a movement they labeled **Chicanismo**—a defiant pride in their heritage and culture.

At the same time, the **United Farm Workers** (UFW) organized the most vulnerable population—migrant workers who picked crops up and down the West Coast. The UFW became a symbol of Latino mobilization. In short, throughout the 1960s and 1970s traditional organizations like LULAC,

Chicanismo: A defiant movement expressing pride in Latino origins and culture in the face of discrimination.

United Farm Workers: An influential union representing migrant farm workers in the West.

activist students, and farm workers all rose up to challenge discrimination. Their efforts prepared the way for contemporary Latino politics—which includes elected officials at every level of government. Today, the central questions for Latino politics turn on immigration, language, and just how the very diverse Hispanic population might mobilize for political action.

The Politics of Immigration

Despite Hispanics' long heritage on the land, Hispanic politics is very much wrapped up with immigration. Although the United States is an immigrant nation, the door to foreigners has historically swung from wide open to shut tight. Since 1965, the United States has experienced an era of high immigration—today one in eight American residents was born abroad.

Immigrants always trigger the same fears: they will undermine American values and culture; they will remain loyal to their own languages, their home countries, and their supposedly un-American ideas; they will take away jobs. As long ago as 1752, Benjamin Franklin worried that there were so many Germans in Philadelphia, "instead of them learning our language, we must learn theirs or live as in a foreign country." Today, some observers have grown alarmed about the *disuniting* of the

● *Cesar Chavez (center), along with Dolores Huerta, organized the farm workers.*

United States. The issue has focused especially on Hispanic Americans, for they are, by far, the largest immigrant group (see Figure 5.6).

Immigration groups fall into three different categories with very different legal claims on civil rights.

1. Those who were born in the United States or have become American citizens (roughly 60 percent of the Latino population) claim the same rights as any citizen. They are in the same protected legal category as African Americans. Any law that singles them out is "suspect" and subject to strict scrutiny by the courts.

2. Foreigners who have not become citizens fall into a second category known as resident aliens. They may work in the United States, they must pay taxes, but they cannot enjoy the benefits of citizenship until they become citizens. Aliens may not vote, and many government programs explicitly exclude them. Legislation in 1996, for example, barred aliens from receiving a range of welfare benefits like food stamps.

3. Some immigrants are unregistered—they are not legal residents of the United States. Many arrived on a temporary visa, got a job, settled down, and simply remained in the country after their legal time in the country expired. Others crossed the borders illegally (327,000 people were caught doing so in

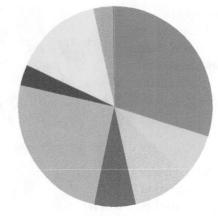

Mexico	11,929,000
Central American	2,989,000
Caribbean	3,749,000
South America	2,740,000
South and East Asia	9,985,000
Middle East	1,384,000
Europe and Canada	5,798,000
Africa and Oceania	1,401,000
Other	37,000

● **Figure 5.6** *US residents born abroad. There are 40,012,000 residents of the United States who were born abroad. Here is where they came from. (US Census)*

2011, down from 1.64 million in 1999). Undocumented aliens have no constitutional rights and, when caught, are liable to immediate deportation. Those who marry an American become eligible for a green card—that is, they can become resident aliens; and anyone born in the United States, even if their parents are undocumented, is a citizen.

The debate over illegal aliens is intense and often angry. Supporters argue that undocumented immigrants are part of the American economy and society. They live in fear of jail and deportation. As a result, they are wary of going to a hospital, visiting their children's school, or reporting crimes against them. American policy, they argue, should offer undocumented people a path to legal status. Opponents respond that the undocumented are breaking the law by their presence. This side opposes any path to legal status (which it labels "amnesty") and urges vigorous prosecution of undocumented aliens and all those who hire or help them.

The issue of undocumented aliens is intensely contested. Even many Hispanic citizens whose families have lived on American soil for many generations consider immigration a defining political issue. It has thrust their community into controversy. It has increased police surveillance. Hispanic immigration is a major part of today's version of the great American question, *Who are we?*

In 2012, President Obama signed an executive order—bypassing a deadlocked Congress—that gave young undocumented aliens temporary work permits and removed the threat of deportation. Tens of thousands lined up to apply for the program the day it went into effect.

The Controversy over Language

Spanish language is another major issue. In 1974, the Supreme Court ruled in *Lau v. Nichols* that equal protection required schools to assist students whose primary language was not English. The Court did not specify a remedy, but many school districts established bilingual education programs—and these eventually generated a backlash. Some observers argue that bilingual education divides the community, undermines the traditional American culture, and disadvantages students who fail to learn English. In 1996, the House of Representatives passed legislation making English the official language of the United States and requiring all official business to be conducted English; the bill has been reintroduced many times since, but the Senate has not approved the measure.

Many Latinos support English-language education—they are eager to give their children a good opportunity to achieve the American dream. At the same time, they worry that behind the English-only movement lies prejudice against the Spanish-speaking population. Won't their children be disadvantaged if no Spanish at all is allowed in the schools? Won't Spanish American voters face problems if all ballots must be printed only in English?

Political Mobilization

Hispanic Americans face many other issues and challenges. More than one in five live below the poverty line—two and a half times the rate for non-Hispanic whites. They are less likely to have health insurance than any major population group. As we have noted, many feel tensions from law enforcement policies.[18]

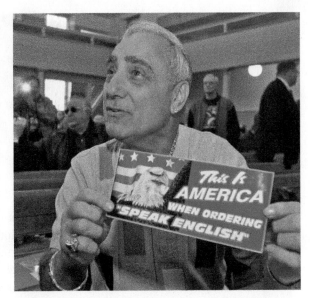

● The owner of Geno's Cheesesteak in Philadelphia announces that customers should speak English. This is a hot issue and always has been. More than 250 years earlier, Ben Franklin complained that all he heard on the streets of Philadelphia was German. Franklin later changed his mind and cheered the immigrants. No word about whether the people at Geno's have changed their minds, too.

One way to address these concerns, of course, is through politics. Latinos face both barriers and advantages in the political arena. The biggest barrier lies in the nature of the Hispanic community itself. In fact, *Hispanic* is a misnomer. Hispanic people come from many different places, each with its own interests and concerns. Figure 5.7 shows the diversity of the Latino community.

For Mexican Americans, concentrated in the Southwest, the politics of immigration looms very large. In contrast, Puerto Ricans, the second-largest Hispanic population, are American citizens by birth; immigration is less relevant to them. Their focus is on economics and, especially in the Northeast, on politics. Cuban Americans offer still another contrast. They have high average incomes and generally do not share the same political concerns as Mexican Americans or Puerto Ricans. In fact, Cuban Americans traditionally stand apart from most Hispanic groups by voting Republican. Salvadorans, now the third-largest Latino group, face the problems of more recent immigrants—poverty, social integration, and community building. Dominicans, in turn, introduce a slightly different spectrum of political concerns. When we talk of Hispanics we are using shorthand that, while sometimes useful, obscures a great many differences.

Is there a common political denominator across this diverse population? Today, a pan-Latino movement seeks to find common ground and mobilize voters around issues that transcend any one country or group. Popular DJs on Spanish radio champion unity. The Hispanic caucus in Congress aims to

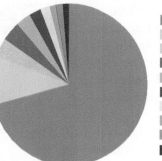

Mexico	31,674,000	65%
Puerto Rico	4,412,000	9%
El Salvador	1,736,000	3.6%
Cuba	1,677,000	3.4%
Dominican Republic	1,360,000	2.8%
Guatemala	1,077,000	2.2%
Colombia	917,000	1.8%
Honduras	625,000	1.2%
Ecuador	611,000	1.2%
Peru	557,000	1.1%

● **Figure 5.7** *Countries of origin— Latinos in America. Most of the 44,646,000 Latinos who live in the United States were born here. This figure shows their national heritage. (US Census)*

speak for Hispanic voters; in 2012, the caucus stood at a record number, with twenty-eight in the House (5.4 percent of the total membership) and three in the Senate. Some Hispanics worry that a pan-Latino construction may lead to the loss of national identity and pride—they point out that you don't see Irish and Italian Americans talking about pan-European heritage. Others respond that finding common cause is an important step to political influence.

In 2006, when the Republican-led Congress proposed tough new legislation focused on undocumented aliens, massive demonstrations sprang up around the United States. A rally in Chicago drew one hundred thousand people, and larger demonstrations followed around the nation. Even veteran observers were surprised by the size and energy of the gatherings, which seemed to echo the great energy and optimism of the civil rights era. In the past, Latino protesters had waved Mexican flags and symbols. This time, they marched under a sea of American flags. Researchers, who were undertaking a major survey of Hispanic Americans during the time period, discovered that the protests made Hispanics feel significantly more American.[19]

In the 2012 election, 71 percent of the rapidly growing Hispanic vote went to President Obama and was a crucial part of his coalition. Leaders of both parties began scrambling to appeal to Hispanic voters. The politics of immigration, which has defined the American past, may very well hold the key to the political future.

THE BOTTOM LINE

- Latinos are the largest immigrant group and one of the fastest-growing populations in the United States today.
- Latinos are a diverse people with many different national identities, histories, cultures, and concerns.
- The great political question is whether Latinos will mobilize around shared interests and concerns. If they do, they will become an even more formidable political force than they are today.

Asian Americans

Asian Americans are the third-largest minority in the United States—after blacks and Hispanics. Unlike Latinos, they do not share a common language; unlike African Americans, they do not share a common historical experience. As you can see from Figure 5.8, Asian Americans range from Indians to Vietnamese, from Koreans to Laotians.

As a group, Asian Americans have the highest education level and the highest median personal income among American population groups (the median is the person right in the middle, with an equal number of people above and below). Members of this group run seven Fortune 500 companies. However, the statistics mask as much as they reveal, for Asian Americans range from Indian Americans with high income and education levels to Hmong from the mountains of Laos with income levels about one-third the US average (Figure 5.9).

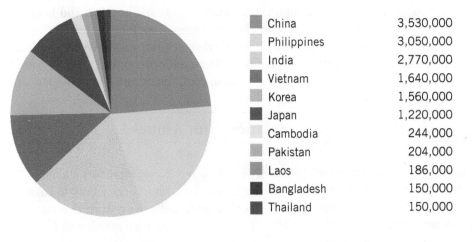

China	3,530,000
Philippines	3,050,000
India	2,770,000
Vietnam	1,640,000
Korea	1,560,000
Japan	1,220,000
Cambodia	244,000
Pakistan	204,000
Laos	186,000
Bangladesh	150,000
Thailand	150,000

● **Figure 5.8** *Countries of origin—Asians in America. Here are the national identities of the 14.9 million residents of the United States who come from an Asian heritage. (US Census)*

● **Figure 5.9** *CEOs of the Fortune 500.*

Nikki Haley, the governor of South Carolina, is one of two Indian American governors—part of a rising generation of Asian American leaders.

The Asian Stereotypes

Asians have a long history of negotiating the complicated American lines between "us and them." The first Asians to arrive were Chinese railway workers in the nineteenth century. When the economy deteriorated in the 1880s, American-born workers turned against these immigrants. Congress passed the Chinese Exclusion Act (1882) barring Chinese immigrants and declaring Chinese people ineligible for citizenship. By 1917 Congress had extended the ban to "all natives of Asia including the whole of India." The California Alien Land Law of 1913 forbade "aliens ineligible for citizenship"—that is, Asian immigrants—from owning land. Each restriction came with painful stereotypes. The Chinese were excluded because, as one California congressman put it, "His ancestors have bequeathed to him the most hideous immoralities. They . . . are so shocking and horrible that their character cannot even be hinted."[20]

After the Japanese attack on Pearl Harbor in 1941, animosity moved from the Chinese to the Japanese. President Roosevelt ordered the army to round up Japanese Americans and place them in cold, flimsy, miserable internment

What Do You Think?

◦•◦ Simple Decency? Or Political Correctness Run Amuck?

In February 2012 Lin-mania captured the American imagination. An obscure NBA player named Jeremy Lin won the opportunity to start for the New York Knicks—and he proved to be fantastic. Suddenly the mediocre Knicks were winning one game after another. Lin was the first Taiwanese American player to suit up for the Knicks. After just one spectacular week, his jersey became the best-selling sports apparel in America.

At the height of the mania, three members of the sports media used the same dubious phrase. All referred to "the chink in his armor." Although each was describing Lin's turnovers—he gave the ball away to the other team far too often—many observers were stunned at what appeared to be a derogatory reference to the Chinese. One individual lost his job over the comment. What do you think?

Yes, this was appropriate punishment	News reporters should know better than to casually use a word that has been an ethnic slur for many years.
No, this was political correctness run amuck.	Words are only words and people should feel free to use whichever words they want—even if they are hurtful.
The deeper question.	What level of basic respect and simple decency do Americans owe each other?

camps. They lost their liberty, their jobs, their property, and their bank accounts. The Supreme Court upheld the internments. In 1968, Congress finally awarded restitution, a payment of twenty thousand dollars to the sixty thousand former inmates who were still alive (about 5 percent of the total).

Perhaps the oddest cultural twist of all is the stereotype that emerged in the 1960s. Many Asian groups—once despised and singled out for exclusion—were perceived as the "model minority": a hardworking group that makes its own way without any demands for rights or privileges. It may seem that this is a "good" stereotype, but of course there is no such thing. By reducing each individual to nothing more than a member of a group, stereotypes demean individuals and stoke social tensions.

The Asian story once again illustrates the enduring clash between America's faith in unalienable rights and its fears for the American way. Immigrants always introduce new forms of diversity—new languages, ideas, and religions. Every generation frets that the latest immigrants are different from the ones that came before. Today, the threat of terrorism has exacerbated that tension, especially for Muslims in America.

THE BOTTOM LINE

- Asian Americans are the third-largest minority group in the United States and now comprise 5 percent of the population.
- Like other minority groups, Asian Americans have faced stereotypes and discrimination—including, today, the image of "a model minority" that, like any stereotype, is simplistic and hurtful.
- Asian Americans are a tremendously diverse group that, on the surface, appear to have little in common with one another. The key to their political effectiveness as Asian Americans lies in finding (and acting on) common interests as well as forging ties to other groups.

Native Americans

The original natives of the United States own the saddest story about rights denied. Before the Europeans arrived, ten million American Indians lived on the land that would become the United States. The colonists brought diseases and a new kind of all-out warfare.

The Lost Way of Life

The dark side of American expansion was the policy of "Indian removal." Again and again, Indian tribes were forced from their homelands as European settlers moved in. Alexis de Tocqueville watched along the banks of the Mississippi as a great tribe of Choctaws—tired, cold, and hungry—were forced westward. He described their journey, in the middle of winter, in the saddest and most moving passages of *Democracy in America*: "It is impossible to imagine the terrible afflictions of those forced migrations.... There is famine behind them, war ahead, and misery everywhere." The sight was so terrible, he wrote, it "will never fade from my memory." He went on to describe the Indians' dogs, who suddenly realized they were being left behind and, with a mournful howl, plunged into the icy river and struggled to swim after their masters.[21] By the time the United States stretched from coast to coast, only about one million of the ten million natives remained.

Recent historians have warned us against simply seeing Native Americans as the passive victims of American westward expansion. The Indians built their own empires and, at times and in places, forced the white settlers to retreat. During King Philip's War (1675–1678), natives sorely tested the New England colonists, destroying all or parts of one in five Massachusetts villages. (The war is named after the the Native American leader, Metacomet, known to the English as "King Philip.") Between 1750 and 1850, the Comanches dominated economic and military life in the Southwest and pulled white settlers, Spanish colonies, and other tribes into what amounted to an imperial system. Still, despite the power and sophistication of the Indians, the final results are familiar: the eventual destruction of their way of life.[22]

● *Red Cloud, Chief of the Oglala Sioux Tribe.*

Indians and the Federal Government

Native Americans have had an ambiguous legal relationship to the United States. In 1831, the Supreme Court ruled that Indian tribes were "**domestic dependent nations**"—essentially, a separate people but without the rights of an independent nation. Native Americans were not considered citizens, protected by the Constitution, until Congress passed the Indian Citizenship Act in 1924. Even today, their legal status remains ambiguous. Of a total population of two million, about a million Native Americans live on tribal reservations, which are independent jurisdictions not subject to state governments. Indians are both American citizens and members of self-governing independent lands, subject to federal regulation and oversight.

The primary connection to American government is bureaucratic rather than electoral. The Bureau of Indian Affairs is responsible for Native American issues. The early placement of the bureau offered a telling symbol of the long and tortured relationship between Indians and the federal government: it was part of the Department of War. Later, Congress moved it to the

Department of the Interior, whose chief purpose is to promote and protect natural resources and public lands.

Social Problems and Politics

Indians face the same social problems as other minority groups. Indian poverty rates are approximately three times as high as the national rates and stand at 32.2 percent—well above any other American group. Life on the reservations is especially difficult, as most are in rural areas with few jobs or resources. Native American life expectancy is about 2.4 years lower than the national average—although it is considerably higher than that for blacks (see Figure 5.10). Native Americans also suffer from low education levels and high infant mortality rates—again, with rates worse than those for whites, Hispanics, and other ethnic groups but somewhat better than those for African Americans.

Native Americans politics divide, roughly, into two camps. The *ethnic minority* perspective argues that Indians should mobilize for rights and equality precisely like other minority groups in the United States. Members of this perspective urge fellow Indians to engage American democracy. The alternative is the separatist *tribal movement*, which advocates withdrawing from American politics and society and emphasizing Native American traditions. The tribal movement (like black nationalism and Chicanismo before it) argues that the best course is separation. Only then, say proponents, can Indians repair their own communal culture.

The civil rights protests inspired some Indians, just as they did so many other groups. Led, in some cases, by the American Indian Movement (or AIM), tribes occupied the Bureau of Indian Affairs in Washington, DC. They "captured" Alcatraz Island in San Francisco Bay. They seized control of the Village of Wounded Knee, the site of a massacre of Indians in 1890, and exchanged gunfire with federal marshals. The goal of the protests was to dramatize the plight of Native Americans—robbed of their ancestral lands, forced onto reservations, relegated to poverty. These grievances, however, come from a long history of government policies and cannot easily be addressed with protests,

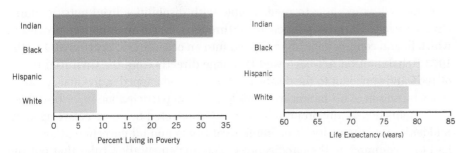

● **Figure 5.10** *American Indians have the highest poverty rate . . . but have life expectancy almost three years longer than black Americans. Notice that Hispanics have the highest life expectancy of any group. (US Census/ Pew Research)*

lawsuits, or changes in existing programs (recall our discussion of de facto discrimination earlier in this chapter).

In recent years, some tribes have used their exemption from state laws to create highly profitable gambling businesses and resorts. The Supreme Court ruled, in 1987, that because tribes are considered sovereign entities, they are free from state prohibitions on gaming. According to the gaming industry, 233 of the nation's 565 tribes run casinos. However, whether this is a positive thing—for the tribes, for the communities around them, and for the United States—is a matter of hot debate.

THE BOTTOM LINE

- Native Americans lost their way of life in the face of disease, armies, and settlers.
- The Supreme Court gave American Indians a special status: a separate people without rights. Although they retain the special status, they became US citizens in 1924.
- Indians debate two different strategies to the problems they face: The ethnic minority approach argues for winning political rights and benefits. The tribal movement approach prefers to withdraw and to emphasize a separate Indian society and culture.

Groups Without Special Protection

As civil rights burst on the American scene in the 1960s and 1970s, the idea of demanding rights spread to other groups that were not mentioned in the Civil Rights Act and have never drawn special scrutiny from the courts.

People with Disabilities

Before 1970, children in wheelchairs did not go to school, and most blind children never learned how to read. People with disabilities lived outside mainstream society. The great political breakthrough came in an unnoticed provision, which liberal congressional staff slipped into an obscure bill. **Section 504** of the 1973 Rehabilitation Act borrowed language directly from the Civil Rights Act of 1964 and applied it to the disabled: "No . . . handicapped individual . . . shall, solely by reason of his handicap, be excluded from participation in, or be denied the benefits of . . . any program or activity conducted by an executive agency." Suddenly, any university receiving federal funds and all government agencies had to accommodate the handicapped. The implementation rules that put the law into effect might normally have been assigned to the obscure rehabilitation bureaucracy that traditionally dealt with handicapped issues; instead, Congress

Section 504: An obscure provision in an obscure rehabilitation act that required all institutions that received federal funds to accommodate people with disabilities.

gave the task to the more powerful Office of Civil Rights in the Department of Health, Education, and Welfare.

Section 504 gave activists a political focus and they immediately made the most of it. When the department was slow to issue regulations, for example, sit-ins at the regional office pushed the matter forward. Notice the dynamic: Congressional staffers dreamed up a change, giving advocates a focus for action. Disabled people and their advocates soon mobilized for widespread change on every level of government. Local health boards, planning agencies, and school officials all began hearing from this new alliance. As disability-rights advocates participated in politics, they exerted more influence. The political pattern resembles African Americans after *Brown v. Board of Education* and feminists after the Civil Rights Act: government action provided new legal rights; the group then organized and demanded further change.

Advocates went from requesting welfare benefits to demanding civil rights. The process culminated in 1990, when Congress passed the Americans with Disabilities Act (ADA). The ADA forbade companies of twenty-five or more employees from discriminating against handicapped people. It also required companies to make "reasonable accommodations" for handicapped people. Unlike racial discrimination, however, a business can avoid making accommodations if it would be expensive or inconvenient to do so. Courts constantly weigh the costs and benefits of making accommodations in specific places. What is reasonable to ask a firm or a store or a university to do to accommodate special needs? Even with this delicate balancing of costs and access, the ADA created what amounts to a massive affirmative action program for people with disabilities. Public transportation, schools, shops, and businesses all must help facilitate a normal, mainstream life for people with special needs.

Sexual Orientation

The movement for same-sex rights began with a riot. In 1969, police raided a New York City gay bar named the Stonewall Inn. Traditionally, gay people responded to such raids with shame. This time, the gay community broke the unwritten rules and erupted into violent protest. The Stonewall riot marks the moment that members of the LGBT community stopped apologizing and announced their identity. Four years later, in 1973, the American Psychiatric Association removed homosexuality from its list of mental disorders.

When activists turned to politics, their first targets were state antisodomy laws, which criminalized gay sex. Chapter 4 discussed the evolution of Court thinking that led, eventually, to *Lawrence v. Texas*, which struck down such laws.[23]

In the early 1980s, gay communities were devastated by a mysterious and deadly plague. At the time, no one knew exactly what the illness was or how it was transmitted—only that it was invariably fatal. In every city, gays organized to confront AIDS; they established links to the medical community,

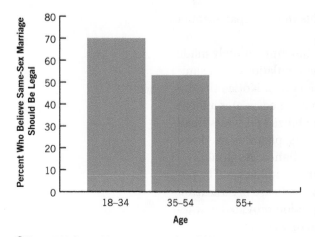

● **Figure 5.11** *Support for same-sex marriage (2011).*

local governments, and social service networks. Some, under the banner of Act Up, took more radical measures to prod politicians and drug companies into action. Around the country, a network of gay groups mobilized and developed political skills. The terrible disease pushed them into local politics.

The demand for same-sex civil rights has been complicated. However, slowly American politics and culture have accepted homosexuality. In 1993, the newly elected Bill Clinton ran into a firestorm in Congress when he promised to open the military to gay men and women. The compromise policy, known as "don't ask, don't tell," permitted gay individuals to serve as long as they kept their sexual orientation hidden. Eighteen years later, the Obama administration ended the policy—the relatively quiet reaction in Congress is a mark of changing cultural norms.

The central controversy today is same-sex marriage. In 2000, Vermont created shock waves with landmark legislation permitting civil unions—giving same-sex couples the same benefits, protections, and responsibilities as married couples. Three years later Massachusetts became the first state to permit marriage. Slowly, other states followed—twelve states and the District of Columbia recognize gay marriage (although not all are issuing marriage licenses as the politics and litigation continue). However, at least thirty states have amended their constitutions to bar gay marriage.

The US Constitution requires states to recognize official acts of other states (under the privileges and immunities clause); however, most states refuse to recognize same-sex marriages performed in other states. Congress protected the reluctant states with the Defense of Marriage Act (DOMA, passed in 1996), which defines marriage as a union between a man and a woman and permits states to reject same-sex marriages performed in other states. The Supreme Court has heard oral arguments but as of this writing has not yet ruled on either DOMA or state laws that that bar gay marriage.

The debates continue. In California the courts ruled that denying same-sex couples the right to marry violates equal protection, the public promptly voted to reject same-sex marriage, and the issue ended up back in court. In Maine, the state legislature approved same-sex marriage and the public agreed in a 2012 referendum. In Massachusetts, the state supreme court struck down the limits on same-sex marriage, and the legislature refused to send a constitutional amendment banning gay marriage to the voters; one longtime opponent of gay marriage changed her vote, she said, after she got to know the gay couple who had moved in next door.

That Massachusetts legislator may signal the future. The most striking thing about this debate is the rapid change in public opinion. In 1996, as Congress was passing DOMA, public approval of same-sex marriage did not rise above 36 percent in any state. In 2010, thirty-six states registered approval levels over 36 percent, and outright majorities approved in fifteen more. Most telling, as Figure 5.11 illustrates, young people overwhelmingly support legal gay marriage (70 percent), while older Americans do not.[24]

The last twenty years has seen a profound change in the legal status and rights of gay Americans. With each passing year they move closer to attaining full civil rights.

THE BOTTOM LINE

- People with disabilities leveraged an obscure bureaucratic rule, used it to mobilize, and eventually won the sweeping rights of the Americans with Disabilities Act. The goal is to mainstream disabled people as much as possible.
- The gay (and lesbian) movements were born in a burst of pride and anger in 1969. Gays were the first to confront AIDS—a harrowing plague (in its early years) that pushed them into politics, health provision, and community building.
- Gay, lesbian, bisexual, and transgender communities have moved from taboo to mainstream. Barriers to military service, civil unions, and marriage have eroded. Nevertheless, the conflict over marriage and childrearing remains a flash point of contemporary culture wars. Few other issues demonstrate as large an age gap.

Conclusion: By the People

The United States is a land of ideas—and arguments about ideas. No American idea is more powerful than the idea of inalienable rights; and none generates more arguments—as you can see from the many 5–4 Supreme Court votes described in this chapter.

Government actions are crucial in settling the arguments about rights. Perhaps the most important lesson to draw from this chapter is the far-reaching consequences of laws and court cases. The Civil Rights Act, for example, ended de jure segregation, focused the women's movement, changed gender relations in schools and workplaces, inspired the disabilities rights movement—and its influence goes on.

Ultimately, however, the quest for rights lies with the public. The *Brown* decision became an enormous force for change only after the civil rights movement seized the possibility. Throughout this chapter, we have seen people rise up to transform the politics of rights—marching into violence in Birmingham, prodding a reluctant government to implement the gender provisions in the Civil Rights Act of 1964, waving American flags over immigrant rights in Chicago, taking over a bureaucrat's office to hurry implementation of disability rules in Washington, or fighting back when the police raided a gay bar in New York City. It was collective action that helped shape the meaning of the legislation and court decisions. Through their passion and their activism, the people are constantly pushing the United States to live up to its founding ideals.

CHAPTER SUMMARY

● The battle for civil rights generally includes seven stages. The group seeking rights must define itself, challenge society, and change the cultural story. The contest for rights spills across federalism; the executive branch can break the ice; Congress is the key to deep social change; the courts are the final arbiters of civil rights.

● The Fourteenth Amendment contains the crucial legal rule for civil rights: "No state shall . . . deprive any person of . . . the equal protection of the laws."

● A great mass movement rose up in which ordinary men, women, and children turned the legal promise of the *Brown v. Board of Education* decision into a practical reality. Protests eventually led to the Civil Rights Act of 1964 and the Voting Rights Act of 1965. The black civil rights movement set the model for future civil rights campaigns by many other groups.

● In order to make up for past discrimination, legislatures and courts turned to affirmative action in the 1960s and 1970s. The courts, and the public, have become increasingly skeptical of these programs.

● Women first won voting rights in the states— across the West—before finally securing the Nineteenth Amendment, guaranteeing the right to vote regardless of gender.

● The Civil Rights Act of 1964 bars gender discrimination. The women's movement organized to take advantage of the legal changes. The results transformed American gender roles in political and professional life.

● Following *Roe v. Wade* (in 1973) and the Equal Rights Amendment (in the mid-1970s), gender politics became especially controversial.

● Latinos are the largest immigrant group and one of the fastest-growing populations in the United States today. Latinos are a diverse people with many different national identities, histories, cultures, and concerns. The great political question is whether they will mobilize around shared interests and concerns. If they do, they will become a formidable political force.

● Asian Americans are the third-largest minority group in the United States and now comprise 5 percent of the population. They are also a tremendously diverse group.

● Native Americans lost their way of life in the face of disease, armies, and settlers. The Supreme Court gave them a special status: a separate people without rights. Though they retain the special status, they became US citizens in 1924.

● People with disabilities leveraged an obscure bureaucratic rule, used it to mobilize, and eventually won the sweeping rights of the Americans with Disabilities Act.

● The gay (and lesbian) movements were born in a burst of pride and anger in 1969. Gays were the first to confront AIDS—a harrowing plague (in its early years) that pushed them into politics, health provision, and community building.

● Gay, lesbian, bisexual, and transgender communities have moved from taboo to mainstream.

Nevertheless, the conflict over marriage and childrearing remains a flash point of contemporary culture wars.

KEY TERMS

1963 March on Washington, 174
Abolition, 164
Affirmative action, 176
Brown v. Board of Education, 172
Civil rights, 159
Civil Rights Act of 1964, 174
Chicanismo, 186
Class action, 184
Compromise of 1850, 165
De facto discrimination, 170
De jure discrimination, 170
Domestic dependent nation, 194
Dred Scott v. Sandford, 165
Emancipation Proclamation, 166

Equal Employment Opportunity Commission (EEOC), 182
Equal protection of the laws, 167
Equal Rights Amendment, 185
Freedom Riders, 173
Free rider problem, 174
Great Migration, 170
Jim Crow, 168
Laws of coverture, 180
Literacy test, 168
Missouri Compromise, 165
National Association for the Advancement of Colored People (NAACP), 171

National Organization for Women (NOW), 182
Plessy v. Ferguson, 168
Quasi-suspect category, 162
Reconstruction, 168
Reframe the issue, 185
Section 504, 196
Seneca Falls Convention, 181
Strict scrutiny, 162
United Farm Workers, 186

STUDY QUESTIONS

1. Name the seven steps involved in civil rights campaigns. Give examples of three, drawing on historical material in this chapter.
2. Describe the Civil War Amendments. Why was the Fourteenth Amendment important?
3. What was Jim Crow legislation?
4. Describe the sit-ins and Freedom Rides of the civil rights movement. What was the point?
5. Describe three effects of the Civil Rights Act of 1964.
6. What is affirmative action?

For further reflection: Write your own Supreme Court decision on affirmative action

in higher education. Would you accept affirmative action in your school? Why or why not?

7. What are undocumented aliens?

For further reflection: What should the United States do about undocumented aliens?

8. What is the Lilly Ledbetter Law?

For further reflection: Why do you think President Obama chose that as the first law to sign as president?

6

Public Opinion and Political Participation

THE EXPLOSION CAME WITHOUT WARNING. A few

minutes before 10:00 p.m. on an ordinary April evening, a bubble of methane gas—at first no larger than a golf ball—squeezed through a thick layer of drilling mud nearly two miles beneath the ocean's surface in the Gulf of Mexico. Shooting past a series of protective barriers and expanding as it rose, the lethal gas erupted with a fiery roar through the Deepwater Horizon offshore oil-drilling rig owned by BP, the giant oil company. Eleven workers on the rig were killed and seventeen others seriously injured.

The explosion burst into public consciousness as well. In the days after the disaster, a horrified nation watched as millions of gallons of crude oil poured out of the destroyed drill's wellhead, deep beneath the ocean. Americans previously little aware of offshore drilling turned against the practice. By early June, as the toxic mess continued to spread, more than 50 percent of the public opposed offshore drilling exploration—up from just 23 percent before the spill.[1] Capturing the popular mood, the Obama administration announced a freeze on new offshore exploration.

After more than three months of gushing oil, federal government and BP engineers managed to cap the spill. Amid severe economic recession, especially on the Gulf Coast, calls increased for a return to offshore drilling exploration. Among the wider public, antidrilling sentiment faded; by early October, with midterm elections looming, opposition to offshore drilling had fallen below 40 percent. President Obama lifted the moratorium, allowing drilling to resume.

Who are we? The world's oldest democracy. The roller-coaster polls, however, pose a dilemma. If the people don't know what they want, how can their views guide the nation?

That question spills over into public policy decisions: *Should* the American public influence a complex, highly technical matter like the risks and benefits of deep-water drilling? The issue of public opinion—what the public says it wants—lies at the heart of self-rule. Somehow, the government must reflect popular views—but how? Government officials constantly balance public opinion and their own best judgment. Yet their responsiveness to popular views is linked to who among the populace is actively participating in our political

● *Deepwater Horizon explosion, April 2010. Public opinion turned sharply against offshore oil drilling in the wake of the Gulf of Mexico oil-spill disaster . . . then shifted again a few months later.*

BY THE NUMBERS *Public Opinion*

Year that "public opinion" was first mentioned by a public official (in France): **1788**
Year the French Revolution began: **1789**
Percentage of the American public unable to name their House member, 1960, 2010: **47, 59**

Percentage of US college students expressing trust in US government, 1961: **74**
Percentage of US college students expressing trust in US government, 1991: **44**
Percentage of US college students expressing trust in US government, 2011: **38**

Highest approval rating recorded by Gallup for any president throughout term (John F. Kennedy): **70.1**
Lowest average approval rating (Harry Truman): **45.4**
Average approval rating for Ronald Reagan and George H. W. Bush, respectively: **52.8, 60.9**

Japanese prime minister Kan approval rating, February 2012: **20**
Russian president Putin approval rating, February 2012: **72**

President Obama approval rating during first month in office (Gallup, February 2009): **71**
President Obama approval rating, February 2011, 2012, 2013: **52, 51, 51**

Percentage turnout of voting-age population, US presidential election, 1840: **80**
Percentage turnout of voting-age population, US presidential election, 1940: **63**
Percentage turnout of voting-age population, US presidential election, 2008: **56**
Proportion of eligible black residents registered to vote, Lowndes County, Alabama, 1965: **0**
Proportion of eligible black residents registered to vote, Lowndes County, Alabama, 2008: **81**

---

system. So, who we are rests, to a large extent, on who is willing to join in, express their views, and become part of our political debate.

Measuring Public Opinion

Professional polling firms like Gallup, major media organizations, partisan outfits, and academic research centers all jostle to provide the most up-to-date polls. Candidates for office commission private polls to tell them how

Table 6.1 Politicians Cannot Avoid the Issues Attracting Most Public Attention

Highest Percentage Who Are Following News Events, Gallup Polls, 1991–2011		
EVENT	DATES	%
Terrorist attacks on New York City and Washington, DC	Sep 14–15, 2001	97
Hurricane Katrina and subsequent flooding of New Orleans	Sep 8–11, 2005	96
War between US and Iraq	Mar 22–23, 2003	95
The sniper shootings in and around Washington, DC	Oct 21–22, 2002	91
The tsunami that struck parts of Asia	Jan 3–5, 2005	89
The situation with Iraq	Jan 3–5, 2003	89
UN inspections for weapons of mass destruction in Iraq	Jan 23–25, 2003	88
News about the oil spill in the Gulf of Mexico	May 24–25, 2010	87
Aftermath of disputed US presidential election	Nov 11–12, 2000	87
Death of Princess Diana	Sep 6–7, 1997	85
Beginning of ground war in Iraq	Feb 24, 1991	84
Situation in Kosovo	Apr 13–14, 1999	84
News about Barack Obama's presidential transition	Nov 13–16, 2008	83
Clinton-Lewinsky matter	Aug 21–23, 1998	83
US military finding and killing Osama bin Laden	May 5–8, 2011	83

they're performing; presidents and governors retain pollsters to gauge public opinion on various policy items. Let's take a look at how good polls are designed, where not-so-good polls cut corners, and—most important—how to recognize each kind.

Polling 101

Imagine that you are hired to conduct a public survey about preferences in the next mayoral election. Where do you start? You could ask a few friends in your American government class whom they plan to vote for, but that would probably not help you predict the winner. Professional pollsters are very careful to define their **sampling frame**—the types of people they plan to survey. If the poll is to reflect public views, your survey respondents must reflect the population: that means they must vary in *age*, *education*, *income*, *race* or *ethnic group*, *gender*, and many other factors, such as their neighborhood of residence. Asking only your classmates would bias the poll toward college-educated and, probably, young people. A good representative survey

Sampling frame: A designated group of people from whom a set of poll respondents is randomly selected.

includes **demographic groups** in rough proportion to their presence in the city's population.

You will also have to make a related sampling decision. Do you want your poll to represent *all* city residents, or only those who will probably turn out and vote? Survey researchers tend to prefer polls of **likely voters**, which more accurately predict the outcome of most elections. Pollsters also often survey likely voters on policy questions, not just election polls.

Before you start knocking on doors or dialing numbers, consider the *timing* of your survey. When do you conduct the poll? If you do it during the day, people with jobs will be away from home or unable to talk; if you conduct a telephone poll on a Friday evening, you're unlikely to find many younger residents at home—skewing your results to older people's opinions.

Once you have chosen your sampling frame and decided when to ask questions, you face an even more important question: What exactly will you ask? If this were a chat with your classmates, you might ask simply, "Whom do you support in the 2012 mayoral election?" But legitimate surveys must take into account **framing effects**: the *way* pollsters ask a question often influences the response.

For example, public support is generally higher when policy is described in terms of its benefit for "lower-income people," as opposed to mentioning specific demographic groups, such as African Americans. In a question about trade policy, public opinion is typically more positive when the surveyors ask about the benefits of "free trade," as opposed to the destructive effects of trade on Americans' jobs. Sometimes these biases can be subtle. In polls on more obscure political races (other than president, governor, or big-city mayor), many respondents prefer the candidate who is named *first*, no matter what party or other identifying details are included in the question.

Frequently, campaign or advocacy groups *want* to skew their survey results—and use framing effects to their advantage. Efforts to directly influence respondents' views, as opposed to legitimate attempts to measure opinions, are termed **push polls**. These "polls" are essentially a form of negative telemarketing; they have more impact on unsuspecting respondents because they are campaign advertisements masquerading as scientific surveys.

One notorious push poll was used during the 2000 Republican presidential primary. George W. Bush was losing his lead in the polls to a surging John McCain, and South Carolina loomed as a decisive primary contest. An anonymous political operative—the Bush campaign denied any involvement—conducted a push poll that asked hundreds of South Carolina voters: "Would you be more likely or less likely to vote for John McCain for president if you knew he had fathered an illegitimate black child?" The question itself was damning, for it implied sexual misconduct and stirred up the complex brew of American racial politics; it contributed to Bush's decisive victory in South Carolina. (Senator McCain and his wife had adopted a daughter from Bangladesh, who was accompanying them on the campaign trail.)

Table 6.2 Comparing Polling Predictions: 2012 GOP Primary

Polling analyst Nate Silver (author of the *538.com* blog) compared a selection of polls taken in presidential primary states one week before the primary election (top table) and on primary day (bottom table). Polls become much more accurate as the election approaches.

POLLING-BASED FORECASTS (538 MODEL), ONE WEEK BEFORE ELECTION			
STATE	PROJECTED	RESULT	ERROR
Iowa	Romney +13.4	Santorum +0.1	13.5
New Hampshire	Romney +26.1	Romney +16.4	9.7
South Carolina	Romney +7.9	Gingrich +12.5	20.4
Florida	Gingrich +7.1	Romney +14.5	21.6
Arizona	Romney +7.8	Romney +20.7	12.9
Michigan	Santorum +1.4	Romney +3.2	4.6
		Average Error	**13.8**

POLLING-BASED FORECASTS (538 MODEL), ELECTION DAY			
STATE	PROJECTED	RESULT	ERROR
Iowa	Romney +2.8	Santorum +0.1	2.9
New Hampshire	Romney +19.9	Romney +16.4	3.5
South Carolina	Gingrich +9.4	Gingrich +12.5	3.1
Florida	Romney +14.7	Romney +14.5	0.2
Arizona	Romney +16.1	Romney +20.7	4.6
Michigan	Romney +0.9	Romney +3.2	2.3
		Average Error	**2.8**

As opinion surveys become ubiquitous in American politics and governance, push polls and other tactical methods have increased as well. Candidates or groups that want to advance a specific point of view are able to manipulate survey questions in ways that support their positions on an issue.[2]

A related concern is the spread of online "polls," such as those you may have seen at your favorite websites. Internet "insta-polls" like these may be harmless enough—but their host sites (and even some media organizations) report them as representative of the entire US public, when they are usually quite skewed. Different websites attract different kinds of people. As a result, online polls violate the polling gold standard: the answer comes from a self-selected group, not from a random sample. Thus, another guide to reading

Quick vote

Do you agree with Rick Santorum that Puerto Rico must have English as its principal language to become a state?

Read Related Articles

| Yes | ‖‖‖‖‖‖‖ | 51% | 49354 |
| No | ‖‖‖‖‖‖‖ | 49% | 48024 |

Total votes: 97378

● *Example of an online poll. CNN offers frequent online polls. These are usually misleading because the sample is not carefully chosen to reflect the whole population.*

● *The pollster's difficult job. Even the best-designed surveys cannot avoid response bias—including some respondents who misrepresent their views on purpose.*

Margin of sampling error: The degree of inaccuracy in any poll, arising from the fact that surveys involve a *sample* of respondents from a population, rather than every member.

Response bias: The tendency of poll respondents to misstate their views, frequently to avoid "shameful" opinions like sexism or racism.

polls: any poll with a sample that selects itself (by surfing to a site, for example) is probably unreliable.

Younger Americans are especially hard to reach and survey. Can you guess why? Many young people use mobile phones rather than land lines. It is now legal for polling firms to dial cell phone numbers at random, but they must hand-dial the numbers—raising the cost of the polls. To save time and money, most professional pollsters use *automated* dialing for land-line calls. Machines dial dozens of numbers at once; when a caller answers, the "robo-dialer" transfers the call to a human surveyor to ask the preapproved polling questions. Today, more than a quarter of Americans of all ages have mobile phones and no land line, a number that continues to increase. Survey researchers must adapt—or face potentially erroneous polls.

Finally you have collected the raw data from all your surveying. Time to tell the world about the details of your poll? Not so fast. You still need to determine your poll's **margin of sampling error**, a statistical calculation for how accurate your results are. By carefully designing their poll, national surveys are able to achieve small errors with as few as 1000–1500 respondents.

Pollsters also must consider **response bias** in publicizing their findings. Studies show that some respondents purposely mislead pollsters. Response bias can reflect animosity towards pollsters or the all-too-human tendency to align with "acceptable" views. Survey questions that might elicit unpopular attitudes, such as racism or sexism, can lead respondents (consciously or unconsciously) to shift their answers in a more socially acceptable direction.

A classic example of response bias arose when Tom Bradley, the first African American mayor of Los Angeles, ran against a white candidate, George Deukmejian, for governor of California in 1982. Bradley had a comfortable double-digit lead in opinion surveys as Election Day approached—but lost the race. Since then, other high-profile campaigns have similarly featured black candidates who had large leads in the polls but lost the election, a result that confounded survey researchers. The apparent inclination of some survey respondents to avoid appearing racist or racially motivated has become known as the "Bradley effect." It's not clear how large this effect is—and some analysts question whether it is significant at all—but it has become part of polling lore in the United States. And it reminds us to pay careful attention to the potential for response bias.

Sample size, framing effects, and margin of error: account for all these, and you're well on your way to conducting a truly scientific public opinion survey. One important reason to understand the design of polls is so that you can distinguish the good from the bad. Table 6.3 summarizes some of the tips in this section.

Do Opinion Surveys Influence Us?

Might the profusion of polls also affect the decisions we citizens make—including how to vote? Evidence suggests that they do. Candidates who are leading in the polls tend to pick up support from voters who were undecided—or who weakly supported the opponent. The **bandwagon effect** in polling varies considerably from place to place and election to election. It can be exaggerated by media coverage.

Bandwagon effect: Tendency of undecided voters to support the candidate who is leading in the polls.

The idea that positive poll results inspire people to support a leading candidate has been around for a long time. Pollsters, however, staunchly resist suggestions that their "objective science" of measuring opinion influences outcomes. George Gallup devoted considerable time and money back in the 1940s to disproving the bandwagon effect of polls. But the fact has stubbornly remained resistant to efforts to dislodge it.

Table 6.3 Five Tips on Reading Polls

1. *Check out the margin of error.* Then reread the poll that figures it in. A 3 percent margin of error means plus or minus 3 percent—turning a 50 percent approval rating into one of 47–53 percent.
2. *What is the timing?* The further away from Election Day, the less meaningful the results. (Take another look at Table 6.2 above.)
3. *The random sample is the gold standard.* If the respondents chose themselves (by deciding to take the survey), then it may be fun to read . . . but it is probably not an accurate picture of the public.
4. *What is the sample size?* Be wary of polls that interview a small number of people.
5. *Compare across polls.* Since every poll has biases, read a range of polls, toss out the extreme findings, and take an average of the rest.

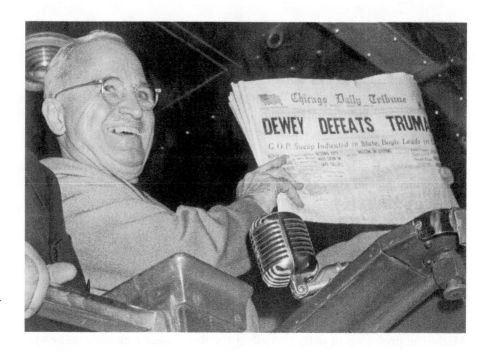

● *Modern polling's Day of Infamy. Even with advanced scientific survey techniques, pollsters make mistakes—none more prominent than this 1948 example. Despite the headline, Harry Truman, holding the newspaper, won by over 3 percent of the popular vote—and by 114 electoral votes.*

Boomerang effect: The discrepancy between candidates' high poll ratings and election performance, caused by supporters' assumption that an easy win means they need not turn out.

Underdog effect: Sympathy for a candidate behind in the polls, contributing to a higher-than-predicted vote total—and sometimes a surprise election victory.

A close cousin of polling's bandwagon effect is the **boomerang effect**. Here, a candidate who has been consistently ahead in opinion surveys performs more poorly than expected on election day. The logic is that supporters see a big lead for their candidate, figure that she will win without any difficulty, and then don't bother to vote.

Scrambling the issue further, some voters also appear to follow the *opposite* of the bandwagon effect. America loves rooting for the underdog—the one we don't expect to win—and this tendency also appears in public opinion polling. The **underdog effect** is invoked when a candidate losing in the polls performs better than expected in the election, sometimes even surprising pollsters with a victory. There's less empirical evidence for this phenomenon than for the bandwagon effect, but enough examples exist that the term has stuck.

THE BOTTOM LINE

- Scientific surveys have come a long way since their origins in 1936. Professionals now design well-specified polls that capture popular views with a high degree of accuracy.
- Indeed, poll results can affect public opinion.
- Sampling errors, response bias, and other potential flaws inevitably confer a measure of uncertainty on any survey.

Sources of Public Opinion

By now you have a sense of the various ways we measure public opinion in modern American society. Where do these public views come from? Why do people hold the political opinions they do? Are convictions firm or open to change?

Public opinion researchers don't yet fully understand how we arrive at our political views. We will review with you the current research about why Americans think the way we do. It is related to our discussion of political participation later in this chapter, but the focus here is different. Instead of asking why we go to the trouble to get involved in politics, here we examine the roots of people's opinions about politicians and policy issues.

Self-Interest: Voting Our Pocketbooks

Some experts believe that we participate in politics largely to advance our personal interests. Economic self-interest matters most. If you're a wealthy businessperson, according to this view, you will try to protect (and increase) your wealth. You are more likely to vote for Republicans, who generally stand for lower taxes and reduced regulations.

One of the first organizations to conduct presidential election polls was the Literary Digest, which relied on postcards sent in by subscribers. In 1936, the magazine predicted a big loss by incumbent president Franklin D. Roosevelt—who went on to win one of the great landslides in history. The *Digest* was so far off base because of its wealthy subscriber list. FDR, to this audience, was a left-wing fanatic. Business leaders expressed bitter sentiments toward the president, and he responded right back at them.

see for yourself 6.1

Go online and listen to excerpts from Roosevelt's fiery campaign speech.

What Do You Think?

Calling the Election Early?

Imagine that you are the news director of a local network TV station. It's election night, one of the biggest days of the year for political news. Reliable exit polling suggests that a local race—for mayor, or state senate, or maybe the US House—is breaking overwhelmingly for one candidate. Your reporters are pushing you to let them announce that result on the air, beating other local stations to the punch. They have the information and accuse you of censoring them. What do you do?

Let the polls close first. If we announce the result before the polls close, some unknown number of voters do not vote, affecting the election outcome. The national TV networks and cable news stations have agreed to hold off announcing results from a specific state until the polls close.

Go for the scoop. It's important to win the television ratings race. Some media organizations report exit polling results while voters are still waiting to cast their ballots.

In a campaign speech at Madison Square Garden in New York, Roosevelt pointed to "organized money" and declared, "They are unanimous in their hate for me—and I welcome their hatred."[3]

In practice, economic interests alone rarely shape political opinions. Wealthy liberals abound, especially in East and West Coast cities like New York and San Francisco. One of the richest Americans, George Soros, backs Democratic candidates, and another, Warren Buffett, calls for higher tax rates on himself and his wealthy friends. On the other hand, many lower-income Americans oppose raising taxes on the rich or other efforts to redistribute wealth in their direction. This latter tendency is striking enough that the economist Thomas Frank wrote a book about it, called *What's the Matter with Kansas?* Frank's title calls attention to the fact that Kansas—with some of the lowest average incomes in the country, especially in its rural sections—is among the most conservative states, represented in Congress exclusively by Republicans. If they focused on their economic interest, argues Frank, they would be more likely to vote for Democrats.

Despite these caveats, wealthier people do, on average, tend to vote Republican. But there are enough exceptions that if we want to understand the roots of public opinion, we can't rely on income and other markers of material interests alone.

Demographic Effects: From Region to Religion

President Lyndon Johnson once remarked, "Tell me where a man comes from, how long he went to school, and where he worships on Sundays, and I'll tell you his political opinions." LBJ, a big-talking Texan, may have overstated the case, but political scientists have repeatedly confirmed his point. Basic demographic details—such as age, religious background, ethnic or racial group, gender, region of residence, and level of education—are strong predictors of people's political outlook. For example, young Jewish individuals or black northeasterners with advanced degrees overwhelmingly vote Democratic. Middle-aged white, male, Christian southerners are very likely to support Republican candidates.

We can see the same demographic effects in specific policy preferences. Take, for example, "English-only" laws that aim to make English the sole language of government. Even in majority Latino areas, supporters argue, street signs or ballots should be printed not in Spanish but exclusively in English. Older, relatively rural voters in the Midwest and South generally support such laws; the strongest opposition, according to an extensive public opinion study, comes "from the college-educated, from women, from non-whites, [and] from residents of urban areas and the coasts."[4]

Demographic forces also tend to work across a range of views. Men and women, for example, have since the early 1980s displayed a **gender gap**—a

Gender gap: Patterned differences in political opinions between women and men.

● *Mayor Rudolph Giuliani shaped reactions to the 9/11 attacks—in New York and around the nation—with both reassuring words to victims and defiant warnings to terrorists—both delivered as he walked the city's streets. Here, the mayor is flanked by Governor George Pataki and Senator Hillary Clinton.*

see for yourself 6.2

Go online to see Jon Stewart resisting Mayor Bloomberg's call to restrict soda sizes. (Flash Required)

on policy matters.[5] After the terrifying 9/11 attacks, millions of Americans watched President George Bush address the nation and New York City mayor Rudy Giuliani speak to (and for) the afflicted city. They each shaped American responses to the terrible event.

The greatest influence is wielded by figures who have the most credibility. Such "experts" on issues may include academics and think tank analysts, news anchors and other familiar sources of commentary, and popular political leaders—especially presidents. (We look further at the role of the media in Chapter 7.) Unpopular presidents are much less likely to influence public opinion. That's another reason smart politicians watch presidents' approval ratings—and why presidents pay close attention as well.

When elites compete to shape members of the public's views on issues, they are trying to *frame* the issue—to give the issue a particular slant. For example, when obesity became a source of widespread popular concern in 1999–2000, policy makers and advocates pushed hard to influence public opinion. What, if anything, should government do in response to sharp increases in Americans' obesity rate? Many leaders—and the food industry— framed the issue as one of personal responsibility: obesity was, they said, a problem of self-control. The solution was simple: eat less, exercise more. Others framed the problem as a toxic food environment—too much high-fat, low-nutrition food is available at low cost in too many places—from fast-food drive-throughs to pharmacies to convenience stores to school cafeterias. As the public health consequences of obesity became clearer, the toxic-food-environment perspective gained traction. The framing battle reached a fever pitch when New York mayor Michael Bloomberg proposed banning sugary drinks larger than sixteen ounces—prompting cheers from public health advocates and a long rant from Jon Stewart. That, in turn, illustrates a theme we will pick up in the next chapter: the media also plays a crucial role in framing issues.

Wars and Other Focusing Events

Sometimes Americans exhibit widespread consensus on political matters, most notably during the outbreak of war. Franklin D. Roosevelt's efforts to provide US support for Britain and other traditional American allies against Germany after World War II broke out in 1939 won at most mixed backing from the American public—until December 7, 1941. The Japanese bombing of Pearl Harbor that day galvanized public support for the war effort. Six decades later, nearly 90 percent of Americans backed the decision to invade Afghanistan a few weeks after the September 11, 2001, terrorist attacks on the World Trade Center and the Pentagon.

Wars inspire a strong sense of "We're all in this together," a nationalist sentiment that has characterized public response to wars in almost every country. But that sentiment typically fades over time. Consider the US conflict in Iraq. When President Bush launched the war, in March 2003, almost 80 percent of the public approved. Four years later, approval for American involvement in Iraq had fallen to barely 30 percent in some polls.

THE BOTTOM LINE

- Our political opinions are influenced by a wide range of factors, from family and friends' views to the power of party identification and of political elites.
- How issues are framed can shift individual and collective views.
- Outside events, especially wars involving the United States, also have a powerful role in shaping our opinions.

Public Opinion in a Democracy

Americans care about public opinion because of the direct connection to democracy—a word that comes from the Greek *demokratia*, and means "rule by the people." For the public to have any meaningful say in ruling, political leaders must listen to their views. Do the people know enough to shape government?

"The masses are asses!" insisted Walter Lippmann in his pathbreaking book *Public Opinion* (published in 1922). Lippmann, a well-known political journalist and cultural critic, dismissed the young "science" of public opinion as undeserving of the name. In his view, the typical American was distracted by celebrities and minor scandals, rarely followed policy issues closely enough to understand the details, and yet readily offered up personal views on any topic. Paying attention to uninformed masses was no way to run a country. Lippman, along with many others, believed that governing involved technical decisions that were best left to well-trained experts.[6]

Many other commentators defend the American public and its role in government. Ordinary Americans, not elite technocrats, are the best judges of what government should do.

Which view most accurately describes Americans? Are we ignorant masses, or a rational collective capable of self-government? The question gets to the heart of what it means to be a democratic nation.

Is the Public Rational?

In 1960, four University of Michigan professors published *The American Voter*. This book hit post–World War II America like a thunderclap. Most citizens interviewed and surveyed in *The American Voter* knew little about the positions

I FORGET. WHO DID YOU SAY I WANTED TO VOTE FOR?

VOTE HERE

POLLSTER

● *The uninformed American voter. Political humorists have long found an easy target in the "ignorant voter." Should public leaders take seriously the views of an often disengaged public?*

Nonattitudes: The lack of a stable perspective in response to opinion surveys; answers to questions may be self-contradictory or may display no ideological consistency.

either political party stood for, or about the main policy issues at the time. Few respondents could name their members of the House or Senate, and fewer still could locate foreign countries—even close allies like Britain, or bitter foes like Russia—on a map.

Even more damning, *The American Voter* described the scientific poll—the instrument widely used to capture public opinion by the 1950s—as all but useless. One of the authors, Philip Converse, later coined the term **nonattitudes** to describe the response of many Americans to polls. When people were asked the same questions at different times, they tended to change their answers—sometimes radically. Moreover, changes in their responses were random: people did not switch their positions in response to new information or in changing contexts, but rather offered up different and even diametrically opposed views for no apparent reason. "Most people don't have real opinions at all," concluded the authors. When interviewers came to the door or called on the phone, people gave "doorstep opinions"—whatever happened to pop into their head at the time. The results—American public opinion—were meaningless.

The American Voter shook confidence in the value of both public opinion and the scientific methods used to measure it. If Americans spewed random thoughts in response to survey questions, what use were opinion polls? This perspective extends right down to the present. Recently, another quartet of political scientists set out to investigate the same territory as that of *The American Voter*; in *The American Voter Revisited*, they drew very similar conclusions: Americans remain politically ignorant.

An alternative view gained traction in the 1980s, most prominently captured in a book-length response to *The American Voter*, called *The Rational Public*.[7] The authors, Benjamin Page and Robert Shapiro, staunchly defended public opinion's legitimate role in policymaking. Yes, most voters were generally inattentive to policy issues and uninformed about many political details.

However, measured across large groups of people, public opinion moves in coherent, stable ways that signal shared views about policy issues, not just random nonattitudes. While a single voter or poll respondent may hold inconsistent or even self-contradictory notions, these are submerged in the collective outlook of tens of millions of voters (or a carefully specified representative sample). Taken as a whole, the public can differentiate among alternative policies, in ways that accurately reflect its shared values and beliefs.

Page and Shapiro's conclusion: the collective public has rational views and the government should pay closer attention to them. It is hard to imagine a starker contrast to the critique described in the previous section. Is there any way to reconcile the two views—ignorant individuals on the one hand, a rational public on the other?

The journalist James Surowiecki recently offered one solution, summarized by the title of his book: *The Wisdom of Crowds*. Even if any one individual does not have clear views, argues Surowiecki, a large crowd, taken together, does add up to a rational public. In fact, a random collection of people, he continues, is actually wiser than a group of experts when it comes to devising the best solution to a policy dilemma.

If public opinion is to guide government, however, three conditions must be met.

1. The people know what they want and seek to guide government decisions.
2. The public can clearly communicate its desires to political leaders.
3. Political leaders pay attention to public views—and respond.

That three-step process reflects the argument for public opinion's vital role in democratic governance. Each step, however, is full of difficulties. Let's consider each in turn.

● *How much does this ox weigh? Ordinary fairgoers' collective guess outperformed agricultural experts, in a famous 19th-century contest—testament to the power of aggregated public opinion.*

Do the People Know What They Want?

Public officials in a democracy aim to reflect majority opinion—while taking the rights and needs of the minority into account. Balancing majority views and minority rights is never easy. Even proponents of strong democracy cannot simply translate public opinion into political decisions.

Moreover, public views are rarely concrete enough to offer a guide for policy makers. For example, in 2009–2010, polls showed a significant majority of Americans were angry with Wall Street banks and other big financial institutions after they led the economy to a near collapse. By large margins, the public favored punitive legislation: slash financial-industry CEOs' pay, throttle back on trading in exotic financial instruments that few people understand, and make the banks pay for the economic mess they helped create.

But when Congress and Obama administration economic advisers tried to translate this public discontent into concrete legislative solutions, popular consensus evaporated. Should we regulate derivatives as we do stocks and bonds so that their trading is transparent? Half the public said yes, half said no. Limit CEOs' pay or the multi-million-dollar bonuses the financial wizards receive each year? Maybe, or maybe not, Americans told surveyors. The public's anger did not extend to the arcane specifics of financial regulations.

What Do You Think?

How Do You Participate?

Which side makes more sense to you: *The American Voter*, which concludes that the public is clueless? Or *The Rational Public*, which insists, on the contrary, that the people are the wisest political actors? The answer to this question is crucial for the practice of democracy.	**I believe the public is thoughtful and informed.** Are you and your friends contributors to a thoughtful American viewpoint, based on your interest in politics or your daily experience?	**I believe the public is clueless.** Or are you more likely to offer clueless "doorstep opinions" that change in unpredictable ways depending on your mood at the time?	**Both.** You believe that both positions have merit. Although many of us are too busy or uninterested to follow political issues closely, taken as a whole the crowd often achieves more insight than an individual expert.

Different polls reported different results. Deep in the details, the crowd did not seem to have much wisdom after all. As one White House official put it, "We're attentive to popular opinion on this, but no one can tell us what the public wants!"[9]

In the end, the bill regulating the financial industry that passed Congress in summer 2010 satisfied few stakeholders, and members of the House and Senate who voted for it rarely mentioned the fact in their campaigns.

Does the public know what it wants? In a general way, it probably does. But political leaders have to supply the policy specifics.

How Do the People Communicate Their Desires?

It is difficult for the people—even a clear majority—to convey its views to policy makers. None of our instruments for adding up and transmitting millions of people's views are particularly effective.

As we have seen, survey research, or scientific measure of popular opinion, is now everywhere in American politics and government. It is a crucial part of the political process and can offer solid impressions of public policy. However, polls have margins of error; they can be spun to advance partisan interests; and they offer general impressions, not a guide to crafting policies and making decisions—as we just saw in the case of the anger at Wall Street.

Mandate: Political authority claimed by an election winner as reflecting the approval of the people.

Of course, democracies also rely on elections. Candidates who win often claim they have a **mandate**: the people have spoken. But it is difficult to translate an election into support for any single policy. President George W. Bush won reelection in 2004 and claimed a mandate to reform Social Security; the effort immediately proved unpopular. Barack Obama thought the 2008 election gave him a mandate to reform the health care system, but that effort also proved unpopular, and, after health reform passed, the backlash helped Republicans make huge gains in Congress during the midterm elections in 2010. In short, it is difficult to translate electoral victory into instructions for any policy area.

Interest groups and political parties also work to collect and transmit popular views.

Do Leaders Respond to the Public?

On the surface, the answer seems to be unambiguous: yes! Our national campaigns collectively spend upward of $1 billion annually on polling. All members of every institution you will read about in this book—senators, presidents, lobbyists, even judges—avidly consume polls about their performance, as well as about the hot issues of the day. **Approval ratings**, which are routinely reported for top US political figures and national institutions, can boost a leader's power when ratings rise and weaken his or her standing when they fall (Figure 6.2).

Franklin D. Roosevelt initiated the practice of private presidential polling, using multiple pollsters to assess public opinion on both election and policy matters. John F. Kennedy was the first president to poll-test specific phrases to describe major policy initiatives. Three decades later, Clinton administration presidential pollsters like Mark Penn were described as having "close to veto power" on some policy decisions.[9] The reliance of the Clinton White House on public opinion went well beyond policies. The president reportedly heard from his polling staff on such matters as where he and his family should go on vacation.

However, attention to public views doesn't necessarily mean that politicians always slavishly follow the poll results. Government officials constantly have to weigh doing what they think is best against doing what the public

Approval rating: A measure of public support for a political figure or institution.

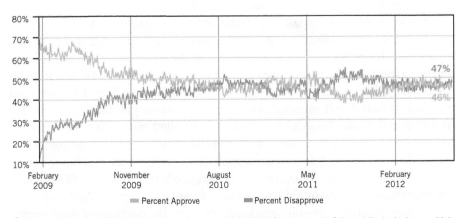

● **Figure 6.2** *President Obama's job approval rating, 2009–2012. Obama roughly followed the typical curve: high positive numbers at the start, decline in years 2 and 3, a rise during year 4. (Gallup)*

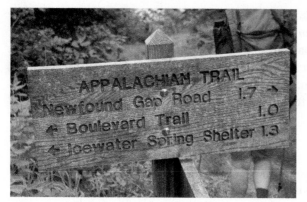

● *A portion of the Appalachian Trail. The Trail's 2,180 miles pass through 14 Eastern Seaboard states. A big shift in public support encouraged Congress to approve the trail's creation a century ago.*

Executive order: A presidential declaration, with the force of law, that issues instructions to the executive branch without any requirement for congressional action or approval.

Policy agenda: The issues that the public considers important, the media covers, and politicians discuss. Setting the agenda is the first step in political action.

desires. (In Chapter 1 we called these two views the trustee and delegate approach to representation.)

Let's return to President Bill Clinton. Despite his poll-happy reputation, he often broke with the findings. For example, in 1994, Mexico faced a major financial crisis. Clinton's economic advisers recommended a multi-billion-dollar loan to the Mexican government—which Americans overwhelmingly opposed. One top Clinton aide warned that the public would blame the president for "pissing billions of dollars down a Mexican rat hole."[10] In the face of strong popular opposition, with no support from Congress, Clinton signed an **executive order** directing the loan to go through—as it turned out, helping to stabilize Mexico's economy.

Recent work on public opinion has discovered that Clinton's action was typical. Political leaders—and presidents in particular—use polling to find the arguments that will resonate with the public. These polls do not determine the president's positions; rather, they guide political leaders in their efforts to persuade the public of the wisdom of those leaders' decisions. Polls help define the language and imagery with which politicians try to persuade the public of their own views—and criticize the opposition and its ideas.[11]

Polls clearly matter in setting the **policy agenda**. Public opinion helps shape what topics governing officials pay attention to in the first place. If the public (and the media, as we will see in the next chapter) thinks something is important, political leaders will usually respond.

Spikes in public opinion have an especially significant effect on Congress. Members are often reluctant to legislate in the face of strong popular opposition. Public views weigh significantly in deciding which items get a hearing. Americans may ignore many topics; but when large numbers of us pay attention to something, politicians generally respond.

Public opinion also enables presidential actions that might otherwise be blocked. Theodore Roosevelt (1901–1909) was a popular president, but he had to abandon his ambitious plans for a national system of protected forest lands in the eastern United States because of public indifference. His less popular successor, William Howard Taft (1909–1913), signed the Forest Reserve Act into law. How did Taft succeed? After a massive forest fire, known as "the Big Burn," raged across three western states and killed more than one hundred young firefighters, public opinion swung decisively in support of environmental protection. If you have hiked on the Appalachian Trail, vacationed in the Smoky Mountains, or gone leaf-peeping in New England, you have benefited from a program made possible by shifting public opinion.

Although collective public opinion holds sway, the opinions of some groups matter more than others. As we have seen, pollsters target the opinions of likely voters—individuals they expect to participate in elections. Social movements, interest groups, and political parties work to collect and transmit their views, and can have a more direct influence on public policies. By participating in the political system, your voice is more likely to be heard.

THE BOTTOM LINE

- If public opinion is to guide politics, three conditions must be met: the public must know what it wants; its views must be effectively communicated; and leaders must pay attention.
- Even strong public opinion may not be specific enough to offer policy guidance.
- United States government officials devote more resources to polling operations than top officials in other nations.
- All government officials constantly have to weigh doing what they think is best against doing what the public desires. Popular views can help set governing agendas. Polls often guide officials, not in selecting a policy, but in determining how best to win over the public to their policies.

Getting Involved: Electoral, Voluntary, and Political Voice

When we do get involved, what are the main avenues to doing so? Unless they are checked out entirely from politics, US residents engage in a variety of participatory practices. Political scientists divide these into three categories: *electoral activities*, of which the most familiar is voting; *civic voluntarism*, ranging from group membership to raising funds for your favorite charity; and *political voice*, which encompasses such expressive acts as sending an e-mail to your local newspaper editor or engaging in protests—like those in the Occupy movements. Let's take up each of these categories in turn.

Electoral Activities

If you have voted in any US election since you turned eighteen, you know the basic drill. First, register to vote, which you can do when you obtain your driver's license. Second, preferably after familiarizing yourself with the candidates, you show up on Election Day at your assigned polling place. Outside Oregon and Washington, the two states that conduct voting primarily by mail, more than 92 percent of Americans vote at a physical location rather than sending absentee ballots. Often, citizens vote in public buildings like schools or fire stations, but voting booths have been housed in barber shops, funeral homes, skating rinks, religious institutions (such as churches, synagogues, and mosques), and even private residences.

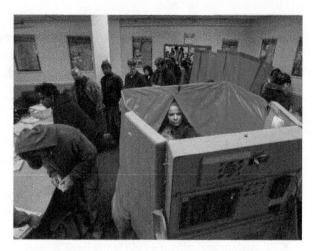

● *Americans vote almost anywhere: in schools and town halls, in churches and mosques.*

Next comes the act of voting. In some locations, you wait in line for a while. Depending on state law, you may then have to provide your identification to the polling workers, who are usually volunteers and not paid for their time—another form of electoral involvement. They will direct you to a voting booth, often adorned with distinctive blue curtains. Inside, you encounter one of many different American voting styles. Some jurisdictions use touch screens, others have you mark paper ballots much as the first US voters did in 1789 (usually in public, back then), and some states use voting machines with levers. These are the source of the familiar phrase "pull the lever" for your preferred candidates. If many different offices are listed on the ballot, perhaps along with an issue referendum or two (which we discuss later in this book), it might take you several minutes to work your way down the ballot and make all your choices. In local elections featuring just a handful of races, you may finish voting in thirty seconds or so.

Compared to other countries, the United States holds more frequent national elections—every two years for House members—and requires elections for a wider range of offices, including many judgeships. This difference helps explain why our **voter turnout**, the percentage of eligible citizens who actually make it to the polls, is among the lowest for the world's developed democratic nations.

Voter turnout: A measure of what proportion of eligible voters actually cast a legitimate ballot in a given election.

Why is US voter turnout so low, compared to that in other democratic countries? As noted just above, we go to the polls more frequently: the sheer number of elections reduces the inclination of some citizens to participate. Another reason is the difficulty working people may have in finding time to make it to their polling place on a Tuesday. Many other nations, in contrast, vote on weekends or national holidays. We return to the question of turnout in more detail in Chapter 8. Given that it is a primary means of engaging in public life, however, relatively low voter turnout in the United States is a source of concern for many observers.

Voting is the most widely recognized form of civic participation. More than 118 million people turned out for the 2012 presidential election. Yet voting can take only a few minutes, and at most we vote twice a year (in primary and general elections, for example). That brief time does little to build the civic habits that help make us healthier, wealthier, and wiser. Beyond voting, Americans (especially the most politically involved) engage in other **electoral activities**. They may work to persuade colleagues to run for office or even launch a campaign themselves. Others post signs on their lawns and bumper stickers on their cars featuring the candidates they support. They donate money to candidates or to their preferred political party. In the 2012 presidential election, more than five million Americans donated funds (some as little as five dollars, others gave millions) to the Obama and Romney campaigns.

Electoral activities: Public engagement in the form of voting, running for office, volunteering on a campaign, or otherwise participating in elections.

Civic Voluntarism

Many Americans—young, middle-aged, and seniors alike—engage in public activity without describing it as politically motivated. They simply volunteer for or contribute money to causes they consider important. Such **civic voluntarism** has a long pedigree. When the young French visitor Alexis de Tocqueville, whom we met earlier in this book, traveled through the United States in 1831–1832, he was struck by Americans' propensity to get involved. In *Democracy in America*, Tocqueville repeatedly remarks on the way Americans join voluntarily to build public institutions like roads, schools, and hospitals; in France, he notes, such projects would require elaborate layers of government approval—and in England, would need the patronage of a lord.[12]

Civic voluntarism: Citizen participation in public life without government incentives or coercion (speaking at a town meeting vs. paying taxes, for example).

Americans still volunteer for causes at higher rates than citizens of other democratic countries. And Generation Y—a group currently in their teens and twenties, including many of your college peers—is the most active in modern US history when it comes to volunteering. Over the past decade, the proportion of teenagers who volunteer has more than doubled. Figure 6.3 displays

● **Figure 6.3** *Americans 15–25: Self-reported reasons for volunteering. (Brookings Institution)*

Makes a Difference	21%
Makes Me Feel Good	24%
Issue Matters to Me	22%
Religious Impetus	14%
Other	19%

What Do
You Think?

Volunteer Globally?

Are you considering volunteer work abroad? Do you have skills that might benefit a community in a developing nation? Do you consider this type of global volunteering as "voluntourism"? What do you think of global volunteering?

Global volunteering is worthwhile. My work in local education, public health, or reconstruction projects could contribute real benefits to the community.

Global volunteering hurts the local community. Well-meaning volunteers can actually crowd local workers out of desperately needed jobs. They may also be able to provide only short-term benefits in an area that requires sustained commitment.

the primary reasons that Gen Y members volunteer. Recent studies suggest that the chief motive for volunteering is rarely padding a résumé for career purposes or university admissions.[13]

Voluntary engagement comes in dozens of different forms. Many people of all ages generously help out in their local communities, in ways that are especially helpful during an economic downturn: working at their local food bank, for example. Volunteers may not see their work as political, and indeed getting involved is often related to a hobby or enthusiasm, rather than public service. Whatever the motivation, however, voluntary activity tends to draw people into the common sphere. And once there, the payoff is clear. If you volunteer, you're more likely to vote, pay attention to political affairs, and otherwise engage in public life. It's best to work with established organizations that know how to maximize the benefits. Visit this book's companion website for a list of US and international organizations that engage volunteers in more positive, sustainable ways. At the same time, many high school and college-age Americans are performing volunteer work overseas.

Political Voice

Political voice: Exercising one's public rights, often through speaking out in protest or in favor of some policy change.

Beyond the drama of electoral campaigns, and apart from volunteering on behalf of a cause, another form of civic participation helps keep a democracy functioning. When you praise or critique a public official (on a blog or in person at a public forum), you're expressing your **political voice**. This type of participation in civic life can be as simple as following the news headlines. If you keep track of leading local, national, and global issues online, or by reading print versions of your favorite newspaper or magazine, and talk over your impressions for a few minutes each day or even just a couple of times each week—at meals with friends, or on Skype with your parents—you are actively exercising your right to voice your views. It may not sound like much, but in

● *Political voice or lawlessness? The office of a Georgia US House member is vandalized after he defends health care reform (2009).*

● *The Boston Tea Party as imagined by an eighteenth-century American artist (December 1773).*

non-democratic systems people can be imprisoned—or worse—for speaking their mind on political matters.

Talking (or blogging or tweeting) about politics and policy is one low-level gateway to expressing your political voice. Another is to join an organization connected to government, such as a political party or interest group. As we'll see in Chapter 9, thousands of US advocacy groups are busy promoting their views, covering every policy issue imaginable.

Some participants register their political voice in more dramatic fashion. Martin Luther King Jr., for example, led civil rights marches in Birmingham, Alabama, on behalf of black Americans. After King was arrested for "agitation," he wrote *Letter from Birmingham Jail* to defend his acts of civil disobedience, an especially inspiring example of political voice. Today, Tea Party activists engage their House and Senate representatives at public forums to express dissatisfaction with government spending. And the Occupy protesters are high-profile cases of speaking one's mind politically.

Sometimes it can be difficult to tell the difference between passionate expressions of political voice and illegal activity. When unidentified opponents of the Affordable Care Act, or "Obamacare," defaced a House member's district office in Georgia after he indicated support for the bill, or threw rocks through a Colorado member's office window, were they taking political action, destroying property—or both? What about the patriots who dumped three valuable shiploads of tea into Boston Harbor in 1773, helping to spark the American Revolution? Today we see them as courageous revolutionaries, but at the time they were mere lawbreakers in the eyes of many British Americans.

Whatever counts as legitimate political voice, exercising this form of participation serves multiple purposes. Remember that better health and career prospects are among the personal benefits accompanying active engagement in public affairs. Here's another plus: government officials are more likely to pay attention when a constituent speaks up—and they really notice when large numbers of people gather to express their views in a focused way. Environmental advocates were active in the United States throughout the 1960s. But when millions of Americans gathered to promote cleaner air and water at the first Earth Day in April 1970, Congress passed major clean-air legislation within a month and a Clean Water Act soon followed. That kind of political-voice activity is the lifeblood of democracy.

Now that you have a handle on what public participation looks like, let's move on to *why* many people get involved in public life. As you read, keep in mind that far more Americans are content to stay on the sidelines.

THE BOTTOM LINE

- Political participation can be categorized in three main ways: electoral activities, civic voluntarism, and political voice.
- Each of these raises vital questions: Why don't more people vote? Does volunteer activity in needy communities serve a valuable purpose, or is it better described as short-lived "voluntourism"? And how can we tell legitimate expressions of political voice from destructive mischief? Political scientists and public officials are still debating the answers.

What Inspires Political Participation?

Humans may be, as Aristotle claimed nearly 2400 years ago, "political animals," but our inclination to get involved politically is not just a question of instinct. Academic studies suggest that the decision to vote, for example, makes little rational sense. As originally described by political economist Anthony Downs, the **paradox of voting** suggests that voting is an essentially irrational act, working against most people's self-interest strictly defined. Thousands or even millions of others share your political views, and the election outcome will almost certainly not be determined by the single vote you cast. Why then go to the time and trouble of learning about the candidates and getting yourself to the voting booth?[14]

Paradox of voting: For most individuals, the cost of voting (acquiring necessary information, traveling to polling site, and waiting in line) outweighs the apparent benefits. Economic theory would predict very low voter turnout, given this analysis.

And yet Americans do get involved, by the tens of millions. Whether we are voting, volunteering, or expressing our political voice, something or someone—and often both—generally helped inspire us to do so. What makes Americans more or less likely to engage in political activity? There are no definitive answers. If there were an easy way to guarantee public participation, democracy's advocates would have discovered and applied it by now. After decades of careful research, however, we do have a heightened sense of which factors are more and less likely to inspire people to get involved.

Four leading influences serve as spurs to individual participation: political education (or "socialization"); the influence of family members or close friends, especially in communities with high levels of **social capital**, or civic engagement and mutual trust; mobilization efforts by advocacy groups and political parties; and—perhaps surprising—receiving benefits from government. Again, we look at each in turn.

Social capital: Relations between people that build closer ties of trust and civic engagement, yielding productive benefits for the larger society.

Political Socialization

Like most countries around the world, the United States features civic education in elementary and secondary grades. When starting school, if you studied in the US, you probably received—whether you were aware or not—a limited diet of political socialization. You engaged with ideas like the desirability of democracy, a free-enterprise system, and personal freedoms, especially individual liberty. You were introduced to the Declaration of Independence, the Constitution, and the founding generation.

The United States is less intensive in its national civic instruction, however, than many other nations. Public school students across France, for example, all study the same subjects in the same order, as determined by the national department of education; a major emphasis is the nature and value of "being French." American education systems are more decentralized: states and local communities have greater freedom to develop curricula and lessons. Perhaps as a result, the United States is unusual among advanced nations in

● *Social capital on the big screen. Characters from* It's a Wonderful Life, *a 1946 film that portrays the power of social networks and civic engagement.*

its lack of sustained educational focus on the importance of political participation. In many American states, no civics course is required at the high school level. When New York State attempted to create such a requirement in the 1990s, some critics labeled civics courses "brainwashing."

Despite the comparative lack of emphasis on political socialization in US schools, our level of education remains a strong predictor of whether we participate in the public sphere. Americans with a college degree are far likelier to be involved than those individuals who did *not* finish or never attended high school. Because many political acts require advanced social, managerial, and bureaucratic abilities—including information processing and English-language mastery—they tend to correlate with higher levels of education. Although K–12 education is far from a centralized national effort to promote American values, success in school does influence the likelihood that one will become involved politically.

Friends, Family, and Social Capital

Another way to predict whether someone will vote or volunteer is to find out whether their parents and closest friends do. On average, someone whose family or peers vote regularly is likely to do so as well. An even more powerful inspiration is being *asked* to vote, volunteer, or otherwise exercise political voice by people close to you. Political science studies find that face-to-face encouragement to participate politically, especially by someone known and trusted, is the most reliable route to political activity. Even being asked to vote by a stranger, as long as it is in person, tends to get results.[15]

Your type of community also seems to make a difference. In areas where neighbors are more trusting, and a general norm or ethic of civic participation is strong, people are more likely to get involved—both in local activities, like block watches or school fundraisers, and in voting for national office. Such communities, organized around a commitment to building social capital, tend to house happier, healthier residents. Through active, open communication and a strong foundation of trust among citizens, Americans can realize the benefits of engagement on a wide scale. Figure 6.4 displays the importance of trust and interpersonal communication in building social capital.

Political scientist Robert Putnam has shown that residents of areas high in social capital tend to be deeply involved in social activities, like book clubs or

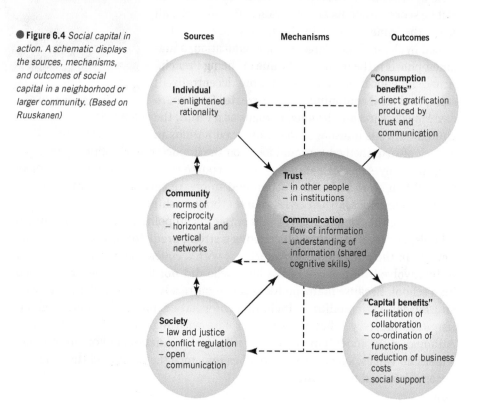

● **Figure 6.4** *Social capital in action. A schematic displays the sources, mechanisms, and outcomes of social capital in a neighborhood or larger community. (Based on Ruuskanen)*

community gardens or bowling leagues, and spend more time connecting informally with one another than in places where people live more anonymously and watch a lot of television. It may sound simple: a key to political participation is to live in a highly participatory community. But transforming a neighborhood into one with strong social capital—or sustaining civic connections once they exist—is no easy task.

In one neighborhood in the city of San Jose, Costa Rica, residents developed their own technique for boosting social capital. The neighborhood had experienced a sharp rise in crime, and residents decided to encourage more extensive connections in hopes of reducing burglaries and other crimes. They pledged to leave for work a few minutes earlier each morning and to take that extra time to greet and talk at least briefly with their neighbors. The practice became informally known as *El Ley del Saludo* (The Law of the Greeting), and it helped reduce crime markedly—as well as boost voting rates and other markers of political participation.[16]

The connection between family and participation may run even deeper. Recent studies suggest that we may *inherit* a tendency to political participation. In other words, your desire to vote or volunteer is determined by your genes—but only partly.[17] Political involvement is shaped by several influences simultaneously, so genetic inheritance, like level of social capital in a community, is one factor among many.

Political Mobilization

The work of **political mobilization** has traditionally been carried out by party organizations. Both major parties remain powerful sources of encouraging millions of people to get involved—especially at election time. (We'll talk about political parties, and the work they do in our political system, in Chapter 9.) On **issue advocacy** campaigns, however, when professional and amateur organizations seek to attract public attention and involvement for a specific cause, interest groups have become our mobilizers in chief.

In the eyes of professional political mobilizers—advocacy groups, campaign strategists, and other members of the enormous "political industry" based in Washington, DC—each of us is a potential resource. If we can be inspired to sign a petition, write our congressional representatives, get out and vote, or otherwise engage politically, we are part of democracy in action.

Political mobilization: Efforts to encourage people to engage in the public sphere: to vote for a particular candidate (and donate money, work on the campaign, etc.) or to get involved in specific issues.

Issue advocacy: Organized effort to advance (or block) a proposed public policy change.

Government Beneficiaries

A fourth significant factor encouraging participation in public life may strike you as odd at first glance—receiving government benefits. If your grandparents get a monthly Social Security check, your older brother or sister was covered by your parents' health insurance past age twenty-one, or you receive a federally guaranteed student loan (which keeps the interest rates low), you are all beneficiaries. Receiving such support can help to boost active participation later in life. Researchers have shown that when the government rewards service—as when returning soldiers receive free or discounted college tuition through the GI Bill—recipients are considerably more likely to get involved as volunteers and to exercise their public voice.[18]

Context

There is a larger backdrop to participation as well. Major shifts in the economy and in politics affect both the intensity and favored types of participation. In the rural South during the 1950s, for example, an infestation of boll weevils (tiny insects that feed on cotton plants) devastated the cotton crop. Many African American subsistence farm workers, their livelihood gone, moved to southern cities—where they became recruits for the civil rights movement. In part because of the boll weevil, they became involved in politics.

Context deeply influences opportunities for political engagement.[19] One dramatic example: during certain historical periods Americans have been more likely to engage in public life than at other times. In fact, these periods of heightened participation seem to occur in regular cycles across US history, with highest-involvement periods separated by intervals of around thirty years.

THE BOTTOM LINE

- Participating in politics and government is influenced both by personal factors: political socializaiton, friends and family, political mobilization, and receiving government benefits.
- Political mobilization is also influenced by the larger social and historiclal context.

● What Discourages Political Participation?

One clue to nonparticipation has to do with who does *not* get involved in politics. What groups of individuals are less likely to vote, to volunteer, or to exercise their political voice?

Age, Wealth, and Education

A substantial proportion of those who tend not to vote or exercise political voice are *young*, aged eighteen to twenty-four. Of US eligible voters who fail to turn out, nearly a third fall into that category. Back in 1960, by comparison, younger Americans made up only 7 percent of the nonvoting population—though this was when the eligible voting age was twenty-one. We return to the participation habits of Generation Y a little later in this chapter.

Along with age, another strong predictor of political participation and, by extension, nonparticipation is related to wealth. Top earners tend to be much more involved in public life than those farther down the ladder in income and wealth. The wealthiest 5 percent of Americans, for example, provide a very high proportion of the dollars contributed by individuals to political campaigns. Or comparing middle-income with lower-income Americans, the latter participate less in every significant way. Poorer people are less than half as likely to vote, attend a political protest, or contact a government official. They are only a third as likely to discuss politics informally in their neighborhoods or to join a political organization. And they are less than 10 percent as likely as middle-income earners to donate funds to political campaigns.[20]

Such class differences in participation strike democratic thinkers as a source of grave worry. In many countries around the globe, concern about the power of concentrated wealth in politics has led to the growth of socialist or labor parties, many of which promote proposals for income redistribution. France, for example, elected in 2012 a Socialist prime minister, turning out a center-right leader; the new leader, François Hollande, campaigned on a promise to reduce inequality, in part by raising income taxes on French millionaires to a 75 percent rate. Such movements are fueled by the idea that the richest citizens constitute a coherent political class, connected by shared interest and ideology, and that serious inequities in policy outcomes are the result.

Americans have traditionally resisted such notions, despite considerable evidence that wealthy people have more access to US political leaders, as well as greater influence over political outcomes. Is the lack of outcry over this imbalance a sign that the rich have successfully brainwashed the rest of us? Or is it less true in America than elsewhere that wealthy people make up a coherent, organized political class? On some issues, the top 1 percent of US wealth holders are deeply divided internally in their political views. For every industrialist seeking to bend policy to suit his or her private interests (pay lower taxes, e.g.), a superwealthy individual like George Soros or Bill Gates donates large sums to the least well-off among us and to political leaders who seek a larger social-welfare safety net.[21]

Along with age and income, what else characterizes the nonparticipants? *Education*, as we saw earlier, is a strong predictor of political involvement—and education level closely tracks income, in a country where college degrees are all but required for salaried positions and where graduate or professional degrees are increasingly necessary for advancement in those positions. Other demographic characteristics—such as race, ethnicity, or gender—have some effect but are less powerful when it comes to predicting participation. Within any group, we see variations in involvement. Many politically apathetic US residents come from the ranks of the well educated, highly paid, and middle-aged. Or consider Latino voters: as noted earlier, in recent years they tended to participate less actively than other groups—but Latinos turned out in record numbers (estimated at 50 percent) and were widely credited with being a key factor in President Obama's reelection.

Ultimately, there is no simple recipe for understanding why one person votes, while her sister who lives in similar circumstances does not, or why one fellow regularly attends town meetings to question local representatives, but his neighbor keeps to himself. Analysts have identified four broad reasons to explain further why many people of all ages, income levels, and educational backgrounds drop out or never join political life in America: alienation, barriers to participation, complacency, and shifting mobilization patterns.

Alienation

Alienation from public life may be described as a feeling of powerlessness, or inability to control one's own political fate. The result is usually abstention from public involvement, although alienation can also lead to intense and even violent protest. A sense of alienation is reported more often in the United States among members of historically excluded groups, especially African Americans.[22] Alienation is also higher among younger people and recent immigrants.

These findings raise a basic question: Do groups of Americans feel alienated because they lack a history of participation? Remember, one predictor of whether a person will get involved in politics is whether his or her parents or peer group are actively engaged. Or is the desire to participate high among immigrants, minorities, or young people, but many become alienated because they are systematically excluded from politics? Researchers have not fully untangled this complicated puzzle.

A sense of alienation from politics and government can also come in less extreme forms. The sheer number of elected offices and the high frequency of US elections can result in public exhaustion and eventually disengagement, especially when campaigns feature seemingly endless negative advertisements. Sharp partisan differences also play a role. In *Why Americans Hate Politics*, journalist and political analyst E. J. Dionne notes a widening gulf between liberals and conservatives in US political debates. The angry debates accompanying this polarization have led many Americans to "hate politics and politicians."[23] This form of alienation, according to Dionne, is driven by a political establishment that focuses on "issues" with little connection to the problems that actually concern people—problems that government leaders seem less interested in trying to solve, compared with protecting their own electoral safety.

In countries with totalitarian or oligarchic rather than democratic political systems, alienation can become pervasive. Large majorities of the population are turned off completely from government or politics. Compared to people in these places, a relatively small portion of the US citizenry exhibits a weaker form of alienation, but the phenomenon is demonstrably present in America.

Institutional Barriers

When Will Walker, a young black farmer, arrived to cast his vote in Tuscaloosa, Alabama, in 1964, he was first required by state law to pass a literacy test, one supposedly designed to prove that he was capable of exercising political judgment. None of the white voters streaming past Will to the voting booths had to take such a test. Will shrugged and turned to the paper before him, brandished by an unfriendly poll worker. He had brushed up on his basic US government facts, and he knew plenty about the candidates for the various offices up for election. Yet no amount of studying could have prepared Will for questions like these:

- The electoral vote for president is counted in the presence of two governmental bodies. Name them: _____ and _____.

- The president is forbidden to exercise his or her authority of pardon in cases of _____.

- If the president does not wish to sign a bill, how many days is he or she allowed in which to return it to Congress for reconsideration? _____ days

- At what time of day on January 2 each four years does the term of the president of the United States end? _____

Go online to view a full list of the questions used in Alabama's mid-1960s literacy test.

Will filled out as many of the twenty questions as he could; he did better than most political science majors might today. But he was turned away from the polls. Alabama allowed only black voters with a perfect score to vote. Owing to this and other deliberate efforts to block participation, many counties across the Jim Crow South featured voting-registration rates among African Americans that approached zero.

Most of these overtly racist obstacles to participation were eliminated during the 1960s. Although some critics continue to point out structural barriers to participation in American public life, other analysts praise the continued expansion of opportunities for engagement. Young Americans who long found it difficult to sign up as new voters, for example, are able to register when applying for a driver's license, thanks to the National Voter Registration Act of 1993, usually referred to as the **motor voter law**. Another longtime limit on public participation involves the difficulty of accessing information. This obstacle is greatly diminished, thanks to the massive amounts of political detail available on the Internet. Many governmental bodies now post reams of data, transcripts, and videocasts of public hearings, along with other types of official information online. National, state, and local governments also make information,

● *Barriers to participation: protesting literacy tests, 1950s. Disenfranchised African Americans protest the literacy test that effectively kept them—but not white voters, however uneducated—from voting from the 1890s until mid-1960s, in many southern states.*

Motor voter law: Passed in 1993, this act enables prospective voters to register when they receive their driver's license.

including ballots, available in multiple languages. Accessibility of this information opens another path to participation for historically excluded prospective voters.

Complacency

A further perspective on nonparticipation grows out of surveys showing that many people find their lives going reasonably well. Without nagging problems or issues they want solved, why bother to get involved? Research shows, for example, that large membership-based interest groups tend to attract more new members and receive a boost in financial contributions when the group's core issues are threatened. After a big oil spill or new warning about global warming, environmental groups attract more public interest. Conversely, when concerns are lessened, citizen groups find it hard to mobilize their followers.

A different view of political apathy comes from the economist John Kenneth Galbraith, who two decades ago coined the phrase "culture of contentment" to describe America. His view was that the upper-middle class, and those at the top of wealth distributions, are determined to secure their gains—and fight hard to sustain their "contented" way of life. Those less well off are increasingly discouraged from political participation, Galbraith argued, since the US polity was organized to continue satisfying the already contented.[24]

Shifting Mobilization Patterns

Before the 1960s, when political parties were Americans' main source of political mobilization, wealthy and poor people were organized to participate in roughly similar numbers. The main focus was on getting people out to vote in elections, so intensive door-by-door canvassing at election time was the norm. A surge in advocacy-group organizing since the 1960s has boosted the public's collective voice in politics. Movements on behalf of consumer rights, the environment, and many other causes represent a major gain in public leverage.

These gains, however, have primarily benefited the relatively well-off, who can devote resources of time and money to public involvement. Political sociologist Theda Skocpol notes that "Americans who are not wealthy or higher-educated now have fewer associations representing their values and interests, and enjoy dwindling opportunities for active participation."[25]

This shift from parties to advocacy groups as the main agents of political mobilization adds up to a **circle of nonparticipation**. If people are so disengaged that they do not affiliate with either of the main US political parties, party organizers are unlikely to reach out to them at election time—because they might vote for the wrong side.

Generation Y and Political Participation

Younger Americans, like the eighteen- to twenty-four-year-olds in many countries, have lower rates of political participation than do older age groups.

Circle of nonparticipation: Resistance by political parties to mobilizing disengaged Americans to vote—because their lack of involvement makes their allegiances to one or the other party suspect.

The exception is in volunteering for organizations that serve the public. From "candy stripers" at hospitals to programs for at-risk kids, young Americans in Generation Y, also termed millennials (born between 1983 and 2001), volunteer at unusually high rates. New forms of civic voluntarism organized through social media, as well as long-established organizations like the Peace Corps, have seen surges in participation among college students and recent graduates.

Rates of participation in electoral or "voice" political activities are much lower among Generation Y members, however. Voting turnout by age remains lowest among young Americans, as shown in Figure 6.5, with the gap among different age groups' voting rates essentially unchanged over the past four decades.

Beyond voting rates, Gen Y members are less likely than previous groups of eighteen- to twenty-four-year-olds to get involved in political campaigns, join or organize advocacy groups dedicated to policy issues, or express interest in politics and government. These findings are worrisome, given that generational trends in participation tend to persist over time. Generation X, roughly those born between 1964 and 1982, was informally described as the "slacker generation" when its members were in college. Today Generation X members' propensity to get involved in public life has remained relatively low, a trend that raises concerns about the viability of America's democratic governance. If their successor generation is even less engaged, those alarms become more urgent still.

The relatively low participation rates of millennials can seem puzzling, given their high engagement as volunteers. But volunteering is generally an

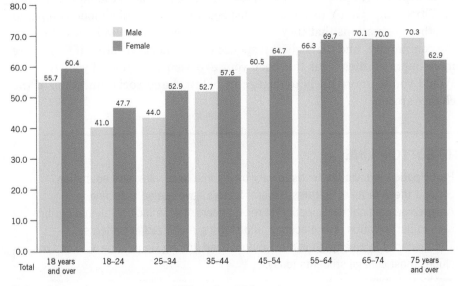

● **Figure 6.5** *Voter turnout by age group, 2008 election. (US Census)*

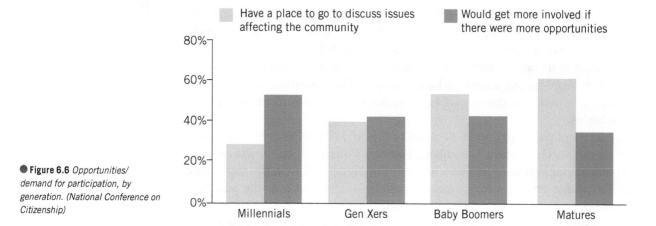

Have a place to go to discuss issues affecting the community

Would get more involved if there were more opportunities

Figure 6.6 *Opportunities/ demand for participation, by generation. (National Conference on Citizenship)*

individual activity. Although you may sign up to volunteer with a friend, you often carry out service work on your own schedule, donating your personal time. Other types of public engagement are more *collective*, and here Generation Y members begin to shrink away from involvement. Late teens and twenty-somethings display relatively low levels of trust in their fellow citizens—a strong marker of inclination to engage in political activities. Responding to a Pew Charitable Trusts poll in 2009, 70 percent of Generation Y members agreed with the statement "Most people look out for themselves," compared to only 40 percent of "matures," or Americans over 65, who agreed. A similar gap was present for the statement "Most people would take advantage of you" (56 percent of Gen Y, compared to 29 percent of matures).

At the same time, Generation Y's members report a desire to participate in political life (Figure 6.6). In a survey conducted by the National Conference on Citizenship, Gen Y respondents displayed the lowest likelihood compared to other generations that they "have a place to go to discuss issues affecting the community" and the highest response to "would get involved if there were more opportunities." Has this been your experience, or that of your friends? Would you be more likely to engage in political and social questions if the chance arose?

THE BOTTOM LINE

- Participation in civic life tends to vary by income level, age, and education.
- Beyond these familiar features, several factors have fueled a decline in Americans' political participation in recent years. These include alienation, barriers to participation, complacency, and shifting mobilization patterns.
- The tendency to disengage is most pronounced among Generation Y, which includes most college students today.

● The Internet, Social Media, and Participation

Another distinguishing feature of Generation Y is that its members are the most "wired" group of Americans in history. They are connected to one another and the wider world through smartphones, social media, and the Internet. What influence have these massive shifts in personal technology had on political participation? The answer may be different from what you expect.

Some political and cultural observers view the Internet, and specifically social media like Facebook and Foursquare, as heralding a revolution in participation. The world has shrunk to a size that was unimaginable just a few years ago—thanks to instantly available information, connectivity across the globe via Skype or Voxer, video links to a huge range of live government hearings and documents, and the ability of organizations to mobilize tens of thousands of members or followers by text or Twitter. Anyone even vaguely interested in participating in public life can do so virtually, accessing practically any cause or social movement on the globe.

Advanced technologies are routinely cited as the force behind such historic political events as the uprising in Iran during the summer of 2009, initially labeled the "Twitter revolution" because young Iranian activists were able to communicate by Twitter to avoid government crackdowns. Cairo's Tahrir Square uprising, which helped launch the "Arab Spring" reforms, is sometimes termed the "Facebook Revolution." Explains Wael Ghonim, a Google marketing manager in Cairo: "This revolution started online . . . when hundreds of thousands of Egyptians started collaborating content. We would post a video on Facebook that would be shared by 60,000 people on their walls within a few hours. I've always said that if you want to liberate a society just give them the Internet."[26]

Similar claims are made about the power of Internet and social media–driven participation in American political life. Clay Shirky, a communications professor, sees the net as fueling ever more dramatic intellectual and political achievements, thanks to vastly reduced barriers to group interaction. In Shirky's view, an emerging "social sector" will stand alongside the private and public sectors as a space for widespread involvement—including in public affairs.[27]

Others see a less exalted role for social media and other forms of interactive communication because of three primary obstacles to extensive public participation online: *central control*, *din*, and the *digital divide*. The fate of Iran's "Green Movement" for change in 2009 illustrates the power of centralized government control even over the chaos of the net. The movement was short-lived, in part because the Iranian authorities, like those in other repressive regimes, were able to severely curb

● *Iran's Green Movement social networks, which arose to bring change . . . have ended in sorrow.*

Twitter and other Internet use. To the extent that Iran's uprising depended on social networks, these were effectively shut down.

Less dramatically, public involvement that depends on wired technology is vulnerable to ordinary interruptions or shutdowns due to system overload or glitches. Hackers are also able to disrupt systems, slowing interaction and endangering users' privacy. Shifting more forms of political participation online could result in severe disruptions of public activity.

With more than 600 million websites on the net, the sheer volume and variety of available information are mind-boggling. The resulting chaos can also be mind-numbing. Becoming informed about a specific topic often involves wading through a forest of anonymous posts, partial information, and deliberate misinformation. One term for this is **din**.

Try googling this chapter's topic, political participation, for example. At last count, we found nearly 3.5 million relevant web sources. Which ones provide valuable or even useable details about participation in the public sphere? Merely to scan each site for one minute would take nearly seven years.

Finally, participation runs up against a **digital divide** between those with and without Internet access. In a democratic political system, forums for public expression are supposed to be open to everyone. As popular engagement with government shifts online, the importance of Internet access—and the social networking sites that help fuel participation—rises accordingly. This is one more way in which less-resourced Americans could be shut out of avenues to public activity.

Use of both the Internet and networking sites is far from equal in the United States. About two-thirds of American adults have reliable online access; thus, one-third are unable to access this tool for public engagement. According to a 2011 study of regular Internet users, nearly 40 percent are not on Facebook, Twitter, or a similar service. Those not participating in social network sites tend to have less education and lower incomes. They are also older: 56 percent of fifty- to sixty-four-year-old Americans do not use a social networking site with any regularity. Certain demographic groups, such as African Americans and Latinos, are underrepresented among social network users, potentially limiting their ability to participate in the public sphere.[28] But the digital divide may be closing. Among those who are online, rates of blogging, texting, and other online forms of engagement are higher among Latinos and blacks than among whites.

The lure of digital democracy is undeniably powerful. Social networking sites that mimic real engagement, such as Second Life or SimCity, generally reach a broader audience than does actual political activity. Young, well-educated Americans typically spend dozens of hours each week online. By comparison, time devoted to engaging in electoral, volunteer, or political-voice activities is minimal. Democratic advocates fear (and initial research seems to confirm) that social media and endlessly available web information are less likely to boost political participation rates or promote public activity than they are to drive us to other pursuits.

Din: Shorthand for the sheer volume of information and noise generated by online sources; can be a disincentive to participate politically.

Digital divide: The gap between those with ready access to the Internet and those without.

THE BOTTOM LINE

- Social networking and political information websites increase opportunities to participate in public life.
- At the same time, the new media may limit collective engagement by creating too many distractions, too much content (some of it malicious), and a digital divide.

Conclusion: Public Opinion and Political Participation in a Digital Age

The Declaration of Independence states a powerful American ideal: the consent of the governed. The Constitution begins "We, the People." Lincoln memorably reaffirmed this national commitment in his Gettysburg Address: "government by the people." Self-rule appears to demand that public opinion guides—or at least influences—the government.

Public opinion surveys are the most widely used effort to understand the popular mind. Scientific techniques have refined polling to a point of remarkable accuracy—especially as an election approaches. However, public opinion often seems whimsical or uninformed. The framers of the Constitution were skeptical of public opinion, and their view is now echoed by those who conclude that the people just do not know enough. Good policy must rely on experts and political leaders.

Others respond that the public must rule, given our foundational commitment to democratic politics in America. Some scholars go on to argue that collective decisions—the wisdom of crowds—are better decisions than even those made by well-trained experts. People from both perspectives agree that the public can be better informed.

How might we encourage the public to become better informed? Can the public gain enough expertise to weigh in on matters like the risks and benefits of deep-water drilling? The answer may lie in improving civic education: provide the public with the tools to determine its own political path.

Yet, as we have seen in this chapter, political participation rates among Americans, especially the less educated and economically worse off, have declined in the twenty-first century. That change owes both to resource challenges and to a sense of alienation from government officials—a sense fueled in part by a decline in efforts to mobilize wide swaths of the citizenry.

Examples from across the globe, including in the United States, testify that excluding nonparticipants—even if not deliberately—often results in profoundly undesirable outcomes. In Weimar, Germany, during the 1920s, for example, leading groups in political life sought to block involvement by poorly educated laborers and unemployed Germans. These previously unengaged voters surged to the polls in 1933, helping provide a large electoral margin for Adolf Hitler. While this example has no direct bearing on present-day America, it starkly affirms the danger of ignoring or marginalizing habitual nonparticipants. They may join the political process suddenly and wrathfully, responding to demagogic appeals when their country faces a crisis.

There is also concrete evidence that political involvement both enhances the collective whole and enhances each participant's personal prosperity, happiness, and health. Perhaps social media will encourage more engagement, especially among the super-wired members of Generation Y. Possibly an expanded roster of government "nudges" will subtly be able to help people help themselves. Whatever the source, expanded participation in politics and government is at the heart of America's democratic aspiration: enhancing the ability to govern ourselves as a free people.

CHAPTER SUMMARY

● Professionals design scientific polls that capture popular views with a high degree of accuracy. However, be cautious when reading polls, such as those without a well-defined sample (for example, online surveys). Always pay attention to the margin of error when interpreting results.

● Many different sources shape public opinion. The most important are family and friends, economic interests, demographics, party affiliation, the view of political elites, and defining events like war.

● In a democracy, public opinion ought to guide the government. But are the people capable of self-rule? Many experts consider public opinion uninformed and unreliable—and therefore a dangerous guide to decision-making. Others respond that the public, taken as a whole, is a rational, reliable source of government decision-making.

● Public officials generally balance public opinion with their own beliefs about the best decisions. Popular views can be especially important in setting the agenda: if something seems important to the public (and the media), politicians respond.

● Whether someone engages in civic life depends on both personal factors—those with politically active family members and close friends, or with higher education levels, are more inclined to participate—and political context. During periodic outbursts of democratic activity, many people who might ordinarily stay on the sidelines are drawn to participate. Inspired by the Occupy movements around the United States, some analysts suggest that we might be entering a time of wider participation now.

● Americans simultaneously get involved in civic affairs, especially in their local communities, and express high dissatisfaction with US government institutions—dissatisfaction that helps to drive down participation rates. Members of so-called Generation Y exemplify this tension: they engage in voluntary public-service activities at record rates but tend to mistrust politics and government. They also increasingly engage with others through social media, a force that is transforming political participation in fast-evolving (and, for the most part, poorly understood) ways.

KEY TERMS

Approval rating, 219
Bandwagon effect, 210
Boomerang effect, 210
Circle of nonparticipation, 234
Civic voluntarism, 223
Demographic group, 206
Digital divide, 238
Din, 238
Electoral activities, 223
Executive order, 220

Framing effects, 206
Gender gap, 212
Issue advocacy, 229
Likely voters, 206
Mandate, 218
Margin of sampling error, 208
Motor voter law, 233
Nonattitudes, 216
Paradox of voting, 223
Policy agenda, 220

Political elites, 213
Political mobilization, 229
Political voice, 224
Push poll, 206
Response bias, 208
Sampling frame, 205
Social capital, 227
Underdog effect, 210
Voter turnout, 222

STUDY QUESTIONS

1. Define the following terms: A push poll. A sampling frame. The margin of error. The Bradley effect.

2. What does it mean to "frame an issue"? Illustrate using the issue of obesity.

3. For further contemplation: Describe another example of "issue framing." You can pick another example from this book, a hot-button issue from news headlines, or an issue that has arisen on your campus or in your community. In each case, describe the alternate frames.

4. "The masses are asses," wrote one observer. He was summarizing a perspective that public opinion is not a reliable guide to government. Some scholars believe that public opinion is a legitimate guide to government. Which of these perspectives on public opinion seems more powerful to you? Do you believe the public is basically ignorant? Or collectively wise? (Yes, it is OK to opt for a bit of both.) Defend your answer.

5. What are some of the benefits of participating in civic and political life?

6. Why do so many Americans—especially younger people, in their teens and twenties—choose not to participate?

7. What features distinguish Generation Y when it comes to participation in civic and political activities?

8. Do you consider social networking sites as a source of enhancing or discouraging participation in public life? What evidence might you consider in support of your claim?

7

The Media

IN THIS CHAPTER, YOU WILL:

○ Learn how the media is changing. ○ Consider the democratic promises and pitfalls of new social media. ○ Explore how the media is (and is not) biased. ○ Understand the rules that channel the media into its current forms. ○ Discover how the media in America is unique. ○ Assess how the media affects politics. ○ See how the media influences campaigns and elections.

IN 1961, the American Medical Association enlisted Ronald Reagan, then an actor, to help fight President John F. Kennedy's health care plan. Reagan cut a record (on vinyl) that the medical association sent (by snail mail) to every physician's home. "If this program passes," warned Reagan, "one day we will awake to find that we have socialism. . . . We will spend our sunset years telling our children and our children's children what it was like in America when men were free." The record asked doctors' wives to invite their friends, serve coffee, play Reagan's message, and then write letters to Congress opposing government health insurance. Congress turned down the program, although another version passed four years later and is now known as Medicare.

In 1993, the Health Insurance Association of America aired television ads opposing President Bill Clinton's health plan. The ads featured "Harry and Louise," a pleasant middle-aged couple, concerned that national health insurance would create a bureaucratic monster and wreck their health care. "They [the Washington bureaucrats] choose," intones a voice at the end of the ad. "You lose." The national media reran the ads on television, described them in newspapers, and discussed them on radio. Congress soon buried the Clinton health proposal.

In 2009, Sarah Palin posted a Facebook entry attacking President Barack Obama's health care plan, then being debated in Congress. "The America I know and love is not one in which my parents or my baby with Down Syndrome will have to stand in front of Obama's 'death panel' so his bureaucrats can decide . . . whether they are worthy of health care. Such a system is downright evil." Palin's "death panel" charge went viral. Talking heads, bloggers, tweeters, radio shock jocks, editorial writers, members of Congress, and citizens all repeated the phrase. Although health reform eventually won, the Palin post helped galvanize opponents who kept right on fighting to repeal the law.

Each snapshot captures the media technology of a different era—and the politics they have channeled. In 1961, a recording reached an elite audience, which responded by mailing letters to Congress. In 1993, a TV ad ran in select markets and then spread via talking television heads. In 2009, a posting

see for yourself 7.1

Go online to hear Reagan's "Operation Coffee Cup" recording.

see for yourself 7.2

Go online to see the Harry and Louise ad.

● *Media reporters swarm a politician.*

instantly reached millions of Facebook friends and Twitter followers, generating reaction in both new formats (blogs, tweets, texts) and traditional ones (newspapers and magazines, radio, TV). Three major changes mark the evolution of issue campaigns across the last half-century:

- First, *the media keeps delivering information faster and faster.*
- Second, *today's media includes many more voices and formats.*
- Third, *the new media permits the public to be much more active.* You can comment on a Facebook posting more easily (and in more ways) than you could respond to a record in 1961 or a TV commercial in 1993.

What is the media?* It is all the ways people get information about politics and the wider world: television, radio, newspapers, Internet searches, blogs,

---

BY THE NUMBERS *The Media*

Number of daily newspapers in print in the United States in 1850: **254**
Number in 1900: **2,226**
Approximate number today: **1,400**
Expected number in 2020, according to the Congressional Research Service: **700**
Estimated number of African American–owned newspapers: **200**
Number of African American–owned newspapers that still print daily editions: **0**

Percentage of Republicans and Democrats who called the media "biased" in 1989: **25**
Percentage of Republicans who say so in 2012: **49**
Percentage of Democrats who say so in 2012: **32**

Number of channels in most homes outside of major cities in 1960: **3**
Number of television channels received by the average home today: **118.6**
Number of households reached by NBC: **112,770,700**
Number reached by the largest Spanish-language network: **57,950,000**
Number reached by the largest Christian network: **68,940,000**
Rank of Walt Disney, Rupert Murdoch's News Corporation, and Time Warner among all the media companies of the world: **1, 2, 3**

Percentages of African Americans, Hispanics, and whites who report being active on social network sites, according to a Pew study on the media: **71, 72, 58**
Percentage of each who report blogging: **22, 13, 14**
Percentage of 18- to 29-year-olds who use the Internet as their major news source: **65**
Percentage of those over 65 who do: **14**

Facebook, Twitter, Tumblr, and more. It is the major information connection between citizens and government.

Every change in the media affects politics. The rise of radio, television, and the Internet each had a profound impact on American politics. Fifty years ago, everyone heard the same newscast and took part in the same debate. Today, each position on the political spectrum tunes in to its own news source and links to its own network. A key question looms above the rising **new media**: Does it enhance democracy? Diminish it? Or perhaps it does some of both?

Who are we? From the very start of this book, we have seen that the United States is an immense, ongoing argument over political ideas. The media is what brings the people into the debates; it is the great link between leaders and citizens. The national media reflects America itself: raucous, fast changing, multilingual, multicultural, forceful, rich, loud, and lucrative. It broadcasts in many languages at home. It broadcasts America to the world.

New media: On-demand access to information and entertainment on digital devices that also features interactive participation with content. Arose in late twentieth century.

American Media Today: Traditional Formats Are Declining

Media technology changes quickly, and each change remakes the connections between citizens and their leaders. The media affects the news we get, the arguments we hear, and the deliberations we engage in.

Where People Go for News

Our lead story is simple. Fifty years ago, three national networks and the daily paper delivered essentially the same news to a largely passive audience. News broadcasts ran once each evening, for a half hour; two networks (later, three) dominated the news, and there were very few differences between their shows. Most households subscribed to one paper. Your grandparents' choices were simple: to tune in or not. Today, new technologies give Americans a host of options that are shaking up both media and government. This story—rapid media change with major consequences for politics and democracy—is nothing new. It has marked media advances throughout American history. Figure 7.1 summarizes where people have been going for their news over the last ten years.

---

* Properly speaking, *media* is the plural of *medium*—usually defined as *the way we convey something*. We use the term, media—meaning mass communication—as a singular noun in keeping with the way the language is evolving.

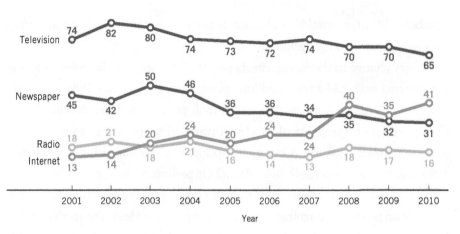

● **Figure 7.1** *Reliable sources. The percentage of Americans who get their national and international news from each medium. (Pew Research)*

As you can see, television remains the top source of news for most Americans. However, the audience is declining; TV was the chief source of news for 82 percent of the public in 2002 and fell to 66 percent by the end of the decade. Newspapers and magazines are crashing; they've lost a third of their readers in the past decade—as well as many of their advertisers. Radio hangs on; almost everyone listens (especially in the car), and a faithful few consider it their major source of news.

The biggest change is the rise of the Internet, which seizes more of the media pie every year. New online technologies expand the net's reach. Almost half the public (47 percent) gets some news through the phone or another mobile device. As you can see, when it comes to delivering the news, every technology is losing ground to the Internet.

The velocity of change is even greater when we focus on different segments of the American audience. The Internet is already the main source of news among adults under thirty, rising past television in 2010. As Figure 7.2 shows, 65 percent of young adults (eighteen to twenty-nine years old) consider the net their main news source. They were allowed to name up to two primary news sources, but only 52 percent chose television. In contrast, not many people over sixty-five (just 13 percent) go online for their news. The media's future rests in the hands (or on the thumbs) of the young—and the young are online.

What do these changes mean for the media, for politics, and for democracy? We can learn more by focusing on the developments in each of the major media.

Newspaper Decline

Newspapers have always been midwives to American democracy. The Federalist Papers (still the most important commentaries on our Constitution) first appeared as newspaper articles in the *New York Independent Journal*.

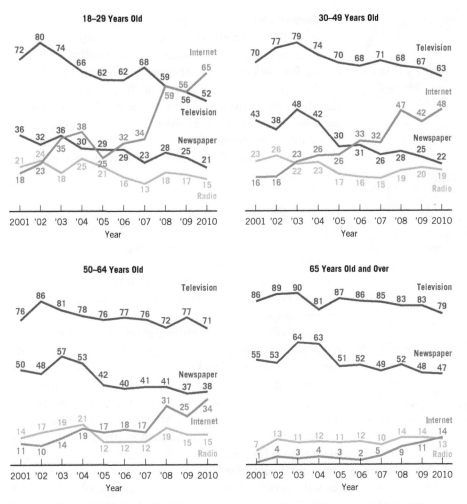

Figure 7.2 *Main news source, by user age. The younger the group, the more they rely on the Internet. Note: Figures add up to more than 100 percent because respondents could volunteer up to two main sources. (Pew Research)*

George Washington subscribed to ten newspapers. His most famous communication, the Farewell Address, was actually a letter addressed to his "fellow citizens" and printed in the papers.

The First Mass Media. In the 1830s, newspapers became the first **mass media**— just when the vote expanded to include all white men. (The definition of mass media is simple: media for the masses.) The papers cost one penny and reflected the raucous and often corrupt politics of the era. The *New York Herald* broke with the stodgy past, hired reporters to go out and dig up facts, and gave the readers just what they wanted—murder, fire, suicide, and crime. That disgusted the old elites but made the *Herald* the most widely read newspaper in the world. One New York rival, the *Tribune*, could boast Karl Marx as a foreign correspondent.

Mass media: Information and entertainment for broad popular audiences— including newspapers, radio, television.

Newspaper influence grew through the nineteenth century. The Spanish-American War, in 1898, is known as the first media war because blaring headlines blamed Spain for sinking an American battleship in Havana Harbor (there was no evidence of this) and helped bully the McKinley administration into the conflict. The papers developed comic strips to stretch their markets to the many immigrants who did not speak English well. By the turn of the century there were more than 2,200 papers in the United States.

The Rise and Fall of the Newspaper Business.

Local advertisers used the papers to reach their customers and generally gravitated to the newspaper with the largest circulation. As a result, most towns and cities had only one newspaper by the mid-twentieth century. Since they charged both the advertisers and the readers, almost every newspaper made money.

Even after the rise of radio and television, newspapers remained the major source for gathering and disseminating news, especially local news. Now, after more than two centuries at the center of the news media, the newspaper era is ending. The advertisers who guaranteed profits have migrated to the web; so have readers. By 2010, more people read their news online than in print—and most of them read it for free.

● *The power of the media, 1898. No one was sure exactly why the American battleship* Maine *exploded. An industrial accident remains likely. But the newspapers left no doubt that it was "Spanish treachery" and pushed a reluctant McKinley administration into war with Spain. Notice the prominent mention of Assistant Secretary Theodore Roosevelt. He would become a hero during the war—and the nation's next president.*

The result is a dramatic decline for big city newspapers. Between 2000 and 2010, American newspapers (and news magazines, also hard hit) slashed 30 percent of their staff. Some major papers stopped printing and moved entirely to the web. At least eight of the twenty largest papers have filed for bankruptcy, in cities from Philadelphia to San Jose. Most emerged from bankruptcy and are still operating, but their finances remain shaky.

Should We Worry?

There is much to celebrate about reading the news online. It is up-to-the-minute and invites active readers who can open a newspaper story, post a comment, click on a link connecting them to a *Huffington Post* report, and then surf over to YouTube for a clip from a TV network—or an eyewitness. The reader, not the editor, chooses the material. The Internet permits readers to respond, to share, to network, and to learn more.

Media analysts, however, see two problems. First, print journalists still do the basic reporting. Web-based outlets add opinions, background, links, and multiple perspectives, but it all begins with stories developed by reporters. If newspapers can't generate revenue, they won't survive. Where will we get the basic facts and stories? Will the reporting function migrate to another media institution?

Second, important stories may get lost. Newspapers always covered the "hot" stories (war, murder, and high school sports) along with less-exciting civic issues (such as school board meetings or wetland controversies). Since it was all one package, the popular stories paid for the civics lessons. As newspapers downsize staff and try to sell their stories by the piece on the web, there may be no way to subsidize coverage on limited-interest (but very important) issues like education.[1]

Radio Holds Steady

The first commercial radio stations sprang up in the 1920s. President Franklin Roosevelt seized the new technology during the Great Depression of the 1930s and delivered a weekly radio address, known as the Fireside Chat. The talks were informal, as if the president were talking to his listeners right by their own firesides. For the first time, the media offered a live connection between elected leaders and the public. Hearing Roosevelt's voice changed the relationship between Americans and their presidents. The people grew to expect a personal link. Indeed, political scientists call this development the rise of the **personal presidency**. The new media technology helped change the presidency itself.

Personal presidency: The idea that the president has a personal link to the public. Made possible by twentieth-century media.

The radio gave new immediacy to wartime reports during World War II—and to baseball games. It accelerated the velocity of news and information. The medium made the nation, and the world, a smaller place.

The radio era lasted just thirty years. By the mid-1950s, television displaced it. However, the radio still has political consequences. Conservative talk radio arose in the late 1980s after the Reagan administration cleared the way (we'll discuss the government connection below). Rush Limbaugh—a talented, loquacious, pugnacious host—syndicated his show, and a stream of other conservatives followed him onto the airwaves. Limbaugh pioneered the argument that became a foundation for conservative talk: the rest of the media is biased, so you have to dial in here. Liberals tried to counter with their

● Roosevelt used the new medium—radio—to speak directly to citizens in their homes. The result: the rise of the personal presidency. The change in the media helped introduce a change in our politics.

own talk shows, but their efforts foundered—perhaps because liberals are less likely to complain that the media is biased.

The main demographic for talk radio is middle-aged, white, male, and conservative.[2] One exception to radio's rightward tilt is National Public Radio (NPR). Its audience, over twenty-seven million listeners a week, is loyal and slowly growing. As news shows fade from the radio dial, NPR, which reaches 99 percent of the US population, takes up the slack. The listeners are older (forty-five to sixty-four), well educated (two and a half times more likely to have a college degree than the general public), and overwhelmingly identify as liberal. Roughly 15 percent of NPR's funds come from the federal government, prompting ferocious criticism from conservatives, who argue that taxpayers should not be supporting radio shows. Supporters respond that rural areas are most reliant on public funds and that they often have no other source of radio news.

Despite its fans and its controversies, radio does not matter much to most Americans. Just over 15 percent of the public call it their major news source and when asked about communications technologies that matter in their lives, the public ranks radio last.[3]

Television: From News to Infotainment

Television came onto the American scene in the 1950s and revolutionized both entertainment and politics. President John F. Kennedy sensed TV's power and gave the first live press conference in February 1961. An incredible sixty-five million people—one in three Americans—tuned in. The young, charismatic president was a natural TV performer, and, once again, a new media technology intensified the link between the people and their president.

The Rise of Cable.   Two networks, CBS and NBC, monopolized the television news business during the 1960s–1970s. Technology broke the monopoly. Cable stations came online in the 1980s and began to reach for small slices of the network audience. They lingered on the fringe of the media until 1991 when an upstart network, CNN, showed live video of allied rockets screaming into Baghdad, the capital of Iraq, at the start of the first Gulf War. CNN introduced a new model: it reported news all day. It gathered footage from local stations around the country, which now had the technical capacity to produce their own videos; in exchange for the feeds, CNN shared its footage of breaking news with local stations. No more waiting until 6 p.m. for the national network news. A new format was born: the twenty-four-hour news cycle. Twenty years ago, the White House staff, and the reporters who covered them, all relaxed when the news cycle ended around 5 p.m. Today, the cycle never ends.

In 1996, Rupert Murdoch launched Fox News, a network with a conservative slant. As Republican viewers headed for Fox, other cable networks (most notably MSNBC) moved to the left and developed shows with a liberal spin.

Eventually, cable channels filled every niche along the political spectrum—Fox on the right, shows like *Hardball* with Chris Matthews in the center, and the *Rachel Maddow Show* and the *Colbert Report* on the left.

Infotainment. Before long, the line between news and entertainment began to evaporate. Late-night talk shows got into the political act. Hosts gleefully lacerated the political losers of the day. Politicians responded by lining up to participate. Senator John McCain, the Republican nominee for president in 2008, announced his candidacy on the *Late Show with David Letterman*—with bandleader Paul Shaffer in pink shades blasting out "Hail to the Chief."

Shows like *Letterman* mix politics and entertainment. One night the Republican frontrunner announces his candidacy for president. Another night it might be an actor like Megan Fox talking about her tattoos. Jon Stewart refined the formula by merging comedy, entertainment, political talk, and savvy media criticism on the *Daily Show*. Stewart himself pointed out the fading line between news and entertainment when he noted that his show airs on Comedy Central and the lead-in features puppets. When asked about their major source of news in a recent Pew poll, young viewers (eighteen to twenty-nine years old) were as likely to tap the *Daily Show* as the network news shows.

The corporate setting helps blur the line between news, politics, and entertainment, a phenomenon now described as **infotainment**. The American news media is part of the entertainment industry. Consider the three national broadcast networks: Walt Disney owns ABC; National Amusements, a theater chain that also runs MTV, controls CBS. NBC is part of a conglomerate that includes Wet 'n Wild—Orlando, Universal Studios, and GM Appliance.

see for yourself 7.3

Go online to see Senator McCain's announcement (check out bandleader Paul Shaffer's pink shades). (Flash Required)

Infotainment: The blurred line between news and entertainment.

● *The line between news and entertainment has blurred. Here, Stephen Colbert (left) and Jon Stewart (right) in the Restore Sanity rally in Washington, DC.*

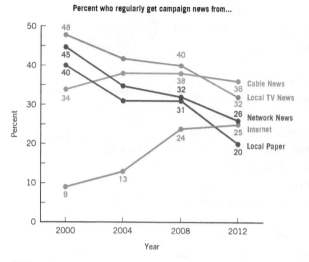

Percent who regularly get campaign news from...

● **Figure 7.3** *Campaign news sources: the Internet grows in importance, cable TV holds steady, and others decline in popularity as sources of campaign news. (Pew Research)*

Univision, which broadcasts in Spanish, is the fifth-largest network and spans TV, radio, music, and websites. The institutional connection helps accelerate the trend to infotainment.

Amid this colorful scene, the network news steadily declines. In 2010, the three network nightly news shows lost 752,000 viewers (3.4 percent), and dropped another 2.2 percent in 2012.

More people report getting their political news from cable than from the networks (see Figure 7.3). Overall, the TV picture reflects the state of the entire American media. A single, shared view of the world has shattered. TV now runs the gamut from left to right and from formal news to frothy entertainment. The lines between entertainment and news continue to vanish.

Movies: Mirroring America

We usually think of cinema as pure entertainment, but it often engages politics. Movies hold a mirror to society. They reflect emerging ideas, construct shared images, promulgate metaphors, and generate support for emerging ideas—sometimes in unexpected ways.

Sometimes a film sets off a great debate about just what Americans believe. In 1989, Oliver Stone set out to satirize investment banking in *Wall Street*. In the movie's classic scene, the master manipulator, Gordon Gekko, gives a speech that ends with a ringing endorsement: "Greed is good. . . . Greed, you mark my words, will save . . . that malfunctioning corporation called the USA." Soon traditional business-news sources—*Newsweek*, *Forbes*, the *Wall Street Journal*—were all debating the proposition. Is greed a social problem or is it the energy at the heart of our economic system? Twenty years later, *The Social Network* used the story of Facebook founder Mark Zuckerberg to raise the old question of greed (this time, for status) among a new generation of entrepreneurs.

What Do You Think?

●.. Movies That Take a Stand

Pick one film and add it to those we've listed. Describe how it takes a stand on some important issue. Is it insightful in its depiction of American politics and culture?

Films that appear to simply entertain—and even exploit—can reflect cultural currents. In 1971, after the civil rights movement had ended, a series of black films came into vogue. Led by *Shaft* and *Sweet, Sweetback's Baadasssss Song*, the films featured all-black casts led by tough, arrogant, highly sexualized characters (male and female) operating in a hazy territory between rough justice and crime. The blaxploitation (a word that combines black and exploitation) genre played to black, urban audiences—with some films crossing over to white audiences—who cheered the cheeky treatment of long-taboo subjects. Black critics both applauded and deplored the blaxploitation genre, but the movies marked a new phase—both angry and liberated—in American racial discourse.

American politics is full of important debates about national identity and values. Films offer a different way to present arguments, project views, and build a collection of shared cultural images. From *Philadelphia* (on homophobia, homosexuality, and AIDS) to *Wag the Dog* (on launching wars to boost presidential popularity), from *Norma Rae* (on union organizing) to *The Hunger Games* (on tyranny in the age of hyped up media spectacle), film can shape the way we talk and think about important issues.

THE BOTTOM LINE

- Thirty years ago, a few outlets—three networks, the local newspaper—delivered roughly the same news. Americans had no real choices about what news media to follow. Today, media outlets cater to every perspective—left, right, and center. Americans no longer share a single source of news.
- In the past, the rise of new media—newspapers, radio, and television—changed the nature of news reporting and altered political institutions like the presidency.
- The traditional newspaper model is in serious decline. This poses a challenge because newspaper reporters still research most of the breaking news. Network television, local television, and cable are all losing ground as the place Americans go for news. The new media is taking their place—especially among young people. What will be the political effects of this change?

The Rise of the New Media

In the spring of 2011, an impoverished street vendor in Tunisia set himself on fire after a government official slapped him and suspended his license. Other people had committed protest suicides with no effect. This time the man's relatives took to the street "with a rock in one hand and a cell phone in another," as one of them put it. They posted videos of their protest—and the brutal police reaction—on Facebook; Al Jazeera, the Arabic television network, picked up the videos and aired them. The images turned small protests into massive demonstrations that eventually toppled the government of Tunisia, then spread to Egypt (where another government fell), Libya (another fallen government), Bahrain, Yemen, Syria, and Iran. The demonstrators told their stories, organized rallies, and communicated with the world through texts, Facebook, and Twitter. The old regimes had held on to power, in part, by ruthlessly controlling news and information. Now, the new social media burst through the censorship.

What effects will the new social media have in the United States? We have already seen how the Internet is shaking up traditional ways of delivering the news. Past media revolutions, from the penny press to radio to cable television, all changed the relationship between the people and the government. What effects will these latest technologies produce?

Some observers predict a new era of citizen participation. Others take a gloomier view and warn about eroding news coverage, fragmented communities, and viral malice.

Scenario 1: Rebooting Democracy

First, new-media optimists begin by pointing out how *active* Internet users are. Television, radio, and newspapers deliver the news to passive audiences. On the Internet, people seek out the news, follow links, and access a world of information. Advocates have a term for the new activism: **clicktivism**—democracy enhanced through the click of a mouse.

Clicktivism: Democracy enhanced through the click of a mouse.

Second, people can easily respond. The web offers multiple opportunities for talking back: tick the "Like" icon, fire off an irate e-mail, launch a blog, or communicate with a network of like-minded people. Democracies, when they're working well, *hear* their people. The new media gives the people many new ways to be heard.

Third, as we have seen, the new media turns everyone into a potential reporter. Traditional news always awaited the arrival of a camera team. Now anyone can record an event on their phone, post it to Facebook or YouTube, and offer it to a media outlet. News items that traditional programs would have missed now feed into the media from every corner of the country. The political equilibrium changes when the public actually sees police officers beating a black motorist or a politician casually tossing off a sexist slur.

Fourth, the web vastly expands the range of commentary. Traditional media limits punditry to a small circle of well-known personalities and authors. Today anyone with something to say can launch a blog, send a tweet to dozens or hundreds (or millions) of followers, or post opinions on Facebook. Some have had terrific success. *Daily Kos*, launched by Markos (Kos) Moulitsas Zúniga in 2003, boasts 2.5 million visitors per month. Nate Silver's 2008 election blog, *fivethirtyeight*, became so popular that the *New York Times* made him a regular contributor. Other familiar sites include *The Drudge Report* (conservative), *The Huffington Post* (liberal), and Glenn Reynolds's *Instapundit* (conservative).

Fifth, the web offers new ways for politicians and parties to reach out. Barack Obama refined the technique and turned his 2008 campaign into a kind of movement. By the 2010 midterms, Republicans—and especially Tea Party conservatives—were using the web to launch a movement of their own.

Finally, new media appears to be overcoming the "digital divide" discussed in the last chapter. At first, minorities appeared to have less access, but online demographics are changing. African Americans have caught up to whites on Facebook and are now more likely to tweet and blog. Latinos still lag, but the gap is closing (see Figure 7.4). A recent study of twelve-year-olds found that the most intense users of the Internet in the United States were African American females.[4]

In sum, optimists argue that new media promotes active users, links people to one another, spreads the news collected by ordinary people, permits citizens to bypass the talking heads and make their own comments, and offers politicians a powerful tool to mobilize, connect, and collect. None of these factors insures that the new media will help refresh American democracy. But they suggest a great deal of promise.

Scenario 2: More Hype and Danger than Democratic Renaissance

All this potential, however, might be squandered. Technological change might not enhance democracy, and, according to some skeptics, is already harming it. Critics level three charges against the new media.[5]

First, the new media relies on old media, which it is choking off. Yes, the new media generates important stories—like Sarah Palin's "death panels" on Facebook or the Tunisian uprising powered by cell phones. But

Figure 7.4 *Who is socially active online? A view by race. (Pew Research)*

Note: Blogging data from Jan. 2010, social networking and Twitter data from May 2010.

these stories—like almost every other story—became important when traditional media ran them. Newspapers, networks, and cable channels still develop and spread most news. The list of top fifteen news websites includes many familiar players: six newspapers, four television networks, and even a radio network (see Table 7.1). True, three of the top six sites—Yahoo!News, Google News, and Huffington Post—are Internet companies. These sites rely heavily on traditional news organizations for their headline stories, however. We clicked on Yahoo!News on a random May 2013 morning. Of the eleven top featured stories—with topics ranging from bombings in Afghanistan's capital to a Washington State bridge collapse to New Jersey bars caught selling rubbing alcohol as whiskey—all eleven were taken from mainstream news sources, like Reuters, Associated Press, National Journal, and ABC News.

Search engines and web portals link largely to stories posted by traditional news sources—the *New York Times*, the *Washington Post*, CNN, and ABC. But here is the bad news: the portals and search engines grab the revenue. The web relies on the same old news sources but avoids paying them. The people who gather the news—for old and new media alike—find it difficult to get paid for their services. As they cut their own costs, news coverage gets

Table 7.1 Most Visited News Websites (May 2013)

RANK	DOMAIN	UNIQUE VISITORS
1	Yahoo! News	110 million
2	CNN	74 million
3	MSNBC	73 million
4	Google News	65 million
5	New York Times	59.5 million
6	Huffington Post	54 million
7	Fox News	32 million
8	Washington Post	25 million
9	Los Angeles Times	24.9 million
10	Daily Mail (UK)	24.8 million
11	Reuters	24 million
12	ABC News	20 million
13	USA Today	18 million
14	BBC News (UK)	17 million
15	Drudge Report	14 million
Source: eBizMBA, Nielsen.		

Selling Old Products via New Media

Once upon a time, if the folks who sold milk wanted to spread the word about their product, they ran an ad in the local paper. Since lots of people read the paper, the ad could be pretty boring and still reach a lot of eyes.

Today there are so many sources of news that it is difficult to grab attention. Imagine you are a dairy producer hoping to boost purchases of milk. Your advertising rep shows up with a new, attention-getting ad for one of milk's newly discovered health benefits. The agency has built a microsite called everythingidoiswrong.org. To attract an audience, they've opted for crude comedy. The site pretends to advise men how to deal with their partner's PMS. The tagline: "Milk Can Help Reduce the Symptoms of PMS."

Do you green-light this, um, unconventional approach? The California Milk Processor Board faced exactly this decision—and decided to give the ad campaign a try. Site visitors were not amused, and they let the advertisers know it. "Wrong," texted one visitor to the web page. "Milk ad campaign blames PMS, insults women." The Board, stung by the backlash, shut down the site and replaced it with an apology. The mainstream media picked up the story and spread it, further embarrassing the campaign's sponsor.

Moral: The crowded new media environment leads to strange antics designed to attract attention. But here's the positive side. The eyeballs can talk back. After just one day, the website disappeared because visitors told the milk people their idea of humor was offensive.[6]

thinner and less reliable—and the old media's downward spiral affects most of the stories that people read on their laptops and cell phones.

Second, the skeptics dismiss the web's promise for elevating new voices. Individuals can write all they want, but few will actually be read. There is no denying the reach of Matt Drudge or *Daily Kos*. But they are rare exceptions. Look again at the measure of Nate Silver's success: his posts now run in the *New York Times*, the essential old media.

Third, the web incubates lies, malice, and falsehood. Rumors start and spread. Our hyperpartisan era puts a premium on running people down—and the Internet makes it easy. For example, even before President Obama was elected, the web buzzed with stories that he is Muslim and that he was not born in the United States. (He is a Christian and was born in Hawaii.) Posting a certified copy of Obama's birth certificate, newspaper announcements of the birth, and a long-form birth certificate did not end the falsehoods flying through cyberspace. Racism, anti-Semitism, misogyny, and character assassination all flourish in the hyperconnected, often anonymous new media. The democratic promise of the web comes with a dark side.[7]

In sum, critics worry that the Internet and the new media will have a corrosive effect on American democracy. They point out that news on the web is still dominated by the same traditional news organizations, which provide content while getting a shrinking share of revenue. Yes, people can post and blog, but not many develop an audience. Finally, the speed and connectivity of the web can lead to misinformation and malice as easily as communication and community.

THE BOTTOM LINE

- The new media is spurring a revolution that is changing the way Americans produce and process news and political information.
- A new era of activism and connection may refresh American democracy. Or troubling developments may diminish it.
- Whether new media enhances our communal life or diminishes it is, ultimately, in our own hands.

Is the Media Biased?

"What you have to do in order to earn the approval of the people in the media," declared Rush Limbaugh, is "to adopt their causes," such as global warming. "And it really helps if you take a position opposite me." Conservative media draws strength from a furious charge: the mainstream media is too liberal (Figure 7.5).[8]

On the other side, liberals also charge the media with bias. In his book *What Liberal Media?* Eric Alterman complains that the news corps rarely challenges the rich, the powerful, or the status quo. The media breathlessly tracks the stock market but rarely tells stories about the rise of inequality. It reports the Washington food fight and ignores labor issues, child poverty, or homelessness. All the Right's hoopla about media bias is, from this liberal perspective, a ruse to cow the mainstream media. And it works: mainstream correspondents respond by leaning over backward to prove they are not biased. One out of three Democrats believes the media is biased against them.[9]

Which is it? A powerful left-wing media out to destroy conservatives? Or timid reporters, editors, and producers, collectively bullied by the Right? We

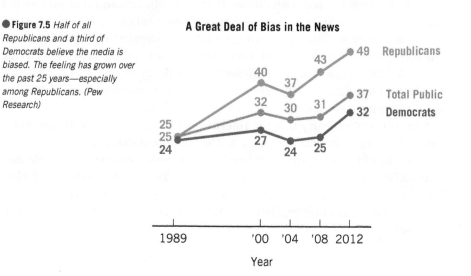

● **Figure 7.5** *Half of all Republicans and a third of Democrats believe the media is biased. The feeling has grown over the past 25 years—especially among Republicans. (Pew Research)*

A Great Deal of Bias in the News

49 Republicans
43
40
37
37 Total Public
32
30 31 32 Democrats
25
25
24
27
24 25

1989   '00 '04 '08 2012

Year

suggest that the media is indeed biased, but not in the way either side imagines. The largest bias comes from the media's real purpose: making money. Media outlets print or say or film things that will draw an audience.

Reporters Are Democrats

Conservatives are correct about the press corps's personal attitudes. Reporters in the mainstream media are more liberal than the country as a whole. Roughly 85 percent of the press corps calls itself liberal or moderate, compared to about 60 percent of the population. Although most reporters call themselves moderates (especially those in the local media, where the number runs well above 60 percent), very few are self-described conservatives. Moreover, the press corps tends to vote for Democratic presidential candidates.

However, dozens of studies about election campaigns fail to show a systematic bias toward Democratic candidates. Scholars have searched for bias in coverage, in statements, and in the kinds of stories that are aired. Some studies in some elections did find favoritism. Overall, however, the media does not lean either to Democrats or to Republicans during election campaigns.

There have been fewer studies of media bias outside of elections. Perhaps reporters' views creep into coverage of policy fights or presidential speeches. We don't have hard evidence about that. However, there is empirical proof of a much deeper bias that runs through the news media—the need to draw a larger audience.

Profits Drive the News Industry

What does the media actually sell? It is not news about government actors or election campaigns. Media sells its audience to advertisers. As a result, the prime directive is to expand the audience. When ratings rise, the media source prospers; when they fall, networks replace anchors and newspapers cut staff. These financial realities give the news media a strong incentive to pitch its own politics near the views of its audience. For the large networks, that means the political center, where most Americans are comfortable. That's why both Left and Right complain about bias; the center *is* to the left of conservatives and to the right of liberals. At the same time, each publication and each network seeks its own audience. More conservative communities usually get more conservative newspapers, and the current media is, as we have seen, divided into strong partisan niches.

In short, the market forces each news source toward the politics of its audience. That pressure, however, is just the start of the market's influence on the media. Other market biases include the search for drama, conflict, and scandal.

Drama Delivers Audiences

There's not much excitement in a school board meeting or a health care proposal. Miners trapped below the earth, on the other hand, pull people to their televisions and radios. A good drama must have a narrative arc with a beginning, middle, and end. It has a protagonist (the miners), pathos (anxious

● *The rule for local news: If it bleeds, it leads.*

spouses), a villain (the coal company or the government regulators), drama (will they be rescued before they run out air?), an ending (tired but jubilant miners hugging their families), and a take-home message (we need to worry about mine safety).

Local news gets much of its drama out of crime. A classic rule of thumb guides the local TV news: "If it bleeds, it leads." Many good things may have happened in the city, but the lead story features the day's most grisly event. The images are familiar to the point of cliché—the breathless reporter live on the scene, yellow tape blocking the area, grim-faced cops or firefighters in the background, weeping relatives in a daze, and perhaps a blank-faced perpetrator blinking into the camera.

The need for drama transforms election coverage as well. It rarely focuses on the issues, an audience turnoff. Instead, it is about the drama of two protagonists, their families, their strategies, their dirty tricks, and their blunders. Elections have a built-in narrative arc with all the familiar features: a *beginning* (the candidates throw their hats into the ring), a *middle* (who is ahead? who had the best week?), a *conclusion* (someone wins), and a *take-home message* (the loser had a fatal flaw that other candidates should avoid).

Check out your favorite news website. Can you see the dramatic narrative that frames the lead story? Pundits criticize the news for lacking substance. However, as a student of political science, you have learned to examine the *institution* and its incentives. The media, seeking a large audience to serve to advertisers, covers whatever attracts most attention. Simply calling for serious coverage will not change the incentives in the media market.

Sex and Scandal

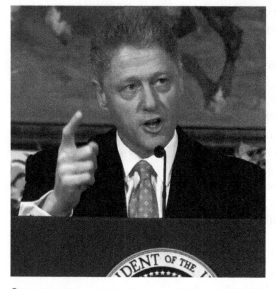

● *President Clinton: "I did not have sexual relations with that woman."*

Nothing attracts an audience like scandals—and the bigger the name attached to it, the bigger the media bonanza. President Bill Clinton's sexual involvement with a White House intern received enormous coverage. A scan of sixty-five newspapers revealed that they averaged more than a story a day for the entire year. During the coverage, CNN quadrupled its average rating. By the end of the year, 97 percent of the public could identify the president's alleged lover, while only 12 percent knew who was chief justice of the United States. Likewise, businessman Herman Cain briefly enjoyed a lead in the polls during the 2012 Republican primaries—but had to withdraw when multiple allegations of sexual harassment made headlines.[10]

The Skeptical Media

Some other media biases have to do less with market and more with the profession of journalism. Two are especially powerful: skepticism and objectivity. Back in the early 1960s, Washington reporters were a small, white, male club with a code that winked at extramarital affairs in the White House or fall-down drunks serving in Congress. Then a series of events transformed the media's stance toward powerful men and women: the moral intensity of the civil rights movement, administration efforts to manipulate the press during the Vietnam War, and the **Watergate scandal** all made the old accommodations seem irresponsible. How could reporters go easy on segregationists or liars?

Watergate was especially significant in fostering skepticism. Reporters investigated a burglary of Democratic Party headquarters that led directly to the White House. President Nixon had secretly taped conversations in the Oval Office and, pursuing the case of the botched burglary, the Supreme Court forced the release of the tapes. Their content stunned Americans. Nixon had always seemed a bit sanctimonious. Now the public could hear him order aides to "stonewall" the Watergate investigations. Even more shocking, the presidential tapes bristled with ethnic slurs, anti-Semitism, and foul language. (The newspaper transcripts were full of the notation, "expletive deleted.")

Reporters redefined their roles. Rather than acting as chummy insiders, they became skeptics, aiming to pierce through official propaganda and find the hidden truth. Relations between press and politician turned adversarial. Each time the members of the press felt misled by an administration, their skepticism grew. For example, Bill Clinton claimed he did not have sex with an intern. (He did.) George W. Bush insisted that Iraq owned dangerous weapons that threatened the United States. (It did not.) The reporter's gold standard became uncovering lies or bad behavior. When reporters find some dirt, the whole media races after the scandal in a breathless pack.

The Fairness Bias

The effort to be fair introduces an unexpected bias. Reporters energetically try to present both sides of each issue. However, when issues do not have two equal sides, the effort creates the impression of a debate that does not exist.

see for yourself 7.4

Go online to listen to two infamous denials: Richard Nixon declares he is not a crook.

Watergate scandal: A failed effort by Republican operatives to break into Democratic Party headquarters in the Watergate office complex in Washington, DC; tapes revealed that President Nixon attempted to cover up the event—costing him the presidency.

see for yourself 7.5

President Clinton claims he did not have sex with "that woman."

THE BOTTOM LINE

- Both conservatives and liberals complain of media bias. However, the media generally reflects the politics of its audience.
- The media's deepest bias comes from the need to win ratings and appeal to advertisers. That puts an emphasis on drama, scandal, and conflict.
- The result emphasizes partisan political divisions.

How Governments Shape the Media

We have seen how technology constantly changes the media which, in turn, changes politics. In this section we examine how political rules shape the development of the media.

Democratic nations organize their media in three different ways: First, the government can fund the media. This **public ownership** model is familiar in many nations—but not the United States (see Table 7.2 next page). Second, the government can *regulate* the media to ensure that it operates in the public interest. Third, the government can stand aside and let the *market* guide the media; the assumption in the market model is that private companies will give consumers (and the advertisers) what they want.

Public ownership: A situation in which media outlets are run by the government and paid for by tax dollars.

The First Amendment Protects Print Media from Government Regulation

You have already encountered the primary political rule governing print media—the *First Amendment*: "Congress shall make no law . . . abridging the freedom of speech or of the press." As we saw in Chapter 4, the Supreme Court has been strict about forbidding government interference with the press. It is very difficult to censor news (known as prior restraint), to convict someone of slander or libel (spoken or written lies), to restrict pornography, or to forbid hate speech.

Market forces impose the limits that do exist. American newspapers, paid for by local advertisers, generally reflect local mores. They are tame compared with, for example, the British tabloids. The Internet, of course, operates in a different kind of market—unmoored to local communities and their values. The result, of course, is a much wilder format—so far, an almost unregulated media frontier.

Regulating Broadcasters

Radio and television fall into a separate category. They have been subject to government regulations from the start. As radio stations spread in the 1930s, their signals began to interfere with one another. In 1934 the Franklin Roosevelt administration created the Federal Communications Commission (FCC) to referee the industry. The agency began with a political philosophy: the airwaves belong to the public. The FCC would license stations on a given frequency—meaning no more overlapping signals—but in exchange, stations were required to be "socially responsible." When a station secured or renewed its license, it had to show that it operated in the public's interest. When television emerged, the FCC expanded its jurisdiction to include it.

In 1949, the FCC issued an important regulation, the **fairness doctrine**. The fairness doctrine required radio and TV stations to give equal time to each side of a public issue.

Fairness doctrine: Regulation that required media outlets to devote equal time to opposite perspectives.

The fairness doctrine reflected the era's expectations: sober, nonpartisan coverage of news and politics. It also reflected the technology, which offered very limited media choices. Finally, the fairness doctrine rested on the New

Table 7.2 Public Television—Abroad and at Home

	DAILY AUDIENCE (BY NATION)	TAXES PAID FOR PUBLIC TV PER PERSON
Most advanced democracies provide public subsidies to media; the US is almost entirely private-market.		
Denmark	69 %	$130
UK (BBC, Ch 4)	50 %	$90 (BBC only)
Germany	40 %	$130
France	30 %	$51
Australia	19 %	$34
Netherlands	35 %	$50
Norway	32 %	$133
Canada	9 % (English speaking) 17 % (French speaking)	$30
Japan	17 %	$54
United States	**1.2 %**	**$3.75**
Source: Benson and Powers, Public Media and Political Independence.[11]		

Deal's philosophy: the airwaves belonged to the public and ought to be guided by the public interest. Each station or channel should offer balanced political coverage and concern itself with the good of the public.

In the 1980s, the Ronald Reagan administration challenged the entire idea of public responsibility enforced by regulatory agencies. It promoted a different political philosophy: end government regulations and let the consumers use the market to enforce what they value. The FCC repealed the fairness doctrine in 1983. When Democrats captured the Senate back from Republicans in 1987, they voted to restore the fairness doctrine, but President Reagan vetoed the legislation.

The consequences were enormous. Under the fairness doctrine, each talk show with a point of view would have to be balanced by another talk show from the opposite perspective. A station that broadcast conservatives like Rush Limbaugh would be required to air an equal amount of liberal programming. Repealing the rule opened the door to conservative talk radio, Fox News, MSNBC, and the rest.

Technology, operating within the new legal rules, transformed the media. Within a decade, changes in both radio (the migration of music to FM freed up the AM band for talk shows) and television (the introduction of cable technology and the proliferation of stations) enabled the media landscape we have today: a rich and raucous menu of news and politics that reaches across the political spectrum.

Protecting Competition

The market model is based on competition. What happens if one corporation captures too much of the market? Might it stifle consumer choice? The question arose when corporations moved to control companies across different media markets—print, radio, and television. Some observers warned that a few companies might come to dominate—and stifle the marketplace of ideas. The top two radio companies, Clear Channel and CBS, control so many stations that they broadcast to a larger audience (263 million strong) than all twenty-four of the remaining radio networks combined. Consolidation, from this perspective, threatens free speech and fair debate.

Those who favor deregulation respond that today's media takes so many different forms, from radio stations to iPads, that stiff competition for consumer attention is inevitable. The **Telecommunications Act of 1996** reflected this second view and permitted many forms of cross-ownership. However, the debate about controlling media consolidation lingers on.

Telecommunications Act of 1996: The major congressional overhaul of communications law that opened the door to far more competition by permitting companies to compete in multiple media markets—radio, television, magazines, etc.

THE BOTTOM LINE

- Democratic nations organize their media in three ways: government ownership, regulation, and markets. The United States has relied on the latter two, regulation and markets.
- The First Amendment protects print media from most government regulation.
- Broadcast media in the United States was originally regulated by agencies like the FCC, which imposed the fairness doctrine—a reflection of a less partisan era.
- Deregulation and the rise of multiple media—interacting with new technology that permitted many channels—have created the spectrum of perspectives and views that mark American media today. This contributes to the high conflict that marks contemporary politics.

● How the Media Shapes Politics

The media influences not just how we talk, but what we talk *about*. It sets the agenda and frames our politics. This section describes how.

News Stories Reinforce Existing Beliefs

Imagine that you're a Republican with lots of Democratic friends. You come across a detailed news story that crushes one of their cherished beliefs. You send it to them with a snide comment—and what happens? Rather than changing their minds, the story simply reinforces what they believe. Researchers have discovered that new information rarely influences people who already have strongly held opinions. Instead, new information reinforces existing opinions regardless of the content of the story. Many people find the conclusion surprising: news stories do not change the opinions of people who pay the most attention to the news.

However, news stories can have an impact on people who have not already made up their minds. About a third of the American public does not have strong political commitments, is less likely to follow the news, and often does not vote. But this group *is* open to influence by the media. Here is a paradox: the news media is most likely to influence the people who pay the least attention to it. Since this group does not follow the news very closely, only news stories with a "**loud signal**" are likely to reach them and influence their views. A loud signal means that a news story gets *broad media coverage* and delivers an *unambiguous message*.

Some stories get wall-to-wall coverage. You cannot turn on a TV or log on without hearing all about them. The examples that began this chapter were all efforts to create such a message during a health care debate: Medicare equals socialism; Obama's health plan means death panels. These stories did not change minds that were already made up—on the contrary, if you supported the plan, the attack likely increased your support. However, these attacks did influence uncommitted, independent voters who were not paying much attention.

● *If a story has a loud signal, they will all be talking about it, as they are here, on* The View. *The stories everyone talks about are the news items that reach undecided voters.*

Loud signal: Media stories with very broad coverage and an unambiguous message.

The Political Agenda

Media outlets may have limited influence on what politically savvy people think, but editors and reporters have enormous influence on what they think *about*. The media leaders listen to the great American political din and pluck out one or two stories to headline and a dozen others for the second tier. Those become the topics that politicians address, Congress investigates, talk shows debate, and you discuss and tweet and blog. When an issue commands such attention, we say it is on the political agenda or **policy agenda**. And this is generally the first step to political action. If something you care about—homelessness, immorality, or animal cruelty—is not being discussed, it is unlikely that political leaders will pay attention to it. The first step to political action is to get your issue onto the national agenda.

The surest route onto the agenda is through the media. Setting the agenda is one of the most important influences the news media has on American politics. Politicians, think tanks, interest groups, citizens, and experts all try to influence the agenda. Sometimes they succeed; far more often they fail. Large demonstrations in major American cities against the

Policy agenda: The issues that the media covers, the public considers important, and politicians address. Setting the agenda is the first step in political action.

Iraq war in 2003 got scant mention. Three years later, another set of demonstrations in support of immigrant rights caught the media's attention. As the news reverberated, the demonstrations multiplied and grew. The coverage put immigration issues squarely on the national agenda. Of course, as we'll see in Chapter 14, getting onto the agenda is only the first step in the long political process. How does the media pick the issues it will emphasize? You already know the answer to that: drama, conflict, a narrative, heroes, villains, and a story that sells.

Does the public focus on an issue because the media covers it? Or does the media cover an issue because the public is focused on it? In a classic study, two political scientists asked subjects what issues they thought were most important. Then the researchers broke the subjects into groups and, over four days, gave each group a different version of the nightly news emphasizing different issues—pollution, defense, inflation, and so forth. For the most part, the issues that the subjects saw on the news became more important in their own minds.[12] When the media focuses on an issue, its importance—or salience—generally rises in the public perception.

Priming the Public

Priming: Affecting voters' or poll respondents' perception of candidates or public officials by raising issues that are perceived to enhance or diminish the candidates.

The issues that rise onto the agenda and dominate the news affect public perceptions of candidates and officials. This influence is known as **priming**. For example, because the Republican Party is identified with smaller government, stories about government incompetence *prime* the public to see the world through Republican eyes. Stories about the plight of the elderly or the hard-working poor get voters thinking along Democratic Party lines.

Priming is a very subtle form of political bias, because media outlets do not need to explicitly favor one side or the other. Rather, they simply run stories on an important topic—which plays to the strength (or weakness) of one party or one candidate. Candidates are evaluated by the kinds of issues that are featured in the news.

Racial images have an especially powerful priming effect. Certain programs—"welfare" or "food stamps"—immediately raise negative, highly racialized associations. When Newt Gingrich, running for the Republican presidential nomination in 2012, termed Barack Obama "the food stamp president," he was widely accused of priming: he hoped to diminish his rival by simply raising the subject of welfare programs and, by implication, race and poverty.

Framing the Issue

Framing: The way an issue is defined; every issue has many possible frames, each with a slightly different tilt in describing the problem and highlighting solutions.

There are many ways to cover an issue, and each offers a slightly different perspective. When the media chooses a particular slant, we say it is **framing** the issue. Obesity offers a simple example. Is obesity the result of individuals with poor self-control? Or does the problem come from the fast-food industry pushing unhealthy calories at children in order to make profits? Perhaps the real trouble lies not in body weight but in American culture's unrealistic (and even dangerous) body norms? Each of these approaches *frames* the issue in a different way. The framing, in turn, brings some solutions into focus and makes others irrelevant. If the problem is individual self-control, then regulating the fast-food industry is not the solution.

Often, media framing is invisible to most people because it simply reflects social conventions. The issue of equality was once framed as a problem concerning white men: Could they achieve the American dream in an industrial system devoted to profits? Later, great social movements rose up and reframed the issue as one that spoke directly to race, ethnicity, and gender.

Sometimes, the framing of an issue becomes part of the debate. For example, the Obama administration issued regulations that required employers to offer contraception as part of their health insurance coverage. Catholic organizations claimed that the ruling violated their religious beliefs. Then the battle over framing began. Republicans charged that the Obama administration was hostile to religion; the Democrats countered that the real Republican purpose was to attack contraception as part of a "war on women" designed to deny women legal access to birth control. The two sides were fighting over how to frame the issue: Was it about religious freedom? Or about an effort to limit contraception? Both sides felt they would benefit politically if they could frame the issue their way.

In short, the frame defines the nature of the problem, organizes potential solutions, and wipes out alternative policies. Media coverage plays a crucial role—often, *the* crucial role—in issue framing.

● *"Kicking Puppies": One way to frame the issue of wealth and poverty.*

THE BOTTOM LINE

- News stories generally do not change minds that are already made up, but a story with a loud, clear signal can influence the undecided.
- The media plays a vital role in setting the national agenda, priming voters to focus on issues that help or harm one side, and framing the way those issues are seen—and resolved.

see for yourself 7.6

Go online to see a long list of late-night political jokes.

● The Media's Electoral Connection

Every aspect of the media's influence on politics is on full display during election campaigns. David Letterman summarized the demand for drama after a primary debate in New Hampshire. "Did you folks see the debate in New

Hampshire over the weekend? Oh my god, dull. I mean they were so dull that today . . . New Hampshire changed its state slogan from "Live Free or Die" to "Please Shoot Me."[13] The usual emphasis on entertainment now places a particular focus on the horse race: Who is winning and why?

The Campaign as Drama

Media coverage has evolved and now devotes much less time to the candidate's speeches. In 1968, the average clip of a candidate speaking on the news, called a **sound bite**, went uninterrupted for over forty seconds. Today, the average clip has fallen to under eight seconds. After those eight seconds, the candidate's speech is simply backdrop for the anchor or the analyst. You might see the candidates gesture and move their lips, but those are just the visual for analysis and interpretation, often centered on (you guessed it!) why the candidate is winning or losing.

Throughout the campaign, reporters' antennae are always up for gaffes and hints of scandal. When one appears, the entire media throngs after it. Every speech and each debate are carefully combed over for blunders. In Chapter 8 we'll explore whether or not this media whirlwind really matters to election outcomes (the short answer is, rarely). However, the issue absorbs talent and energy. Effective campaigns develop rapid-response teams that can deal with whatever crisis gusts through the media on that day. George W. Bush dealt with allegations of cocaine use with a simple, firm answer: "When I was young and foolish, I was young and foolish." Newt Gingrich briefly vaulted to the top of the Republican pack in the 2012 primary when he turned a potential scandal (his second wife alleged that he asked her for an open marriage) into a raking assault on the media. "I think the destructive, vicious, negative nature of much of the news media," he said to roars of approval at one CNN debate, "makes it harder to govern this country, harder to attract decent people to run for public office, and I am appalled that you would begin a presidential debate on a topic like that." Gaffes and scandals are part of life on the campaign trail, and effective politicians learn how to blunt them—or even turn them to advantage.

Candidate Profiles

Campaign coverage often features a powerful narrative. The media sketches a profile of each candidate—simplistic, exaggerated, and very hard to escape. That image then shapes future coverage. Once the portrait develops, it reverberates through the world of infotainment. Behavior that "fits" immediately gets airtime, reinforcing the narrative.

The media first pictured Barack Obama as cool—"no drama Obama"—and later "cold and aloof." John McCain was old (David Letterman: "I don't want to say McCain looked old but when he tried to leave the funeral home he had to show his ID"). The press played Mitt Romney as an out-of-touch rich guy; the *Washington Post* and the *Wall Street Journal* ran columns listing the "top

Sound bite: A short clip of speech taken from a longer piece of audio. Often refers to a brief excerpt from a speech by a candidate or politician.

see for yourself 7.7

Go online to see Gingrich deflect comments about his personal scandal.

ten Romney wealth gaffes," leading off with his quip that he appreciated American cars because his wife "drives a couple of Cadillacs."[14] Comments that would have been ignored in other campaigns rushed to the top of the news with a "There he goes again."

Narratives about woman candidates often fall into gender stereotypes. Hillary Clinton was, for a time, the front-runner in the 2008 Democratic campaign for the presidency; she was cast as the grind, the shrew, the scold, the harpy, and the emasculator. The Democratic leader in the House, Nancy Pelosi, shared a similar image. Sarah Palin, the Republican vice-presidential candidate, was portrayed as a ditz, a diva, a hysteric, or a dim but charming beauty queen.

Campaigns constantly try to reset the frame. Hillary Clinton famously choked up during the New Hampshire primary when a supporter asked her how she managed. "This is very personal for me," she responded, creating a video image that cut through the official narrative and the reporters. When she came from behind in the polls to win the New Hampshire primary, many analysts speculated that the very personal image, looping repeatedly in the weekend before the vote, made the difference, by shifting the media narrative about her.

Campaigns respond to the shrinking sound bite by creating visual images that will speak louder than the inevitable punditry. Waving flags, cheering throngs, or bales of hay down on the farm all convey images—regardless of media voiceovers. But campaigns have to step cautiously, for there is a fine art to creating persuasive visuals. Some photo opportunities only underscore the candidate's weakness. President George W. Bush seemed to offer a heroic picture when he landed in a flight suit on an aircraft carrier, the USS *Abraham Lincoln*, and declared that major military operations in the Iraq war had concluded. A banner produced by the White House proclaimed "Mission Accomplished." When the war dragged on, the photos became an ironic rallying point for its critics.

Campaigns spend extraordinary sums on advertising. Some ads have become classics, usually because of their wicked stings. The Democrats painted Republican Barry Goldwater in 1964 as an extremist, with a spot that featured a little girl plucking the petals off a daisy suddenly interrupted by an ominous countdown and a fiery mushroom cloud.

Political advertisements become especially effective if they seep into the news coverage and become part of the campaign narrative. That can amplify the signal enough to reach the voters in the middle who are not paying much

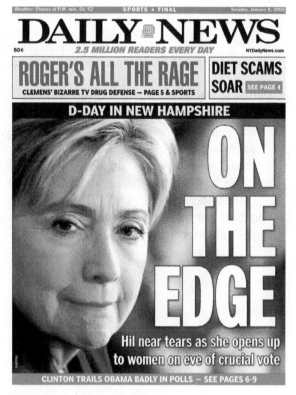

● *Are the rules different for women? Hillary Clinton briefly chokes up during the New Hampshire primary, and the story echoes through the media.*

see for yourself 7.8

Go online to see Hillary Clinton's human response to a personal question.

see for yourself 7.9

Go online to see some of the most famous fear-driven advertisements—starting with the little girl and the atom bomb in 1964. (Flash Required)

Does the Media Enhance Democracy?

Return to the question that opened this chapter. When you think about the American media, what do you see for the future of democracy and politics? Are you with the optimists or the pessimists?

Agree. A booming media enhances American democracy. Media offers new ways to process news, build networks, and interact with leaders. Clicktivism works as a robust new form of political action.

Disagree. Media harms democracy. The Babel of voices hastens national decline by chasing sensation and fomenting conflict. New media in particular erodes our news-producing capacity, increases inequalities, and offers dark corners that incubate malice.

Unsure. Of course, the answer may lie somewhere in the middle, but keep the range of possibilities in mind as you monitor the media in the years ahead.

attention. As in every other aspect of politics, the new media raise the prospect of great changes in campaigning. Facebook and Twitter give candidates a targeted way to circumvent the mass media and speak directly to supporters. Online messaging creates a sense of movement, of belonging. It offers a way to mobilize supporters behind a cause without relying on traditional media coverage. Ironically, the mainstream media eagerly reports on successful new media campaigns—amplifying that success by publicizing it.

THE BOTTOM LINE

- Media coverage of campaigns reflects the general patterns of the contemporary media. It emphasizes drama, conflict, and the horse race narrative.
- Campaigns attempt to influence the media, or bypass it and speak directly to supporters. These efforts in turn become part of the media coverage.

Conclusion: At the Crossroads of the Media World

The media reflects the United States—and broadcasts it to the world. It has many critics. Conservatives blast the mainstream media's bias; liberals lament Fox News and Rush Limbaugh; still others criticize the violence or the vulgarity on prime time. Also remember what makes the American broadcast media distinctive: it has always been a commercial enterprise. For better or for worse, whatever draws an audience survives and flourishes.

America's media reflects the nation and its people. The fifth-largest network in the United States is the Spanish-language Univision. Univision beats all the major networks on both Wednesday and Friday nights among young adults (eighteen to thirty-four-year-olds, the demographic that advertisers most seek), and in early 2013 passed NBC's audience for nightly newscasts. In fact, the seven Spanish-speaking networks can boast a total of 258 affiliates. Together, they reach more local stations than any one of the major networks. Nor does the foreign-language media stop at Spanish. In San Francisco, Comcast offers 35 foreign-language channels, and the Dish satellite menu includes 100 foreign-language stations. Sixty million Americans (including one of your authors) have at least one parent born abroad, and the media reflects that reality.

What else does the media tell us about who we are? Here's another important indicator: the ten largest religious networks have 338 affiliates. The largest, the Worship Network, reaches an estimated 69.9 million households (by way of comparison, Fox reaches 112 million).

As we have seen, television in every demographic is being squeezed by the web and the new media. And, in this booming new category, it is America's young people that drive the change—pioneering novel technologies, picking winners and losers among sites and applications. Generation Y's members are the most wired in history (though watch out for the under-12 "Gen Z" set!), with major implications for our politics and governance that will play out in coming years.

Pessimists lament the collapse of our national community. Every political side now has its own news shows; Americans don't just disagree about their values—they don't even hear or see the same reality. Mainstream newspapers and networks are losing money, and, as a result, their capacity to collect the news is declining. The hard news media cut staff and lay off reporters. As the details about national and international events get sketchier, the void is filled by loud, ill-informed opinions. The entire news apparatus dashes after drama, conflict, and scandal. Important issues like education, the environment, and impartial analysis of the health care system cannot survive in this chase for audience where victory goes to the loudest or the most outrageous.

To pessimists, the new media only hastens the demise of the old reflective politics that permitted leaders to work together, to forge compromises, and to address our national problems. Today's media—fragmented, declining, sensationalist—exacerbates the conflicts in American politics.

In contrast, optimists see a thriving democracy where people are active and engaged. Debates in Washington may be long and loud, but that only reflects an energetic nation undergoing enormous change. As media outlets expand, people's choices grow richer. Today, the United States has a broad lineup of news, information, and analysis. Members of the traditional media try to present objective reports as best they can. Cable channels and radio stations get partisans excited about their ideas and their parties. And new media—Internet-based outlets like Facebook and Twitter—permits people, especially young people, to engage in political dialogue like never before. The media stirs up the best feature of American politics: broad participation and strong opinions, which leaders cannot help but hear.

All of these features add up to a nation at the crossroads of the media world. The United States consumes programs and programming in hundreds of languages. All that content offers one answer to our question, *Who are we?* The United States is multinational and multicultural, bustling with changes and beaming its images to the world—through television, cinema, blogs, and tweets.

CHAPTER SUMMARY

● The media links people to information about politics and the wider world. It includes television, radio, newspapers, the Internet, Facebook, Twitter, and more.

● Media technology changes very rapidly, and each change reshapes the connections between citizens and their leaders—a crucial criterion for democracy. A big question, however, runs through this chapter: Does today's media strengthen American democracy or weaken it?

● News sources are changing. Newspapers, television, and radio are all declining. Online news is rising fast. It is the number-one source of news for people under thirty. The enormous number of news sources blurs the line between entertainment and news, and report from across the political spectrum.

● The new social media changes news and information. On the upside, users are more active. They can choose, respond, report, comment, and share. Candidates and parties have new ways to connect. On the downside, online media are destroying print journalism, still the most important way to develop and spread the news. The new media

environment means that we as a society do not share the same news. It facilitates the spread of rumors.

● Yes, the media is biased. Reporters in the mainstream press are less conservative than the general population, but they do not seem to tilt election coverage. The deepest bias—across the entire news-media spectrum—comes from the media's purpose: they are businesses that need audiences to generate revenue. That means that the news emphasizes drama, conflict, and scandal.

● Media stories affect public opinion among people who do not have strong opinions. Since those people tend to pay less attention to the news, stories with strong signals (heavy coverage, a strong perspective) will change opinion.

● The media—and the stories it chooses to emphasize—helps set the political *agenda*, *prime* the electorate, and *frame* issues. This influence gives it considerable power over American politics.

● In many ways, the media reflects America. What we watch and hear tells us who we are.

KEY TERMS

Clicktivism, 254
Fairness doctrine, 262
Framing, 266
Infotainment, 251
Loud signal, 265

Mass media, 247
New media, 245
Personal presidency, 249
Policy agenda, 265
Priming, 266

Public ownership, 262
Sound bite, 268
Telecommunications Act of
    1996, 264
Watergate scandal, 264

STUDY QUESTIONS

1. Where do most Americans get their news? From local television, network television, newspapers, or the web?

2. What source do young Americans (eighteen to twenty-nine) rely on most for their news?

3. Name two problems most analysts see in the decline of print journalism. Do you agree that these are problems? Why or why not?

4. How is the American media biased? Describe three of its biases.

5. Choose a newspaper and look at today's headlines. Can you find a "media narrative" in the story? Do you see a narrative arc, drama, conflict, good guys and bad guys? Can you come up with a more objective way to present the story?

6. Research a potential presidential candidate for 2016. What does she or he stand for? Now, design a campaign commercial for that candidate. Put him or her in the best possible light using visuals and voiceovers. Post your creation on YouTube.

7. Pick a story. Read the coverage in the *New York Times*. Now compare the coverage with two other sources: the BBC and Al Jazeera. Identify at least one difference in the way the other two media covered the story.

8

Campaigns and Elections

The WALL of CHAMPIONS

HE WAS TOO OLD to run for president. Too conservative. Too intellectually lightweight. Too clueless. "They say hard work never hurt anyone," he quipped, "but, I figure, why take the chance?" When his staff tried to project a different image and released a packed workday schedule, the press corps called it his work *month*. He thoughtlessly launched his presidential campaign in Albany, Mississippi—where three civil rights workers had been murdered fifteen years earlier—and analysts wondered if he was sending a secret signal to racists. The pundits agreed: there was no way that sixty-nine-year-old Ronald Reagan could defeat a sitting president—until he did, in a landslide. Ronald Reagan won the White House the way all presidents do—through a long, hard, successful campaign. With a wink and a smile, he deflected all the charges made against him. "There you go again," he kept saying during the one presidential debate, calmly shaking his head as if he just couldn't believe the things that his rival, President Carter, was saying.

Sometimes, it seems as if presidential campaigns barely matter. Econometric models predict the party that will take the White House. The winner seems obvious from day one. Reagan's campaign illustrates how campaigns do matter. The long race for president takes a large number of candidates—fourteen Republicans participated in the primaries in 2012—and winnows them down until the United States has its president. Meanwhile, hundreds of thousands of other races take place—from US senators to judges to municipal drain inspectors. Elections make American government.

Who are we? A nation of elections. The Declaration of Independence focused on representation more than any other topic. Two hundred thirty-seven years later, Americans vote more often and for more officers—on every level of government—than the people of any other nation. Through elections, Americans chose leaders, guiding philosophies, programs, policies, and even the nation's attitude toward the rest of the world.

see for yourself 8.1

Go online to see Governor Reagan's "There you go again" retort.

● *Mitt Romney on the campaign trail. The campaign to win the White House takes years and requires speech after speech to audiences big and small.*

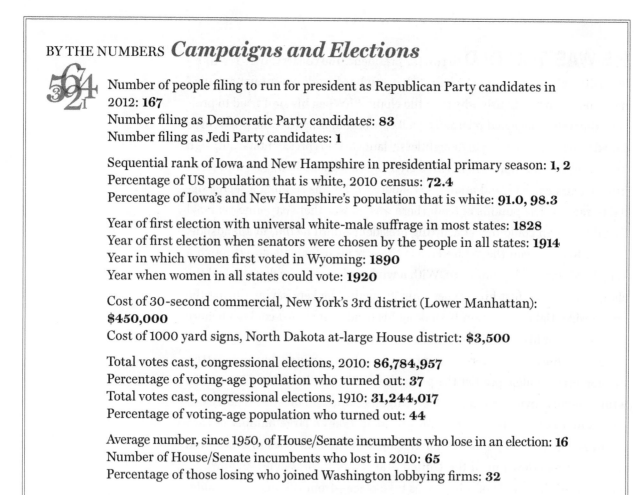

BY THE NUMBERS *Campaigns and Elections*

Number of people filing to run for president as Republican Party candidates in 2012: **167**
Number filing as Democratic Party candidates: **83**
Number filing as Jedi Party candidates: **1**

Sequential rank of Iowa and New Hampshire in presidential primary season: **1, 2**
Percentage of US population that is white, 2010 census: **72.4**
Percentage of Iowa's and New Hampshire's population that is white: **91.0, 98.3**

Year of first election with universal white-male suffrage in most states: **1828**
Year of first election when senators were chosen by the people in all states: **1914**
Year in which women first voted in Wyoming: **1890**
Year when women in all states could vote: **1920**

Cost of 30-second commercial, New York's 3rd district (Lower Manhattan): **$450,000**
Cost of 1000 yard signs, North Dakota at-large House district: **$3,500**

Total votes cast, congressional elections, 2010: **86,784,957**
Percentage of voting-age population who turned out: **37**
Total votes cast, congressional elections, 1910: **31,244,017**
Percentage of voting-age population who turned out: **44**

Average number, since 1950, of House/Senate incumbents who lose in an election: **16**
Number of House/Senate incumbents who lost in 2010: **65**
Percentage of those losing who joined Washington lobbying firms: **32**

How Democratic Are American Elections?

Time, place, and manner clause: The constitutional clause that delegates control of elections to the state governments.

The Constitution leaves most election details to the states. For example, states choose the **"time, place, and manner"** for electing members of Congress. Right from the start, the Constitution produces fifty slightly different election systems.

Government by the people can be measured along multiple dimensions: How often do people vote? How many positions do they vote for? What role does money play in the process? The American electoral process is distinctive along each of these dimensions.

● *Elections as a symbol of democracy. Here, women in Iraq display the ink that means they have voted—their first chance to participate in an election.*

Frequent and Fixed Elections

One way to hold public officials accountable to the people is to require them to frequently face the public. The United States holds elections for national office more often than most other democratic countries. With House members chosen every two years and presidents every four years, we troop to the polls at a record pace. Add in our regular state and local elections (for governor, mayor, state legislature, city council, and so on), and there is never a year in the United States without multiple major statewide elections.

Do you see any drawbacks to this practice of frequent elections? Some analysts worry about the constant electoral preoccupation of politicians. All that campaigning consumes a great deal of public officials' time, as well as scarce resources (we'll get to the cost of elections in a few pages). Critics also worry that it is more difficult to focus on policymaking when House members are constantly running for reelection. As a Canadian prime minister once remarked: "In your system, you guys campaign for 24 hours a day, every day for two years. You know, politics is one thing, but we have to run a government."[1]

Number of Elected Officials

Not only are American elections unusually frequent compared to most countries, but the *number* of positions filled by elections is enormous. From presidents to municipal drain inspectors, Americans chose their public officials. And the roster of elected positions continues to expand. The United States was the first nation to choose its chief executive by popular election—even if the Founders hedged by adding the Electoral

College. American judges were also the first to face the voters, more than a century ago. Today thirty-nine states elect judges. Most other countries would not dream of electing judges since they are meant to be impartial officials. Instead, most nations appoint all judges.

To better grasp the number of elective offices, look at Table 8.1, which lists elected officials representing the residents of Iowa City, Iowa.

Table 8.1 Who Do You Vote for in Iowa City?

NATIONAL OFFICIALS	
1 US president	
2 US senators from Iowa	
1 US representative from Iowa's 2nd District	
STATE OFFICIALS	
1 Iowa governor	
1 Iowa lieutenant governor	1 Iowa secretary of state
1 Iowa attorney general	1 Iowa state treasurer
1 Iowa agriculture secretary	1 Iowa state auditor
1 Iowa state senator	1 Iowa state representative
COUNTY OFFICIALS	
1 county supervisor	1 county sheriff
1 county treasurer	1 county attorney
1 county auditor	1 county recorder
TOWNSHIP/CITY OFFICIALS (IOWA CITY IS BOTH A CITY AND A "TOWNSHIP")	
1 township clerk	
3 township trustees	
7 school board members	
4 education agency directors	
7 city council members (who in turn elect one member as Iowa City mayor)	
9 agriculture extension members	
1 soil and water conservation commissioner	
7 Iowa Supreme Court justices (appointed for one year by governor, then must win a public "retention election" every eight years).	

Too Many Elected Positions?

| Yes, there are too many elective positions. The public is asked to vote too often. Few voters can learn about so many races. The US should appoint more experts to handle the technical aspects of government. | No, we need to encourage people to vote more often. With US voting rates so low, reducing the number of elected officials would be unhealthy for our democracy. Voting permits the people to hold their public officials directly to account. |

Count them up: there are fifty-eight elected officials for Iowa City alone. That number is one measure of democracy in action. Some argue, however, that this is *too much* democracy. From Anchorage, Alaska, to Zapata, Texas, there are over 520,000 elective offices at the local, state, and national level. That's roughly 1 for every 420 Americans eligible to vote. Too many? What do you think?

Financing Campaigns: The New Inequality?

In a democracy, all voters should have an equal say in selecting the winner. Legally, each registered American voter can show up at the polls only once per election. But there is growing concern about the ever-larger sums of money flowing through US elections. Do big contributors have more influence over elections?

Too Much Money? Candidates for national office (presidency and Congress) spent an estimated $6 billion on their campaigns in 2012, a new standard. The 2010 congressional elections also set a record for midterm spending, at $3.6 billion. Both in overall cost and in per-candidate expense, American federal campaigns are by far the world's most expensive. Do we spend too much? Many critics say yes. Nonprofit organizations like Democracy 21 and the Sunlight Foundation devote their energies to reducing the costs of campaigns, saying that the ever-rising price tag violates norms of equal influence.

Figure 8.1 reports spending by candidates for the presidency, House, and Senate, as well as funds from political parties and from corporate and advocacy groups.

Polls consistently run up lopsided majorities against the role of money. Table 8.2 shows the public opinion landslide against the rising tide of campaign cash.

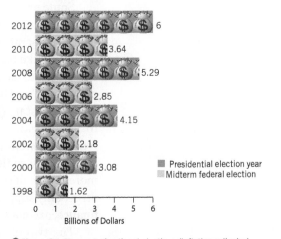

● **Figure 8.1** *The cost of national elections (inflation-adjusted dollars). Every federal election breaks the record for money spent. (Federal Election Commission and Opensecrets.org)*

Table 8.2 The Cost of State Elections

Think for a moment about elections in your state. Overall, would you say that candidates who run for office in your state spend too much money on their election campaigns, about the right amount of money, or not enough?			
	TOO MUCH	ABOUT RIGHT	NOT ENOUGH
Democrats	71	22	3
Republicans	66	25	3
Independents	73	17	2
Source: The Demos Foundation, January 2006.			

Election Spending in Context.   The numbers sound huge but let's put election spending in context. The total amount spent on all congressional races (435 House and 34 Senate) in 2010 was around $3.6 billion. That's less than half of what Americans paid for potato chips that same year, and under a fifth of the estimated amount spent for online pornography. Is electing our national legislature really so expensive, compared to the dollars we devote to salty snacks and smut?

Beyond the sheer cost, critiques of election spending raise further questions about democracy and fairness. Are America's wealthy—individuals, corporations, organized groups like labor unions—able to "buy" elections, or at least gain unequal influence over outcomes? This concern is divided into two parts: first, that one political party unfairly stacks the deck in its direction; and second, that influence (exercised by individuals or corporations) is unevenly distributed in ways that add up to dangerous inequities.

Some groups of professionals, spurred by ideology or other partisan influences, contribute mainly to one party. For example, labor unions financially back Democrats (by a ten-to-one margin, in recent elections), and some industries—like oil and gas companies—largely support Republican candidates. But most business sectors split their donations about evenly between the two major parties. The biggest-spending group of corporate donors, finance/insurance/real estate (FIRE) companies, gave 50 percent of their donations in 2010 to Republican candidates for Congress, and 46 percent to Democrats. (The remainder went to independent or third-party candidates.) Two years earlier, in 2008, those figures were essentially reversed: Democrats received slightly more than half of FIRE industry donations. Thus, conventional views that Wall Street only supports Republicans, who have long been seen as the party of high finance, are not true. Most corporations want a seat at the table in both parties.

The two major parties have also spent at roughly equal levels in recent elections. In 2010, Democratic candidates for House and Senate spent $1.82 billion, while Republican office-seekers spent $1.77 billion.

Looking beyond partisan balance, do some people or companies gain unfair advantages because of the large amounts of money they give to future officeholders? A tiny proportion of Americans provides most personal donations to candidates. In 2010, only about 0.35 percent of the US voting-age population donated more than two hundred dollars to one or more candidates. That relatively small group (about eighty-two thousand people) provided more than two-thirds of the total funds raised by candidates. Figures like this, argue campaign finance reform advocates, demonstrate that a handful of wealthy people wield outsized influence in politics through their financial contributions. Figure 8.2 summarizes the sources of the 2012 presidential campaign for Obama and Romney.

Major Donors: PACs, Super PACs and Beyond. Although the US system sets strict limits on individual donations (no one may contribute more than $2,500 to any individual candidate), some wealthy donors—often Washington lobbyists—are legally able to deliver unlimited amounts of money to a presidential or congressional candidate they support. They do so through **bundling**: shorthand for the process of convincing dozens of colleagues and friends to donate at or near the maximum amount, then delivering all the checks. In 2012, the Obama and Romney campaigns each collected more than $100 million through bundlers. Each candidate had well over five hundred bundlers working on their behalf.

The small pool of individual donors who contribute hundreds or thousands of dollars, as well as the even smaller group who bundle campaign checks, are joined in financing campaigns by various institutional donors. Many corporations and advocacy groups form **political action committees** (**PACs**) to make legal donations to candidates. PACs, which by law must comprise fifty or more contributors, may legally contribute higher dollar amounts

Bundling: A form of fundraising in which an individual persuades others to donate large amounts that are then delivered together to a candidate or campaign.

Political Action Committee (PAC): An organization of at least fifty people, affiliated with an interest group, that is permitted to make contributions to candidates for federal office.

● **Figure 8.2** *Sources of funds, by type of contributor, 2012 presidential campaign (as of July 31, 2012). (Opensecrets.org)*

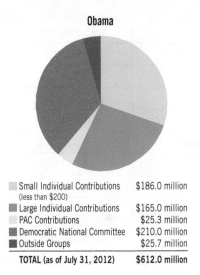

Obama

Small Individual Contributions (less than $200)	$186.0 million
Large Individual Contributions	$165.0 million
PAC Contributions	$25.3 million
Democratic National Committee	$210.0 million
Outside Groups	$25.7 million
TOTAL (as of July 31, 2012)	**$612.0 million**

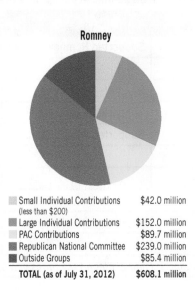

Romney

Small Individual Contributions (less than $200)	$42.0 million
Large Individual Contributions	$152.0 million
PAC Contributions	$89.7 million
Republican National Committee	$239.0 million
Outside Groups	$85.4 million
TOTAL (as of July 31, 2012)	**$608.1 million**

Super PACs: Organizations that are permitted to raise and spend unlimited amounts of money to promote a candidate or publicize a cause. However, they may not directly contribute to a candidate or coordinate with a campaign.

527 groups: Organizations governed by Section 527 of the federal tax code; they are allowed to raise and spend unlimited amounts for "issue advocacy"—but are forbidden to coordinate their efforts with any candidate or campaign, and their ads cannot mention a candidate, favorably or unfavorably.

than may individuals. In 2012, the limit on a PAC donation was five thousand dollars per candidate in a given election cycle. (Candidates can actually collect up to two times the limit from an individual or PAC, since they typically run twice: in a primary and general election.[2])

New to presidential politics in 2012 are so-called **super PACs**, formally known as "independent expenditure-only committees." Created in 2010 after a federal court ruling, super PACs are allowed to raise unlimited sums of money from virtually any source—business firms, unions, or individuals—and spend as much as they like to openly support or oppose political candidates. Unlike traditional PACs, super PACs cannot donate money directly to political candidates. They seemed to have considerable influence in the 2012 campaign. Over 500 super PACs were registered in 2012; forty-one super PACs spent more than $500,000 and the seven largest had spent over $256 million by the end of August. The Romney-supporting "Restore our Future" and "American Crossroads" and the Obama-backing "Priorities USA Action" led the way (Table 8.3).

Still another source of campaign-related funds are **527 groups**, which are forbidden from advocating directly on behalf of any candidate's election. They can accept and spend unlimited amounts for "issue advocacy." They may not explicitly support or oppose a candidate, but the ads they run can be indirectly supportive—or scathing. "Senator Jones is a tree killer who hates the environment" is an acceptable message a 527 group may broadcast; "Vote against Senator Jones" is not.

Table 8.3 "Super PAC" Funds, 2012 National Elections

Super PACs that raised and spent more than $5 million during the 2012 campaign include:			
SUPER PAC	CANDIDATE	AFFILIATION	TOTAL $
Restore Our Future	Supported Romney	Conservative	$96,700,000
American Crossroads		Conservative	$56,800,000
Winning Our Future	Supported Gingrich	Conservative	$23,907,272
Priorities USA Action	Supported Obama	Liberal	$35,600,000
Red, White & Blue	Supported Rick Santorum	Conservative	$8,346,179
Club for Growth Action		Conservative	$13,800,000
AFL-CIO Workers' Voices PAC		Liberal	$7,100,000
American Bridge 21st Century		Liberal	$8,600,000
Make Us Great Again	Supported Rick Perry	Conservative	$5,585,945
Congressional Leadership Fund		Conservative	$6,500,000
Sources: Center for Responsive Politics, Federal Election Commission (as of August 31, 2012).			

Presidential and congressional campaigns have been affected by 527 involvement. "Swift Boat Veterans for Truth," for example, spent over $22 million on the 2004 election and managed to redefine Democratic senator John Kerry from a war hero to a traitor—a brutally effective advertising campaign that helped defeat Kerry.

PACs, bundlers, 527s, super PACs: Altogether, outside groups raised an estimated $970 million to go along with the roughly $2 billion raised by the Obama and Romney campaigns in 2012. Each innovation raises a fresh round of questions about democracy and campaign spending. Does contributing funds to a legislator "buy" anything valuable for donors? Should the system be changed to reduce the influence of monetary contributions? We'll take up both questions at the end of this chapter. Critics raise a final point: members of Congress spend a great deal of time and energy raising money—it may prove a major distraction from governing. (We will consider this problem in Chapter 10 when we study Congress.)

THE BOTTOM LINE

- Are American elections truly democratic? Americans vote more often than the citizens of most democracies.
- Americans vote for more offices—from state judges to school board members—than the people in other democracies. Some critics suggest we vote on too many offices.
- The most familiar question about American democracy today fixes on the role of money in election campaigns. PACs, super PACs, and 527s have become fixtures in national elections.

Presidential Campaigns and Elections

The presidency is the greatest electoral prize. Presidential candidates receive a crush of media and public attention. Front-runners attract large audiences wherever they go, and candidates become an instant campaign case study if they win their party's nomination. Small wonder that every four years, so many political leaders catch "presidential fever" and declare their candidacy. Fourteen hopefuls considered themselves serious contenders for the 2012 Republican nomination.

Who Runs for President?

Onetime candidate Morris "Mo" Udall, who ran in 1976, said afterward, "You have to be a little crazy to run for president." Along with the positive aspects (if you like attention, that is), seeking the presidency is expensive, privacy shredding, and exhausting. Yet in every campaign, dozens take up the challenge.

● GOP primary candidates, 2012. The Republican field, before a Michigan debate. From left to right: former senator Rick Santorum (PA), former House Speaker Newt Gingrich (GA), Representative Michele Bachmann (MN), eventual nominee Mitt Romney, Texas governor Rick Perry, Representative Ron Paul (TX), businessman Herman Cain, and former Utah governor Jon Huntsman

Some are third-party hopefuls, representing various ideologies or causes. Norman Thomas ran under the Socialist Party banner a record six times from 1928 to 1948; Princess Christina Gerasimos Billings-Elias, who ran in 2008 and 2012, vowed to apologize for all past US "wrongful actions."

Serious presidential candidates generally have experience as elected officials—and, in the last half century, both parties always have nominated only candidates with one of three offices on their resume—vice president, governor, or senator. Three points stand about successful candidates (see Table 8.4):

Senators usually lose. Barack Obama was the first in forty-eight years to win running from the Senate. Five senators ran and lost between 1964 and 2004.

Vice presidents have a better record than those in the other two offices. Seven sought the White House in the last fifty years; all won their party's nomination, and three went on to win the presidency.

Governors are the new winners. Before Jimmy Carter won in 1976, no governor had won the presidency since Franklin Roosevelt in 1932. In fact, only two governors had been elected in the entire twentieth century. Since 1976, however, four out of our six presidents have come from governors' mansions. What changed? As we have seen again and again, after the upheaval of Vietnam, civil rights, and Watergate, Americans lost their confidence in Washington, DC, and its insiders. Governors from both parties win by claiming they were successful state executives untainted by the mess in DC.

No one else gets elected. Every election season, people from other positions toss their hats into the ring. There is almost always a member of the House and often a businessperson. Here's the sad truth: they never win modern elections. The last president to come directly out of the House of Representatives? Andrew Jackson back in 1828. Businesspeople with no experience in elected office? It has never happened. It takes enormous political

Table 8.4 The President's Resume

YEAR	WINNER	PREVIOUS POSITION	LOSER	PREVIOUS POSITION
1960	John Kennedy	Senator	Richard Nixon	Vice president (53–61)
1964	Lyndon Johnson	Vice president (1961–63)	Barry Goldwater	Senator
1968	Richard Nixon	Vice president (1953–61)	Hubert Humphrey	Vice president (1965–69)
1972	Richard Nixon	Incumbent	George McGovern	Senator
1976	Jimmy Carter	Governor	Gerald Ford	Vice president/Incumbent
1980	Ronald Reagan	Governor	Jimmy Carter	Incumbent
1984	Ronald Reagan	Incumbent	Walter Mondale	Vice president (1977–81)
1988	George H. W. Bush	Vice president (1981–89)	Michael Dukakis	Governor
1992	Bill Clinton	Governor	George H. W. Bush	Incumbent
1996	Bill Clinton	Incumbent	Bob Dole	Senator
2000	George W. Bush	Governor	Al Gore	Vice president (1993–2001)
2004	George W. Bush	Incumbent	John Kerry	Senator
2008	Barack Obama	Senator	John McCain	Senator
2012	Barack Obama	Incumbent	Mitt Romney	Governor

talent to run the contemporary gauntlet from primaries through the general election and into the White House. In the past half century, newcomers to the political process have not been able to negotiate it.

Presidential Campaigns Have Three Phases

Presidential campaigns involve distinct stages. First, the *nominating process*, in which each party chooses its contender, is often drawn out over years of campaigning followed by some six months of state-by-state **primary elections, caucuses**, and conventions. Second, the two major *party conventions* take place during late summer of an election year. Finally, the *general election* features the final battle for the White House and kicks off in earnest after the conventions. Each stage requires very different political strategies, played out amid the white-hot lights of national—and global—media coverage.

Winning the Nomination

Presidential candidates must master the nominating process's elaborate rules and primary-election calendar to have any hope of success. Complicating matters further, both the rules and the calendar change for every presidential election. Remember that each state determines its own primary-election calendar—carefully negotiated with the national parties. Every four years,

Primary election: an election that determines which candidate will represent a political party.

Caucus: A local meeting at which registered members of a political party meet to select delegates representing presidential candidates.

What Do You Think?

Why Iowa and New Hampshire?

Starting around two years before each presidential election, the nation's most powerful politicians and skilled campaign advisers start traveling to two small states. By tradition, Iowa's caucuses and New Hampshire's primary are the first two presidential contests held every four years—giving them an outsized influence in the process. If you win, or perform better than expected, in one or both, you're launched toward the nomination. If you do badly in both, your campaign is in trouble. These states are less populated and not very diverse: Iowa ranks thirtieth in population and is 91 percent white, New Hampshire forty-second in population and is 98 percent white. Should they continue to have such an important say in choosing a president?[3]

Yes. Proponents answer that the small states test the candidates' ability at one-to-one meetings with small groups—a very different kind of test than the media campaigns that follow in large states.

No. Opponents point out that two unrepresentative states eliminate many candidates before any large state has even had a chance to vote.

Super Tuesday: The date on the primary calendar when multiple states hold primaries and caucuses.

Winner-take-all: The electoral system used in US general presidential as well as many primary and other elections. The candidate receiving a simple majority (or, among multiple candidates, a plurality) receives all electoral votes or primary delegates. Sometimes also called "first-past-the-post."

Proportional representation: The allocation of votes or delegates on the basis of the percentage of the vote received; contrasts with the winner-take-all system.

states jockey to schedule their balloting near the front of the line. Holding a primary early in the process, before the nomination is decided, attracts attention—and gives the voters an important say in selecting the nominee. Back in 1992, the national party leaders began scheduling multiple elections on a single date, known as **Super Tuesday**—hoping to keep the contest from dragging out too long; in 2012, that "Super" day was March 6, when eleven states held primaries or caucuses. By then twelve states—nearly a quarter of the total—had already voted.

Both parties require that a winning candidate amass a certain number of delegates, assigned proportionately based on state population. In 2012, for example, California had 172 delegates; New Hampshire had just 12. Traditionally Republicans used a **winner-take-all** system, under which the winning candidate receives all the delegates for that state. Democrats, in contrast, have generally employed a system of **proportional representation**, allocating delegates based on the proportion of the vote a candidate wins. In 2012, most GOP primaries also shifted to proportional representation. Why? Party activists thought the previous nomination had been decided to soon—before their candidate had been fully tested. Sure enough, the new rules appeared to extend the contest.

In the 2012 New Hampshire Republican primary, for example, Mitt Romney won with 39 percent of the votes, followed by Ron Paul's 23 percent and third-place Jon Huntsman's 17 percent. Based on complicated proportional rules, Romney received 8 of the state's 12 delegates, Paul got 3, and

Huntsman received 1. The remaining candidates all won under 10 percent of the votes and were awarded no delegates. Three weeks later, in Florida, which used winner-take-all rules, Romney's 46 percent of the primary vote netted him all 50 of the state's delegates. Newt Gingrich, finishing second with 32 percent, received none.

Primary-season candidates must make strong first impressions, compete well in state after state, avoid errors or outrageous statements in a dozen or more debates, and manage a campaign team that, as the contests continue, can swell to thousands of people. They also may have to carefully calibrate their issue positions. Far fewer Americans turn out for primary than for general elections, and those who do tend to be more ideologically driven than the more middle-of-the-road fall electorate. Conventional political wisdom holds that candidates must therefore run more to the extreme—farther left for Democrats, farther right for Republicans—to capture the nomination, and then move back to the middle for the fall election. Though this tendency may be overstated,[4] the end of primary season generally enables both nominees to reintroduce themselves—while their opponents will try to define them in a negative way (a job that is much easier with relatively unknown candidates).

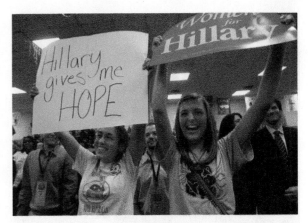

● *Hillary Clinton came very close to becoming the first woman to win a major-party nomination for president. The rules, which divided the delegates from each state, meant that after she failed to compete in a series of small states, she could not catch up despite winning many of the large states.*

Organizing the Convention

Political party conventions showcase the party's presidential nominee on a national stage; they also gather party insiders from across the United States for several days of meetings and celebration. Advocacy groups and corporate interests flock to the conventions as well: everyone jockeys to be noticed by a potential future president and his or her closest advisers.

When it works well, the convention can provide the nominee an **electoral bounce**, a boost in the polls that lasts from a few days to several weeks. The 2012 Democratic convention, held in Charlotte, North Carolina, presented a clear, tightly scripted message, united Democrats, and gave President Obama a bounce that broke open what had been considered a very close race. Conversely, a divided party or uninspiring nominee can squander the opportunity or, in the worst cases, broadcast undesirable images to a watching nation.

Electoral bounce: The spike in the polls that follows an event such as a party's national convention.

The General Election

Until the past decade, presidential nominees typically took a break for vacation after the conventions, held in July or early August, and resumed campaigning after Labor Day weekend (in early September). Since 2000, however, the campaigns have continued with virtually no pause. With just three months

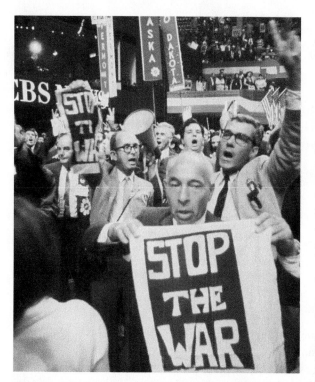

● *Chicago—1968 Democratic Convention. Angry protests both in and outside the hall created an image of disarray and crisis. Democrats had won nine of the previous eleven presidential elections, but this convention symbolized the collapse of the old Democratic coalition. Republicans would take the White House in five of the next six elections.*

between convention and Election Day, every hour matters. Campaigns lose no opportunity to stage a media event, approve a Facebook post, criticize the opposing candidate, or meet with donors to gather more cash.

General elections usually feature two or three debates between the nominees, as well as, in most years, a vice-presidential debate. These contests are among the most widely watched political events on the political calendar. Debates, like the party convention, might make a difference to the November outcome: a slip-up might turn off some wavering voters, whereas a strong performance can attract more support to a candidate's side.

The first televised presidential debate, held in 1960, featured Republican Richard Nixon (the sitting vice president) and Senator John F. Kennedy, the Democratic nominee. More than seventy million Americans tuned in—some two-thirds of the adult population at the time. Though listeners who heard the debate on the radio told pollsters that Nixon had won narrowly, on TV the charismatic Kennedy seemed the winner. Watch the debate for yourself—both candidates are stiff by today's standards—and see if you agree with conventional wisdom: television made Kennedy the winner.

At each stage of the election, style can matter as much as substance. As we saw in the previous chapter, some critics blame the media for providing primarily "horse race" coverage, or paying attention only to which candidate is rising or falling in the polls.

Winning Presidential Elections

Along with the candidates themselves—their speeches, gaffes, debate performances, and responses to the many unexpected events on and off the campaign trail—a variety of factors help determine the winner. Some are under candidates' control, like raising sufficient funds to mount a worthy campaign; others are a matter of luck and circumstance.

Economic Outlook.   Economic factors, like the unemployment rate, economic growth (or decline), and stock market trends, have a powerful place in many voters' minds. Bill Clinton's headquarters in 1992 featured a whiteboard displaying a reminder to campaign staffers: "The Economy, Stupid." As his opponent, President George H. W. Bush, found out the hard way, if the economy is performing poorly, the party holding the presidency is likely

see for yourself 8.2

Go online to see excerpts from the 1960 Nixon-Kennedy debate.

Kennedy and Nixon launch the televised campaign age, 1960.

The Clinton campaign "War Room," 1992.

to suffer. As Arkansas governor, Clinton had virtually no influence over national economic performance. But by criticizing Bush's policies and offering his own blueprint for economic revival, Clinton kept national focus on economic performance and became the first Democrat to win the White House in sixteen years.

Mitt Romney also emphasized the sputtering US economy in his 2012 campaign, touting his business background to suggest he knew how to generate jobs and blaming incumbent Barack Obama for failing to revive employment. However, the charges did not appear to affect voters. While the economy was depressed at the start of the campaign, it improved in the year leading up to the election. This was especially true in the important Midwestern states like Ohio where the unemployment rate declined a full percent. Moreover, the Obama administration claimed credit for the improving economy in the Midwest by emphasizing its bailout of the auto industry, which was prospering by late 2012. The Democrats also turned the economic issue back on Governor Romney, slamming his experience running a private equity firm as "vulture capitalism," blaming Republican ideas for ruining the economy before the Democrats came to power, and highlighting Governor Romney's criticism of the auto industry bailout. By the end of the campaign, the Democrats had neutralized the Republicans' core economic argument.

Demographics. Each party works to build a winning coalition, relying on its base of likely supporters and reaching out to undecided groups. In the 2012 fall campaign, Mitt Romney targeted white voters, a constituency that had not given a Democratic nominee more than 43 percent of the vote in thirty-five years. Although Romney had not polled well among strong conservatives during the GOP primaries, he won them over in the

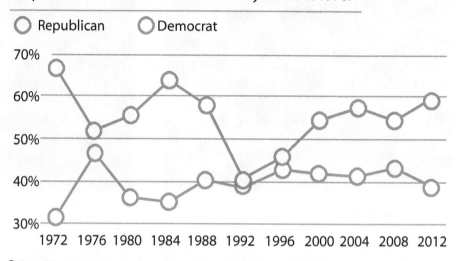

No Democratic presidential candidate has won more than 43 percent of the white vote since Jimmy Carter in 1976.

○ Republican   ○ Democrat

● **Figure 8.3** *Percentage of white vote won by major-party candidates, 1972–2012.*

general election and ended up winning a lopsided 59 percent of the white vote. Despite that, observers attributed the president's victory to what NBC news described as a "demographic time bomb": the white vote is a shrinking part of the electorate while President Obama ran up big margins in the fastest growing populations: Latinos (an estimated 71 percent supported the president), Asian Americans (73 percent), African Americans (93 percent), and young people eighteen to twenty-nine years old (60 percent voted for President Obama). Together the four groups now add up to 45 percent of the voting population and the president's large margins among them assured his victory. Defeated Republicans quickly began debating how to appeal to the rising demographic groups.

War and Foreign Policy. Most Americans pay closer attention to domestic issues—especially those that touch their pocketbooks. Occasionally, foreign policy issues become pivotal, especially when the nation is at war. Barack Obama's campaign highlighted the president's decision to launch a daring raid that killed Osama bin Laden, mastermind of the 9/11 terrorist attacks (see Chapter 11 for a discussion). Democrats used the raid as an example of the candidate's toughness. Governor Romney tried to challenge this narrative, arguing that President Obama had not been tough enough on China, Iran, and Libyan terrorists and that he sowed confusion among allies by "apologizing for America."

Projecting toughness can backfire if it is not convincing. When Michael Dukakis opposed George H. W. Bush in 1988, he climbed into an M1

see for yourself 8.3

Go online to see the Obama campaign's political spot focusing on the killing of Osama bin Laden.

see for yourself 8.4

Go online to see the Dukakis/tank campaign advertisement.

Abrams tank for a photo opportunity; clad in a helmet several sizes too large and peeking out of the tank created an unintentionally comical image—and gave voters pause about Governor Dukakis's readiness to serve as commander-in-chief.

Domestic Issues. Every presidential candidate has a list of favorite programs and strategies. Bill Clinton talked about education, energy, Medicare, and Medicaid so often that his staff started calling his campaign E2M2. The candidate's issues are important, not because they will decide the election (highly unlikely), but because they set the agenda for the presidency. In 2012, Republicans extensively criticized "Obamacare," the health reform legislation that passed in 2010. President Obama insisted on raising taxes on the wealthy through out the campaign. When he won, he claimed a popular mandate to implement his health reform and succeeded in raising taxes on those making more than $450,000 a year.

The Campaign Organization. One truism that every would-be president knows: it is essential to assemble a team of talented, loyal advisers capable of charting a plan for victory. Yet this obvious task can be immensely difficult in practice. Hillary Clinton began the 2008 campaign comfortably ahead in every poll. She had the resources and experience to attract many of the most experienced Democratic operatives to her side. Yet, as Barack Obama began to climb in the polls, and then defeated Clinton in the initial contest in Iowa, the Clinton campaign was inundated with internal sniping and disorganization.[5]

There is no fail-safe recipe for winning a presidential election. They occur so rarely—since World War II, only seventeen times—and involve such an immense array of influences that journalists, academics, and political professionals spend the next several years making sense of the outcome. Our ability to explain why one candidate or another won a race is exceeded in difficulty only by predicting that outcome in advance.

Predicting Presidential Elections

Social scientists have developed sophisticated models predicting presidential elections. Some even go so far as to say all the campaign excitement is irrelevant: their models will accurately predict which party will control the White House in all but the closest elections. Prediction models generally look at the economy, the popularity of the current president, and how long the current party has held the White House (one party has controlled the White House for more than two successive terms just once in the past sixty years).

The models apply only to the general election, when the field is already down to two candidates. Primaries—with multiple candidates, competing across many states—are too complicated for predictive models.

THE BOTTOM LINE

- Presidential elections, despite their grueling intensity and duration, attract many aspirants every four years.
- Nearly all of the serious candidates are experienced politicians. Senators tend to run most frequently, but vice presidents and governors are likeliest party nominees, in recent decades. Since 1976, governors have won most often.
- The three phases of the campaign—nominating process, party conventions, and general election—require different political strategies.
- Election outcomes are influenced by many factors—notable among them: economic performance, war and peace, advisers and organization, the coalition of supporters, and the candidate's own personality and performance. Add to this the role of accident and luck, and election outcomes are difficult to predict.

Congressional Campaigns and Elections

In contrast to the focus on two presidential candidates, congressional elections feature a colorful kaleidoscope of races across the country. Every two years, all 435 House districts hold an election, with an additional 33 or 34 Senate seats in play as well. The result is a political junkie's dream.

Candidates: Who Runs for Congress?

The 2012 congressional races featured, among other colorful characters, a New York City street preacher, an environmental activist known as "No Impact Man," a former professional wrestling executive, and a retired Secret Service agent. None of that quartet made it to Congress, but the wrestling executive, Linda McMahon, won the Republican nomination for Connecticut's Senate election—as she had in 2010.

Almost anyone can seek a seat in Congress. Convicted felons, although prohibited from voting in many states, can still run for Congress—and occasionally win. Apart from the age, citizenship, and residency requirements outlined in Table 8.5, there are virtually no limits on candidacy.

Table 8.5 Requirements for Running for Congress

Age	Successful House candidates must be at least 25 years old to take office; senators must be at least 30.
Citizenship	House candidates must have been a US citizen for at least 7 years—9 for the Senate.
Residence	Candidates must live in the state, though not necessarily the House district, where they are seeking election.

Contending seriously for a seat in Congress is a different story. Winning an average House race costs well over one million dollars; to make it to the Senate, you'll need on average seven million dollars. (These figures differ depending on district and state, of course.) Most successful candidates must be wealthy—or have a lot of well-connected friends who can help them raise money. The time required to mount a legitimate race requires freedom from the long working hours that most jobs demand. The personality traits that inspire candidates to run for Congress—self-confidence, leadership ability, interest in politics—increase as people move up the ladder of educational and economic success.

Even so, Congress is not a rich person's club. Most members are not from blue-collar backgrounds; however, in contrast to many democracies, congressional races attract relatively few top American business leaders, wealth holders, or celebrities. It's hard to imagine Mark Zuckerberg, Warren Buffett, or Oprah in Congress. The sociologist C. Wright Mills noted long ago that House and Senate races represent the "middle levels of power" in America. And, when the famous or wealthy mount a run, they don't always win. Meg Whitman, then eBay's CEO, spent an eye-popping $175 million of her own money in a failed race for governor of California; Linda McMahon spent $100 million

● *Connecticut's GOP nominee for US Senate, 2010 and 2012. Former CEO of World Wrestling Entertainment Linda McMahon climbs into the ring.*

on her two failed senate races in 2010 and 2012; talk show host Jerry Springer pulled out of the Ohio Democratic primary for Senate in 2004. Each time one party targeted a Senate candidate, the other party matched the resources; the price tag for Senate races ran up to $70 million (in Massachusetts), $38 million (Ohio), and $32 million (in Virginia). The results reflected what political scientists have long found: the money did not guarantee the Senate elections.

If neither money nor celebrity guarantees a seat, here's a more promising shortcut to Congress: be related to a member. Plenty of representatives and senators have followed relatives into office. Back in 2004, nearly a fifth of the forty-one new House members traced their family legacies to members of Congress or other high national office. Add in President Bush, reelected that year; he was grandson of a senator, son of a president, and brother of a governor. The current Congress features more than two dozen such family ties. All these dynastic connections can lend Capitol Hill the air of a royal court—minus the powdered wigs. House Republican Rodney Frelinghuysen is the latest in a long line of Frelinghuysens, dating back to the 1790s, to represent north-central New Jersey. He comments: "You sort of get it in your blood."[6]

Despite the uptick in famous names, political amateurs still dominate the crop of House challengers today. Typically, about one in six non-incumbents running for the House is an elected official, usually from the state legislature; another ten percent or so serve in non-elected government positions—often they are former Congressional staff. The remaining candidates—generally around three quarters of the total—are new to government service. Senate candidates, because they run statewide, tend to be more experienced. Most are political veterans.

As for demographic considerations, women are on average just as likely as men to win elections to Congress—but fewer run. The parties are slower to recruit them to run and women are less likely to decide to do so. One recent study shows that when a woman announces her intention to run, she is more likely to draw primary challengers than a man is.[7] Members of large minority groups (African Americans, Latinos, and Asian Americans) tend to run much less often than Caucasians, proportionate to population, but their ranks are rapidly growing (as we discussed in Chapter 5).

Talent and experience are vital in congressional races. Party leaders know that recruiting skilled candidates—more political background, better education—gives them a leg up in the contest between Democrats and Republicans for power in Congress. A candidate's background also has an impact on the quality of representation in Washington. How well Congress carries out its work depends on the political ability of its members.

The Power of Incumbency

If you talk to sitting members of Congress about reelection, you will see the worry wash over their faces. House and Senate officeholders face a more volatile American electorate than they did a quarter-century ago: voters are less predictable and harder to reach through traditional advertising. Now that virtually every utterance is digitally preserved, candidates have to be more careful about what they say. The popular senator George Allen of Virginia, cruising with a twenty-point lead in 2006 against little-known Democratic challenger James Webb, was caught on videotape at a campaign rally calling an Indian American Webb staffer "macaca," a slang racial insult. The clip ran everywhere from CNN to the *Colbert Report* to *Letterman*. Allen tried to deny it, laugh it off, and apologize, but he could not shake the media storm and wound up narrowly losing—dooming his 2008 presidential aspirations as well. Allen never recovered. In 2012 he again ran for the Senate, this time against former governor Tim Kaine. Outside groups poured $50 million into the election (the majority for Allen) but the Republican lost again.

Despite this more treacherous electoral environment, most incumbent House and Senate members fare very well in their quest for reelection. Even in 2010, when Republicans won back the House in the largest Republican landslide since 1890, more than nine of every ten incumbents won another term. At first glance, this **incumbency advantage** is a mystery. As we will explore

see for yourself 8.5

Go online to hear Senator George Allen's "macaca moment."

Incumbency advantage: The tendency for members of Congress to win reelection in overwhelming numbers.

in Chapter 10, Americans overwhelmingly give Congress a thumbs-down. The 112th Congress (which took over in 2011) recorded the lowest approval ratings in modern history, sinking as low as 9 percent in one poll. Yet in 2012, incumbents running for reelection won 90 percent of the races in the House and 91 percent in the Senate (Figure 8.4).

How can this be? For one thing, members have become very skilled at running *against* Congress. They position themselves as reasonable individuals fighting against a dysfunctional institution. And the way Congress operates—stalemate on the big issues, lots of little favors to constituents—makes the stance an easier sell. "I'm for expanding aid to needy children," say liberal members, "but I can't get it past the Republicans on Capitol Hill. Oh, and how about that new aquarium I funded?" GOP members have a similar story. Members are attentive to constituents, raise a great deal of money, and already have staff and name recognition. Most win reelection.

Congressional Election Results

Along with incumbents' tendency to win reelection, congressional elections feature additional intriguing patterns. One of these concerns **midterm elections**, or those held in a nonpresidential year. In most elections the president's party loses Congressional seats. In the last twenty-two midterm elections (eleven each in the House and Senate), the president's party picked up seats in either chamber of Congress only four times—and only a few seats each time. In contrast, the president's party lost double-digit House seats seven of eleven times—including huge swings in 2010, 1994, and 1974 (63, 54, and 48 seats respectively). (See Table 8.6.)

Midterm elections: National elections held between presidential elections, involving all seats in the House of Representatives, one-third of those in the Senate, 36 governors, and other positions.

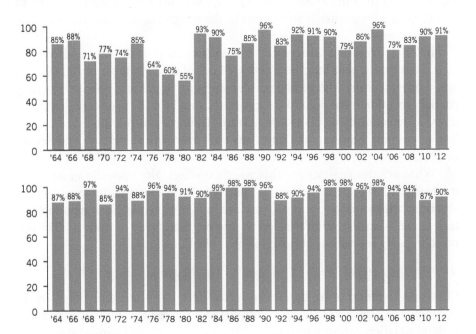

● **Figure 8.4** *Senate (top) and House (bottom) reelection rates, 1964–2012.*

Table 8.6 Midterm Congressional Election Results, 1970–2010

		SEAT GAIN	
ELECTION YEAR	PRESIDENT	HOUSE	SENATE
2010	Obama (D)	R+63	R+6
2006	GW Bush (R)	D+30	D+6
2002	GW Bush (R)	R+8	R+2
1998	Clinton (D)	D+5	(No chg.)
1994	Clinton (D)	R+54	R+8
1990	GHW Bush (R)	D+8	D+1
1986	Reagan (R)	D+5	D+8
1982	Reagan (R)	D+26	(No chg.)
1978	Carter (D)	R+15	R+3
1974	Nixon (R)	D+48	D+3
1970	Nixon (R)	D+12	R+1

The president's party has won seats in a midterm election only four times in the past forty years.

Another intriguing pattern concerns America at war. Although we might expect voters to "rally around the flag" and support the president's party, in fact the opposition usually wins seats in the congressional election following a war's outbreak.

In 1992, President George H. W. Bush swiftly won the first Gulf War in 1991. Less than a year later he was tossed out of office in favor of Bill Clinton and the Democrats, who picked up seats in both House and Senate. The only partial exception is the second George Bush, who held the presidency in 2004, a year after committing US troops in Iraq. His party was pummeled in the following election, however, as Democrats took over both the House and Senate in 2006.

What are the reasons for this wartime effect, the opposite of what we might expect? It appears that a war's patriotic "rally effect" fades away swiftly. Wartime brings anxiety, tension, sacrifice, and even panic. Such emotions attach to the administration that led us into conflict, fairly or unfairly. The opposition party capitalizes at congressional-elections time.

Redrawing the Lines: The Art of the Gerrymander

Fifty-one Democrats in the Texas House left the state and holed up in Oklahoma in May 2003. The legislative leaders called the Texas Rangers, the Federal Aviation Administration, and the Department of Homeland Security to "round 'em up and bring 'em home." What was going on?

Republicans had won control of the Texas legislature, and they immediately whipped out their red pens to redraw the congressional districts. Democrats claimed that Tom DeLay (R-TX), the Republican majority leader in the US House, had masterminded a plan to stack new districts to assure Republican winners. Because the Democrats in Texas knew they were going to lose a vote that they considered unfair, they took off to deny the majority a quorum (the number of members a legislature needs to have present in order to do official business).

Indeed, when the Democratic state legislators finally limped home, they lost the vote over redistricting. As a direct result, five Democrats lost their seats in the US House in the 2004 election. Classic political hardball helped keep Congress in Republican hands for another two years.

Membership of the House of Representatives has been fixed at 435 for over a century. The American population keeps shifting, and after every ten-year census, each state has the job of redrawing the boundaries of the election districts. In a **gerrymander**, the party in power draws the lines to help itself. See Figure 8.5 for a hypothetical example of how it works.

Imagine a state called PoliSciLand, which has two districts that are 100 percent Republican (A and B) and one district that is 100 percent Democratic (C): PoliSciLand thus sends two Republicans and one Democrat to Congress. Then, an enterprising Republican on the redistricting committee says, "Hey, we're the majority in this PoliSciLand legislature. Let's redraw the congressional districts our way."

Can you see the result? By drawing the district lines horizontally instead of vertically, Republicans took the Democratic district and split its voters into three different congressional districts. Instead of one district with 100 percent Democratic voters and two that are 100 percent Republican, PoliSciLand now has three districts, each 33 percent Democratic and 66 percent Republican. Without a change of mind by a single voter, our imaginary PoliSciLand state now has three House Republicans . . . and no Democrats.

The term *gerrymandering* goes back to 1812, when Massachusetts governor Elbridge Gerry signed a bill that redrew the districts to help his party. One of Gerry's new districts looked like a salamander, which at that time was seen as a sort of mythical dragon. "Gerry" + "salamander" = "gerrymander," and a great American contribution to the art of politics was born.

Today, with sophisticated information technology, state legislatures can carefully craft political boundaries. Two main techniques are "packing," or

● *President Wilson declares US entry into World War I. A year and a half later, his Democratic Party would be punished in congressional midterm elections.*

Gerrymander: Redrawing an election district in a way that gives the advantage to one party.

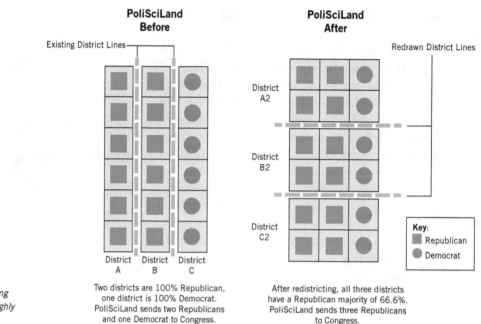

PoliSciLand Before

Existing District Lines

District A   District B   District C

Two districts are 100% Republican, one district is 100% Democrat. PoliSciLand sends two Republicans and one Democrat to Congress.

PoliSciLand After

Redrawn District Lines

District A2

District B2

District C2

Key:
■ Republican
● Democrat

After redistricting, all three districts have a Republican majority of 66.6%. PoliSciLand sends three Republicans to Congress.

● **Figure 8.5** *How gerrymandering works. A hypothetical case of highly political redistricting.*

THE GERRY-MANDER.

● *The original gerrymander: Massachusetts, 1812.*

placing all the like-minded voters into one district, and "cracking," or spreading them out so that they form a minority in many districts. Our imaginary PoliSciLand cracked the Democratic district.

Savvy political observers carefully watch who wins the state legislatures in the round years ('10, '20, '30, . . .), because those results determine the majority that gets the job of redrawing the lines after the census numbers are announced. This is especially difficult if your state is losing population. After the 2010 census, ten states were forced to rearrange their districts after losing population and therefore at least one House seat (New York and Ohio each lost two). In the 2012 House primaries, several sitting members were forced to run against each other, after their districts were combined.

In contrast, eight states were population gainers, led by Texas, which picked up four new congressional seats, and Florida, which got two more. Both winners and losers engaged in a messy, politically charged redistricting process. In several states the parties took each other to court—by now almost as familiar a practice as redistricting itself. The effect of gerrymanders in 2012: Republicans won the popular vote by 7 percent across ten states but gained 76 percent of the seats in those states. Many results look at least as bizarre as the original gerrymander. See, for example, Maryland's newly drawn arrangement post-redistricting, in Figure 8.6.

Nonpartisan Districting and Minority Representation

Some reformers would like to put the whole process of drawing electoral districts into the hands of a nonpartisan commission that would divide states into natural communities and not tilt to any political side. California passed a law to do just that after the 2010 census. State legislative districts were redrawn by a "Citizens' Redistricting Commission" rather than by elected politicians, who naturally seek to protect their personal and partisan interests. The result was compact, contiguous districts faithful to existing geographic communities—and a lot of angry legislators at the state and US House level, as they scrambled to figure out their new district lines. Ten other states have commissions that make some effort to draw nonpartisan lines. For the rest of the country, redistricting is left to the political process. Thus, the election contest usually begins in earnest—long before anyone starts running—when the state legislature sits down to draw the district.

After the 1990 census, some states used the process to enhance the number of black representatives. They created majority-minority districts packed with African American voters, and these districts proved very likely to send African American representatives to Congress. White Republicans strongly supported the effort because packing black Democratic voters into some districts left the surrounding areas more Republican. The overall effect was an increase in Republican representatives, alongside the expected increase in black legislators.

Was that a good deal for African American Democrats? For black Democrats, it was an anguishing call because it split the two sides of their

● **Figure 8.6** *Gerrymandering today: Maryland's congressional districts, 2012.*

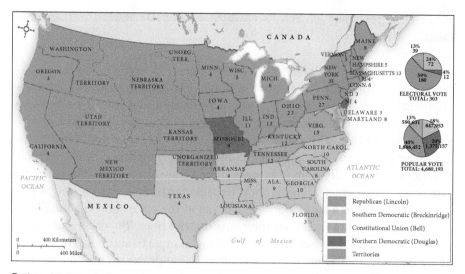

● **Figure 8.7** *Some elections are known as "critical elections" and appear to reverberate for many years. One example is the critical election of 1860. With four candidates running in the chaotic general election, Lincoln's recently created Republican Party captured electoral strongholds in the North and West, building a majority that would endure through the Civil War and for 15 years after. (Abraham Lincoln blog)*

political identity. It gave them more black representatives, but fewer Democrats. Given the long, painful heritage of racial exclusion, many African Americans saw a good argument for pursing majority-minority districts. In 1995, the Supreme Court ruled that race could not be the predominant factor in creating congressional districts, and this packing was halted.[8] Despite dire predictions, the black congressional caucus continued to grow, from twenty-nine House members (in 1995) to forty-four after the 2012 election.

THE BOTTOM LINE

- Every two years, all 435 House seats and a third of the Senate seats are up for election.
- Very few restrictions govern who may run—and some candidates are true characters.
- House and Senate incumbents have powerful built-in advantages when running for reelection.
- The president's party generally loses House and Senate seats during the mid-term election following the president's victory. Presidents who declare war also tend to see their party lose seats in the subsequent election.
- Decennial redistricting of House seats can result in some strangely shaped—and politically motivated—districts known as gerrymanders. Redistricting tends to further increase the advantage of incumbency.

How to Run for Congress

Having mastered the broad outlines of US national campaigns and elections, perhaps you are pondering your own race for a local position or even for Congress. How can you make that first run a successful one? Here we highlight four keys to winning a congressional election—*money, organization, strategy*, and *message*. Even if you are not planning to be a candidate, remember these as you watch House and Senate races shape up in coming months.

Key 1: Money. First and foremost, you will need funds to mount a legitimate challenge—at least a million dollars in many House districts, and five or six times that if you are running for Senate. Where does all the money go? TV advertising, along with radio and print ads, takes a big chunk, followed by everything from staff salaries to yard signs. Unless you are wealthy (or married to a rich person), you are going to have to "dial for dollars." Your staff will prepare **call lists** for any downtime you might have, as you desperately seek to pack your war chest.

To boost your chances of winning and reduce the cost of campaigning, you may want to wait and run for an **open seat**—one with no incumbent running, because of a sitting member's retirement or death. Taking on an incumbent costs more each election cycle (Figure 8.8).

Key 2: Organization. You will also need a well-constructed team to run for Congress. Somebody has to recruit and train all those speechwriters and fundraisers, supportive community leaders, get-out-the-vote experts, and volunteer envelope stuffers. Until the advent of candidate-centered politics in the 1980s, parties took care of most of that work. The local Republican or Democratic organization provided the knowledge and manpower to mount a campaign. Today, challengers like you usually have to build your own

Call list: A long list of potential donors whom candidates must phone.

Open seat: A seat in Congress without an incumbent running for reelection.

● **Figure 8.8** *Cost of beating a House incumbent, 1974–2012. (Center for Responsive Politics)*

CAMPAIGN LINGO

If you're running for Congress, you will want to know what your advisers are talking about. Here are a few insider terms from the campaign trail.

• **Robocall**: Automated phone call used to contact thousands of voters simultaneously; may feature a recorded message by the candidate or a popular party leader—or an attack on the opponent.

• **Advance team**: Campaign staffers who arrive at a major event site ahead of time to organize the site and build crowds.

• **Retail campaigning**: Attracting supporters or votes one by one, through door-to-door visits or small meetings. More efficient is *wholesale* campaigning, reaching hundreds or thousands at once through a speech or targeted advertisement—or robocall.

Name recognition: An advantage possessed by a well-known political figure, a political celebrity.

organization from scratch. Yes, the parties get involved in a handful of high-profile races, pumping in funds where possible and providing occasional strategic advice. But most often the candidate and core supporters build an organization.

When Jon Corzine decided to mount a Senate race from his home state of New Jersey in 2000, he quickly realized that he needed "a different paradigm: I couldn't do this with a small team from the office."[9] Corzine, a former senior executive at the investment firm Goldman Sachs, took a straightforward approach to developing a good campaign organization: he bought one.

There is a side benefit to the expense of assembling a talented campaign organization. Political insiders see hiring established pollsters, media experts, and so forth as the sign of a competitive campaign. Funders, recognizing a possible winner, will start directing more money your way. Although most new congressional candidates publicly decry the "professionalization" of campaign politics, they usually hire at least some established members of the Beltway insiders' club.

Key 3: Strategy.   A fat bankroll and seasoned organization can't compensate for a common rookie-congressional-candidate mistake—the lack of a well-conceived campaign strategy. Uncertainty is a central fact in every election, given fast-shifting political winds, opponents' moves, and the power of unexpected events. Incumbent members tend to stick to the strategy that got them there last time; you will have to invent a strategy that plays well to your political and personal strengths.

Two elements of successful congressional campaign strategies are vital: building a coalition of supporters and connecting with voters. Every state or district includes "influentials," such as local business leaders, political activists, religious leaders, and spokespeople for identity groups. Strategically attracting some of them—and, presumably, their voting followers—is essential to victory. A coalition-building strategy also targets broader groups likely to vote for a party's candidate. During the 1980s and 1990s, House Republican candidates in district after district forged coalitions of conservative, middle-aged, white, Protestant, relatively affluent voters. By 2006, this reliable lineup had fragmented in many places, and Democrats won forty-seven of forty-eight contested House seats to retake control of the chamber. By 2010, the Republican coalition was back, now fueled by Tea Party activists. By 2012, it had faded again. Notice how fast the winds shift in contemporary electoral politics.

Candidates primarily contact voters through the media. Candidate strategies need to include plenty of high-profile events, such as speeches before substantial crowds and press conferences engaging new ideas for helping the district or state. All of these can attract reporters without cost to the candidate. If you cannot build crowds because of your low **name recognition**, you may resort to more creative approaches. For example, Democrats call on Bruce Springsteen, Republicans on Clint Eastwood.

Paid advertising is also a cornerstone of any successful strategy, but marketing a House or Senate candidate involves more than big-budget TV ads. In the 2012 South Carolina presidential primary, 70 percent of voters reported the Internet as their main source of news. Your campaign will need a smart social media strategy, as outlets like Facebook and Twitter are inexpensive ways to reach large numbers of potential voters.

Be careful not to fall into the "technology trap," though: campaign professionals insist that "old-fashioned politicking" is still essential to victory. As a House challenger in 1974, Bill Clinton announced his intention to "shake every hand in the district." Clinton lost that race but employed the strategy in his next race for Arkansas governor, which he won. Said one voter, "I'd go to the store—there was young Bill Clinton. Go to the movies—there he was at the entrance, hand out. Eventually I told him I'd vote for him if I just didn't have to shake his hand anymore!"[10]

Another traditional approach will have to receive attention from your trusted strategists, **negative campaigning**. This usually involves strewing doubt in voters' minds about your opponent's policy positions, ethics, and character. Much as you may find this repugnant, without "going negative" you will have a hard climb to victory. Expect that the other side's opposition researchers will strive to portray you in the least flattering light possible. It is a lot easier to play offense than to defend against attacks, no matter how unfair.

> **Negative campaigning:** Running for office by attacking the opponent. An unpopular tactic that is, nevertheless, very effective.

Key 4: Message.   Meeting the voters, either virtually through technology or firsthand, is important. But they also need a reason to vote for you. Candidates with a clear, powerful rationale for why they are running can sometimes topple better-financed and more elaborately organized opponents.

In the relatively rare case that a first-time challenge like yours is victorious, what can you expect as a freshman member of Congress? (Yes, *freshman*: the term is the same as in high school or college, and the learning curve is surely as steep!) What comes next?

A *new campaign*, starting immediately. For House members, election looms just two years away. Senators have a more relaxing six years—but must run statewide, which in high-population or sprawling states is very time-consuming. Winning election to become a congressional "sophomore" can be especially difficult. The legendary House Speaker Sam Rayburn told each incoming House freshman class that "a member of Congress can be elected by accident, but seldom reelected by accident." Voters back home will watch a first-term member especially closely, as will his or her colleagues on Capitol Hill.

As a sitting representative or senator, you may join your colleagues in denouncing Washington as corrupt and in need of reform. Such a message has short-term electoral appeal, but it has corroded Americans' support for their national legislature in recent decades. And this decline in support raises an important concluding question: Is the American electoral system in need of reform?

THE BOTTOM LINE

- To run successfully for Congress, you need to follow a few vital steps: raise sufficient funds (then raise more), organize a talented and loyal team, develop a strategy that plays to your strengths, and hone your message.
- If you and your team do a splendid job and luck is on your side, you may be a first-time congressional victor; well done! Next up: starting all over again, with a new campaign.

● Conclusion: Reforming American Elections

Does the US electoral system work? In this chapter we have highlighted a variety of concerns—from gerrymanders to incumbency rates to the influence of money in politics. Is it a problem that we keep sending the same representatives back to Congress, up to 98 percent of the time? Is it a problem that big spenders often win? Many reforms have been proposed to address problems like these.

Start with *gerrymanders*. We could end partisan battles over House districts and ask neutral panels to draw the lines—as California did after the 2010 census. Reformers praise the idea of moving away from bluntly partisan gerrymanders designed to pad the majority party. Why not create rational, compact, community-based districts? The proposals are often defeated by a simple problem: whom can we trust to draw the districts? In many states, voters have been skeptical of non-partisan experts and prefer to leave the issue to state legislatures or governors, who are after all accountable to the public. The debate continues, however, heating up each time one party draws up another outrageous election district.

Next comes *money*. Do we really want our legislators spending hours each day, every day, raising funds? Do we want them piling up so much cash that no one can afford to run against them? Although the system is highly unpopular there is little agreement about how to change it. Many reformers call for publicly financed elections, where (as in most other advanced democracies) the government provides equal funding to each candidate and allows relatively small donations from the public, typically under two hundred dollars. This would create a much more even playing field between incumbents and challengers. Three states—Arizona, Connecticut, and Maine—currently have full public funding in place for congressional and other statewide elections, although Arizona's system was struck down by the Supreme Court in 2011 and is undergoing revisions.

We also saw concerns in this chapter that money buys donors unfair influence. How about co-chairing a fundraiser? Surely that earns a House or

Senate member's heartfelt gratitude. Or perhaps you sign on as a bundler, pulling in tens of thousands of dollars for a presidential or congressional candidate. Surely they will owe you once they reach office. The connection seems obvious to many critics.

Nevertheless, political scientists, examining the data from every angle, have a very hard time proving anything like direct "pay-to-play" schemes—contributing to a campaign expecting a policy payoff after the election. The best that analysts have been able to show is that big donors enjoy better personal access to a House member or senator. Tracing actual votes, or other legislative favors, to contribution patterns has so far come up empty. Money makes it difficult to upset incumbents and it takes up enormous time and energy. Large donors can help protect incumbents who support their perspective. However, research suggests that it does not directly buy votes or favors.[11]

Campaign finance reform polls well, but it also has strong critics. They argue that contributing to campaigns is a form of free speech. If a candidate excites you, why shouldn't you send money? When Barack Obama and Hillary Clinton ran in the 2008 primaries against each other, their campaigns caught the imagination of millions of people, and the dollars poured in.

The greatest disagreement rests on who can spend: Should we give large organizations—like corporations and labor unions—the same right to free speech as citizens? The Supreme Court in 2009 reaffirmed the argument that corporate or labor union contributions to campaigns are protected as a form of free speech. Another concern is that a single very wealthy individual can simply bankroll a candidate—as appeared to happen in the 2012 primaries. Congress has been reluctant to move boldly toward finance reform, with Republicans especially skeptical. The debate remains intense but the institutional barriers to finance reform—in both Congress and the courts—have gotten steeper.

Along with redistricting and campaign finance reform, some analysts have proposed *term limits*. The president is limited to two terms, as are many governors. Why not limit members of Congress to, say, twelve years of service? The problem with this reform is that good legislating takes skill. Term limits clear out legislators just when they have learned how to become effective. A steady infusion of fresh blood makes for an inexperienced legislature, transferring power to lobbyists—who do not have term limits and can build up memory and help "guide" the steady flow of rookie legislators. Term-limits proponents reply that we must find some way to restore Congress to the people. Incumbents become most savvy at staying in office—term limits would open up Congress to fresh ideas and talent.

These are three of the most popular reform ideas. Individual states have tried versions of each, but nationally we still have gerrymandering in most states, only weak limits on campaign spending, and no term limits for Congress. Candidates for national office must raise millions of dollars to be seen as serious contenders—and (as a result) almost everyone wins reelection to a partisan

Congress that often bogs down in stalemate—and receives worse grades than almost any other institution in American life.

Is the system broken? Or is it doing what it has always done: muddling through just fine? We will look at this issue in far more detail when we study Congress (in Chapter 10) and the presidency (Chapter 11).

Whether the system needs reform or not, campaigns and elections provide avenues to participation for the many groups in American society. Every system—and every change—creates a new configuration of winners and losers. Each generation of Americans decides whether to shake up the system of campaigns and elections—or to leave things in place. Every election brings new excitement, new voters, and new ideas into American politics. We hope that you get engaged with our electoral system—it is the one and only way to ensure government by the people.

CHAPTER SUMMARY

● Elections—free, fair, competitive elections—define democracies. They give the people a say over who governs them.

● The most important question in the chapter is this: Are American elections democratic enough?

● American electoral systems are unique because:

- The number of positions that we vote for is huge—over 520,000.

- We vote often compared to other nations.

- Federal elections for the House of Representatives take place every even-numbered year.

- In some places, there are elections every single year.

● The Constitution puts the states in charge of running elections, instructing them to manage "the time, place, and manner."

● In the last sixty years, presidents have had one of just three jobs on their résumés: vice president, governor, or senator.

● The road to the White House passes through three stages: primaries, the convention, and the general election.

● The most familiar question about American democracy today involves the role of money in election campaigns. PACs, super PACs, and 527s have become fixtures in national elections.

● Econometric models have become fine predictors of which party will control the White House. They cannot predict primary winners and often fall short at predicting close elections or Electoral College results.

● The only constitutional limits to running for Congress are age, citizenship, and residency in the state.

● Winning a race for Congress takes money, organization, constituent service, name recognition, and a good knowledge of the district.

● Every ten years, the state legislatures redraw the congressional districts to keep up with changes in the population. The *gerrymander* is a district that is redrawn to help one party. Across time, some striking patterns have emerged in congressional elections: the president's party loses seats in the midterm, results have grown more volatile (with the party in power shifting often), and war spells trouble for the president's majority.

KEY TERMS

527 groups, 282
Bundling, 281
Call list, 301
Caucus, 285
Electoral bounce, 287
Gerrymander, 297
Incumbency advantage, 294

Midterm election, 295
Name recognition, 302
Negative campaigning, 303
Open seat, 301
Political action committee (PAC), 281
Primary election, 285

Proportional representation, 286
Super PACs, 282
Super Tuesday, 286
Time, place and manner clause, 276
Winner-take-all, 286

STUDY QUESTIONS

1. For further study: Is the American system of elections democratic enough for the twenty-first century? Defend your position by pointing to features that make it more (or less) democratic.
2. Who decides about who can vote?

First describe what the Constitution says about the matter in the "time, place, and manner" clause.
Next, consider the role of constitutional amendments in the voting process.

3. Describe the American system of campaign finance. What are PACs? How about super PACs?
4. For further study: What is campaign finance reform? Make an argument for or against campaign finance reform. If possible, explain how recent research supports your argument.

5. Describe the three stages of the presidential campaign.
6. You have decided to run for Congress. What four things will your campaign need in order to be successful?
7. What is negative campaigning? Why do candidates rely on it so heavily?
8. For further study: If you were running for Congress, would you use negative campaign ads on your opponent? Why or why not?
9. Describe three reforms that have been suggested for campaigns and elections in the United States. Now, pick one and argue for or against it. Be sure to defend your position.

9

Interest Groups and Political Parties

YOU HAVE BEEN HIRED as a new congressional staffer—and today is your first day at work on Capitol Hill. (Congratulations!) You arrive during a wildly busy legislative season. The office is bustling, and nobody has time to get you oriented. In fact you barely know where you are assigned to sit . . . and now the legislative director has asked you to prepare a detailed analysis of a huge bill that you have never heard of—by tomorrow morning.

Where to begin?

Quick, call the Congressional Research Service, the research arm of Congress. They're glad to help you out, they say—but it will take a few weeks. *Weeks?* You have hours, at best.

You feel like slinking out of the office before anyone notices, and disappearing into a completely different career. Then salvation arrives on your desk, in the form of an elegantly bound, meticulously researched report on the bill. All the details you need are laid out clearly. You wonder whether to cry or laugh with relief. Who *wrote* this? You look around to thank your angel of an officemate. Not here, your colleagues smile: over on **K Street**. An interest group lobbyist sent it directly to you. As this chapter displays, that elegant and timely report is at the heart of what interest groups do in Washington.

Interest groups have become so central to American government that it is difficult to imagine our system without them. At the same time, lobbyists and the interest groups they represent consistently receive among the lowest approval ratings of any professionals, in or outside politics (Figure 9.1).

Who are we? We are a nation of too many lobbyists and special interests. Or are we? Pause for a moment and consider: How many lobbying groups work in Washington on behalf of *your* interests? None, you say? Or perhaps one or two advocate for causes you care about—like the environment or tax relief or the Catholic Church? In fact, like most Americans, you are represented by dozens of groups. Advocates who push for clean air, safe food, cheap cell phone service, and most everything else you care about. Your college or university probably has representatives who lobby to promote the school's concerns—at the state capital and in Congress. Your student fees or tuition may help pay for their work. The United States Student Association

K Street: A major street in downtown Washington, DC, that is home to the headquarters for many lobbying firms and advocacy groups—and thus synonymous with interest group lobbying.

● *Lobbyists in action. Health care lobbyists pack the Senate Finance hearing room during a crucial committee debate on the Affordable Care Act.*

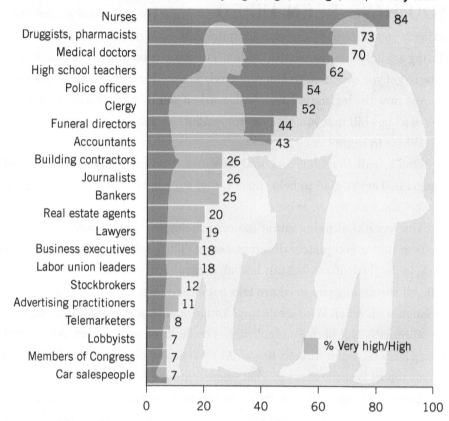

Please tell me how you would rate the honesty and ethical standards of people in these different fields — very high, high, average, low, or very low?

Field	% Very high/High
Nurses	84
Druggists, pharmacists	73
Medical doctors	70
High school teachers	62
Police officers	54
Clergy	52
Funeral directors	44
Accountants	43
Building contractors	26
Journalists	26
Bankers	25
Real estate agents	20
Lawyers	19
Business executives	18
Labor union leaders	18
Stockbrokers	12
Advertising practitioners	11
Telemarketers	8
Lobbyists	7
Members of Congress	7
Car salespeople	7

● **Figure 9.1** *Lobbyists—and members of Congress—rank at the bottom of Americans' approval ratings for various professions, tied for last with car salespeople.* (Gallup)

and the National Association of College Students lobby directly on behalf of undergraduates; they promote policies like expanding college access and opposing cuts in federal student-loan programs. Many intercollegiate sports programs retain their own lobbyists. Whether you know it or not, you are a participant in what one expert terms our "interest-group society."[1]

While the explosion of interest groups is a relatively recent American political phenomenon, parties were there from the beginning. We have always been a deeply partisan people and many of us form lifelong attachments as Republicans or as Democrats. Yet we are also quick to denounce partisanship and to dream up reform after reform to diminish party conflict.

In short, Americans have a love/hate relationship with the major institutions that champion their political views—interest groups and parties. Even if you do not think of yourself as a member of an interest group or a party, you have agents in Washington representing your views and interests.

BY THE NUMBERS *Interest Groups and Political Parties*

Number of lobbyists who registered with Congress, 2012: **11,890**
Percentage of registered lobbyists who serve only public interest clients: **33**

Total spending reported by health care lobbying groups, 2011: **$670,904,815**
Total spending on lobbyists reported by the city of Portland, Oregon, 2011: **$235,000**

Number of groups registered to lobby on homeland security spending, 2011: **1,874**
Number of groups registered to lobby on behalf of homeless people, 2011: **86**
Percentage of former members of Congress who work as Washington lobbyists: **41**

Total amount donated to "527" groups for issue advocacy, 2010 election:
$490,000,000
Estimated spending by "Super PAC" organizations, 2012 election: **$629,000,000**

Number of "sponsored trips" (usually paid by interest groups) taken by members of
Congress, 2011: **1617**

Registered Democrats, 2011: **72 million**
Registered Republicans, 2011: **55 million**
Registered independents, 2011: **42 million**

Number of people who dropped registration in Democratic and Republican
Parties between 2008 and 2012: **2.5 million**

Percentage of Americans who identified with Democrats, Republicans, and independents, respectively, in a Pew poll (July 2012): **32, 24, 38**
Percentage of voting-age Americans who join a political party: **61**

Percent favorable/unfavorable rating of Republican Party, August 2011: **34/59**
Favorable/unfavorable rating of Republican Party, August 2001: **48/47**

Favorable/unfavorable rating of Democratic Party, August 2011: **43/50**
Favorable/unfavorable rating of Democratic Party, August 2001: **54/40**

Although Americans do not feel warm and fuzzy about interest groups
and political parties, they play a vital role in our society. A political party is *an
organization, with a public following, established to win elections, generally
by promoting a set of principles.* Political parties organize American government around competing ideas. Interest groups also organize Americans based
on their ideas and interests. But unlike political parties, interest groups play

many different kinds of roles in American politics. We begin by drawing a distinction between the types of interest groups and what they do.

What Interest Groups Do

Maybe you don't think of college wrestlers or clean-air activists or Baptists when you imagine interest group lobbyists in action. But all of these—and virtually every other set of Americans you can imagine—are in fact interest groups. We define **interest group** as an organization whose goal is to influence government.

There are two important elements in that definition. The first is *organization*: a collection of wheat farmers begins to resemble an interest group only when they meet regularly to jointly discuss and manage their concerns. The second is *influence government*: plenty of organized groups have no contact with public officials. When those wheat growers join the American Farm Bureau Federation and press Congress for subsidies to keep crop prices stable, then they are an interest group.

James Madison warned against interest groups—he called them "factions"—in Federalist no. 10, calling them the "mortal diseases" that had always killed off popular government. His solution? *Increase* the number of interest groups. That way, none would become too powerful and they would have to work together to accomplish anything. Increase the number of groups? That is one piece of advice the United States has certainly taken.

At least two hundred thousand interest groups are active in American politics today. About three-quarters of those are public-advocacy or citizen groups; the remainder represents private (usually corporate) interests. Many interest groups hire **lobbyists** to promote their cause. Some lobbying professionals work full-time, paid by clients to influence lawmakers. Plenty of other people occasionally try to influence government—like college students who fan out across their state capital each year, asking legislators to oppose higher student fees or appropriate more funding for science labs.

Public Advocacy Groups

Public interest groups aim to represent Americans' collective interests, such as environmental protection or consumer product safety. For example, the Association of Community Organizations for Reform Now (ACORN) is among the nation's largest advocates for low- and moderate-income families: they work on voter registration, health care, affordable housing, and other social issues. Public interest groups may also represent the interests of a group of citizens.

The American Association of Retired Persons (AARP), for example, is a **membership group** that represents nearly forty million Americans over age

Interest group: An organization whose goal is to influence government.

Lobbyist: A person who contacts government officials on behalf of a particular cause or issue.

Membership group: An interest group primarily organized around voluntary members: often a nonprofit or public advocacy organization.

fifty. AARP provides many benefits to its members, from disseminating information about health issues for older Americans to providing discounts at hotels or car rental agencies. It also lobbies on a wide range of issues affecting seniors, from Social Security benefits to disability insurance. In 2006, when President Bush tried to add a new prescription-drug benefit to Medicare, Democrats thought they had the votes to block the legislation on Capitol Hill. Then AARP threw its weight behind the bill—and it passed.

Let's take a closer look at what these interests group do.

● *One example of an environmental interest group mobilization effort.*

What Public Interest Groups Do for Their Members. Interest groups like AARP perform three main functions for their members. First, groups *inform members about political developments.* The American government is sprawling—every House member represents some seven hundred thousand people. Interest groups have become a primary link between the public and its government. Groups provide access through which members (such as animal rights activists or Future Business Leaders of America) learn details about Washington, DC, or state or local governments. Most of us have little time to keep up with the huge range of policies, even those affecting our career or personal interests. That's where lobbyists, who monitor topics that matter to their clients or members, can help.

The channel of access runs two ways. A second main role interest groups play is to *communicate members' views to government officials.* These members can be corporate or other private actors, or they can be collections of Americans interested in a topic. Join a citizen group, and its Washington representatives will convey your opinions directly to public officials—in all three branches of the government.

Third, interest groups *mobilize the public,* that is, they get groups of people to act politically. They come up with TV ads, Mailgram alerts, Facebook postings, or tweets that are meant to provoke action.

Many Americans care deeply about abortion policy, for example. They usually are not satisfied merely by voting every two or four years for candidates who share their position. Pro-life and pro-choice groups offer their supporters frequent opportunities to *do something* on this issue of personal concern. Contributing funds, writing letters, joining protests, exchanging ideas with others of similar views, even winning an occasional audience with policy makers: interest groups facilitate all these means of political participation.

When groups mobilize their members, they're often pushing their own specific angle, of course. A few years ago, the Food and Drug Administration proposed regulations to reduce teen smoking. Tobacco-company lobbyists mounted a big "education" campaign, aimed at both the public and lawmakers—about the dangers of a giant, out-of-control federal bureaucracy meddling with people's freedom to smoke. Public health groups pushed right back with graphic advertisements showing the ravages of smoking—amputations, voice boxes, and death.

How well represented by lobbying groups are your specific political concerns? If you care about something that is already on the government agenda, groups are very likely promoting your view in Washington. More obscure topics—and less powerful interests—may be less likely to get a hearing. However, if you have strong opinions about a policy that seems to be overlooked, do not despair. American political history is full of "crackpots" who believed in outlandish things—ending segregation, cleaning up polluted rivers, putting airbags in every car, ending tobacco use in public places—that eventually won out.

Public Interest Groups and the Free Rider Problem. Advocates representing membership groups face a challenge. They must attract, and retain, enough supporters to promote their cause: fight global warming or reduce immigration or ensure safer food. Facing competition from dozens of other groups pursuing similar aims, nonprofit groups can have trouble staying alive. Most public interest organizations face the problem of free riders: why would anyone join a membership group when they can leave the hard work to others and still enjoy the results?

Log on to the website for a public interest group you find appealing—Greenpeace or the National Rifle Association (NRA) or Habitat for Humanity, which builds homes for needy people around the globe. Alongside the rhetoric about global warming or the right to bear arms, you'll see quite a bit of swag available. Tote bags, trips to Yosemite, gun-safety videos, teddy bears, Habitat travel mugs—all free or discounted for joining. (Ironically, the NRA also offers its members accidental death insurance.)

In political science terms, these **material benefits** are a key part of what membership groups provide. Such benefits help attract new members, whose dues provide part of the funds needed to keep the lights on and lobbyists on board. Others join because of **expressive benefits**: the group expresses values that its members share, such as social justice or individual freedom. Still other people may join an interest group for **solidary benefits**. Think of your own experience as a Girl Scout or fraternity member: it can feel very powerful to be part of the group. Interest-based organizations tap into that feeling, and attract and hold members based on shared social fellowship.

Private Interest Groups

Private interest groups often represent economic actors such as corporations, trade associations, professional organizations, unions, or entire

Material benefits: Items distributed by public interest groups as incentives to sign up or remain a member.

Expressive benefits: Values or deeply held beliefs that inspire individuals to join a public interest group.

Solidary benefits: The feeling of shared commitment and purpose experienced by individuals who join a public interest group.

● Wikipedia goes dark. When Congress proposed legislation to curb Internet privacy, the online community feared censorship and launched a successful campaign to stop the bill. The popular information-sharing site Wikipedia shut down for 24 hours, replacing its page with this banner.

industries. You have probably heard of the American Medical Association (AMA). The American Medical Association advocates for medical liability reform to protect physicians. It also works to change the way Medicare pays physicians. Like public interest groups, the AMA works to inform its members of political developments and communicate views to government officials. However, it spends fewer resources on mobilization of the public and more on lobbying in Washington DC.

What is a **lobbyist**? Put simply, a lobbyist is a person who contacts government officials on behalf of a particular cause or issue. Some lobbying professionals work full-time, paid by clients to influence lawmakers. Plenty of other people occasionally try to influence government.

Private interest groups might lobby individually or join forces. For example, after months of carefully laying the groundwork, members of a **lobbying coalition** comprising entertainment industry groups—TV networks, record companies, Hollywood studios—were poised to win antipiracy legislation protecting their products against illegal downloading and copying. Because the bill featured restrictions on Internet use, new media companies—including Google, Facebook, Reddit, and eBay—charged that it was censorship. At the last minute, the new media companies formed a coalition of their own, and sprang into action. Wikipedia went dark for twenty-four hours with a simple request on its home page that users contact members of Congress and oppose the bill. The strategy was an extraordinary success. The popular outcry, carefully coordinated by lobbyists for new media companies, buried the legislation.

Lobbyist: A person who contacts government offi cials on behalf of a particular cause or issue.

Lobbying coalition: A collection of lobbyists working on related topics or a specific legislative proposal.

> **THE BOTTOM LINE**
> - Interest groups, or organizations that seek to influence government, employ lobbyists to pursue benefits for their clients or members.
> - Some interest groups advocate for the public good or groups of citizens while others represent private concerns.
> - Interest groups serve members by communicating political information to them, analyzing and relating members' views to policy makers, and mobilizing people to make their voices heard.

● Interest Groups, Representation, and Power

Concern about special interests has surged periodically since Madison published his famous warning about the danger of fractions. Jacksonian Democrats, Progressives, New Dealers, 1960s radicals: many of the reformers we saw in earlier chapters expressed a fear that a few select groups (usually big business) were getting fat off the rest of us. All the outcry, however, obscures the basic truth: interest groups aren't just "them"— they're us.

But how well is the entire public represented in the interest group system? Do special interests have too much power? It is to these questions that we now turn.

Interest Groups and Representation

Pluralism: An open, participatory style of government in which many different interests are represented.

Whether our interest group system represents all (or most) people is a red-hot debate, both among political scientists and across the public. Some, in a view called **pluralism**, hold that as long as the American political process is open to a wide range of different groups, then government policies should roughly correspond to public desires. No single set of interests dominates our system, pluralists insist, and all the different groups pushing and tugging allows the collective good to shine through. You might see this as a latter-day update of James Madison's argument in Federalist no. 10 that began this chapter: the answer to the problem of interest groups is—more interest groups.

Demosclerosis: The collective effect of the sheer number of Washington lobbyists in slowing the process of American democratic policymaking.

Two pessimistic theories respond to the pluralists. First, hyperpluralists fear that there are so many interests and so many groups that the entire system is bogging down in stalemate. Any time a group proposes a new project—education reform, a new highway, privatizing Social Security, or updating the electric grid—there is always another group ready to oppose it because they don't want to pay the taxes, or fear harm to the environment. Hyperpluralists fear gridlock. The journalist Jonathan Rauch coined the term **demosclerosis** to describe the sheer number of lobbyists at work in Washington. *Demo* is

Power elite theory: The view that a small handful of wealthy, influential Americans exercises extensive control over government decisions.

● *Too many lobbyists in Washington? Critics say too many professionals are involved in the influence-seeking business; defenders list positive contributions interest groups make to American government.*

the Greek root meaning "of the people" (think *demo*cracy). *Sclerosis*—well, we should all keep our arteries clear of dangerous sclerotic plaque and other hardening agents. Rauch, echoing the hyperpluralists, suggests that the American body politic is endangered by the sheer buildup of lobbyists.[2]

Others worry that the playing field is tipped too far toward the richest and most powerful people. This **power elite theory** portrays a group of wealthy, influential Americans—mostly from the corporate sector—who mingle with one another regularly and thus are able to promote their shared ("class") interests in government. Most of the power elites live and work in cities other than Washington, DC, so business lobbyists do the day-to-day work of influencing government on the elite's behalf.

"Power elite" analysts look at events like the $125 billion US government bailout of big banks in 2008–2009—using public tax dollars—and conclude that corporations get a special deal in American government. Nobody bailed out the more than one million property owners who lost their homes during the worst of the economic crisis, most of them because of the same subprime-mortgage crisis that devastated the banks. One recent analysis by three political scientists carefully counted the number of lobbyists and how much they spent and came up with numbers that gave new life to the elitist perspective: lobbying, they discovered, is dominated by business: 53 percent of the lobbying organizations and 72 percent of the expenditure represents business interests. In contrast, public interest lobbying weighs in at about 5 percent of lobbying effort. And groups supporting the less privileged employ just 2 percent of the lobbyists in Washington. The results, they suggest, reflect the conclusion of a famous political scientist back in 1960: this is a chorus that "sings with a decidedly upper-class accent."

Which view—pluralist, hyperpluralist, or power elite—is correct? Political scientists can't say for sure. It is difficult to tell whether big business or other powerful groups successfully turn policies in their direction on a regular basis. For every example like the bank bailout, affirming the power of elites in the American system, another story seems to suggest the opposite—that small business or retired people or environmental advocates prevail. The best guess: all three of these theories sometimes capture the truth.

When President Reagan began his second term in 1985, he called for "fair, simple, and sweeping" tax reform. Congress got to work, with the House Ways and Means Committee and Senate Finance Committee holding extensive hearings and marking up legislation. Lobbyists by the dozens clamored for tax favors to help their clients, a spectacle that aroused familiar alarms about interest group influence. The bipartisan tax-reform bill that ultimately passed included almost no special favors for business interests. That tax reform episode remains an answer to the cynical argument that corporate power always wins in Washington. The tax reform bill is but one episode in the daily stream of political battles. Let's now take a broader look at how we measure and restrict the influence of lobbies.

Interest Groups and Power

Tens of thousands of lobbyists, all chasing members of Congress and their staffs as well as White House and executive-branch officials: many commentators see that as decisive evidence of interest group influence. When health reform was atop the national agenda during 2009–2010, one report calculated that six lobbyists were engaged on the issue for each member of the House and the Senate.[3] That's more than 3,200 lobbyists, all clamoring to be heard on a single topic.

Ultimately, if you measure the power of lobbyists by simple numbers, then this sector is certainly powerful. Do the rising numbers suggest overbearing power? Not necessarily. They mean only that interest group lobbyists have become a central part of the operation of national, state, and local government.

Lobbyist Spending

Lobbyists rarely visit lawmakers just to offer a cheerful greeting. Interest groups big and small, from Wall Street financial interests to Michigan asparagus growers, spend an estimated eight billion dollars each year attempting to influence Washington policymaking (Figure 9.2). This doesn't include spending on political campaigns.

This eight-billion-dollar figure is inexact. Official Senate and House records indicate that *registered* lobbyists reported spending nearly four billion dollars on lobbying activities in 2012. Many of those seeking to influence Congress never bother to register. Analysts estimate that total spending is about twice the amount indicated in lobbying registrations.

Clients of private groups and members of public groups together provide those billions of dollars, spent on lobbyists' salaries, research costs (remember that neatly bound report!), the expense of running a Washington office, travel, and so forth. Table 9.1 lists the top-spending lobbying clients for 2011. Note the various sectors represented: health care, oil/gas, telecommunications, military contractors, real estate, and even American seniors. Most of

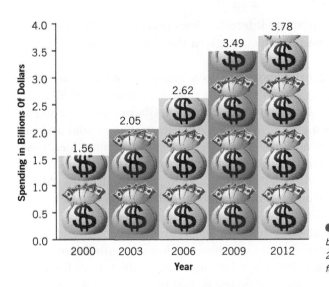

● **Figure 9.2** *Trends in spending by registered lobbyists, 2000–2012, in billions of dollars. (Center for Responsive Politics)*

Table 9.1 Biggest-Spending Lobbying Clients, 2011

LOBBYING CLIENT	TOTAL
US Chamber of Commerce	$66,370,000
General Electric	$26,340,000
National Association of Realtors	$22,355,463
American Medical Association	$21,490,000
Blue Cross/Blue Shield	$20,985,802
ConocoPhillips	$20,557,043
American Hospital Association	$20,482,147
AT&T	$20,230,000
Comcast	$19,260,000
Pharmaceutical Research & Manufacturers	$18,910,000
National Cable & Telecommunications Assn.	$18,530,000
Boeing Company	$16,060,000
Verizon Communications	$15,470,000
AARP	$15,170,000
Lockheed Martin	$15,166,845
Source: Center for Responsive Politics	

these big spenders are corporate interests: Does that fuel the "power elite" view? Or is it merely a waste of money, given that business loses plenty of policy battles?

When an issue of great importance to a group or industry arises in Washington, affected groups tend tvo boost their spending. In 2009–2010, a climate-change bill was promoted by President Obama and debated in Congress. The legislation aimed to reduce Americans' use of coal and oil. Sharp spending increases on lobbying were reported by oil companies, coal-mining industries, and electric utilities, which burn thousands of tons of coal each year to produce electricity. The largest lobbying firm for utilities, Edison Electric Institute, spent around $7 million in 2008, then jumped to $10.5 million in lobbying expenses in 2009—a 50 percent increase.

Some analysts look at these hikes in spending and conclude that they prove interest groups' extensive political influence. But the truth is more complicated. We might ask, for example, what the energy industry got for all its spending. Although no climate-change law passed in 2010 (or 2011, or 2012), was this lack of success due to lobbying opposition?

Our conclusion about all that money: it probably did not influence very many votes. On a high-profile issue like climate change, most members of Congress have very strong views: liberals fiercely support the legislation (unless they think it does not go far enough); conservatives are equally strongly against it. You can predict most of the votes. What are the lobbyists spending funds on, then? They are supporting the members that agree with them, or trying to "soften up" the few members who might be persuadable on this topic. If members need facts for the debate, lobbyists are there to provide background. That's why, in our chapter-opening story, that invaluable report landed on your desk. The lobbyists who back your member of Congress knew exactly when you would need that report.[4]

A clearer sign of lobbying heft may be an adjustment in a policy or specific bill. Energy companies, for example, successfully pushed to include an "offset program" in climate-change legislation: they could invest in projects to remove carbon dioxide from the atmosphere if they were unable to meet

What Do You Think?

Assessing the Influence of Lobbyists

We have discussed numbers and money as indicators of the power of interest groups in American government. In what other ways might we determine the extent of their influence? Count up the meetings between lobbyists and legislators? Trace the complicated connections between campaign donations from an interest group and a Congress member's vote on specific legislation? Scholars have been working for years to answer this question—and are still trying. Can you imagine any other ways to better assess lobbyists' influence in American policymaking?

reduced emissions targets. This technical policy change underlines an important truth: the more obscure the provision, the better the chances of winning it. The less the public is aware of a topic, the more room Congress has to deliver favors.

Regulating Interest Groups

All this talk of influence leads naturally to questions about how interest groups are regulated. What are lobbyists forbidden to do in pursuit of their policy goals? For a long time, the answer was "not much." Until 1946, there were no real limits on lobbying action, though out-and-out bribery—clearly exchanging votes for money or other favors—was prohibited. That year, Congress passed the **Federal Regulation of Lobbying Act**, which required lobbyists seeking influence in the House or Senate to:

- *Register with Congress.* An office was opened in the Capitol—today registration is online—for lobbyists to fill out forms (first annually, and eventually every three months) listing all clients on whose behalf they sought to influence Congress.

- *Report the amount and sources of income derived from lobbying Congress.* This line-by-line list is supposed to include all a lobbyist's clients and how much they paid, but some lobbyists exploit the rules to keep their clients out of sight.

Notice the absence of any restrictions on lobbying activity. In theory, a lobbyist could accept a large sum from one client and pass those funds on to a member of Congress as a "gift." The 1946 law merely required interest group representatives to identify both themselves and the source/amounts of their payments for lobbying.

Tighter restrictions on gift giving were imposed in 1995, following public clamor about presents, meals, and travel "junkets" for Congress members, paid for by interest groups. The House banned virtually all gifts. On the Senate side, inexpensive items like T-shirts and other trinkets were still allowed—up to fifty dollars per year for any senator from a given lobbyist. This **gift ban** law was designed to make it more difficult to "buy" favors from a member of Congress than in the past. Members and lobbyists insisted that gifts were simply tokens of friendship and esteem; critics thought otherwise.

Loopholes in the 1995 law swiftly appeared. The House prohibition on lobbyists' buying meals for congressional members or their staff was clarified to cover only meals consumed while sitting down, presumably at a restaurant. "Finger food," such as hors d'oeuvres eaten standing up at parties, was a legitimate expense—enabling lobbyists to continue attending or even sponsoring fundraising events for congressional members.

Stories like the "finger food exception" inspired a fresh round of popular outrage, sparking Congress to revisit interest group lobbying reform. In

Federal Regulation of Lobbying Act: The initial US statute spelling out requirements on lobbyists active in Congress, passed in 1946.

Gift ban: A regulation that eliminates (or sharply reduces the dollar amount of) gifts from interest groups to lawmakers.

2007, a new Democratic majority closed many of the loopholes in the gift ban and barred senators from lobbying their former colleagues for two years after leaving the Senate.

THE BOTTOM LINE

- A long debate between pluralist, hyperpluralist, and power elite theorists continues about whether the collective public is well represented by interest groups.
- Because of the difficulty in directly measuring interest group influence in government, researchers turn to metrics like number of lobbyists and funds they spend on lobbying.
- Beginning in the mid-1960s, an advocacy explosion saw lobbyist numbers climb dramatically. Resources devoted to lobbying also rose sharply beginning in this period.
- Despite their extensive presence and billions of dollars in spending, lobbyists are not likely to change congressional minds on high-profile votes; their role is more akin to supporting the members on their side. Votes on more obscure or highly technical topics are another matter.
- Regulations on interest group activity are relatively limited in the United States. They have been tightened lately but loopholes remain.

Lobbying the Federal Branches of Government

Iron triangle: The cozy relationship in one issue area between interest group lobbyist, congressional staffer, and executive-branch agency.

The traditional model of Washington power brokers depicted a closed process dominated by **iron triangles**—tight, durable links among powerful interest groups, congressional committee chairs, and administration officials.

Consider one example: *farm subsidies*. For decades, many American farmers—growing crops from corn to tobacco—have received "price supports," or subsidies worth millions of dollars, from the US government. Critics charge that this practice is a huge giveaway of taxpayer dollars. With minor tweaks, the system remains in place.

In some accounts, a classic iron triangle explains the staying power of farm subsidies. Congressional staffers on the Agriculture Committees in the House and Senate (point A on Figure 9.3) developed close relationships with lobbyists for various farm groups (point B), who encouraged them to appropriate funds managed by Agriculture Department bureaucrats (point C). The lobbyists made sure to establish friendly connections with Agriculture officials as well. But if the executive branch (C) balked at implementing subsidies, they might find their congressional appropriation cut the following year—so they usually kept

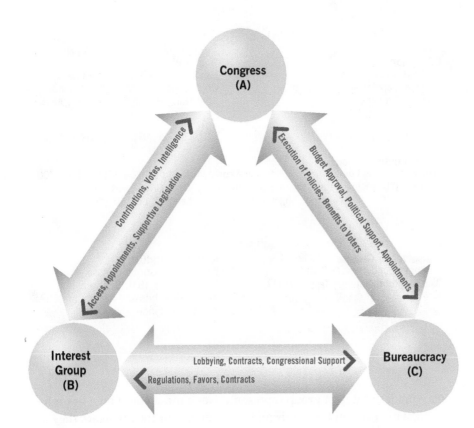

● **Figure 9.3** *Iron triangle. The classic image of interest group power features the close relationship between Congress, special interest groups, and federal government bureaucracy.*

the programs humming along. The combination of executive branch, legislative branch, and lobbyists—the iron triangle—was unstoppable.

Iron triangles proliferated around Washington into the 1960s, given the relatively closed environment of national policymaking. The subsequent "advocacy explosion" initially brought more lobbyists in closer contact with Capitol Hill staffers, which ensured the triangles' survival for a while.

Rise of the Issue Network

Over the past thirty years, however, iron triangles have given way to a very different image—of loose, open **issue networks**. More and more lobbyists representing more and more positions, in addition to growing numbers of congressional staffers, have broken apart the cozy triangles. Political scientist Mark Peterson charts a "radical change" in the 1980s, as triangles dissolved into a "far more diverse and open system" that featured "looser, less stable, less predictable, and more diverse patterns of interaction and decision."[5]

Figure 9.4 illustrates an example of an issue network, in telecommunications policy. Notice how much more complicated than a simple triangle this network is. Welcome to the life of a Washington lobbyist today! To negotiate these networks—to faithfully represent members or to attract new

Issue network: Shifting alliances of public and private interest groups, lawmakers, and other stakeholders all focused on the same policy area.

● **Figure 9.4** *Issue network. Today scholars generally see a more extensive network of actors influencing policy than the classic iron triangle. Here, the issue network that influences telecommunications policy. (Based on Kiyohara 2008; Berry and Wilcox 2007.)*

Education
Teachers union, National PTA, Schools, Department of Education, Catholic Education Groups

Social Welfare
Liberal Groups, Community Based Organizations, Benton Foundation, ALA, Rural Health Clinics, RAC, AHA

Telecommunications
Local telephone companies, Long distance companies, USTA, COMPTEL, NCTA, FCC, USAC, NTIA, White House, Commerce Committees, CBO, CRS, Court, Department of Justice, FTC, Cellphone companies, VoIP providers, Lawyers, Lobbying firms

Conservative Groups
Heritage Foundation, PFF, CES, Cato Institute, National Taxpayers Union

High-tech Industry
Wireless Infrastructure Association (PCIA), Apple, IBM, Software Information Industry Association (SIIA), Gates Foundation

clients—modern interest group representatives cannot count on a few reliable contacts, with a committee chair and a bureaucrat or two. Instead, they must cultivate connections across Capitol Hill and in multiple executive departments and agencies.

Intergovernmental and Reverse Lobbying

Intergovernmental lobbying: Attempts by public officials in one part of the government to influence their counterparts elsewhere—in another branch, or at a different (state or local) level.

Reverse lobbying: Attempts by government officials to influence interest groups on behalf of their preferred policies.

Public officials are not simply passive recipients of lobbying appeals: they also make those appeals themselves. Some engage in **intergovernmental lobbying**, pushing their counterparts in other branches to support their policy aims. When President Lyndon Johnson promoted a civil rights program in the mid-1960s, he made more than 150 telephone calls a day to members of the House and Senate, urging them to pass his legislative package. When mounting a full-blown effort on behalf of his goals, a president can be the most powerful lobbyist in Washington.

Government officials also lobby interest groups, an activity termed **reverse lobbying**. Members of Congress and White House officials regularly reach out to groups aligned with their legislative efforts, coordinating efforts by lobbyists to promote their programs with the public and other lawmakers. These efforts can be controversial. In 2001, Vice President Dick Cheney headed an energy task force that included six cabinet members—plus oil, gas, coal, and other industry executives and lobbyists. They met privately (no names released, no public record of the discussions). Public interest groups protested and sued, demanding a list of names. They charged that the administration had invited oil executives to come in and help shape energy policy to their own benefit—reverse lobbying run amuck.

White House and congressional leaders alike regularly convene closed-door meetings of a wide range of affected interest groups before moving forward on a policy proposal. Hearing from the various sides can generate a broad scope of information and ideas, and also may establish a compromise that wins enough support to push legislation through. Barack Obama used this approach to health reform in 2009–2010, when he directed advisors to meet secretly with groups representing the insurance industry, pharmaceutical companies, hospitals, physicians, and other primary stakeholders. On the positive side, the usual lobbying opposition to health reform was muted: the insurance industry, which had run ads against the Clinton health plan, largely stayed out of the fight over Obama's. When details of these deals were disclosed, however, Obama faced strong criticism from his own party and eventually turned to attacking the insurance companies he had courted earlier in the policy battle.

Lobbying the Courts

Iron triangles and issue networks portray lobbyists engaging with the two elective branches, Congress and the presidency. What about the courts, which—as you will see in Chapter 13—have a major role in federal and state policy making? Do interest groups successfully penetrate the cloistered sanctums of the federal judiciary?

Most lobbyists would seize the opportunity to talk directly to Supreme Court or other federal justices, trying to influence them through direct persuasion. But by law and custom, interest groups have almost no access to Supreme Court justices and very little connection to other federal (or senior state) judges. As one lobbyist writes, rather forlornly: "No one came to the Supreme Court to lobby. . . . The mere mention of a pending case at a cocktail party was forbidden."[6]

This separation of judges from direct lobbying influence fuels a view of the judiciary as independent, floating in the refined air of principles and theories, relatively free of the swamp of regular politics. But lobbyists still manage to weigh in on judicial decision-making, even without seeing judges in person to make their case. They do so in three main ways.

● *Choosing a justice. Supreme Court nominee Elena Kagan arrives for her Senate hearings, in a room filled with lobbyists for interest groups—many of which spent millions of dollars seeking to influence the confirmation battle. In the end, Kagan was confirmed by a wide margin.*

Lobbying on Judicial Confirmations. One way to shape court decisions is to influence the central players—to help determine who gets appointed as Supreme Court or federal judges in the first place. Each federal judge is approved by the Senate. That process used to be routine—the two longest-serving Supreme Court justices were both approved unanimously. Then, in 1987, the process suddenly changed. The Reagan administration nominated legal scholar Robert Bork, an unapologetic conservative, to replace a moderate justice. Liberals felt that everything from a woman's right to choose to the protection of civil rights would be threatened. Interest groups sprang into action to oppose the nomination. Conservative interest groups mobilized in response. After a high-publicity battle the nomination was defeated. We'll look at the case in more detail in Chapter 13; for now, the crucial point: after Bork, every Supreme Court nomination has immediately prompted a multi-million-dollar confirmation fight. Interest groups spend heavily on public campaigns, to influence the presidents who choose judges and the senators who confirm—or block—a president's choice.

Filing Amicus Curiae ("Friend of Court") Briefs.   Groups interested in a pending case are permitted to—and sometimes invited by a court to—write up legal memos, or "briefs," arguing their position in the case. Major cases attract dozens of such documents: in 2003, when the Supreme Court reviewed affirmative action, in a case involving the University of Michigan, 107 groups and individuals filed amicus curiae briefs. There is no guarantee that judges will take these briefs seriously (or even read them), but anecdotal evidence suggests that the briefs have an "agenda-setting" role. Based on groups' arguments, and sometimes the volume of briefs, they help influence what cases do and do not get heard.

Sponsoring Litigation.   It can be very expensive to take a case to court. Researching the relevant issues, paying the lawyers, and pursuing litigation through multiple appeals can cost millions of dollars. Interest groups often take up a legal cause, contributing both financial resources and expertise. When the Supreme Court agreed to review "establishment clause" rules about what counts as state sponsorship of religion—for example, whether government funds can go to Catholic schools, or whether a state courthouse can post the Ten Commandments—interest groups like the American Civil Liberties Union (liberal) and the Federalist Society (conservative) provide substantial expertise and financing.

One form of sponsorship that was pioneered by public interest advocates in the 1960s is class-action lawsuits. This form of legal action allows a group to sue on behalf of hundreds or even thousands of affected people in the same "class"—for example, all those exposed to asbestos at work or discriminated against in segregated schools. The famous *Brown v. Board of Education* case of 1954 was a class-action suit, sponsored primarily by the National Association for the Advancement of Colored People. Class-action suits transformed many aspects of American society—workplaces, schools, welfare offices—in the 1960 and 1970s, although recent rule changes have made them more difficult to file.

Political scientists and legal scholars dispute whether interest group involvement in court decisions makes much difference. Whatever the scholarly conclusion, lobbyists unwilling to leave any stone unturned in their advocacy efforts will continue to include legal action as a vital part of their campaigns to promote government activity. Such well-planned, wide-ranging efforts are an essential part of any successful lobbying strategy. But other ingredients matter as well.

THE BOTTOM LINE

- Lobbyists working in specific areas sometimes still form "iron triangles" with congressional staff and executive-branch officials.
- More fluid "issue networks," featuring lobbyists as central players, increasingly characterize today's complex policy-making environment.
- Lawmakers also lobby: they seek to persuade other public officials (intergovernmental lobbying) or secure assistance from interest groups (reverse lobbying).
- Interest groups also lobby the judicial branch, through funding confirmation battles, filing amicus curiae briefs, and financing litigation.

Political Parties and US Government

Two main political parties have long dominated American elections and government. The Democrats (originally Democratic-Republicans) won the White House for the first time in 1800 with the election of Thomas Jefferson and generally stand for enhancing political and economic equality. The Republican Party (also known as the **Grand Old Party**, or GOP) has been campaigning for "free labor" or "free markets" or "less government" since 1856. The parties are so familiar that their symbols—donkeys and elephants, respectively—are enough to represent them in the media. Third parties have often tried to break in, but they have never lasted very long. In contrast to most other democracies, the United States is a two-party system.

Grand Old Party (GOP): Long-standing nickname for the Republican Party; ironically, bestowed early in the party's history in the 1870s.

What the Parties Do

Love them or hate them, political parties are an essential part of American government. They do five major jobs:

Parties Select Candidates. The parties choose the candidates who will run for election. The Republicans began with twelve contenders running for president in 2012 and voted, state by state, until they had selected Mitt Romney.

● *Donkeys and elephants square off. Since the late nineteenth century, Republicans have been symbolized by the elephant (powerful, venerable, never forgets) and Democrats by the donkey (strong, hardworking, stubborn).*

The parties select candidates to run for office at every level of government—except local government, which as we will see often relies on **nonpartisan elections**.

Parties Champion Ideas. The United States reverberates with ideas, and every candidate takes a position on scores of issues. How do voters keep them all straight? In effect, parties create a brand that gives people an easy way to find candidates who roughly share their views. If you strongly support action to counter global warming, and to achieve a path to citizenship for undocumented immigrants, robust social programs, a woman's right to choose, public radio, and high-speed rail, you are probably a Democrat. If, on the other hand, you care more about lowering taxes, reducing the size of government, rolling back regulations, supporting morality, strong traditional families, a robust military, and outlawing abortion, you are probably a Republican. You want to mix and match from the lists? You're likely an independent that belongs to neither party. Each party has its language and symbols. Do people in a group raise their voices when they say "under God" in the Pledge of Allegiance? They're likely to be Republicans, participating in a party ritual.

Parties Mobilize Voters. The parties work to get the people to vote for their candidates. The parties raise money, hire consultants, craft advertisements, take polls, and organize phone banks. They have also become adept at suppressing the other side's votes through negative advertising.

Parties Organize Governing Activity After the Election. Once the election is over, each party works to enact its signature programs. The parties, and their leaders, propose action, line up votes, and organize government activity in Congress (as we will see in Chapter 10), in presidential administrations (Chapter 11), and in the state governments (as we saw in Chapter 3).

Parties Help Integrate New Groups into the Political Process. They are important agents of **political socialization**, transmitting basic lessons about politics and government (the details may differ, depending on the party). Parties have introduced immigrants, young voters, evangelical Christians, high-tech entrepreneurs, and many more into the American polity. Parties provide a crucial communication link between 320 million Americans, spread across a continent, and their elected leaders.

Political parties provide an efficient, effective solution to these five issues.[7] Is there anything especially distinctive about the American **party system**? Yes: the United States is unusual in relying on only two parties.

Nonpartisan election: An election where candidates run as individuals, without any party affiliation. Many towns and cities feature nonpartisan elections.

Political socialization: Education about how the government works and which policies one should support; provided by family, friends, schools, parties, and other national institutions.

Party system: The broad organization of US politics, comprising the two main parties, the coalition of supporters backing each, the positions they take on major issues, and each party's electoral achievements.

Two-Party America

All 435 members of the House of Representatives, 98 out of 100 senators, and 49 out of 50 governors are either Democrats or Republicans. Why is the United States so resolutely devoted to the number "two" when it comes to party politics?

One reason for this two-party tradition draws on American ideas. As we saw in Chapter 1, Americans long ago embraced a set of national ideals, including liberty, self-rule, and equality. Recall that these ideas tend to divide into different, hotly disputed, philosophies. Each side of these great debates is typically associated with one of the two major parties. For example, most Republicans see liberty as freedom from government; most Democrats fight for programs that will help free needy people from want. The two parties each seize a classic definition of liberty—what we described as negative and positive liberty, respectively.

As you know by now, institutions invariably reinforce ideas. In this case, the winner-take-all electoral rules, described in the previous chapter, keep third parties out. A party that wins 20 percent of the national vote but doesn't actually win any states or districts is blanked in both Congress and the Electoral College.

Most other democracies operate multiparty systems. Proportional representation systems, described in the last chapter, give small parties an incentive to compete. The European Green Parties (who are environmentalists) or free market parties (known as neoliberals) often win seats in the legislature if they receive a certain percentage of the vote—usually 5 percent. Once they win representatives, they introduce legislation, generate publicity, and—most important—provide key support on close votes, after negotiating concessions for their cause. Anyone trying to start those parties in the United States will have a more difficult time. America's winner-take-all system gives a party no seats at all for coming in second. The Green Party, for example, could win 25 percent of the vote across the nation and not take a single seat in Congress.

● Parties socialize new groups into politics. When evangelical Christians started getting involved in politics in the 1970s and 1980s, Republican leaders were there to show them the ropes. Here, President Ronald Reagan speaks to evangelical leaders.

● *Election posters in multiparty Japan.*

The result is simple and dramatic: the rules push every group to join the major parties. The free market advocates generally go to the Republicans, the environmentalists join the Democrats. If candidates try to run on their own, they are accused of being "spoilers"—attracting voters from the party that is more sympathetic to their cause and, as a result, throwing the election to the party that does not share their philosophy at all.

This is precisely what happened in the 2000 presidential election. In Florida, Republican George Bush won 48.847 percent of the vote; Democrat Al Gore won 48.838 percent of the vote; and Green Party candidate Ralph Nader won 1.635 percent of the vote. Even though Bush won by only 0.0001 percent—winner take all—he commanded all twenty-five Electoral College votes and won the presidency. What did disappointed Democrats say? Ralph Nader and the Green Party had drawn just enough liberals away from the Democrats to throw the election to the Republicans—who were far less sympathetic to Nader's causes. The Florida experience only reinforced the great institutional lessons: work within the two parties.

Additional institutional forces help keep the two main parties at the center of American politics. State laws determine who gets on the ballot, and they often make it very difficult for a minor-party candidate to be listed. In Florida, for example, after reforms in 2011 that *eased* restrictions, a third party still needs to collect more than 112,000 notarized signatures simply to list its candidate on a presidential-primary ballot—a high bar for a small party. Officials defend the rules by arguing that without them, voters would face a confusing mess of multiple candidates.

Similarly, the three presidential debates in 2012 featured only President Obama and Mitt Romney. The rules specified that third-party candidates could appear only if they averaged 15 percent national support in public opinion polls—too high for candidates from little-known third parties like the ones listed in Table 9.2.

There is a great advantage to America's two-party style. It is predictable and stable. In a system with many parties, each election is followed by negotiations among the parties trying to form a majority. Today, in Germany the majority coalition has two parties, in Israel five, and in India thirteen. Sometimes a single group pulls out of the governing coalition—and forces a new election.

There are also disadvantages to the two-party dominance in the United States.[8] For starters, it is less representative. In 2010, 38.8 percent of the voters in Massachusetts voted for Republican congressional candidates. Is it fair to end up with ten Massachusetts Democrats—and no Republicans—in

Table 9.2 National Parties Nominating Presidential Candidates, 2012

• Americans Elect
• American Third Position Party
• America's Party
• Constitution Party
• Democratic Party
• Green Party
• Justice Party
• Libertarian Party
• Party for Socialism and Liberation
• Prohibition Party
• Reform Party USA
• Republican Party
• Socialist Equality Party
• Socialist Party USA

Congress? Voters in Germany or Japan or other proportional representation systems generally have more choices for national or local office; people passionate about a cause—immigration, the environment, religion—often find a party devoted to the cause. But perhaps you're wondering if we have ever made room for additional parties?

Third Parties in American Politics

Theodore "Teddy" Roosevelt was one of the most colorful Figures in US political history: a military hero who suffered from asthma, a big-game hunter who adopted an orphaned bear cub (giving rise to the familiar "Teddy Bear").

Riding a wave of popularity, Roosevelt retired from the presidency in 1908 and handed the reins over to his political ally William Howard Taft. Soon, however, the restless Roosevelt broke with Taft and aimed to retake the White House in the 1912 election. Forming a new Progressive Party, Roosevelt campaigned enthusiastically—and came in second, far behind winner Woodrow Wilson, who won 435 electoral votes to Roosevelt's 88.

Roosevelt did manage to outperform his former ally Taft, becoming the only third-party candidate ever to finish second in a presidential election. Table 9.3 lists all the third-party presidential contestants gaining more than 5 percent of the popular vote or more than ten electoral votes since 1840. It's a short list without a single candidate who came close to winning.

Table 9.3 The Most Successful Third-Party Presidential Contenders, 1840–2012

ELECTION	THIRD-PARTY CANDIDATE(S), PARTY	PERCENTAGE OF POPULAR VOTE (NO. OF ELECTORAL VOTES)
1856	Millard Fillmore, American (Know- Nothing) Party	22% (8)
1860	John Bell, Constitutional Union Party	12.6% (39)
1892	James Weaver, People's Party	8.5% (22)
1912	Theodore Roosevelt, Progressive Party Eugene Debs, Socialist Party	27.4% (88) 6% (0)
1924	Robert LaFollette, Progressive Party	16.6% (13)
1948	Strom Thurmond, States' Rights (Dixiecrat) Party	2.4% (39)
1968	George Wallace, American Independent Party	13.5% (45)
1980	John Anderson, independent, National Unity Party	6.6% (0)
1992	Ross Perot, independent, United We Stand Party	18.9% (0)

Just as no presidential aspirant from a minor party has found success, no third party has lasted for very long at the national level. Roosevelt's Progressive Party, for example, elected some fifteen members to Congress and spearheaded important reforms. However, it had dissolved within four years. Minor parties have remained active in some states: in Minnesota, for example, the "Farmer-Labor Party" was powerful enough in the 1930s–1940s that it merged with the Democrats. To this day, Minnesota electoral contests are between Republican candidates and those of the "DFL," or Democratic-Farmer-Labor.

Minnesota also marks one of the occasional third-party gubernatorial successes in modern American politics. Jesse Ventura, a former professional wrestler (known as "The Body"), rode his blend of outsized personality and

● *Wrestler-turned-governor Jesse Ventura, Reform Party.*

blunt commonsense to the governor's mansion as a Reform Party candidate in 1998. In the last quarter-century, only four other states have elected governors outside the major parties: Alaska (1990), Connecticut (1990), Rhode Island (2010), and Maine (1994, 1998). All four winners were independents rather than representatives of third parties.

Despite this limited record of electoral success, minor parties are valuable contributors to American government. Since Democrats and Republicans generally compete to win "swing" voters in the political center, the differences between the two major parties can become blurred. Third-party movements have often injected strong and controversial views into the major parties. They have fought for the abolition of slavery, the direct election of senators, votes for women, laws eliminating child labor, the prohibition of drinking, the income tax, limits on immigrants, and—in the case of the Tea Party Patriots—smaller government. Typically the major parties absorb and then champion policy proposals from the minor parties.

Third parties, especially those with a national following, can also provide a vehicle for people to express alternative views. This helps dissidents get a hearing, expands civic engagement, and perhaps minimizes the potential of anger and violence that arise when people see their cause as ignored.[9] Third parties shake up a government system that can be resistant to change.

THE BOTTOM LINE

- America's two-party style has endured for over two hundred years, with Democrats and Republicans the main standard-bearers since 1856.
- The foundational American ideas and the organization of our elections help explain the dominance of the two parties.
- Third parties arise periodically to challenge two-party dominance, but none has ever managed to break through.

How Parties Are Organized

When Barack Obama emerged as the Democratic Party's presidential nominee in summer 2008, he became the de facto head of the party. Though no one had elected Obama as party chief—in fact, the then Democratic Party chairman, former Virginia governor Tim Kaine, remained in place—it was Obama who represented Democrats in the media, Obama who headlined Democratic fundraisers, and Obama who placed his trusted advisers in positions of power within the party's apparatus.

What type of organization did the new party leader represent? American parties have three parts: the party-in-government, the party organization, and the party in the electorate. And, like most American institutions we have studied in this book, each of these parts has a national, a state, and a local dimension. By now you will recognize the classic feature of American political institutions: a very complicated organizational chart. Let's take a closer look.

Party-in-Government

Party-in-government:
The portion of a political party's organization that comprises elected officials and candidates for office.

The **party-in-government** is made up of candidates, officeholders, and their top staffers. The presidential candidate or (for the losing side) the highest-ranking elected official unofficially heads the party-in-government. House Speaker John Boehner informally led the Republican Party but stepped aside when Mitt Romney became the GOP nominee for president in 2012; when Romney lost, Boehner again became the Republican leader.

The party-in-government promotes the party's issues and fights its policy battles in both Congress and the executive branch. On Capitol Hill, party leaders include the whips, who are tasked with keeping their party's members in line and voting with the party (see Chapter 10). Each party's House and Senate members separately caucus (meet as a group) to discuss strategy and build consensus. Similar caucus meetings take place in most state legislatures, sometimes with national "talking points" sent from central party committees: these are adapted to individual state political needs.

A constant struggle for influence takes place within each party-in-government. When John Boehner took over the Speaker's gavel in January 2011, other prominent Republicans also commanded national attention—Senate Republican minority leader Mitch McConnell; some well-known GOP governors like Rick Perry of Texas and Haley Barbour of Mississippi; and the men and women who were already running for the Republican nomination for president in 2012.

Some individuals compete to become the party's public face because they believe their vision is best suited to lead to a long-term victory. Others seek to advance a specific ideological vision. Some may seek power for its own sake,

● Changing of the party-leader guard. As presidential nominees emerge, they assume the unofficial mantle of "party-in-government leader," often superseding congressional leaders. Mitt Romney stands behind House speaker John Boehner, ready to take over as Republican leader just as President Obama assumed leadership from the Democratic leaders of Congress, Harry Reid and Nancy Pelosi in 2008.

or crave public attention. Whatever their motivation, the most prominent officeholders and national candidates compete to put their stamp on the party-in-government—and to get the rest of the party to follow them.

Party Organization

The **party organization** provides support for a party's candidates and elected officials. The party organization includes national, state, and local party officials, as well as political professionals supporting the party: fundraisers, pollsters, and PR experts. Party organizational leaders rarely have much of a public profile. Can you name the official chairs of the Democratic or Republican Party? (Debbie Wasserman Schultz and Reince Priebus, respectively.) Even most political scientists flunk that question. They may be unknown, but they are vitally important for they coordinate the party across fifty states.

The central organization for both parties is a national committee—the Republican National Committee, or RNC, and the Democratic National Committee, or DNC. These committees raise funds for the party, coordinate election strategies, decide which local races to fund, organize a national convention every four years, and prepare the **party platform**—the party's statement of purpose and its position on issues. If you are a candidate for a prominent office—from senator to mayor—your success may rest in large part on your ability to persuade the party organization to contribute funds to your campaign.

The committees also issue and enforce the party's rules for primary elections, from the presidential level downward. Important members of the DNC and RNC include the state party chairs and vice chairs, who make up two hundred of the most faithful activists in each party.

Congress also has extensive party organizations, employed both to win elections and to advance the party's policy priorities on Capitol Hill. Democrats and Republicans each have party hierarchies in both the House and the Senate. You will learn more details in Chapter 10, on Congress.

Another set of party committees in each chamber—the Republican Senatorial Campaign Committee, for example—organizes strategy and, like the DNC and the RNC, collects funds. For the 2010 midterm elections, the Democratic Congressional Campaign Committee (known as the "D-Triple-C," or just "D-Trip," in Washington) raised $164 million for Democratic House candidates. Their counterpart, the National Republican Congressional Committee, hauled in $132 million—but won far more House seats, suggesting that money isn't everything in election results.

Party in the Electorate

What is left after the officeholders and the party organizations? We are! The largest sector of each party—and, to the frustration of Democratic and Republican officials, the least active or organized—are We, the People, at least

Party organization: The portion of a political party that includes activists, state/local leaders, and affiliated professionals like fundraisers and PR experts.

Party platform: The written statement of a party's core convictions and issue priorities. Generally revised every four years, in time for the national party convention.

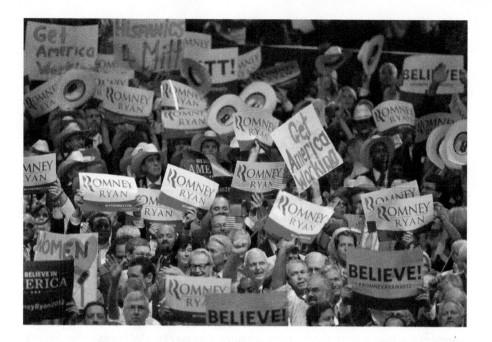

● *Party in the electorate. The Republican faithful gather in Tampa, Florida, in 2012 and cheer their nominee.*

Party in the electorate:
The largest (and least organized) component of a political party, drawn from the public at large: registered members and regular supporters.

those who are registered party members. Each party's followers make up the **party in the electorate**.

Members of the electorate attach themselves, with varying degrees of commitment, to one or the other party. The parties are enormous: roughly 72 million Democrats and 55 million Republicans, with another highly prized 40 million citizens registered as independents. Recently the public has begun to drift from registering with a party to registering as independents—although this effect is more pronounced in opinion polls than in actual registrations. With such large numbers and declining allegiance, it is never easy for party leaders to predict how many of their members will participate, contribute, or vote.

The Big Party Tents

The media generally focuses on the famous party names—Barack Obama or Mitt Romney. Political parties thrive, however, when all their elements—the officeholders, the organization, and the public supporters—work together. That means sharing the same message, getting enthused about party principles, and even embracing the party symbols—right down to the bumper stickers.

Although coordinating the three parts of the party—elected officials, party officials, and supporters—may sound simple, American federalism makes it complicated. Local officials run the party in each state. Democrats in a conservative state like Alabama often have more in common with many Republicans than they do with liberal Democrats in San Francisco or New

York City. The same is true, of course, for the more liberal Republicans in New York or Massachusetts—which posed a strategic problem for former Massachusetts governor Mitt Romney as he ran for the Republican Party nomination. Romney's problem illustrated the essential dilemma of two parties competing in fifty very different states. Southern Democrats (or northern Republicans) constantly plead with their colleagues to moderate their stance so that the party can make inroads in their own states.

Federalism pushes each of the two major parties to adopt a "big tent" approach: spread themselves wide, embrace followers of divergent views, and hope any resultant ideological muddle doesn't turn off too many party members. This tactic creates more varied (and often clashing) subgroups within each of the parties. In multiparty nations, the different elements of each party might form parties of their own. The American system keeps pushing very disparate groups—from very different parts of the country—together into the big tents of the Democrats and Republicans.

THE BOTTOM LINE

- The parties include three separate groups: (1) the party-in-government, consisting of elected politicians, their staffs, and affiliated political professionals; (2) the party organization, consisting of party chairs, the national committees, and the state party leaders; and (3) the party in the electorate, consisting of the millions of people who identify with the party.
- American parties are highly decentralized: President Obama or Speaker Boehner may win media attention and national organizers issue party platforms, but state and local party leaders largely run their own organizations, independent of national headquarters.
- Each major party must work to unite different perspectives under one "big tent."

America's Party Systems: Origins and Change

Today's Republican and Democratic Parties compete in a very different environment than their predecessors did. At regular intervals, the party system undergoes an electoral realignment: the coalitions, the issues, and the relative strength of the parties shift—sometimes very suddenly. We can identify at least six distinctive "party systems" stretching across American history. Understanding the previous systems helps illuminate what is typical and what is unique about party politics today.

Beginnings: First Party System (1789–1828)

After the revolution, the battle over ratification drew almost everyone into the argument between pro-Constitution Federalists (who supported a stronger central government) and their Anti-Federalist opponents (who thought power should remain with the states and communities). The first administration, under President George Washington, saw a continuation of the same conflict: Secretary of the Treasury Alexander Hamilton and Vice President John Adams pressed for a strong national government (and eventually dominated the administration).

Representative James Madison and Secretary of State Thomas Jefferson resisted central power. Factions supporting and opposing the administration formed in the House and Senate; talented writers pressed each group's case in newly established national newspapers—and political parties were born.

Candidates for the first Congresses identified as either Federalists (strong national government) or Democratic-Republicans (states' rights and limited national power).

In 1800, Democratic-Republican candidate Thomas Jefferson won a bitter, razor-thin victory over President John Adams. This was the first time the White House changed party hands. For the rest of the first party period, the Democratic-Republicans dominated national politics, winning the next six presidential elections and controlling both chambers of Congress for twenty-four years (see Table 9.4).

Rise: Second Party System (ca. 1828–1860)

When Andrew Jackson won the presidency in 1828, some twenty thousand Democrats (many of them angling for government jobs) swarmed into Washington for his inauguration. Supreme Court Justice Joseph Story, watching the spectacle, spoke for many old-style gentry: "The reign of King Mob seemed triumphant."[10] Instead, it was the birth of modern party politics.

● Dueling in the first party. Despite a general convention of elaborate courtesy, the first party system also featured bitter disputes—spilling over, in this case, into a famous duel that ended Alexander Hamilton's life.

Table 9.4 Overview of the Six Party Systems

Notice that the sixth party system—our own—is very unusual in one way: no party dominates. This is especially true in recent times. Democrats have a small edge in the House, Republicans a small edge in the Senate, and the Republicans dominate/have an edge in the White House.

| | YEARS IN CONTROL | | | | | |
	PRESIDENT		HOUSE		SENATE	
	FEDERALIST	DEM REPUB	F	DR	F	DR
1. 1789–1828	12	28	8	26	12	22
	DEMOCRAT	NAT REPUB/ WHIG	DEM	NR/WHIG	DEM	NR/WHIG
2. 1829–1860	24	8	24	8	28	4
	DEM	REPUBLICAN	DEM	REPUB	DEM	REPUB
3. 1861–1896	8	28	6	30	14	22
4. 1897–1932	8	28	10	26	6	30
5. 1932–1968	28	8	32	4	32	4
6. 1969–2012	16	28	30	14	25	17
a) **recent 1992–2014**	**14**	**8**	**6**	**16**	**10**	**12**

In just three decades, political parties had evolved into a form that we would recognize today. Party competition grew fierce; leaders no longer pretended to be neutral public servants above the fray; voting rights expanded; enthusiastic party members threw themselves into politics. These hallmarks of America's second party system remain the backbone of our party practices.

Party names changed along with the institutional shifts. The Federalists had vanished. Jefferson's old Democratic-Republicans split into two factions in the 1820s. Supporters of Andrew Jackson adopted the "Democratic" half, while a separate faction aligned with a brilliant young Kentucky politician, Henry Clay, called themselves "Whigs"—a British term associated with opposition to tyranny—in this case, "King Andrew."

Both parties foundered on the question of slavery. Neither, however, could duck the issues. As the United States spread west, every new territory and state raised the same terrible question: Should slavery be permitted to spread as Americans moved westward? Factions formed within each party. In the early 1850s, the Whigs, who had attracted the strongest opponents of slavery, collapsed under the issue. Out of the Whigs' demise the Republican Party and a new party system rose up—and clarified the future of slavery in the United States.[11]

War and Reconstruction: Third Party System (1860–1896)

Republican Party candidate Abraham Lincoln won the presidential election of 1860; the southern states feared the end of slavery and the nation soon entered its terrible Civil War.

After the war, Republicans drew on the party to help rebuild the nation. "Radical Republicans" promoted black rights, helping to boost many former slaves into Congress and statehouses under the Republican banner. Democrats, fighting back in the South, denounced Reconstruction's "excesses" and often resorted to explicitly racist tactics that tried to limit the freedom of the former slaves to travel, to vote, or to seek employment.

After winning the war, Republicans dominated elections between 1864 and 1880. Not until Grover Cleveland broke through in 1884 would Democrats again hold the White House—and he was the only Democratic occupant between 1860 and 1912. The Republicans controlled the House of Representatives for thirty of the next thirty-six years.

With the end of "Radical Republican" rule in 1877, each party developed a strong regional identity, with Democrats controlling the "solid South" of former Confederate states and Republicans strongest in the Northeast and Midwest. Large numbers of European and Asian immigrants streamed into the cities during the 1870s and 1880s; city governments featured well-developed **party machines**—powerful political organizations. Managed by a

Party machine: A hierarchical arrangement of party workers, often organized in an urban area to help integrate immigrants and minority groups into the political system. Most active in the late nineteenth and early twentieth centuries.

● *Reconstruction featured a hotly fought battle between the parties. While Republicans promoted images of new racial harmony and national economic health, Democrats warned of impending doom. This caricature was part of the racist campaign designed to show that the former slaves were not prepared for freedom—a false charge backed by violence that eventually helped defeat efforts at racial reconstruction.*

party boss, party machines provided immigrants with such basic services as food, shelter, jobs, contacts, and a sense of belonging. In exchange, the party could count on a block of all-important votes, once immigrants became naturalized citizens. The machines grew notorious for bribery and corruption. In some places they paid men to vote, stuffed ballot boxes, permitted repeat voters, and engaged in terrible brawls on Election Day.

Reformers eventually cleaned up city politics (although the hardiest machines lasted well into the twentieth century) through a series of institutional reforms that included banishing the parties themselves from urban elections. Thus, today parties remain crucial on the national and state level, but many cities have nonpartisan elections. In fact, you can measure how strong the urban reformers have been in any city by checking whether the parties still operate in local elections.

Party boss: The senior figure in a party machine.

● *The story of Jack and the Beanstalk with President Theodore Roosevelt, brandishing the sword of "public service," as Jack confronting corrupt "giants" of Wall Street like banker J. P Morgan.*

Business and Reform: Fourth Party System (1896–1932)

After twenty years of Republican dominance (1860–1880) neither party won the White House for two successive terms; two candidates lost the popular vote but squeaked into the White House through Electoral College victories (which we will discuss in Chapter 11). Suddenly, in 1896, the party system changed again and a renewed Republican Party, now known as the "millionaires party," swept back into control. However, McKinley was assassinated in 1901, and his vice president, Theodore Roosevelt, stepped into the White House and challenged the "millionaires' club."

The great debates of the fourth party system featured support for the status quo and business, on the one side, and pressures for political and economic equality (championed by the Progressive movement) on the other. Should women win the vote? Should the government regulate emerging corporate giants, like Standard Oil or the Central Pacific Railroad? Should judges be elected? On the state level, should the government regulate child labor? Should it limit the workday for men and women? Should it provide funds for the blind or the aged? To the Progressive reformers, led by Theodore Roosevelt, the answer was yes, yes, yes.

The 1920s became a boom time, marked by rising new industries like advertising, automobiles, and electricity. Then the economy collapsed in 1929–1930 and, amid the economic wreckage, a new party system rose up.

Depression and New Deal: Fifth Party System (1933–1968)

Another President Roosevelt, Teddy's distant cousin Franklin, helped define the fifth party system. The Great Depression (1929–1941) unhinged party politics, crippling a Republican Party associated with the economic crash.

After three years of economic misery, FDR's uncompromising inaugural address swept in a new politics. Roosevelt frankly blamed the "unscrupulous money changers" and "self seekers"—the old "millionaires' club"—for the nation's "dark days." Roosevelt's **New Deal** focused on jobs, infrastructure, government aid to the elderly (Social Security), temporary assistance for the needy (unemployment insurance, welfare), and new federal government agencies to manage it all. Roosevelt's Democratic Party reaped the electoral rewards, reshaping party coalitions.

The Democratic Party coalition included an unusual mix of interests. It had controlled the South since Reconstruction, when defeated Confederates rejected their Republican military conquerors. The big-city machines, with their ethnic supporters, also voted reliably Democratic (occasionally cheating at the ballot box to offset rural Republicans). To this reliable base, Roosevelt added labor unions (the Democrats sponsored legislation that permitted the movement to grow); farmers who saw agricultural prices rise under FDR; and—perhaps most surprising—African Americans.

African Americans had been loyal to the GOP since Lincoln signed the Emancipation Proclamation. However, Democratic presidents Franklin Roosevelt (1932–1945), Harry Truman (1945–1953), John Kennedy

New Deal: Broad series of economic programs and reforms introduced between 1933 and 1936 and associated with the Franklin Roosevelt administration.

What Do You Think?

Does the 2012 Election Suggest a New Party Period?

What do the results of the 2012 presidential election tell us about the immediate future of the party system? Is one party or another poised to establish dominance and break away for a long period of time?

Yes. President Barack Obama's reelection means that Democrats have won the White House in four out of the last six elections—and the party won the popular vote in a fifth election (in 2000), only to lose a disputed count in Florida. At least in the presidency, the electorate seems poised to break away from the long string of very close elections.

Probably not. Republicans held onto House control in 2012, while Democrats continued to hold the presidency and Senate. Since the early 1980s, neither party has been able to control all three for more than a short period.

No. The government is still divided and close elections still look like the order of the day. Changing demographic trends may herald a new period in the future, but no clear signs exist yet.

(1961–1963), and Lyndon Johnson (1963–1969) proposed far-reaching legislation on everything from racial desegregation to national health insurance.

As the Democrats embraced civil rights, southern Democrats turned into Republicans. As the Democratic coalition began to crumble, a new generation of Republicans rose up with fresh ideas for America.

The Sixth Party System: The Parties at Equal Strength (1969–Present)

Richard Nixon (1969–1973) and, later, Ronald Reagan (1981–1989) developed a "southern strategy" to win middle-class white votes. They emphasized small business, limited government, and a more market-oriented vision. The Republican Party had always had a conservative wing, but now this wing rose to dominance. By the 1980s, the parties lined up in their contemporary ways: on economic and social issues alike, Democrats leaned left, Republicans right.

Republicans had controlled the fourth party period, and Democrats the fifth. The new party era introduces something new: neither party is in control. Instead, very close elections swing party control back and forth. Very close elections, year after year, have sharpened the partisanship.

Perhaps the United States will experience close elections for a long time to come. Or perhaps one party or the other is poised to break away, establish dominance, and start a new party era. We will return to this question when we study the presidency.

THE BOTTOM LINE

- Two main parties have always dominated US party politics—and since 1856 it has been the same two parties, Republicans and Democrats.
- The two parties—and the contest between them—regularly reboots into a new party system. Each change in party system means a change in the voters making up each party, and in the ideas that inspire them.
- Historians count at least six party systems since the US founding. We believe that the United States entered a sixth party system sometime around 1968: the system of very close elections, especially after 1990.

● Party Identification . . . and Ideas

You have been reading about the two main political parties (and some minor ones). Most Americans consider themselves Republicans, Democrats, or independents. However, even with just two parties to choose from, Americans are more likely to express a strong party preference than are people in most other democratic countries. That powerful attachment to one party is called **party identification**.

Party identification: Strong attachment to one political party, often established at an early age.

Building Party Identification

Where does our unusually powerful sense of party identification come from? And does strong party identification make a difference in American politics and government? Our party identification often begins in childhood. Many of us maintain allegiance to a religious denomination or sports team because of parents, family members, or close friends. Republican or Democratic Party loyalty often starts in the same way. Mark Losey, running for a US House seat in 2006, told his Ohio audiences how he chose his party. As a child, he used to go for walks on his grandfather's farm. "On one of those walks," recalled Losey, "I asked, 'Grandpa, are we Democrats or Republicans?' My Grandpa, who grew up on a farm during the height of the Great Depression, paused. 'Before Roosevelt became president, our family almost starved to death,' he replied. Grandpa Wren is still a Democrat. So am I."[12]

Of course, political views may change. Senator Orrin Hatch, a Utah Republican, was raised a staunch Democrat. During college, however, as Hatch recalls: "I learned that personal responsibility and a government closer to the people was supremely better for businesses and individuals than an intrusive federal government that led to personal dependency."[13] Republicans were more closely identified with these perspectives, and Hatch switched his party allegiance.

Party identification is also shaped by personal identity. Race and ethnic background are often strongly correlated with party ID: African Americans, Mexican Americans, Puerto Ricans, and women tend to vote Democratic—and the trend for each group has been rising. Whites, men, Cubans, and evangelical voters tend to be Republicans—although in 2012 Cuban voters narrowly supported Obama (Figure 9.5).

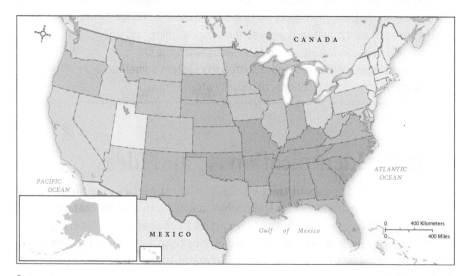

● **Figure 9.5** *Evangelical voter proportions. Darker colors indicate a higher proportion of evangelical residents; lighter colors indicate a lower proportion. More evangelicals tends to mean more Republican votes.*

Other traits, like personality, help explain the strength of party feelings. Recent studies suggest that people who exhibit more "openness" (eager to explore new experiences) and "agreeableness" (very social in outlook) are more likely to be strong Democrats. Those who measure high in "conscientiousness" (strong sense of duty, discipline, impulse control) and "emotional stability" (even-tempered) tend to be stronger supporters of the Republican Party.[14] Think about your own personality: Does it fit with this recent political science wisdom?

Another influence on the strength of party ties is political context—put simply, what's happening in national politics when a voter forms attachments. As we saw in the last section, certain "critical elections" involve large shifts of voters into one or another party. Each party strives hard for the magic formula: find the right combination of hot-button issues, nominate the right charismatic figure (for example, Barack Obama or Ronald Reagan) to run for president, and hope that a big shift in party identification takes place. When the magic strikes, the party can benefit for many years (and elections). Democrats hoped in 2008 that Barack Obama might be such a transformative figure—and after a tough election victory in 2012, analysts will be watching to see if Obama and the Democrats are able to build a sustained majority.

Although we are always looking for a sea change, no mass shift in party identification has shown up for the last twenty-five years or so. The relative proportion of Republicans, Democrats, and independents bumps around a little, but each hovers at around a third of the electorate. Currently, Democrats poll at around 33 percent and Republicans between 24 percent and 29 percent, depending on the poll. But recently one thing appears to be changing—the surge in independents, weary of both parties. Recent polls put them at around 38 percent. Why? One reason may be the intense conviction among the party faithful.

The Power of Party Attachment

Three key aspects of public involvement are shaped by party identification: voting/political participation, "filtering," and ideology.

What Do You Think?

•.. Personality and Party

Consider your own personality and party preference. Does recent political science research help predict your view— and the views of the people around you?	**Yes.** I believe that Democrats are more likely to seek new experiences and Republicans are more likely to emphasize duty and discipline.	**No.** I think there are different traits that explain party identification. (Please specify which traits you think matter most.)	**Interests, Not Personality.** I don't believe personality predicts politics. We are rational creatures pursuing our own self-interest regardless of personality.

Voting/Participation. Your Democratic or Republican party ID tends to be a very strong predictor of your voting habits. In 2008, for example, 91 percent of Democrats voted for Obama for president, while 79 percent of Republicans voted for McCain. Analysts measuring the strength of party attachment find that strong partisans tend to be very loyal **straight-ticket voters**, sticking with their party's candidates right down the ballot. Their opposite? **Split-ticket voters**, who choose candidate by candidate. Political scientists showed the link between party identification and voting more than fifty years ago, and the "standing decision" of party members about how to cast their ballots has not changed since. Partisan attachment also helps determine whether a voter will turn out in the first place: voting rates are higher among those with strong party identification than among the rest of the public. Beyond voting, strong partisans are much more likely than the general population to volunteer as campaign workers, attend rallies, donate money, and run for office themselves. The key to every election is turning out the party's **base voters**, making sure they actually show up at the polls, while winning over the independents.

Ideology. People in other nations, especially those in multiparty systems, see the Democrats and Republicans as pretty much alike. However, Americans see vast—and growing—differences. Given the dizzying array of issues facing government, party identification provides a simple framework for understanding issues and forming opinions.

Straight-ticket voter: One who votes for the same party for all offices on a ballot.

Split-ticket voter: One who votes for at least one candidate from each party, dividing his or her ballot between the two (or more) parties.

Base voters: Party members who tend to vote loyally for their party's candidates in most elections.

● **Figure 9.6** *Declining Republican support for tougher environmental laws. The percentage of party members who support stricter laws and regulations to protect the environment has been on the decline, especially among Republicans. (Pew Research)*

● *Tea Party members rally. They are one part of the large coalition of views that make up the Republican Party—but, for a while at least, their energy gave the entire party a boost. The danger: very strong views can threaten the support of the independents.*

Recent studies suggest that party ideology may be growing stronger. On one issue after another, members of the two parties have become more polarized. Take support for environmental legislation, for example. Twenty-five years ago, members of both parties supported tougher environmental laws—93 percent of Democrats and 86 percent of Republicans. In fact, Republican president Richard Nixon was especially effective at passing green policies. Today 93 percent of Democrats continue to support tougher environmental legislation (no change in twenty-five years) while support has crashed among Republicans— falling to 47 percent by 2012. On one issue after another, members of the parties have begun to take radically different views.

Both Democrats and Republicans publish an official statement of party positions during every presidential campaign. These statements are known as the *party platform*. Why a platform? Back in the late 1840s, abolitionist William Lloyd Garrison demanded that each party include an antislavery "plank" in its "platform." Neither party did, but Garrison's carpentry metaphors survived, and parties have used the terms ever since.[15] Not many people actually read the platforms. But people do identify with a party because its ideas—its platform—speak to them.

THE BOTTOM LINE

- A substantial majority of voting-age Americans identify strongly with one of the two major parties. Others declare themselves independents.
- Our powerful sense of party ID is a result of many factors, including parental influence, political context, and even personality type.
- Party ID in turn helps shape our voting patterns, the ways we filter political information, and our bedrock ideas about politics and government.
- Each party features several ideological factions, with most politically aware Americans aligning with one or two of these.

◗ Party Competition . . . and Partisanship

Parties began to lose their influence over politics and government in the mid-1960s. Interest groups muscled in on party territory, mobilized voters, and shaped issue positions. Americans began to identify with movements and organizations—civil rights, environmentalism, right to life, libertarians. The parties floundered. By the 1970s and 1980s, political observers were publishing books like *The Party's Over* and *The Decline of American Political Parties*.[16] The central role of parties in organizing elections also slipped, with the rise of the "candidate-centered election" that we met in the preceding chapter.

Parties Rise Again

Just as political science analysts declared the death of parties, however, their revival began. During the 1980s, changing congressional rules shifted power from committee chairs back to party leadership, strengthening the party-in-government. A huge influx of money into politics further revitalized party organizations, buoyed by the widespread adoption of political action committees (PACs) in the 1980s, "527" committees in the 2000s, and super PACs in the 2010s. The DNC and RNC, along with the congressional campaign organizations, became the chief recipients of campaign funds—and directed them in turn to candidates, who became more dependent on the parties as a result.

The parties also became ideologically purer. Conservative southern Democrats switched to the GOP. Liberal Republicans moved—or were pushed—to the Democrats. Each party was now organized around a clear set of ideas and principles. Each side could concentrate on defeating its foes—rather than on negotiating the differences within its own ranks.

Competition Intensifies

Today the two parties are thriving, contesting very close national elections. The three presidential elections between 1996 and 2004 featured the closest trio of successive races since the 1880s. One marker of the intensity of Democratic-Republican competition today: control of the White House and Congress has been switching back and forth between the major parties at a rapid pace. Table 9.5 traces party control of the three elective national institutions since 2000.

Seven shifts in party control (two presidential, three Senate, two House) across the three institutions in a single decade is an unusually high rate of change—it matches the change in the previous forty years (1960–2000). Today's strong competition means that neither party can pull away and dominate; neither can break through and remake the electoral landscape. These close elections are what marks the sixth party system.

Table 9.5 Party Control of US National Institutions Since 2000

ELECTION YEAR	CONTROL OF PRESIDENCY	PARTY IN CONGRESSIONAL MAJORITY (SIZE OF MAJORITY)	
		SENATE	HOUSE
2000	**R (Bush)**	**50-50 (later +1 D)***	R (9 seats)
2002	R (Bush)	**R (2 seats)****	R (24 seats)
2004	R (Bush)	R (10 seats)	R (29 seats)
2006	R (Bush)	**D (2 seats)**	**D (37 seats)**
2008	**D (Obama)**	D (19/20 seats)	D (79 seats)
2010	D (Obama)	D (6 seats)	**R (49 seats)**
2012	D (Obama)	D (10 seats)	R (32 seats)

*After May 2001, when Senator Jeffords switched parties, Democrats controlled the Senate.
**BOLD indicates that party control switched after that year's election.

Partisanship and Its Discontents

During the decline of party power in the 1970s–1980s, many analysts wondered if strong partisanship was diminishing as well. Today, Americans worry about the opposite problem: too much partisanship.

In the past, partisan differences on Capitol Hill were blurred by factions within each party. Democrats were so bitterly divided they could barely hold a **party caucus** during the 1950s–1960s. Democratic liberals were in the vanguard of the civil rights and gender-equality movements, while Southern Democrats fiercely defended segregation. Republicans were divided between relatively liberal members from the Northeast and forceful conservatives in the heartland.

Today those differences within the parties have almost disappeared. Party factions remain, but party members are far less diverse in their views. The strongest divisions are now between the two parties. By 2010, the most left-leaning Republican in the US Senate was to the right (in terms of voting record) of the most rightward Senate Democrat. For the first time, ideological conflict in both House and Senate breaks down perfectly along party lines. This partisan divide makes the political contest—over ideas, programs, even the meaning of America—louder and angrier than it has been in more than a century.

Party caucus: A meeting of all House or Senate members of one or the other main party, usually to discuss political and policy strategies.

No matter where you look, partisanship within government is rising. It is also increasing among the public.[17] It is not clear who influences whom. Are partisan officials fanning the flames of party difference among Americans? Or do activists within each party push their leaders to take stronger positions against the opposition? Or perhaps media outlets like Fox News and MSNBC, catering, respectively, to conservatives and liberals, have driven us into our party corners? The answer is probably yes to all three.

Should we worry? Is the rise in partisan differences dangerous? Does it make governance worse? Public opinion surveys repeatedly report Americans' dismay at partisan disagreement, even while we fan the flames of party polarization. What is it that Americans are so worried about?

First, the argument goes, party divisions lead to gridlock—a slowdown in government's ability to get things done. Second, bitter partisanship, as one commentary put it, "breeds bad public policy."[18] Third, a toxic partisan climate is said to drive more public officials away from government service, because less-partisan members of Congress retire early in the face of incivility and relentless conflict. And fourth, it leads to disenchantment among the public.

Is partisanship really generating these types of bad government outcomes? Some political scientists break with popular wisdom and argue that the fears of partisan breakdown are exaggerated: American government—with checks, balances, and federalism—was designed to move incrementally. Delay is part of the normal process. Although parties are more polarized today than in the recent past, they argue, it is not clear that American policy-making is slower or less effective than it was thirty or fifty years ago. Whether or not you like the results, President Obama's first two years yielded policy achievements that rival any congressional session over the past forty years including health reform, economic stimulus, and financial regulations. **Divided government** (when at least one house of Congress is controlled by a party different from that occupying the White House) has always been loud, divisive—and unexpectedly productive.[19]

Finally, congressional retirements in the 2000s actually lagged behind the pace for the 1980s or 1990s, and the average length of House or Senate service rose slightly in the 2000s. Is partisan rancor driving the "best and brightest" out of politics? The argument is not supported by counting up years of service.

Other political scientists contest this optimistic view. When the Democrats controlled both Congress and the presidency, legislation passed; even so, the debate continued almost unabated—in the courts and on the state level. When Republicans took over the House, the inability to compromise led to paralysis. Even if divided government worked in the past, the partisan differences have grown too intense to be good government. Moreover, the partisan intensity drives away everyone but the shrinking party bases—as the millennial generation's experience grimly testifies.

Divided government: Periods during which at least one house of Congress is controlled by a party different from the one occupying the White House.

Which side is right? We'll return to this argument in more detail when we study Congress in Chapter 10. For now, be aware that there are two sides to the argument about whether rising partisanship is harming American government.

THE BOTTOM LINE

- After declining thirty to forty years ago, the main political parties are both thriving—and highly competitive. Recent national elections feature narrow margins of victory in presidential races and frequent shifts in party control.
- This competition has helped fuel a rise in partisan differences, evident among both national policy makers and the US public.
- Most Americans—and many social scientists—believe that partisanship is affecting the quality of American government. The intensity of the conflict, they believe, will weaken our institutions.

Conclusion: A Party System Ripe for Reform?

As we have seen, Americans have passed laws in an attempt to ensure that wealthy and powerful groups do not have undue influence on public policy. Through the years, Americans have also considered reforms to our political party system. Here are three of the most commonly voiced proposals. As always, we invite your own ideas.

1. Proportional representation. As we saw earlier, America's winner-take-all system elects the highest vote recipient in each of 435 single-member House districts—and that reduces to almost zero the number of House or Senate members who are not from one of the two major parties. A PR system provides minor parties with representation equivalent to their electoral support. You would soon have representatives of the environmental party, the pro-immigration

What Do You Think?

Winner Take All

If it were up to you, how would you vote?	**Introduce proportional representation.** I believe that this approach would give voters more choices and increase voter participation.	**Keep things as they are.** "Winner take all" has been working for more than two centuries. Why change it?

What Do You Think?

:. Third Parties

If it were up to you, how would you vote on the subject of third-party representation in American government?

Make it easier for third parties. It should be easier for minor parties to be listed on the ballot and take part in the national debates leading to the election. Change will be difficult to implement if third-party voices are continually silenced on the national stage. Besides, adding new voices might lessen the level of conflict between the parties.

Keep things as they are. Giving innumerable third parties an equal voice would create a babble of conflicting views and little consensus on important issues. Moreover, it might make agreement even more difficult on topics such as health care, gun control, and national defense.

On second thought . . . Since the two parties are not going to step aside, only deeper institutional changes—like proportional representation—would really give third parties a serious chance.

● After the near-fatal shooting of Rep. Gabrielle Giffords (D-AZ), US Senators broke with tradition for the State of the Union address. Rather than all Democrats and all Republicans sitting in separate groups, pairs of senators sat together. One "odd couple" pictured here: liberal Charles Schumer of New York and conservative Tom Coburn of Oklahoma.

party, the anti-immigration party, and the libertarians. Would this change be a good thing?

Supporters claim that it would give voters more choices, possibly increasing voter turnout. It would also enhance policymaking, by ensuring that a wider spectrum of options is considered, better reflecting the nation's ideological and civic diversity. Many advocates predict that more women and minority-group representatives could be elected.[20]

2. Reduce the barriers to third-party competition in elections. If not a wholesale switch to a PR system, why not make it easier for minor parties to be listed on the ballot? Why not let them join major-party candidates onstage in debates? Multiple parties might reduce the level of conflict and force groups to compromise and reach out across party lines. They might bring change and fresh ideas into American politics.

On the other hand, perhaps the two parties have effectively managed the head-spinning diversity of America. Opening the floodgates to numerous minor parties might make it even more difficult to achieve consensus.

3. Reduce partisanship in government.   Reformers promoting this approach sometimes call for a "postpartisan" American politics. Ideas include limiting negative campaigning (unfortunately, this is hard to do, because negative campaigning works), reducing the role of outside advocacy groups in campaigns (attempts to do so have been struck down by the Supreme Court), adopting public financing (implemented in a few places, but without notable reduction in partisan polarization), and finding creative ways to bridge the party divide in government. One small effort to boost cooperation, introduced after the nearly fatal shooting of Representative Gabrielle Giffords (D-AZ), had opposing-party pairs sit together at the president's annual State of the Union address.

So far, the attempts at unity have been swamped by disagreements. If partisan differences are to decline in intensity, the change is likely to originate with our public officials—or with voters who punish partisan-style governance at the next election. Neither governors nor governed have shown much inclination to change their practice of decrying partisanship, while fiercely embracing their party and its ideas.

Here is a slightly different way to think about parties and partisanship. Consider the rich history of party politics in America that we have traced across six party systems. Those 225 years have often seen a spirit that the Greeks called *agonistic*—a willingness to disagree with your adversaries, while acknowledging their views as legitimate. This spirit means engaging wholeheartedly in a process of argument. In a democracy, successful political ideas must not just be good. We must also contest them, and we do this through party competition.

After all, the United States has always been a nation based on ideas—and intense disagreements about what they mean. The great debate that now occupies the parties has been going on for more than two hundred years. The important goal is that as many citizens as possible all join in. The greatest dangers come, not from strongly held views but from the apathy of the citizens. That, in the long run, might be the greatest risk of our charged partisan times.

What Do You Think?

Partisanship

| Should we be trying to diminish partisanship? | **Yes, partisanship is harmful.** Partisanship leads to paralysis. Worse, it is turning people off from politics, and that will create problems for us in the long run. | **No, partisanship is healthy.** The problems of partisanship originate with strong ideas and close elections. The arguments are useful and just part of the democratic process. We should encourage intense views and strong arguments—that's what introduces bold new ideas. |

CHAPTER SUMMARY

● Interest group lobbying has long been a vital feature of US government and politics. Lobbyists are deeply engaged in all parts of our policymaking system, and groups have sprung up to represent virtually every imaginable professional, personal, and identity-based interest, providing their members with information about federal policies and conveying those members' concerns to Washington.

● Americans hold lobbyists in very low regard.

● Lobbyists are active in all three branches of government; in each, they both seek and provide information—the currency of politics. They also work on (and help finance) political campaigns and are closely intertwined with leadership of both Republican and Democratic Parties.

● America's two-party style has endured for over two hundred years, with Democrats and Republicans the main standard-bearers since 1856.

● The foundational American ideas and the organization of our elections help explain the dominance of the two parties. So do the electoral rules.

● Third parties arise periodically to challenge two-party dominance, but none has ever managed to break through.

● Each major party must work to unite under one "big tent" their key figures and followers. These include the *party-in-government* (elected politicians, their staffs, and affiliated political professionals); the *party organization* (party chairs, the national committees, and the state party leaders);

and the *party in the electorate* (the millions of people who identify with the party).

● American parties are highly decentralized: state and local party leaders largely run their own organizations, independent of national headquarters.

● The system of two parties—and the contest between them—regularly reboots into new party systems. Each change in party system means a change in the voters making up each party, and in the ideas that inspire them.

● Historians count at least six party systems since the US founding: the Federalist era, the Jacksonian era, Civil War and Reconstruction, business's rise and Progressive reform, the New Deal, and (beginning around 1969), a contemporary period of roughly equal balance between the two major parties.

● A substantial majority of voting-age Americans identifies strongly with one of the two major parties. Others declare themselves independents.

● The powerful sense of party ID is a result of many factors, including parental influence, political context, and even personality type.

● Party ID in turn helps shape our voting patterns, the way we filter political information, and our bedrock ideas about politics and government.

● Most Americans—and many social scientists—believe that partisanship is affecting the quality of American government. The intensity of the conflict, they believe, will weaken our institutions.

KEY TERMS

Base voters, 346
Demosclerosis, 316
Divided government, 350
Expressive benefits, 314
Federal Regulation of Lobbying
    Act, 321
Gift ban, 321
Grand Old Party, 327
Interest group, 312
Intergovernmental lobbying, 324
Iron triangle, 322
Issue network, 323

K Street, 309
Lobbying coalition, 315
Lobbyist, 312
Material benefits, 314
Membership group, 312
New Deal, 342
Nonpartisan election, 328
Party boss, 341
Party caucus, 349
Party identification, 343
Party in the electorate, 336
Party-in-government, 334

Party machine, 340
Party organization, 335
Party platform, 335
Party system, 328
Pluralism, 316
Political socialization, 328
Power elite theory, 316
Reverse lobbying, 324
Solidary benefits, 314
Split-ticket voter, 346
Straight-ticket voter, 346

STUDY QUESTIONS

1. There are three main theories about the effects of interest groups: pluralism, hyperpluralism, and elitism. Describe each.

2. After reading the chapter, which of the theories in Question 1 seems to you most accurate? Justify your answer.

3. Describe the traditional iron triangle. Explain the issue network that has now replaced it in large part.

4. What is the free rider problem? Name three kinds of benefits that interest groups provide to overcome the free rider problem.

5. What are the two main reasons American politics is usually limited to two political parties?

6. What is proportional representation?

7. For further contemplation:
   a) Would you support introducing proportional representation in Congress?
   b) What would be the effects?
   c) Explain why these would help or harm American democracy.

8. Describe four functions that parties serve in the American electoral process.

9. What are the three separate parts of the party organization? Explain what each part is responsible for.

10. What is party identification? Name three factors that influence party identification.

11. For further contemplation:
    a) What does partisanship mean?
    b) Explain why many Americans worry about partisanship.
    c) The authors suggest the fears of partisanship may be exaggerated. Do you agree with this suggestion or not? Explain why.

12. What kind of interest group would represent you best? Is it a group that works on a specific issue, like gun control or lower taxes? Or one representing a specific "identity" group, like women or Latinos or LGBT people? Or a geographically based organization concerned with the interests of Texans or New Englanders or Mountain States residents? Or, to take still another example, is the group organized around a partisan or ideological perspective, from libertarian to progressive? Why is that kind of group your preferred representative?

10

Congress

PASSING LEGISLATION through the US Congress is remarkably difficult. Consider the long and winding road that confronted health care reform.

Action kicked off in the House of Representatives in March 2009. Over four months, three different House committees produced two different bills. The Speaker of the House, Nancy Pelosi (D-CA)—the first woman Speaker in American history—worked to combine elements of both bills into a single "Affordable Health Care for America Act." Pelosi and her top lieutenants spent the summer and early fall meeting one by one with different **congressional caucuses** in the House: conservative Blue Dogs, the liberal Progressive Caucus, the Congressional Black Caucus, the Hispanic Caucus, abortion opponents, and others. Each wanted to add to or subtract from the bill. All kinds of hot issues came up. Some legislators demanded that coverage of abortion be excluded, others charged that doing so would lead to back-alley abortions; some insisted that undocumented aliens be explicitly rejected, others objected that this was cruel. While the members negotiated, all kinds of interest groups lined up to lobby the Speaker's team. After months of dealing, the House version of the bill emerged.

The health reform bill then went to the House Rules Committee, which sets the rules that guide the debate whenever a measure goes to the full House of Representatives for a vote. The rules—each piece of legislation gets its own—specify things like the time allotted for debate and whether amendments can be tacked on. By now it was late October—and after seven feverish months of activity the legislation had still not reached the House **floor**. All the action had been in committees or behind the scenes. On Saturday, November 7, the House finally considered the measure, and after a fierce debate that lasted all day (with sparks flying about whether abortion would be covered), the legislation squeaked through by a vote of 220–215 as the clock moved toward midnight. Only one Republican voted for the legislation.

The House proceedings were the easier part of the process. The Senate (with one hundred members) also began deliberating in March 2009. Two

Congressional caucus: A group of House or Senate members that convene regularly to discuss common interests; they may share demographic characteristics, geography, or issue concerns.

Floor: The full chamber, either in the House of Representatives or Senate. A bill "goes to the floor" for the final debate and vote.

● *John Dingell Jr. (D-MI) swings the gavel that had been used to conclude voting the day the House passed health care reform in fall 2009. The same gavel had signaled the passage of Medicare in 1965. Dingell, the longest-serving House member ever (57 years and counting), voted for both bills.*

committees produced two *more* bills—making five different versions so far, each one topping a thousand pages. On the Senate Finance Committee, Democrats and Republicans negotiated for seven months—until November— before the Republicans dropped out and left the Democrats to vote the proposal through the committee on a straight party vote. The Senate majority leader, Harry Reid (D-NV), then hammered out a compromise Senate-style: Reid met not with separate coalition groups but one-by-one with individual senators, searching for the magic sixty votes that would prevent a legislation-killing filibuster.

That sixtieth vote did not come easily. One moderate Democrat, Ben Nelson of Nebraska, held out for weeks, finally securing a health benefit for his state that was valued at some one hundred million dollars. Stakeholders in other states were incensed by this "Cornhusker kickback," but other senators quietly lined up to try and negotiate their own special deals.[1] Senator Joe Lieberman (Ind-CT) went on CBS's *Face the Nation* and simply announced that he would not support the legislation unless an important provision (negotiated by liberal Democrats) was dropped—a whole section of the bill had to be crossed out to secure his vote. After days of debate, negotiating, and compromise, an exhausted Senate voted yes at 7:15 a.m. on December 24 to version

● New GOP senator spells doom for health reform? Scott Brown's victory in the January 2010 special election to replace deceased senator Ted Kennedy (D-MA) reduced the Democratic seat margin in the Senate to 59–41— one short of the number needed to break a filibuster.

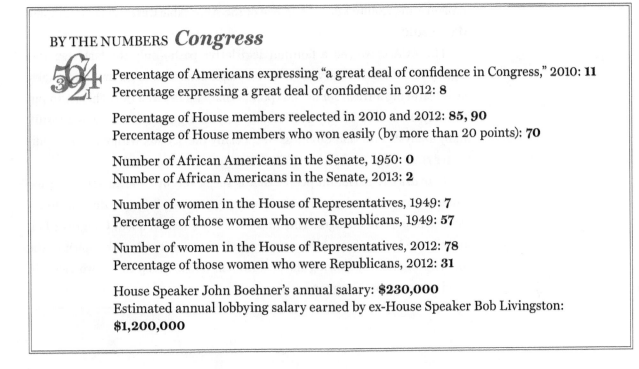

BY THE NUMBERS *Congress*

Percentage of Americans expressing "a great deal of confidence in Congress," 2010: **11**
Percentage expressing a great deal of confidence in 2012: **8**

Percentage of House members reelected in 2010 and 2012: **85, 90**
Percentage of House members who won easily (by more than 20 points): **70**

Number of African Americans in the Senate, 1950: **0**
Number of African Americans in the Senate, 2013: **2**

Number of women in the House of Representatives, 1949: **7**
Percentage of those women who were Republicans, 1949: **57**

Number of women in the House of Representatives, 2012: **78**
Percentage of those women who were Republicans, 2012: **31**

House Speaker John Boehner's annual salary: **$230,000**
Estimated annual lobbying salary earned by ex-House Speaker Bob Livingston: **$1,200,000**

no. 6 of the "Patient Protection and Affordable Care Act" (notice that even the title was not the same as the legislation that had passed the House). Senate Majority Leader Harry Reid was so tired he mistakenly voted nay and—as everyone laughed—he sheepishly changed his vote. All forty Republicans voted against the bill.

Advocates cheered this passage, but the legislation was still not ready. Since the House and Senate had passed substantially different versions of the law, leaders of each chamber began appointing members to a **conference committee** to iron out the differences. That stage would introduce a fresh round of negotiating, lobbying, and debating—this time between the two chambers. With the holiday break at hand, Congress agreed to come back late in January 2010 and finish its work.

Instead, the legislation met another dramatic twist. A special election in mid-January to fill a Senate seat in Massachusetts resulted in a surprise victory for Republican candidate Scott Brown, whose campaign platform prominently featured stopping "Obamacare." Brown's victory appeared to be the death of health reform—since the Democrats no longer had sixty votes in the Senate to break off a filibuster. However, several weeks of parliamentary

Conference committee: A temporary collection of House and Senate members, appointed to work out a compromise version of legislation that passed both chambers in different forms.

maneuvering resulted in the passage of the Affordable Care Act (ACA), in late March 2010.

The ACA traversed a familiar legislative path—only the last step was slightly out of the ordinary. Nearly every significant law faces multiple stages, each featuring a fresh set of veto points that can derail a bill. This is, to put it mildly, an excruciatingly difficult way to pass legislation. Partly as a result, many analysts now dub Congress—especially the Senate, with its archaic filibuster rules—the "broken branch" of American government.[2]

Who are we? A vibrant people that is suspicious of government. Congress builds that suspicion right into its governing process: it is very difficult to introduce important changes. This raises the key question about Congress: Is it indeed "the broken branch of government"? Or does it reflect the spirit of the American nation by slowing the government down? Keep these two views in mind as we explore Congress.

Introducing Congress

The Constitution put Congress at the center of American government. The document's first and longest article provides a detailed accounting of legislative organization and authority (Table 10.1).

This is a formidable set of powers. For most of American history, Congress ruled. After the Civil War, a weak but obstinate President Andrew Johnson brooded in the White House while Congress passed bill after bill redefining the nation, including the postwar constitutional amendments ending slavery and guaranteeing voting rights to black Americans—which President Johnson ineffectually opposed. A half-century later, when Senator Warren Harding won the presidential election of 1920, one of his old Senate buddies told him to "sign whatever bills the Senate sends you . . . and don't send bills for the Senate to pass."[3]

By the middle of the twentieth century, however, Congress had become increasingly deferential to the White House, especially in foreign affairs. Today, the nation looks first to the president to manage the economy, deploy troops, address crises, and pursue policy objectives.

Still, Congress remains near the center of American government. As President Obama discovered during the health care debate, presidents may command more public attention, but they need cooperation from the House and Senate to advance their policies. We judge presidents in part on whether their programs win approval from Congress, as you will see in the next

Table 10.1 Constitutional Powers of Congress

From article 1, section 8 (unless otherwise noted).*
Financial. Power to raise revenue through taxes and borrowing, to pay national debts and "provide for the common defense and general welfare"; regulate trade and commerce among the American states and with other countries.
Legal. Establish US citizenship laws. Regulate bankruptcy laws, issue US money, and punish counterfeiters. Establish a patent system ("to promote the progress of science and useful arts"). Fix national weights/measures standards. Enact laws subject to presidential approval.
Institutional. Organize judicial and executive branches; establish postal system (article 2, sec. 2). Set up and control the national capital—since 1797, in Washington, DC. Admit new states and exercise control over US territories (article 3, sec. 3).
National defense. Declare war and regulate rules for prisoners of war. Raise and fund US Army, Navy, and other defense forces.
Additional congressional powers are provided by constitutional amendment. For example, the Thirteenth (1865), Fourteenth (1868), and Fifteenth (1870) Amendments authorize Congress to enforce African Americans' civil rights, as you read in Chapter 5.

chapter. Moreover, Congress's importance extends far beyond the vital responsibility of lawmaking. As much as any other actor or institution in US government, it is Congress that answers the question, *Who are we?*

Two Houses, Different Styles

Congress reflects two faces of the American people in its basic makeup. Like most other national legislatures, Congress is bicameral—comprising "two houses." The *House of Representatives* is the larger chamber and includes 435 members, divided among the states based on population size, along with six nonvoting delegates from Washington, DC, Puerto Rico, American Samoa, Guam, and other US territories. All 441 House members serve two-year terms and each represents a district of around 700,000 people.

The House is organized around a relatively clear set of rules and procedures. The majority party wields centralized control, through a powerful leadership team. In the **113th Congress**, Republicans are in the majority; this permits the GOP leader, Speaker of the House Boehner, to control what issues reach the floor, and frequently to get them passed.

The smaller Senate is made up of just 100 members, two from each US state, each elected for a six-year term. In its organization, the Senate reflects Americans' liberty-loving, individualistic side. Back in the nineteenth century, an old truism (sometimes attributed to Mark Twain) declared "every

113th Congress: The Congress elected in 2012. The first Congress met in 1789–1790. Each Congress is elected for a two-year session and numbered consecutively.

Legislative hold: An informal way for a senator to object to a bill or other measure reaching the Senate floor. The action effectively halts Senate proceedings on that issue, sometimes for weeks or longer.

Filibuster: Rule unique to the US Senate that allows any senator to hold the floor indefinitely and thereby delay a vote on a bill to which they object. Ended only when sixty senators vote for cloture.

see for yourself 10.1

Go online to see Senator Smith's noble filibuster celebrating the lone brave voice.

senator a little king"; the old quip still resonates today.[4] Each woman and man in the Senate possesses a remarkable degree of autonomy, especially compared to the average House member. Any senator—even the most junior—is able to halt the entire body's consideration of a bill merely by placing a **legislative hold** on it.

Let's consider a typical example. Before the US military can promote an officer, the Senate must vote its approval. Normally this is a routine formality. In 2003, however, Senator Larry Craig (R-ID) quietly put a hold on all Air Force promotions. No Air Force officer could advance to the rank of major, colonel, lieutenant general, or anything else. The Senate tabled—put aside—every proposed promotion. What had upset Senator Craig? The Air Force had promised to station some planes in Idaho, and Craig charged that they had reneged on their promise. So he did what any senator is permitted to do—bring action on an issue to a halt with a one-man veto.[5]

Popular American culture, in films such as *Mr. Smith Goes to Washington* or the *West Wing* TV episode featuring a noble **filibuster**—"democracy's finest show"—celebrates the lone senator standing up bravely for justice. But much of the time these stands involve narrow-minded issues, like Senator Craig's—even if the consequences are large. Certainly they seemed so, to those Air Force officers whose careers were stalled.

The two congressional chambers present a familiar contrast in the United States. Americans, we saw in Chapter 1, embrace direct democracy—and the centralized House can move swiftly on national legislative priorities. Americans also fear government power and seek stability: enter the independent senators, slowing legislation down with filibusters and holds. Legend has it that Thomas Jefferson, who had been in Paris during the Constitutional Convention, asked George Washington why the Constitution established two chambers in Congress. "Why," responded Washington, "do you pour your tea into the saucer?" "To cool it," replied Jefferson. "Just so,"

What Do You Think?

Senate Filibusters

Should senators be allowed to hold up legislative initiatives indefinitely, or until their opposition can round up sixty votes to stop their stalling action? What do you think?	**Yes.** Filibusters ensure independence and protect minority rights. Slowing government down is a good idea.	**No.** The sixty-vote rule makes a mockery of simple majority rule and causes gridlock, slowing policymaking to a crawl. It is time to rewrite Senate rules and end the filibuster.	**Not Sure?** You may want to ponder this question as you read the rest of the chapter.

returned Washington, "we pour House legislation into the senatorial saucer to cool it." Whether or not the exchange actually took place, it neatly captures the contrast between House and Senate.[6] The key question for us now is whether the Senate is too good at this task—cooling legislation. Do we need a more nimble and responsive government in the twenty-first century? Or is the senatorial function—slowing things down—more important than ever?

● *Facing the Senate Judiciary Committee. Supreme Court nominee (now Justice) Sonia Sotomayor at her hearing in 2009. Presidential nominees face only Senate, not House, review.*

The House and Senate Have Some Unique Roles

The Constitution also gives each branch some unique authority. All budget measures must originate in the House. Now that the Senate is also directly elected by the people, however, this rule has become less important. The House also has the power to impeach public officials—including the president—for "high crimes and misdemeanors." After the House impeaches (or indicts) an officeholder, the Senate holds a trial and decides whether to remove him or her. For its part, the Senate has exclusive authority over two important matters. The president negotiates treaties with other countries, but the Senate must approve by two-thirds majority. Sixty-seven votes is a very high bar in today's politics, and, as we will see in the next chapter, presidents have found some creative ways around it.

The Senate also has sole power to review presidential appointments—the Constitution calls it "advice and consent." Each nominee for the Supreme Court, for example, goes before the Senate Judiciary Committee and then must win confirmation from the full Senate.

THE BOTTOM LINE

- Congressional powers, as granted under the Constitution, are extensive and very clearly defined.
- America's Congress is bicameral: the House has 435 members (plus six nonvoting members) who are elected every two years. The one hundred senators serve six-year terms.
- The two houses of Congress reflect different national priorities. Populists appreciate the responsive House; advocates of stability embrace the more deliberate Senate where rules like the filibuster make it more difficult to pass legislation.

Congressional Representation

Members of Congress represent their constituents in multiple ways. They live in the same state or district—which is known as *geographic* representation. They share views about the political issues—or *substantive* representation. Another angle is *descriptive* representation—which measures the extent to which they look like the people they represent in terms of race, ethnicity, gender, age, national origin, and so on. Geographic representation is required—members must live in their state or district. However, citizens often have to choose between descriptive representation (she is the same gender, race, ethnicity and/or religion as I am) and substantive representation (she does not look like me but believes what I believe).[7]

Trustees and Delegates

see for yourself 10.2

Go online to access an interactive map of African Americans in the House and Senate through US history.

Each member of Congress—in fact, every representative in any organization—faces the same conundrum: Do what you think is right? Or, do what your constituents want? As we saw in Chapter 3, theorists have wrestled with that question over the years.

Do the Right Thing. On the one hand, representatives owe us their best judgment. They sit in the House or Senate, with considerably more information than their constituents. Just like your doctor or your lawyer, your House and Senate members' job is to pursue what is best for you. And, if you disagree with the result, you can always vote for their opponent. This perspective is known as the *trustee* view of representation.

On a lot of issues, members of Congress must rely on their best judgment, or that of their staff: constituents have no strongly held views, or express "doorstep opinions," as we saw in Chapter 6. Most people care little whether their senators voted to approve the president's choice for deputy undersecretary of commerce.

Do What the People Want. Another view holds that true representation involves House or Senate members faithfully following popular preferences. A lot of choices before Congress have to do with basic values. You do not need more information to know how you feel about the right to own guns. Or whether health care is a universal human right. A legislator, according to this view, should take his voting instructions directly from his constituents. This is the *delegate* view of representation.

Political scientists recognize that the rules help tilt individuals one way or another (here is the institutional perspective again). When the constitutional framers required members of the House to run every two years, they favored the delegate view: pay close attention to the people, or you will be out of a job. The Senate has six years between elections; the rules practically instruct them to be trustees, to act as they think best.

What ultimately makes for good representation? The theoretical answer is simple: *representatives effectively pursue their constituents' substantive interests.* The trick comes in figuring out what those interests are and promoting them through the complicated legislative process. Eventually, at election time, the people will judge whether their members of Congress effectively pursued their interests. To political scientists, this is how a well-operating representative system works.

This theorizing barely registers on the radar screens of most members of the House and Senate. They come to Congress with a clear perspective that informs nearly all of their important votes. They rarely stay up late at night pondering what stand to take on gun rights or on national health insurance. The answers are part of their basic philosophy, forged years before they arrived in Congress. Most politicians do not pander—at least not on large, visible issues. They know what they believe and—despite popular wisdom—they rarely say merely what they think their audience wants to hear.[8] However, a great outcry from the constituency over an issue will often back a member off. It is always safer to do nothing—and blame the other members.

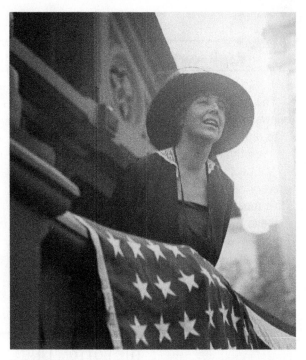

● *Jeannette Rankin, first woman in Congress. Representative Rankin addresses a women's-suffrage meeting in Washington, DC. She was first elected in 1917—before the Nineteenth Amendment legally enfranchised women in all states. Among underrepresented groups, the number of women in Congress has grown most rapidly—but today still adds up to just 20% of the members.*

What Do You Think?

●●● Who Really Represents You?

| Which do you consider more important—descriptive or substantive representation? | **Descriptive Representation.** Race, ethnicity, gender, and class are crucial to representation. Someone cannot really speak for me if he or she has not experienced the world as I have experienced it. | **Substantive Representation.** It doesn't matter if someone looks like me as long as he or she effectively represents my views. Someone who does not share my views is not going to represent me well no matter what he or she looks like. | **On the other hand.** There may be no right answer to this question—political theorists have long argued about which to emphasize. Think about how you might combine these two positions. |

Two Views of Representation

The trustee and the delegate views are both legitimate ways to represent people. Do what you think best—or do what the people tell you to do. On every issue, each representative must decide how to weigh these two key factors. Take a moment and ask yourself how you would act as a member of the Senate or House.

Delegate. I am more apt to be a delegate and take my voting instructions directly from my constituents.

Trustee. I am more inclined to be a trustee and simply do what I believe to be the right thing on behalf of my constituents.

Unsure. Maybe the choice is not so black and white. Perhaps the answer depends on the issue. If you take this middle ground, think about the kinds of issues that would make you a delegate or a trustee.

THE BOTTOM LINE

- Members of the House and Senate represent Americans in multiple ways. These include:
  - *Geographic representation*: The election rules say members must live in the state or district.
  - *Descriptive representation*: Does the assembly look like the people?
  - *Substantive representation*: Do members of Congress effectively pursue constituent interests?
- Along with these different styles of representation, members can act as delegates or trustees. Representatives can faithfully follow what the people want, or do as their political experience, instincts, and core principles dictate.

Elections: Getting to Congress—and Staying There

How do members of Congress spend their days? From occasional glimpses of C-SPAN you might imagine Congress as a sustained feast of debates, but members of the House and the Senate spend relatively little time in floor sessions. Table 10.2 displays the typical workweek of a member of the House, taken from a 2008 survey. Not a lot of time left for quietly contemplating the major issues of the day, is there?

Congressional Elections

Congress spends a great deal of time campaigning. House members face the voters every two years—more frequently than most other national legislatures around the world. Even senators, with a more comfortable six years between races, must keep their campaign operation—especially fundraising—humming along. Notice, in Table 10.2, that the members spend as much time raising money as they do on committee meetings or floor action. Does this constant pressure to attract donations and remind voters of their virtues turn off members of Congress, or potential candidates? As we saw in Chapter 8, most of them stay in office a long time. And, when a seat in either chamber opens because of retirement or death, the list of eager office seekers from both parties is almost always a long one.

It was always clear at the Constitutional Convention that the United States would have an elected national legislature. But a major dispute involved the extent of popular participation in choosing members of Congress. Recall the original compromise: House members would be elected directly, while senators were to be insulated from the whims of public opinion and chosen by state legislatures.

As western states joined the Union, their legislatures turned the Senate elections over to the people (the westerners also gave women the vote); the entire nation began voting for senators in 1913 when the Seventeenth Amendment was ratified. Did the state legislatures pick more elevated senators than the people (as the constitutional framers expected)? Not necessarily. In the very first congressional elections, for example, Virginia's legislature passed over James Madison for the Senate; the people of his district had better

Table 10.2 Division of Time of a Member of the House

Meeting with staff (mostly in Washington)	19%
Meeting with constituents (mostly in district)	19%
Ceremonial events (in district; some in DC)	15%
Fundraising calls/meetings	8%
Committee meetings (hearings, member meetings)	8%
Floor action (votes, debates, morning business)	7%
Office work (e-mail, reading, legislative drafting)	7%
Informal talks (with colleagues, lobbyists, media)	6%
Caucus meetings (all-party or subgroup gatherings)	5%
Other (miscellaneous)	5%

sense and elected him to the House, where he immediately pushed through the Bill of Rights (discussed in Chapter 2).

Reapportionment: Reorganization of the boundaries of House districts, a process that follows the results of the US census, taken every ten years. District lines are redrawn to ensure rough equality in the number of constituents represented by each House member.

Another important influence on US House elections is **reapportionment**. As we discussed in Chapter 7, every ten years the US census determines which states have gained or lost population, and since each district is the same size, House seats are reapportioned accordingly. In 2010, Texas gained four new seats, Florida gained two, and New York and Ohio each lost two. The new districts are drawn by the state legislature, and, as we saw in Chapter 8, fierce political battles surround the way the lines are drawn. Savvy political observers pay special attention to elections for the state legislatures in a census year (the next one is 2020), since the majority party in the state legislature often skews the districts in its own favor—advantaging either Democrats or Republicans in the effort to control Congress.

A Government of Strangers

In the past—before jets, advanced technology, and modern campaigns—Congress members stayed in Washington. Senators or representatives worked together during the day and socialized at night and over the weekends. In fact, a bar for members—called the Hole in the Wall—was located between the House and Senate chambers.

Today, most legislators are not in Washington long enough to get to know one another very well. They dash in, spend three days packed with congressional business, and dash back home. This schedule makes it very difficult for Congress to get things done, because it is now a collection of strangers. The tortured process—described at the start of this chapter—is further complicated by the lack of personal relations.

Why do the members insist on rushing home each week? In fact, when political scientists build models to explain and predict congressional behavior, they often assume that reelection is a member's primary goal. We consider this an exaggeration. Many members are genuinely pursuing their political ideals. But there is no denying that the pressure for reelection dominates congressional behavior.

THE BOTTOM LINE

- Members of Congress are always running for office. Fundraising takes a particularly important amount of time and attention.
- Members pay special attention to their home style: most go back to the constituency every week—compressing normal congressional business into Tuesday through Thursday.
- Congress has become an institution of strangers who do not know one another. Most members focus most intensely on reelection.

Congress at Work

When members of the House and Senate do gather in Washington, they have a staggering to-do list: managing the nation's legislative business, investigating executive-branch activities, staging public hearings about everything from auto safety to US aid to Zimbabwe. And, of course, raising money. How—and where—do they accomplish all that work?

The City on the Hill

The huge Capitol building is perched on an actual hill; its majestic marble dome dominates the Washington skyline. Traditionally, no building in the District of Columbia except the Washington Monument may be taller. The Capitol building is also the heart of a small "city within a city." Six grand office buildings house the members and their staff; the newer buildings feature offices the size of basketball courts. Three ornate structures house the Library of Congress, which has mushroomed from Thomas Jefferson's personal book collection to the largest library in the world.

Inhabitants of this "city" include the 535 members of Congress, along with more than 25,000 staff members, who range from well-paid senior policy experts to temporary interns; the Capitol police force, 250 members strong; and the US poet laureate, a Congress-appointed position whose occupant receives a beautiful office in the Library of Congress. And don't forget the 75,000 or so lobbyists. It all adds up to a very busy place.

How much are members paid? As of 2012, the rate is $174,000 for House and Senate members—more than four times the average American's annual earnings (see Table 10.3). Leaders earn a slightly higher salary; House Speaker Boehner is the best paid, at $223,500. Constituents frequently complain that congressional salaries are too high. Note, however, that most members of Congress have to maintain two residences, one in Washington—among the most expensive real estate markets in the United States—and one back in their home district or state. And comparable leaders in other areas—from business to academia—make much higher salaries. If your primary professional aim is to make money, running for Congress is not your best bet.

The congressional staff members are a major presence in this company town. Until 1893, most members of the House had no staff support and senators were allotted one part-time staffer (beginning in 1891), paid six dollars per day. Congress's professionalization meant a steady increase in assistants, researchers, committee experts, legal counsel, and the like. By the 1990s, the congressional staffs leveled off at around 27,000 total members.

Each House and Senate member has a chief of staff, a legislative director, a press secretary, a scheduler, and a host of others, including legislative correspondents (LCs) who handle the huge volume of constituent requests that pour into each member's office. Many graduates take entry positions (like the

Table 10.3 Annual Average Salaries by Profession

CEO, top 500 company	$12.9 million
NBA player	$5.6 million
NFL player	$1.9 million
US president	$400,000
Four-year university president/chancellor	$385,909
Physician, ophthalmology	$250,500
Senior US executive-branch official	$196,700
Member of Congress	**$174,000**
Pharmacist	$106,000
Personal financial advisor	$90,900
IT professional	$80,500
Social worker	$54,220
Plumber	$48,700

Note: All figures as of 2012
Source: Data from Bureau of Labor Statistics and U.S. Office of Personnel Management.

LC), since there are generally opportunities to move up quickly. Legislative staffs are dominated by young men and women often right out of college.

In addition, each summer thousands of college students descend on Capitol Hill to work, usually without pay. One of us worked as a congressional intern: it is not glamorous activity, but congressional offices hum with excitement and offer a ringside seat on one of the most fascinating institutions in the world.

Capitol Hill life runs on a unique rhythm. Congress usually remains in session from the beginning of January through early August; members return after Labor Day and rush to finish for the year in early October during election (or, even-numbered) years—since they are anxious to focus on their campaigns. In nonelection years, the session lasts longer—this chapter opened with a discussion of the 2009 session, which lasted until December 24. When in session, the Hill buzzes with action Tuesday through Thursday. Staffers work late into the night, while lobbyists and media swarm around the Capitol.

Minnows and Whales: Congressional Leadership

When Lyndon Johnson (D-TX) served as Senate majority leader in the 1950s, he divided colleagues into two camps: "whales," who could enact landmark

● *Congressional staff at work. Staff members (standing) brief their House bosses before the start of a Budget Committee hearing.*

legislation, and "minnows," who dutifully followed others. Most "whales" are chairs of important committees or part of the formal leadership structure.

The House and Senate feature very different leadership styles. The smaller, more collegial Senate—where any member can request a hold and bring the entire body to a halt—usually requires patient, consensus-minded leadership. Majority leaders do not so much lead as manage Senate procedures, cajoling and pleading proud senators to move legislation along. The larger House, run on majoritarian principles, permits much tighter central control from the Speaker and other top leaders.

House Leadership.   Democrats and Republicans each choose a party leader from their ranks. When a new Congress opens after an election (in January of odd-numbered years), the majority party votes its leader to the top post in Congress, the Speaker of the House. In 2010, the Republicans captured the House and John Boehner (R-OH) replaced Nancy Pelosi as Speaker. The Speaker serves as the public face of the House. He or she is simultaneously an administrative officer, a political spokesman, and a party leader.

As chief administrative officers of the House, Speakers preside over the chamber on special occasions (for example, when a president delivers the State of the Union message to Congress). They rule on procedural issues, choose members for committees, assign legislation to committees, and "maintain order and civility"—although civility is sometimes difficult to maintain.

● *Speaker Boehner assumes the gavel. In a powerful symbolic moment, outgoing Speaker Nancy Pelosi passes the gavel to new Speaker John Boehner, who is momentarily overcome with emotion.*

King of the Hill rule: A special rule governing floor consideration of a bill. A series of amendments on the same topic may all win majority approval, but only the last amendment receiving a majority vote—the "king of the hill"—is incorporated into the bill.

As political leaders, Speakers set the House's agenda, determining which bills are considered and when. They negotiate with the Senate and executive branch. And they help manage the Rules Committee, which, as we saw at the start of the chapter, guides the floor action for all legislation. Speakers sometimes work with Rules to invent ways to hold the majority together on important votes. In 1981, for example, Speaker Tip O'Neill, a colorful Massachusetts Democrat, worried that House Democrats would feel pressured to support measures backed by the very popular new president, Ronald Reagan. O'Neill huddled with Rules Committee Democrats and came up with a new rule, the **King of the Hill**. It permitted Democrats to vote for amendments that Reagan favored and—at the same time—alternative amendments preferred by O'Neill and the Democrats. The last vote is the King of the Hill—the vote that counts.

As party leaders, Speakers lead the majority party, promoting legislative priorities of their side. They help spin issues in their party's favor and serve as the party's public face. Popular Speakers help their party. That leads the opposition to try and diminish them—to portray them as partisan or ruthless. It takes a nimble politician to juggle the different roles the Speaker must play.

The House majority leader is the second in command. He or she acts as the majority party's floor manager, negotiator, and spokesperson. The majority leader also serves as the Speaker's eyes and ears, tracking party members' actions and preferences. Eric Cantor (R-VA), the current majority leader, was a rival of John Boehner for the Speakership. Congress watchers closely track the subtle competition between the two. In contrast, Nancy Pelosi had been the undisputed Democratic leader.

The number-three position is the majority-party whip. The *whip*, currently Kevin McCarthy (R-CA), is responsible for party discipline—ensuring that Republicans vote the way the leadership wants them to. The term whip comes from the British Parliament which long ago borrowed the term from fox hunting, where the "whipper-in" was responsible for keeping the pack of hounds together—and yes, those fox hunters did the job by cracking whips. The majority whip leads a team of nine deputy whips, each responsible for members from a different region.

The minority generally has the same leadership structure, with one big difference: no Speaker. House whips have a challenging time persuading their proud, talented colleagues to vote the way they want them to. They do a lot of arm twisting and deal cutting—and they have to be creative. Back in the 1970s, minority whip Leslie Arends (R-IL) needed one more GOP vote to win an important agriculture bill. One Ohio Republican, knowing the bill was unpopular with his constituents, simply flew home. When Arends discovered his crucial vote was missing, he called an Ohio radio station and persuaded the DJ to announce, every fifteen minutes: "If anybody spies Representative Jones, who should be representing us in Washington but isn't, tell him he's supposed to be in Washington tomorrow for an important vote." Jones flew back the next morning and sheepishly voted with his fellow Republicans.

Senate Leadership. When you think about the Senate, take all the difficulties involved in managing the House—and quadruple them. Senate rules like the filibuster and the hold give each individual a great deal of autonomy—recall how one senator scuttled an entire section of the health reform bill. The Senate leadership must turn to personal skills, especially an ability to negotiate with colleagues.

The senators elect a majority leader—currently Harry Reid (D-NV). However, the Senate leader does not even formally preside over the chamber. The Constitution gives that job to the vice president. In practice, vice presidents rarely show up in the Senate—appearing mainly for very important votes (the VP can break a tie) and on ceremonial occasions. Similarly, the **president pro tempore** (currently Patrick Leahy, D-VT) has presiding authority at certain formal occasions. Otherwise, every senator presides in turn over the body, serving rotating half-hour stints. A staff member stands by the presiding member's side, helping him or her negotiate the complex rules.

President pro tempore: Majority-party senator with the longest Senate service.

After Hillary Rodham Clinton, elected to the Senate from New York in 2000, served her first half-hour in the Senate's presiding chair, she told colleagues it was "the most difficult thing I'd ever done in politics."[9] Considering that she helped design a national health reform package during her storm-tossed eight years as First Lady (1993–2000), those rules must indeed be tortuous.

Senate whips from both majority and minority parties serve the same functions as in the House—though they command much less power to demand party discipline, again owing to the Senate's individualistic ways. This difficulty extends right up to the majority leader. It is hard to set the Senate's agenda or command floor action, for example, in a context of unlimited debate and amendments, with the constant threat that any one senator will place a hold on legislation or mount a filibuster. The best that majority leaders and their team can muster is to influence which policies will be considered on the Senate floor, and in what order—though that is usually done in consultation with the minority leader. If the minority leader indicates that an item will be subject to a filibuster or a hold, the majority leader normally passes over it and moves to the next item on the agenda.

Committee chairs, though important figures in the House and Senate, do not serve as part of the formal leadership team. Chairs are appointed by leaders in each chamber, rather than elected by a majority of members—though traditional norms of seniority often mean that the longest-serving committee member from the majority party becomes chair.

Committees: Workhorses of Congress

The regular duties of congressional lawmaking play out mainly in committees. As instruments of policymaking, House and Senate committees are center stage; party leaders or presidents sometimes struggle to overcome their decisive influence. Presidents often watch as the legislation they care about disappears forever into the maze of committee deliberation. Table 10.4 lists the types of committees, which have not changed in more than a

Table 10.4 Congressional Committee Types

- *Standing committees*: Permanent bodies, with fixed jurisdiction. (Table 10.5 lists them all.) House and Senate standing committees vary widely in prestige: the oldest are traditionally the most influential, though some newer ones (like Intelligence, created after 9/11 in both chambers) deal with significant topics. Standing committees are further divided into multiple *subcommittees*, organized around areas of expertise.

- *Select committees*: Created to investigate a particular issue; these exist for a defined period of time. Also called *special committees*. A select committee to investigate the causes of 9/11 was convened from 2002 to 2003, for example.

- *Joint committees*: Made up of both House and Senate members, organized to address topics of continuing importance. Can remain in place for decades; the Joint Committee on Taxation has existed since 1971, for example. *Conference committees*, introduced earlier in this chapter, are temporary joint committees that iron out differences in legislation after it has passed in both House and Senate.

Table 10.5 House and Senate Permanent Committees, 113th Congress

US HOUSE COMMITTEES	US SENATE COMMITTEES
Agriculture	Aging (Special)
Appropriations	Agriculture, Nutrition, and Forestry
Armed Services	Appropriations
Budget	Armed Services
Education and Labor	Banking, Housing, and Urban Affairs
Energy and Commerce	Budget
Financial Services	Commerce, Science, and Transportation
Foreign Affairs	Energy and Natural Resources
Homeland Security	Ethics (Select)
House Administration	Environment and Public Works
Intelligence (Permanent Select)	Finance
Judiciary	Foreign Relations
Natural Resources	Health, Education, Labor, and Pensions
Oversight and Government Reform	Homeland Security and Governmental Affairs
Rules	Indian Affairs
Science and Technology	Intelligence (Permanent Select)
Small Business	Judiciary
Standards of Official Conduct	Rules and Administration
Transportation and Infrastructure	Small Business and Entrepreneurship
Veterans Affairs	Veterans Affairs
Ways and Means	

century. In fact, legislative committees were invented in the very early days of the United States: the British Parliament still has nothing resembling the extent and power of congressional committees.

The committee system is yet another way American government separates powers. It means that Congress winds up with multiple centers of authority; the process is slower and harder for the public (and the media) to follow. But the division of labor allows an institution—with distracted, busy members—to accomplish more. By dividing their labor, Congress is able to dispatch more than ten thousand items of business each year.

The standing committees provide a main avenue to get favored services, or "pork," home to the district. Members on the Appropriations

Earmark: A legislative item, usually included in spending ("appropriations") bills, that directs Congress to fund a particular item in one House district or senator's state.

Committee—which decides how US funds are spent—are known as "cardinals," like the ruling cadre in the Vatican. Other members approach them, hat in hand, to request **earmarks** in the form of items in appropriations bills: a dam in this district, funds for highway construction in that one.

The committee system makes Congress far more efficient. But there is also a harsher reality: it fragments Congress into fiefdoms, hides action from public view, makes it relatively easy to do little favors for well-placed constituents (a tax break or a phone call to back off a pesky regulator), and makes it extremely difficult to pass major legislation or to address large national problems.

The organization of Congress raises, once again, the dilemmas of American democracy: Is the system biased toward the powerful? Does the bias against action frustrate the popular will or simply reflect the American wariness of government (or both)? What do you think?

Leadership and Assignments

House Republicans gathered late in the 1999 session to celebrate another year in the majority, with several representatives rising in humorous spirit to toast Speaker Denny Hastert (R-IL), who'd replaced disgraced Speaker Newt Gingrich earlier that year. Together they sang in rhyme:

> *I love Speaker Hastert, his heart is so warm;*
> *And if I love him he'll do me no harm.*
> *So I won't sass the Speaker, not one little bitty . . .*
> *And then I'll wind up on a major committee.*

Congress members' idea of fun may be a little different from yours. An important truth lies beneath the hilarity, though. The Speaker assigns members (and chairs) to each committee—a vital decision, given all the power committees wield. Over in the Senate, the decision involves more give-and-take but ultimately rests in the majority leader's hands. Minority party assignments are recommended by minority leaders in both chambers.

Members compete fiercely for assignment to the most influential committees. Once they are on a committee, representatives and senators often stay for many years—gaining power and influence, and aspiring to become chair. Members also seek to join committees that reflect the concerns of their district. When Representative David Price (D-NC) joined Congress after an upset victory in 1993, he requested committee assignments not because of his intellectual interests—although, as a political science professor, he had plenty of those. Instead, Price judged the House Banking (now Financial Services) Committee to be vital to North Carolina and his district in particular, because of all the banks and other financial centers in the area.[10]

Skilled committee chairs are able to broaden the jurisdiction of their committee by claiming pieces of bills that are referred to many different committees. President Clinton's health-reform proposal went to ten different House and Senate committees in 1994. Each committee has its own process. It can bury the bill, change it completely, or report a modified version. Often, as we saw with the Affordable Care Act in 2009–2010, multiple committees produce different bills.

Jurisdictional squabbles can erupt into battles for influence between committees, when their responsibilities overlap. The House and the Senate each have different committees for Homeland Security, for Intelligence, and for Foreign Affairs. Sometimes they all hold hearings on the same issue; and, since legislation is assigned to every committee that has jurisdiction over the topic, overlapping authority means multiple committees wrestling to shape the same legislation.

THE BOTTOM LINE

- Congress is a like a small city. Its citizens include the 535 members of Congress, 25,000 staff, and an army of lobbyists. The city includes its own amenities, traditions, and slang.
- Congressional leadership in the House includes a Speaker, majority and minority leaders, and ten whips. Successful leaders in the House impose discipline on their party members. The Senate allows far more individual action. Party leaders and whips have fewer institutional tools with which to impose discipline.
- Congressional committees are the workhorses of Congress. They have proved efficient and adaptable over the years. However, the committee system also fragments Congress, hides action from public view, advantages well-placed constituents looking for individual favors, and makes it difficult to pass major legislation.

Legislative Policymaking

As the Affordable Care Act's convoluted passage testifies, congressional lawmaking can be boiled down to five words: ***Complex process. Difficult to win***. The last ten years (or, as you now know to call it, the last five sessions of Congress) saw an average of 4,239 bills submitted each year. How many made it all the way through the process? An average of 4.2 percent.

Why even bother? There are other ways to make policy. As we will see in the following chapters, presidents can issue executive orders (Chapter 11), bureaucrats can write regulations (Chapter 12), and activists can go to the courts (Chapter 13). But nothing else has the status—symbolic as well as legal—of an act of Congress. That's why the proposed bills keep coming despite the long odds. What happens once a bill is proposed?

The Importance of the Legislative Process

Americans complain about the nation's failure to face up to global warming. Or our broken public education system. Or our inability to ban abortion, regulate handguns, or reduce the federal budget deficit. Pundits explain these failures by invoking "American attitudes" or "American culture" or "powerful lobbyists." Here's a more accurate explanation: congressional rules make it very hard to do any of these things—even when a majority of legislators (and of the nation) are in support.

Drafting a Bill

Anyone can petition Congress to consider a bill, but only members of the House and Senate have the right to introduce one. Every piece of legislation needs at least one primary sponsor, whose name is publicly inscribed on the first page.

Bills can feature any number of cosponsors, or members who agree to have their names listed as supporters. The main sponsors usually try to sign on many members, especially powerful ones like committee chairs, as cosponsors. A loose rule of thumb: the more cosponsors a bill has, the higher the likelihood of passage.

Anything can be introduced as legislation—no matter how far out of the box. Congressman Ron Paul (R-TX) once introduced a bill mandating that the Treasury buy a one-inch-wide strip of land stretching down the middle of the United States from Canada to Mexico. All goods or people crossing that line would be charged a toll, declared Representative Paul, eliminating the need for any other taxes or government fees. The bill has not made it out of committee—at least not yet.

see for yourself 10.3

Go online to view an example of a congressional bill, its description, supporters, and status.

● *President Bush seeks congressional approval for Iraq war. Like previous presidents, including his father, President Bush took his case for war to Congress. Here, flanked by Vice President Cheney and House Speaker Pelosi, Bush appeals to both chambers for continued support of the war, nearly four years after hostilities began.*

Table 10.6 Examples of Creative Legislative Titles

• "Greener America Act" (2007): Protect West Virginia coal industry against stronger environmental regulations.
• "Pass a Budget Now Act" (2012): Cut congressional pay for each day that a budget resolution (overview of spending/revenue targets for the coming year) fails to pass.
• "Personal Responsibility in Consumption Act" (2006): Immunize fast-food companies against lawsuits by obese consumers.
• "What Really Happened Act" (2002): Require instant TV replay in all major sports.
Note: None of these passed.

The sponsors rarely write the legislation themselves. Some bills include language taken from state legislation, or even foreign governments. Congress members "borrow" legislative language from each other, adapting colleagues' bills for their own use. Most serious bills go to the experts at the Congressional Research Service (CRS) for drafting help. Bill drafters also consult with outside experts, including executive-branch officials, lobbyists, and academics. And members especially enjoy copying themselves: it's something of a ritual in many congressional offices, as a new year begins, to dust off and reintroduce bills that failed in the previous session.

Once the bill is drafted and the cosponsors have signed on, it is ready for the next step: submission.

Submitting the Bill

The more traditional Senate typically introduces bills as the legislative day opens, around noon on Tuesdays, Wednesdays, and Thursdays. Let's take a peek inside the chamber.

The presiding officer taps his or her gavel, bringing the stir of conversation to a halt. Members pause as the Senate chaplain recites a prayer. A swirling bustle breaks out as the chaplain concludes. Routine administrative motions (like approving records of the previous day's proceedings) are followed by morning-hour statements—short speeches that celebrate home-state achievements. A constituent is turning one hundred years old, or a softball team has won the state title.

Watch carefully: a senator snaps her fingers. A page (usually a high school student, specially trained for this role) dashes down the aisle, takes the senator's document, and places it in a flat wooden tray beside the bill clerk. The clerk writes a number on the first page (bills are numbered serially, starting each session with S.1), notes the senator's suggestion for committee referral, and places it in a tray. That night it is printed. A bill has been born!

● *Celebrity congressional witnesses include . . . Elmo! The Muppet Elmo "testifies," with the help of Rep. Duncan Hunter (R-CA), before the House Education Appropriations subcommittee in support of funding for school music programs.*

Committee hearing: The primary means by which committees collect and analyze information as legislative policymaking gets under way. Hearings usually feature witnesses providing oral testimony, along with questioning of the witnesses by members of Congress.

The House is less ritualized, in keeping with its democratic spirit—but bill introduction continues an old-fashioned practice. Representatives carry proposed bills themselves, down to the rostrum. They hand their legislation to the clerk or drop it in a mahogany box, called the "hopper." From there, bills are delivered to the Speaker's office, where they are assigned a number—starting each session with H.R. 1—and referred to committee.

Committee Action

As we have seen, committees are the congressional workhorses. The House leadership normally assigns the proposal to committees with authority (or jurisdiction) over the area affected by the proposed legislation—recall that the health care bill went to five different committees. Once they get a bill, the committees perform four major tasks.

1. Committees Hold Hearings on Policy Topics. Witnesses submit written testimony (for staff members and reporters to read); unless they are really important, they are limited to a five-minute presentation before the committee. When they begin, a little green light goes on; at the four-minute mark, a yellow light goes on. At five minutes, a red light blinks. Nervous rookies stop mid-sentence; veterans ignore the lights and talk serenely on—until the chair bangs the gavel.

The staff carefully puts together a list of who is testifying at each **hearing**. Witnesses generally include White House officials and cabinet heads—each of whose testimony has to be cleared with the Office of Management and Budget (OMB; introduced in the next chapter as "the agency that says no"). At many hearings, officials try to stick to their authorized script while critical Congress members pummel them—knowing full well that the government witness cannot express any views that were not already cleared by OMB.

2. Committees Prepare Legislation for Consideration on the House or Senate Floor. They are the primary source of policy development in Congress. Members and committee staff, drawing on their collective knowledge, assess and revise a bill.

Major rewrites of bills occur in **markup sessions**, when the committee gathers to work through the legislation's language, line by line. The result, called a "chairman's mark," is hot property among lobbyists, public advocates, and other interested parties; it contains many of the details that will become law if the legislation wins approval.

Following markup, the committee holds a vote on whether to report a bill to the full House or Senate. When the Senate Finance Committee considered economic stimulus legislation in 2009, it voted down more than one hundred amendments before passing the bill on party lines, 13–10. All that work is in just one Senate committee—and remember that at least one other committee (and usually more) is negotiating another version of the same legislation.

Committee votes are pivotal moments in a bill's career, as important as roll-call votes on the floor. If a bill is voted down in committee—not reported, in Congress-speak—it is usually dead. Those voted up by a narrow margin probably face tough sledding on the floor and the Speaker may decide never to bring it up for a vote—the bill dies even though it won a majority vote in committee.

3. Committees Also Kill Legislation, Deleting Items That Are Judged Less Important or Not Particularly Urgent—or Not Politically Viable. Of the more than four thousand bills referred to the forty House and Senate standing committees each year, about one in eight sees any action at all. Well into modern times, bills were often quietly deleted in committee, without any public acknowledgment of how members voted. A key reform of the 1970s required all committees to keep full records of important votes.

4. Committees' Work Extends Beyond Legislation, to Oversight. Congress monitors the executive branch, making sure cabinet departments and agencies perform their roles properly. Oversight can be high-stakes activity: oversight hearings investigate scandals like Watergate in the 1970s, review major issues like the 9/11 terrorist attacks, or evaluate presidential appointees like President Obama's 2009 Supreme Court nominee, Sonia Sotomayor. Committees also continue to monitor the programs that it has passed.

We will talk more about oversight in Chapter 12, on the executive bureaucracy. Note that, as with lawmaking, the committees of Congress are the front lines in this vital interplay between the legislative and executive branches.

Floor Action

A successful bill makes it through committee markup (where it was amended, but remains recognizable) and is approved by one or more committees. Next stop: the House or Senate floor. Once it gets here, your measure's chance of becoming law has increased dramatically. Of bills that make it to the floor, more than half are enacted. But legislation may take a long time to get there—leaders rarely call up a bill until they know they have the votes to win.

Floor procedures in the House and Senate are very different from one another. After a Senate committee approves a bill, it is placed on the "business calendar," from which it will be called up for consideration on a timing schedule worked out by the majority and minority leaders. Only bills that receive **unanimous consent**—agreement by all senators—can be brought to the floor. One nay and the bill is put on hold.

Committee markup session: A gathering of a full committee to draft the final version of a bill before the committee votes on it. Markups open to the public are often standing-room only.

Unanimous consent: A Senate requirement, applied to most of that body's business, that all senators agree before an action can proceed.

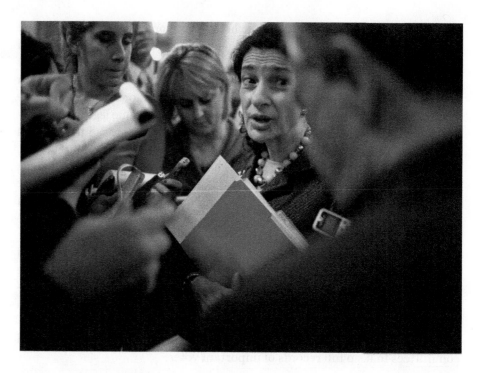

● Senator Olympia Snowe, a now-retired Maine Republican, explains her vote after a Finance Committee hearing on health reform.

In the House, the majority-party leadership exerts more control over what issues make it to the floor. They may have to start by rewriting the legislation—sometimes because multiple committees have passed different chairman's marks and cannot come to agreement among themselves. Other times, the Speaker, majority leader, and fellow leaders must rewrite a bill to get the measure through.

As we saw earlier, President Obama's push for health reform in 2009 yielded two very different bills coming out of the three House committees. "Blue Dog" (moderate) Democrats tried to scale back the scope of reform in the Energy and Commerce Committee, whereas progressive Democrats advocated more sweeping changes. Before House floor action began, members went home for their summer recess—and, like their Senate counterparts, they ran into furious constituents at town hall meetings.

As angry people shouted down their Congress members, a heavily compromised health-reform effort escalated into a populist battle about how liberal (or conservative) America was going to become. "We want our country back," chanted Tea Party members at anti-"Obamacare" rallies. Many Democrats in conservative districts ran for cover—leaving House leaders to rewrite a plan that had already undergone months of negotiation in the three committees.

Once it confirms the language of the bill, the House Rules Committee issues a directive about what type and how many amendments it will permit. The membership of the Rules Committee is usually stacked to favor the majority party, and the committee chair works closely with the Speaker to ensure that floor action will follow the leadership's wishes. The Senate, in contrast, allows virtually unlimited consideration on the floor; amendments of all kinds just keep on coming.

In both chambers, once bills make it to the calendar, they can get stuck there—for an entire session, in some cases. A logjam of legislation may be the reason. Or it might be the result of coordination issues between House and Senate, given the requirement that legislation has to move through both chambers.

Eventually the calendar clears, and a bill's moment for floor consideration arrives. Often advocates hope their measure will be taken up in the House and Senate roughly at the same time, although plenty of legislation makes it only to one or the other chamber during a session—another form of death sentence. A bill to prohibit any taxpayer funding for abortion and another that capped government spending each sailed through the House in 2012—and both disappeared when the Senate failed to act.

In both chambers, floor action on legislation follows the same broad procedures.

First, a bill is assigned a floor manager—usually the legislation's main sponsor, but on big issues the chair of the committee or subcommittee that reported the bill takes up this role. The manager handles amendments as they come up, and controls the time for debate. Majority and minority party members each have a certain number of hours and minutes to discuss the legislation, determined in the Senate by agreement between party leaders and in the House by the Rules Committee.

Then the political maneuvers really start. In both House and Senate, floor action involves amendments, procedural moves, eventually a final vote—and

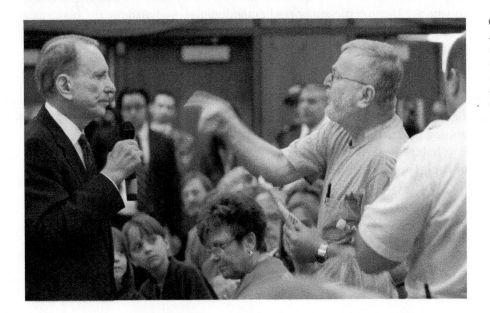

● Constituents confront Congress. A "town hall" meeting about health reform turns confrontational; Senator Arlen Specter, a Pennsylvania Republican who subsequently switched parties, is at left.

a lot of talk along the way. Members rarely change any votes with their eloquence. But floor speeches are not empty oratory. Congress watchers know that who chooses to speak, and what they say, matters. "I rise to support H.R. 835" is very different from "I rise to thank my good friend for introducing this excellent bill, H.R. 835; I have just a few questions about it." Each signals valuable clues about the likely outcome. Whips listen especially closely and adapt their floor strategies to secure a majority in support of party-approved amendments and the final vote for passage.

The real audience for much of the speechmaking is the constituency back home eager to see their representatives fight for (or against) an issue. At times, however, the members snap at one another. Members of the minority express frustration at the hardball tactics of the leadership. Representative David Obey (D-WI)—a leading member of the Democratic minority—became angry after Republican leadership amendments added controversial new items like oil drilling in the Arctic National Wildlife Reserve (ANWR) to a carefully negotiated compromise. "Once again the orderly legislative process has been corrupted by a couple of muscle men in the Congress," charged Obey. When the Democrats took the majority the following January, the Republicans were soon criticizing the tough tactics of Democratic Speaker Nancy Pelosi.

The rules in the House permit leaders to introduce creative strategies to get their legislation through. Earlier we saw the King of the Hill rule worked out by Speaker O'Neill with Rules Committee Democrats in 1981. Republican Speaker Newt Gingrich faced losing a vote in 1995 because some Republican House members feared opposing Democratic proposals that were popular in their districts. With only a slender margin of House seats, even a handful of GOP "no" votes would deliver a victory to the opposition. Gingrich's innovative response? Create a special *Queen* of the Hill rule, which allowed Republicans to vote for Democratic-supported amendments—and also for the majority's desired alternative. The version that won the most votes (the Queen) would ultimately be adopted . . . and the GOP members could explain back home that they'd voted "yea" on the Democratic alternatives, protecting their political capital.

Senate leaders, far from inventing new rules, are more likely to breathe a sigh of relief after steering a bill past the potential member "holds" and simply getting it to the floor. There, a related danger lurks: the filibuster. A senator may halt all activity by refusing to yield the floor and the only way to stop him or her is through a **cloture vote** which requires the approval of three-fifths of the Senate—sixty votes.

Filibusters used to be rare events. Between 1927 and 1960, there were only 18 efforts to break a filibuster (or cloture filings); not a single one succeeded in *invoking cloture* or stopping the filibuster and permitting a vote on the issue. As you can see in Figure 10.1 the effort to "invoke cloture" became more common in the 1970s (which averaged thirty-two filibusters every two year session) and became a familiar tactic in the 1990s (averaging seventy-two

Cloture vote: The Senate's only approved method for halting a filibuster or lifting a legislative hold. If sixty senators—three-fifths of the body, changed in 1975 from the original two-thirds —vote for cloture, the measure can proceed to a vote.

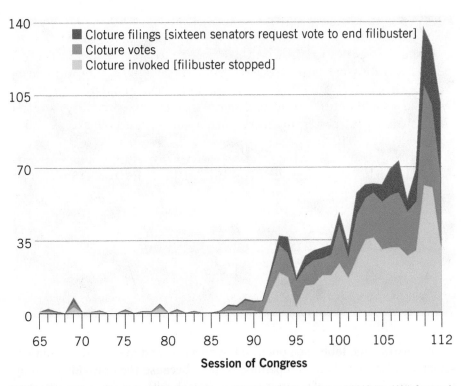

Cloture filings [sixteen senators request vote to end filibuster]
Cloture votes
Cloture invoked [filibuster stopped]

Session of Congress

● **Figure 10.1** *Cloture voting in the US Senate, between 1919 (the 65th Congress) and 2010 (the 111th Congress). Filibusters, and the effort to end them by "invoking cloture," used to be rare events. Now they are part of every day Senate business. (United States Senate)*

a session). Both Democrats and Republicans, when in the minority, resorted to the filibuster to stop action or exact concessions.

In the past three sessions, sixty votes has effectively become the new Senate threshold for passing legislation. During the 111th Congress, in 2009–2010, minority Republican senators threatened a filibuster on every major bill brought up by majority Democrats, requiring a cloture vote on each.

Once amendments are voted down or adopted, the time for speeches has expired, and the leadership reckons it has a winning majority, it's time for a final floor vote. On uncontroversial matters, a **voice vote** of all members is sufficient. But several dozen votes each session are judged important enough to require a **roll-call vote.** In the Senate, a clerk still calls the roll, alphabetically scrolling through senators by last name, with each responding "yea" or "nay" (or "present," if they wish to abstain). Because the much-larger House would take hours to proceed in this way, roll calls are done electronically. Representatives use a card about the size of a credit or ATM card that they plug into kiosks located around the House chamber.

Roll-call votes on major bills are among the most important public acts a member of Congress performs. These votes attract a great deal of attention,

Voice vote: A congressional vote in which the presiding officer asks those for and against to say "yea" or "nay," respectively, and announces the result. No record is kept of House or Senate members voting on each side.

Roll-call vote: A congressional vote in which all members' votes are recorded, either by roll call (Senate) or electronically (House).

● *Conference committee in action. With staffers at the ready and media recording every utterance (and lobbyists crowded in the halls outside), a Senate-House conference committee works to resolve differences on a bill.*

from constituents, lobbyists, potential opponents, and media alike. Political scientists also find them compelling, in part because they provide a handy data source (hundreds of votes each session, each with a clear yes/no alternative). Despite years of roll-call analyses and some elaborate theories, we aren't very good at predicting vote outcomes. Whips and other nose-counters in Congress perform better than most academic models.

Conference Committee

Legislation must pass the Senate and House in identical form to be ready for presidential signature. If different versions of a bill pass—and technically a single comma, in a five-hundred-page bill, counts as a "difference"—a conference committee must reconcile them. These special sessions, made up of lawmakers from both chambers, provide a golden opportunity for disgruntled members or attentive lobbyists to revisit a bill. Interested parties who failed to get a favorite item included during committee or floor action now have another chance.

House-Senate conferences, if successful, yield a single version of a bill. Each chamber then has an "up-or-down" floor vote—no further amendments permitted. Opponents in the Senate may launch another filibuster hoping to win over new members who object to the compromises made with the House. If the majority beats the filibuster in the Senate and a majority of both houses votes in favor, the bill has passed Congress.

Presidential Action: Separated Powers, Once More

Even after all that, the bill has still another hurdle. No bill becomes law until the president signs it. On important issues, the signing ceremony often takes place in the White House Rose Garden. Presidents sign multiple copies of the bill, handing out pens to the original sponsors and other high-ranking congressional members in attendance.

Presidents can also **veto** legislation. Here's yet another place a bill can falter. If the president says no, Congress has one more shot at passing the legislation. It's a high bar, though. To deny or override a veto, both chambers need a two-thirds majority: at least 67 senators and 291 members of the House have to say no to the president. Only in this way can a bill become law without a presidential signature.

We will cover more details about veto practices in the next chapter, on the presidency. Fortunately for most legislative advocates, presidential opposition is rare: George W. Bush vetoed just twelve bills during his eight years as president, and Barack Obama was even more sparing, vetoing only two bills during his first term.

Veto: The constitutional procedure by which a president can prevent enactment of Congress-passed legislation.

THE BOTTOM LINE

- Transforming a policy idea into a federal law is highly complex—but the power of an officially sanctioned law inspires the introduction of thousands of bills in Congress each year.
- Bills often have creative titles and multiple authors inside and outside Congress—but only a member may introduce a bill.
- Congressional committees are the central actors in legislative policymaking, holding hearings and marking up (or deleting) bills to prepare them for floor action.
- Floor procedures are another intricate part of the process. Once passed by House and Senate, legislation may still face a conference committee, a presidential veto, or both.

Why Is Congress So Unpopular?

Congress, the "people's branch," might be expected to win the most public approval among our three national governing institutions. Yet it is by far the least-popular branch. For a half-century, polls have reported the popularity of Congress, the sitting president, and the Supreme Court, along with other institutions. Since the 1970s, Congress has come in last in virtually every survey—often by a great margin. Today, Congress is less popular than at any time in modern history, and less popular than most other political figures and institutions—including celebrity Paris Hilton and the idea of America going Communist (Figure 10.2).

Constituents tend to like their own representatives and senators, who receive far higher approval numbers and, as we saw in Chapter 7, are reelected at very high rates. We vote for our own members of Congress—yet despise the institution

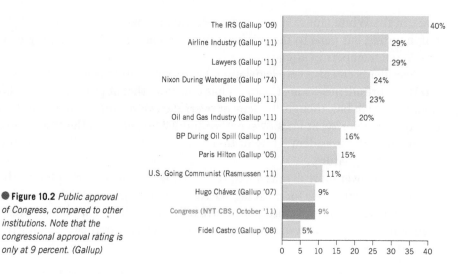

The IRS (Gallup '09) — 40%
Airline Industry (Gallup '11) — 29%
Lawyers (Gallup '11) — 29%
Nixon During Watergate (Gallup '74) — 24%
Banks (Gallup '11) — 23%
Oil and Gas Industry (Gallup '11) — 20%
BP During Oil Spill (Gallup '10) — 16%
Paris Hilton (Gallup '05) — 15%
U.S. Going Communist (Rasmussen '11) — 11%
Hugo Chávez (Gallup '07) — 9%
Congress (NYT CBS, October '11) — 9%
Fidel Castro (Gallup '08) — 5%

● **Figure 10.2** *Public approval of Congress, compared to other institutions. Note that the congressional approval rating is only at 9 percent. (Gallup)*

they serve in. Why? Based on opinion surveys and other research, here is what we know: the public dislikes partisan fighting and gridlock. Let's look more carefully at each complaint.

Partisan Polarization in Congress

Congress has exhibited partisan differences since its origins. Strong party disputes, fueled by the regional contention that ultimately sparked civil war, led many senators and representatives to carry swords, pistols, or Bowie knives while in the Capitol. Following a rousing antislavery speech by Senator Charles Sumner of Massachusetts in 1856, a Southern House member, Preston Brooks, slipped onto the Senate floor and beat Sumner unconscious with a cane. Sumner was unable to resume his Senate duties for nearly three years.

Subsequent combat in the House or Senate was mostly—but not entirely—limited to rhetorical, rather than physical, disagreement. During the 1950s and 1960s, Democratic majorities in both chambers largely masked differences—mostly between southern conservatives and liberals from other regions of the country—within the Democratic caucus. Cross-party sniping rose during the 1980s, as Republicans became more competitive within Congress. When the GOP won control of the Senate in 1980, it marked the first time they held a majority in either chamber since 1955.

The fault lines cracked open further after 1990, when House Republicans elected Newt Gingrich, a former history professor, as their leader. Gingrich orchestrated a series of legislative maneuvers designed to defeat or at least embarrass the Democratic majority; his "guerrilla-style" moves helped usher in an era of incivility and partisan difference. A few months into Gingrich's tenure, the veteran Senate majority leader Bob Dole passed a group of younger Republican House members and jokingly saluted them: "Hello, gentlemen; what are we against today?" "We don't know yet, sir," one shot back. "But we're

What Do You Think?

Is a Partisan Congress a Good Thing?

Should Congress seek more cross-party agreement? The answer might not be so obvious—especially if you view politics in terms of principles and high ideas, not merely the pursuit of self-interest. The modern "partisan" Congress features a significant ideological divide between conservative Republicans and progressive Democrats. Partisanship is the way members pursue the things they believe in and try to persuade the public of their perspectives. What do you think?

Yes, a partisan Congress is a good thing. It permits the public to choose between different political philosophies. The two parties represent different visions of America. That's better than two parties that basically say the same things.

No, Congress has gotten too partisan. The parties may disagree with one another, but they do not reflect most Americans. Most people are moderates who do not feel well-represented by the strong party views on either side.

It Depends. The context matters. For example, in times of economic suffering, people should put aside their political philosophy (whether pro- or antigovernment) and legislate relief.

going to make damn sure it doesn't happen!" Partisanship rose largely because the Republicans were challenging the Democrats for control of the House for the first time in almost forty years.[11]

Political scientist Barbara Sinclair has shown that the proportion of House votes in which a majority of Democrats voted against a majority of Republicans increased by more than 50 percent during the 1990s and early 2000s.[12] By another measure, party cohesion—the proportion of each party's House or Senate members who vote with the party majority—remained at or above 90 percent each year after 1990, after historically varying from the mid-60s to the low 80s. In other words, the parties in Congress were digging in against each other, with fewer and fewer members willing to look for middle ground or vote with the other side.

Partisan tensions continued to run high after Democrats retook control of Congress in 2006 and extended their seat margins in 2008. President Obama's call for increased civility and bipartisanship did not travel very far down Pennsylvania Avenue. During a presidential address to the House and Senate on health care, with millions watching on TV, House member Joe Wilson (R-PA) shouted, "You lie!" after President Obama claimed no undocumented aliens would get care under the reform—a dramatic breach of decorum (Wilson later apologized) that revealed the raw feeling on multiple issues: health, immigration, and trust between the parties.

Titles and subtitles of recent books about Congress underscore the point: *How Partisanship Is Poisoning the House of Representatives*, or *The Broken Branch: How Congress Is Failing America and How to Get It Back on Track*, or *Republic, Lost: How Money Corrupts Congress*, or *It's Even Worse Than It Looks: How the American Constitutional System Collided with the New Politics of Extremism*.[13]

Divided Government

A second source of legislative gridlock is divided government, when each party holds at least one of the three nationally elected branches: the presidency, the House, or the Senate. Include state governments and the courts, and the gridlock gets even worse. One or both houses of Congress led by a party opposed to the president, the argument goes, will result in a legislative standoff—as well as more aggressive congressional investigations of the White House. The argument makes intuitive sense, but many scholars disagree.

Political scientists David Mayhew and Keith Krehbiel have separately shown that divided government is actually no less productive of legislative achievements than is unified government—when the presidency and both houses of Congress are in the same party hands.[14] Neither scholar denies the existence of gridlock or policy stalemate; they do not attribute it to divided government. When the chips are down, they each argue, the political

● *Congressional partisanship, Civil War era–style. A Northern cartoonist renders the 1856 caning of Senator Sumner in vividly imagined fashion.*

SOUTHERN CHIVALRY — ARGUMENT versus CLUB'S.

process works. Disruptions and breakdowns occur, but usually in the short term. The crises, writes Mayhew, are "short-term, limited, tolerable and correctable."

Other political scientists disagree. Sarah Binder, a scholar at the Brookings Institution, questions the results. Divided government, she argues, leads directly to stalemate. Others argue that, whatever the historical record, the recent polarization has brought "the virtual disappearance of regular order in Congress."[15]

The conclusion is simply that careful scholars disagree. As you observe Congress in the future, keep both perspectives in mind. Watch to see if, after all the dramatics and the finger pointing, the two sides quietly agree on legislation—especially toward the end of the sessions. If so, it reflects the optimists: divided we govern. If not, you'll know the pessimists made the right prediction and Congress has proven to be "the broken branch."

THE BOTTOM LINE

- Congress has grown more partisan. The parties themselves are more ideologically consistent. This makes for sharper conflict, but it also gives people clearer choices.
- Does divided government lead to more gridlock? Political scientists disagree. Some argue that it does not; "Divided we govern," they insist. Others argue that recent developments—the growing ideological purity of the parties, the regular use of the filibuster—signal that divided government now means an inability to solve America's problems.

● Conclusion: Congress and the Challenge of Governing

The story of this chapter can be summed up like this: Congress, as an institution, does some important things very well—and others not very well at all. Representatives and senators look after the American public, as individuals, remarkably well. Direct constituent service, at home in the district and state, is often superb. That's why reelection rates are so high.

But as our individual needs have become better supported, solving the big societal problems—immigration, health care, government spending, inequality, global warming, an attractive business climate—has suffered. By any measure, Americans' collective concerns are at least as important as our personal aims. The great question we have asked throughout this chapter is whether the

US Congress has lost its ability to do the big collective things well, or whether it still muddles through precisely as the constitutional framers intended.

In the past, the Congress has certainly proven capable of remarkable collective achievements. Medicare and Social Security, to take two of the largest congressional programs, have cut the rate of poverty among elderly Americans by more than half and provided seniors with what is generally recognized as the most generous health benefits across the globe.

Genuine democratic, popular government can be chaotic, muddled, and sometimes repugnant. But it is essential. Our national legislative branch, our representatives in Congress, must continue to fulfill their democratic duties—and be rewarded by the public for doing so—if we are to manage democracy and live in freedom together.

CHAPTER SUMMARY

● America's Congress is bicameral: the House of Representatives has 435 members elected every two years; in the Senate, 100 Senators serve six-year terms.

● The two chambers of Congress reflect different national priorities. Populists appreciate the responsive House; advocates of stability embrace the more deliberate Senate.

● Members of the House and Senate represent Americans in multiple ways. These include:

- *Geographic representation*: The election rules say members must live in the state or district.

- *Descriptive representation*: Does the assembly look like the people?

- *Substantive representation*: Do members of Congress effectively pursue constituent interests?

● Members of Congress are always running for office. Fundraising takes a particularly important amount of time and attention.

● Congressional leadership in the House includes a Speaker, majority and minority leaders, and ten whips. Successful leaders in the House impose discipline on their party members. In the Senate, party leaders and whips have fewer institutional tools with which to impose discipline.

● Congressional committees are the workhorses of Congress. They have proved efficient and adaptable over the years. However, the committee system also fragments Congress, hides action from public view, advantages well-placed constituents looking for individual favors, and makes it difficult to pass major legislation.

● Floor procedures are another intricate part of the process. Once passed by House and Senate, legislation may still face a conference committee, a presidential veto, or both.

● Congress has grown more partisan. The parties themselves are more ideologically consistent. This makes for sharper conflict, but it also gives people clearer choices.

● The difficult path to legislation raises the key question about Congress: Should we cheer the difficult process as a way to limit government? Or worry that the institution is not up to addressing America's vital problems?

KEY TERMS

113th Congress, 361
Cloture vote, 384
Committee hearing, 380
Committee markup session, 381
Conference committee, 359
Congressional caucus, 357

Earmark, 376
Filibuster, 362
Floor, 357
King of the Hill rule, 372
Legislative hold, 362
President pro tempore, 373

Reapportionment, 368
Roll-call vote, 385
Unanimous consent, 381
Veto, 387
Voice vote, 385

STUDY QUESTIONS

1. Discuss the following reforms:

   A. There should be public financing for all congressional elections. Even if it means raising taxes.
   B. The Senate filibuster should be abolished.
   C. There should be more limits on lobbyists.

2. How did Congress lose so much power to the president? Are there ways to get some of that power back? Should power be more balanced between the two branches?

3. Why is Congress so partisan? Can you think of ways to reduce partisanship? Are there any advantages to drawing strong partisan lines between Republicans and Democrats?

4. Should it be easier to pass laws through Congress than it is presently? What, if any, benefits do all the checking and balancing provide?

5. Why is Congress so unpopular with the American people? In your view, does Congress deserve its low approval ratings?

11

The Presidency

IN THIS CHAPTER, YOU WILL:

- See how the Constitution defines the presidency.
- Focus on presidential power. Learn what presidents do.
Reflect on presidential popularity—and greatness. Consider
the personal side of the office. Tour the Executive Office of the
President, and meet the team around a president.

GEORGE WASHINGTON, the first president of the United States, faced a problem. He had to find a way to persuade thirteen independent-minded states to think of themselves as one unified nation. Washington decided to foster unity by touring the new country—a grueling journey in the 1790s. He set out with assistants, slaves, horses, and dogs. As the party approached each town, the president mounted a great white steed and cantered handsomely into the cheering throngs, his favorite greyhound trotting at his side. Washington named the dog Cornwallis, after the British general who surrendered to end the Revolutionary War. Poor Cornwallis the greyhound died while touring the southern states, but his name reminded the people that they were part of a proud and independent nation. Everywhere Washington went, the people greeted their president with ringing bells, cheers, songs, speeches, parades, and flags. The crowds felt, at least for a day, like Americans.[1]

Who are we? Each president offers a different answer. Washington may be our greatest president, not because of his domestic programs or foreign policies: critics were scathing about both. Instead, Washington embodied the new nation. He championed American ideals, spoke to national aspirations, introduced new ideas, and personified the nation's sense of identity—both to Americans and to the world. All presidents do the same—some more successfully than others. Each offers a different answer to the question, Who are we?

The president's role is difficult partly because Americans rarely agree about who we are. The United States are often the *Un*-United States. Washington took slaves on his unity tour. Didn't slavery violate the new nation's ideals? Many Americans knew that it did.

Two hundred twenty-two years after Washington's tour, President Barack Obama received a report from the Central Intelligence Agency (CIA). The agency had tracked down Osama bin Laden, the mastermind of the 9/11 attacks, living in a compound in Pakistan. At least seven different agencies gathered information, gamed scenarios, and offered advice. The president could order an air strike and bomb the compound to rubble. He could inform our ally, the Pakistani government, and coordinate a joint raid. Ultimately, Obama and his team chose a very risky option. Helicopters slipped under Pakistani

● *The president has many advisors but has to make the tough decisions alone. Here, President Obama prepares his remarks to the nation about the raid on bin Laden's compound in Pakistan.*

radar and ferried Navy SEALs into the compound. The team stormed buildings, shot and killed bin Laden and four others, grabbed computers, handcuffed his wives and children for local officials, and disappeared in less than an hour. The president and his aides monitored the dramatic operation in real time. They did not inform the Pakistani government, Congress, or the American people until the raid was over. Obama had many agencies and advisors to guide him, but ultimately he had to make the call alone. The president, as George W. Bush liked to say, is "the decider."

The raid demonstrates the extensive power of the modern presidency. Today, the American executive can approve the death of an enemy on the other side of the world. The power and reach of the office raise the same question the delegates debated at the Constitutional Convention. How much authority should the president have? Or, to translate the question for modern times: Has the president grown too powerful for a democratic republic? Or is this exactly the "energy in government" that Alexander Hamilton and James Madison were seeking back in 1787?

Washington's tour and Obama's raid illustrate three essential features about the American president:

> *The president personifies America.* More than any individual, presidents tell us who we are—and what we are becoming.

> *The president injects new ideas into American politics.* Our discussion of Congress emphasized the institution, the rules of the game; the presidency puts more focus on individuals and ideas.

> *The president has enormous powers.* That authority raises a fundamental question: Is the president too powerful for a democratic republic? Or is the office too weak to do what Americans demand of it? Perhaps the same president can be both too strong and too weak at different points. Keep this question of authority in mind as you read the chapter.

Defining the Presidency

A time traveler from the nineteenth century would easily recognize today's Senate or the Supreme Court. However, the modern White House would stun her. The presidency is the branch of the federal government that has changed the most.

BY THE NUMBERS *The Presidency*

Number of presidents in the last 100 years: **18**
Number of Democratic presidents in the last 100 years: **8**

Length, in months, of shortest presidency (William Henry Harrison): **1**
Length, in months, of longest presidency (Franklin Roosevelt): **145**

Number of years by which Franklin Roosevelt's lifespan was shorter than that of the average person at the time: **12.4**
Number of presidents younger than Barack Obama when they were elected: **2**

Election year of last president without a college education (Harry S. Truman): **1945**
Election year of last president with no formal schooling (Andrew Johnson): **1865**

Birth year of first president to be born in a hospital (Jimmy Carter): **1924**

Year in which first woman (Victoria Woodhull) ran for president: **1872**
Year in which women could first vote for president nationwide: **1920**

Number of presidents who lost the popular vote but still won the election: **4**
(John Quincy Adams, Rutherford B. Hayes, Benjamin Harrison, George W. Bush)

Number of presidents who were sons or nephews of prior presidents: **4**
(John Q. Adams, Benjamin Harrison, Franklin Roosevelt, George W. Bush)

Percent average winning margin in the popular vote in the last 20 elections: **9.8**
Percent average winning margin in the Electoral College vote: **52.2**

Highest presidential approval ratings (percent) ever recorded by Gallup (for Harry Truman, George H. W. Bush, and George W. Bush, respectively): **91, 89, 89**
Lowest approval ratings recorded by Gallup at end of a full term (for Harry Truman, Jimmy Carter, and George W. Bush, respectively): **31, 34, 34**
Highest approval ratings at end of a full term (for Bill Clinton, Ronald Reagan, and Dwight Eisenhower, respectively): **66, 63, 59**

Estimated proportion of presidents who had affairs: **1 in 3**

Number of presidents to hold a patent: **1** (Abraham Lincoln, for an invention to free boats trapped on a sandbar)

One hundred fifty years ago Americans could walk right in the front door of the White House and greet the president. In 1829, during President Andrew Jackson's inauguration, supporters mobbed the mansion and forced the president to climb out a window for his own safety; aides filled tubs with whiskey and orange juice on the lawn to lure the crowds outside. When William

● *A different era. After the inauguration, presidents held an open house. Here, Americans crush into the mansion to shake hands with President Jackson—who had to escape through a window.*

Henry Harrison won the presidency in 1840, so many men milled about the White House hoping to get a government job that the president-elect could not find an empty room to meet with his cabinet. After Warren Harding was elected in 1920, his old Senate colleagues brusquely advised him not to bother them with legislative proposals.

Today there are no more mobs in the White House or curt orders from Congress. The presidency is a different institution. Presidents have redefined their roles and renegotiated their powers. To this day, each president has the opportunity to reshape the office. One reason the presidency is so fluid lies in the job description. By now, you know where to look for that: the Constitution.

Defined by Controversy

The Constitutional Convention faced three tough questions when they defined the office (for more detail, see Chapter 3). First, *should the United States even have a president?* Traditional republics feared executive power; after all, strong executives defined monarchies and empires. The founders feared the English king as too powerful; they also worried that the state governments were too weak. Their job was to find a happy medium. In the end, they selected a single president and established simple qualifications for the post: a natural-born citizen at least thirty-five years old who had lived in the United States for fourteen years.

Second, *how long should the president serve?* Delegates debated many options: four, six, seven, eight, eleven, and fifteen years as well as a life long term. They settled for four years; in 1945, the twenty-second amendment limited presidents to two terms.

Third, *how should the United States choose its president?* This was the toughest question of all. Delegates believed that the public could not be trusted, the state legislatures were too self interested, and that Congress would become too powerful if it got the task. They settled on a round about method, which you encountered in Chapter 8. The states would each get electoral votes equal to their congressional delegation. Political scientists still debate the merits of the Electoral College because it distorts the popular vote—and has put the loser in the White House four times.

The President's Powers

Article 2 of the Constitution, which defines the presidency, seems puzzling at first glance. Article 1 meticulously defines everything Congress is empowered to do: the instructions run for fifty-two paragraphs. In contrast, Article 2 says very little about who the president is and what the president does, devoting

Table 11.1 The President's Powers Are Balanced by Congress

The president is commander in chief of the army, navy, and state militias. But Congress has the power to declare war, set the military budget, and make the rules governing the military.
The president can grant pardons and reprieves for offenses against the United States.
The president can make treaties (with the approval of two-thirds of the Senate), appoint ambassadors (with the advice and consent of the Senate), and select Supreme Court justices and other officers (again, with Senate approval).
The Constitution also authorizes presidents to solicit the opinions of his officers (the cabinet members) and requires presidents to report on the state of the Union.
The president may sign or veto laws after Congress passes them. Congress may override a veto with a two-thirds vote of both chambers.

only thirteen paragraphs to the office. This vague constitutional mandate is one reason why the office keeps evolving.

The Constitution is especially concise when it gets to the heart of the presidency: the powers and duties of the chief executive. It grants the president a limited number of **expressed powers**, or explicit grants of authority. Most are carefully balanced by corresponding congressional powers. Table 11.1 summarizes this balance.

Expressed powers: Powers the Constitution explicitly grants to the president.

The president draws real authority from a simple phrase at the end of the section: "take care that the laws be faithfully executed." Congress votes on legislation, then sends it to the executive branch to put into effect. In other words, Congress grants **delegated powers** to the president. For example, Congress passes legislation that aims to improve hospital care. It delegates power to the executive branch, which issues a rule saying that hospitals will receive lower federal payments if patients develop infections after surgery.

Delegated powers: Powers that Congress passes on to the president.

Modern presidents claim a third source of authority: **inherent powers of the presidency.** These are not specified in the Constitution or delegated by legislation but are implicit in the vague article 2 phrase "The executive power shall be vested in a president." During crises, presidents have often seized new "inherent" powers. During the Civil War, for example, President Lincoln took a series of unprecedented military actions with no clear legal basis. He imposed censorship, ordered a naval blockade, and took other actions while Congress was not in session. After the 9/11 attacks, President Bush exercised inherent powers to engage in foreign surveillance, to detain enemy combatants without hearings, and to authorize coercive interrogation (which critics called torture). Presidents claim inherent powers; the Supreme Court then weighs whether they have overstepped the constitutional boundaries of their authority.

Inherent powers of the presidency: Powers assumed by presidents, often during crisis, on the basis of the constitutional phrase "The executive power shall be vested in the president."

The result is a very fluid definition of presidential power. Presidents define their roles, negotiating the limits of the office through their actions at home and abroad. Crises generally expand the presidential role. More than any other institution, the presidency is a constant work in progress. The arc of presidential history begins with a modest constitutional grant of power that has grown enormously through the years.

This discussion brings us back to the question we posed at the start of the chapter: Has the president become too powerful? We turn to that question in the next section.

An Imperial Presidency?

The constitutional framers wrestled with the same issue we debate today: *power.* How much authority do presidents need to protect the nation and get things done? How much power goes so far as to violate the idea of limited government?

During George Washington's national tour, a few Americans fretted about his nine stallions, gold-trimmed saddles, personal attendants, and all that adulation. Washington, they whispered, was acting more like a king than the president of a homespun republic. They were articulating a constant American theme: the president has grown too mighty. Flash forward two centuries. Today, the president travels with a cast of hundreds: lawyers, secretaries, cooks, speechwriters, baggage handlers, doctors, aides, snipers, bomb-sniffing dogs, and armored cars. When President Clinton visited China, it took thirty-six jumbo jets (each holding 145 tons of cargo) to carry the presidential team and all its baggage. When the second President Bush visited England, the imperial trappings of the presidential entourage (five hundred members strong) reportedly surprised the Queen.[2]

Presidents have constantly redefined the authority of their office—setting off the critics who charge that they have gone too far. Washington's successor, President John Adams, did not have to worry about cheering crowds. Critics mocked the chubby second president as "His Rotundity." Adams attracted so little attention that he regularly swam naked in the Potomac River (until a woman reporter allegedly spied him, sat on his clothes, and demanded an interview). Even Adams, however, aroused widespread fears about executive power when he signed the Alien and Sedition Acts, which gave the executive broad powers to deport "dangerous aliens" and punish "false, scandalous, and malicious" speech. The president seemed to be trampling the First Amendment by silencing criticism.

Some presidents—most notably, George W. Bush—have stretched the limits of the office by aggressively advancing a **unitary executive theory**. This view holds that the Constitution puts the president in charge of executing the laws, and therefore no one—not Congress, not the judiciary, not even the people—may limit presidential power when it comes to executive matters. Many executive decisions demand swift, decisive, and sometimes secretive action: only an empowered president, the argument goes, can make those instantaneous calls.

The unitary executive theory is controversial. Opponents fear that it upsets the Constitution's intricate checks and balances and tips power from

Unitary executive theory: The idea that the Constitution puts the president in charge of executing the laws; therefore, no other branch should limit presidential discretion over executive matters.

Congress (to pass laws) to the presidency (to sign and then execute them). Proponents respond that they are simply breathing new life into Hamilton's plea in the Federalist Papers: to be a great power, the United States must have a robust executive capable of vigorous action.[3]

Arthur Schlesinger Jr., a celebrated historian, warned of an **imperial presidency**. Very powerful presidents, he feared, become like emperors: they run roughshod over Congress, issue secret decisions, unilaterally deploy force around the world, and burst past the checks and balances limiting presidential power. Critics have charged that Presidents Lyndon Johnson, Richard Nixon, and George W. Bush all displayed imperial traits; others worry that imperial features have become part of the presidency itself.

At issue are two vital principles: We need a president who is strong enough to lead the country and face our problems. But if presidents become too strong, we lose our republican form of government. This is a deep paradox in American politics: *we need powerful leaders; we fear powerful leaders.*

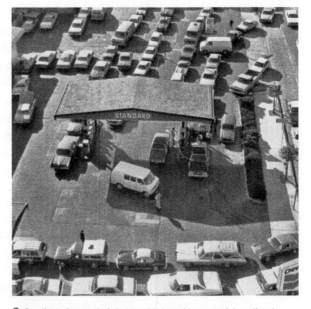

● *Gas lines. A case study in a troubled presidency: an international energy crisis led to long lines at gas stations during the Jimmy Carter years. Presidents take the blame for many events they cannot control—like this one.*

A Weak Office?

At the same time, the presidency can also seem very weak. Every modern president has complained about his inability to get basic goals accomplished. Congress, courts, the opposing political party, the media, interest groups, and bad luck can all humble a president. In the last half century, only four (of ten) presidents completed two full terms. What kind of "imperial" presidency is that?

The presidents can seem weakest when they face domestic issues. Even under the best of circumstances, as we saw in the previous chapter, it is difficult to get major legislation through Congress. The president nominally runs the executive branch, but the bureaucracy is immense and often difficult to control. Other institutional actors refuse to go along with presidential priorities. Moving the American political process can be extremely difficult, even for the savviest presidents.

For a case study in the weak presidency, take Jimmy Carter. Congressional relations turned frosty early in his term, when Carter unexpectedly vetoed a spending bill. Congress was stung at the abrupt rejection. Carter's major legislative proposals quickly ran into trouble on Capitol Hill. Then the economy turned bad. Interest rates spiraled toward 20 percent and unemployment topped 10 percent. Gas prices also soared, forcing customers in some regions to wait in long lines at gas stations.

Imperial presidency: A characterization of the American presidency that suggests it is demonstrating imperial traits, and that the republic is morphing into an empire.

Carter did not seem to have an answer to all the woes besetting the nation. A few months later, militant Iranian students took fifty-three Americans hostage at the US embassy in Tehran and held them for 444 days. A weak president seemed to be completely overwhelmed by events all around him.

Back and forth goes the debate. Is the president getting too powerful and breaking free from popular control? Or is the president not up to the job of governing a superpower? Striking the right balance between presidential power and popular control is one of the most important issues for American democracy.

THE BOTTOM LINE

- The president has three kinds of powers: expressed in the Constitution, delegated by Congress, and inherent in the role of chief executive.
- Americans want a powerful president; Americans fear a powerful president.
- The executive branch has grown far stronger over time, especially when it comes to foreign policy.
- At the same time, presidential power is limited, especially when it comes to solving domestic problems.

● What Presidents Do

Over time, presidents have taken on many jobs. Some are described in the Constitution. Others spring up during national crises. Presidents seized still others as they jockeyed for political advantage. By now, the president has accumulated an extraordinary number of hats (and helmets). In this section we will review the many things the president does—starting with commanding the armies.

Commander in Chief

The Constitution lays it out simply: "The president shall be the Commander-in-Chief of the Army and Navy of the United States and the militia of the several states, when called into the actual service of the United States." Congress declares war and presidents manage it.

For many years, the United States had a small standing army and called men and women to service in wartime. The size of the army jumped thirty-eight-fold during the Civil War and thirty-six times during World War I. After the wars, the army quickly demobilized. This approach reflected classical theory. In great republics like Athens and Rome, citizens took up arms when enemies loomed and then returned home when the crisis had passed—just as George Washington had done during the revolution. Peacetime armies were, according to the traditional perspective, a recipe for empire or monarchy.

This tradition changed after World War II, when the United States faced off against the Soviet Union in the so-called Cold War. An army of around 250,000 (after World War I) grew into a force of over two million and spread across the globe. Back in 1835, Tocqueville mused that the Constitution gave the president "almost royal prerogatives which he has no occasion to use." Now the occasion had arrived, and the president's power grew.

Today, America's active-duty force numbers 1.4 million, with another 1.4 million in reserve (Figure 11.1). Supplying the military involves a sprawling military-industrial complex. The defense budget runs over $750 billion—not including spending on wars, the Department of Veterans Affairs, Homeland Security, intelligence agencies, and other related efforts. The military operates 750 installations that span the globe. In short, the commander in chief oversees the world's largest fighting force. That role, by itself, makes the president one of the most powerful individuals in the world.

Meanwhile, checks on the commander in chief have faded. The Constitution authorizes Congress to declare wars, but, since the nuclear age dawned in 1945, presidents have rarely waited for Congress to act. Facing the doomsday threat of nuclear missiles, military response time is measured in minutes—too fast for congressional deliberation.

In an effort to regain some of its authority, Congress passed the War Powers Act in 1973, requiring congressional approval after troops had been deployed for sixty days. That is a far weaker check than the constitutional power to declare war. It concedes the president's authority to unilaterally deploy troops; Congress does not get its say until American men and women are already in combat—when it is very difficult to vote no. Moreover, presidents have been contemptuous of the War Powers Act. "I don't have to get the permission from some old goat in the United States Congress to kick Saddam Hussein out of Kuwait," President George H. W. Bush told the Texas Republican Convention—even though Bush did seek congressional approval before launching the first Gulf War.[4] Presidents

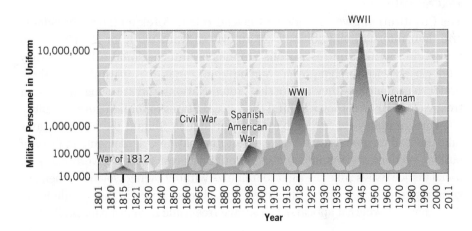

● **Figure 11.1** *The military and how it grew, 1820–2011: active-duty military. Traditionally, the United States called soldiers to war and then demobilized after the war. However, troop levels never went back down to prewar levels. The United States began to play a global role after the Spanish-American War. (Historical Statistics/ Statistical Abstracts)*

slip around the War Powers Act by not starting the clock on the sixty days specified in the War Powers Act.

Today, the president generally asks Congress for a resolution supporting major military action. In October 2002, for example, President George W. Bush asked for and received congressional authorization to use force against Iraq if and when he felt it was necessary.

Presidential powers have always waxed during wartime. Franklin Roosevelt's attorney general once commented, "The Constitution has not greatly bothered any wartime president."[5] However, when wars drag on and become unpopular, the president's powers seem to fade: Congress holds hearings and threatens the budgets; public approval ratings decline; protests spring up.

Presidents are deeply engaged by their military role. They start each day with a security briefing that reviews all the dangers stirring around the world; they have a large national security staff; and—the great symbol of our nuclear age—they are never more than a few feet away from "the football."

If you see the president in person, or a wide-angle shot on television, you will glimpse a military officer standing about twenty feet away and clutching a medium-size black briefcase, known as "the football." What's in the bag? The answer is classified information, but over the years the public has learned that it is a mobile communications center locked into the American nuclear arsenal. Every minute of every day the American president is steps away from a kit that would enable him or her to launch an attack that could obliterate any nation from the face of the Earth.

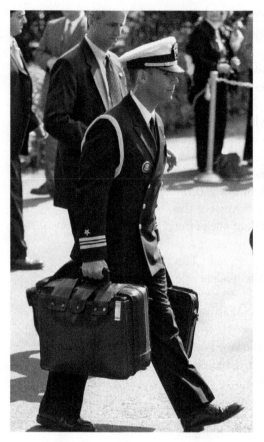

● *A uniformed officer with "the football"— a briefcase that contains launch codes for the nuclear arsenal. The football is always a few feet away from the president.*

Top Diplomat

The Constitution gives presidents the lead role in foreign affairs. Presidents and their international advisers set an overall framework for the US role in the world. Some administrations emphasize international alliances; they work closely with foreign powers and build multinational institutions. Others prefer to go it alone—they ignore the United Nations and are reluctant to sign treaties for fear that they will bind the United States to foreign governments.

Foreign policy issues bombard each president. Should the United States take the lead on global warming, or reject international agreements in favor of bulking up domestic manufacturing? Should we press foreign governments on social justice issues (like the right to unionize without facing violence) when negotiating trade agreements? Should we try to broker peace in the Middle East? Stop genocide where it appears? Encourage free trade in South America? What should be done about rogue states with nuclear weapons? Presidents and their team constantly meet, discuss, threaten, and negotiate with nations near and far.

Foreign diplomacy is not just about trouble spots. The State Department manages 305 embassies, consulates, and diplomatic missions around the world. Presidents must hash out American relations with nearly 200 nations that range from "special friends" to distant allies to avowed enemies. Intricate questions arise about how to approach each country: Should the president shake hands with our nation's enemies? Every smile or snub sends a diplomatic message. A president sets the tone and the policy for all these relationships.

Global statecraft is full of unexpected snares. When newly elected President Obama met British prime minister Gordon Brown for the first time, the English press howled about "humiliation." Brown had given Obama a valuable pen carved from the timbers of a nineteenth-century British warship; Obama's gift was a pile of DVDs. Did the popular president really mean to humiliate the relatively unpopular prime minister? Certainly not; the new administration had slipped up. On the international stage, every presidential action is magnified, analyzed, and blogged about.

● *International diplomacy on the court. President Obama signals American closeness to Britain with this all-American night of college basketball. Prime Minister David Cameron is just to the right of the president.*

Two years later, the Obama administration had learned its lesson. When new prime minister David Cameron came calling, Obama whisked him via Air Force One ("the first foreign leader to ride on the presidential aircraft," cheered the English press) to a courtside seat at the first round of the NCAA basketball championship.

Foreign policy crises differ vastly from everyday domestic politics. Passing laws is a long, complicated process full of compromise and constraint. During international crises—hostage situations, terror attacks, the outbreak of wars—all eyes turn toward the president and his team. Often presidents must make fast decisions with immediate consequences. John F. Kennedy captured the intensity, a few weeks after taking office, in a late-night phone call to former vice president Richard Nixon during his first international crisis. "It really is true that foreign affairs is the only important issue for a president to handle, isn't it? I mean who gives a shit if the minimum wage is $1.15 or $1.25 compared to something like this?"[6]

The First Legislator

The Constitution includes presidents in the legislative process. It authorizes them to *recommend measures* for Congress's "consideration," report to Congress *information on the state of the Union*, and *veto legislation* they oppose.

Recommending Measures. Until modern times, presidents generally avoided legislative affairs. In 1840, William Henry Harrison devoted his inaugural address—the longest in history—to denouncing the insatiable love of power creeping into the presidency. He pledged to honor congressional authority by avoiding legislative involvement. Dwight Eisenhower (1953–1961) was the last president to try and leave legislation to Congress. His cabinet officers complained, and before long Eisenhower was recommending measures—and blasting Congress when they failed to approve his proposals.

Today presidential candidates define the legislative agenda long before they arrive in office. As the 2016 election begins to shape up, click on candidate websites for proposals to deal with issue after issue: economic policy, health care, education, energy, budgets, taxes, and the list will go on. In our fast-paced media environment, silence on any topic invites criticism. At every news conference and debate, candidates joust over their proposals. Listen carefully: amid all the talk lie a handful of issues that a candidate is passionate about. Presidents-elect generally try to advance these once in office. For President George W. Bush, it was tax cuts, education reform, and privatizing Social Security. Candidate Barack Obama emphasized economic improvement, health reform, and global warming. Each president arrives in office with a few legislative priorities. However, they are soon enmeshed in many other issues. Campaign promises require attention. Top advisers lobby for their favorite programs. And unexpected issues constantly spring up and require presidential attention.

State of the Union. The Constitution invites the chief executive to report on the state of the Union "from time to time." Today the SOTU address, as insiders term it, is an annual event, delivered with great fanfare before Congress, Supreme Court justices, official Washington, and a national television audience. The State of the Union speech is also the annual focal point of the cabinet members and other White House officials, who compete to get their

● The State of the Union address: one of the great pageants on the Washington calendar—and a great victory for the agencies that get their programs mentioned.

favorite programs mentioned in the message. All submit their proposed ideas months in advance, and the president's staff picks the winners (or substitutes its own favorites).

The president then declares his legislative program for the year in the speech. What you hear is a long and often dull list of programs: for the president's team, however, each little bullet point is a triumph for one person or department and a defeat for all those pushing programs that failed to make the cut.

Following the SOTU address, each issue undergoes a second round of debates within the administration: Does it really fit our budget? Can we make it work smoothly? Did Congress cheer or yawn when the boss rolled it out? What was the public reaction? Most policies have friends and enemies in the administration—and if you get your favorite program I may not get mine. The process is a polite version of a knife fight. Proposals that survive go up to Capitol Hill, where they face the long, complicated congressional process we described in the last chapter.

Presidential "Batting Average."   Only members of Congress can formally propose a law, so presidents rely on supporters in each chamber to submit their bills. The White House has a congressional liaison team to negotiate and cut deals. Generally hidden from public view, the liaison is a key role in the modern presidency. No matter how talented a liaison might be, frustration inevitably sets in. To the executive branch, legislators seem overly parochial as they focus on their states and districts. Still, most presidents quickly learn the same lesson: work closely with Congress. Managing that is one of the most important presidential skills.

We can measure each president's legislative success—generally referred to as the batting average (Figure 11.2). There are many different ways to keep score: all the bills the president endorses, the most important bills, or bills that the other party opposes. You can see that when the same party controls the White House and Congress, known as unified government, the batting average is much higher—usually around .800. When the opposition party controls Congress (divided government), the average usually falls below .500. Some political scientists have argued that divided government makes for a more effective legislative process. But notice how divided governments (the red lines) have been yielding less agreement in recent years. As we saw in previous chapters, the two parties are much more uniformly opposed to one another than in the past, when each party had both conservative and liberal wings.

Veto.   When Congress passes a law, presidents have the authority to sign or **veto** (*veto* means "I forbid," in Latin). A veto blocks the legislation unless two-thirds of both chambers vote to **override** it, a very high bar to achieve. Presidents have ten days to return the legislation to Congress with a message explaining why they have rejected it. If the president does nothing, the bill becomes law in ten days.

Veto power: The presidential power to block an act of Congress by refusing to sign it.

Override: The process by which Congress can overcome a presidential veto with a two-thirds vote in both chambers.

President	Party	Years in Office	Congressional Control	% Congressional Support
Dwight Eisenhower	R	1953–1954	Republicans Control Congress	86.0
Dwight Eisenhower		1955–1960	Democrats Control Congress	67.7
John F. Kennedy	D	1961–1963	Democrats Control Congress	84.6
Lyndon Johnson	D	1963–1969	Democrats Control Congress	82.2
Richard Nixon	R	1969–1974	Democrats Control Congress	64.3
Gerald Ford	R	1974–1977	Democrats Control Congress	58.3
Jimmy Carter	D	1977–1981	Democrats Control Congress	76.6
Ronald Reagan	R	1981–1986	Mixed Control (R Senate, D House)	67.4
Ronald Reagan	R	1987–1989	Democrats Control Congress	45.4
George H. W. Bush	R	1989–1993	Democrats Control Congress	51.8
Bill Clinton	D	1993–1994	Democrats Control Congress	86.3
Bill Clinton	D	1995–2000	Republicans Control Congress	48.1
George W. Bush	R	2001–2006	Republicans Control Congress	80.9
George W. Bush	R	2007–2008	Democrats Control Congress	43.0
Barack Obama	D	2009–2010	Democrats Control Congress	92.0
Barack Obama	D	2011	Mixed control (D Senate R House)	57.1

● Figure 11.2 *Presidential batting average, measuring the proportion of Congressional bills on which the president took a position that passed.*

President's party controls Congress
Opposition party controls Congress
Congress split

The veto is a formidable weapon. In the last eighty years presidents have rejected more than 1,400 bills. Congress managed to override just sixty times: a congressional "batting average" of 4 percent. Recently the veto has become a more partisan weapon, as conflict between the parties has escalated. Franklin Roosevelt, Harry Truman, and Jimmy Carter all flourished the veto pen against a Congress controlled by their own party; in their first two years the three presidents struck down seventy-three, seventy-four, and nineteen bills, respectively. In contrast, the most recent presidents—Clinton, Bush, and Obama—*combined* for a total of two vetoes against their own party majorities in their first two years (Figure 11.3).

A president's veto rarely comes as a surprise. As Congress works on a law, the president's congressional liaisons are ever-present. Administration officials may threaten a veto to shape the legislation in favorable ways. When negotiations get especially intense, the president can also go public and threaten Congress. Congressional leaders in turn can threaten to bury a bill the president wants, or openly defy a president to veto popular bills. After all the back-and-forth, presidents have developed yet another strategy: they can voice their displeasure while signing bills into law.

Signing Statements. Bill signing has become a great Washington ritual, especially for popular legislation. Congressional sponsors flank the president, who has a big pile of pens to hand out to the program's key supporters while cameras capture the smiling moment.

In recent decades, presidents increasingly issue **signing statements** as they are signing a bill into law. These statements may offer their administration's interpretation of the law—one sometimes at odds with Congress's expressed ideas. President George W. Bush, reflecting his strong view of the unitary executive, used signing statements to challenge, limit, or reject an estimated 1,200 sections of congressional bills—roughly twice as many challenges as all previous presidents combined. Late in the Bush presidency, the American Bar Association condemned the practice as an undue expansion of federal authority.[7] President Obama, like most Democrats, criticized the signing statements. Once he was in office, however, he continued the practice. Unless the Supreme Court rules on the matter, this may become another example of the pattern: presidents redefine their own office and expand its powers.

Signing statements: A president's declarations commenting on the bill that is signed into law.

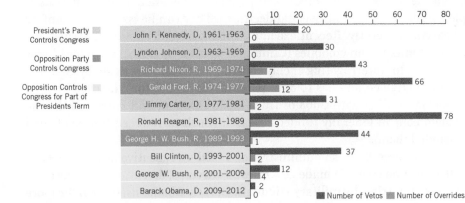

	President's Party Controls Congress
	Opposition Party Controls Congress
	Opposition Controls Congress for Part of Presidents Term

John F. Kennedy, D, 1961–1963 — 20 / 0
Lyndon Johnson, D, 1963–1969 — 30 / 0
Richard Nixon, R, 1969–1974 — 43 / 7
Gerald Ford, R, 1974–1977 — 66 / 12
Jimmy Carter, D, 1977–1981 — 31 / 2
Ronald Reagan, R, 1981–1989 — 78 / 9
George H. W. Bush, R, 1989–1993 — 44 / 1
Bill Clinton, D, 1993–2001 — 37 / 2
George W. Bush, R, 2001–2009 — 12 / 4
Barack Obama, D, 2009–2012 — 2 / 0

■ Number of Vetos ■ Number of Overrides

● **Figure 11.3** *Presidential vetoes and overrides. Note that vetoes were far more common fifty years ago, even when the same party controlled Congress and the White House; Congress rarely manages to override a presidential veto.*

● *President Obama signs the health care bill, surrounded by congressional sponsors. To his right is a young man whose mother, dying of cancer, vocally supported the president's bill so that others would be afforded the treatment she was denied. Sitting on the president's left is Congressman Dingell, whose father introduced the first national health insurance bill 70 years earlier.*

Chief Bureaucrat

The Constitution gives the president the power to appoint the men and women of the executive branch of government, subject to confirmation by the Senate. President Washington took the top officers of the major departments and organized them into a cabinet to advise him. The original cabinet included four officers: the secretaries of war, Treasury, and state, and the attorney general. By 1800 the executive branch included two hundred officeholders.[8]

Today, the executive branch includes fifteen departments and 2.7 million employees—or more than 4 million, counting active-duty military. Presidents appoint some four thousand **political appointees** who direct the executive agencies; the rest of the staff are **civil servants** who remain from one administration to the next. We will explore these officials and their agencies in the next chapter, on the executive bureaucracy.

As chief executive, presidents wield powers that do not need to go through Congress. They can sign **executive orders**, with the force of law, setting guidelines for federal agencies. Contemporary administrations issue around forty to fifty executive orders a year. Some are simply instructions for operating the executive branch: setting up a new council or office, for example. Others involve controversial decisions. They can be issued with fanfare or executed secretly. Recent executive orders have declared wilderness areas off-limits to snowmobiles (Clinton, rewritten by Bush); introduced new guidelines for interrogating enemy combatants (Bush, rewritten by Obama); required large companies to offer parental leave (Clinton); blocked companies from trading with Cuba or Iran (Bush, Obama); and regulated the use of stem cells in federally funded research (Bush introduced limits; Obama rescinded them).

The George W. Bush administration relied on executive orders to prosecute its war on terror. It made new rules on wiretaps, detention of enemy combatants, and trials by military tribunals. Barack Obama used them for more technical purposes until the Republicans took control of the House in 2011. The Obama team, then blocked in Congress, began to make policy through executive orders. For example, when Congress voted down the Dream Act, which

Political appointees: Top officials in the executive agencies appointed by the president.

Civil servants: Members of the permanent executive-branch bureaucracy who are employed on the basis of competitive exams and keep their positions regardless of the presidential administration.

Executive order: A presidential declaration, with the force of law, that issues instructions to the executive branch without any requirement for congressional action or approval.

offered a path to citizenship for some undocumented aliens, President Obama issued an executive order designed to stop deportation (and allow work permits) for young, undocumented men and women who had been brought to the United States as children—one provision in an act that Congress had refused to pass. The administration has been blunt: if partisan gridlock blocks important action, the executive will use other tools. Some observers worry that in the process, Congress is slowly losing authority while presidents—from both parties—use a traditional form of executive authority to further expand the scope and authority of their office.

Economist in Chief

Economic authority is one power the Constitution definitely does *not* grant the president. The power of the purse—taxing, spending, borrowing, and regulating commerce—is all in congressional hands. However, during the Great Depression of the 1930s, the Roosevelt administration seized responsibility for putting the nation back to work, launching one recovery program after another. "Take a method and try it," insisted Roosevelt. "If that fails, try another. . . . Above all try something."[9]

The idea soon took root: the president was responsible for a smooth-running economy. The year after Roosevelt died, Congress legislated a Council of Economic Advisers (CEA) to help guide presidents' efforts to oversee the economy. Today, the president and a host of advisors monitor economic conditions. White House economists vet every plan and proposal for its impact on American prosperity. Every new administration crowds more economists into its ranks. When Obama won reelection in 2012, among his first moves was to announce the revamped White House economic team—stocked with both formal and informal advisors. Presidential popularity and, as we saw in Chapter 8, the party's chances of holding onto the office in the next election are heavily influenced by economic conditions.

The Head of State

Most nations have a ceremonial head of state who stands above partisan politics and represents the nation. The queen of England, the emperor of Japan, and the president of Israel all play this nonpolitical role while their prime ministers make the policies that govern their countries. Citizens of the British Isles do not need to check their political affiliation when they sing "God Save the Queen"—she represents them across the political spectrum. In contrast, the presidents of the United States play both roles. They stand for the nation even while they represent one party in political debate.

Presidents spend a lot of time in their ceremonial role. They throw out the first pitch during the World Series, spare a turkey every Thanksgiving, light the White House Christmas tree, smash a bottle of champagne across the bow of a new aircraft carrier, congratulate national heroes, host championship sports teams, and embody America every time the Marine Corps Band plays "Hail to the Chief." When presidents travel abroad they represent all Americans, not just their party or their supporters.

During George W. Bush's presidency, a group of diplomats from across Asia gathered in Bangkok to greet a new US ambassador to the region. The American ambassador raised his glass and offered a traditional toast: "To George W. Bush." The foreign diplomats felt uncomfortable. They respected the United States but vehemently disagreed with the administration's handling of the war on terror. They wanted to toast the United States (which President Bush represented) but not the administration's policies (which President Bush led).

This tension arises in every administration. It comes from the dual role presidents play: they stand for the nation and they also represent a party and a point of view. The clash between ceremonial and political becomes especially vivid when presidents are running for reelection. Everything they do echoes back on the campaign.

Combining both roles adds to the office's prestige and, therefore, the president's power. Bruising policy battles are balanced out by the pomp and circumstance that many other nations reserve for royalty. No rival in Washington can match that.

Party Leader

George Washington repeatedly warned the country against political parties and the strife they brought. However, by his second term, rival parties were not so quietly emerging. As suffrage spread beyond landowning gentlemen, parties grew into the largest political organizations in America. They created yet another role for the president: party leader.

This role sharpens the tension we raised in the last section. There is a very fine line between leading the nation (and standing for everyone) and leading the Democrats (which means defeating Republicans). The tension becomes acute during war. As the Cold War developed, Senator Arthur Vandenberg (R-MI) famously declared that party "politics stop at the water's edge"—the nation had to be united to defeat Communism. That idea, never fully honored, collapsed in the debate over Vietnam. Almost everything the president does, home and abroad, is now part of the great American political debate.

Ronald Reagan hosted a reception at the White House to celebrate Democratic legislators who had switched allegiance to his Republican party. Bill Clinton astonished everyone at his prowess—rivals called it shamelessness—at raising money for Democratic candidates; Republicans charged that the president rewarded big donors with a night in the Lincoln Bedroom. When George W. Bush took over, Democrats complained that the president was using the war on terror to defeat Democrats and build a permanent Republican majority. Republicans, in turn, accused Barack Obama of leaking classified information about the death of bin Laden for political gain. Each side accuses the other of taking politics to unprecedented extremes.

President Obama took office determined to dial down the party conflict. He offered Republicans important positions in his administration, like secretary of defense; he tried a bipartisan Super Bowl party; and he negotiated long and hard to win over at least a couple of Senate Republicans to his health plan. The efforts failed. When Democrats began calling the Republicans "the Party of No," the Republicans defiantly responded that they were the party of "Hell No!" Voters rewarded the sentiment in 2010 with a midterm Republican landslide.

Can anything tamp down the partisan conflict? Yes: the secret ingredient is fear. When a president grows very popular, opponents will often go along out of fear that the voters might punish them if they do not. Presidents who get more votes in a district than a House member of Congress, or more votes in the state than a senator, can be very persuasive—as long as their poll numbers remain high.

The Bully Pulpit: Introducing Ideas

President Theodore Roosevelt was bursting with ideas, opinions, exhortations, and warnings. He called the presidency itself a "bully pulpit" (today we might say "awesome platform"). Roosevelt knew that an active president has the country's ear, an opening to introduce and promote new ideas.

● *Theodore Roosevelt called the presidency a "bully pulpit." No other office is more effective for introducing new ideas Here, TR takes full advantage of his pulpit.*

Most presidencies are marked by a few big ideas. In his inaugural, John F. Kennedy called the nation to public service. "Ask not what your country can do for you," said Kennedy. "Ask what you can do for your country." As the second-youngest president in history (after Theodore Roosevelt), Kennedy projected youthful energy and vigor. The president's ideas seemed part and parcel of the man himself. Ronald Reagan championed a very different idea when he called government the source of our national problems; individuals pursuing the American dream and trying to get rich were, he declared, the real source of national vitality. Successful presidents arrive in office with powerful ideas—and persuade the public to embrace new visions of our political life.

Where do the grand themes come from? Presidents develop them on the way to the White House. Ideas reflect a president's personal experience or fire up an important constituency. They bubble up from allies, intellectuals, policy networks, think tanks, and old friends. Big ideas move political mountains because they inspire followers and sustain movements.

A sign of a fading party is a cupboard bare of ideas. When Jimmy Carter won the White House in 1976, a member of his transition team wrote a strange memo. The new administration, he said, must educate its appointees about President-elect Carter's "goals and philosophy." The Democrats of that era were so vague about their ideas that the president's staff thought it necessary to instruct its troops about what their new leader stood for.[10]

More than any political office in America, the presidency rises and falls on ideas. "The power of the presidency," as one scholar famously put it, "is the power to persuade."[11] Persuasion involves the ability to put something new before the public, the power to take an unfamiliar notion and get the whole nation talking about it. Throughout this book, we have focused on the power and importance of ideas in American politics. The presidency is the institution best geared to inject new ideas into our great national conversation.

The Impossible Job

How can anyone juggle so many different presidential roles? The honest answer is that no one can. Even great presidents cannot handle all their jobs well all of the time. Still, this is what we demand of our presidents.

Each presidential role requires different strengths and skills. No person will have them all. However, the bully pulpit can help. Bold ideas bring together the many threads of this huge task. They make a presidency coherent. Without that, presidents may seem overwhelmed by the job, skittering from one task to another without a broader sense of purpose and vision.

Finally, note one theme that has run through every role: presidential authority has grown in every aspect of the office. The president's many roles are one more way to measure the swelling power and importance of the office. That brings us back again to the central paradox of the executive: the presidency grows ever more powerful, yet the role has grown so large that no one person can perform every aspect of it well.

THE BOTTOM LINE

- The president wears many hats and helmets. Some are specified in the Constitution. Others have developed over time.
- Presidential roles include commander in chief, top diplomat, first legislator, head bureaucrat, economist in chief, head of state, and party leader. Presidents are also uniquely situated to introduce new ideas—tying together these many different roles.
- The president's authority has grown in every one of these roles. At the same time, it is difficult to do so many different things effectively.

Presidential Leadership: Success and Failure in the Oval Office

Presidents try to manage perceptions of their performance. They address the public, use (and bypass) the media, schedule eye-catching events, and rely on polls to hone their message. How do we know if they have succeeded? We'll examine three different measures: polls, historical rankings, and the great cycles of political time.

Managing the Public

As the only nationally elected official (excepting the vice president, who is elected as a package with the president), presidents develop a relationship to the people, which they cultivate by **going public**—directly addressing citizens in order to win support. Each new form of media—radio, television, Twitter—shifts the way presidents go public.

John F. Kennedy demonstrated the full power of the media when he held the first live, televised press conference in February 1961. It was a smash with the sixty-five million who watched; Kennedy's approval ratings climbed to 75 percent and stayed high for sixteen months. As we saw in Chapter 7, the first live press conference was an important milestone on the way to the personal presidency. Kennedy had shifted how presidents connect to the public: people saw him, watched him, and related to him directly.

Today, presidents continue to look for ways to relate directly to Americans. They call town hall meetings, travel across the country, and give speeches before large crowds. They speak directly to the camera from the Oval Office. Their office tweets supporters. You can follow them on Facebook. Each is an effort to win the public over—sometimes for a specific policy, sometimes for a broad presidential agenda.

Presidents "go public" primarily through the media. Each effort—from the town hall meeting with a small group to the speech in front of thousands—is designed to control the spin that filters out through newscasts, talk shows, and Twitter feeds.

Images are often more important than words. Presidents hug disaster victims, play basketball with the troops, or wave to cheering throngs holding American flags in a foreign nation. The image can turn negative in an instant. President Johnson playfully lifted his beagle by the ears in front of the press (cruel!). President Ford slipped and fell in public

Going public: Directly addressing the public in order to win support for oneself or one's ideas.

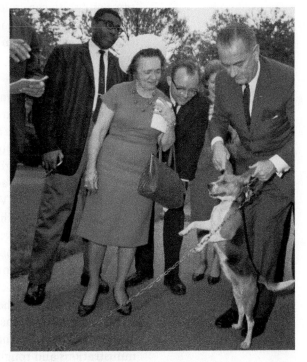

● *Lyndon Johnson lifting his beagle by the ears. The president was trying for a lighthearted moment but quickly felt the backlash from outraged pet lovers.*

see for yourself 11.1

Go online to see President Ford's unfortunate stumble. (Flash Required)

(clumsy!). President George H. W. Bush threw up at a state dinner in Japan (you can imagine!). In a complicated world, a single picture can distill popular perception. Images have an impact—positive or negative—when they seem to reveal the president's true strengths or weakness. The key point is simple: *Presidents constantly try to manage their image in the public eye.*[12]

Our 24/7 media era, as you saw in Chapter 7, complicates the effort to touch the public. On the one hand, it is easier than ever to communicate. However, the velocity of the news cycle means that most efforts only linger a few hours before they are displaced by the next story. A generation ago, an important presidential address might dominate the news for several days. Now, the sheer volume of information flowing through the media means that only the most important events will command attention for long. The president's message now requires constant repetition, amplification, and—to grip viewers—a touch of novelty and drama. Going public is a rapidly changing art form.

The White House runs a sophisticated polling operation that guides its outreach efforts. The president's daily schedule frequently includes briefings from the administration's pollster. The president's team scrutinizes the findings, not to develop new policies but to recalibrate the ways it presents its message. President Bush doubled down on the war in Iraq and Social Security privatization despite polls that told him it was unpopular; President Obama did the same on health care reform. An administration's goals may not change, but the language and the pitch is heavily poll tested in the constant search for the most effective way to communicate to the public.[13]

Approval Ratings

Every week, another wave of polls report how Americans view the president's performance. These are used widely, inside and beyond Washington, as a rough barometer of the administration's success. Any one poll can be misleading (as we saw in Chapter 6), but if you eliminate the outliers—the occasional polls that are much higher and lower than the others—and scan the rest you'll have a snapshot of the administration's ratings that are reverberating through the media and around Washington.

A president riding high in the polls finds governing easier. The press corps and Washington insiders are slightly more deferential. Members of Congress watch the president's popularity in their own states and districts; when presidents are popular, members think twice about opposing them. As the president's approval sinks, criticism rises. Congressional allies back away. Press coverage turns sour. The late-night talk shows serve up mockery.

All administrations run through polling cycles; no president stays above 50 percent approval for an entire term. Average out differences across administrations and roughly the same pattern emerges: high approval scores at the start, usually above 60 percent; a slow decline that bottoms out midway through the second year; a gradual ascent and peak toward the end of the fourth year (see Figure 11.4). With luck, it rises above 50 percent in time for reelection. Each individual administration offers its own unique variations—with general economic performance especially affecting the approval level.[14]

Dramatic events create spikes in approval (or disapproval). The two highest ratings on record boosted George H. W. Bush after a quick, dramatic victory in the first Gulf War, and his son George W. Bush after he responded to terrorist attacks on the World Trade Center in September 2001 by standing defiantly on the rubble with a bullhorn, surrounded by cheering firefighters and cleanup crews. Each Bush peaked at 89 percent approval rating in Gallup polls. Such spikes in popularity are usually temporary. A year after his military triumph,

see for yourself 11.2

Go online to see President George W. Bush's dramatic bullhorn speech at Ground Zero.

● **Figure 11.4** *Presidential job approval. Every administration goes through polling cycles—rising and falling in public esteem. Note how approval ratings are affected by important events and political decisions. (Gallup)*

George H. W. Bush's approval rating had fallen below 40 percent and he lost his reelection campaign. The younger Bush narrowly won reelection but ended his time in office tied for the lowest ratings after a full term.

Polls offer immediate public feedback, but they do not reflect an administration's historical importance or long-term success. For that we can turn to a different kind of poll.

Presidential Greatness—and Failure

Back in 1948, historian Arthur Schlesinger Sr. asked a panel of historians to rank the presidents. Their choice for the top three: Abraham Lincoln, George Washington, and Franklin Roosevelt. Poll followed presidential poll. We list five different versions in Figure 11.5. In each, a different panel of historians and political scientists rank order the presidents from the greats to the mediocre to the failures.

Greatness in Context: The Rise and Fall of Political Orders

Presidents are by no means masters of their destiny. The times make the presidents as much as they make the times. Individual presidents fit into national cycles of politics and power. Presidential scholar Stephen Skowronek describes each presidency as part of a great historical pageant: the rise and fall of **political orders**. A political order is a set of ideas, institutions, and coalitions that dominate an era.[15] On Skowronek's telling, orders rise and fall in three steps. Every president fits somewhere in the cycle.

Political order: The set of institutions, interests, and ideas that shape a political era. Great presidents reconstruct the framework launching a new order.

Step 1: A New Order Rises.   Outstanding leaders take over the presidency and shake up the political system. An Abraham Lincoln, Franklin Roosevelt, or Ronald Reagan introduces a fresh philosophy of government. He leads a political party with new allies and new ideas into power. The public responds enthusiastically to this bold break with old political ways.

Step 2: The Order Refreshed.   Every governing coalition eventually grows tired. The great president who boldly articulated its themes is gone. Many of the original goals are won. New problems arise that have nothing to do with the philosophy that fired up the party in the first place. The ideas begin to look out of date; the great coalition begins to unravel. In fortunate times, a new leader will come along and infuse the party with a fresh variation of the old philosophy, renewing the aging order.

Step 3: The Old Order Crumbles.   No order lasts forever. Over time, the party finds its ideas increasingly irrelevant. The old order feels outdated, a political dinosaur.

Every president comes to Washington with fresh hope and promise. Political historians look back and see that they operate within a cycle. Some (Lincoln, Roosevelt, Reagan) take office as the head of a new coalition with

	SCHLESINGER ['48]	SCHLESINGER JR. ['96]	WSJ [2005]	SIENNA ['10]	USPC ['11]
George Washington	2	2	1	4	3
John Adams	9	11	13	17	12
Thomas Jefferson	5	4	4	5	4
James Madison	14	17	17	6	14
James Monroe	12	15	18	7	13
John Q. Adams	11	18	25	19	20
Andrew Jackson	6	5	10	14	9
Martin Van Buren	15	21	27	23	27
William H. Harrison	—	—	—	35	—
John Tyler	22	32	35	37	37
James Polk	10	9	9	12	16
Zachary Taylor	25	29	35	33	33
Millard Fillmore	24	31	36	38	35
Franklin Pierce	27	33	38	40	39
James Buchanan	26	38	40	42	40
Abraham Lincoln	1	1	2	3	2
Andrew Johnson	19	37	37	43	36
Ulysses Grant	28	24	29	26	29
Rutherford Hayes	13	23	24	31	30
James Garfield	—	—	—	27	—
Chester Arthur	17	26	26	25	32
Grover Cleveland	8	13	12	20	21
Benjamin Harrison	21	19	30	34	34
William McKinley	18	16	14	21	17
Theodore Roosevelt	7	6	5	2	5
William H. Taft	16	22	20	24	25
Woodrow Wilson	4	7	11	8	6
Warren Harding	29	39	39	41	38
Calvin Coolidge	23	30	23	29	28
Herbert Hoover	20	35	31	36	26
Franklin Roosevelt	3	3	3	1	1
Harry Truman	—	8	7	9	7
Dwight Eisenhower	—	10	8	10	10
John F. Kennedy	—	12	15	11	15
Lyndon B. Johnson	—	14	18	16	11
Richard Nixon	—	36	32	30	23
Gerald Ford	—	28	28	28	34
Jimmy Carter	—	27	34	32	18
Ronald Reagan	—	25	6	18	8
George H. W. Bush	—	24	21	22	22
Bill Clinton	—	20	22	13	19
George W. Bush		—	—	39	31

● Figure 11.5 **Rating the presidents.** Here are the results of five independent polls by historians and political scientists (you can find dozens of them). Historian Arthur Schlesinger polled historians in 1948; his son, Arthur Schlesinger Jr., repeated the exercise with historians and political scientists in 1996; the Wall Street Journal did a "balanced poll" of both liberals and conservatives—note that liberals and conservatives do not disagree very much on the presidential rankings; Sienna College polled 750 professors in 2010; and the US Presidency Centre at the University of London offers the perspective of British scholars of the US presidency.

fresh ideas. Others come to Washington at the end of an era (Herbert Hoover, Jimmy Carter). They face a far more difficult governing challenge. To some extent, the rankings we saw above reflect each president's place in political time.

THE BOTTOM LINE

- Presidents try to manage public perceptions of the job they are doing. They get immediate feedback from polling. A president's place in history, however, usually does not emerge right away.
- Great presidents change the way Americans see themselves. They change what government does. They forge a new answer to the question, *Who are we?*
- Individual presidents don't completely control their own destiny. They operate in the historical cycle of political orders.

● The President's Team: A Tour of the White House

When Herbert Hoover moved into the Oval Office in 1929, he presided over a presidential staff of four administrative assistants, plus thirty-six typists, clerks, and messengers. That was it. No speechwriter, no press secretary, no congressional liaison; no chief of staff, no drug czar, no budget director. Today, the presidency is more than a man or an idea or a party. It is a bureaucracy staffed by thousands of people.

The Political Solar System: Presidential Appointments

Every time a new president is elected, thousands of people hope for a job. College professors who've always dreamed of government service, college students who worked on the campaign, business executives looking for a plum on their résumé, and supporters who believe the president-elect will make America a better place: all want to work for the new administration.

To get a job in a presidential administration, do not start by being modest. You must campaign: one executive angling to be a senior Treasury Department official a few years back tasked four subordinates to do nothing but promote his name to the administration's transition team in charge of selecting top appointees (yes, he got the job).

This section highlights those officials working directly for the president. A crucial opening point: power is always measured by proximity to the president. The executive branch is like the solar system, with the president as the sun and everyone else rotating around him. A trump card in any Washington, DC, conversation: "When I was talking to the president . . . ." Most people who work for the president are in an orbit somewhere past Pluto: they never get any face time. Let us look at some who do.

The Vice President

Traditionally, the vice president's primary job was to stand in the wings in case the president died. That awful transition happened eight times in American history, four times by murder. Thus, almost one in five presidents came to office after the death of his predecessor. There were at least four more close calls: assassins fired point-blank at Andrew Jackson (the gun jammed), Franklin Roosevelt (the shooter missed the president, killed the mayor of Chicago), Gerald Ford (a bystander grabbed the gunwoman's arm, diverting the shot), and Ronald Reagan (the bullet lodged less than an inch from his heart).

Besides standing by in case of catastrophe, vice presidents preside over the Senate and cast a vote in case of a tie. There is not much power in presiding; it is more like being a parliamentarian than a majority leader, and the vice president only appears in the Senate chambers on special occasions.

Otherwise, a vice president's responsibilities are entirely up to the president. For a long time, the role

● *Vice President Cheney was a savvy Washington operator who developed a reputation for wielding formidable power during the first term of the George W. Bush administration (2001–2005). With time, his power waned and, by the end of the administration, he often found himself isolated within the cabinet.*

was meager. Franklin Roosevelt's first vice president, John Nance Garner, offered the most famous assessment of the post when he said the job was "not worth a pitcher of warm piss."

The weak vice presidency continued well into the twentieth century. Harry Truman had barely met with President Roosevelt when FDR's death in 1945 catapulted him into the Oval Office. "Boys," he said when he met the press the next day, "if you ever pray, pray for me now." In 1960, reporters asked President Eisenhower what ideas Vice President Nixon, who was running to succeed him, had contributed. "If you give me a week," quipped the president nastily, "I might think of one."

The vice presidency became an important office during the Carter administration (1977–2001). From Carter through Obama, five of the last seven presidents were Washington outsiders who had never held a federal job; every newcomer chose a longtime federal government insider as his vice president, relying on him as advisor, confidant, and envoy. Slowly but surely, vice presidents gathered the emblems of power: a seat at cabinet meetings (1950s), an office in the White House (1970s), a vice-presidential jet (Air Force 2, in the 1970s), a growing staff, and—perhaps most important in status-obsessed Washington—regular meetings with the president.

In recent years, vice presidents are put in charge of major administration efforts: Dick Cheney's office effectively managed the war on terror for President Bush, and Joe Biden has been a major voice on foreign policy for Barack Obama. Even with these changes, vice presidents' power and influence still depend on the president.

The Cabinet

Members of the cabinet have two primary roles: they run executive-branch departments, and they meet to discuss policy with the president in cabinet meetings. Once the cabinet served as a president's governing team. As we saw earlier, Washington's initial cabinet had four members. By Abraham Lincoln's time, there were seven. Today the cabinet has grown to fifteen members; add the vice president and other important officers on the president's staff, and meetings are too large to serve as a real decision-making body.

We discuss the cabinet, and the hundreds of thousands of federal bureaucrats who work under cabinet secretaries in the executive agencies, in the next chapter. Today, cabinet meetings have become largely ceremonial occasions.

In most administrations, a handful of cabinet officers rise above the rest and shape administration policy. Political scientists call them the "inner cabinet": the secretaries of State, Defense, Treasury, and Justice—precisely the quartet in Washington's original cabinet. Most other cabinet secretaries operate far from the centers of power. Departments like Transportation and Energy have vital roles to play. But, unless they have personal connections or unusual responsibilities, they are rarely part of a president's inner circle.

● President Obama runs a cabinet meeting. As you can see, today's cabinet has become too large to make important decisions.

Cabinet secretaries often come to see issues from the perspective of their own bureaucracy rather than the administration or the party. After all, they are surrounded by tens of thousands of employees who do a lot of work with limited resources and look to the secretary to champion their causes. Richard Nixon's close adviser John Ehrlichman groused that the administration chose solid, budget-cutting conservatives to run the cabinet departments—and then watched their appointees run off and "marry the natives." They abandoned the administration's priorities, complained Ehrlichman, and began to think like their subordinates about the importance of their agency's work.

Presidents must manage the tension between senior cabinet officials and the circle of presidential advisors in the White House. At one cabinet meeting during the Carter years, the secretary of Housing and Urban Development summed up her frustration by blurting out: "We can move government forward by putting phones in the White House staff offices and then using them." Translation: No one in the White House even returns my phone calls. The president's inner circle (and the power of proximity) had shifted from the cabinet to the White House staff.[16]

The Executive Office of the President

In modern times, influence over the president has leaked steadily into the **Executive Office of the President** (EOP), made up of agencies that help a president manage his daily activities. These administrators and advisors surround the chief executive. President Franklin Roosevelt organized the EOP in 1939; it now has about 1,700 employees. Many are experts who stay on from one administration to the next. Presidents who have been most adamant about expanding the EOP are conservatives frustrated that the cabinet agencies did not pursue their values. Richard Nixon created or revamped four of the EOP offices, Ronald Reagan added three more. Today every president—left, right, or center—relies on them.

> Executive Office of the President (EOP): The agencies that help the president manage daily activities.

In the Executive Office of the President, a familiar clash gets especially intense. On one hand, most EOP employees are experts on specific issues—drug policy, health care, or the budget. On the other, they have to serve each president's political philosophy (not to mention reelection prospects). Slowly the balance between these goals has tipped toward politics.[17] Let's visit the most important offices in the EOP.

The Office of Management and Budget (OMB). This is the most powerful agency in the executive branch—known (not very fondly) as "the agency that says no." The OMB uses its authority over the federal budget to manage the entire executive branch. During the Reagan administration, the agency acquired its most powerful weapon—**central clearance**: the power to review and "clear" (or OK) anything a member of the administration says or does in public. All members, from the secretary of defense to an analyst in the Small Business Bureau, must submit every speech they make, opinion piece they write, congressional

> Central clearance: The OMB's authority to review and "clear" (or okay) anything a member of the administration says or does in public.

testimony they deliver, and policy they propose to OMB for its approval. Until they get OMB's nod, they may not say or publish a word.

The OMB vets every administration proposal. When Congress passes a bill, OMB coordinates various White House officials' recommendations about signing or vetoing the legislation. Officials at the OMB often get the last word as well. Imagine how frustrating it is for energetic new secretaries to take over their departments, only to learn they must clear all their formal statements and policy proposals with the budget office.

Notice a slow change in our political process, over the last thirty years or so: *economic thinking rules*. Pundits describe the tension between experts (crunching numbers) and political appointees (pushing the president's agenda and big ideas). An enduring change is the way the entire system tilts toward and empowers the economic perspective.

Before the Nixon administration organized the OMB (in 1971), fiscal control was much looser. President Lyndon Johnson famously low-balled his economic estimates. One day, instructing a young senator from Massachusetts named Ted Kennedy, Johnson warned him not to let economic projections slow up his favorite bills and illustrated the point with Medicare. "The fools [at the Bureau of the Budget] had to go projecting [Medicare] down the road five or six years, and when you project it the first year it runs $900 million."[18] Those anticipated costs, complained LBJ, cost him votes in Congress; he advised the new senator to stop economists from interfering with important proposals. Today, OMB requires cost-benefit analyses for all White House policy moves. The era of simply suppressing cost estimates is long past. Still, the future is never certain and every savvy political operator knows plenty of ways to massage the numbers.

The Council of Economic Advisers (CEA).   Meet another clutch of economists. The council and its chair keep an eye on the whole economy, private as well as public. This office does economic analysis for the president: unemployment predictions, productivity measurements, economic forecasts, and all the rest.

The National Security Council (NSC).   The NSC brings together the powerful officers who make national security policy: secretaries of state, defense, intelligence, and treasury (economists again); the chair of the Joint Chiefs of Staff; and others that the president selects. The national security advisor directs the council and must work for consensus across all the different perspectives and formidable personalities: diplomatic, military, and economic. In some administrations, the national security advisor is as influential as the secretaries of state or defense. Empowering the NSC has tightened White House control over foreign policy, as we will see in more detail in Chapter 14.

Table 11.2 illustrates the basic logic of the Executive Office of the President. The list of offices reflects the hats and helmets that the president wears. Organizing a new EOP office is one way for administrations to

Table 11.2 Offices in the Executive Office of the President

OFFICE	EMPLOYEES	YEAR ORGANIZED	ORGANIZED BY
White House Office	406	1939	Franklin Roosevelt
Office of the Vice President	24	1972	Nixon
Office of Management and Budget	521	1921/1971	Harding/Nixon
Office of Administration	212	1977	Carter
Council of Economic Advisors	28	1946	Truman
Council on Environmental Quality	22	1969	Nixon
Office of Policy Development	32	1970	Nixon
Executive Residence	95 (full-time)	—	—
National Security Staff	54	1947	Truman
Office of National Drug Control Policy	102	1988	Reagan
Office of Science and Technology	28	1976	Ford
Office of the US Trade Representative	212	1963	Kennedy
Homeland Security Council	16	2001	G. W. Bush

signal the things they consider most important. Nixon added the Council on Environmental Quality, George W. Bush an office for his Faith-Based Initiatives.

The Heart of Power: The White House Office (WHO)

Our tour ends at the heart of power. The White House Office is part of the Executive Office of the President, but it also stands apart. This group of four hundred or so advisors, aides, and associates work directly for the president, most of them in the West Wing. At the center is the **Chief of Staff**, the president's gatekeeper, traffic cop, and coordinator. Other important offices include speechwriters, White House counsel (the president's official lawyer), and the legislative affairs team.

Chief of Staff: The individual responsible for managing the president's office.

Until President Obama, the two parties organized their White House Offices very differently from one another. Franklin Roosevelt set a mixed example for future Democrats: creative chaos. Roosevelt surrounded himself with gifted intellectuals, gave them overlapping tasks, and let them freelance from issue to issue. In theory, bold ideas would flow from an office full of talented, loosely organized thinkers. Many Democratic administrations tried to mimic Roosevelt. John Kennedy valued broad-minded intellectuals and encouraged them to weigh in on any subject. So did Bill Clinton; early

SPEAK LIKE A BUREAUCRAT

Want to learn to talk like a Washington bureaucrat? Start practicing now. Casually toss off something like: "I'm given to understand that WHO is the real force in the EOP." Those are two indecipherable acronyms (the more the better) and, of course, the passive voice: you don't want to risk revealing your sources!

in his administration, staffers would jump in and out of meetings and conversations regardless of their assigned tasks. The bull sessions went on deep into the night. People would wander into any meeting and throw in their "two cents' worth."

In contrast, Republicans like clearly defining organization and tasks. You'll find no vague or dotted lines on their personnel tables. The Republicans usually model their organization on the military or traditional business: crisp lines of authority go from the president to the Chief of Staff. Everyone has a clearly defined role.

Democrats often dismiss their rivals' style as unimaginative, stifling, and conformist. Republicans answer that good organization avoids confusion and error and that the Democrats are disorganized and undisciplined. Each style has advantages and drawbacks.

In either style, the Chief of Staff makes the White House run. He or she directs traffic through the president's office, oversees the schedule, sums up the decisions that are made, and follows up to see that those decisions are understood and implemented. The office requires a strong, talented, smooth, competent administrator familiar with the levers of power. Occasionally, a president will try to act as his own Chief of Staff (Jimmy Carter) or bring in a political neophyte (Bill Clinton); when that happens chaos generally follows. The other extreme is equally dangerous. If the Chief of Staff seems arrogant, aloof, or rude, the White House loses support and cooperation.

The White House staff is like a little village, full of odd folkways and habits that reflect the way the president wishes to run the country. For example, Ronald Reagan put special emphasis on his speechwriting team; they spent hours watching his past speeches to learn his rhythms and his way of thinking. The president reworked their draft speeches with great care. Reagan's successor (and vice president), George H. W. Bush, found this process artificial. He thought the president should speak plainly. He demonstrated the new order by stripping the speechwriting team of its White House Mess (dining hall) privileges. The village recognized a major demotion.

When a new president comes to town, attention focuses on his cabinet selections. The wise observer knows to track more subtle appointments to the White House Office. After all, no matter how brilliant the secretary of labor or how experienced the secretary of HHS, they will have to rely on unseen advisors in the White House to convey their ideas, programs, and problems to the president.

Officials located farther from the West Wing—like cabinet secretaries, in their giant departments scattered around Washington—can seem desperate in seeking presidential attention. Cabinet meetings can be a circus, with every member anxious to get a minute alone with the president. But busy presidents are deft at vanishing. The route to influence—the path to "yes" on any program—runs through the White House Office staff.

Unlike the high-ranking members of the cabinet agencies, most EOP staffers are not subject to Senate confirmation. They are elected by no one, overseen only by the Chief of Staff, and often have regular access to the president's ear. Should the president's advisors, rather than the experienced cabinet secretaries confirmed by the Senate, run the executive branch? Again, we confront the fundamental question: power and control versus democracy and enhanced accountability. Perhaps the twenty-four-hour media cycle forces presidents to keep power and expertise right at their fingertips. Perhaps granting authority to White House staff makes the whole federal leviathan more responsive to the will of the people. Most advanced democracies are, ultimately, ruled by experts. American government is run in part by men and women with a sharp eye on winning the next election.

One final feature of the White House staff strikes most newcomers: it is young—much younger than the staff running other governments, large corporations, universities, or major nonprofit organizations. Cabinet secretaries with years of experience often complain that their access to the president is governed by young people in their twenties and thirties.

The First Spouse

One team in the White House Office does not fit any traditional political category: the office of the president's spouse. Traditionally, the "First Lady" role was simply that of hostess. Eleanor Roosevelt broke the traditional mold and pioneered a new role, the First Lady as activist. She discovered a batch of love letters between her husband, Franklin, and his secretary, Lucy Mercer. Rather than split up, the couple became energetic political partners. Eleanor was a powerful liberal activist, a popular symbol of the New Deal, and a forceful advocate for Franklin and his policies. In effect, she became a one-woman campaign for liberal social policy. A *New Yorker* cartoon captures the First Lady's spirit of tirelessly campaigning for social and labor reform. Deep underground, two sooty coal miners stop their labors as one remarks with surprise: "For gosh sakes, here comes Mrs. Roosevelt!"

"For gosh sakes, here comes Mrs. Roosevelt!"

Few First Ladies were as active or committed as Eleanor Roosevelt, but she set a pattern of policy engagement that her successors have followed. Lady Bird Johnson chose "beautification" of American cities and highways. Nancy Reagan became a spokesperson for the war on drugs. Mrs. Reagan was the first to achieve that mark of status, an office in the West Wing. Bill Clinton assigned his wife, Hillary, the signature policy initiative of his presidency, national health care reform. In fall 1993, Hillary Clinton's virtuoso performance in a series of congressional hearings appeared to signal success for national health insurance. The legislation failed, but Mrs. Clinton went on to her own successful political career—and established a new ceiling for First Ladies' contribution to presidential action.

By the time Michelle Obama came to the office, expectations were high. Here was a charismatic First Lady with a Harvard Law degree and a successful career independent of her husband. With some fanfare, Mrs. Obama focused on childhood obesity, a prominent policy issue. She is honorary chair of President Obama's signature White House Council for Community Solutions, and she plays a very visible role as "First Mother"—an emblem of the American family. Political scientists—especially those interested in gender and power—have begun to pay particular attention to the role of the First Spouse.

THE BOTTOM LINE

- Each president directs a massive organization—the executive branch of the federal government.
- Cabinet secretaries manage the great bureaucracies of the executive branch of government but only a few have influence in the White House.
- Over time, executive-branch policymaking has migrated from the cabinet to the Executive Office of the Presidency—the network of offices that help the president manage the government.
- The president's innermost circle is the White House Office. These close advisors—often relatively young—include the Chief of Staff, speechwriters, legislative liaison, and the office of the First Lady.

● Conclusion: The Most Powerful Office on Earth?

President Obama took office with soaring hopes. He was a symbol of American aspiration: after centuries of racial struggle, the United States had elected an African American leader. Like all presidents, Obama put a new set of ideas, proposals, and priorities before the American people.

Obama traveled around the world—London, Ankara, Port of Spain, Moscow, Accra, Cairo—drawing a sharp line with his predecessor. "We must embrace a new era of engagement based on . . . mutual respect," Obama told the United Nations."[19] The United States would no longer act unilaterally, without regard for other nations' views. Ten months after his inauguration he was awarded the Nobel Peace Prize—a sign of how world leaders cheered a pivot away from the go-it-alone American attitude.

The new president shifted America's policymaking. The issues he cared about became those in the news and before Congress: health care reform, college loans, education, and clean air. Obama removed American troops from Iraq and expanded the number in Afghanistan, while setting a definite withdrawal date—all controversial actions. The Oval Office reverberates with power and responsibility.

From another angle, it is full of limitations, checks and balances. The economy remained weak—and sapped President Obama's popularity. Congress rejected some of his signature reforms. It blocked him from closing the military prison at Guantánamo. He won health care reform—an extraordinary achievement—but never managed to persuade the public of its merits, to the great advantage of the Republicans who had been united against it. In 2010, Obama's Democratic Party lost its House majority in the party's largest midterm defeat in a century. The most powerful office on earth was hemmed in by checks and balances.

The Obama record raises, once again, the fundamental question about the presidency. It is a far more powerful office than it was a century ago. Has it grown too powerful for a republic? Or, on the other side, is it too hobbled to carry out the mandate of the public? Or would it be most accurate to say that the same president can be too powerful or too weak, depending on the issue, the circumstances, and the incumbent?

Now President Obama heads into a second term. He begins by working with Congress to avoid a "fiscal cliff" of deep automatic budget cuts, and then sets out policy priorities for the months ahead. New State Department officials adjust the US foreign policy stance towards the world. Before long, familiar questions are renewed: Into its sixth year, is the Obama administration too powerful? Or not powerful enough?

Who are we? The president offers us an answer—actually, several different answers. Americans seek a powerful, confident figure at the government's center. At the same time, we fear strong executives and hem them in through a labyrinth of checks and balances. We want our collective democratic voice ringing in the ears of our national leaders—but also want our security protected in ways that may require secrecy and fast, decisive choices. We are a people that demands small government—yet complains when every need isn't speedily met by the executive branch. We are a complicated, diverse, paradoxical people—like the presidency that reflects and serves us.

see for yourself 11.3

Go online to see Obama's 2009 address to the United Nations.

CHAPTER SUMMARY

● *The president personifies America.* More than any individual, the president tells us who we are—and what we are becoming.

● *The president injects new ideas into American politics.* Our discussion of Congress emphasized the institution, the rules of the game; the presidency puts more focus on individuals and ideas.

● The president has three kinds of powers: those expressed in the Constitution, those delegated by Congress, and those inherent in the role of chief executive.

● The executive branch has grown far more powerful over time, especially when it comes to foreign policy.

● The office of the president constantly raises the same fundamental question: *Is the president too powerful for a democratic republic? Or, on the other hand, is the office too weak to do what Americans demand of it?* Or, perhaps, the president is both too strong and too weak at the same time.

● The president wears many hats and helmets. The presidential roles include commander in chief,

top diplomat, first legislator, head bureaucrat, economist in chief, head of state, and party leader. The president's authority has grown in every one of these many roles. At the same time, it is difficult to do so many different things effectively.

● Presidents try to manage public perceptions of the job they are doing by going public and getting feedback from polls. Individual presidents don't completely control their own destiny. They operate in the historical cycle of *political orders*.

● Over time, executive-branch policy has flowed from the cabinet secretaries to the Executive Office of the Presidency—the network of offices that help the president manage the government.

● The president's innermost circle is the White House Office. These close advisors—often relatively young—include the Chief of Staff, speechwriters, legislative liaison, and the office of the First Lady.

KEY TERMS

Central clearance, 423
Chief of Staff, 425
Civil servants, 410
Delegated powers, 399
Executive Office of the President (EOP), 423
Executive order, 410
Expressed powers, 399
Going public, 415
Imperial presidency, 401
Inherent powers of the presidency, 399
Override, 407
Political appointees, 410
Political order, 418
Signing statements, 409
Unitary executive theory, 400
Veto power, 407

STUDY QUESTIONS

1. Some people have suggested changing the president's term to one seven-year term without the possibility of reelection. What do you think?
2. Should we abolish the Electoral College?
3. What do you think: Is the president too strong? Or too weak? Defend your opinion.
4. Name seven different roles the president plays. Which do you consider the most important right now? How well do you think the president is carrying out this role today?

5. How well do you think President Obama "goes public"—appealing to the American public to support his policies? Do *you* respond positively to his speeches and legislative requests?
6. Explain the role of the OMB. What does this agency do? What perspective was it designed to bring to the policy debates?

7. Describe the role of a First Lady. Despite getting involved in policies, the First Ladies are often more popular than the presidents. Why do you think that is so?

8. Describe the three stages of every political order. Where do you think we stand today in the great cycle of presidential political time?

12

Bureaucracy

IN THIS CHAPTER, YOU WILL:

Learn how the bureaucracy developed, how it is meant to work—and why things sometimes go wrong. See how federal agencies do their job. Examine the different kinds of agencies that comprise the public service. Consider who—if anyone—controls the bureaucracy. Review possible reforms.

IN *THE PERFECT STORM*, actor George Clooney plays a real-life fishing boat captain who ignores US Weather Service warnings and heads his boat into impossibly high seas—and death for all the men aboard. Another captain, Linda Greenlaw, obeys the alert, steams for shore, and saves her crew. Five years later, Clooney wrote, directed, and starred in *Good Night, and Good Luck*, which tells the story of Senator Joseph McCarthy's search for Communists allegedly working in the US State Department. A counsel for the US Army, Joseph Welch, along with CBS anchor Edward R. Murrow, helped expose McCarthy's witch hunt. And, in the 2009 feature *Men Who Stare at Goats*, Clooney plays the former head of a special American military unit tasked with training "psychic spies." Each of these George Clooney vehicles highlights the work of government bureaucrats.

The National Ocean and Atmospheric Administration (NOAA)—part of the Department of Commerce—issued those weather bulletins in *The Perfect Storm*. With a budget of about $5.5 billion, NOAA provides detailed weather predictions across the globe. The US Coast Guard—part of the Department of Homeland Security—performed a daring rescue of a family aboard a sailboat that had strayed into the same storm. Senator McCarthy caused an uproar in the State Department—today, an agency with 19,000 employees staffing 305 embassies and consulates around the world. He was eventually humiliated on national television by a lawyer working for the largest bureaucracy in America, the US Army. And, although the "goat starers" are figments of a screenwriter's imagination, the federal bureaucracy does include intelligence agencies in the Departments of State, Energy, Treasury, Justice, and Defense (which has twelve separate intelligence agencies spread across the four military branches) as well as the Central Intelligence Agency (CIA) and the Federal Bureau of Investigation (FBI).

One of Hollywood's leading men seemed to be celebrating the good works of government bureaucracy. Surprising? Of course it is. Most Americans hold a very low opinion of the federal government. Only 19 percent of the public "trust the government to do what is right always or most of the time," according to Gallup polls (Figure 12.1). Politicians often run for office against the faceless bureaucrats. Republican candidates promise to cut whole agencies—although they rarely do so

● *George Clooney, as seen in the film* The Perfect Storm. *Clooney seems to like making movies with connections to government bureaucracy.*

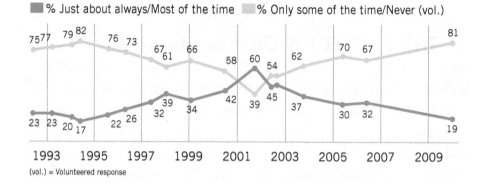

% Just about always/Most of the time   % Only some of the time/Never (vol.)

Figure 12.1 *This poll tracks Americans' response to the question "How often can you trust government in Washington to do what is right?" Notice how trust (blue line) peaked after the 9/11 attacks. Today, more than four in five Americans have a negative view (green line). (Gallup)*

(vol.) = Volunteered response

when they win office; Democrats join right in and promise to shrink government programs "that do not work," as President Obama put it in his first inaugural address. And, indeed, it is easy to find examples of hapless bureaucracies doing foolish things.

This chapter tells a different story about the federal bureaucracy—one that you might not expect. Bureaucrats, despite their terrible reputation, perform valuable, even life-saving services. The bureaucracy is what makes government run.

The criticism of generic bureaucrats generally melts away when pollsters ask about specific agencies. For example, 68 percent of the public give high marks to the Environmental Protection Agency; 80 percent of frequent fliers approve the Federal Aviation Administration; and 84 percent of medical professionals have a great deal of confidence in the Food and Drug Administration.[1] The bureaucrats look a lot better when we focus on what they actually do.

Who are we? In many ways, the government bureaucracy is us—or at least many of us: it employs 2.7 million civilians (and over 4 million men and women if you include active duty military). State and local governments employ 19 million more Americans. These numbers add up to 23 million people on government payrolls. Moreover, the federal bureaucracy is the part of American government that most resembles the population it serves. Remember that Congress is overwhelmingly white, male, and middle-aged (Chapter 10); the White House staff is mostly white and young (Chapter 11). But the 2.7 million people who make up the US civilian bureaucracy are as diverse as the nation (Figure 12.2).

Does its diversity make the bureaucracy more democratic? Not necessarily. One of the great challenges posed by the bureaucracy is how to synchronize

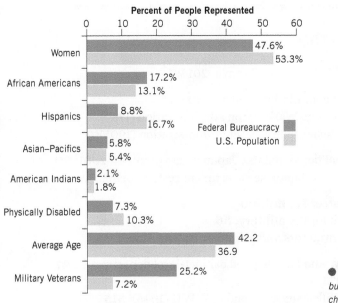

Percent of People Represented

Women	47.6% / 53.3%
African Americans	17.2% / 13.1%
Hispanics	8.8% / 16.7%
Asian–Pacifics	5.8% / 5.4%
American Indians	2.1% / 1.8%
Physically Disabled	7.3% / 10.3%
Average Age	42.2 / 36.9
Military Veterans	25.2% / 7.2%

Federal Bureaucracy ▇
U.S. Population ▇

● **Figure 12.2** *US civilian bureaucracy: demographic characteristics. (US Census)*

it with the people's will. The same question we raised in the last chapter—does presidential power threaten popular rule?—returns in this chapter in a slightly different form: Can a bureaucracy of 2.7 million unelected federal workers govern democratically? It is an important and difficult question. The federal bureaucracy is essential to good government. Can we make it fit with democratic governance?

● Bureaucracies in an American Democracy

Predicting storms near Miami, keeping tabs on the government of Liberia, and tracking terrorists in London take large, well-coordinated bureaucracies—as NOAA, the State Department, and the Central Intelligence Agency try to be. In this section, we will look at where the US bureaucracy came from, how bureaucracies are structured, and some of the problems that can make them fall short.

How the Bureaucracy Grew

In the nineteenth century, US government jobs were political prizes. Men got their posts—as officers in the army, postmasters in rural towns, or tax

---

BY THE NUMBERS *The Bureaucracy*

Number of cabinet departments, US executive branch, 2013: **15**

Number of agencies/independent commissions today: **500**
Number of agencies during the George Washington administration (1789): **4**
Number of agencies during the Theodore Roosevelt administration (1905): **7**

Number of ministries (like cabinet departments), Japanese government, 2001: **20**
Number in 2002, following extensive Japanese government restructuring: **12**

Total federal bureaucracy workforce: **4.4 million**
Percentage of that total who work for the military: **36**
"Hidden workforce" of federal contractors and grantees: **10.7 million**

Number of women, in US history, who have headed cabinet-level departments: **27**
Number of those named since 1975: **24**
Total cabinet secretary positions filled since the end of WWII (1945): **315**

Miles of hallways in the largest US federal building, the Pentagon: **17.5**

Average salary of a civil servant, 2009: **$71,206**
Maximum annual salary earned by a civil servant (GS-15, top of scale): **$129,517**
Number of GS categories, which specify earnings ranges within each category: **15**

Average layers of upper management in large US cabinet departments: **64**

---

collectors in the ports—because they helped politicians win elections. When George Washington Plunkitt, a colorful New York politician, decided to enter politics, he went to the local boss with what he called a marketable commodity: votes. He got his start in politics by delivering the votes of all his friends and neighbors.[2]

As you can imagine, this system was inefficient, unfair, and corrupt. New Yorkers in George Washington Plunkitt's day did not get help from their government if they voted for the wrong party (that is, if they were not Democrats), if they had the wrong skin color (not white), or if they belonged to the wrong ethnic group (not Irish). Senator William Marcy (another New Yorker) gave the system its name when he declared, "To the victor belong the spoils." After he made his comment, giving jobs to political friends became known as the **spoils system**.

Reformers fought long and hard to break this corruption. Jobs, they believed, should be distributed on the basis of merit, not political connections. The reformers championed what we now call **universalistic politics:** a government

Spoils system:
Government jobs given out as political favors.

Universalistic politics:
Government by universal rules, impartially applied.

of impartial rules that apply equally to everyone. That ideal was the basis for bureaucratic government in the United States.

A great political battle erupted between the reformers and the politicians, with their spoils system. In 1883, a crazed office seeker assassinated President James Garfield. Suddenly, the reformers had a martyr for their cause. The spoils system, they said, had caused the president's assassination. Popular outcry pushed a reluctant Congress to pass the **Pendleton Civil Service Act**, which required the federal government to hire well-qualified individuals, who must take exams to qualify for their posts. It was the first step toward building the professional bureaucracy that runs the government today.

Reformers fighting for a more efficient government had a big advantage: There were jobs that needed doing. As the society and economy grew more complex, the spoils system failed to answer the nation's needs. Five important national needs pushed the United States toward a more efficient—and more bureaucratic—government.

War.   Each time the United States mobilized for war, the government grew. Wartime was no time to rely on political hacks; each effort spurred a new search for competent administrators and new bureaus and offices. After each war, government maintained some of the new jobs it had taken on. The number of civilian employees doubled during World War I and tripled during World War II. Wartime mobilization, more than any other force in American history, created the large national bureaucracy we have today.[3]

Morality.   Nineteenth-century observers often noted that the United States had an underdeveloped government; however, they often added, the government was very active in regulating morality. Enforcing moral rules required the creation of increasingly sophisticated agencies. For example, the fight against obscenity—pornography, prostitution, birth control, and abortion—led to the creation of new bureaus, from the post office (which confiscated fifteen tons of "lustful" books in a decade) to the FBI (whose first major task was protecting women who had been forced into prostitution). Likewise, the effort to outlaw all liquor (under Prohibition, which lasted from 1920 to 1933) created a powerful new law enforcement agency in the Department of the Treasury.[4]

Economics.   Over time, the federal government took over responsibility for economic performance. This created many new government offices—commissions designed to regulate business (starting in the 1887 with the railroads), the Federal Reserve to stabilize banking (created in 1913 after a series of financial panics), and a host of new offices and agencies after the Great Depression (in the 1930s).

Geography.   The United States spread rapidly across the continent. Keeping the far-flung nation together led to a more sophisticated postal service

Pendleton Civil Service Act: The 1883 law that shifted American government toward a merit-based public service.

● *Moral reformer Anthony Comstock launched a quest in the 1870s–80s to stamp out any signs of smut. His effort helped build a sophisticated postal bureaucracy.*

"Your Honor, this woman gave birth to a naked child!"

(including, briefly, the famous Pony Express); new forms of transportation; the distribution of public lands to homesteaders; and endless military actions against Native Americans.

Race and Immigration. The issue of slavery and civil rights constantly engaged the federal government—leading, most dramatically, to the Civil War and the occupation of southern lands by the federal army. Likewise, immigration debates required new federal officials, charged with deciding who could settle in the United States.

Americans may not like government. For a long time, politicians resisted a centralized bureaucracy—preferring the spoils. However, each of these forces— war, morality, economics, geography, and questions of race and immigration— pushed the United States toward more efficient national bureaus and agencies. The Pendleton Act of 1883 laid the cornerstone for the civil service; by 1900 (after the Spanish-American War), the United States had an emerging national bureaucracy; and by 1946 (after World War II) the country had developed the bureaucracy that governs America to this day.

The Bureaucratic Model

What is a bureaucracy supposed to look like? The German sociologist and political economist Max Weber (1864–1920) reduced it to five characteristics that, in theory, mark all modern bureaucracies—including the American civil service. Let's consider these one at a time. And, remember, this is the way the bureaucracy is *supposed* to operate—not the way it always does.[5]

Hierarchy. All bureaucracies have a clear chain of command. Each individual reports to the person above her all the way up to the president—or the queen, or the pope, or the chancellor of the university. A clear chain of command specifies every individual's superiors and subordinates. Weber noted that the desire to move up the ladder makes most individuals sensitive to their superior's orders. In this way, the efforts of thousands of people can be coordinated.

Figure 12.3 shows the hierarchy of the US Department of Energy (DOE), starting with the cabinet secretary and moving down through an elaborate subset of assistants, deputies, and associate administrators. This chart lists only the top 48 positions—16,000 men and women work in the agency (and 84,000 more work under contracts with the DOE). The principle of hierarchy allows the leaders to coordinate the work of all their subordinates.

Division of Labor. Bureaucracies divide complex tasks and assign each piece to an individual or a group. The members of the agencies become experts at their own specialized tasks. The hierarchy coordinates all these specialists into a smoothly working operation. For example, the division of labor permits the State Department to have specialists in each area, each language, and each country.

● **Figure 12.3** *Organizational chart for the Department of Energy. (Dept. of Energy)*

Fixed Routines.   Rather than making things up as they go along, bureaucrats are expected to follow well-specified codes of conduct called Standard Operating Procedures (SOPs).

Have you ever applied for food stamps or unemployment compensation? If you do, you'll face forms, details, and visits to different offices. This is bureaucratic routine in action, designed to treat everybody the same way. If you've been stopped for speeding, you'll ruefully recall the ritual that police officers follow, from requesting your license and registration to checking your plates for outstanding warrants. That's a fixed routine, too, and each step has a purpose.

Equal Rules for All.   The ideal is always the same: the rules apply equally to everyone. In the spoils system, it was all about whom you knew. In contrast, the bureaucratic official is not supposed to care whose daughter you are or what special story you have to tell.

Technical Qualifications.   Since bureaucracies operate on the basis of expertise, people get their jobs only on the basis of their qualifications. For example, take another look at Figure 12.3. Near the middle of the organization chart you'll find an Office for High Energy Physics (among other things, it maintains accelerators for research into the origins of the universe). George Washington Plunkitt got his job by rounding up votes for the Democratic Party of New York; however, the staff in the office for High Energy Physics got their jobs thanks to their scientific expertise.

Bureaucratic Pathologies

These five characteristics look good on paper. However, the real world can be an entirely different story. Examples are never hard to find.

Early in 2010, news reports revealed that eight-year-old Mikey Hicks, an ordinary American boy with no ties to terrorism, was stopped, searched, and interrogated every time he and his family boarded a plane. The Transportation Security Authority (TSA) explained that his name was on the agency's no-fly list (because a real suspect had a similar name). Despite his family's complaints, it took the TSA months to remove Mikey from the list. And, while the TSA agents were grilling Mikey, a *real* terrorist, Umar Farouk Abdulmutallab, boarded a Northwest Airlines flight and unsuccessfully tried to blow it up. No one asked him any questions, even though two months earlier his father, a prominent business person, had reported that his son was training at an Al Qaeda camp for terrorists in Yemen.

Why do these errors happen? Because every feature of the ideal bureaucracy has its potential downside—call it too much of an efficient thing. The problems that develop are known as **bureaucratic pathologies**. Familiar pathologies include:

Bureaucratic pathologies: The problems that tend to develop in bureaucratic systems.

- **Rote.** Rote implies slavishly following old standardized routines despite new developments. The failure to adjust (with the excuse of "I'm just doing my job") can lead to problems, even tragedies. When members of an organization get too used to following standard procedures, they avoid responsibility—and potential blame—by hiding behind their assigned routines.

- **Imperialism**. Bureaucracies compete just like private companies. They want bigger budgets and better staffs. They want to avoid the budget cuts that will make life more difficult for them. These attitudes lead them to grow too big and to engage in turf wars.

- **Turf war**. Agencies often find that they are doing overlapping jobs. This replication leads to tensions about who is responsible for what. For example, there are at least nineteen intelligence agencies in the federal government. If the agencies view each other as competitors, they will fail to share information. The FBI and the CIA, for example, are notorious for their turf wars.

- **Lack of coordination.** Even agencies that are good at doing their own job often have no smooth mechanisms for cooperating with other agencies. That's because their routines are internal to the agency and doesn't apply to other organizations. If the agencies are imperialistic or fighting a turf war, the problem can become acute.

- **Clientelism**. Sometimes an agency develops routines (SOPs) that favor some constituents over others. For example, if the Department of Agriculture sends out multiple, complicated forms to qualify for loans, they will favor agricultural corporations (which have bookkeepers and secretaries) over small family farms where there is little time for fifty-page forms. The bias may not be explicit, but it is built into the routines. And, since the favored clients—the big farms—don't complain, the routine continues.

● *A threat to national security? Mikey Hicks was subjected to intense questioning every time he flew—thanks to a glitch in the no-fly list. Bureaucratic pathologies—such as an inability to break routines—are an exaggerated form of exactly what make bureaucracies effective. Call it too much of a good thing.*

What was the problem for Mikey? Primarily, the problem of rote. Once his name was on the watch list, the agency kept running through its routine and questioning him. Meanwhile, there was no simple routine for removing names. Because the agency would be in serious trouble if it removed a real terrorist, the routine for removing names is slower, with more checkpoints and approvals, than the routine for adding a name. Why did the real terrorist slip through? Here, the problem lay in different security agencies that competed over turf and failed to coordinate. The father contacted one agency, which failed to pass the information to another.

In popular culture, the story of bureaucratic pathology has completely eclipsed every other aspect of the subject. This is a mistake. We could not run the military, deliver the mail, operate an airport, process Social Security checks, or predict the weather without bureaucratic agencies. The key question for all governments—for all organizations, including your college or university—is this: How do we produce the benefits of bureaucracy while minimizing the pathologies?

The Democratic Dilemma

Bureaucracies have an inherently difficult fit with democracy. Democracy works from the bottom up. Citizens express their opinions about what the government should do. The Congress and the presidency are essentially democratic institutions because each claims its authority directly from the people.

In contrast, bureaucracy runs on expertise. The deputy secretary of Civilian Radioactive Waste Management in the DOE relies on highly specialized knowledge regarding radioactive waste. The security agencies have classified information about potential terrorists. NOAA specialists monitor scientific data. None of these jobs is primarily responsive to public sentiment.

The difference between elected office and bureaucratic posts creates a clash of cultures. Democracy collects general views from many ordinary citizens regardless of whether they are well-informed. Bureaucracy, when it runs properly, operates on the basis of specialized information. The enduring question for American government is how to manage the tension between these two polarities.

Before we think about democratic controls of the bureaucracy, let's take a more detailed look at what bureaucrats actually do.

THE BOTTOM LINE

- Before the rise of the bureaucracy, government jobs were distributed as spoils, or political rewards. Reformers challenged this system and eventually built a national bureaucracy.
- The ideal bureaucracy has five characteristics: hierarchy, division of labor, fixed routines, equal rules for all, and technical expertise.
- Bureaucracies are prone to pathologies like hewing too closely to a routine, fighting over turf, favoring some clients over others, and refusing to coordinate. These are all exaggerations of the very features that make bureaucracies efficient.
- Because they rely on specialized expertise and information, bureaucracies pose a dilemma for democratic governance.

What Bureaucracies Do

After Congress passes a law or the president issues an executive order, the bureaucracy puts it into effect. This involves making many judgments, since inevitably there are gaps in the law. Sometimes Congress sidesteps difficult questions to avoid a conflict—or an unpopular decision; sometimes the laws are vague because they were written in a hurry or amended at the last minute; and sometimes legislation involves technical details that Congress simply leaves to the bureaucratic experts. There are two steps to the bureaucratic process of putting a law into practice: rule making and implementation.

Rule Making

Rule making showcases classic bureaucratic principles in action: a fixed process with multiple steps always carried out in the same way (Figure 12.4). First, the agency studies the law and proposes a "rule" that spells out how the new program will operate; the details must make clear to the thousands of businesses and individuals exactly what they are required to do. For example, many cities and states require restaurants to list on the menu board or placard the calories of an item, right next to its price.

Sounds simple, right? It is not. What restaurants must post calorie labels? Does the rule apply to hot dog carts? Movie theaters? Soup kitchens for people without homes? In what size fonts should they make their labels? If the font is

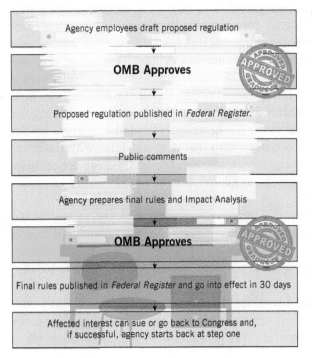

Agency employees draft proposed regulation

↓

OMB Approves   APPROVED

↓

Proposed regulation published in *Federal Register.*

↓

Public comments

↓

Agency prepares final rules and Impact Analysis

↓

OMB Approves   APPROVED

↓

Final rules published in *Federal Register* and go into effect in 30 days

↓

Affected interest can sue or go back to Congress and, if successful, agency starts back at step one

● **Figure 12.4** *Rule making in practice. Government rule making showcases classic bureaucratic principles in action: a fixed process with multiple steps always carried out in the same way. (Office of Management and Budget)*

Reduced-Fat Banana Chocolate Chip Coffee Cake
380 cal
$1.95

● *Many cities and states now require restaurants to list calories of an item on the menu or with the item itself. Writing the rules that put these mandates into effect is not easy.*

not specified, some companies might be tempted to put the calories in tiny numbers that no one will notice.

After the agency has devised the rule, it sends the rule to the Office of Management and Budget (OMB) for approval. (You know from our tour of the White House in the last chapter that OMB has the power of central clearance—it gets a chance to say "no" to almost anything.) After OMB gives its okay, the agency publishes the **proposed rule** in a document called the *Federal Register*, the daily journal of the federal government. Anybody who is interested can comment. Who reads the *Federal Register*? In theory, any citizen can read it online or at a library. In practice, most people don't know it exists, while lobbyists and lawyers pore over it as if it were the latest hot novel. The day we wrote this chapter, for example, the *Federal Register* included proposed rules controlling twenty-three toxic chemicals (from the Environmental Protection Agency) and proposed rules on inspecting poultry slaughterhouses (from the Food Safety and Inspection Service). You can be sure that lawyers and lobbyists for chemical companies and chicken producers will be bombarding the agencies with comments and questions (which are also published in the *Federal Register*). Environmental and consumer groups also take part. As you might guess, the actual details of the proposed rule and the comments are extremely technical.

The agency reviews all the public comments, makes changes, and proposes a **final rule** along with an analysis of the likely impact of the new rule. Back it goes to the OMB, which has thirty days to review the final rule. Then, the final rule is published in the *Federal Register*. Typically thirty days later, the regulation goes into effect. The final rule is not necessarily the end of the process. An individual citizen, group, or corporate firm that does not agree with the result can sue the agency for misinterpreting Congress's intent. Or it can appeal to its allies in Congress and try to get the legislators to criticize the rule and push the agency to restart the process.

In practice, lobbyists for the industry negotiate with the agency as the proposed and final rules are being written. They offer advice and threaten to sue. The experts in the agency push back and decide when to call the industry's bluff. Consumer groups often get into the action as well, trying to balance the views of the industry.

As you can see, we are describing a major political debate about a very narrow slice of American life (like inspecting chickens) that takes place every day, far from the public eye. Congress gets plenty of media coverage when

Proposed rule: A draft of administrative regulations published in the *Federal Register* for the purpose of gathering comments from interested parties.

Final rule: The rule that specifies how a program will actually operate.

it considers legislation. But the debates over how laws will work take place deep in the shadows, where only the most knowledgeable experts have an idea about what is going on.

Implementation

After the rules are in place, the bureaucratic agencies have to implement the new policies. Those chickens have to be inspected or the chemicals regulated.

Implementation is the last step in a long process: the president proposed the law; then Congress passed it, the courts upheld it, and the bureaucratic agency published draft rules, gathered comments, and published final rules in the *Federal Register*. Although the process ends up in bureaucratic hands, the bureaucrats are active at every stage in the process. For example, they often propose programs; they help write the legislation (after all, they are experts on the topic); and they testify before congressional committees that are considering the law.

Sometimes, as you might expect, executive bureaucrats develop close alliances with members of Congress as well as with interest group lobbyists. A specialist in the Environmental Protection Agency might spend years working with "green" members of Congress, as well as environmental groups and the industries that are most affected by the regulations. As another example, the Bureau of Alcohol, Tobacco, Firearms and Explosives works closely with gun makers and members of Congress who care about guns.

When the connections among bureaucrats, members of Congress, and the industry become too cozy, the result is called an iron triangle (see Chapter 9). Today, the concern about iron triangles is fading. It is difficult for a small group to quietly dominate the process; there are usually other interest groups, members of Congress, and bureaucrats from a different agency to challenge the cozy arrangements. The take-home message, however, has not changed: the bureaucracy is not walled off from other actors in government. It is part of the process every step of the way.

see for yourself 12.1

Go online to view a video about the history and operation of the *Federal Register*.

THE BOTTOM LINE

- Once a law is passed or an executive order is signed, the program goes to the bureaucracy to be put into effect.
- The bureaucrats propose rules, publish them in the *Federal Register*, gather comments, rewrite the rules, and publish the final version. The law or executive order is now in effect.
- At every step of the process, lawyers and lobbyists interact with the bureaucracy; these interactions typically take place far from the political limelight.
- Top bureaucratic officials often take part in every step of the political process—from proposing legislation to putting it into effect.

How the Bureaucracy Is Organized

Each presidential administration names the heads of the government bureaucracy—about four thousand people known as political appointees. The Senate must approve these men and women, including cabinet secretaries, their assistants and deputies, the ambassadors to countries around the world, and other top figures. The appointees' role is to steer their agencies in the direction charted by the president—and the voters.

Under these four thousand appointees toil some 2.7 million **civil servants** (the number fluctuates from day to day) who work at their jobs regardless of which party is in the White House. Imagine the tensions when a new political appointee (often a campaign official) arrives eagerly touting the new president's philosophy to an office of career officials. The bureaucrats usually have more expertise than the political appointee who has just been named as their boss. The civil servants know that before long (on average, a bit more than three years) the eager new appointee will move on, to be replaced by another. These agency professionals are acutely aware of the rules, regulations, and SOPs that guide their agency. They literally tell their new bosses what they can do, how they should do it, and the many things that they might want to do but that could land them in trouble because they fall outside the rules, clash with another agency's mission, or raise a sore point with a powerful member of congress.

The organizational chart of the federal government includes four different kinds of agency: the cabinet departments, autonomous bureaus, independent regulatory agencies, and the bureaucracy's service organizations. Let's take a closer look at each type.

Civil servants: Members of the permanent executive-branch bureaucracy who are employed on the basis of competitive exams and keep their positions regardless of the presidential administration.

The Cabinet Departments

President George Washington's cabinet had just four departments: State, Treasury, War (now called Defense, which sounds a little less aggressive), and the Office of the Attorney General (later called the Justice Department). Over time, presidents added new departments till the cabinet reached its current size—fifteen departments. Table 12.1 lists each, the year it was founded, and how large it is today. Notice how the military dominates the government's personnel count. The Department of Defense claims over 2.4 million employees, including the men and women in uniform, and manages facilities that take up thirty million acres around the world; no other organization in the United States comes close. If we add the second two largest cabinet agencies—Veterans, which takes care of retired military personnel (235,000 employees), and Homeland Security (191,000)—America's defense establishment is larger than the rest of the government combined.

The Challenge of Governing.   Naming a cabinet secretary is part of the fanfare of new administrations. The event is full of optimism and promise as the

Table 12.1 US Executive Bureaucracy: How the Bureaucracy Grew

CABINET DEPARTMENT	FOUNDING	CURRENT EMPLOYEES
State	1789	19,000 (plus 31,000 foreign nationals)
Treasury	1789	120,000
Defense	1789	771,000 civilians (1.6 million active military)
Justice	1789	115,000
Interior	1849	75,000
Agriculture	1862	98,000
Commerce	1903	45,000
Labor	1913	16,500
Health & Human Services (originally "Health, Education and Welfare")	1953	83,700
Housing & Urban Development	1965	9,818
Transportation	1966	60,000
Energy	1977	16,600 (93,000 working under contract)
Education	1979	5,000
Veterans Affairs	1989	235,000
Homeland Security	2002	191,000
ADDITIONAL FEDERAL AGENCIES (NON-CABINET)		
Social Security Administration		70,270
Environmental Protection Agency		19,737
NASA		19,000
General Services Administration		12,000
Other independent agencies		68,000
US Postal Service (a semi-independent federal agency since 1971)		736,000
Total Federal Service		**2,838,000**
Estimated number of federal contractors and grantees		**10,700,000**

Source: Curtis Copeland, Congressional Research Service, The Federal Workforce, Characteristics and Trends, *April 2011.*

● Jack Lew, center, the White House Chief of Staff (and now the Treasury Secretary), speaks during a cabinet meeting in the Cabinet Room of the White House, January 31, 2012. Notice the little plaque affixed to his chair—each cabinet chair has one specifying the agency and the year it was founded. President Obama is to the right at the very center of the cabinet table looking over the shoulder of then-Secretary of Defense Leon Panetta. (Official White House Photo by Pete Souza)

president sings the nominee's praises and the media speculates about fresh policy directions. Then, the difficulties begin. Imagine what hurdles you face if you are in the secretary's shoes.

First, you go before the Senate for confirmation; in the increasingly partisan Washington environment, any past indiscretion may surface and force you to withdraw. If all goes well, you take office when the president does on a cold Washington day in late January.

Next, you have to select your staff—your team is not yet in place. The presidential transition group sends you boxes of résumés. You pick names for your deputies, your assistants, and the leaders of the dozens of offices in your agency; some you know, others the president's advisors recommend, and still others have impressive résumés. Then, you send your selections over to the White House for a thumbs-up. Because White House staffers may have their own favorites, you'll have to negotiate about some of your choices. Next, the FBI examines every nominee's background. After that, each nominee goes to the Senate for confirmation.

If you are lucky, the White House doesn't ask a thousand questions, nothing embarrassing turns up in the FBI's detailed check, and no senator objects to the appointment. You might then have your political appointees in place by August. However, if you get caught in a bottleneck—at the White House, the FBI, or (most likely) in Congress—it will be a year or more before members of your team are in place and ready to go. Remember, there are fifteen cabinet departments—in addition to dozens of federal agencies—and all are scrambling to get their people through the neck of the bottle. By August 2009, more than seven months after taking office, the Obama administration had only 43 percent of its senior people in place; the previous administration, under George W. Bush, did not have most of its security team in office when the 9/11 terrorists attacked the World Trade Center—eight months after Inauguration Day. As Washington has grown more partisan, the confirmation process has become more difficult. And remember that a single senator can put a hold on one of your appointments if you, your department, or your nominee has provoked him or her.

Getting leaders into their offices is just the first challenge. The secretaries face the more fundamental problem of managing a large bureaucracy that they know very little about. Cabinet secretaries are accomplished individuals, but they are unlikely to have much experience with the many facets of their departments. For example, Obama's secretary of the Department of Homeland Security (DHS), Janet Napolitano, had been governor of Arizona. On the one hand, she was familiar with some homeland-security issues, like those surrounding immigration; on the other hand, she probably did not know much about the Office of Cybersecurity, the Coast Guard, or the Animal and Plant Inspection Service—all bureaus under her direction. Almost all secretaries face the same problem. And, with a new administration in town, a huge to-do list of policy goals awaits each new executive.

Many critics wondered why President Obama asked the Bush administration's Secretary of Defense, Robert Gates, to stay on as Obama's first term began in 2009. After all, the president-elect had fiercely criticized Bush's defense policy. Now you know the answer: Obama could not afford a slow transition at Defense because he planned to take immediate action—in Iraq, Afghanistan, and Guantánamo Bay. He chose someone who already knew how to operate the levers at the Pentagon. Since President Obama and Secretary Gates shared many ideas and goals, the president chose a fast start over the luxury of naming his own person. Gates stepped down in 2011, succeeded by Leon Panetta and, in 2013, former Senator Chuck Hagel—another Republican.

The Rotating Bureaucracy. The turnover at the top rung of the US bureaucracy is unique. No other democracy works in this way—nor does any other major institution. No private company, nonprofit organization, or university routinely asks thousands of outsiders to take over for an average of 3.3 years and then expects them to step aside and make way for an entirely new crop of leaders. Meanwhile, the political appointees scrambling to catch up are in charge of a huge bureaucratic leviathan. Thousands of civil servants toil away at the agency's tasks, working from one administration to the next.

Management consultants would run screaming from the room if you suggested setting up a business in this way. And, here, we cannot look to the Constitution because it does not describe a cabinet or a bureaucracy. Many political scientists, however, think the bureaucracy does work. The civil service does its job, often quite well. And the political leadership, for all the problems of the transition, comes to the job with a definite philosophy, based on a president's central ideas.

Each administration tries to impose its philosophy on the great bureaucracy. Conservative presidents select people who share their outlook to run the departments and agencies. Those appointees try to steer a mammoth like the Department of Defense or Health and Human Services in a more conservative direction. When a Democrat wins, more liberal appointees try to adjust the department in the other direction. It is never easy because of the hurdles we have described: difficulties in appointing a team, the resistance of career bureaucrats to many changes, the long process of instituting reforms (draft rules, OMB clearance, final rules), and the many actors who leap into the process (congressional committees, interest groups, consumer advocates, program beneficiaries, and so on).

Despite all the barriers, new administrations can have a powerful influence on their agencies. An example is the Federal Emergency Management Agency (FEMA), which responds to natural disasters. President Bill Clinton transformed the agency into a decentralized, authority-sharing outfit with a very proactive approach. When floods hit the Midwest in 1993, the new FEMA won widespread applause for its swift, well-organized assistance. People might despise federal bureaucrats, but FEMA officials drew high praise at the time.

When the George W. Bush administration came to office, FEMA was on its list of target agencies. Why? From a conservative perspective, FEMA had become *too* proactive. Republican members of Congress charged that the agency had gone into the flood plains and bought out homeowners to avert disaster the next time the river flooded. That sounded to critics like a big government welfare program in action. The Bush administration restored the old FEMA policies. The routines were further complicated when the Congress moved the agency into the new, and very large, Department of Homeland Security.

In this case, the changes led to political disaster. In part owing to the restoration of a rule-bound, elaborately hierarchical structure, and in part to an inexperienced (but politically connected) director, FEMA responded feebly to Hurricane Katrina, a massive storm that flooded New Orleans in 2005. The tragedy played out in real time as the media depicted widespread desperation—and no federal response in sight. The agency's director, Michael Brown, lost his job, and President Bush's popularity ratings tumbled.

The FEMA example illustrates an important point about the federal bureaucracy. Calling for smaller government sounds promising on the campaign trail. However, each nook and cranny of the sprawling government establishment has a job to do; almost all deliver services that some people rely on. That responsibility makes cutting government agencies difficult in actual practice. In addition, bureaucratic reorganizations that few people care about—like where to site FEMA—can have serious consequences for delivery of services.

The great debate that began at the Constitutional Convention rages on today. Do we want an energetic and efficient government? Or one that is more responsive to the people? When it comes to the cabinet, the United States leans toward being responsive rather than efficient. But neither approach is easy in a bureaucracy so large or a system so complicated.

Other Agencies

Most of the federal bureaucracy—about 1.8 million civilians—work in the cabinet agencies. There are three other categories of federal workers, however, and each offers a different twist to the life of the bureaucracy.

Executive Agencies. Independent executive agencies have more focused jobs than the cabinet departments. The Social Security Administration, for example, is responsible for running the Social Security program, which provides pensions for people over sixty-five. The Environmental Protection Agency is entirely focused on the difficult job of overseeing the environment. In contrast, the Interior Department (a cabinet agency) has responsibilities that include—among many other things—supervising Indian affairs, national parks, geological surveys, oceans and energy, and surface mining.

The independent executive agencies perform a wide range of jobs: among them, they land astronauts on the moon (NASA), send Americans around the world to perform service projects (the Peace Corps), gather intelligence (CIA), manage the banking system (the Federal Reserve), monitor elections (the Federal Election Commission), and investigate violations of civil rights in the workplace (Equal Employment Opportunities Commission).

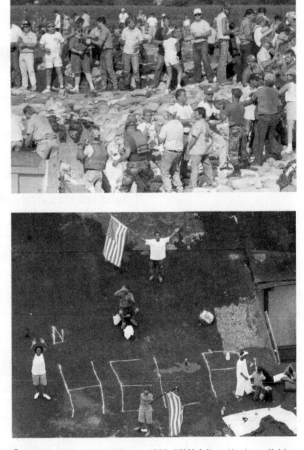

● *FEMA success: Midwest floods, 1993. FEMA failure: Hurricane Katrina, 2005.*

Independent Regulatory Commissions. Another kind of bureau emerged to regulate business. The first one set the organizational template. In the 1880s, farmers and small business complained bitterly that they were at the mercy of the railroads, which could make or break them with their arbitrary freight rates. The farmers pleaded for government controls. However, reformers faced a problem. The railroad owners were so wealthy and powerful that they dominated the state legislatures and Congress. How could consumers be protected against these powerful "robber barons"? Reformers decided to organize a regulatory agency, the Interstate Commerce Commission (ICC), that would operate independently from Congress and the White House. Reformers hoped that the agency's independence would permit it to regulate industry—free from corrupting lobbyists and politics. Table 12.2 lists all the independent regulatory commissions that eventually followed the ICC.

The independent regulatory commissions had the authority to issue regulations, enforce laws, and settle disputes—essentially combining legislative,

Table 12.2 Independent Regulatory Commissions (listed in order of creation)

IRC	YEAR CREATED	SHUT DOWN
Interstate Commerce Commission	1887	1995
Federal Trade Commission	1914	—
Federal Communications Commission	1928	—
Federal Power (later Federal Energy Regulatory) Commission	1930	—
Securities and Exchange Commission	1935	—
National Labor Relations Board	1935	—
Civil Aeronautics Board	1940	1985
Atomic Energy (later Nuclear Regulatory) Commission	1954	—
Federal Maritime Commission	1961	—
Equal Employment Opportunity Commission	1965	—
Consumer Product Safety Commission	1972	—
Federal Election Commission	1975	—

executive, and judicial powers in one agency. A set of commissioners, nominated by the president and confirmed by the Senate, ran the agency for a fixed term that did not overlap with the president's term—still another way to minimize political influence. The hope, beginning with the ICC, was that modern management methods rather than politics would guide regulatory policy.

By now you know enough about American politics to recognize the reformers' naïveté: independent agencies were no less political than any other branch of government. As we saw when we examined the rule-making process, regulating an industry inevitably involves plenty of back-and-forth negotiations between regulators and the industry.

In the past thirty years, a new generation of reformers has come up with a solution to **regulatory capture**: deregulation—that is, abolishing the agencies altogether and letting free market competition protect consumers. The original Interstate Commerce Commission (ICC) was dismantled in 1995. The Civil Aeronautics Board, another regulatory commission, which protected the airline industry by limiting competition, was abolished in 1985, leading, directly or indirectly, to all kinds of consequences, good and bad—frequent-flier programs, fewer airlines, huge fluctuations in fares, and inedible food.

Regulatory capture: The theory that industries dominate the agencies that regulate them.

Deregulation brings us full circle. The farmers and small business pleaded for relief from predatory markets. Now, a new generation of reformers offers a solution to problems with the regulatory agencies: return to the markets.

An Army of Their Own. A small support army maintains and services the massive office buildings housing the executive branch. Imagine supplying 2.7 million workers; imagine the job of hiring, paying, reviewing, promoting, and sometimes firing all those workers. These details require still another type of institution in the US bureaucracy: independent **central service agencies**, most notably the Office of Personnel Management (OPM) and the General Services Administration (GSA).

Central service agencies: The organizations that supply and staff the federal government.

Do you want to work for the US government, as a civil servant? OPM manages the giant "USAJobs" website, listing hundreds of thousands of federal bureaucracy job openings each year. Once you apply for your position, your application will be read and screened by OPM staff. When you are hired, your employment materials (pay level, vacation-time details, health benefits) will come from them. And, when you are ready to leave government service, you'll talk to OPM about the government pension you may have accumulated.

Private Contractors. One final category of government workers does not work for the government at all. They work for private companies that provide goods and services under contract to the government. **Private contractors** now perform many of the jobs that once were handled directly by government employees. For example, the military increasingly relies on private firms to provide meals, transportation, security services, and even commando teams. For the first time in American history, there were more private contractors (about 200,000) than uniformed military personnel (about 190,000) in the war zones in both Iraq (2003–2012) and Afghanistan (2001–2014). Beyond war, private companies provide a full range of government services, including homeland security, international diplomacy, prison management, and garbage collection.

Private contractors: Private companies that contract to provide goods and services for the government.

Executive-branch agencies and commissions all face leadership challenges similar to those faced by the cabinet departments. The appointment

● Private contractors, like Blackwater Worldwide, provided military services in Iraq and Afghanistan. Here, a private contractor is part of the security detail for L. Paul Bremer, who oversaw the American operation in Iraq.

process is cumbersome and complicated by politics. New appointees have to scramble to learn the bureaucratic ropes, even as the to-do list piles ever higher. And the administrative team takes longer to get into place.

How can the nation's agencies operate effectively when their leaders are on the way in and just learning the ropes or are on the way out and operating as lame ducks? For an answer, we need to confront the complicated question of just who is in charge of the American bureaucracy.

THE BOTTOM LINE

- The federal bureaucracy includes five different types of agencies. The fifteen cabinet departments, forming the largest group, employ roughly 1.8 million civilians.
- The government includes four other kinds of bureaucracies: executive agencies focus on one type of issue like environmental quality; independent regulatory commissions oversee specific industries; central service agencies staff, stock, and supply the entire bureaucracy; and private contractors are licensed to provide goods and services for the government. Different kinds of agencies face different kinds of political problems and challenges.
- The president appoints a small number of executives; the rest are members of the permanent civil service.
- The cabinet and other appointed executives provide political direction; the civil servants provide expertise and continuity.
- Among the many challenges to a smoothly functioning system is the time—typically more than a year—that it takes a new administration to get its leadership team in place.

Who Controls the Federal Bureaucracy?

Controlling 2.7 million bureaucrats, 1.6 million military personnel, and more than 10 million private contractors is a daunting leadership responsibility—and a giant management headache. It is also crucial for democracy. Self-rule requires mastering the bureaucracy. But who is in charge?

The People

In a democracy, the federal government must, ultimately, respond to the people. Most executive departments trumpet something like *We Serve the People* on their websites. However, real popular control faces the problem we have discussed throughout this chapter: much of what the bureaucracy does is too technical for direct public engagement.

How does the IRS figure tax penalties for S corporations wrongly electing to amortize anticipated losses with write-downs? What is the maximum engineering pendular sway ratio on truss-style bridges? Does the chemical compound bisphenol-A, widely used in plastics, leach into bottled drinking water—and, if it does, how dangerous is it to public health? Americans do not have the time or the knowledge to develop opinions about such matters. We need someone else to act on our behalf.

The President

In theory, the president controls the bureaucracy. The Constitution is clear on this issue: "the executive Power shall be vested in a President of the United States of America." The president is the bureaucrat in chief. The form of bureaucratic control that follows from this declaration is known as **overhead democracy**: the people elect the presidents who, through their appointees, control the bureaucracy from the top.

In practice, most presidents are frustrated in their efforts to manage the millions of men and women under their command. Harry Truman put it famously when he commented on his successor, General Dwight D. Eisenhower. "He'll sit here and he'll say 'Do this!' and 'Do that!' *And nothing will happen.* Poor Ike, it won't be a bit like the army. He'll find it very frustrating."[6]

When presidents appoint the directors of the executive branch, they quickly discover that the bureaucracy has its own preferences, processes, and routines. Before long, many executives begin to see the world through the eyes of their agencies—rather than from the perspective of the White House. President Richard Nixon, a Republican, bluntly expressed his frustration: Democrats had run the government for twenty-eight of the previous thirty-six years, and Nixon believed that many of the career civil servants were simply Democrats waiting for the next liberal administration. "If we don't get rid of these people," Nixon wrote, "they will sit back on their well-paid asses and wait for the next election to bring back their old bosses."[7]

Congress

Although bureaucrats "belong" to the executive branch, the legislative branch wields a surprising amount of authority. Congress shapes the bureaucracy through four powers.

- *Funding.* Most important, Congress funds nearly all executive-branch programs, since it determines and votes on the budget. If Congress doesn't like a bureaucratic proposal, or if some agency head falls out of favor with a powerful subcommittee, that program or department may find its budget slashed by congressional appropriators.

- *Oversight.* Congress has oversight power to supervise the executive branch, including both White House and federal bureaucratic operations. Policing department and agency actions is normally a routine

Overhead democracy: A system by which the people elect the presidents, who, through their appointees, control the bureaucracy from the top.

operation—making sure that funds are properly expended or programs achieve their stated goals. But Congress can extend its oversight authority into major investigations of executive-branch actions. The mere mention of oversight hearings is a major threat to the bureaucracy.

- *Authorization.* Of course, Congress passes the laws and often has to reauthorize them after a specified number of years. Although we have seen that recent administrations have increasingly relied on executive orders, Congress wields the power to amend programs or even deny their reauthorization.

- *Reorganization.* Finally, Congress can change the structure and nature of executive-branch organizations. In the wake of the September 11, 2001, attacks, President George W. Bush called for creation of the Department of Homeland Security. Three years later, Congress finally approved his request—but added many rules about things like employee pay and unionization rules.

These four sources of power add up to extensive congressional influence. Agency heads and cabinet secretaries are often more responsive to Congress—with its power of the purse and oversight authority—than to the president. Bureaucratic leaders regularly lobby Congress for additional funding or authority. They also frequently complain, however, about congressional "micromanagement."

Congressional power is also circumscribed, of course. The power to shape or influence is still a far cry from the power to command or control. Presidents and congressional leaders sometimes clash over who controls the bureaucracy. Meanwhile, another powerful set of players—interest groups—quietly exert influence as well.

Interest Groups

Interest groups closely engage bureaucrats as they administer the laws. As we saw earlier (in Chapter 9), lobbying groups comment extensively on proposed rules. They offer information about the needs and capacity of the affected industry. As bureaucrats finalize the rules and implement programs, they often engage the industry, whose cooperation may be necessary to make the program work smoothly. Bureaucratic officials, trade groups, and consumer alliances often share expertise and interests. Over time, they can develop close relations, which make the interest groups influential in the day-to-day operations of the executive agencies. The interest groups—often fighting among themselves—can also complain, report back to Congress, or sue. The result is another set of influences on bureaucrats in action.

Bureaucratic Autonomy

Partly because they have so many would-be masters, bureaucrats wind up with considerable autonomy in how they do their work. Many public officials have strong views about their fields—protecting the environment, enforcing the civil rights laws, or keeping the homeland safe. They also have an interest in increasing their own autonomy—applying their best judgment to the problems they face.

This search for autonomy is especially true for the government officials who deal directly with the public. These **street-level bureaucrats** are administrators at the bottom of the government organization who interact with the public—welfare officers, police, teachers, or poultry-plant inspectors. General policies are formulated in the higher administration, but it is the street-level bureaucrats who actually run the programs, constantly using their own judgments. The police officer may write you a speeding ticket—or let you off with a warning.[8]

Consider a more complicated case. The Women, Infants, and Children program (WIC) provides vouchers for meals to low-income families with children. On the national level, Congress debates the funding and the administration determines the rules for eligibility. On the local level, the street-level bureaucrats constantly make judgment calls about exactly how strictly to apply the rules. For example: this woman makes too much money on paper, but her ex-husband is not paying his child support. That woman was ill and missed the application deadline—do you give the EBT card (for buying food)? This family has broken the rules again and again but if you cut off their program benefits, the children will suffer. The street-level bureaucrats have enormous influence in deciding just how strictly to apply the rules. Program beneficiaries quickly learn about the power of street-level bureaucrats.

Moreover, at the street level, every program has its own tone. Some programs (like Social Security) treat their beneficiaries with respect; others (like Temporary Assistance for Needy Families) take a more disciplinary stance.[9]

> **Street-level bureaucrats:** Public officials who deal directly with the public.

Democracy Revisited

Many agents—the president, Congress, and interest groups—exert some control over the bureaucracy. Each does so on behalf of others: the White House tries to speak for the public, Congress for voters in a state or district, and interest groups on behalf of clients who might range from a business sector to the environmental or civil rights community. Bureaucrats try to maximize their own discretion to do what they think is best. The essential question is the one we started with: Do these clashing forces add up to democratic control?

The answer is yes and no. At times, these different forms of democratic control offer a rough form of popular oversight. Administrations that focus on delivering services can have considerable success;

● *A street-level bureaucrat in action! A local official in the Modesto California Health Department, part of the Women, Infants, and Children program, measures the growth of a young client.*

presidents who seek to change the direction of federal policy can, if they stick to it, have some success; congressional oversight often improves responsiveness. But all the levers for democratic control are blunt instruments. They take hard work, constant attention, and considerable luck. In the next section, we examine three reform proposals that might enhance popular control of the bureaucracy.

THE BOTTOM LINE

- In a democracy, the public must ultimately control the government bureaucracy. The question is how.
- Different actors exert some control on the bureaucracy: the president (who names the leaders), Congress (through funding and oversight), and interest groups.
- Bureaucrats still operate with considerable autonomy—applying their own judgment to policy problems. "Street level" bureaucrats are especially likely to exercise their own discretion.

🔵 Reforming the Bureaucracy

The bureaucracy's reputation for being expensive, slow-moving, and scandal-ridden has attracted a long history of reform efforts. Let's consider three popular proposals.

Open Up the System

The public's faith in government tumbled in the late 1960s and the early 1970s, after an unpopular war in Vietnam, civil rights unrest, and President Nixon's shocking behavior during the Watergate scandal. One response was a concerted attempt to make the executive bureaucracy more transparent. Sunshine laws require public hearings and citizen input; they open up bureaucratic debates to public view. The **Freedom of Information Act** extends citizen access to agency and department deliberations. Any individual or news organization may file a Freedom of Information Act request to see an unreleased government document (the legislation created a new verb, "to FOIA" a document). Today, every federal agency has its own website that tries to explain just what it is doing.

Freedom of Information Act: A 1966 law that facilitates full or partial disclosure of government information and documents.

Reinventing Government

During the 1980s and 1990s, some bureaucratic reformers began to stress responsiveness. Departments should treat the public as customers and make their services more efficient and user friendly. Early in the Clinton administration, Vice President Al Gore took charge of a sweeping "Reinventing

Government" project—designed to cut bureaucratic delays, increase efficiency, reduce costs, decentralize management, and empower employees to make decisions.[10] The efforts continued into President George W. Bush's administration with a special emphasis on *deregulation*—leaving businesses and private citizens freer to look after themselves.

Some success stories emerged. In fact, many of the measures of bureaucratic effectiveness that were developed under the "Reinventing Government" project remain in place today.

Privatization

If the bureaucracy seems slow and inefficient, perhaps private companies can do the job more efficiently. As we have discussed, the most powerful trend in government has been outsourcing public services to private firms. For-profit companies collect garbage, manage prisons, protect the homeland, cook for the troops, and launch commando raids abroad.

● *An employee of Immigration and Customs Enforcement's Stewart Detention Center in Lumpkin, Georgia, waiting for the front gate to be opened. The detention center is operated on contract by Nashville-based Corrections Corporation of America.*

The movement for privatizing federal (and many state) programs took flight in the 1970s and received a boost from President Reagan in the 1980s. His administration turned some forty thousand government jobs over to private contractors, for reported savings of more than six hundred million dollars. As we noted above, more than ten million private contractors are working for national, state, and local governments today.

Private firms often can do the job for less. But the savings are at least partly offset by the need to supervise the private companies. What happens when a private contractor—worrying, as they must, about the bottom line—cuts corners or violates rules? For example, the Blackwater corporation did many indispensable jobs for the US military in Iraq. However, they also created multiple headaches. Poorly trained operators who killed Iraqi civilians created waves of protests—critics charged the company with 195 shooting incidents. The firm also experienced chronic cost overruns. As criticism grew, the company quietly changed its name to "Xe" and then changed its name again to "Academi. "

Private providers can also walk away from their government services when they are no longer making a profit—or when they go out of business. In New York City, Mayor Rudolph Giuliani (1992–2001) privatized many school bus services. When the private company that had won the contract defaulted, the city had to scramble to find buses and prepare drivers in time for the start of the school year.

The benefits of privatization are still debated, like the other reforms we've discussed here. Research in this area suggests that *competitive contracting* (requiring more than one bid from outside contractors who want to provide government services) can save money and boost quality. However, the most important calculation, often overlooked by reformers, is factoring in a way for government officials to supervise the private contractor. Careful oversight is a critical dimension of making privatization work.

> **THE BOTTOM LINE**
> - Some critics of bureaucratic performance recommend "sunshine" reforms to publicize agencies' work.
> - Others call for reinventing government to make it more constituent-friendly, or privatizing some bureaucratic functions.

Conclusion: The Real Solution Lies with You

President Kennedy came to office with a burst of idealism and declared, "Ask not what your country can do for you—ask what you can do for your country." Inspired by the young president, the early civil rights movement, and the general optimism of the era, many college graduates streamed into public service. Today, fewer Americans are attracted to government service. Can this trend change? What would draw *you* into government?

The ultimate answer to the problems of bureaucracy, we believe, lies in the interest and commitment from a new generation. We are deeply concerned that men and women like you and your classmates—a well-educated group interested in political science—will bypass government altogether.

Indeed, politicians from both parties take shots at the bureaucrats. They freeze pay, downsize departments, and disparage millions of individuals. However, a closer look suggests that the bureaucracy performs many jobs we need and value—from warning sailors about storms to defending the United States. Ultimately, our government—our democracy—is only as good as the bureaucracy that puts public policy into effect. This brings us back to you and your generation's commitment to public service. And what public officials can do to foster it.

CHAPTER SUMMARY

● Within the executive branch, the US federal bureaucracy does a vast amount of work in governing—and more closely resembles the nation's population than any other segment of our national government. However, Americans express deep ambivalence about our bureaucracy, generally rating it very low in opinion polls.

● The American bureaucracy was established in reaction to the spoils system (1828–1901).

● In theory, bureaucracies operate with five characteristics: hierarchy, division of labor, fixed routines, equal rules for all, and technical qualifications.

● Bureaucrats, in the United States as in other countries, perform a wide range of functions—from managing the nation's defense and national economy to organizing and providing food stamps and tax cuts. The bureaucracy is specifically charged with implementing the laws passed by Congress and signed by the president. This typically involves an administrative rule-making process as well as actual delivery of services and carrying out of programs.

● Since the 1930s, the federal bureaucracy has grown to about 4.4 million employees—roughly half civilian and half military. This growth has occurred despite anti-"big government" sentiment among Americans; helping to overcome this sentiment have been forces like war, morality, and economics. Organizing such a sprawling set of cabinet departments and agencies, populated by civil servants and political appointees, is an immense job.

● It is not readily apparent who is in charge of managing the bureaucracy. Many different players have a role, including the public, the president, Congress, and interest groups. Even with—or perhaps because of—all those masters, bureaucrats have considerable discretion in how they carry out their work. This freedom can lead to serious tensions between Americans' democratic ideals of representative accountability, and an unelected, often *unaccountable* workforce of civil servants.

● Public disapproval of the bureaucracy arises from several different complaints. Reform efforts include enhancing transparency of bureaucratic practices, reinventing government to improve responsiveness and reduce layers of management, and privatizing government services.

KEY TERMS

Bureaucratic pathologies, 440	Overhead democracy, 455	Spoils system, 436
Central service agencies, 453	Pendleton Civil Service Act, 437	Street-level bureaucrats, 457
Civil servants, 446	Private contractors, 453	Universalistic politics, 436
Final rule, 444	Proposed rule, 444	
Freedom of Information Act, 458	Regulatory capture, 452	

STUDY QUESTIONS

1. Look back at the Department of Energy's (DOE's) organizational chart on p. 537 of this chapter. Does it seem useful to describe how different DOE offices relate to each other? Why or why not? If you were in charge of the DOE, how strict would you be about adhering to this chart—would you allow some wiggle room? Or would reporting authority go up the lines and boxes described here?

2. Is the US federal bureaucracy too large? Do we need 4.4 million people working for the government—in addition to another ten million or so hired under federal contracts? If you'd like to see it smaller, where should we start cutting workers?

3. Who runs the bureaucracy? Do bureaucrats have too much discretion in how they perform their duties? What are the respective merits of a "street-level" or "top-down" management style?

4. Let's say you have just learned about some unsavory doings in your bureaucratic agency or department. Do you blow the whistle—report the problem? Or do you keep quiet? What would affect your decision?

5. Based on what you now know about the US bureaucracy, should we mount a major push for reform? What type(s) of reforms would be most useful? Or are the various parts of the bureaucracy working pretty well the way they are?

13

The Judicial Branch

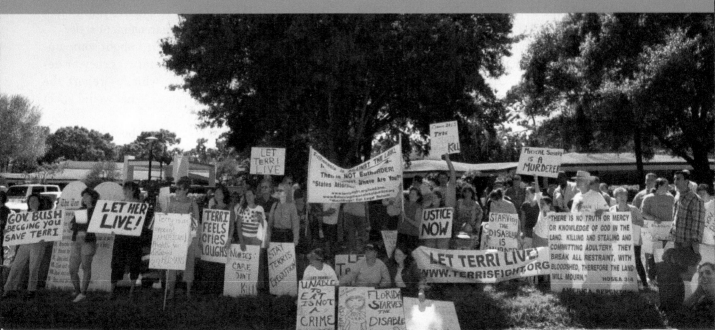

TERRI SCHIAVO, a twenty-six-year-old woman, collapsed in her home in St. Petersburg, Florida, went into a coma, and then lingered in what her doctor called "a persistent vegetative state." She exhibited no brain activity and was kept alive by a feeding tube. After eight years, her husband, Michael, decided to remove the tube and allow Terri to die. He filed a petition with the court requesting permission to remove the feeding tube; her parents went to court to stop the removal—and the political frenzy began. Politicians, disability rights groups, pro-life organizations, and the national media all leapt into action, issuing moral judgments, medical opinions, and political threats. William Frist, the Senate majority leader and a former heart surgeon, declared that he saw "signs of life" in a videotape of Terri. Demonstrations and counterdemonstrations raged outside the courthouse.

The Florida legislature passed "Terri's Law," signed by Governor Jeb Bush, which ordered the hospice to reinsert the feeding tube. The US Congress passed its own bill authorizing Terri's parents to go to federal court and claim that her federal rights had been violated. President George W. Bush flew to Washington from his Texas ranch and, with maximum media exposure, signed the legislation. Amid all the intense activity, however, it soon became clear that Terri Schiavo's fate was entirely in the hands of the courts.

After almost three years, in February 2000, a local Florida court ruled that the tube could be removed, and in April 2000 the state **appellate court** upheld the ruling. Four years of legal maneuvers followed, but both state and federal courts upheld the decision to remove the tube. Various Florida courts also struck down "Terri's Law" and other legislative efforts to stop the courts from permitting the tube removal; an appellate court and finally the Supreme Court backed up the decision by repeatedly refusing to hear the case. Finally, in March 2005—after almost seven years of legal wrangling—the Supreme Court refused to intervene one last time, Terri Schiavo's feeding tubes were removed, and she died.

By the end of the fight, all sides were focused on the judicial system. "I'm glad the courts are in charge of this, not Congress or [Florida governor] Jeb Bush," one Florida resident told a reporter.[1] A protester outside Terri's hospice

Appellate courts: The system of federal justices, organized into district courts and circuit courts, who hear appeals from lower courts, culminating in the Supreme Court.

● *Outside Terri Schiavo's hospice.*

clutched a sign that expressed the opposite view: "Hey Judge," his poster read. "Who Made You God?"

Alexander Hamilton predicted that the judiciary "will always be the least dangerous" and "the weakest" branch of government, for, he reasoned, it has "no influence" over "the sword" (the president controls the army) or "the purse" (Congress is in charge of the budget).[2] Yet, as the Schiavo case illustrates, the US judiciary has accumulated sweeping powers—including the ability to overrule state legislatures and Congress, governors, and even presidents. The courts have the authority to strike down any laws, rules, or regulations that violate the Constitution—as the courts interpret it.

We have seen in earlier chapters the great reach and power of the Supreme Court—for example, when it struck down compromises and protected slavery (in *Dred Scott*, 1857); when it cracked the entire edifice of segregation (*Brown v. Board of Education*, 1954); and when it swept away a state network of laws prohibiting abortion (*Roe v. Wade*, 1973). More recently, the Supreme Court decisively stopped the vote counting in the disputed 2000 election—making George W. Bush president (*Bush v. Gore*); rejected bipartisan efforts to limit money flowing into American elections (*Citizens United*); and riveted national attention in 2012 when it considered the signal achievement of the Obama administration, the Affordable Care Act, and upheld it (we'll explore the health care case later in this chapter). These last three decisions were all the more controversial because each was decided by a single vote—5 to 4.

At least on the surface, judicial authority can seem breathtaking. The previous two chapters, on the presidency and bureaucracy, asked whether those institutions still fit a democratic framework. The question becomes even more pointed for the federal courts. Unelected officials with lifetime appointments wield the power to overrule the long, hard, democratic process of forging legislation. The Founders believed that the more political branches of government—the president and Congress—needed the courts to check them. Has that check now grown too powerful? Has it grown too political? These are the momentous questions that guide our examination of the courts.

Who are we? A nation founded on the world's oldest constitution, which directly or indirectly governs almost every aspect of our collective life. "Without the Constitution, there would be no America," observes one historian.[3] The courts ultimately rule on how the Constitution applies to the problems we face. Small wonder that the United States is—and always has been—a nation of courts, lawyers, and people ready to sue.

We will begin with the basics. What does the court system look like? How does it make decisions? How did it amass so much power over our politics, our government, and our daily lives? The answer starts with the basic character of the American people: *who we are.*

BY THE NUMBERS *The US Judiciary*

Original number of Supreme Court justices: **5**
Largest number of justices (1863–1866): **10**

Number of Supreme Court justices appointed, 1882–1910: **18**
Number of Supreme Court justices appointed, 1982–2010: **9**

Number of years John Marshall was chief justice of the United States: **34**
Number of years served by his successor, Roger Taney: **28**
Number of chief justices in American history: **16**
Number since 1953: **4**
Number of US presidents since 1953: **11**

Total number of Catholic justices on Supreme Court, 1789–1910: **3**
Number of Catholic justices currently serving on Supreme Court: **6**

Total number of cases heard by Supreme Court, 1987–1988 term: **155**
Total number of cases heard by Supreme Court, 2011–2012 term: **69**

Vacancies on the Supreme Court during Eisenhower presidency (1953–1960): **5**
Vacancies on the Supreme Court during Carter presidency (1977–1980): **0**

Salary, federal district court judge, 2010: **$169,300**
Average salary, first-year associate, New York City law firm, 2010: **$163,000**
Supreme Court chief justice salary: **$223,500**
Supreme Court associate justice salary: **$213,900**
Median annual income for all lawyers: **$112,000**
Average salary, NBA player, 2010: **$5,600,000**

Charge for filing a civil case (anyone can do so) in federal district court: **$350**
Estimated number of Americans who served on juries, 2012: **344,500**

Total fine charged in jury trial to Minnesota woman for illegal downloads, 2009: **$1,900,000**
Total number of songs she illegally downloaded: **24**

⬤ Who Are We? A Nation of Laws...and Lawyers

The United States relies on courts to resolve more matters than most nations. The result is a deeply legalistic political culture.

Embracing the Law—and Lawsuits

Litigation: The conduct of a lawsuit.

Lawsuits, or **litigation**, are a near-constant feature of American public life. Courts are routine sites for settling private and public disputes alike. Advocacy groups, private citizens, and corporations go to court as a "first-strike" option. Litigation is an essential part of the rule-making process (discussed in the previous chapter). Business competition spills into the courts. Most other industrial nations rely more on **mediation** in noncriminal cases; citizens and groups are also more likely to defer to civil servants. In contrast, Americans sue. The total number of legal actions—from murder trials to traffic violations—approaches 100 million a year. Only a few other nations—most notably, Great Britain and Denmark—have as many suits per capita as the United States does.

Mediation: A way of resolving disputes without going to court, in which a third party (the mediator) helps two or more sides negotiate a settlement.

America is not only a people of litigation but also of lawyers. The number has risen fourfold since 1960, six times faster than population growth. The nation now has one lawyer for every 275 people—far outstripping Canada (one in every 450), India (1,200), France (1,403), and every other nation (see Figure 13.1). As early as 1835, Alexis de Tocqueville could comment, "There is hardly any political question in the United States which does not, sooner or later, turn into a judicial one."[4]

Declining Trust

Traditionally, lawyers and courts enjoyed high prestige. Tocqueville described lawyers as democracy's natural aristocrats and noted that the American people trusted them. Not anymore.

⬤ **Figure 13.1** *Number of lawyers, per capita, by nation. The shorter the bar, the larger the number of lawyers relative to the population. Japan is a society based on consensus and has only 22,000 lawyers in a nation of 127 million people. The United States is at the other extreme with one lawyer for every 275 citizens.*

United States	275
Brazil	326
United Kingdom	401
Canada	450
Germany	593
India	1,200
France	1,403
Japan	5,772

0   1000   2000   3000   4000   5000   6000

Today, law, lawyers, and the legal system all face shrinking reputations. The Supreme Court recently received its lowest favorable ratings in at least twenty-five years (see Figure 13.2).

Even when the judiciary's prestige ebbs, it still generally ranks roughly the same as the president and towers over Congress. In summer 2012, one poll pegged confidence in the three institutions at 37 percent for the Supreme Court, 35 percent for the presidency, and just 12 percent for Congress, which as usual was the lowest-rated national institution.

Courts in American Culture

Images of law and lawyers run through American culture, with the image alternating between heroism and cynicism. On one side, in *To Kill a Mockingbird*, Gregory Peck's Atticus Finch wins the African American community's respect when he passionately defends a black man unjustly accused of rape: "In our courts all men are created equal," he proclaims at the film's climax. "That's no ideal to me. That is a living, working reality."

On the other side, the scripts are also familiar: eager young lawyers complete law school, join a firm—and have the idealism crushed out of them. Films that offer variations on the theme include *The Firm*, *Presumed Innocent*, and its 2010 sequel, *Innocent*. Another critical storyline portrays the corrupting power of money in the law. In *The Insiders*, *A Civil Action*, and *The Lincoln Lawyer*, a team of high-priced legal talent fights a worthy cause or character.

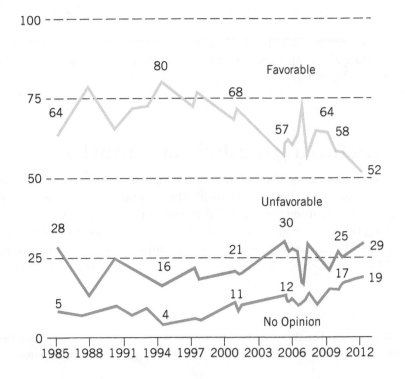

● **Figure 13.2** *The Supreme Court declines in public esteem. After the Bush v. Gore decision (in 2000), Democrats gave the court low rankings, but Republicans didn't. Today, the skepticism is rising among Democrats, Republicans, and independents. Recent polls put the approval rating at 52 percent (shown here), 45 percent, (Pew Research), and 37 percent (Rasmussen).*

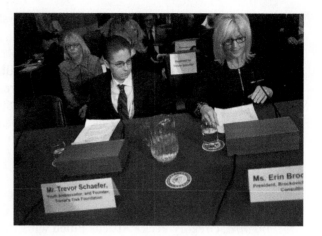

● Erin Brockovich, a law clerk without any legal training, whose tireless, extraordinary effort resulted in a major environmental legal victory. Here she testifies before Congress.

In American culture, as in politics, the law is a place where our highest ideals are on display—and where we simultaneously fear that corruption runs rampant. We will return at chapter's end to proposed reforms of the legal system. First let us explore how that system works in practice.

THE BOTTOM LINE

- The United States relies on courts and litigation more than most other nations—a political reality reflected in both the number of lawsuits and the number of lawyers.
- Trust in the Supreme Court has declined in recent years.
- Law continues to play an important role in American popular culture—portrayed in both idealistic and cynical terms.

● Organizing the Judicial Branch

The Constitution offers detailed instruction for Congress (article 1) and vague rules for the executive branch (article 2). The judiciary gets the least attention of all. The Constitution vests judicial power in the Supreme Court, without specifying the number of justices, and empowers Congress to design the rest of our federal court system. This section examines how the courts are organized. As usual, there's a distinctive look to how Americans run this branch of government.

Divided We Rule

By now you know the story: when Americans see government power, they divide it. Two chambers of Congress, with layers of committees and subcommittees;

an executive branch split into departments, agencies, commissions, and White House offices; and a federalist system of national, state, and city officials all co-operating, competing, and overlapping. Court powers are also divided.

Most other nations feature a single, unitary system of courts. In contrast, the United States exhibits *judicial federalism*. Both federal and state court systems are further divided into three layers, as Figure 13.3 displays: lower courts conduct trials; appellate courts hear appeals; and a supreme court in both state and federal systems renders a final verdict. The national Supreme Court is the ultimate arbiter for all cases. However, millions of cases are filed each year; the Supreme Court only reviews around seven thousand lower-court cases and, in recent years, accepts and hears eighty or fewer. That leaves a great deal of authority in the lower ranks of the judiciary.

State and Local Courts

Local trial and state appeals courts are the workhorses of the judiciary, handling most of the nontraffic cases in the United States each year. State courts are responsible for all cases that arise under state law; they rule on everything from antitrust disputes to murder cases and from medical malpractice to marijuana possession. States organize their judicial system in their own way—so there is considerable variation around the nation.

The first stop in most cases is a state trial court; appeals usually are handled in state appellate courts. In high-profile cases, appeals from state courts may be heard by the US Supreme Court. Many landmark cases originate—and sometimes reach settlement—in state courts. The 2012 decision to uphold the "Obamacare" health reform law began as a state decision, as did *Roe v. Wade* (which struck down a Texas law banning abortion), *Bush v. Gore* (settling the disputed presidential ballots in Florida), and the Terri Schiavo case that opened this chapter. However, very few of the millions of state cases ever reach a federal judge—as these cases all did.

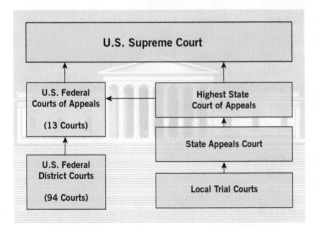

● **Figure 13.3** *Organization of the US federal courts system.*

Judicial Selection

Do you think you might like to become a state judge? There are surprisingly few formal criteria for selection. You may not even need a law degree: twenty-two states require no formal training before judges start hearing cases. Most judges do first make their name as lawyers, though many come from government or academic positions. If you plan to lobby a governor to ensure your judicial appointment, make sure you pick the right state: only seventeen states authorize their governor to select judges, and two leave selection to the state legislature. Most states (thirty-one) elect judges. Judges' terms range, depending on the state, from two to fourteen years, and these are usually renewable.

The idea of electing judges is controversial. After all, the courts are meant to be above partisan politics, protecting rights and weighing evidence separate from political pressures. Elections, say the critics, undermine the courts' ability to stand up to a majority intent on denying the rights of the minority. Moreover, campaign contributions could lead to bias and even corruption on the state benches. Former Supreme Court justice Sandra Day O'Connor has been an especially vocal critic of the political pressures that encroach on elected judges; she calls the campaigns "tawdry and embarrassing."[5] Still, the

What Do You Think?

How Should States Select Their Judges?

Which of these three arguments about judicial selection in the states seems most persuasive to you?

Let the people vote. The people are the best guardians of their own welfare. Let them decide who should be their justices. No matter how courts are organized, it is naive to think that politics can be kept out of the equation. Today, 75 percent of the public thinks that justices sometimes let their own political views influence their rulings (see Figure 13.7). Since politics is inevitable, the public should have a direct voice in judicial selection.

Appointment by a governor. A state governor (with the advice and consent of the state senate) will have valuable information about the candidates and can keep better track of which justice is doing a good job. With selection by public officials, the problems of campaigning and raising funds (with their possible corruption) will not filter into the courts.

Merit committees. Courts must be above politics. They must defend the rights of minorities and unpopular views. The only way to ensure such fairness is to let impartial merit commissions make the selection. The commission's nominees can then be voted up or down by the legislature.

Unsure. You will probably have a stronger opinion by the end of the chapter.

United States is the land of five hundred thousand elected officials. The American ideal—government by the people—leads many states to insist that judges stand directly accountable to the public. Voters tend to agree: in 2010, Nevada's voters decisively rejected a referendum that would have ended judicial elections (57 percent voted no).

Federal Courts

Federal courts hear three kinds of cases. First, they handle crimes that violate federal laws, issues that involve federal treaties, or cases touching on the Constitution. Examples range from the dramatic to the mundane: terrorism, immigration, organized crime, civil rights, patents, insider trading, or flag burning. Second, they decide disputes that spill across state lines—for example, interstate drug trafficking or conflicts between parties in different states (with at least $75,000 in dispute). Third, after state courts have ruled on a case, the parties can appeal to federal courts.

● *Judicial elections: emblem of democracy—or path to corruption?*

Most federal cases begin in one of the ninety-four **district courts**, which house just under seven hundred judges. Every state has at least one district court, and the larger states (like California and Texas) have as many as four. District courts determine the facts of the case (did John Smith try to blow up a federal building?), they build a record detailing the evidence, and they then apply the law to reach a ruling. Cases at this level are heard by a single district judge.

District courts: The first level of federal courts, which actually try the cases. Each decision is based not on a statute but on previous judicial decisions.

District court judges, like all federal judges, are appointed by the president, subject to "advice and consent" review by the Senate, and hold their office for life. Until recently, the Senate routinely approved nearly all judicial appointments, sometimes with very little scrutiny. In today's hyperpartisan Congress, however, the opposition party generally challenges judicial nominations—slowing them down in the hopes that their party will take the presidency and fill the empty seats. By the Obama administration's fourth year, a full 9 percent of the federal bench was vacant, creating an alarming backlog of cases.

Above the ninety-four district courts are thirteen federal appellate courts, known as **circuit courts**. A party that loses in district court can appeal to this next level. Three circuit court judges hear each case, usually to determine whether the district court made the correct ruling. They rule on the basis of the record established on the lower level: there is no jury and no cross-examination. Some 180 judges serve these circuit courts, collectively ruling on nearly 70,000 cases in a typical year. Like district courts, the circuit courts are organized geographically and referred to by their number: Figure 13.4 displays the current organization. Cases from Florida—like the Terri Schiavo

Circuit courts (US Court of Appeals): The second stage of federal courts, which review the trial record of cases decided in district court to ensure they were settled properly.

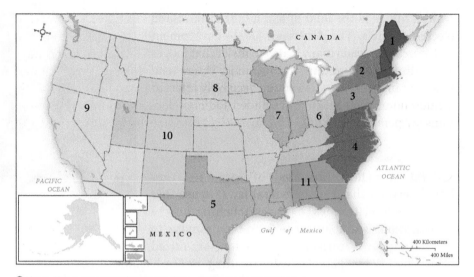

● **Figure 13.4** *A map of the federal circuit courts. (Federal Judicial Center)*

case—go to the Eleventh Circuit Court of Appeals, which is based in Atlanta. Some kinds of cases (like those involving patents or international trade) go directly to a court known as the US Court of Appeals for the Federal Circuit.

Sometimes multiple versions of a case reach different district and circuit courts. Cases challenging the Affordable Care Act as unconstitutional were filed in forty state courts across the United States. Nineteen different district courts considered the matter. On the next level, seven circuit courts eventually accepted appeals. Of these, one—the Eleventh Circuit's ruling that the individual mandate to buy insurance was unconstitutional—was ultimately heard by the Supreme Court, which issued the definitive ruling. Other cases have a more difficult time making it into federal court: for example, four different federal courts—two district, one circuit, and the Supreme Court—refused to hear an appeal to the Florida Supreme Court's decision to allow removal of Terri Schiavo's feeding tube.

Specialized Courts

The federal judiciary also includes a set of specialized courts, each covering a specific subject. These include military justice, tax disputes, and bankruptcy. In recent years bankruptcy claims have risen to more than 1.5 million annually. There is also a secret court, ruling on federal government requests to conduct electronic surveillance of suspected spies.

Judges on all these courts are appointed by the president and are subject to Senate confirmation. Unlike other federal judges, however, they do not serve for life. Bankruptcy judges, for example, serve renewable fourteen-year terms; federal magistrates, who handle certain types of civil trials, are appointed to renewable eight-year terms.

The US military runs its own separate court system, addressing breaches of justice by members of the armed forces. These courts have been a source of controversy in recent years, after President George W. Bush called for military tribunals to try defendants charged with terrorism against the United States, many of them held as "enemy combatants" in Guantánamo Bay, Abu Ghraib, or other detention centers around the globe. The Obama administration first suspended the military trials; but after Congress resisted moving the trials to civilian courts, the administration reinstated the tribunals with some changes in their rules. In rare cases, tribunals are permitted under the Constitution. The last large-scale use of military tribunals occurred after World War II, to try Nazi war criminals.

Together, these specialized courts, ranging from bankruptcy to military, constitute something of a "third judiciary" alongside state and federal courts. Periodically, critics advance proposals for a new type of special court, usually to deal with some technical area of law they believe regular citizen juries cannot handle adequately. The latest proposals focus on medical malpractice, where multimillion-dollar damage suits turn on ambiguous "medical errors." Overall, specialized courts provide a further example of the complexity characterizing the divided, fragmented US judicial branch—as Figure 13.5 vividly demonstrates.

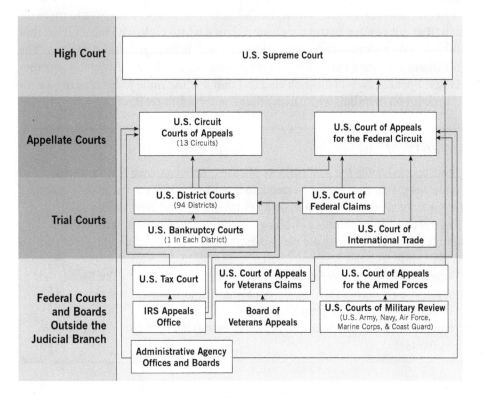

● **Figure 13.5** *Special courts within the federal system. A more detailed snapshot of the federal system illustrates that it is, in reality, far more complicated than the simple tripartite system of district, circuit, and supreme courts.*

What Do You Think?

•ₒₒ Identity on the Bench

As Justice Sotomayor's comment (below) suggests, a person's life experience can deeply inform his or her judgment about politics, culture, and other matters.

How important is it to reflect race, ethnicity, and gender in the lifetime appointments to the federal judiciary? Are there other traits—class? religion? age?—that also merit representation?

Diversity in the Federal Judiciary

Do federal judges reflect America's population? No. Just above one-quarter of judges are women, and more than 80 percent are white. Eleven percent of federal judges are African American (compared to 12.2 percent of the population), 7 percent are Hispanic (compared to 16.3 percent), and only 1 percent are Asian American (compared to 4.7 percent). Does it make a difference if the judge presiding over a federal case is female, or Latino?

Supreme Court Justice Sonia Sotomayor suggested that it did, ten years before she was appointed to the Court. "I would hope that a wise Latina woman," Sotomayor said, "with the richness of her experience would more often than not reach a better conclusion than a white male who hasn't lived that life." In other words, personal experience will inform judicial decisions. The comment provided cause for reflection—and also raised controversy. Former House Speaker Newt Gingrich claimed that a white male judge making a similar claim on behalf of white men would be forced to resign.[6]

THE BOTTOM LINE

- State courts handle the vast majority of cases. Although each state's judiciary system is distinctive, all are divided into three levels: trial courts, appeal courts, and a state supreme court. A majority of US states elect their judges.
- Federal courts rule on cases involving constitutional questions, federal laws, and federal treaties. They are divided into ninety-four district courts, eleven appeals courts, and the Supreme Court.
- Federal justices are selected by the president and confirmed by the Senate, and they hold their position for life. Party polarization in Congress has created a serious problem of unfilled judgeships.
- Numerous additional federal courts handle everything from bankruptcy to military matters.

The Courts' Role

Alexander Hamilton's assurance that the judiciary would play a minor role in American government did not last long. John Marshall, still the longest-serving chief justice in US history—he held the office from January 1801 to July 1835—helped establish the US courts as unusually powerful. How did Marshall do it?

Judicial Review

The breakthrough came in the landmark case *Marbury v. Madison*. Marshall asserted that the Supreme Court has the authority to overrule any act of Congress that violates the Constitution.

The case arose after John Adams lost the 1800 election and, during his last hours as president, made "midnight appointments" that installed his supporters in judicial positions. The new president, Thomas Jefferson, came to office with very different political views and vehemently opposed the last-minute appointments. Jefferson directed his secretary of state, James Madison, to destroy the appointment letters—including one naming William Marbury as justice of the peace for the District of Columbia. The Judiciary Act of 1789, which established the position, referred disputes directly to the Supreme Court. Marbury duly petitioned the Court and requested that it require Madison to deliver his commission. This action constituted a high-stakes early test of the Court's authority.

Marshall and his fellow justices faced a trap. On the one hand, if the Court ruled in favor of Marbury, the recently elected President Jefferson might very well ignore the Court—and diminish its importance in the new federal government. On the other hand, Marshall did not wish simply to accept President Jefferson's defiance. Marshall found an ingenious way around the dilemma—and vastly expanded the role of the Court in the process.

Led by Marshall, a unanimous Court ruled that Congress, in drafting the Judiciary Act of 1789, had erred in granting the Supreme Court the direct authority (or "original jurisdiction") to decide the question. The Constitution implied that the Supreme Court should rule on such cases only on appeal from the lower courts. However, the Constitution was silent on what would happen if Congress passed a law that clashed with the Constitution. Marshall filled in the blank with a dramatic move: "It is emphatically the province and duty" of the Court, wrote Marshall, to judge "if a law be in opposition to the Constitution." With that, Marshall established the court system's mighty power of **judicial review**—even though that authority is never mentioned in the Constitution itself.

The Court decided the case by striking down section 13 of the Judiciary Act of 1789—the section that referred cases like this one directly to the Supreme Court. Since that was the basis of Marbury's petition, the Court

Judicial review: The Court's authority to strike down acts that violate the Constitution and to interpret what the Constitution means.

ruled that it had no constitutional authority to force the administration to deliver the petition. President Jefferson opposed Marshall's clever move; he vigorously denounced the "despotism" and "oligarchy" by which unelected officials "usurp[ed]" control of the Constitution from elected ones. But what could Jefferson do? In asserting the Court's authority, Marshall had sided with the president and denied Marbury his petition. By apparently relinquishing power, Marshall permanently strengthened the federal judiciary.[7]

Marshall deftly addressed a basic issue in American government, with profound implications that reverberate in the present day. When there is doubt about what the Constitution holds or implies, the Supreme Court makes the call.[8]

Activism Versus Restraint

The Supreme Court was slow to wield the power it had asserted. It did not overrule another act of Congress for fifty-four years, until the *Dred Scott* decision struck down the Missouri Compromise and declared that black people were "so far inferior that they had no rights which the white man was bound to respect." That decision brought the issue of slavery to a boil in 1857—and established a pattern: many of the most intense disputes in American politics wind up decided in court.

Recently the judiciary has stepped up the pace with which it overrules Congress. In the 150 years following *Marbury*, it struck down just 22 federal laws; in the 21 years between 1990 and 2011, it struck down 42 acts of Congress, including acts designed to ban flag burning, guns near school yards, child pornography, and violence against women.

Today, the Supreme Court is embroiled in many intense debates: May the United States hold "enemy combatants" at Guantánamo Bay without charge or trial? May Congress limit campaign contributions? Is the right to bear arms so fundamental that it may not be curtailed by state or local governments? Does the right of privacy forbid states from banning abortions? Each of these questions was removed from the realm of public opinion, or the jurisdiction of elected officials, and settled by the Supreme Court—generally by a 5–4 vote.

The Supreme Court also reviews state and local statutes. This power required far less subtle maneuvering to establish. The Constitution's "supremacy clause" declares that "this Constitution and the laws of the United States . . . shall be the supreme Law of the Land" (article 6). The Judiciary Act of 1789, which established the federal court system (yes, the same act that created William Marbury's position) granted the Court the authority to enforce the supremacy clause and to strike down state laws that clash with the Constitution or with federal statutes. The judiciary has been more active on this level, striking down state actions at about six times the rate it overturns federal laws. Over time, federal courts have struck down more than one thousand state and local laws.

Many landmark cases struck down state laws that established segregation, outlawed abortion, or established school prayer. As the federal appeals court majority put it during the *Schiavo* case: "when the fervor of political passions moves the Executive and the Legislative branches to act in ways inimical to basic constitutional principles, it is the duty of the judiciary to intervene."[9]

The rising pace of judicial action overturning legislation leads to an enduring question: How energetic should courts be in reviewing cases? **Judicial activists** take a vigorous approach to reviewing the other branches of government; the courts must be vigilant in protecting rights. Between the 1950s and the 1970s, liberal activists were in the Supreme Court majority. The Court struck down segregation, forbade school prayer, and found a right to privacy in the penumbra (or shadow) of the Constitution (see Chapters 4 and 5 for a discussion of these cases).

> **Judicial activism:** A vigorous or active approach to reviewing the other branches of government.

Judicial restraint holds, on the contrary, that the courts should overturn the elected branches of government reluctantly and as a last resort. The terms—*activism* and *restraint*—are easily politicized. Conservatives bitterly attacked liberal judicial activism; as the courts turned conservative, however, liberals began to criticize activist judges for being eager to overrule the will of the people's representatives.

> **Judicial restraint:** Reluctance to interfere with elected branches, only doing so as a last resort.

The idea of activism is, in many ways, similar to the discussion in Chapter 2 about how to read the Constitution. Is it a living and evolving document, as the pragmatists believe? Or should we insist on going back and reconstructing the original meaning, as originalists think we should do? As we noted in Chapter 2, the difference between these positions is less stark than it might appear. The Constitution can be ambiguous; it often requires a nimble analysis to apply it to a contemporary case—as Marshall illustrated when he first asserted the right of judicial review. Even staunch originalists might very well disagree with one another about the Constitution's meaning and how it applies in any individual case.

The Judicial Process

The judiciary's role goes far beyond weighing constitutionality. Legal cases constantly raise the question of how a law should be applied in a specific dispute. The court has the job of determining legislative intent. We saw this in the last chapter, in the case of the bureaucratic rule-making process. If farm lobbyists do not like the new regulations for inspecting poultry slaughterhouses, they can go to court and claim that the regulatory agency has mistaken what Congress intended when it authorized those inspections. Ultimately, the court has to rule on what Congress meant to do—perhaps in the distant past. Because lawsuits are a regular feature of policymaking, federal courts stay very busy interpreting the intent of the other branches.

Often there is no legislative record or executive action to settle a case. The American colonists introduced an English system known as **common law**. Common law (also known as *case law*) is a system of law developed by judges

> **Common law:** A system of law developed by judges in deciding cases over the centuries.

in deciding cases over the centuries. Since legal judgments should be consistent from case to case, each time a court settles a case it sets a **precedent** that will guide similar cases in the future. Over the years, the common law offers a rich legal heritage to guide judges in settling disputes. In countries without a common law tradition, like France, judges may not rule unless there is a statute or regulation to guide them.

American courts hear two different kinds of cases. **Civil law** handles cases between two parties. William Marbury sues James Madison for his commission; a young man sues his Catholic diocese because a priest molested him; a major corporation sues a local pizza chain for borrowing its corporate logo. **Criminal law** involves cases where someone is charged with doing something prohibited by the government.

The party who complains—Marbury, the man who was molested, or the government coming down on an alleged criminal—is called the **plaintiff**; the party that is sued is the **defendant**. In court cases, the plaintiff is listed first and the defendant second; thus, the case is called *Marbury* (the plaintiff) *versus Madison* (the secretary of state who did not deliver the commission).

Precedent: Judicial decisions that offer a guide to similar cases in the future.

Civil law: Cases that involve disputes between two parties.

Criminal law: Cases in which someone is charged with breaking the law.

Plaintiff: The party that brings the action in a lawsuit.

Defendant: The party that is sued in a court case.

Too Much Power? . . . or Still the "Least Dangerous" Branch?

Keep in mind the key question about the Court: Should nine unelected, lifetime appointees wield this much power in a twenty-first-century democracy? Although the courts are undeniably powerful, every institution faces limits.

The courts operate with four different kinds of restraints.

First, the federal courts have *no electoral base*. Their prestige and mystique are balanced by a lack of democratic authority. This has made some past courts careful about confronting elected officials. For example, the Supreme Court delayed the ruling in *Brown v. Board of Education* (striking down segregated schools) for almost two years while the justices struggled to reach unanimity. Chief Justice Earl Warren felt that such an important case—challenging segregation laws across many states—should have the backing of all nine members.

Second, courts have relatively *limited resources* compared to other units of government. The judicial branch commands small budgets.

Third, courts are by definition *reactive decision makers*. Executive-branch agencies or legislators can tackle problems and devise solutions. Courts await disputes; cases must come to them. True, most major issues do wind up before the courts—but, unlike the other branches, they do not define the problem or shape the question that is being disputed.

Finally, the courts must rely on other branches for *enforcement*. Judges rules. Other actors—in and out of government—implement the decision. The Supreme Court could strike down school desegregation; it could not, however, enforce the decision, which was blocked for years by intransigent state and local officials. President Andrew Jackson made the point dramatically. When the Supreme Court struck down a Georgia law governing relations with the Cherokees, he reputedly said, of the chief justice: "John Marshall has made his decision, now let him enforce it."[10]

THE BOTTOM LINE

- Chief Justice John Marshall asserted the Court's authority to review acts of Congress for their fit with the Constitution in *Marbury v. Madison*. The Judiciary Act of 1789 authorized the Court to review state laws.
- The Court has not often struck down acts of Congress, but it began to do so at a quicker pace beginning in the 1990s.
- There are two general approaches toward defining the courts' role in government: *activists* believe in a vigorous judiciary scrutinizing the other branches; judicial *restraint* holds that courts should intervene rarely and reluctantly.
- The vital overarching question remains the same one that Chief Justice Marshall and President Jefferson crossed swords over more than two centuries ago: is the Court acting in ways that are indispensable for democracy? Or in ways that threaten it?

The Supreme Court and How It Operates

Tucked away at the top of the majestic marble Supreme Court building on East Capitol Street, among all the justices' offices and conference rooms and libraries lined with leather law books, is . . . a small basketball court. Known as the "highest court in the land," the court is used exclusively by Supreme Court insiders: the justices' clerks, both current and former; a few staff members; and occasionally one of the justices joins a game. We can imagine the basketball court as symbolic of the Supreme Court itself: exclusive, little known, and open to a tiny membership on a lifetime basis. The basketball court is open for play except when the Court is hearing oral arguments.

Hearing Cases

The Supreme Court is in session for approximately nine months each year, by tradition opening on the first Monday in October. The justices are generally out of public view, except when the Court meets to hear *oral arguments*—the presentation of a case that the Court has agreed to review. Arguments are usually scheduled on Monday, Tuesday, and Wednesday mornings. If you are visiting Washington, DC, on a day when oral arguments are occurring, do attend. These fascinating sessions are free and open to the public, on a first-come, first-served

● *A formal portrait of the Supreme Court. Standing, from left: Sotomayor, Breyer, Alito, Kagan. Seated: Thomas, Scalia, Roberts, Kennedy, Ginsburg.*

see for yourself 13.1

Go online to listen to oral arguments on the Obama health care plan.

Amicus curiae: A brief submitted by a person or group that is not a direct party to the case.

Rule of four: The requirement that at least four Supreme Court judges must agree to hear a case before it comes before the Court.

basis. (We recommend that you get to the Court early to wait in line and bring something to read—perhaps this book!)

Supreme Court oral arguments do not resemble the courtroom scenes on TV. Rather than dramatic arguments by lawyers to juries, or fierce cross-examination of witnesses, the Supreme Court features justices as the sole audience: no jury is present, and no witnesses are called. Any case that the Supreme Court agrees to hear has already been thoroughly aired by at least one lower court, except in rare instances. Normally, cases are heard in one hour, and each side's lawyer—called "counsel" in Court-speak (whether it is one lawyer or many)—is granted thirty minutes to make his or her best argument.

Before the hearing, the parties submit written briefs spelling out the details of their argument. Other interested parties may submit their own briefs, endorsing the side they favor. The outside contributions are known as ***amicus curiae*** (Latin for "friend of the court") briefs.

Are oral arguments important? Perhaps not. Justice Clarence Thomas told one interviewer that they influence his colleagues "in five or ten percent of the cases, maybe, and I'm being generous there." Chief Justice John Roberts added in a lecture, "The judges are debating among themselves and just using the lawyers as a blackboard."[11] What matters far more are the written briefs that the counsel submit.

Selecting Cases: Formal Requirements

How do the justices decide which cases to hear? Losing parties in lower courts are permitted, depending on the nature of the case, to file a petition with the Supreme Court—stating the facts of the case and setting out detailed arguments as to why the Court should hear the case. At least four judges have to vote to hear a case for it to make it to the Supreme Court; that requirement is known as the **rule of four**.

When the justices agree to hear a case, the Supreme Court issues a *writ of certiorari* (legal-speak for "to be informed") demanding the official record from the lower court that heard the case. Roughly eight thousand petitions are filed with the Supreme Court each year, and some eighty are accepted—barely 1 percent. How do cases make it into that elite group? That remains one of the great mysteries of American government. The Court never gives any formal explanation for why it decided to grant certiorari to this case and not that one.

Formally, a case must meet three conditions before it is even eligible for the Supreme Court—or any other court, for these requirements apply at all judicial levels. The case must involve a *legitimate controversy*—that is, an actual dispute between two parties. Supreme Court justices do not deal with hypothetical matters; no court offers "advisory opinions."

● *Crowds gather to demonstrate for and against the Affordable Care Act ("Obamacare") as the Supreme Court deliberates on the matter. Frequent demonstrations reflect the politicization of the Court.*

Second, the parties bringing a case must have *standing*: they must prove an actual harm (or imminent harm) to receive a hearing. Merely being distressed or concerned about a far-off environmental disaster's effect is not enough to bring a lawsuit, for example; you must prove that the oil spill or pollutant is directly affecting your livelihood (or your health or your property).

Finally, if the Court's proceedings will no longer affect the issue at hand, it is considered *moot*—irrelevant—and the case is thrown out. A famous example comes in *Roe v. Wade*, where a federal district court dismissed the case as moot because the plaintiff, "Jane Roe" (real name: Norma McCorvey), had already delivered her child. The Supreme Court rejected this view, noting that the typical length of legal appeals processes meant that pregnancies would usually conclude too soon for a court decision to be reached.

see for yourself 13.2

Additional oral arguments for the Obama health care plan.

Conference Sessions and Written Decisions

What do the justices do when they are not on the bench, hearing oral arguments? There is plenty of work to occupy them. Justices keep busy writing opinions (usually with substantial assistance from their clerks, who prepare drafts and discuss details with their boss); deciding which cases to hear in the future; and reading briefs for upcoming oral arguments. And, most intriguing of all, the justices meet in conference.

Justices discuss the cases recently heard in oral argument, indicating their voting preferences, and the chief justice assigns the job of writing the **majority opinion** in each decided case. This is the official statement of the Court. Any justice who wishes to can issue a **concurrent opinion**, explaining why he or she voted in favor of the majority outcome—different justices come to the same opinion for different reasons. Justices who disagree about

Majority opinion: The official statement of the court.

Concurrent opinion: A statement that agrees with the majority opinion.

Dissent: A statement on behalf of the justices who voted in the minority.

● *To Bork: To turn down a competent nominee for political reasons. Justice Robert Bork was a conservative nominee rejected by the Senate in 1987.*

● *Elena Kagan's confirmation hearing in 2010. Today, hearings are major events on the Washington political calendar.*

the outcome write a **dissent** indicating why they voted against the majority. Some dissents become celebrated after the fact—or form the basis for future rethinking of the issues by the Court.

Confirmation Battles

Given the lifetime tenure and the immense influence often wielded by the Supreme Court justices, one of the most significant moments on the American political calendar is the appointment of a new justice. Confirmation hearings have become unusually heated, with strong partisanship apparent both in Senate Judiciary Committee hearings on a nominee and among a wide range of interested groups across the US population.

THE BOTTOM LINE

- The Supreme Court generally hears cases on the basis of petitions requesting a review of lower-court decisions. Four justices have to vote to hear a case before it becomes part of the 1 percent that come before the Court.
- To be heard in federal court, a case must meet criteria involving: controversy, standing, and mootness. Other factors that make it more likely that the case will be heard include the scope of the question, a clash between lower courts, the justices' own interests, and requests from the solicitor general.
- Cases involve oral arguments, written briefs, and conferences with only the justices present. The chief justice assigns a majority opinion; others write concurring or dissenting opinions for the record.
- Confirmation to the federal bench—and especially to the Supreme Court—was once a polite affair that largely involved questions of competence. Today, confirmations are some of the most politically charged dates on the political calendar. This discord raises an important question: How does the charged politics that surrounds the Court affect its own workings—and its standing with the public?

JUDGE	APPOINTED BY (PRESIDENT)	SELECTED FROM	YEAR	SENATE VOTE		PUBLIC OPINION*		
				YES	NO	YES	NO	NO OPINION
Elena Kagan	Obama	U.S. Solicitor General	2010	63	37	44	34	22
Sonia Sotomayor	Obama	US Court of Appeals	2009	68	31	56	36	9
Samuel Alito	G. W. Bush	US Court of Appeals	2006	58	42	54	30	16
John Roberts	G. W. Bush	US Court of Appeals	2005	78	22	60	26	14
Stephen Breyer	Clinton	US Court of Appeals	1994	87	9	—	—	—
Ruth Bader Ginsburg	Clinton	US Court of Appeals	1993	96	3	53	14	33
Clarence Thomas	G. H. W. Bush	US Court of Appeals	1991	52	48	58	30	12
Robert Bork	Reagan	US Court of Appeals	1987	42	58	38	35	26
Anthony Kennedy	Reagan	US Court of Appeals	1988	97	0	—	—	—
Antonin Scalia	Reagan	US Court of Appeals	1986	98	0	—	—	—
*Results of Gallup Poll, when available.								

● **Figure 13.6** *Supreme Court nominations and confirmations. Nomination votes have gotten closer. Before the Bork appointment, qualified justices were easily confirmed. Notice that both Kennedy (a moderate) and Scalia (a conservative) won unanimously. After Bork, unanimous votes disappear and the hearings have gotten more contentious. Debates become especially heated when a swing vote is up for replacement. It is much easier to replace a liberal with a liberal or a conservative with a conservative.*

● Judicial Decision-Making and Reform

How do judges reach their decisions in a case? Social scientists emphasize four different perspectives.

The Role of Law

In theory, justices decide cases on the basis of the legal facts as laid out in the documents submitted. They read the law, consider the intent of those who framed the law, and place it in the context of the Constitution.

According to long-established principle, justices generally abide by previously decided cases. This is known as **stare decisis** (literally, "stand by the

Stare decisis: Deciding cases on the basis of previous rulings or precedents.

things decided"). Occasionally (but rarely), the Supreme Court concludes that the precedents were wrongly decided and overrules a past decision. In general, however, legal theory suggests that the Supreme Court rules on the facts, guided by precedent. As Chief Justice John Roberts put it at his confirmation hearing, "Judges are like umpires. Umpires don't make the rules; they apply them. . . . My job is to call balls and strikes."[12]

The umpire metaphor is appealing. However, legal cases are very often ambiguous. Applying the Constitution, 235 or more years later, is rarely simple or straightforward. Political scientists who analyze Supreme Court decisions have found another perspective with a good deal of analytic power.

Ideology and Partisanship

Ideology provides another guide to the judicial mind. Political scientists have generally found that the justices' beliefs are the most powerful predictor of how they will vote, especially on the difficult cases. Some studies look at the party identification of the justices; others at their ideology prior to confirmation; and still others at the views of the presidents who appointed them. No matter how ideology is measured, one study after another suggests a very strong relationship between the justices' beliefs and their votes. In brief, we can predict the justices' votes, over time, with considerable accuracy, based on their political orientation.[13]

The idea that the Court often rules on the basis of politics poses a dilemma for the logic of American government. The Court is designed to stand above

● **Figure 13.7** *Most think justices' ideology plays a role in decision making. Scholarly analysis generally backs up this popular opinion. (Kaiser Family Foundation)*

In General

Do you think the Supreme Court justices usually decide their cases based on legal analysis without regard to politics and ideology, or do you think they sometimes let their own ideological views influence their decisions?

17% Usually decide cases based on legal analysis
9% Don't know/Refused
75% Sometimes let own ideological views influence decisions

In Case Challenging Affordable Care Act's Mandate

In ruling on this case, do you think the Supreme Court justices will base their decision on legal analysis without regard to ideology or politics, or do you think they will let their own ideological views influence their decision?

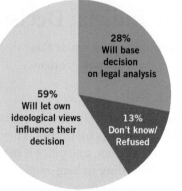

28% Will base decision on legal analysis
13% Don't know/Refused
59% Will let own ideological views influence their decision

politics. That they rule on the basis of political ideology—and are widely seen as doing so—raises a problem for the legitimacy of this powerful institution. This is precisely what John Paul Stevens predicted would happen when the court stopped the recount in Florida with its *Bush v. Gore* decision (decided 5–4, along the predictable partisan lines).

Collegiality and Peer Pressure

Collegiality, or more bluntly *peer pressure*, is a third factor that shapes decisions. Supreme Court justices (in fact, all federal court judges) spend a lot of time together, hearing cases and discussing their decisions. They exert some influence on one another's outlook and decision-making.

Another angle on the idea of "peer pressure" arises from the larger legal community. A few hundred people—law professors, law students, legal bloggers, congressional members, committee staff on the House and Senate Judiciary Committees, interest group activists—make up the attentive audience for most judicial decisions. The audience's judgment about a specific judicial opinion can be laudatory or scathing. Harvard law professor Frederick Schauer demonstrated that judges—especially Supreme Court justices, the most scrutinized of all judicial figures—seem to notice. Analyzing a large dataset of Court decisions, Schauer found that "judicial reputation" played an important part in explaining why justices moved left or right on an ideological scale during their service on the Court.[14]

Institutional Concerns

Finally, justices sometimes appear to think about the interests of the Court as an institution. They spend many years on the bench and are aware of the outside forces that might affect the standing of the Court—public opinion, a hostile Congress, or a skeptical executive. We saw a prime example in the early years of our nation with *Marbury v. Madison*. Marshall was thinking about the role and standing of his institution as he crafted his complicated opinion. Some recent studies underscore the importance of this perspective.[15]

THE BOTTOM LINE

- Four different perspectives help explain how justices make their decisions.
- First, we should pay attention to their own explanation: they follow precedent and the facts of the case.
- Political scientists are more likely to find that ideology is the best predictor in the long run. Recently, the public has also taken this view. It poses a dilemma for American governance: an institution designed to be above politics is increasingly seen as essentially political. That perception has helped turn confirmation hearings volatile.
- Two final factors also play a role: collegiality and institutional protection.

Nineteen Cases You Should Know

The history of American court cases includes a long list of famous—and occasionally infamous—decisions, from *Marbury v. Madison* forward. Here we list nineteen cases, organized chronologically, that every student of American government should be familiar with, to help you understand our political system and the impact of the judiciary.

1. *Marbury v. Madison* (1803)

Without Marshall's momentous decision, we might not have judicial review—or courts so deeply engaged in US government and policymaking. You read about this one earlier in this chapter.

2. *McCullough v. Maryland* (1819)

James William McCullough was an obscure clerk who worked for the Baltimore branch of the National Bank of the United States. The state of Maryland levied an annual tax on all banks "not chartered by the state" of Maryland; at the time the National Bank was the only one. On behalf of the bank, McCullough refused to pay the Maryland tax and sued. The Maryland Supreme Court ruled against McCullough, arguing that the Constitution said nothing about establishing a bank—the national bank was unconstitutional in the first place.

Taking a loose interpretation of the Constitution (rather than a strict construction that would have limited Congress to doing only what was explicitly allowed), Chief Justice Marshall upheld the constitutionality of the bank. Marshall argued that Congress had every right to establish a national bank under the Constitution's necessary and proper clause (which, as you saw in Chapter 2, authorizes Congress to do anything that is "necessary and proper" for "carrying into execution" the powers it was granted).

Furthermore, declared the Court, Maryland was forbidden to tax the national bank. "The power to tax," declared Marshall for the unanimous majority, "involves the power to destroy."[16] The states had no such power over federal institutions since the collective American citizenry had established a national government with the Constitution's ratification. The Court's action affirmed the federal government's superiority to state governments in all specific instances named by the Constitution; this decision marked a significant advance toward American nationhood.

● *Daniel Webster argued 223 cases before the Supreme Court, including* McCullough v. Maryland *and* Dartmouth College v. Woodward. *He would go on to become one of the outstanding senators in American history.*

3. *Dartmouth College v. Woodward* (1819)

New Hampshire's legislature sought to extend control over the college, effectively converting it from a private to a public institution. The Court's decision—again written by Marshall—reaffirmed Dartmouth's private charter; Marshall redefined contracts as transactions involving private property rights (rather than "political relations between the government and its citizens"). The Court extended contract rights to private corporations, providing a foundation for free enterprise as we know it today.

4. *Dred Scott v. Sandford* (1857—discussed in Chapter 4)

As tensions mounted over the spread of slavery into the West, Chief Justice Roger Taney inserted the Supreme Court squarely into the middle of the debate. Writing for a 7–2 Court majority, Taney ruled that Dred Scott, a Missouri slave who was taken to a free state and later back to Missouri, was still a slave.

The Court went on to rule that Congress did not have the power to prohibit slavery in the territories. The bottom line: slavery could not be restricted in any western territory.[17] Many constitutional historians choose *Dred Scott* as the worst Supreme Court decision in American history.

5. *Santa Clara Co. v. Southern Pacific Railroad* (1886)

Santa Clara Co. v. Southern Pacific Railroad was a routine tax case, decided unanimously without much notice—but it reverberates through our politics today. California had forbidden corporations from deducting their debts from their taxable property. The Court ruled that California had acted improperly, because corporations should be treated as persons and afforded the Fourteenth Amendment right of equal protection. The case established a precedent—later expanded—that enhanced the power of corporations. The bottom line: *Santa Clara* set a precedent that, with time, gave corporations all the legal benefits of individual citizens.

6. *Plessy v. Ferguson* (1896—see Chapter 5)

The Civil War resulted in freedoms for black Americans. After a turbulent period of "Reconstruction," the South (followed, if less blatantly, by other sections of the United States) set about reasserting second-class status for African Americans. Across the region, state legislatures passed explicit laws mandating segregated facilities.

One 1890 Louisiana statute, "Law 111," required (among other restrictions) that railroads maintain separate cars for black and white ticket holders. Homer Plessy deliberately challenged the law by refusing to move to the "colored car" on an East Louisiana Railroad train. The case eventually reached the Supreme Court, where Plessy's lawyers argued that

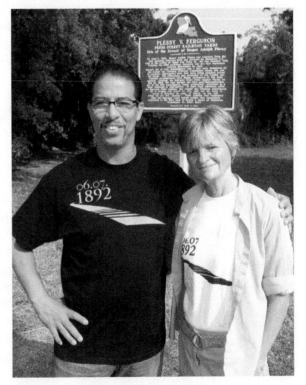

● *Keith Plessy and Phoebe Ferguson, descendants of the two men named in the famous case, have become friends and formed a foundation to promote new and innovative ways to study civil rights. As their own experience testifies, the battle for civil rights is passed on from generation to generation. Now, it is in your hands.*

see for yourself 13.3

Go online to see a discussion of the *Plessy* case.

the segregation violated his Fourteenth Amendment rights. (Remember that the Fourteenth Amendment guaranteed to all Americans "equal protection under the law.") The Court rejected Plessy's argument and upheld Louisiana's law, cementing the infamous doctrine of "separate but equal" for nearly sixty years (until *Brown v. Board of Education*). The decision permitted racial segregation, and in the next ten years the Jim Crow system went firmly into place with the Supreme Court's blessing.

7. *Lochner v. New York* (1905)

The rise of mass industry and manufacturing in the late nineteenth century bred strong demands for worker protection. Several states passed laws limiting working hours and banning child labor. New York State's worker protections, passed in 1897, included a "Bakeshop Act" that prohibited anyone from working more than ten hours a day, or sixty hours a week, in a bakery.

Joseph Lochner, a bakery owner in Utica, was fined for requiring employees to exceed the sixty-hour weekly limit. He took his case to court, insisting that the Fourteenth Amendment protected his right to establish free contracts with his workers, independent of state influence.

Two New York courts denied Lochner's appeals. In a 7–2 ruling, the Supreme Court reversed the New York decisions, holding that the Bakeshop Act was an invalid exercise of the state's power. The decision ushered in a thirty-year **Lochner era**, during which courts repeatedly struck down state economic and labor regulations, including minimum-wage laws, in the name of individual economic liberty. Governments could not interfere with the private right to contract by introducing worker protections.

Lochner era: A period from 1905 to 1937, when the Supreme Court struck down laws (like worker protection or minimum wage) that were thought to infringe on economic liberty or the right to contract.

8. *Muller v. Oregon* (1908)

Oregon limited the number of hours women could work. Whereas Lochner ruled that the state could not regulate men's hours, this case found that women were different from men. The Court ruled that "the difference between the sexes does . . . justify a different rule respecting a restriction of the hours of labor." It went on to say that the concern about "healthy mothers" justified the state intervention.

The case is particularly important for gender readings of the law. Yes, women won labor protections, but notice how: the case supported the idea that a woman was different from a man and, more to the point, that her role as childbearer and mother was more important than her role as worker.

9. *Schenck v. United States* (1919—discussed in Chapter 4)

Charles Schenck, the secretary of the US Socialist Party, printed and distributed leaflets expressing opposition to a US military draft in World War I. Schenck was convicted under the Espionage Act of aiding the enemy during wartime. Insisting that he was exercising his First Amendment free speech rights, Schenck took his appeal to the Supreme Court.

For the first time, the Court formally marked out boundaries around protected speech: as Holmes wrote, words presenting a "clear and present danger" were legitimate subjects of legislative prohibitions. The **clear and present danger** test guided the court for fifty years—it was rewritten in 1969. (Recall that a "test" is a general principle designed to guide future court decisions on a topic.)

Clear and present danger: Court doctrine that permits restrictions of free speech if officials believe that the speech will lead to prohibited action like violence or terrorism.

10. *National Labor Relations Board v. Jones and Laughlin Steel Corporation* (1937)

Jones and Laughlin was the nation's fourth-largest manufacturer of steel—an industry that had very aggressively opposed unions. The company fired ten workers who tried to unionize and was sued by the labor board for violating the Wagner Act (of 1935), which protects the right to unionize. The company responded that the Wagner Act violated the Constitution. The lower courts both agreed that precedent was on the company's side.

In a 5–4 decision, Chief Justice Charles Evans Hughes reversed the lower-court decisions and held that Congress had the power, under interstate commerce, to regulate the company's treatment of its workers. This decision broadly expanded congressional power to regulate economic matters.

Along with another case, *West Coast Hotel Company v. Parrish* (also decided 5–4 in 1937), the courts now permitted legislatures to regulate relations between business and workers. The cases meant the end of the "Lochner era."

● *Fred Korematsu refused to enter a Japanese internment camp. Today his lifelong fight on behalf of civil liberties is commemorated by the "Fred Korematsu Day of Civil Liberties and the Constitution."*

11. *Korematsu v. US* (1944)

During World War II, President Roosevelt's executive order forced Japanese Americans out of their homes and into hastily constructed internment camps. Fred Korematsu, a California native, was arrested for defying the order. The Court ruled 6–3 that the need to defend against espionage during wartime justified the order—and its violation of equal protection. The case was one of the first to use the **strict scrutiny** of government actions: the Court is primed to strike down any law that singles out a race or ethnicity unless there is a very strong reason for doing so (see Chapter 5 for discussion). In this case, the Court ruled, the government's action met the standards of strict scrutiny. The case has become infamous for its mistreatment of Japanese Americans.

Strict scrutiny: The tendency to strike down as unconstitutional any legislation that singles out race or ethnicity unless the government has a compelling interest in such legislation.

12. *Everson v. Board of Education* (1947)

Recall from Chapter 2 that the First Amendment erects what Thomas Jefferson termed a "wall of separation" between church and state.

Arch Everson, a New Jersey resident, sued the state for its policy of reimbursing the costs of public school transport to parents of both public and private school children. Because nearly all the private schools were Catholic, Everson argued that the reimbursement constituted government support, violating the establishment clause.

Everson lost his argument in New Jersey's courts; in a 5–4 decision, the US Supreme Court agreed. While a "wall of separation" had to remain, wrote Justice Hugo Black for the majority, the reimbursement was constitutionally acceptable because it was offered to all students, whether or not they practiced a religion.

Even though *Everson* permitted the New Jersey reimbursement, it forbade any action that might seem to favor religion. The decision eventually led courts to ban Christmas scenes from public parks and the Ten Commandments from courtrooms.

13. *Brown v. Board of Education* (1954—discussed in Chapter 2 and Chapter 5)

This landmark decision, decided unanimously, declared that segregating schools for black and white children violated the equal protection clause of the Fourteenth Amendment. As Supreme Court Justice Earl Warren put it, "separate schools are inherently unequal." The decision boosted the civil rights movement and led the way to an end to legal segregation. It overturned *Plessy v. Ferguson*, described above.

14. *Mapp v. Ohio* (1961—discussed in Chapter 4)

Cleveland police received a tip in 1959 that local resident Dollree Mapp was harboring a suspected bombing fugitive, and they swarmed her house without a search warrant. The police found no fugitive—but did find obscene material, at the time legally forbidden in Ohio. Mapp was arrested and convicted. She appealed. The Supreme Court reversed her conviction and, drawing on the Fourth Amendment (prohibiting unreasonable searches and seizures), devised the "exclusionary rule"—illegally obtained evidence cannot be admitted in a criminal trial. The Roberts Court has recently rolled back the exclusionary rule.

15. *Gideon v. Wainwright* (1963—see Chapter 5)

Perhaps you've read *Gideon's Trumpet*. If so, you'll never forget the story of Clarence Gideon, accused (unjustly, as it eventually was proved) of a minor theft from a Florida pool hall. Lacking funds to hire a defense attorney, Gideon represented himself at his trial—relatively common practice into the early 1960s. He was swiftly convicted, but he appealed his sentence based on the state's failure to provide a competent defense lawyer.

The Supreme Court held that Gideon was wrongly convicted, and ordered a new trial. The *Gideon* legacy: anyone charged with a serious criminal offense has the right to an attorney. Moreover, the state must provide a lawyer to any defendant unable to afford legal counsel. *Gideon* was the first in a series of landmark judicial decisions upholding the rights of defendants in criminal proceedings, including the so-called *Miranda rights* to counsel during police questioning. Recently, the Court has strengthened the right to counsel, holding that it applies to plea bargain cases where a defendant is offered a deal: plead guilty, avoid a trial, and receive a lighter sentence.

16. *Roe v. Wade* (1973—discussed in Chapter 4)

The *Roe v. Wade* decision, written by Justice Harry Blackmun, struck down a Texas statute outlawing abortion—and expanded the personal right to privacy under the Constitution. The right to privacy, wrote Blackmun, is "fundamental" and "broad enough to encompass a woman's decision whether or not to terminate her pregnancy." The *Roe* decision—since qualified by other cases discussed in Chapter 4—remains one of the great dividing lines in American politics and a "litmus test" for most federal judicial nominations.

17. *US v. Nixon* (1974)

This case revolved around the **Watergate scandal** and the white-hot political debate that ensued. President Nixon refused to turn over audiotapes of White House conversations, along with other requested materials, to the special prosecutor investigating Watergate, on the ground of "executive privilege," a sweeping claim of presidential immunity. In a unanimous 8–0 decision, Chief Justice Warren Burger (appointed by Nixon five years before) upheld the doctrine of executive privilege but concluded that presidents could not invoke it

Watergate scandal: A failed effort by Republican operatives to break into Democratic Party headquarters in the Watergate office complex in Washington, DC; tapes revealed that President Nixon attempted to cover up the event—costing him the presidency.

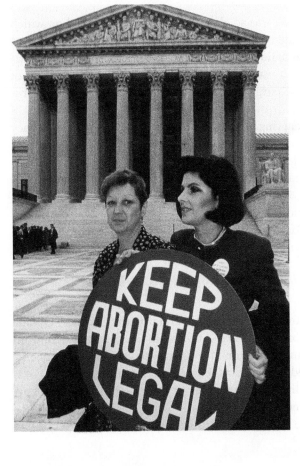

● *Norma McCorvey (at left in photo), the woman known as Jane* Roe *in* Roe v. Wade. *McCorvey later converted to Catholicism and became a pro-life activist.*

What Do You Think?

Name Another Landmark Case

Why didn't we take our list to a nice round number? To leave room for your choice. Think about the many cases we have already discussed in this book. Then pick one that you would add to the list: What would it be?

Hint: Some cases that are frequently seen as landmark cases include *Citizens United* (striking down campaign finance legislation, discussed in Chapter 8), *Miranda* (the right to remain silent, Chapter 4), *Tinker* (student free speech, Chapter 4), *Bakke* (affirmative action, Chapter 5), *Arizona v. United States* (on state authority over immigration control, Chapter 3) or . . . now it is your turn. Choose a case, add it to the list, and explain why you consider it a landmark.

see for yourself 13.4

Go online to listen to the Supreme Court oral argument for *Bush v. Gore* (2000).

in criminal cases to withhold evidence. Nixon acquiesced—and resigned as president a month later.

18. *Bush v. Gore* (2000)

The 2000 presidential election was so close that the results hinged on which candidate would win the state of Florida. High drama surrounded a recount of some of Florida's disputed ballots, stretching well past the November 7 election. On December 8, Florida's supreme court ordered a manual recount of ballots in selected districts; George W. Bush's lawyers, fearing this would result in an advantage for Vice President Gore, appealed the decision to the US Supreme Court. The Court, acting with unusual speed because of the urgency of the issue—a presidential election hung in the balance—halted the recount the very next day. Two days later, on December 11, the Court scheduled time to hear from both side's lawyers. Less than twenty-four hours later, Chief Justice Rehnquist handed down a 5–4 ruling that no constitutionally valid recount could be completed by Florida's December 12 deadline for certifying election results. The long presidential contest of 2000 was over. George Bush won Florida's twenty-five electoral votes and, with them, the presidential election.

19. *National Federation of Independent Business v. Sebelius* (2012)

This blockbuster decision took on two controversial features of the Obama administration health reform law. The Affordable Care Act required all Americans to buy health insurance or face a fine (paid with their income taxes); it also expanded Medicaid, a joint federal and state program, to cover all Americans under sixty-five who were poor or near poor (the federal government would pay 90 percent of the costs).

Can the federal government require individuals to carry health insurance? Proponents said yes: Congress has the power to regulate interstate commerce (see case number 10, above, *NLRB v. Jones and Laughlin*). Chief Justice Roberts and the four conservative justices ruled that Congress does *not* have the power under interstate commerce to require that people buy health insurance. Then, very dramatically, the chief justice broke with the conservatives and ruled that Congress does have the power to tax—and this is a tax. The Obama reform was upheld. However, Roberts got Supreme Court watchers buzzing. Conservatives have long wanted to curtail the congressional use of interstate commerce. Was Roberts handing conservative jurisprudence a victory—perhaps a return to the Lochner era that conservatives have been calling for—even while upholding the Obama health care law? Time will tell.

In the other part of the case, the Court ruled 7–2 that Congress could not change the rules of the Medicaid program and require states to expand their Medicaid program. It could only offer the funds and encourage the states to participate. Was this, wondered analysts, a new rollback of the federal government's power over federalism? Again, future cases will tell. The true scope of a case like this often takes years to reveal itself.

● **Figure 13.8** *Honesty/ethical standards of various professions. (Gallup)*

● Reforming the Judiciary

Americans hold a decidedly mixed view of the judicial branch. We go to court more frequently than most nations. But we are dubious about the legal system in general and give poor reviews to its main actors: lawyers, juries, and (increasingly) justices.

An independent judiciary has deep roots, in both our colonial English heritage and in the classical liberal tradition (as you saw in Chapter 1). Yet despite its appetite for litigation, the public also expresses deep concerns about our legal system. Those worries have been growing in recent years. Four common critiques include the high cost of litigation, the legal system's perceived bias against the less powerful, expanding judicial authority, and the possibility of corruption.

Ideas for Reform: More Resources

Given this national love-hate relationship, many suggestions for improving the judiciary have been advanced. One of the most prominent reform proposals would grant the courts more resources.

Key actors in the US judicial system talk about a "quiet crisis" in the American judiciary, stemming from an increasing difficulty in attracting top legal and political talent to seek judgeships. One reason is a long-term decline in judges' pay, which has fallen dramatically relative to that of other professionals inside and outside the legal system. Figure 13.9 compares federal district court judges' average salary to that of law professors and law-school deans, across a forty-year period. As you can see, judges in 1969 made substantially more than their academic counterparts at Harvard, the highest-paying law school. Today they make half as much as senior professors—and barely a third as much as deans.

Academics are at the lower end of the legal world's salary spectrum. Brand-new lawyers who work for law firms in large US cities earn more in their first year of practice than most experienced federal district judges. If smart law school graduates are discouraged from seeking judgeships because they can make much more elsewhere, the system is in trouble. Chief Justice Roberts has warned that "if judicial appointment ceases to be the capstone of a distinguished career and instead becomes a stepping stone to a lucrative position in private practice, the framers' goal of a truly independent judiciary will be placed in serious jeopardy."[18]

The US court system runs on a very small budget, relative to other governing institutions—much smaller than the private sector's. Many state courts are staggering under the burden of cases—and coping with strategies like pushing through plea bargains in the vast majority of criminal cases. As we saw in Chapter 4, public defenders have impossible caseloads consisting of hundreds of cases. The tensions of underfunding run throughout the court system. If court decisions are reshaping American policy and government, perhaps courts should receive more resources. On the federal level, it may even be worth thinking about developing a research capacity to evaluate the potential impact of court rulings.

Term Limits

Large public majorities (and increasing numbers of legal academics) express support for the idea of judicial term limits.[19] In a broad sense, limiting federal judges' terms—to fifteen or eighteen years, the two most commonly proposed periods—helps address the fear of "unelected judges" ruling without any brake on their decisions. Judicial term limits would greatly reduce the high level of contention around judicial appointments, especially to the Supreme Court. It would wipe away the prospect that a forty-year-old justice will sit on the bench for three decades or more—which now provokes enormous political battles. It would still keep the Court insulated from political tumult—eighteen years is a long time—while providing for a regular circulation of new judges with fresh perspectives. One version of this proposal would permit the president to nominate a Supreme Court justice every two years so the Court would always have a balance of new ideas and experienced hands.

"Life tenure" takes on a different meaning in modern times, when healthy adults remain productive into their eighties. When the Constitution was ratified in 1789, the typical adult life span was closer to sixty years. Between 1789 and 1970, the average term a justice served on the Supreme Court was just under 15 years. Since 1970, that figure has nearly doubled, to 28.5 years.

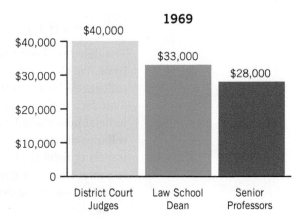

Data based on information received from Harvard Law School; Professors' salaries based on a 9-month teaching schedule.

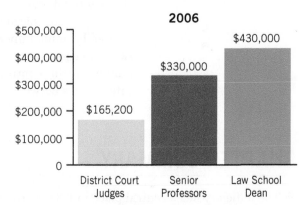

Based on informal and confidential survey of law school administrators and most recent available data. Professors' salaries based on 11-month teaching/research schedule.

● **Figure 13.9** *Falling judicial salaries, compared to law school figures. (Administrative Office of the US Courts/Federal Judiciary)*

THE BOTTOM LINE

- The courts face four popular criticisms: cost, bias, power, and corruption.
- *Reform proposal #1:* Direct more resources to the judicial branch—in both the state and federal courts.
- *Reform proposal #2:* Introduce term limits to the federal bench. Supreme Court justices would serve eighteen years, a time frame permitting each president a judicial nomination every two years.

🔵 Conclusion: Democracy and the Courts

The debates about the judiciary's proper influence in a democracy will continue. We have seen in this chapter that US courts wield an unusual amount of influence—far more than courts in most other nations, perhaps too much in a modern democratic society. We have also seen that there are clear limits to judicial power—from the reactive nature of the judicial process to the courts' reliance on others to implement decisions. Perhaps expanding resources and imposing term limits would modernize the courts and enhance their ability to serve American government by doing what they do at their best: faithfully reflecting—and consistently enforcing—the constitutional rules that guide our public life.

Reforms can only go so far. The powerful role of the courts in a democracy will always be vexing for a simple reason: the courts are designed to serve as a check, ultimately, on "We, the People." The courts, when they are acting properly, stop the people and their representatives from violating the Constitution or from harming minority rights. However, as the steady parade of 5–4 decisions discussed in this chapter indicates, what exactly the Constitution means is often a highly controversial matter. As a result, the courts always face a delicate balance between enforcing the Constitution (as a majority on the Court sees it) and deferring to democracy (and the majority of the country).

CHAPTER SUMMARY

🔵 The judiciary has a central place in US government and politics—as well as in our legalistic national culture.

🔵 Americans express uneasiness about their judicial system, despite their faith in the rule of law. This dichotomy leads to a complex dynamic: respect for judges and their rulings on the one hand, concerns that the legal system is biased and too costly on the other.

🔵 Compared to other advanced democratic nations, US courts possess a great deal of influence over our politics and government. This owes primarily to the power of judicial review, asserted long ago by Chief Justice John Marshall. Once again, Americans found a way to separate and fragment power—continuing the work begun in the Constitution.

🔵 Alongside their uncommon influence, courts are hemmed in by restrictions like limited resources, stare decisis requirements, and their lack of an electoral base (at the federal level).

🔵 The judiciary has affected a vast range of areas through its Constitution-interpreting authority, from religion and race to economic regulations and even presidential election outcomes. This impact is evident through a set of landmark cases—each of which typically arouses great controversy, leading to renewed calls for limits on judicial activism. Originalist and pragmatist schools have very different views of what constitutes such "activism."

🔵 The Supreme Court marks the pinnacle of judicial—and constitutional—authority in the United States. Its operations, often carried out behind closed doors, are the subject of fascinated speculation: How do nine justices decide? The leading theories: they follow the rule of law; they are guided by their ideology; they are moved by peer pressure; and they are concerned about the institution of the courts.

● Given the combination of the power of the courts and Americans' uncertainty about how it should be wielded, a set of reforms is put forth each year. Two in particular deserve careful attention: whether federal judges' current life terms should be limited, and whether the judiciary's expansive responsibilities should be rewarded with more resources—especially to continue attracting our finest legal minds to judgeships.

KEY TERMS

Amicus curiae, 480
Appellate courts, 463
Circuit courts (also known as US Court of Appeals), 471
Civil law, 478
Clear and present danger, 489
Common law, 477
Concurrent opinion, 481

Criminal law, 478
Defendant, 478
Dissent, 481
District courts, 471
Judicial activism, 477
Judicial restraint, 477
Judicial review, 475
Litigation, 466

Lochner era, 488
Majority opinion, 481
Mediation, 466
Plaintiff, 478
Precedent, 478
Rule of four, 480
Stare decisis, 483
Strict scrutiny, 489

STUDY QUESTIONS

1. Should the judiciary have less power in American government and politics? How would you propose to restrain judicial authority in practice?
2. The Supreme Court is currently 33 percent women, around the same proportion as women in other federal courts (district and circuit). Does that seem unjustly low to you, given that women make up nearly 52 percent of the US population? What about the fact that none of the nine justices is Protestant, in a country that is around 51 percent Protestant? Should we care about the religious preferences of Supreme Court justices?
3. Do Supreme Court clerks—and other federal judges' clerks—have too much influence, given their relatively young ages? Should they serve for longer than one year, given the importance of the work they do?
4. Should we mandate more transparency for judicial operations? Televise Supreme Court oral arguments, for example? Require that Court conferences be transcribed and publicized? Are there any benefits to the secrecy that characterizes the federal judiciary?
5. Do either of the reforms raised in this chapter appeal to you? Why or why not? Might they be most successful if offered as a package? (Term limits, appealing to critics of judicial activism, combined with higher judicial pay and more resources for the courts, which might make term limits palatable to current and future judges.)
6. Should the federal judiciary be the last line of defense in protecting Americans' constitutional rights and liberties? Why or why not? And if not, what other institution or group of people should have this responsibility? Be specific: How would another actor or group protect rights and liberties better than federal judges, and ultimately the Supreme Court, do today?

14

Domestic and Foreign Policy

SUMMER 2011 was unusually hot in Washington, DC, and partisan tempers were flaring. President Obama had proposed an increase in the **debt ceiling**, a dollar-figure cap (currently around $16.4 trillion) on US borrowing. Congressional approval is required to raise the ceiling, which allows the Treasury Department to cover spending on everything from Social Security checks to the war in Afghanistan. Over the past four decades, such requests have been granted more than seventy times, under both Democratic and Republican presidents.

This time, however, many House and Senate Republicans refused to go along with the debt-ceiling increase. Long negotiating sessions, stretching through July, ended in recriminations and finger pointing. Officials around the globe warned that inaction threatened US default on its fiscal obligations, a potential calamity. Finally, on July 31, a deal was struck—but too late for nervous financial markets. A few days later, an independent agency reduced America's credit rating. Stock prices plunged around the world, threatening the fragile global economic recovery.

The president and Congress were debating not just a number but *what government should do.* In other words, they were debating public policy. Exchanges like these about policy decisions have far-reaching implications, affecting tens of millions of Americans and many more millions around the world. Policy debates also return to this book's familiar chapter-opening question: *Who are we?*

Perhaps Americans are best described in terms of the policies we enact—and those that we reject or abandon. Why do we seize privately owned land to protect spotted owls and flying squirrels? Provide expansive military support to anti-government rebels in Libya but not in Syria? Imprison one in nine young black men? Closely regulate sex but not violence in movies? Keep secret the details of drone strikes against America's enemies? These and thousands of other policy decisions contribute to the kaleidoscopic portrait of who we are.

All the actors introduced in this book—interest groups, Congress, the media, executive-branch officials, military leaders and diplomats, the courts, and

Debt ceiling: A congressionally mandated limit on how much the national government can borrow to finance federal spending.

● *President Obama and House Speaker Boehner attempt to reach a deal on the debt-ceiling impasse in 2011. Though a temporary solution was eventually reached, by 2013 the issue had cropped up again—threatening to paralyze Washington once more.*

BY THE NUMBERS *US Domestic and Foreign Policy*

Number of laws passed, 112th Congress (Jan. 2011–Jan. 2013): **283**
Number of laws passed, 80th Congress (Jan. 1947–Jan. 1949; labelled the "Do-Nothing Congress" by President Truman): **906**

Number of new rulemaking proposals initiated, 2010: **2,920**
Total number of federal agencies, departments, and boards engaged in rulemaking: **277**
Percentage of proposed federal rules required by OMB to include cost-benefit analysis, 2011: **94**

Fiscal year 2012 US federal budget deficit: **$1,316,000,000,000**
Spending on Social Security, Medicare, and Medicaid in FY 2012:
$2,124,000,000,000
Percentage reduction in the deficit if Congress cut all nondefense discretionary spending: **2.2**

US military spending as percentage of all the military spending in the world: **55**
Percentage spent by China: **6**
Percentage spent by Russia: **4**

Percentage of US federal budget spent for defense, 1960: **52**
Percentage in 2012: **19**

more—come together to make public policy. We will see how government officials craft our domestic and foreign policies.

● Public Policymaking in Five (Not-So-Easy) Stages

Policies often take the form of laws, but they can also be regulations, presidential executive orders, funding formulas (determining who gets how much), informal norms, or action plans. Think of an issue you care about: clean drinking water, infant mortality, or protection against terrorist acts. All these, like every political issue reaching government officials' attention, play out through public policymaking—whether in controlling waterborne pollutants, encouraging prenatal care and mandating safe infant delivery rooms, or devising effective antiterrorism efforts.

Recall the seven basic American political ideas we explored in Chapter 1. For example, consider *limited government* or *self-rule*: both are at stake whenever we launch new domestic or international programs that expand federal government authority. At the same time, Americans' sense of *equality* is embedded in a whole range of policies, from low tax rates on investment income to welfare rules requiring recipients to find work.

There are five stages to the policy process. Figure 14.1 displays the stages graphically. We will organize our trip through the public policy system by exploring each of these in turn.

1. Agenda Setting

Policymaking doesn't begin in earnest until public officials recognize that something is a problem worthy of government attention. Beginning in the late 1980s, for example, American obesity rates increased rapidly. Physicians and some public health workers tried to respond, but only after more than a decade did obesity become an item on the **policy agenda**. Though no single actor writes the agenda down formally in one place, as we saw in Chapter 7, a combination of media coverage, attention, and legislative proposals from members of Congress and the executive branch indicate that a topic is prominent enough to be considered part of the national agenda.

In the case of obesity, that change came about after the public release of a series of maps charting the rise in obesity rates among adults, portrayed state by state and year by year, issued early in 2000 by the Centers for Disease Control and Prevention (CDC). The public's widespread attention to obesity affirmed the maps' release as a **"focusing event,"** as defined by political scientist John Kingdon.

Policy agenda: The issues that the media covers, the public considers important, and politicians address. Setting the agenda is the first step in political action.

Focusing event: A major happening, often of crisis or disaster proportions, that attracts widespread media attention to an issue.

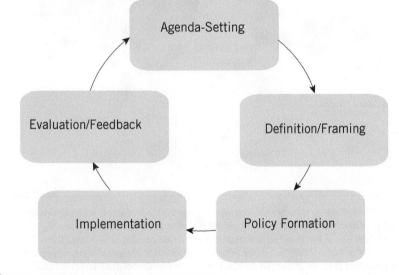

● **Figure 14.1** *The five stages of domestic policymaking.*

The obesity maps (see Figure 14.2) appeared on CBS News and quickly went viral. Within a few weeks policy makers across the country were discussing ways to address rising obesity, especially among children. Obesity, like other issues that achieve agenda status, was widely discussed, often in alarmed terms. National agenda items are the policy topics that we dispute at the dinner table, that trend on Twitter, and that you discuss in class.

Whether deliberate plans (like obesity maps) or dramatic accidents (like the Deepwater Horizon oil-platform explosion you read about in Chapter 6), focusing events are critical to shaping policy agendas. Those agendas are typically the source of fierce competition, since the policy system can emphasize only a few priorities at any given time.

2. Framing

In translating agenda items into proposed policy solutions, questions arise. What are the root causes of the problem? How bad a problem *is* this? How should public officials respond, if at all? Most agenda issues involve such questions of framing (which we discussed in Chapter 7); the answers are far from obvious, and they can differ greatly depending on who is making the argument.

Let's consider an example from education policy. As Table 14.1 displays, American secondary school students continue to lag behind counterparts from many other advanced countries in science, math, and reading tests. When the latest round of results was released, school performance dominated

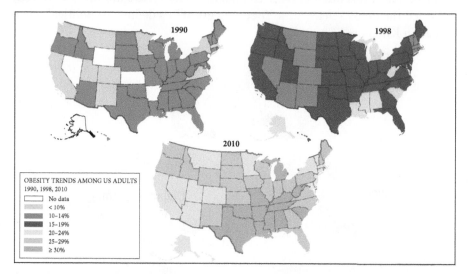

● **Figure 14.2** *Growth of obesity, state by state. This summary displays the swift growth in average obesity rates across the 50 US states. In 1990, no state had 15 percent or more of its adults considered obese. Eight years later, nearly all states were in the 15–20 percent range, and several (tan color) had passed the 20 percent mark. And a dozen years after that, in 2010, tan was the best that the nine states with lowest obesity rates could boast; at least that many had topped the 30 percent mark. (Centers for Disease Control and Prevention, 2010)*

Table 14.1 Framing School Education Policies: Poor US Student Performance

Top ten countries and the United States in overall scores for reading, math, and science in 2009*					
READING	OECD AVERAGE SCORE: 493	MATH	AVG. 496	SCIENCE	AVG. 501
1. Shanghai-China	556	Shanghai-China	600	Shanghai-China	575
2. South Korea	539	Singapore	562	Finland	554
3. Finland	536	Hong Kong-China	555	Hong Kong-China	549
4. Hong Kong-China	533	South Korea	546	Singapore	542
5. Singapore	526	Taiwan	543	Japan	539
6. Canada	524	Finland	541	South Korea	538
7. New Zealand	521	Liechtenstein	536	New Zealand	532
8. Japan	520	Switzerland	534	Canada	529
9. Australia	515	Japan	529	Estonia	528
10. Netherlands	508	Canada	527	Australia	527
17. United States	**500**	**31. United States**	**487**	**23. United States**	**502**

*Testing is done every three years.
Source: Highlights from PISA 2009: Performance of U.S. 15-Year-Old Students in Reading, Mathematics, and Science Literacy in an International Context, *Washington DC, National Center for Education Statistics, publication 2011004, 2010.*

local and national policy agendas. Parents, teachers, and businesses anxious to hire well-trained employees in a globally competitive market all agreed: scores had to improve. That goal merely placed the issue on the agenda. Then disputes about defining the problem began. Was it that American kids were poorly prepared for the tests, compared to children in other countries? Or that many US classrooms were overcrowded, with too few teachers to provide pupils with personalized instruction? Were officials in the Department of Education better positioned to address the problem of mediocre test scores, or should solutions come from the local level, where children attend school?

On and on the discussion raged, along familiar lines. Federal officials had no official say in education policy until the mid-1960s, when Congress established an extensive program of national funding through the Elementary and Secondary Education Act. The US Department of Education wasn't created until 1979. Champions of local control of education have fought to limit federal activity ever since. In the 2012 presidential primary, Republican candidates unanimously insisted that the Department of Education was a big part of the problem. To them, it had to be restructured—or shut down altogether. In its place, several of the GOP candidates and their allies offered policy solutions like **school vouchers**, long popular among conservatives. Other conservative thinkers, along with some moderates, supported **charter schools**. These public-private hybrids, usually without unionized teachers, are often generously funded by private donors. In this view, the less the federal government is involved, the better.

Progressives and moderate Democrats instead insisted that national education officials had to step in to reduce inequities in school financing, so that the richest districts in a state—able to provide more resources—do not leave schoolchildren in lower-income areas far behind. Many Democrats supported the Obama administration's "Race to the Top" initiative, which awards federal support to states with promising plans for public school improvement. They also favored expansion of federal programs like Head Start, designed to help lower-income children perform well through individualized instruction in their early years.

National or local? Charter schools and vouchers or government programs like Head Start? Would progressive solutions reduce inequity or mostly amount to federal government "meddling"? Do conservative solutions address poor instruction—due, some insist, to unionized teachers allowed to remain in classrooms despite poor results—or are they an unjustified assault on public schools? These different ways of "framing" issues, also called problem definition, have big consequences: they help determine which policy responses the government considers. As issues are framed and reframed, policy actors translate their preferred solutions into law, propelling policymaking to a third stage.

3. Policy Formation

After a problem reaches the policy agenda, and struggles to define it settle into one or two primary frames, proposed solutions must be evaluated—and adopted or discarded. This process of policy formation is again a sprawling, complicated one. Members of Congress and, often, state and local legislators engage in the myriad activities you studied in Chapter 10: drafting bills, holding hearings, and hammering out compromises in committee meetings and floor debates. Executive-branch experts weigh in, all the way up to the president if the issue is sufficiently high-profile. Advocacy groups and industry lobbyists swarm around lawmakers, judicial rulings reshape the policy debate, and media experts opine through print, broadcast, the blogosphere, and Twitter.

Analyzing Policy, *Ex Ante*.   Competing ideas, rhetorical displays, deft procedural moves, power plays: these features underpin policy formation in every society, as they have for hundreds of years. Recently, more technical work has also become vital to policy success. Policy analysis involves constructing scientific measures of a proposed policy's costs and benefits *ex ante*—before it passes and

School voucher: A cash payment that enables children to apply to private schools, sometimes outside their immediate neighborhood.

Charter school: A privately run school under town or city supervision; usually free to public school children who qualify for admission.

● *Educational reform: the lighter side. Programs like Head Start, No Child Left Behind, and Race to the Top respond to education policy makers' worries about US students' performance—which can be exaggerated, as captured in this humorous cartoon.*

goes into effect. This is a central feature of contemporary policymaking in the United States and other advanced industrial nations.

A relatively straightforward approach to analyzing a proposed policy involves **cost-effectiveness** studies. Here, analysts compare several policy alternatives that deliver the same overall benefit. Thus they can measure which one does so at the *lowest cost*. Let's say a local government decides to repaint the town hall. Different painting companies bid for the job. Presumably they all provide the same basic service, perhaps with minor differences in paint color or warranty. City officials can compare these similar vendors based on proposed costs alone, and ask which provides the most cost-effective service.

> **Cost effectiveness:** The projected costs of a proposed policy, as revealed by a relatively simple study.

Not many policy decisions are that straightforward, however, especially when they reach the national agenda. In 2008, a commission appointed by then-president Bush recommended a hike in the federal gasoline tax, both to pay for highway maintenance and to reduce Americans' oil consumption. Since 1993, the national gas tax has remained at 18.4 cents per gallon, after slowly rising over the preceding sixty years from a penny per gallon. To illuminate the likely effects of this policy shift—and to help estimate the range of an ideal tax increase—experts performed a **cost-benefit analysis**. This elaborate form of *ex ante* evaluation is carried out by trained analysts, some of them working in government and others in academia, lobbying firms, or think tanks.

> **Cost-benefit analysis:** A more complex study of the projected costs and benefits associated with a proposed policy.

The primary costs and benefits of a gas-tax increase are listed in Table 14.2. Once such a list is clear, analysts then estimate dollar values for each of the main costs and benefits, using a complicated formula. Sample results for the gas tax are shown in Table 14.3.

From Cost-Benefit Analysis to Politics.   Cost-benefit and other *ex ante* evaluations are widely used in policymaking, with significant impact on both legislative votes and judicial decisions. They alone, however, do not determine policy. In the gas tax example, lawmakers from both parties recognized that a hefty tax hike would arouse furious opposition. Instead, some congressional Democrats proposed a phased-in sequence of higher gas taxes, rising incrementally from

Table 14.2 Gas Tax Costs/Benefits

GAS TAX COSTS
• Direct cost of the tax to drivers (those in rural areas, and with lower incomes, are hardest hit)
• Higher price of services dependent on transportation, like shipping goods by truck
GAS TAX BENEFITS
• Reduced urban air pollution (thereby improving public health)
• Reduced CO_2 emissions (slowing the pace of climate change)
• Reduced US dependence on imported oil
• Diminished traffic congestion (saving drivers' time)
• Reduced traffic accidents (because people drive less or switch to mass transit)

18.4 cents to 40 cents per gallon by 2014. This policy was set aside during the debate over the Affordable Care Act (ACA), which stretched from summer 2009 into March 2010; once Congress returned to the gas tax issue, 2010 midterm elections were approaching. Democrats, fearing the electoral penalty of any tax increase they advocated, quietly abandoned the plan. Political considerations routinely trump even a clearly positive policy analysis.

4. Policy Implementation

With a new law on the books, policymaking passes to the implementation stage. As you read in Chapter 12, this process is not so visible or well

Table 14.3 Cost-Benefit Valuation of a Proposed Gas Tax

COSTS OF GAS TAX	VALUE*	BENEFITS OF GAS TAX	VALUE*
• Direct cost to drivers	$0.23	• Public health (air pollution)	$0.40
• Transportation services	$0.52	• Climate (CO_2 emissions)	$0.11
		• Reduced oil imports	$0.12
		• Time saved (less traffic)	$0.58
		• Reduced accidents	$0.55
TOTAL	**$0.75**		**$1.76**
*Values are estimated per gallon of gas. Source: Authors' calculation, combining several existing models.			

understood. During policy formation, televised congressional hearings, action-urging White House speeches, and cliff-hanger House and Senate floor votes keep the attentive public engaged. Afterward, however, the glare of media attention moves on. Implementing national policies is primarily handled by the executive bureaucracy, which labors mostly out of public view. Does this shift in visibility mean that the work of policy implementation is less politicized? Many American political thinkers and actors have agreed, dating back at least to Woodrow Wilson, who as a political scientist in 1887 described bureaucratic activity as "a technical science." Wilson insisted that "administrative questions are not political questions."[1]

As Wilson learned upon becoming president thirty years later, implementing public policy is in fact a highly political event. Implementation involves two main steps: working out the specifics of the law, primarily through the rulemaking process introduced in Chapter 12, and then delivering the government services or enforcing the new regulations. Both these steps attract intense interest—and, inevitably, political fighting—from the communities most affected by the policy change.

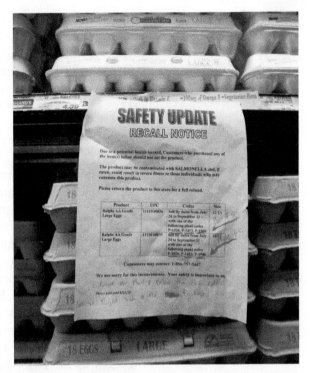

● *Tainted food and top-down policy response. When reports are received about possibly dangerous tainted food products, the Food and Drug Administration, along with the Department of Agriculture, spearheads a national top-down response.*

Rulemaking Revisited.   Once the Affordable Care Act (ACA) passed in late March 2010, the national health bureaucracy went to work. The Department of Health and Human Services (HHS) quietly established a "war room," comprising a few dozen staffers dedicated to ACA rulemaking. Their task: translating the act's often vague language into a blueprint for putting health reform into effect. Remember, each aspect of a new law requires a separate rule, and each rule requires a wealth of detail, painstakingly spelled out. For example, one part of the law mandates that dependents up to age twenty-six remain eligible for health insurance through their parents; the previous cutoff age was eighteen, or twenty-one for students enrolled in college. In the ACA as written by Congress, this requirement took only a couple of sentences. However, the HHS rule specifying details—who was eligible, under what circumstances, penalties for violation, and so forth—ran to more than twenty-five single-spaced, tiny-print pages in the *Federal Register*.[2]

Top-Down Delivery.   Once the final rule setting out a policy's details has been reviewed and published, it is time to provide the benefits or regulations that the law was designed to achieve. As American national government stepped up its level of domestic policy activity following World War II, delivery of public services was established as a "top-down" process. Confident in the wake of victory, American and British architects of the new science of public policy proclaimed that the executive branch, working from clear goals and strategies, could deliver government services in a coherent, transparent manner. They saw cabinet secretaries and agency heads as firmly in charge of the process. Lower-level bureaucrats and "policy clients" (the people government was serving) were mainly concerned with *compliance*, or doing what they were told to do.

Many policy planners still promote this top-down model of delivering government benefits and services. It can work when a policy is relatively simple, with clear, well-specified goals that are not difficult to meet. Imagine a national ban on sales of a food product found to be tainted by potentially fatal bacteria, for example. A high-ranking figure, like the secretary of agriculture or head of the Food and Drug Administration, issues a public warning. Government inspectors then ensure that the dangerous product is removed from grocery shelves, law-enforcement officials investigate the cause of the outbreak, and prosecutions may follow. The public's role is simple: avoid the tainted product. The policy aim is clear, as are the lines of authority.

Bottom-Up Delivery. For complicated policies, "bottom-up" provision of public services or regulations can be more effective than top-down efforts to command and control outcomes. Bottom-up service delivery starts with **street-level bureaucrats**, who work directly with recipients of government benefits. Examples include the social worker who calls on needy families to make sure their food stamps have arrived; the IRS agent who checks to confirm that your charitable claims are all legitimate donations; or the air-traffic controller who brings your flight in for a safe landing. All these policy providers and regulators work directly with the public, and they can exercise discretion in making decisions. Certainly a hierarchy is still in place, with cabinet secretaries and agency heads at the top. But when street-level officials are allowed a measure of autonomy, or at least some input into decision making, government services are often delivered more efficiently and regulations are put in place with less disruption. Sometimes, these street-level actors may even ignore superiors' orders and do what they consider best, based on experience.

Street-level bureaucrats: Government officials who deal directly with the public.

5. Policy Evaluation and Feedback

Let's imagine that a policy problem has made it onto the agenda and been framed successfully. A solution has been formulated, passed into law, and implemented: the new service is being delivered or regulation put in place. Do these accomplishments mean our policymaking story has ended? Not at all. It is still essential to confirm whether a new benefit or regulation actually works.

This is the stage of policy evaluation. Does a program need tweaking in practice because its benefits are not reaching many people? Should we abandon an ineffective regulation and try something else? Moreover, nearly every policy of significance, once adopted, "feeds back" into the policy process, shaping public agendas. Sometimes that feedback process creates new policy problems in turn. In short, policymaking never really ends.

Policymaking proceeds in a context of uncertainty: even armed with *ex ante* analyses, no one can be sure how a policy will play out in practice. Therefore it is essential to evaluate programs after implementation, or *ex post*, to determine how well they're working and make adjustments. The outcome may include devising yet another new policy to address changes rippling out from one recently put in place.

Ex Post Policy Evaluations

Ideally, evaluators would check every new government benefit or regulation, once in place, to see how well it works. Although, due to resource constraints, that usually does not happen, many policies are subjected to at least occasional *ex post* evaluations. These tend to follow a prescribed sequence. An evaluator compares a policy program to the original goals that Congress and executive-branch rule makers had in mind, according to an established set of criteria. The evaluator could be a government agency, an academic or think tank analyst, an interest group, or a court-appointed independent authority—or sometimes all of these, as prominent programs often attract multiple evaluations. The evaluator collects and assesses relevant information, using data where available, makes a judgment about program effectiveness, and issues recommendations.

Do these steps sound like a reasonably objective effort? If a policy is performing more or less in line with its designers' goals, it should be left alone. If not, a good *ex post* evaluation will point out places where the policy could be tweaked to improve performance. But rarely is policymaking that straightforward.

When a law is first drafted, advocates fight hard to frame the policy change positively, advance it through Congress, and win the president's signature. Many of them remain engaged during the rulemaking process to make sure it is rolled out as they expected. Now imagine an *ex post* evaluation that suggests the policy is not working so well. These supporters probably will not agree that all their energy was misspent. Instead, they may criticize the evaluation for flawed methodology and commission a competing evaluation. Similarly, in the face of a positive evaluation, the opposition—which fought against the new policy, all the way from framing to rulemaking—rarely gives up and admits that its criticisms were wrong.

New policies, once implemented, do not just play out in a vacuum. They in turn shape and constrain future policymaking, as a growing body of political science research shows. This is the process scholars term "policy feedback."

A program that distributes benefits will attract loyal supporters, who push for its extension. Lawmakers seeking to reform or cancel the program (perhaps based on an *ex post* evaluation) can find their efforts thwarted by these grateful recipients. More subtly, as a policy is rolled out, actors of various types will adapt to the policy, making it difficult to change. Bureaucrats get organized to administer a benefit; businesses rework their economic forecasts to account for a new regulatory framework. The political scientist Paul Pierson describes these tendencies as **path dependence**: once a policy is established, possibilities for reform or change are constrained by the "path" it has followed through implementation and service delivery.[3]

Path dependence: The tendency of policy makers to follow established routines in thinking about or acting on a specific topic.

A classic example of a policy with powerful feedback effects is Social Security, passed in 1935. By introducing a language of "entitlement," the designers of Social Security achieved far-reaching effects. Senior citizens feel that they have earned their right to receive old-age government benefits. Millions of Americans to this day organize their investment decisions and retirement planning around the path created by Social Security. This view makes it virtually untouchable by policy makers, even as the program has grown into a $750 billion behemoth.

THE BOTTOM LINE

- US policymaking may be described in terms of five stages. Policies do not proceed neatly from one to the next, but the "stages" idea is a useful way of distinguishing among different actions carried out by policy officials.
- The first of these is agenda setting, whereby concerns receiving widespread attention become policy issues.
- A second stage is problem definition and framing, featuring debates about how to describe an issue and which solutions are most viable.
- A third stage is policy formation, a process of legislative and executive activity to develop the policy idea in concrete terms.
- A fourth stage is policy implementation, marked by rulemaking and service delivery.
- Fifth includes evaluation and policy feedback, steps that help determine whether a policy works—and that often start the debate all over again.

US Social Policy

Public policy comes in many forms, as the various examples above attest. *Fiscal policy* has to do with matters of finance, like monetary supply and taxes; we will address fiscal matters later in this chapter, when we look at federal budgeting. *Foreign policy* covers topics like wars and defense, diplomacy, and trade agreements; we devote the next section to those. Most other issues are grouped together as *social policy*, having to do with people's individual or group well-being. Health, housing, education, employment, criminal justice, child welfare, and old-age security: all these vital areas make up social policy. Also under this heading are controversial topics like abortion, gay marriage, and recreational drug use.

Compared to industrialized western European countries, most of which developed modern social policies in the late nineteenth century, the United States was slow to adopt these at a national level. Old-age insurance, for example, was provided in Germany as far back as 1883, and in Great Britain in 1911; not until the mid-1930s and Franklin Roosevelt's New Deal was a similar policy (Social Security) established here. Many advanced democracies enacted universal health insurance starting in the 1880s; the United States still does not guarantee health care to all its citizens. Americans' embrace of self-help individualist doctrines and long-standing resistance to "big government," along with a federalist structure that provides a patchwork of benefits through state and local officials, helps explain the distinctive (and slow) growth of social policymaking in the United States.

From colonial days onward, "poor relief" offered support for needy Americans, inspired by both religious tenets and laws inherited from Elizabethan England. Benefits were limited, however—and came with a price. People on relief sometimes faced the loss of their personal property and the right to vote. The able-bodied unemployed were often forced to work or were jailed, although laws varied from state to state. Even with all these conditions, until the Civil War, poor relief was the largest single budget item in most American towns and cities.[4] And the term was still used well into the twentieth century, especially during the Great Depression.

Wars and Social Policy

Wars and their aftermath were the source of most major social policy advances during the first century and a half after the Constitution was ratified. The Revolutionary War gave rise to the earliest state-level efforts to administer organized benefits. In New York, for example, a "Committee on Superintendence of the Poor" was created to aid people who lost their homes during the fighting. In the wake of the Civil War, national government benefits flowed at unprecedented levels to soldiers and their families. The first old-age pensions were provided to Union army veterans during the late nineteenth century. Their mothers, widows, and children later received some state support, including monthly welfare payments and regulations on child labor—sons and daughters of sacrificed soldiers should not be forced to work, the argument went.

A more recent instance of a policy that grew out of wartime is the GI Bill, passed in 1944 to reward American troops returning from World War II with a heavily subsidized college education. The bill's designers expected that soldiers would benefit personally from attending college; a secondary hope was

● During the Great Depression, new federal social policies were created at a rapid clip. Traditional policies, like "poor relief," were expanded as well, in response to social need.

that US labor markets would be able to adjust slowly to millions of newly returned soldiers, as universities absorbed many of the veterans.

What policymakers did not expect is that American higher education would be transformed, as colleges and universities expanded to meet the needs of 4.4 million soldiers turned students—many of them with fewer family resources than the traditionally better-off young men and women who attended US colleges before 1945. Moreover, many GI Bill beneficiaries, political scientist Suzanne Mettler has shown, went on to become unusually civic-minded Americans.[6] College attendance continued to grow in subsequent years, aided by a host of new government programs (policy feedback again!) stretching from Pell Grants and low-interest student loans, both established in the 1960s, to the American Opportunity Tax Credit, passed in 2010 and providing an estimated $181 billion in benefits in 2012.

War's domestic equivalent is grave economic hardship, and the Great Depression starting in 1929 helped lead to more extensive federal social policies, many arising from Franklin Roosevelt's New Deal. Among the numerous social programs run or financed by the US government today, let us look at three of the longest lived and most extensive.

● The GI Bill's postwar effects: housing students on the quad. The GI Bill brought a surge of World War II veterans to college and university campuses; often, makeshift housing had to be devised, as in these temporary Quonset huts erected on the University of Wisconsin–Madison's quad in 1947.

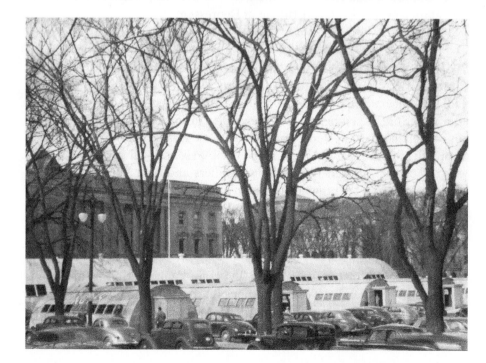

Old-Age Insurance: Social Security

Since its 1935 enactment, Social Security has provided Americans sixty-five and older—provided they
have lived in the United States at least five years—
with a monthly living stipend. The minimum age
was recently raised to sixty-six, and Congress has
discussed increasing it by another year or two. Social
Security payments vary with income: a worker who
retires making $65,000 a year would currently re-
ceive $1,609 per month. The original act also created
an unemployment insurance program (more on that
below), paid benefits to disabled workers and their
families, and offered financial assistance to low-income families with children. Financing comes from
a payroll tax on all eligible workers, today as in the
original act.

As initially passed, the Social Security Act excluded a wide range of occupations from the program, effectively limiting benefits (and payroll-tax
contributions) to white males. In subsequent years,
such jobs as teachers, nurses, domestic helpers, li-
brarians, and agricultural laborers were added to the
act's coverage, effectively creating the first universal social policy in American history. Although the
program began small—only 53,000 beneficiaries in
1937, the first full year of implementation, who to-

The first Social Security check. Ida May Fuller, the first recipient (in
1940) of a monthly retirement Social Security check, for $22.54. A legal
secretary, Fuller contributed payroll taxes to Social Security during her
last three years of employment, with contributions totaling $24.75, before
retiring at age 65. Because she lived to be 100, she received nearly
$23,000 in Social Security benefits over her remaining years.

gether received a little over $1.2 million in benefits—it grew rapidly. In 2011,
Social Security paid some $700 billion to 57 million workers, supported by
payroll taxes from 158 million employees. At around 4.5 percent of the nation's **gross domestic product** (GDP), Social Security is the largest single federal government program.

Although the old-age benefits provided by Social Security have helped
lift many seniors out of poverty, for decades alarms have been sounded about
financially supporting the program—and concerns continue today, as Social
Security moves inexorably toward a $1 trillion annual cost. Efforts to privatize
or otherwise change the system of universal contributors and beneficiaries are
routinely rejected, however. Social Security's sacrosanct status has given rise
to a colorful metaphor, borrowed from electrified train lines: touch the "third
rail" surging with electricity, and you will receive a fatal shock. Politicians refer to Social Security as the "third rail of American politics": propose major
changes, and electoral penalties will swiftly follow.

Gross domestic product:
The value of all the goods
and services produced in a
nation over a year.

Unemployment Benefits

As the Great Depression stretched into the 1930s, some 34 million Americans
(more than a quarter of the 122 million population) lived in households with

no full-time wage earner. Across the United States, unemployment rates reached shocking levels, topping out at 80 percent of able-bodied adults in Toledo, Ohio, for example. In 1932, Wisconsin became the first state to provide cash assistance to temporarily jobless residents. Three years later, the Social Security Act included a provision for joint federal-state unemployment benefits, funded like old-age insurance through a payroll tax on employees. States administer the program, with federal oversight and funding assistance.

During the recent major recession, unemployment levels rose from less than 4 percent in 2008 to above 10 percent in 2009. A federal supplement to laid-off workers extended eligibility for unemployment benefits from the twenty-six weeks that most states provide to ninety-nine weeks. Costs soared accordingly, and Republicans sought to scale back the extra federal assistance. With unemployment rates dipping only slowly through 2012, job creation—and the cost of benefits for unemployed workers—was a central issue in the presidential and congressional elections.

Health and Disability: Medicare/Medicaid

In the early 1960s America ranked as the wealthiest nation in the world, but barely half of the nation's seniors had health insurance. Even with Social Security, an estimated third of those over sixty-five lived in poverty, in significant part because of the cost of health care.

Lyndon Johnson, fresh from a landslide election victory in 1964, promoted health insurance coverage for all Americans over sixty-five as part of his Great Society plan. Critics fought hard against the proposed new social benefit. Johnson's Republican opponent in that election, Arizona senator Barry Goldwater, tapped into a long-lived American vein of disapproval for handouts: "Having given our pensioners their medical care in kind, why not food baskets, why not public housing accommodations, why not vacation resorts, why not a ration of cigarettes for those who smoke and of beer for those who drink?"[7]

After some fancy footwork in Congress, Medicare was passed in 1965, as an amendment to the Social Security Act. As with old-age and unemployment benefits, Medicare was financed through a payroll tax on all employees. And like Social Security, the program grew rapidly after it was implemented in 1966. Today some 49.4 million Americans receive Medicare benefits; by the late 2020s the program is expected to serve nearly 80 million people, as the last of the baby boomer generation (born between 1945 and 1964) retire. The program's costs currently exceed $500 billion each year and are projected to grow to nearly $750 billion by 2030.

Paying this giant tab became more difficult after 2006, when a new Congress-authorized prescription-drug benefit for seniors went into effect. Rising health care costs put constant pressure on this popular program.

As the battle over Medicare raged in 1965, a companion measure to provide health insurance to disabled and low-income people, dubbed "Medicaid," was quietly passed. Each state was encouraged (but not required) to establish a Medicaid program of its own; Arizona was the last state to sign on, in 1982. Over time, a variety of additional benefits were added to Medicaid, including dental and nursing home coverage.

Distinctive among these large American entitlement programs, Medicaid was established as a "means-tested" program, with benefits provided only to those below a certain income level—which varies by state. The Affordable Care Act (ACA) initially included a requirement that all states provide Medicaid funding to everyone whose income is below 133 percent of the **federal poverty line**. The Supreme Court's historic 2012 decision to uphold the ACA as constitutional, described in Chapter 13, also repudiated the universal Medicaid funding requirement. Instead, each state is allowed to decide whether it will adopt the 133 percent standard.

Like Social Security and Medicare, Medicaid has grown rapidly, both in the number of people it serves and the associated expense. During its early years, only a few thousand beneficiaries sought Medicaid assistance for their health care. In 2012, more than 50 million Americans received some Medicaid coverage, at a cost of more than $260 billion.

Figure 14.3 displays projected costs for Social Security, Medicaid, and Medicare in the years ahead, measured as a percentage of the expected US gross domestic product (GDP). Taken together, these **entitlement programs** will require some very tough choices about spending on other programs and about tax rates to raise the revenue required to fund them.

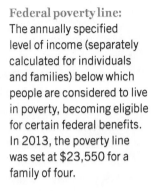

Federal poverty line: The annually specified level of income (separately calculated for individuals and families) below which people are considered to live in poverty, becoming eligible for certain federal benefits. In 2013, the poverty line was set at $23,550 for a family of four.

Entitlement program: A government benefit program whose recipients are *entitled* by law to receive payments. Social Security, Medicare, and Medicaid are the three largest.

● **Figure 14.3** *Spending on the three big entitlement programs totals a little under 9 percent of US GDP. That figure is projected to double over the next 30-plus years. That, in turn, puts significant pressure on actors to devise viable reforms. (Congressional Budget Office)*

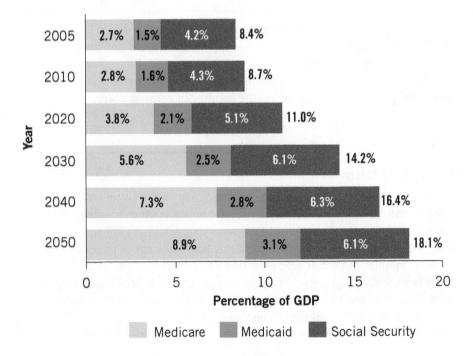

What Do You Think?

Should We Reform Social Security and Medicare?

Social Security and Medicare are perhaps the two most fiercely defended US government programs. Any hint of a cut in either and senior citizens respond vehemently, as do the House and Senate members who represent them. Are you braver than most American elected officials: Are you willing to tackle cutting Social Security and Medicare (and, while you are at it, Medicaid)?

Yes, reform Social Security and Medicare programs. The budget savings of even minor adjustments—such as raising the eligibility age—would be immense.

No, leave Social Security and Medicare intact. The political fallout would certainly be furious, but so would the impact on the lives of seniors. Suggesting such reforms could also have long-term political consequences because the opposing party would sound the alarm immediately.

Unsure. To better understand the situation, think through the reasons that seniors (like your grandparents or other over-sixty-five people you may know) would be upset to have the rules of the game changed as they come to expect health coverage and an older-age pension. Can you think of any ways to improve these programs with lesser consequences for older Americans?

On the plus side, the growth of American social policies like these has greatly reduced the number of people—especially seniors and children, arguably our most vulnerable citizens—living in dire need. Balancing those needs against the budget pressures of continued program growth is among the most important policy challenges facing the country in coming years.

THE BOTTOM LINE

- Social policymaking in the United States is typically more controversial, and features less expansive coverage, than social policies in other advanced industrial nations.
- Wars, along with severe economic downturns, have been major sources of expansions in American social policies across US history.
- Three large social programs—old-age insurance, or Social Security; unemployment insurance; and health/disability benefits, or Medicare and Medicaid—are especially significant in US politics and government.

The Federal Budget Process

"It's a good policy idea, but we just don't have the budget room to pursue it." Variations on that phrase have been repeated countless times in Washington in recent years, as American policymaking has become more oriented around the budget. This bottom-line focus owes primarily to the US **federal budget deficit**—the gap between how much our national government spends and how much we take in through taxes and fees (Figure 14.4). The defiict is currently around $900 billion, or 5.5 percent of our gross domestic product. Though a declining percentage, that figure still inspires lawmakers to search for ways to reduce spending or increase revenues to restore the budget to balance—including dramatic ideas like sequestration, or across-the-board budget cuts.

Federal budget deficit: The gap between revenues received by the national government (primarily through individual income and corporate taxes) and spending on all public programs.

Federal deficits were recently at historic highs for three main reasons. First, our most expensive trio of entitlement programs—Social Security, Medicare, and Medicaid—continue to grow rapidly. Together they now cost an annual $2.1 trillion, more than half the entire US budget. Second, US conflicts in Iraq and Afghanistan have also rung up a high cost. Although spending totals are disputed, they exceeded $400 billion each year until troops began departing in 2011.[8] Third, federal revenues declined after large tax cuts were enacted in 2001, a trend accelerated by the economic crisis beginning in September 2008, as both corporate and individual income shrank.

Can the historic deficits of recent years be reversed? To tackle budget reform, it is essential first to grasp the basics of how national government budgeting works. As we will see, much of American domestic policymaking is organized around our budget process.

Budget politics, like US policymaking more generally, progresses more or less in stages (Figure 14.5). Formally, three primary stages are established by a pair of laws: the Budget and Accounting Act of 1921, passed in an age of much smaller American national government; and the Congressional Budget and Impoundment Control Act, passed in 1974 during a time of political turmoil and economic recession. The process begins with the White House.

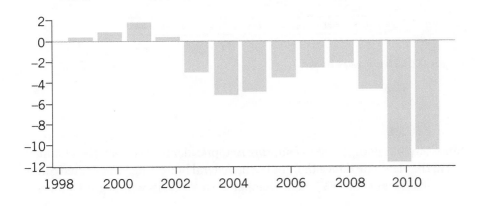

● **Figure 14.4** *US government budget (as proportion of GDP), 1998–2011. (TradingEconomics .com/US Treasury)*

● **Figure 14.5** *US federal budget process.*

Fiscal year: In budget calculations, the "new year" beginning October 1 and ending the following September 30. Organized many decades ago, for accounting purposes.

The President's Budget Proposal

Since the 1921 Budget and Accounting Act, presidents have been the first movers in the elaborate dance that makes up federal budgeting. The United States starts its **fiscal year** (FY) each October 1, so FY 2014 will begin October 1,

2013. For each approaching fiscal year, the White House is expected to submit to Congress in early February a proposed budget. This document details projected federal spending for thousands of different government programs.

The president's budget proposal lacks any statutory authority; Congress is free to ignore it completely. Its release by the White House, however, is a major event. Advocacy groups howl when funding for their pet projects is cut, and businesses jockey to minimize the costs of new regulations or taxes. Congressional committees with budget responsibilities schedule hearings to question cabinet heads and senior presidential aides, and media organizations compile helpful charts. With the president's proposal publicized, digested, and (often) repudiated by Congress—in 1996, the Senate held a symbolic vote on adopting President Clinton's budget, which was rejected 99–0—the action then shifts to Capitol Hill.

Congressional Budget Resolution

While executive-branch analysts compile figures to feed into the White House budget proposal, congressional budget experts are similarly working toward their own blueprint for spending and revenues, known as a **budget resolution**. Like the president's proposal, congressional budget resolutions are not binding laws, and they do not require a presidential signature. Instead, they provide a general "sense of Congress" about budgetary expectations and are meant to guide the committees responsible for finishing the budget during summer and fall.

Budget resolutions are less detailed than the president's several-hundred-page proposal. They set out overarching spending expectations in nineteen broad categories, known as "budget functions." Budget committees in both House and Senate, created by the 1974 budget act, carry out the bulk of this work. Each committee spends several months assembling a budget resolution, which must pass the full chamber. Senate and House versions are inevitably different, and they must be reconciled in a conference committee. The joint outcome, formally known as a "concurrent budget resolution," is supposed to be approved by April 15 of each year. Owing to political battles, these resolutions are almost always late. Over the past thirty-seven years, Congress has only six times approved a budget resolution on schedule. In 2012, for the fifth time in the past ten years, Congress was unable to pass a resolution a all. Given such a stalemate, the previous year's budget resolution remains in effect.

Budget resolution: A joint House-Senate creation that outlines targets for federal spending, revenue levels, and the resultant budget deficit (or surplus) for the coming fiscal year.

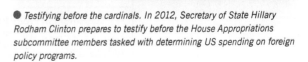

● *Testifying before the cardinals. In 2012, Secretary of State Hillary Rodham Clinton prepares to testify before the House Appropriations subcommittee members tasked with determining US spending on foreign policy programs.*

Appropriations Committee Action

As the Budget Committees prepare a resolution they hope will pass, another set of twenty-six committees—thirteen in each chamber—is hard at work filling in the specifics. How much should the State Department spend on aid to developing countries? Should we fund the Agriculture Department's full request for food-stamp spending?

Members of the Appropriations Committees make those tough decisions, program by program. Back in 1921, the US split up budget authority into thirteen separate areas. National defense is one area, for example; health, education, human services, and labor (Americans on the job) are combined into another sprawling area. Both the House and Senate Appropriations Committees are divided into thirteen subcommittees—one to handle budget planning for each area (see Table 14.4).

If everything works smoothly, each subcommittee completes its spending bill (most are several hundreds of billions of dollars) by mid-September and sends it to the president for his signature. That allows all spending to be in place for the new fiscal year, beginning October 1.

Unfortunately, budget complexities and old-fashioned political infighting mean that appropriations bills are rarely finished on time. Instead of passing appropriations bills, Congress adopts a continuing resolution to enable our

Table 14.4 Appropriations Subcommittees: Areas of Jurisdiction

• Agriculture; Food and Drug Administration
• Departments of Commerce; Justice; and State
• Department of Defense
• District of Columbia
• Energy and Water Development
• Foreign Operations
• Department of Interior
• Departments of Labor; Health and Human Services (HHS); and Education
• Legislative Branch
• Military Construction
• Department of Transportation
• Department of Treasury; US Postal Service
• Department of Housing and Urban Development; the Veterans Administration

federal government to keep functioning. All those 4.4 million workers continue the previous year's spending plan, with little opportunity to fund new programs or reassign spending to high-performing areas.

You can see how Congress is proceeding with the current fiscal year's budget by following a link for this chapter at the book's companion website. Has the budget resolution passed on time? Are appropriations bills moving at a steady pace? If the answer is no, you will know that another round of political disagreements has erupted.

You can also track the size of the US budget deficit—how much more we are spending than we take in through tax revenues and borrowed funds. Though the US has the world's largest budget deficit, as a proportion of our giant economy it is smaller than many other advanced democracies' deficits.

All big decisions are affected by the budget, because every government action has significant financial implications. And because most budget decisions have winners and losers—since more money for my program means less for yours—this is one of the most political aspects of policymaking. Who gets what, when, and how? In the United States, we make those decisions in significant part through our budget process.

Budgeting also underscores many of this book's basic lessons about politics and government. Separated powers slow the process by encouraging bargaining, battling, and compromise. The central place of economic efficiency in policymaking is reinforced by a politics organized around budgeting. Cost-benefit calculations are made in monetary terms, after all. Ultimately, budgeting involves the fundamental choices that help define how we Americans see ourselves.

THE BOTTOM LINE

- The US budget process, when on schedule, runs from early February through October 1 and encompasses a presidential proposal, concurrent budget resolution, and appropriations bills.
- In practice the process rarely runs on time, and various "fixes" like omnibus bills and continuing resolutions have been invented to keep the budget system functioning.
- Although the details can be obscure, budget battles in Washington are almost always among the most dramatic features of US policymaking because of the high stakes that are involved.

American Foreign Policy Goals

Three goals guide foreign policy—security, prosperity, and the spread of American values. These goals often clash with one another: pursuing one can mean sacrificing another. As we describe each goal, think about which seems most important to you.

● *Is global warming a security threat? Here, a polar bear family clings to a vanishing ice cap.*

Goal No. 1: Security

First, the United States must defend itself. *Security means protecting important national values from external threats.* No other nation or group can be allowed to threaten American lives or liberty. But security comes at a cost. How much should the United States spend on its military? And does protecting security require us to focus on non-military challenges like global warming or the international drug trade?

Traditional security threats have come from hostile nations. The terrorist attacks of September 11, 2001, brutally demonstrated how today's threats can come not just from other nations but from loosely organized terrorist groups like Al Qaeda, which planned the attack on the World Trade Center. In the twenty-first century, the United States faces security threats from many different directions: hostile nations, international terrorism, global warming, health pandemics, cyberwarfare, the drug trade, modern pirates, and economic meltdowns around the world.

American policy makers must decide which dangers to emphasize. Should we focus on terrorists? China's rising military power? Or is economic decline the biggest danger? Every threat requires a different approach.

Political attitudes play an important role in defining threats. Everyone worries about terrorists. However, liberals also emphasize problems that the world community faces together: global warming, health epidemics, and how poverty and injustice breed violence. Conservatives are more likely to focus on the specter of nuclear attacks by nations like Iran or North Korea, the international drug trade, and the dangers to American borders posed by illegal immigrants. Herman Cain, running for the 2012 Republican presidential nomination, drew both cheers and jeers when he proposed an electrified fence on the Mexican border with the warning "*It will kill you.*"

Goal No. 2: Prosperity

The second goal of foreign policy is to ensure prosperity. A nation's power ultimately rests not on its armies but on its economic engine.

Today, the US economy is the largest in the world—it makes up more than a fifth of the entire global economy. American foreign policy engages economic issues in a number of ways: It aids local business in developing foreign markets. It protects the energy supply and searches for alternative energy sources. It uses its wealth to reward nations with foreign aid or to punish them with economic sanctions. It supports open markets around the globe. Beneath all the activity lies a serious concern: What does America's economic future hold—growth or decline?

Free Trade. American economic policy champions **free trade**—*the idea that goods and services should move across international boundaries without government interference.* Until the twentieth century, most governments tried to protect their own industries. They slapped tariffs on foreign goods—special taxes that made imports more expensive than local products. Governments also boosted local business with subsidies and tax breaks. This favoritism is called **protectionism**, because it is designed to protect local business from foreign competition.

For the past fifty years, American policy makers have worked to break down the protectionist policies that have kept American goods and services out of other countries. A quarter of all our economic activity involves imports or exports. In theory, free trade helps consumers in every country, since it offers more choices and lower prices. If Detroit can make better cars at a lower price, consumers from Kansas to Kazakhstan should be able to buy them. In theory, once the trade barriers fall, each nation will gravitate to the kinds of industries it can produce best.

In 1994, international negotiations produced the World Trade Organization (WTO), which oversees trade discussions among nations and the resulting rules. The current round of trade talks was launched in 2001 in Doha, the capital of Qatar, in the Persian Gulf (it is therefore called the Doha Round). Officials from more than 140 countries have met annually ever since, with no agreement in sight.

Global trade talks like the Doha Round could be very beneficial to the world economy. Economists estimate the value of a successful free-trade pact that reduces trade barriers worldwide at hundreds of billions of dollars. Yet these talks have repeatedly collapsed, often when poorer countries join to veto the agreements. Why?

In 1994, the Clinton administration championed the North American Free Trade Agreement (NAFTA), which created a free trade zone spanning the United States, Canada, and Mexico. The pact passed Congress, although a majority of Democrats voted against it in both House and Senate. In 2011, the Obama administration won approval of free trade pacts with three more nations—South Korea, Panama, and Colombia. This time less than a third of the Democrats in the House voted for the agreements. The Democratic presidents had to round up Republican votes to win the agreements. Why did so many Democrats vote against free trade pacts?

Challenges to Free Trade

Every administration, every team of economic advisors, and almost every policy textbook agree: free trade makes everyone better off. However, many citizens fiercely oppose the idea. Free trade faces three challenges.

First, critics of free trade charge that it is cheaper to produce goods in nations that outlaw unions, reject safety standards, and don't worry about

Free trade: Goods and services moving across international boundaries without government interference.

Protectionism: Efforts to protect local business from foreign competition.

Fair trade: Trade that includes environmental and labor protections in agreements so nations do not get unfair advantages by exploiting workers or harming the environment.

pollution. Jobs will move to those nations. The critics suggest an alternative to free trade. **Fair trade** reduces trade barriers but, at the same time, negotiates worker protections and environmental regulations right into the trade agreements. In these ways, say proponents, the workers of all nations will compete with the same rules.

Second, free markets cause social displacement, at least in the short run. Free trade in agriculture, for example, pushes small farmers in poor nations like Nigeria off their farms and into megacities like Lagos with massive slums.

Third, as international markets have opened, they have grown volatile. In 2008, American banks invested heavily in housing mortgages and sold the investments to foreign banks. When the American housing market collapsed, the crisis flashed around the globe. Three years later, a European financial crisis bounced right back to the United States.

A Nation in Decline?   Will the United States retain its economic power? If we compare national economies, the United States certainly does not look like a country on the skids. It accounts for almost a quarter of the entire world's economic output—two and one-half times as much as China, over four times as much as Germany, and more than 163 other nations *combined* (see Figure 14.6A). Every nation uses American dollars for trade, and English has become the language of international affairs.

Although the US economy remains by far the largest, others may be catching up. Turn to economic performance over the last five years, and the winners and losers look very different (Figure 14.6B). America's growth ranked tenth among the world's fifteen largest economies. China grew more than nine times faster, Brazil five times faster, and Canada and Germany both 25 percent faster. In little more than a decade, China vaulted ahead of Japan and

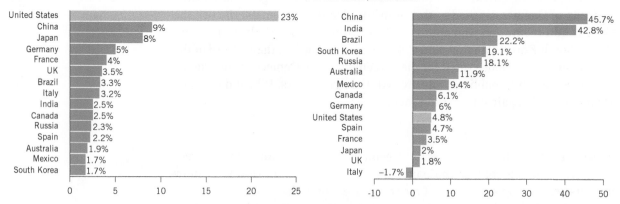

● **Figure 14.6** *World economies. A. The world's 15 largest economies. Notice that despite all the talk of decline, the US is still, by far, the largest economy. (International Monetary Fund) B. Rise in GDP, 2005–2010. However, the US has been growing more slowly than most other large economies. (World Bank)*

● *Nineteenth-century artists imagined a spirit of providential destiny that guided America. Here, America flies forward, the star of Empire on her forehead, Learning and Technology in either hand, as Native Americans and wild beasts flee before the irresistible civilization. The painting, by John Gast, was widely copied and reprinted.*

now has an economy almost 40 percent of the United States'. If that trend continues (a very big if), the United States will soon have a genuine economic rival with a large and dynamic economy.

The United States buys more from other nations than it sells to them. This imbalance, known as a **trade deficit**, has existed every year since 1975. Is it a problem that Americans import more than they export? Economists differ. Most believe that the nation cannot continue buying more from other nations than it sells to them without this eventually threatening the economy.

Some critics also worry that the United States is failing to invest in its *infrastructure*—its roads, train tracks, air terminals, and public transportation. Travelers to Asia marvel at the sleek airports and railroads. Does the Chinese growth of the past decade mean that authoritarian governments are more efficient at organizing the economy than America's democracy?

Which is it? A nation in decline? Or an entrepreneurial dynamo setting the pace for the world? You can keep your own score in the years ahead by watching just one measure of world power: the size of the American economy relative to the rest of the world.

Trade deficit: The deficit arising when a nation imports (or buys) more goods from foreign nations than it exports (or sells) to them.

Goal No. 3: Spreading American Ideals

Most people believe that every nation's foreign policy goal can be described simply: blunt self-interest. However, explaining American action only in terms of power or prosperity misses something important.

In the very first inaugural address, in 1789, President George Washington declared that the new nation had a special mission: "The sacred fire of liberty and the destiny of the republican model of government are . . . entrusted to the hands of the American people." This, he told his countrymen, might even be liberty's best and final chance.[10] From the very start, American leaders believed that the United States had a special role in the world—to champion liberty.

American leaders often justify foreign policy action in terms of promoting values such as liberty and democracy. The United States entered World War I, said President Woodrow Wilson, because "the world must be made safe for

Is America Exceptional?

Every nation is unique in many ways. But is the United States exceptional in the way that George Washington and many others have claimed?

Yes. The United States is exceptional in that it makes sacrifices to spread values like freedom and democracy around the world. It does not ignore self-interest but equates it with the spread of liberty and democracy.

No. Americans may like to think that they are acting purely on principle. But, like every nation, the United States pursues its own self-interest. It is dangerous and misleading to insist that we are helping others when, in reality, we are helping ourselves.

It depends. Americans pursue their self-interests. They also pursue values like democracy and rights. Some leaders get the balance right and are cheered around the world. Others are less effective. It depends on the leader and the situation.

democracy." America is "privileged to spend its blood," he continued, for "a universal dominion of right." Forty years later, President Jimmy Carter called for "a foreign policy that is democratic, that is based on fundamental values, and that uses power and influence . . . for humane purposes."[11]

American Exceptionalism. The belief that the United States plays a special role in world affairs is known as **American exceptionalism**.

American exceptionalism: The view that the United States is unique, marked by a distinct set of ideas such as equality, self-rule, and limited government.

Is the United States exceptional? Many American leaders believe it is "a nation like no other," as former presidential candidate Newt Gingrich put it, with "a sacred commitment" to our founding principles. Foreign observers, however, often warn that American exceptionalism is a myth, sometimes a dangerous myth. It can lead Americans to reduce complicated reality into a simple clash between good and evil.

THE BOTTOM LINE

- The first goal of American foreign policy is security, but not all policy makers agree on what are security threats.
- The second goal of foreign policy is to to protect prosperity. Economic strength is the ultimate source of power on the world stage.
- American economic policy has been guided by pursuit of free trade—the dropping of barriers to international commerce.
- The United States tries to spread its own values, of democracy and freedom—sometimes creating goodwill, at other times a backlash. This is a rare goal for a nation's foreign policy.

Foreign Policy Strategies Over Time

Ron Paul, the long-shot Republican presidential candidate in 2008 and 2012, drew whoops from supporters when he repeated his foreign policy: "America does not interfere militarily, financially, or covertly in the internal affairs of other nations. Period."[12] This statement may sound strange coming from a man who wishes to be commander in chief of the most powerful army in history, but Paul is following in the footsteps of the first commander in chief, George Washington.

Many Americans still hold this view, now known as **isolationism**—the desire to avoid interfering in other nations' affairs. In contrast, most contemporary foreign policy analysts are **internationalists**. They believe that America's interests are best protected by actively engaging the world. American leaders create an overall framework to meet the challenges of the time. Their **grand strategy** includes everything from a military doctrine to ways of seeing and interpreting the world. The United States has adopted four different grand strategies over the past century, culminating today in the fight against terror. Once the strategy is in place it can be very difficult to change—until a dramatic event breaks up the old order.

> **Isolationism:** The doctrine that a nation should not interfere in other nations' affairs and should avoid all foreign commitments and alliances.
>
> **Internationalism:** The belief that national interests are best served by actively engaging and working with other nations around the world.
>
> **Grand strategy:** An overarching vision that defines and guides a nation's foreign policy.

Strategy 1: Standing Alone (1918–1939)

World War I was horrific. The fighting bogged down into trenches in eastern France, and hundreds of thousands of men died moving the line back and forth a few miles. After Europeans on both sides had bled their armies for three years, the United States entered the war and quickly tipped the balance. In a little more than a year, the United States led England and France to victory over Germany and Austria.

President Woodrow Wilson championed a new international order after the war. The United States would spread democracy to every nation and join with other countries in a collective security organization called the League of Nations. Wilson's dream was, he said, "to correct the evil," and to "purify . . . every process of our common life."

Wilson's highly moral and multilateral vision met furious opposition. Many Americans were scornful of the European leaders who had blundered into the terrible war. Some became isolationists and wanted nothing more to do with international affairs. Many others became unilateralists. They were willing to act abroad, but only on American terms.

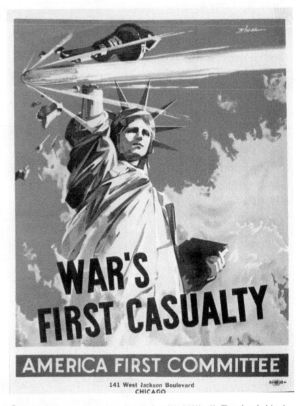

● An isolationist poster from just before World War II. The view is blunt: going to war threatens American liberty. The attitude vanished when the United States was attacked at Pearl Harbor. However, today the sentiment has returned.

If the League of Nations decided to send troops to keep the peace, Americans would not get involved unless Congress decided to do so. In November 1918 the Republicans won both houses of Congress, and they took a strong unilateral position. When President Wilson refused to compromise his multilateral approach, Congress voted down his peace treaty and refused to join the League of Nations.

In the years following World War I, American grand strategy was simple. The United States would intervene, unilaterally, only when its own interests were threatened. The United States sent ships and troops around the world—to Russia (during and after the Bolshevik Revolution), Mexico, Panama, Turkey, China, and many other places. It almost always acted independently and minded its own interests.

Strategy 2: The Cold War (1945–1991)

When World War II began in 1939, many Americans wanted nothing to do with another foreign war. "America first," they said. This position changed in

● **Figure 14.7** *Europe during the Cold War. For fifty years, American foreign policy, operating with its allies (through the North Atlantic Treaty Organization, or NATO) focused on containing the Soviet Union in its sphere. The US military prepared itself for a land war in Europe.*

December 1941, when Japan attacked the US navy base at Pearl Harbor, sank eleven ships, and killed 2,400 men. On that day, the era of standing alone ended.

Less than four years later, large swaths of Europe and Asia lay in rubble. Untiold millions of soldiers and civilians were dead (the mind-numbing estimates vary from thirty-eight million to seventy million). When the war ended, in September 1945, the only rival to the United States was the Soviet Union, whose armies occupied the nations of central Europe. Many observers warned that the Soviets were poised to extend their control. If anyone was going to lead the free world against the Soviet Union, it had to be the United States.

The Truman administration decided to accept the Soviets' current sphere of influence but to oppose every effort to expand it, a policy known as **containment**. The crucial test came in February 1947. The Democratic administration asked a Republican Congress to pour funds into Greece and Turkey to stop them from turning to Communism. Legend has it that the chair of the Foreign Relations Committee, Senator Arthur Vandenberg (R-MI), promised to support Truman but gave him a word of advice about rallying the nation: "You are going to have to scare the hell out of the American people."[13] This Truman proceeded to do in a famous speech before Congress.

While the United States retained economic and military primacy, it joined with other nations in **multilateral organizations** dedicated to opposing communism and spreading democracy and capitalism. It broke with its own past to help establish multiple organizations: the United Nations (formed in 1945), the Organization of American States (OAS, 1948), the North Atlantic Treaty

Containment: American Cold War strategy designed to stop the spread of Communism.

Multilateral organization: International body of three or more nations organized around a common goal.

● One of history's turning points: jubilant Berliners climb the Berlin Wall as Communism collapses. Suddenly, American foreign policy makers needed an entirely new grand strategy.

Organization (NATO, 1949), and the Southeast Asia Treaty Organization (SEATO, 1954). Senator Vandenberg gave the era its famous slogan when he quipped that American party politics "stopped at the water's edge." In other words, Democrats and Republicans would no longer disagree about international affairs.

All the same, the era posed new and difficult questions for American leaders. Should the United States support brutal dictators if they joined us in fighting Communists? Should it resist popular, democratic movements if they seemed to tilt toward the Communists? Where and when should we send troops? Each of these questions eventually escalated into an angry debate. Conservatives defended the fight against "the Evil Empire," as some of them dubbed the Soviet Union. Liberals began to charge that an increasingly knee-jerk fight against the fading threat of Communism was leading the United States to repress democratic movements around the world (Figure 14.7).

The debate grew heated. However, with thousands of American and Soviet missiles still threatening a nuclear holocaust, the Cold War framework remained in place—until Soviet Communism suddenly collapsed.

Strategy 3: The New World Order (1989–2003)

Around the world, people gaped at the incredible television footage in November 1989. Germans were clambering onto the Berlin Wall and ripping it apart. For almost thirty years, the Wall—running through Berlin and separating Communist and democratic Germany—had been the symbol of the Cold War. Communist guards had shot people trying to leap to freedom. President John Kennedy had looked out at the Wall and declared, "All free [people], wherever they may live, are citizens of Berlin." Ronald Reagan had stood on the same spot and challenged the Soviet leader, "Mr. Gorbachev, tear down this wall." Now the East German guards stood awkwardly by, uncertain what to do, as the delirious mob hammered the Wall to pieces. Within two years, the entire Soviet empire collapsed. The framework that had guided American foreign policy for more than fifty years was suddenly irrelevant. What next?

see for yourself 14.1

Go online to see footage of the joyous destruction of the Berlin Wall in 1989.

President George H. W. Bush proclaimed "a new world order." He touted an active, multilateral march toward free markets and democracy. On his right, the neoconservatives began to press for a more muscular foreign policy. The United States should use its unchallenged military strength to make the world more peaceful, democratic, and secure. If allies did not want to get on board, they should just get out of our way.

On the left, many Democrats took a more modest posture. The United States finally had an opportunity to scale back its military-industrial complex and shift national resources into "a peace dividend"—money for education, highways, health care, and a balanced budget. Liberals denounced the idea that military force could spread either peace or democracy.

Isolationism, which had been on the fringe during the Cold War, now made a comeback on both left and right. Some conservatives began to warn that "a new world order" was nothing more than code for international organizations that would imperil American independence. Bipartisan foreign policy had been shaky for decades. Now it collapsed. Politics no longer stopped at the water's edge.

The loud debate about how the United States should relate to the world suddenly ended on September 11, 2001.

Strategy 4: The War on Terror (began 2001)

The 9/11 attacks killed almost three thousand people. The attacks shut down American institutions from coast to coast—financial markets in New York, Disney World in Florida, the great arch in St. Louis, and air travel across American airspace (for five days). In the stunned aftermath, the George W. Bush administration constructed a formidable new foreign policy framework that stands to this day. To define the attacks as a crime would have brought in the American justice system. Instead, the administration declared them an act of war and responded with a "war on terror." That choice changed America's role in the world.

The war on terror targeted terrorists, nations that harbored terrorists, and any organizations that assisted terrorists. The war's architects took firm action to protect the homeland. They focused intensively on security. Opponents soon rose up and charged that a war on terror would become an endless conflict against an amorphous foe and would, in the long run, weaken the United States by undermining its bedrock values—liberty and the rule of law (we discussed the debate in Chapter 4, on civil liberties).

At first, most nations rallied to support the United States. *Le Monde*, a liberal French newspaper, ran a column on September 12, 2001, that ended with a ringing phrase: "We are all Americans now."

see for yourself 14.2

Go online to read the *Le Monde* "We are all Americans now" column.

Preemptive War. During the Cold War, the United States operated on the theory of *deterrence*: build a military so overpowering—including nuclear weapons—that other nations will be afraid to attack. Deterrence is aimed at other governments. However, the strategy does not work with extremists who are willing to sacrifice their lives for a cause.

What can be done against such fanatics? President George W. Bush defined what came to be known as the Bush Doctrine—the strategy of preemptive war. As the president explained it at West Point, "Deterrence—the promise of massive retaliation against nations—means nothing against shadowy terrorist networks with no nation or citizens to defend." The United States, he continued, had to eliminate threats "before they emerge." Our military "must be ready to strike in any dark corner of the globe"—before a nation or group directly threatens us.[14] We would attack them before they could strike us.

The Bush Doctrine was immediately controversial. Those who disagreed responded that it is immoral to strike nations and groups that have not attacked us. In the first place, that's one thing that makes us different from the terrorists. And in the second, launching the American military around the globe generates new resentments and creates new enemies. It only multiplies security problems. When the Obama administration came to office, talk of preemptive wars stopped, but we shall see that many features of the Bush Doctrine have remained in place.

On the surface, the debate was about national security. But below the surface lay a clash about American principles. Those who supported President Bush argued that American interests are the same as the interests of all other people who love peace and justice. That is what the United States stands for, they said. Opponents responded that, when push comes to shove, every nation acts in its own self-interest, even the United States, and that, as a result, American policy makers should work with other nations rather than simply taking unilateral action.

War in Afghanistan.   American leaders quickly traced the 9/11 attacks to Al Qaeda. The terrorist network had found sanctuary in Afghanistan, a nation

What Do You Think?

Terrorists and the Rule of Law

In this chapter, we have described the debate between two foreign policy goals: bolstering security and projecting American values. That tension has taken a new form in recent times. Which of the following policies would you choose in pursuing the war on terror in the future?

Hunt down terrorists. The United States has no choice but to chase after terrorists with every weapon at its disposal. Terrorists are evil and kill innocent people. We must interrogate terrorism suspects using any method that can elicit information, hunt down those who plan to do us harm, and attack nations that harbor terrorists before they can attack civilian populations around the world. A strong emphasis on national security is the only way to keep the United States—and the world—safe.

Let the law prevail. America has always stood for the rule of law. Permanent security lies not in hunting terrorists but in inspiring people around the world with the power of our ideas— democracy, equality, and equal protection under the law. We proclaim our view of justice to the world when we give even our worst enemies a fair trial. The war on terror undermines our Constitution, subverts our values, and makes us weaker.

Unsure. Maybe the truth lies in between these choices. Perhaps you can design your own policy somewhere between these positions.

ruled by the **Taliban**, a fundamentalist Islamic group. The United States organized antigovernment militias in Afghanistan and helped them swiftly overthrow the Taliban government. Most American allies, as well as many nations in the region, supported the campaign. After the quick victory over the Taliban government, American and Afghani forces tried to capture or kill Al Qaeda leaders—some took shelter next door in Pakistan. The United States and its allies also worked to pacify Taliban insurgents, build democracy in Afghanistan, and stabilize Pakistan and keep it as an ally. After more than ten years of fighting, funding, and diplomacy, Al Qaeda is a shadow of its former self and most of its leaders are dead. However, the other goals—democracy in Afghanistan, stability in Pakistan, pacifying the Taliban—have not been met.

War in Iraq. The Bush administration followed the strike against Afghanistan with a fateful decision to topple Saddam Hussein in Iraq. Officials argued that Saddam had "weapons of mass destruction," such as atomic weapons or poison gas. Since he was a sworn enemy of the United States, he might turn those weapons over to terrorists. Neoconservatives saw war with Iraq as the first big test of their approach. The United States, they believed, should deploy its unrivaled power to depose a dictator, free a people, and wipe out another potential state sponsor of terrorism.

There was, however, a problem. Iraq had not actually attacked the United States. This would be America's first preemptive war. To complicate matters, UN inspectors were already in Iraq, looking for weapons of mass destruction. Although they had followed every lead from US intelligence, they found none. Even such close allies as Brazil and Mexico suggested giving the UN inspectors more time to do their job; other allies advised the Bush administration not to attack a nation that had not attacked us first. Despite the failure to persuade important allies, the United States launched its attack on Saddam Hussein's government in March 2003.

World public opinion turned decisively against the United States. The goodwill that had followed 9/11 evaporated. American policy makers reasoned that a free, democratic, and prosperous Iraq would soon silence critics. Success—and grateful Iraqis—would vindicate the administration's strategy. The military easily toppled the dictator. But Iraq burst into violence. Religious sects and tribes attacked one another; some turned their guns and explosives on the United States. The death toll rose among both American troops and Iraqi civilians. Iraqi society teetered on the edge of chaos. Arab nations and European allies, who had opposed the war, now blamed the United States for the carnage. And, to make matters still worse, no weapons of mass destruction were ever found.

The Obama administration hoped to pivot away from the war on terror and establish a new grand strategy. This has proved difficult. As we have seen so often, institutions—once established—are hard to undo. The key question

Taliban: A fundamentalist Islamic sect that took control of Afghanistan in 1996 and gave shelter to the Al Qaeda terrorist network.

confronting Americans is the same one that the Obama administration struggled with: What sort of grand strategy should the nation pursue now?

THE BOTTOM LINE

- The United States forged four grand strategies in the twentieth century.
- It stood alone and acted unilaterally (1918–1939), it led the democratic nations in multilateral coalitions during the Cold War (1945–1991), it debated a new world order after the Cold War (1991–2001), and it launched a war on terror.
- The Obama administration called for a move away from the war on terror but found that difficult to do.

● Conclusion: Reforming US Policymaking

By now you have a better handle on the complex realm of US policymaking, both foreign and domestic, and budgeting. If you are like many Americans, your increased knowledge may lead you to imagine a few changes to the policy process. Most would-be reformers address specific policies. We have seen many examples in this chapter, from addressing rising obesity rates to fighting terrorism at home and abroad.

Where do new policy ideas come from? It is natural to assume that Congress and executive-branch administrators generate them all, or perhaps that established interest-group activists are the primary source. In fact, a substantial proportion of innovative public-sector ideas comes from people outside government and beyond the ranks of lobbyists residing in Washington, DC.

In recent years, the term "policy entrepreneur" has been applied to these outsiders—those who generate new ideas, help move them up policy agendas, translate them into workable proposals, and often help implement them as well. Not infrequently, these entrepreneurs are young, frequently just out of college. They have not been part of the regular policymaking system long enough to be subject to "groupthink," the tendency to recycle familiar (and sometimes stale) ideas.

What do we know about these innovative individuals? The literature on this subject is relatively thin, but a few common characteristics have emerged.[15] For one, policy entrepreneurs are willing to invest time and resources to achieve their aims, often at risk to their own comfort and financial well-being, in hopes of future return in the form of policy change. These innovators also tend to be talented storytellers, able to convey complex policy information through simplified stories and scenarios. Recall from earlier in this chapter, as well as from Chapter 6, the importance of powerful narratives in successful policy framing. Such tales help convey to policy makers what the problem is and what a promising solution might be. Though some policy entrepreneurs may engage in a lonely struggle for change, most successful efforts involve a network of entrepreneurs, diffusing policy ideas across towns, cities, and states.

Over the years American government has proved resistant to large-scale changes in individual policy areas—in part because the existing ways of carrying out policy have become institutionalized. Once again, strong path-dependent practices tend to reinforce the status quo. Although this trend can be discouraging to would-be reformers, remember from our discussion of interest groups in Chapter 9 that a great virtue of the US policy system is its remarkable stability. Those who can pursue policies within a context of predictable rules may achieve the most long-lasting reforms. That flexible combination may also help explain how America's system of policymaking has endured for so long.

THE BOTTOM LINE
- Policy entrepreneurs, drawn from all walks of life, seek to devise innovative solutions for public policies.
- Although novel policies are hard to push through to completion, the contest over agenda setting and problem definition is relatively open. As in the business or the nonprofit sector, a persistent policy entrepreneur can realize rewards.
- The most successful entrepreneurs tend to develop compelling narratives about their preferred issue, willingly risk creature comforts to pursue policy change, and develop networks to diffuse and test their ideas.

CHAPTER SUMMARY

● Public policymaking inevitably involves choices: Should we reduce the interest rate on student-loan repayments? Launch a manned mission to Mars? Ban automatic weapons in the wake of a tragic shooting? Understanding those choices is the essence of politics and government in America.

● Five stages mark the process of devising domestic policies. These are not a recipe or blueprint for action, but most policy achievements pass through all these.

- *Agenda setting* describes the transformation of an idea into a policy issue, as public attention expands.

- Once a topic is on the agenda, it must be *defined*—What is this issue about?—and *framed*: how lawmakers and public talk about an agenda item often determines whether it will move forward or gather dust.

- A third stage, *policy formation*, involves the legislative and executive activities that translate talk into concrete statutory language.

- Once a policy has been passed into law, it must be *implemented*, involving rulemaking and then delivery of public services.

- Finally, policies are *evaluated*; once implemented, they create a *feedback* process that affects future policymaking in that area.

● The largest US policy programs, in terms of spending and numbers of people served, are social policies like Social Security, Medicare, Medicaid, and unemployment insurance. The longtime American resistance to big government helps to explain the slow growth of these and other social policies. That same resistance has encouraged a turn toward privatization—shifting public services to the private sector.

● Attention to efficiency, combined with harder economic times, has elevated the importance of budgeting in American politics and government. The congressional budget process is a complicated, slow-moving machine, which rarely meets its key deadlines—largely because the financial stakes are so high.

● The three goals of American foreign policy are security, prosperity, and spreading American values.

● Twentieth-century grand strategies included standing alone (1918–1939), primacy in a coalition of anti-Communist nations (1946–1989), the search for a new world order (1991–2001), and the War on Terror (since 2001).

● Policy entrepreneurs who succeed tend to tell memorable stories, sacrifice comfort and resources to advance their policy efforts, and work collaboratively with like-minded reformers. Engaging in the policy process, though it moves slowly and incrementally, can be immensely fulfilling.

KEY TERMS

American exceptionalism, 526
Budget resolution, 519
Charter school, 504
Containment, 529
Cost-benefit analysis, 505
Cost effectiveness, 505
Debt ceiling, 499
Entitlement program, 515
Fair trade, 524

Federal budget deficit, 517
Federal poverty line, 515
Fiscal year, 518
Focusing event, 501
Free trade, 523
Grand strategy, 527
Gross domestic product, 513
Internationalism, 527
Isolationism, 527

Multilateral organization, 529
Path dependence, 510
Policy agenda, 501
Protectionism, 523
School voucher, 504
Street-level bureaucrats, 508
Taliban, 533
Trade deficit, 525

STUDY QUESTIONS

1. What is "public policy"? Why is it so important to the work of government?
2. How do items get on the policy agenda?
3. Think of an issue you care about. How is it currently *framed* in national discussions about the issue? How would you frame it?
4. Why does policy formation—translating a topic from "good idea" into a bill ready for a congressional vote—take so long?

5. What is the difference between an *ex ante* and *ex post* policy evaluation? How are both useful in helping shape a government program?
6. Why are our largest entitlement programs—Social Security, Medicare, and Medicaid—so expensive?
7. Why does Congress have to pass continuing resolutions at the end of most budget years?

8. How important, in your view, is balancing the US budget?

9. Name the three foreign policy goals that the United States pursues. Discuss the relative importance of each goal. If you had to stress one, which would it be?

10. What four grand strategies did the United States pursue in the twentieth century? Describe each.

11. If you could change any aspect of the American policymaking process, what would it be?

APPENDIX I

The Declaration of Independence

When in the course of human events, it becomes necessary for one people to dissolve the political bands which have connected them with another, and to assume, among the powers of the earth, the separate and equal station to which the Laws of Nature and of Nature's God entitle them, a decent respect to the opinions of mankind requires that they should declare the causes which impel them to the separation.

We hold these truths to be self-evident, that all men are created equal, that they are endowed by their Creator with certain unalienable Rights, that among these are life, liberty and the pursuit of happiness. That to secure these rights, governments are instituted among men, deriving their just powers from the consent of the governed; that whenever any form of government becomes destructive of these ends, it is the right of the people to alter or to abolish it, and to institute new Government, laying its foundation on such principles and organizing its powers in such form, as to them shall seem most likely to effect their safety and happiness. Prudence, indeed, will dictate that Governments long established should not be changed for light and transient causes; and, accordingly, all experience hath shown, that mankind are more disposed to suffer, while evils are sufferable, than to right themselves by abolishing the forms to which they are accustomed. But when a long train of abuses and usurpations, pursuing invariably the same object evinces a design to reduce them under absolute despotism, it is their right, it is their duty, to throw off such government, and to provide new guards for their future

security. Such has been the patient sufferance of these colonies; and such is now the necessity which constrains them to alter their former systems of government. The history of the present King of Great Britain is a history of repeated injuries and usurpations, all having in direct object the establishment of an absolute tyranny over these States. To prove this, let facts be submitted to a candid world:

He has refused his assent to laws, the most wholesome and necessary for the public good.

He has forbidden his governors to pass laws of immediate and pressing importance, unless suspended in their operation till his assent should be obtained; and, when so suspended, he has utterly neglected to attend to them.

He has refused to pass other laws for the accommodation of large districts of people, unless those people would relinquish the right of representation in the legislature, a right inestimable to them and formidable to tyrants only.

He has called together legislative bodies at places unusual, uncomfortable, and distant from the depository of their public records, for the sole purpose of fatiguing them into compliance with his measures.

He has dissolved representative houses repeatedly, for opposing with manly firmness his invasions on the rights of the people.

He has refused for a long time, after such dissolutions, to cause others to be elected; whereby the legislative powers, incapable of annihilation, have returned to the People at large for their exercise; the State remaining in the mean time exposed to all the dangers of invasion from without, and convulsions within.

He has endeavored to prevent the population of these States; for that purpose obstructing the laws for naturalization of foreigners; refusing to pass others to encourage their migrations hither, and raising the conditions of new appropriations of lands.

He has obstructed the administration of justice, by refusing his assent to laws for establishing judiciary powers.

He has made judges dependent on his will alone, for the tenure of their offices, and the amount and payment of their salaries.

He has erected a multitude of new offices, and sent hither swarms of officers to harass our people, and eat out their substance.

He has kept among us, in times of peace, standing armies without the consent of our legislatures.

He has affected to render the Military independent of, and superior to, the civil power.

He has combined with others to subject us to a jurisdiction foreign to our constitution and unacknowledged by our laws; giving his assent to their acts of pretended legislation:

For quartering large bodies of armed troops among us;

For protecting them, by a mock trial, from punishment for any murders which they should commit on the inhabitants of these States;

For cutting off our trade with all parts of the world;

For imposing taxes on us without our Consent;

For depriving us, in many cases, of the benefits of Trial by Jury;

For transporting us beyond Seas to be tried for pretended offences;

For abolishing the free System of English Laws in a neighbouring Province, establishing therein an Arbitrary government, and enlarging its Boundaries so as to render it at once an example and fit instrument for introducing the same absolute rule into these colonies;

For taking away our charters, abolishing our most valuable laws, and altering fundamentally the forms of our governments;

For suspending our own legislatures, and declaring themselves invested with power to legislate for us in all cases whatsoever.

He has abdicated government here, by declaring us out of his protection and waging war against us.

He has plundered our seas, ravaged our coasts, burnt our towns, and destroyed the lives of our people.

He is at this time transporting large armies of foreign mercenaries to complete the works of death, desolation and tyranny, already begun with circumstances of cruelty and perfidy scarcely paralleled in the most barbarous ages, and totally unworthy the head of a civilized nation.

He has constrained our fellow citizens taken captive on the high seas to bear arms against their country, to become the executioners of their friends and brethren, or to fall themselves by their hands.

He has excited domestic insurrections amongst us, and has endeavored to bring on the inhabitants of our frontiers, the merciless Indian savages, whose known rule of warfare, is an undistinguished destruction of all ages, sexes and conditions.

In every stage of these oppressions we have petitioned for redress in the most humble terms; our repeated petitions have been answered only by repeated injury. A prince whose character is thus marked by every act which may define a tyrant, is unfit to be the ruler of a free people.

Nor have we been wanting in attentions to our British brethren. We have warned them from time to time of attempts by their legislature to extend an unwarrantable jurisdiction over us. We have reminded them of the circumstances of our emigration and settlement here. We have appealed to their native justice and magnanimity, and we have conjured them by the ties of our common kindred to disavow these usurpations, which, would inevitably interrupt our connections and correspondence. They, too, have been deaf to the voice of justice and of consanguinity. We must, therefore, acquiesce in the necessity, which denounces our separation, and hold them, as we hold the rest of mankind, enemies in war, in peace friends.

We, therefore, the representatives of the United States of America, in general Congress, assembled, appealing to the Supreme Judge of the world for the rectitude of our intentions, do, in the name, and by the authority of the good people of these colonies, solemnly publish and declare, that these united colonies are, and of right ought to be free and independent states; that they are absolved from all allegiance to the British Crown, and that all political connection between them and the state of Great Britain, is and ought to be totally dissolved; and that, as free and independent states, they have full power to levy war, conclude peace, contract alliances, establish commerce, and to do all other acts and things which independent states may of right do. And for the support of this declaration, with a firm reliance on the protection of Divine Providence, we mutually pledge to each other our lives, our fortunes and our sacred honor.

APPENDIX II

The Constitution of the United States of America

We the People of the United States, in Order to form a more perfect Union, establish Justice, insure domestic Tranquility, provide for the common defence, promote the general Welfare, and secure the Blessings of Liberty to ourselves and our Posterity, do ordain and establish this Constitution for the United States of America.

Article I
Section 1

All legislative Powers herein granted shall be vested in a Congress of the United States, which shall consist of a Senate and House of Representatives.

Section 2

The House of Representatives shall be composed of Members chosen every second Year by the People of the several States, and the Electors in each State shall have the Qualifications requisite for Electors of the most numerous Branch of the State Legislature.

No Person shall be a Representative who shall not have attained to the Age of twenty five Years, and been seven Years a Citizen of the United States, and who shall not, when elected, be an Inhabitant of that State in which he shall be chosen.

Representatives [and direct Taxes]* shall be apportioned among the several States [which may be included within this Union, according to their respective Numbers, which shall be determined by adding to the whole Number of free Persons, including those bound to Service for a Term of Years, and excluding Indians not taxed, three fifths of all other Persons].** The actual Enumeration shall be made within three Years after the first Meeting of the Congress of the United States, and within every subsequent Term of ten Years, in such Manner as they shall by Law direct. The Number of Representatives shall not exceed one for every thirty Thousand, but each State shall have at Least one Representative; and until such enumeration shall be made, the State of New Hampshire shall be entitled to choose three, Massachusetts eight, Rhode-Island and Providence Plantations one, Connecticut five, New York six, New Jersey four, Pennsylvania eight, Delaware one, Maryland six, Virginia ten, North Carolina five, South Carolina five, and Georgia three.

---

*Modified by the Sixteenth Amendment.
**Negated by the Fourteenth Amendment.

When vacancies happen in the Representation from any State, the Executive Authority thereof shall issue Writs of Election to fill such Vacancies.

The House of Representatives shall choose their Speaker and other Officers; and shall have the sole Power of Impeachment.

Section 3

The Senate of the United States shall be composed of two Senators from each State, chosen [by the Legislature thereof]* for six Years; and each Senator shall have one Vote.

Immediately after they shall be assembled in Consequence of the first Election, they shall be divided as equally as may be into three Classes. The Seats of the Senators of the first Class shall be vacated at the Expiration of the second Year, of the second Class at the Expiration of the fourth Year, and of the third Class at the Expiration of the sixth Year, so that one third may be chosen every second Year, [and if Vacancies happen by Resignation, or otherwise, during the Recess of the Legislature of any State, the Executive thereof may make temporary Appointments until the next Meeting of the Legislature, which shall then fill such Vacancies].**

No Person shall be a Senator who shall not have attained to the Age of thirty Years, and been nine Years a Citizen of the United States, and who shall not, when elected, be an Inhabitant of that State for which he shall be chosen.

The Vice President of the United States shall be President of the Senate, but shall have no Vote, unless they be equally divided.

The Senate shall choose their other Officers, and also a President pro tempore, in the Absence of the Vice President, or when he shall exercise the Office of President of the United States.

The Senate shall have the sole Power to try all Impeachments. When sitting for that Purpose, they shall be on Oath or Affirmation. When the President of the United States is tried, the Chief Justice shall preside: And no Person shall be convicted without the Concurrence of two thirds of the Members present.

Judgment in Cases of Impeachment shall not extend further than to removal from Office, and disqualification to hold and enjoy any Office of honor, Trust or Profit under the United States: but the Party convicted shall nevertheless be liable and subject to Indictment, Trial, Judgment and Punishment, according to Law.

Section 4

The Times, Places and Manner of holding Elections for Senators and Representatives, shall be prescribed in each State by the Legislature thereof;

---

*Changed by the Seventeenth Amendment.
**Modified by the Seventeenth Amendment.

but the Congress may at any time by Law make or alter such Regulations, except as to the Places of chusing Senators.

[The Congress shall assemble at least once in every Year, and such Meeting shall be on the first Monday in December, unless they shall by Law appoint a different Day.]*

Section 5

Each House shall be the Judge of the Elections, Returns and Qualifications of its own Members, and a Majority of each shall constitute a Quorum to do Business; but a smaller Number may adjourn from day to day, and may be authorized to compel the Attendance of absent Members, in such Manner, and under such Penalties as each House may provide.

Each House may determine the Rules of its Proceedings, punish its Members for disorderly Behaviour, and, with the Concurrence of two thirds, expel a Member.

Each House shall keep a Journal of its Proceedings, and from time to time publish the same, excepting such Parts as may in their Judgment require Secrecy; and the Yeas and Nays of the Members of either House on any question shall, at the Desire of one fifth of those Present, be entered on the Journal.

Neither House, during the Session of Congress, shall, without the Consent of the other, adjourn for more than three days, nor to any other Place than that in which the two Houses shall be sitting.

Section 6

The Senators and Representatives shall receive a Compensation for their Services, to be ascertained by Law, and paid out of the Treasury of the United States. They shall in all Cases, except Treason, Felony and Breach of the Peace, be privileged from Arrest during their Attendance at the Session of their respective Houses, and in going to and returning from the same; and for any Speech or Debate in either House, they shall not be questioned in any other Place.

No Senator or Representative shall, during the Time for which he was elected, be appointed to any civil Office under the Authority of the United States, which shall have been created, or the Emoluments whereof shall have been increased during such time; and no Person holding any Office under the United States, shall be a Member of either House during his Continuance in Office.

Section 7

All Bills for raising Revenue shall originate in the House of Representatives; but the Senate may propose or concur with Amendments as on other Bills.

---

*Changed to January 3 by the Twentieth Amendment.

Every Bill which shall have passed the House of Representatives and the Senate, shall, before it become a Law, be presented to the President of the United States: If he approve he shall sign it, but if not he shall return it, with his Objections to that House in which it shall have originated, who shall enter the Objections at large on their Journal, and proceed to reconsider it. If after such Reconsideration two thirds of that House shall agree to pass the Bill, it shall be sent, together with the Objections, to the other House, by which it shall likewise be reconsidered, and if approved by two thirds of that House, it shall become a Law. But in all such Cases the Votes of both Houses shall be determined by yeas and Nays, and the Names of the Persons voting for and against the Bill shall be entered on the Journal of each House respectively. If any Bill shall not be returned by the President within ten Days (Sundays excepted) after it shall have been presented to him, the Same shall be a Law, in like Manner as if he had signed it, unless the Congress by their Adjournment prevent its Return, in which Case it shall not be a Law.

Every Order, Resolution, or Vote to which the Concurrence of the Senate and House of Representatives may be necessary (except on a question of Adjournment) shall be presented to the President of the United States; and before the Same shall take Effect, shall be approved by him, or being disapproved by him, shall be repassed by two thirds of the Senate and House of Representatives, according to the Rules and Limitations prescribed in the Case of a Bill.

Section 8

The Congress shall have Power

To lay and collect Taxes, Duties, Imposts and Excises, to pay the Debts and provide for the common Defence and general Welfare of the United States; but all Duties, Imposts and Excises shall be uniform throughout the United States;

To borrow Money on the credit of the United States;

To regulate Commerce with foreign Nations, and among the several States, and with the Indian Tribes;

To establish an uniform Rule of Naturalization, and uniform Laws on the subject of Bankruptcies throughout the United States;

To coin Money, regulate the Value thereof, and of foreign Coin, and fix the Standard of Weights and Measures;

To provide for the Punishment of counterfeiting the Securities and current Coin of the United States;

To establish Post Offices and post Roads;

To promote the Progress of Science and useful Arts, by securing for limited Times to Authors and Inventors the exclusive Right to their respective Writings and Discoveries;

To constitute Tribunals inferior to the supreme Court;

To define and punish Piracies and Felonies committed on the high Seas, and Offences against the Law of Nations;

To declare War, grant Letters of Marque and Reprisal, and make Rules concerning Captures on Land and Water;

To raise and support Armies, but no Appropriation of Money to that Use shall be for a longer Term than two Years;

To provide and maintain a Navy;

To make Rules for the Government and Regulation of the land and naval Forces;

To provide for calling forth the Militia to execute the Laws of the Union, suppress Insurrections and repel Invasions;

To provide for organizing, arming, and disciplining the Militia, and for governing such Part of them as may be employed in the Service of the United States, reserving to the States respectively, the Appointment of the Officers, and the Authority of training the Militia according to the discipline prescribed by Congress;

To exercise exclusive Legislation in all Cases whatsoever, over such District (not exceeding ten Miles square) as may, by Cession of particular States, and the Acceptance of Congress, become the Seat of the Government of the United States, and to exercise like Authority over all Places purchased by the Consent of the Legislature of the State in which the Same shall be, for the Erection of Forts, Magazines, Arsenals, dock-Yards, and other needful Buildings;—And

To make all Laws which shall be necessary and proper for carrying into Execution the foregoing Powers, and all other Powers vested by this Constitution in the Government of the United States, or in any Department or Officer thereof.

Section 9

The Migration or Importation of such Persons as any of the States now existing shall think proper to admit, shall not be prohibited by the Congress prior to the Year one thousand eight hundred and eight, but a Tax or duty may be imposed on such Importation, not exceeding ten dollars for each Person.

The Privilege of the Writ of Habeas Corpus shall not be suspended, unless when in Cases of Rebellion or Invasion the public Safety may require it.

No Bill of Attainder or ex post facto Law shall be passed.

[No Capitation, or other direct, Tax shall be laid, unless in Proportion to the Census or enumeration herein before directed to be taken.]*

No Tax or Duty shall be laid on Articles exported from any State.

No Preference shall be given by any Regulation of Commerce or Revenue to the Ports of one State over those of another; nor shall Vessels bound to, or from, one State, be obliged to enter, clear, or pay Duties in another.

No Money shall be drawn from the Treasury, but in Consequence of Appropriations made by Law; and a regular Statement and Account of the Receipts and Expenditures of all public Money shall be published from time to time.

No Title of Nobility shall be granted by the United States: And no Person holding any Office of Profit or Trust under them, shall, without the

---

*Modified by the Sixteenth Amendment.

Consent of the Congress, accept of any present, Emolument, Office, or Title, of any kind whatever, from any King, Prince, or foreign State.

Section 10

No State shall enter into any Treaty, Alliance, or Confederation; grant Letters of Marque and Reprisal; coin Money; emit Bills of Credit; make any Thing but gold and silver Coin a Tender in Payment of Debts; pass any Bill of Attainder, ex post facto Law, or Law impairing the Obligation of Contracts, or grant any Title of Nobility.

No State shall, without the Consent of the Congress, lay any Imposts or Duties on Imports or Exports, except what may be absolutely necessary for executing it's inspection Laws: and the net Produce of all Duties and Imposts, laid by any State on Imports or Exports, shall be for the Use of the Treasury of the United States; and all such Laws shall be subject to the Revision and Control of the Congress.

No State shall, without the Consent of Congress, lay any Duty of Tonnage, keep Troops, or Ships of War in time of Peace, enter into any Agreement or Compact with another State, or with a foreign Power, or engage in War, unless actually invaded, or in such imminent Danger as will not admit of delay.

Article II
Section 1

The executive Power shall be vested in a President of the United States of America. He shall hold his Office during the Term of four Years, and, together with the Vice President, chosen for the same Term, be elected, as follows:

Each State shall appoint, in such Manner as the Legislature thereof may direct, a Number of Electors, equal to the whole Number of Senators and Representatives to which the State may be entitled in the Congress: but no Senator or Representative, or Person holding an Office of Trust or Profit under the United States, shall be appointed an Elector.

[The Electors shall meet in their respective States, and vote by Ballot for two Persons, of whom one at least shall not be an Inhabitant of the same State with themselves. And they shall make a List of all the Persons voted for, and of the Number of Votes for each; which List they shall sign and certify, and transmit sealed to the Seat of the Government of the United States, directed to the President of the Senate. The President of the Senate shall, in the Presence of the Senate and House of Representatives, open all the Certificates, and the Votes shall then be counted. The Person having the greatest Number of Votes shall be the President, if such Number be a Majority of the whole Number of Electors appointed; and if there be more than one who have such Majority, and have an equal Number of Votes, then the House of Representatives shall immediately choose by Ballot one of them for President; and if no Person have a Majority, then from the five highest on the List the said House shall in like Manner choose the President. But in choosing the President, the Votes shall be taken by States, the Representation from each State having one Vote; a quorum for this purpose shall consist of a Member or Members from two thirds of the States, and a Majority of all the States shall be necessary to a Choice. In every Case, after the Choice of the President, the Person having the greatest Number of Votes of the Electors shall be the Vice President. But if there should remain two or more who have equal Votes, the Senate shall choose from them by Ballot the Vice President.]*

The Congress may determine the Time of choosing the Electors, and the Day on which they shall give their Votes; which Day shall be the same throughout the United States.

No Person except a natural born Citizen, or a Citizen of the United States, at the time of the Adoption of this Constitution, shall be eligible to the Office of President; neither shall any Person be eligible to that Office who shall not have attained to the Age of thirty five Years, and been fourteen Years a Resident within the United States.

In Case of the Removal of the President from Office, or of his Death, Resignation, or Inability to discharge the Powers and Duties of the said Office, the Same shall devolve on the Vice President, and the Congress may by Law provide for the Case of Removal, Death, Resignation or Inability, both of the President and Vice President, declaring what Officer shall then act as President, and such Officer shall act accordingly, until the Disability be removed, or a President shall be elected.

The President shall, at stated Times, receive for his Services, a Compensation, which shall neither be increased nor diminished during the Period for which he shall have been elected, and he shall not receive within that Period any other Emolument from the United States, or any of them.

Before he enter on the Execution of his Office, he shall take the following Oath or Affirmation:—"I do solemnly swear (or affirm) that I will faithfully execute the Office of President of the United States, and will to the best of my Ability, preserve, protect and defend the Constitution of the United States."

Section 2

The President shall be Commander in Chief of the Army and Navy of the United States, and of the Militia of the several States, when called into the actual Service of the United States; he may require the Opinion, in writing, of the principal Officer in each of the executive Departments, upon any Subject relating to the Duties of their respective Offices, and he shall have Power to grant Reprieves and Pardons for Offences against the United States, except in Cases of Impeachment.

He shall have Power, by and with the Advice and Consent of the Senate, to make Treaties, provided two thirds of the Senators present concur; and he shall nominate, and by and with the Advice and Consent of the Senate,

---

*Changed by the Twelfth and Twentieth Amendments.

shall appoint Ambassadors, other public Ministers and Consuls, Judges of the supreme Court, and all other Officers of the United States, whose Appointments are not herein otherwise provided for, and which shall be established by Law: but the Congress may by Law vest the Appointment of such inferior Officers, as they think proper, in the President alone, in the Courts of Law, or in the Heads of Departments.

The President shall have Power to fill up all Vacancies that may happen during the Recess of the Senate, by granting Commissions which shall expire at the End of their next Session.

Section 3

He shall from time to time give to the Congress Information of the State of the Union, and recommend to their Consideration such Measures as he shall judge necessary and expedient; he may, on extraordinary Occasions, convene both Houses, or either of them, and in Case of Disagreement between them, with Respect to the Time of Adjournment, he may adjourn them to such Time as he shall think proper; he shall receive Ambassadors and other public Ministers; he shall take Care that the Laws be faithfully executed, and shall Commission all the Officers of the United States.

Section 4

The President, Vice President and all civil Officers of the United States, shall be removed from Office on Impeachment for, and Conviction of, Treason, Bribery, or other high Crimes and Misdemeanors.

Article III
Section 1

The judicial Power of the United States shall be vested in one supreme Court, and in such inferior Courts as the Congress may from time to time ordain and establish. The Judges, both of the supreme and inferior Courts, shall hold their Offices during good Behaviour, and shall, at stated Times, receive for their Services a Compensation, which shall not be diminished during their Continuance in Office.

Section 2

The judicial Power shall extend to all Cases, in Law and Equity, arising under this Constitution, the Laws of the United States, and Treaties made, or which shall be made, under their Authority;—to all Cases affecting Ambassadors, other public Ministers and Consuls;—to all Cases of admiralty and maritime Jurisdiction;—to Controversies to which the United States shall be a Party;—to Controversies between two or more States;—[between a State and Citizens of another State];—between Citizens of different States;—between Citizens of the same State claiming Lands under

Grants of different States, [and between a State,] or the Citizens thereof, [and foreign States, Citizens or Subjects].*

In all Cases affecting Ambassadors, other public Ministers and Consuls, and those in which a State shall be Party, the supreme Court shall have original Jurisdiction. In all the other Cases before mentioned, the supreme Court shall have appellate Jurisdiction, both as to Law and Fact, with such Exceptions, and under such Regulations as the Congress shall make.

The Trial of all Crimes, except in Cases of Impeachment, shall be by Jury; and such Trial shall be held in the State where the said Crimes shall have been committed; but when not committed within any State, the Trial shall be at such Place or Places as the Congress may by Law have directed.

Section 3

Treason against the United States, shall consist only in levying War against them, or in adhering to their Enemies, giving them Aid and Comfort. No Person shall be convicted of Treason unless on the Testimony of two Witnesses to the same overt Act, or on Confession in open Court.

The Congress shall have Power to declare the Punishment of Treason, but no Attainder of Treason shall work Corruption of Blood, or Forfeiture except during the Life of the Person attainted.

Article IV
Section 1

Full Faith and Credit shall be given in each State to the public Acts, Records, and judicial Proceedings of every other State. And the Congress may by general Laws prescribe the Manner in which such Acts, Records and Proceedings shall be proved, and the Effect thereof.

Section 2

The Citizens of each State shall be entitled to all Privileges and Immunities of Citizens in the several States.

A Person charged in any State with Treason, Felony, or other Crime, who shall flee from Justice, and be found in another State, shall on Demand of the executive Authority of the State from which he fled, be delivered up, to be removed to the State having Jurisdiction of the Crime.

[No Person held to Service or Labour in one State, under the Laws thereof, escaping into another, shall, in Consequence of any Law or Regulation therein, be discharged from such Service or Labour, but shall be delivered up on Claim of the Party to whom such Service or Labour may be due.]**

---

*Altered by the Twelfth Amendment.
**Repealed by the Thirteenth Amendment.

Section 3

New States may be admitted by the Congress into this Union; but no new State shall be formed or erected within the Jurisdiction of any other State; nor any State be formed by the Junction of two or more States, or Parts of States, without the Consent of the Legislatures of the States concerned as well as of the Congress.

The Congress shall have Power to dispose of and make all needful Rules and Regulations respecting the Territory or other Property belonging to the United States; and nothing in this Constitution shall be so construed as to Prejudice any Claims of the United States, or of any particular State.

Section 4

The United States shall guarantee to every State in this Union a Republican Form of Government, and shall protect each of them against Invasion; and on Application of the Legislature, or of the Executive (when the Legislature cannot be convened), against domestic Violence.

Article V

The Congress, whenever two thirds of both Houses shall deem it necessary, shall propose Amendments to this Constitution, or, on the Application of the Legislatures of two thirds of the several States, shall call a Convention for proposing Amendments, which, in either Case, shall be valid to all Intents and Purposes, as Part of this Constitution, when ratified by the Legislatures of three fourths of the several States, or by Conventions in three fourths thereof, as the one or the other Mode of Ratification may be proposed by the Congress; Provided that no Amendment which may be made prior to the Year One thousand eight hundred and eight shall in any Manner affect the first and fourth Clauses in the Ninth Section of the first Article; and that no State, without its Consent, shall be deprived of its equal Suffrage in the Senate.

Article VI

All Debts contracted and Engagements entered into, before the Adoption of this Constitution, shall be as valid against the United States under this Constitution, as under the Confederation.

This Constitution, and the Laws of the United States which shall be made in Pursuance thereof; and all Treaties made, or which shall be made, under the Authority of the United States, shall be the supreme Law of the Land; and the Judges in every State shall be bound thereby, any Thing in the Constitution or Laws of any State to the Contrary notwithstanding.

The Senators and Representatives before mentioned, and the Members of the several State Legislatures, and all executive and judicial Officers, both of the United States and of the several States, shall be bound by Oath or Affirmation, to support this Constitution; but no religious Test shall ever be required as a Qualification to any Office or public Trust under the United States.

Article VII

The Ratification of the Conventions of nine States, shall be sufficient for the Establishment of this Constitution between the States so ratifying the Same.

The Word, "the," being interlined between the seventh and eighth Lines of the first Page, the Word "Thirty" being partly written on an Erazure in the fifteenth Line of the first Page, The Words "is tried" being interlined between the thirty second and thirty third Lines of the first Page and the Word "the" being interlined between the forty third and forty fourth Lines of the second Page.

Attest William Jackson Secretary

Done in Convention by the Unanimous Consent of the States present the Seventeenth Day of September in the Year of our Lord one thousand seven hundred and Eighty seven and of the Independence of the United States of America the Twelfth In witness whereof We have hereunto subscribed our Names,

G°. WASHINGTON

Presidt and deputy from Virginia

Delaware
Geo: Read
Gunning Bedford jun
John Dickinson
Richard Bassett
Jaco: Broom

Maryland
James McHenry
Dan of St Thos. Jenifer
Danl. Carroll

Virginia
John Blair
James Madison Jr.

North Carolina
Wm. Blount
Richd. Dobbs Spaight
Hu Williamson

South Carolina
J. Rutledge
Charles Cotesworth
    Pinckney
Charles Pinckney
Pierce Butler

Georgia
William Few
Abr Baldwin

New Hampshire
John Langdon
Nicholas Gilman

Massachusetts
Nathaniel Gorham
Rufus King

Connecticut
Wm. Saml. Johnson
Roger Sherman

New York
Alexander Hamilton

New Jersey
Wil: Livingston
David Brearley
Wm. Paterson
Jona: Dayton

Pennsylvania
B Franklin
Thomas Mifflin
Robt. Morris
Geo. Clymer
Thos. FitzSimons
Jared Ingersoll
James Wilson
Gouv Morris

Articles

In addition to, and Amendment of the Constitution of the United States of America, proposed by Congress, and ratified by the Legislatures of the several States, pursuant to the fifth Article of the original Constitution.

(The first ten amendments to the U.S. Constitution were ratified December 15, 1791, and form what is known as the "Bill of Rights.")

Amendment I

Congress shall make no law respecting an establishment of religion, or prohibiting the free exercise thereof; or abridging the freedom of speech, or of the press; or the right of the people peaceably to assemble, and to petition the Government for a redress of grievances.

Amendment II

A well regulated Militia, being necessary to the security of a free State, the right of the people to keep and bear Arms, shall not be infringed.

Amendment III

No Soldier shall, in time of peace be quartered in any house, without the consent of the Owner, nor in time of war, but in a manner to be prescribed by law.

Amendment IV

The right of the people to be secure in their persons, houses, papers, and effects, against unreasonable searches and seizures, shall not be violated, and no Warrants shall issue, but upon probable cause, supported by Oath or affirmation, and particularly describing the place to be searched, and the persons or things to be seized.

Amendment V

No person shall be held to answer for a capital, or otherwise infamous crime, unless on a presentment or indictment of a Grand Jury, except in cases arising in the land or naval forces, or in the Militia, when in actual service in time of War or public danger; nor shall any person be subject for the same offence to be twice put in jeopardy of life or limb; nor shall be compelled in any criminal case to be a witness against himself, nor be deprived of life, liberty, or property, without due process of law; nor shall private property be taken for public use, without just compensation.

Amendment VI

In all criminal prosecutions, the accused shall enjoy the right to a speedy and public trial, by an impartial jury of the State and district wherein the crime shall have been committed, which district shall have been previously ascertained by law, and to be informed of the nature and cause of the accusation; to be confronted with the witnesses against him; to have compulsory process for obtaining witnesses in his favor, and to have the Assistance of Counsel for his defence.

Amendment VII

In Suits at common law, where the value in controversy shall exceed twenty dollars, the right of trial by jury shall be preserved, and no fact tried by a jury, shall be otherwise re-examined in any Court of the United States, than according to the rules of the common law.

Amendment VIII

Excessive bail shall not be required, nor excessive fines imposed, nor cruel and unusual punishments inflicted.

Amendment IX

The enumeration in the Constitution, of certain rights, shall not be construed to deny or disparage others retained by the people.

Amendment X

The powers not delegated to the United States by the Constitution, nor prohibited by it to the States, are reserved to the States respectively, or to the people.

Amendment XI

Passed by Congress March 4, 1794. Ratified February 7, 1795.

Note: Article III, Section 2, of the Constitution was modified by Amendment XI.

The Judicial power of the United States shall not be construed to extend to any suit in law or equity, commenced or prosecuted against one of the United States by Citizens of another State, or by Citizens or Subjects of any Foreign State.

Amendment XII

Passed by Congress December 9, 1803. Ratified June 15, 1804.

Note: A portion of Article II, Section 1, of the Constitution was superseded by the Twelfth Amendment.

The Electors shall meet in their respective states and vote by ballot for President and Vice-President, one of whom, at least, shall not be an inhabitant of the same state with themselves; they shall name in their ballots the person voted for as President, and in distinct ballots the person voted for as Vice-President, and they shall make distinct lists of all persons voted for as President, and of all persons voted for as Vice-President, and of the number of votes for each, which lists they shall sign and certify, and transmit sealed to the seat of the government of the United States, directed to the President of the Senate;—the President of the Senate shall, in the presence of the Senate and House of Representatives, open all the certificates and the votes shall then be counted;—The person having the greatest number of votes for President, shall be the President, if such number be a majority of the whole number of Electors appointed; and if no person have such majority, then from the persons having the highest numbers not exceeding three on the list of those voted for as President, the House of Representatives shall choose immediately, by ballot, the President. But in choosing the President, the votes shall be taken by states, the representation from each state having one vote; a quorum for this purpose shall consist of a member or members from two-thirds of the states, and a majority of all the states shall be necessary to a choice. [And if the House of Representatives shall not choose a President whenever the right of choice shall devolve upon them, before the fourth day of March next following, then the Vice-President shall act as President, as in case of the death or other constitutional disability of the President.—]* The person having the greatest number of votes as Vice-President, shall be the Vice-President, if such number be a majority of the whole number of Electors appointed, and if no person have a majority, then from the two highest numbers on the list, the Senate shall choose the Vice-President; a quorum for the purpose shall consist of two-thirds of the whole number of Senators, and a majority of the whole number shall be necessary to a choice. But no person constitutionally ineligible to the office of President shall be eligible to that of Vice-President of the United States.

Amendment XIII

Passed by Congress January 31, 1865. Ratified December 6, 1865.

Note: A portion of Article IV, Section 2, of the Constitution was superseded by the Thirteenth Amendment.

Section 1

Neither slavery nor involuntary servitude, except as a punishment for crime whereof the party shall have been duly convicted, shall exist within the United States, or any place subject to their jurisdiction.

Section 2

Congress shall have power to enforce this article by appropriate legislation.

Amendment XIV

Passed by Congress June 13, 1866. Ratified July 9, 1868.

Note: Article I, Section 2, of the Constitution was modified by Section 2 of the Fourteenth Amendment.

Section 1

All persons born or naturalized in the United States, and subject to the jurisdiction thereof, are citizens of the United States and of the State wherein they reside. No State shall make or enforce any law which shall abridge the

---

*Superseded by Section 3 of the Twentieth Amendment.

privileges or immunities of citizens of the United States; nor shall any State deprive any person of life, liberty, or property, without due process of law; nor deny to any person within its jurisdiction the equal protection of the laws.

Section 2

Representatives shall be apportioned among the several States according to their respective numbers, counting the whole number of persons in each State, excluding Indians not taxed. But when the right to vote at any election for the choice of electors for President and Vice-President of the United States, Representatives in Congress, the Executive and Judicial officers of a State, or the members of the Legislature thereof, is denied to any of the male inhabitants of such State, being twenty-one years of age,* and citizens of the United States, or in any way abridged, except for participation in rebellion, or other crime, the basis of representation therein shall be reduced in the proportion which the number of such male citizens shall bear to the whole number of male citizens twenty-one years of age in such State.

Section 3

No person shall be a Senator or Representative in Congress, or elector of President and Vice-President, or hold any office, civil or military, under the United States, or under any State, who, having previously taken an oath, as a member of Congress, or as an officer of the United States, or as a member of any State legislature, or as an executive or judicial officer of any State, to support the Constitution of the United States, shall have engaged in insurrection or rebellion against the same, or given aid or comfort to the enemies thereof. But Congress may by a vote of two-thirds of each House, remove such disability.

Section 4

The validity of the public debt of the United States, authorized by law, including debts incurred for payment of pensions and bounties for services in suppressing insurrection or rebellion, shall not be questioned. But neither the United States nor any State shall assume or pay any debt or obligation incurred in aid of insurrection or rebellion against the United States, or any claim for the loss or emancipation of any slave; but all such debts, obligations and claims shall be held illegal and void.

Section 5

The Congress shall have the power to enforce, by appropriate legislation, the provisions of this article.

---

*Changed by Section 1 of the Twenty-sixth Amendment.

Amendment XV

Passed by Congress February 26, 1869. Ratified February 3, 1870.

Section 1

The right of citizens of the United States to vote shall not be denied or abridged by the United States or by any State on account of race, color, or previous condition of servitude.

Section 2

The Congress shall have the power to enforce this article by appropriate legislation.

Amendment XVI

Passed by Congress July 2, 1909. Ratified February 3, 1913.

Note: Article I, Section 9, of the Constitution was modified by Amendment XVI.

The Congress shall have power to lay and collect taxes on incomes, from whatever source derived, without apportionment among the several States, and without regard to any census or enumeration.

Amendment XVII

Passed by Congress May 13, 1912. Ratified April 8, 1913.

Note: Article I, Section 3, of the Constitution was modified by the Seventeenth Amendment.

The Senate of the United States shall be composed of two Senators from each State, elected by the people thereof, for six years; and each Senator shall have one vote. The electors in each State shall have the qualifications requisite for electors of the most numerous branch of the State legislatures.

When vacancies happen in the representation of any State in the Senate, the executive authority of such State shall issue writs of election to fill such vacancies: Provided, That the legislature of any State may empower the executive thereof to make temporary appointments until the people fill the vacancies by election as the legislature may direct.

This amendment shall not be so construed as to affect the election or term of any Senator chosen before it becomes valid as part of the Constitution.

Amendment XVIII

Passed by Congress December 18, 1917. Ratified January 16, 1919. Repealed by Amendment XXI.

Section 1

After one year from the ratification of this article the manufacture, sale, or transportation of intoxicating liquors within, the importation thereof into, or the exportation thereof from the United States and all territory subject to the jurisdiction thereof for beverage purposes is hereby prohibited.

Section 2

The Congress and the several States shall have concurrent power to enforce this article by appropriate legislation.

Section 3

This article shall be inoperative unless it shall have been ratified as an amendment to the Constitution by the legislatures of the several States, as provided in the Constitution, within seven years from the date of the submission hereof to the States by the Congress.

Amendment XIX

Passed by Congress June 4, 1919. Ratified August 18, 1920.

The right of citizens of the United States to vote shall not be denied or abridged by the United States or by any State on account of sex.

Congress shall have power to enforce this article by appropriate legislation.

Amendment XX

Passed by Congress March 2, 1932. Ratified January 23, 1933.

Note: Article I, Section 4, of the Constitution was modified by Section 2 of this amendment. In addition, a portion of the Twelfth Amendment was superseded by Section 3.

Section 1

The terms of the President and the Vice President shall end at noon on the 20th day of January, and the terms of Senators and Representatives at noon on the 3d day of January, of the years in which such terms would have ended if this article had not been ratified; and the terms of their successors shall then begin.

Section 2

The Congress shall assemble at least once in every year, and such meeting shall begin at noon on the 3d day of January, unless they shall by law appoint a different day.

Section 3

If, at the time fixed for the beginning of the term of the President, the President elect shall have died, the Vice President elect shall become President. If a President shall not have been chosen before the time fixed for the beginning of his term, or if the President elect shall have failed to qualify, then the Vice President elect shall act as President until a President shall have qualified; and the Congress may by law provide for the case wherein neither a President elect nor a Vice President shall have qualified, declaring who shall then act as President, or the manner in which one who is to act shall be selected, and such person shall act accordingly until a President or Vice President shall have qualified.

Section 4

The Congress may by law provide for the case of the death of any of the persons from whom the House of Representatives may choose a President whenever the right of choice shall have devolved upon them, and for the case of the death of any of the persons from whom the Senate may choose a Vice President whenever the right of choice shall have devolved upon them.

Section 5

Sections 1 and 2 shall take effect on the 15th day of October following the ratification of this article.

Section 6

This article shall be inoperative unless it shall have been ratified as an amendment to the Constitution by the legislatures of three-fourths of the several States within seven years from the date of its submission.

Amendment XXI

Passed by Congress February 20, 1933. Ratified December 5, 1933.

Section 1

The eighteenth article of amendment to the Constitution of the United States is hereby repealed.

Section 2

The transportation or importation into any State, Territory, or Possession of the United States for delivery or use therein of intoxicating liquors, in violation of the laws thereof, is hereby prohibited.

Section 3

This article shall be inoperative unless it shall have been ratified as an amendment to the Constitution by conventions in the several States, as provided in the Constitution, within seven years from the date of the submission hereof to the States by the Congress.

Amendment XXII

Passed by Congress March 21, 1947. Ratified February 27, 1951.

Section 1

No person shall be elected to the office of the President more than twice, and no person who has held the office of President, or acted as President, for more than two years of a term to which some other person was elected

President shall be elected to the office of President more than once. But this Article shall not apply to any person holding the office of President when this Article was proposed by Congress, and shall not prevent any person who may be holding the office of President, or acting as President, during the term within which this Article becomes operative from holding the office of President or acting as President during the remainder of such term.

Section 2

This article shall be inoperative unless it shall have been ratified as an amendment to the Constitution by the legislatures of three-fourths of the several States within seven years from the date of its submission to the States by the Congress.

Amendment XXIII

Passed by Congress June 16, 1960. Ratified March 29, 1961.

Section 1

The District constituting the seat of Government of the United States shall appoint in such manner as Congress may direct:

A number of electors of President and Vice President equal to the whole number of Senators and Representatives in Congress to which the District would be entitled if it were a State, but in no event more than the least populous State; they shall be in addition to those appointed by the States, but they shall be considered, for the purposes of the election of President and Vice President, to be electors appointed by a State; and they shall meet in the District and perform such duties as provided by the twelfth article of amendment.

Section 2

The Congress shall have power to enforce this article by appropriate legislation.

Amendment XXIV

Passed by Congress August 27, 1962. Ratified January 23, 1964.

Section 1

The right of citizens of the United States to vote in any primary or other election for President or Vice President, for electors for President or Vice President, or for Senator or Representative in Congress, shall not be denied or abridged by the United States or any State by reason of failure to pay poll tax or other tax.

Section 2

The Congress shall have power to enforce this article by appropriate legislation.

Amendment XXV

Passed by Congress July 6, 1965. Ratified February 10, 1967.

Note: Article II, Section 1, of the Constitution was affected by the Twenty-Fifth Amendment.

Section 1

In case of the removal of the President from office or of his death or resignation, the Vice President shall become President.

Section 2

Whenever there is a vacancy in the office of the Vice President, the President shall nominate a Vice President who shall take office upon confirmation by a majority vote of both Houses of Congress.

Section 3

Whenever the President transmits to the President pro tempore of the Senate and the Speaker of the House of Representatives his written declaration that he is unable to discharge the powers and duties of his office, and until he transmits to them a written declaration to the contrary, such powers and duties shall be discharged by the Vice President as Acting President.

Section 4

Whenever the Vice President and a majority of either the principal officers of the executive departments or of such other body as Congress may by law provide, transmit to the President pro tempore of the Senate and the Speaker of the House of Representatives their written declaration that the President is unable to discharge the powers and duties of his office, the Vice President shall immediately assume the powers and duties of the office as Acting President.

Thereafter, when the President transmits to the President pro tempore of the Senate and the Speaker of the House of Representatives his written declaration that no inability exists, he shall resume the powers and duties of his office unless the Vice President and a majority of either the principal officers of the executive department or of such other body as Congress may by law provide, transmit within four days to the President pro tempore of the Senate and the Speaker of the House of Representatives their written declaration that the President is unable to discharge the powers and duties of his office. Thereupon Congress shall decide the issue, assembling within forty-eight hours for that purpose if not in session. If the Congress, within twenty-one days after receipt of the latter written declaration, or, if Congress is not in session, within twenty-one days after Congress is required to assemble, determines by two-thirds vote of both Houses that the President is unable to discharge the powers and duties of his office, the Vice President shall continue to discharge the same as Acting President; otherwise, the President shall resume the powers and duties of his office.

Amendment XXVI

Passed by Congress March 23, 1971. Ratified July 1, 1971.

Note: Amendment XIV, Section 2, of the Constitution was modified by Section 1 of the Twenty-Sixth Amendment.

Section 1

The right of citizens of the United States, who are eighteen years of age or older, to vote shall not be denied or abridged by the United States or by any State on account of age.

Section 2

The Congress shall have power to enforce this article by appropriate legislation.

Amendment XXVII

Originally proposed Sept. 25, 1789. Ratified May 7, 1992.

No law, varying the compensation for the services of the Senators and Representatives, shall take effect, until an election of representatives shall have intervened.

APPENDIX III

The Federalist Papers 1, 10, and 51

By Alexander Hamilton, James Madison, John Jay

The debate over ratifying the Constitution in 1787–8 was very close, especially in New York. To persuade the people of the state, Hamilton, Madison, and Jay wrote eighty-five newspaper essays arguing for ratification. Three of the most influential, reproduced here, are Federalist Papers 1, 10, and 51.

FEDERALIST No. 1
General Introduction
For the Independent Journal. Saturday, October 27, 1787

HAMILTON
To the People of the State of New York:

AFTER an unequivocal experience of the inefficacy of the subsisting federal government, you are called upon to deliberate on a new Constitution for the United States of America. The subject speaks its own importance; comprehending in its consequences nothing less than the existence of the UNION, the safety and welfare of the parts of which it is composed, the fate of an empire in many respects the most interesting in the world. It has been frequently remarked that it seems to have been reserved to the people of this country, by their conduct and example, to decide the important question, whether societies of men are really capable or not of establishing good government from reflection and choice, or whether they are forever destined to depend for their political constitutions on accident and force. If there be any truth in the remark, the crisis at which we are arrived may with propriety be regarded as the era in which that decision is to be made; and a wrong election of the part we shall act may, in this view, deserve to be considered as the general misfortune of mankind.

This idea will add the inducements of philanthropy to those of patriotism, to heighten the solicitude which all considerate and good men must feel for the event. Happy will it be if our choice should be directed by a judicious estimate of our true interests, unperplexed and unbiased by considerations not connected with the public good. But this is a thing more ardently to be wished than seriously to be expected. The plan offered to our deliberations affects too many particular interests, innovates upon too many local institutions, not to involve in its discussion a variety of objects foreign to its merits, and of views, passions and prejudices little favorable to the discovery of truth.

Among the most formidable of the obstacles which the new Constitution will have to encounter may readily be distinguished the obvious interest of a certain class of men in every State to resist all changes which may hazard a diminution of the power, emolument, and consequence of the offices they hold under the State establishments; and the perverted ambition of another class of men, who will either hope to aggrandize themselves by the confusions of their country, or will flatter themselves with fairer prospects of elevation from the subdivision of the empire into several partial confederacies than from its union under one government.

It is not, however, my design to dwell upon observations of this nature. I am well aware that it would be disingenuous to resolve indiscriminately the opposition of any set of men (merely because their situations might subject them to suspicion) into interested or ambitious views. Candor will oblige us to admit that even such men may be actuated by upright intentions; and it cannot be doubted that much of the opposition which has made its appearance, or may hereafter make its appearance, will spring from sources, blameless at least, if not respectable—the honest errors of minds led astray by preconceived jealousies and fears. So numerous indeed and so powerful are the causes which serve to give a false bias to the judgment, that we, upon many occasions, see wise and good men on the wrong as well as on the right side of questions of the first magnitude to society. This circumstance, if duly attended to, would furnish a lesson of moderation to those who are ever so much persuaded of their being in the right in any controversy. And a further reason for caution, in this respect, might be drawn from the reflection that we are not always sure that those who advocate the truth are influenced by purer principles than their antagonists. Ambition, avarice, personal animosity, party opposition, and many other motives not more laudable than these, are apt to operate as well upon those who support as those who oppose the right side of a question. Were there not even these inducements to moderation, nothing could be more ill-judged than that intolerant spirit which has, at all times, characterized political parties. For in politics, as in religion, it is equally absurd to aim at making proselytes by fire and sword. Heresies in either can rarely be cured by persecution.

And yet, however just these sentiments will be allowed to be, we have already sufficient indications that it will happen in this as in all former cases of great national discussion. A torrent of angry and malignant passions will be let loose. To judge from the conduct of the opposite parties, we shall be led to conclude that they will mutually hope to evince the justness of their opinions, and to increase the number of their converts by the loudness of their declamations and the bitterness of their invectives. An enlightened zeal for the energy and efficiency of government will be stigmatized as the offspring of a temper fond of despotic power and hostile to the principles of liberty. An over-scrupulous jealousy of danger to the rights of the people, which is more commonly the fault of the head than of the heart, will be represented as mere pretense and artifice, the stale bait for popularity at the expense of the public good. It will be forgotten, on the one hand, that jealousy is the usual concomitant of love, and that the noble enthusiasm of liberty is apt to be infected with a spirit of narrow and illiberal distrust. On the other hand, it will be equally forgotten that the vigor of government is essential to the security of liberty; that, in the contemplation of a sound and well-informed judgment, their interest can never be separated; and that a dangerous ambition more often lurks behind the specious mask of zeal for the rights of the people than under the forbidden appearance of zeal for the firmness and efficiency of government. History will teach us that the former has been found a much more certain road to the introduction of despotism than the latter, and that of those men who have overturned the liberties of republics, the greatest number have begun their career by paying an obsequious court to the people; commencing demagogues, and ending tyrants.

In the course of the preceding observations, I have had an eye, my fellow-citizens, to putting you upon your guard against all attempts, from whatever quarter, to influence your decision in a matter of the utmost moment to your welfare, by any impressions other than those which may result from the evidence of truth. You will, no doubt, at the same time, have collected from the general scope of them, that they proceed from a source not unfriendly to the new Constitution. Yes, my countrymen, I own to you that, after having given it an attentive consideration, I am clearly of opinion it is your interest to adopt it. I am convinced that this is the safest course for your liberty, your dignity, and your happiness. I affect not reserves which I do not feel. I will not amuse you with an appearance of deliberation when I have decided. I frankly acknowledge to you my convictions, and I will freely lay before you the reasons on which they are founded. The consciousness of good intentions disdains ambiguity. I shall not, however, multiply professions on this head. My motives must remain in the depository of my own breast. My arguments will be open to all, and may be judged of by all. They shall at least be offered in a spirit which will not disgrace the cause of truth.

I propose, in a series of papers, to discuss the following interesting particulars:

THE UTILITY OF THE UNION TO YOUR POLITICAL PROSPERITY THE INSUFFICIENCY OF THE PRESENT CONFEDERATION TO PRESERVE THAT UNION THE NECESSITY OF A GOVERNMENT AT LEAST EQUALLY ENERGETIC WITH THE ONE PROPOSED, TO THE ATTAINMENT OF THIS OBJECT THE CONFORMITY OF THE PROPOSED CONSTITUTION TO THE TRUE PRINCIPLES OF REPUBLICAN GOVERNMENT ITS ANALOGY TO YOUR OWN STATE CONSTITUTION and lastly, THE ADDITIONAL SECURITY WHICH ITS ADOPTION WILL AFFORD TO THE PRESERVATION OF THAT SPECIES OF GOVERNMENT, TO LIBERTY, AND TO PROPERTY.

In the progress of this discussion I shall endeavor to give a satisfactory answer to all the objections which shall have made their appearance, that may seem to have any claim to your attention.

It may perhaps be thought superfluous to offer arguments to prove the utility of the UNION, a point, no doubt, deeply engraved on the hearts of the great body of the people in every State, and one, which it may be imagined, has no adversaries. But the fact is, that we already hear it whispered in the private circles of those who oppose the new Constitution, that the thirteen States are of too great extent for any general system, and that we must of necessity resort to separate confederacies of distinct portions of the whole. This doctrine will, in all probability, be gradually propagated, till it has votaries enough to countenance an open avowal of it. For nothing can be more evident, to those who are able to take an enlarged view of the subject, than the alternative of an adoption of the new Constitution or a dismemberment of the Union. It will therefore be of use to begin by examining the advantages of that Union, the certain evils, and the probable dangers, to which every State will be exposed from its dissolution. This shall accordingly constitute the subject of my next address.

PUBLIUS

FEDERALIST No. 10
The Same Subject Continued (The Union as a Safeguard Against Domestic Faction and Insurrection)
From the Daily Advertiser. Thursday, November 22, 1787.

MADISON
To the People of the State of New York:

AMONG the numerous advantages promised by a well constructed Union, none deserves to be more accurately developed than its tendency to break and control the violence of faction. The friend of popular governments never finds himself so much alarmed for their character and fate, as when he contemplates their propensity to this dangerous vice. He will not fail, therefore, to set a due value on any plan which, without violating the principles to which he is attached, provides a proper cure for it. The instability, injustice, and confusion introduced into the public councils, have, in truth, been the mortal diseases under which popular governments have everywhere perished; as they continue to be the favorite and fruitful topics from which the adversaries to liberty derive their most specious declamations. The valuable improvements made by the American constitutions on the popular models, both ancient and modern, cannot certainly be too much admired; but it would be an unwarrantable partiality, to contend that they have as effectually obviated the danger on this side, as was wished and expected. Complaints are everywhere heard from our most considerate and virtuous citizens, equally the friends of public and private faith, and of public and personal liberty, that our governments are too unstable, that the public good is disregarded in the conflicts of rival parties, and that measures are too often decided, not according to the rules of justice and the rights of the minor party, but by the superior force of an interested and overbearing majority. However anxiously we may wish that these complaints had no foundation, the evidence, of known facts will not permit us to deny that they are in some degree true. It will be found, indeed, on a candid review of our situation, that some of the distresses under which we labor have been erroneously charged on the operation of our governments; but it will be found, at the same time, that other causes will not alone account for many of our heaviest misfortunes; and, particularly,

for that prevailing and increasing distrust of public engagements, and alarm for private rights, which are echoed from one end of the continent to the other. These must be chiefly, if not wholly, effects of the unsteadiness and injustice with which a factious spirit has tainted our public administrations.

By a faction, I understand a number of citizens, whether amounting to a majority or a minority of the whole, who are united and actuated by some common impulse of passion, or of interest, adversed to the rights of other citizens, or to the permanent and aggregate interests of the community.

There are two methods of curing the mischiefs of faction: the one, by removing its causes; the other, by controlling its effects.

There are again two methods of removing the causes of faction: the one, by destroying the liberty which is essential to its existence; the other, by giving to every citizen the same opinions, the same passions, and the same interests.

It could never be more truly said than of the first remedy, that it was worse than the disease. Liberty is to faction what air is to fire, an aliment without which it instantly expires. But it could not be less folly to abolish liberty, which is essential to political life, because it nourishes faction, than it would be to wish the annihilation of air, which is essential to animal life, because it imparts to fire its destructive agency.

The second expedient is as impracticable as the first would be unwise. As long as the reason of man continues fallible, and he is at liberty to exercise it, different opinions will be formed. As long as the connection subsists between his reason and his self-love, his opinions and his passions will have a reciprocal influence on each other; and the former will be objects to which the latter will attach themselves. The diversity in the faculties of men, from which the rights of property originate, is not less an insuperable obstacle to a uniformity of interests. The protection of these faculties is the first object of government. From the protection of different and unequal faculties of acquiring property, the possession of different degrees and kinds of property immediately results; and from the influence of these on the sentiments and views of the respective proprietors, ensues a division of the society into different interests and parties.

The latent causes of faction are thus sown in the nature of man; and we see them everywhere brought into different degrees of activity, according to the different circumstances of civil society. A zeal for different opinions concerning religion, concerning government, and many other points, as well of speculation as of practice; an attachment to different leaders ambitiously contending for pre-eminence and power; or to persons of other descriptions whose fortunes have been interesting to the human passions, have, in turn, divided mankind into parties, inflamed them with mutual animosity, and rendered them much more disposed to vex and oppress each other than to co-operate for their common good. So strong is this propensity of mankind to fall into mutual animosities, that where no substantial occasion presents itself, the most frivolous and fanciful distinctions have been sufficient to kindle their unfriendly passions and excite their most violent conflicts. But the most common and durable source of factions has been the various and unequal distribution of property. Those who hold and those who are without property have ever formed distinct interests in society. Those who are creditors, and those who are debtors, fall under a like discrimination. A landed interest, a manufacturing interest, a mercantile interest, a moneyed interest, with many lesser interests, grow up of necessity in civilized nations, and divide them into different classes,

actuated by different sentiments and views. The regulation of these various and interfering interests forms the principal task of modern legislation, and involves the spirit of party and faction in the necessary and ordinary operations of the government.

No man is allowed to be a judge in his own cause, because his interest would certainly bias his judgment, and, not improbably, corrupt his integrity. With equal, nay with greater reason, a body of men are unfit to be both judges and parties at the same time; yet what are many of the most important acts of legislation, but so many judicial determinations, not indeed concerning the rights of single persons, but concerning the rights of large bodies of citizens? And what are the different classes of legislators but advocates and parties to the causes which they determine? Is a law proposed concerning private debts? It is a question to which the creditors are parties on one side and the debtors on the other. Justice ought to hold the balance between them. Yet the parties are, and must be, themselves the judges; and the most numerous party, or, in other words, the most powerful faction must be expected to prevail. Shall domestic manufactures be encouraged, and in what degree, by restrictions on foreign manufactures? are questions which would be differently decided by the landed and the manufacturing classes, and probably by neither with a sole regard to justice and the public good. The apportionment of taxes on the various descriptions of property is an act which seems to require the most exact impartiality; yet there is, perhaps, no legislative act in which greater opportunity and temptation are given to a predominant party to trample on the rules of justice. Every shilling with which they overburden the inferior number, is a shilling saved to their own pockets.

It is in vain to say that enlightened statesmen will be able to adjust these clashing interests, and render them all subservient to the public good. Enlightened statesmen will not always be at the helm. Nor, in many cases, can such an adjustment be made at all without taking into view indirect and remote considerations, which will rarely prevail over the immediate interest which one party may find in disregarding the rights of another or the good of the whole.

The inference to which we are brought is, that the CAUSES of faction cannot be removed, and that relief is only to be sought in the means of controlling its EFFECTS.

If a faction consists of less than a majority, relief is supplied by the republican principle, which enables the majority to defeat its sinister views by regular vote. It may clog the administration, it may convulse the society; but it will be unable to execute and mask its violence under the forms of the Constitution. When a majority is included in a faction, the form of popular government, on the other hand, enables it to sacrifice to its ruling passion or interest both the public good and the rights of other citizens. To secure the public good and private rights against the danger of such a faction, and at the same time to preserve the spirit and the form of popular government, is then the great object to which our inquiries are directed. Let me add that it is the great desideratum by which this form of government can be rescued from the opprobrium under which it has so long labored, and be recommended to the esteem and adoption of mankind.

By what means is this object attainable? Evidently by one of two only. Either the existence of the same passion or interest in a majority at the same time must be prevented, or the majority, having such coexistent passion or interest, must be rendered, by their number and local situation, unable to concert and carry into effect schemes of

oppression. If the impulse and the opportunity be suffered to coincide, we well know that neither moral nor religious motives can be relied on as an adequate control. They are not found to be such on the injustice and violence of individuals, and lose their efficacy in proportion to the number combined together, that is, in proportion as their efficacy becomes needful.

From this view of the subject it may be concluded that a pure democracy, by which I mean a society consisting of a small number of citizens, who assemble and administer the government in person, can admit of no cure for the mischiefs of faction. A common passion or interest will, in almost every case, be felt by a majority of the whole; a communication and concert result from the form of government itself; and there is nothing to check the inducements to sacrifice the weaker party or an obnoxious individual. Hence it is that such democracies have ever been spectacles of turbulence and contention; have ever been found incompatible with personal security or the rights of property; and have in general been as short in their lives as they have been violent in their deaths. Theoretic politicians, who have patronized this species of government, have erroneously supposed that by reducing mankind to a perfect equality in their political rights, they would, at the same time, be perfectly equalized and assimilated in their possessions, their opinions, and their passions.

A republic, by which I mean a government in which the scheme of representation takes place, opens a different prospect, and promises the cure for which we are seeking. Let us examine the points in which it varies from pure democracy, and we shall comprehend both the nature of the cure and the efficacy which it must derive from the Union.

The two great points of difference between a democracy and a republic are: first, the delegation of the government, in the latter, to a small number of citizens elected by the rest; secondly, the greater number of citizens, and greater sphere of country, over which the latter may be extended.

The effect of the first difference is, on the one hand, to refine and enlarge the public views, by passing them through the medium of a chosen body of citizens, whose wisdom may best discern the true interest of their country, and whose patriotism and love of justice will be least likely to sacrifice it to temporary or partial considerations. Under such a regulation, it may well happen that the public voice, pronounced by the representatives of the people, will be more consonant to the public good than if pronounced by the people themselves, convened for the purpose. On the other hand, the effect may be inverted. Men of factious tempers, of local prejudices, or of sinister designs, may, by intrigue, by corruption, or by other means, first obtain the suffrages, and then betray the interests, of the people. The question resulting is, whether small or extensive republics are more favorable to the election of proper guardians of the public weal; and it is clearly decided in favor of the latter by two obvious considerations:

In the first place, it is to be remarked that, however small the republic may be, the representatives must be raised to a certain number, in order to guard against the cabals of a few; and that, however large it may be, they must be limited to a certain number, in order to guard against the confusion of a multitude. Hence, the number of representatives in the two cases not being in proportion to that of the two constituents, and being proportionally greater in the small republic, it follows that, if the proportion of fit characters be not less in the large than in the small republic, the former will present a greater option, and consequently a greater probability of a fit choice.

In the next place, as each representative will be chosen by a greater number of citizens in the large than in the small republic, it will be more difficult for unworthy candidates to practice with success the vicious arts by which elections are too often carried; and the suffrages of the people being more free, will be more likely to centre in men who possess the most attractive merit and the most diffusive and established characters.

It must be confessed that in this, as in most other cases, there is a mean, on both sides of which inconveniences will be found to lie. By enlarging too much the number of electors, you render the representatives too little acquainted with all their local circumstances and lesser interests; as by reducing it too much, you render him unduly attached to these, and too little fit to comprehend and pursue great and national objects. The federal Constitution forms a happy combination in this respect; the great and aggregate interests being referred to the national, the local and particular to the State legislatures.

The other point of difference is, the greater number of citizens and extent of territory which may be brought within the compass of republican than of democratic government; and it is this circumstance principally which renders factious combinations less to be dreaded in the former than in the latter. The smaller the society, the fewer probably will be the distinct parties and interests composing it; the fewer the distinct parties and interests, the more frequently will a majority be found of the same party; and the smaller the number of individuals composing a majority, and the smaller the compass within which they are placed, the more easily will they concert and execute their plans of oppression. Extend the sphere, and you take in a greater variety of parties and interests; you make it less probable that a majority of the whole will have a common motive to invade the rights of other citizens; or if such a common motive exists, it will be more difficult for all who feel it to discover their own strength, and to act in unison with each other. Besides other impediments, it may be remarked that, where there is a consciousness of unjust or dishonorable purposes, communication is always checked by distrust in proportion to the number whose concurrence is necessary.

Hence, it clearly appears, that the same advantage which a republic has over a democracy, in controlling the effects of faction, is enjoyed by a large over a small republic,—is enjoyed by the Union over the States composing it. Does the advantage consist in the substitution of representatives whose enlightened views and virtuous sentiments render them superior to local prejudices and schemes of injustice? It will not be denied that the representation of the Union will be most likely to possess these requisite endowments. Does it consist in the greater security afforded by a greater variety of parties, against the event of any one party being able to outnumber and oppress the rest? In an equal degree does the increased variety of parties comprised within the Union, increase this security. Does it, in fine, consist in the greater obstacles opposed to the concert and accomplishment of the secret wishes of an unjust and interested majority? Here, again, the extent of the Union gives it the most palpable advantage.

The influence of factious leaders may kindle a flame within their particular States, but will be unable to spread a general conflagration through the other States. A religious sect may degenerate into a political faction in a part of the Confederacy; but the variety of sects dispersed over the entire face of it must secure the national councils against any danger from that source. A rage for paper money, for an abolition of debts, for an equal division of property, or for any other improper or wicked project, will be less apt to pervade the whole body of the Union than a particular member of it; in the same proportion as such a malady is more likely to taint a particular county or district, than an entire State.

In the extent and proper structure of the Union, therefore, we behold a republican remedy for the diseases most incident to republican government. And according to the degree of pleasure and pride we feel in being republicans, ought to be our zeal in cherishing the spirit and supporting the character of Federalists.

PUBLIUS

FEDERALIST No. 51
The Structure of the Government Must Furnish the Proper Checks and Balances Between the Different Departments.
For the Independent Journal. Wednesday, February 6, 1788.

MADISON
To the People of the State of New York:

TO WHAT expedient, then, shall we finally resort, for maintaining in practice the necessary partition of power among the several departments, as laid down in the Constitution? The only answer that can be given is, that as all these exterior provisions are found to be inadequate, the defect must be supplied, by so contriving the interior structure of the government as that its several constituent parts may, by their mutual relations, be the means of keeping each other in their proper places. Without presuming to undertake a full development of this important idea, I will hazard a few general observations, which may perhaps place it in a clearer light, and enable us to form a more correct judgment of the principles and structure of the government planned by the convention.

In order to lay a due foundation for that separate and distinct exercise of the different powers of government, which to a certain extent is admitted on all hands to be essential to the preservation of liberty, it is evident that each department should have a will of its own; and consequently should be so constituted that the members of each should have as little agency as possible in the appointment of the members of the others. Were this principle rigorously adhered to, it would require that all the appointments for the supreme executive, legislative, and judiciary magistracies should be drawn from the same fountain of authority, the people, through channels having no communication whatever with one another. Perhaps such a plan of constructing the several departments would be less difficult in practice than it may in contemplation appear. Some difficulties, however, and some additional expense would attend the execution of it. Some deviations, therefore, from the principle must be admitted. In the constitution of the judiciary department in particular, it might be inexpedient to insist rigorously on the principle: first, because peculiar qualifications being essential in the members, the primary consideration ought to be to select that mode of choice which best secures these qualifications; secondly, because the permanent tenure by which the appointments are held in that department, must soon destroy all sense of dependence on the authority conferring them.

It is equally evident, that the members of each department should be as little dependent as possible on those of the others, for the emoluments annexed to their offices. Were the executive magistrate, or the judges, not independent of the legislature in this particular, their independence in every other would be merely nominal.

But the great security against a gradual concentration of the several powers in the same department, consists in giving to those who administer each department the necessary constitutional means and personal motives to resist encroachments of the others. The provision for defense must in this, as in all other cases, be made commensurate to the danger of attack. Ambition must be made to counteract ambition. The interest of the man must be connected with the constitutional rights of the place. It may be a reflection on human nature, that such devices should be necessary to control the abuses of government. But what is government itself, but the greatest of all reflections on human nature? If men were angels, no government would be necessary. If angels were to govern men, neither external nor internal controls on government would be necessary. In framing a government which is to be administered by men over men, the great difficulty lies in this: you must first enable the government to control the governed; and in the next place oblige it to control itself. A dependence on the people is, no doubt, the primary control on the government; but experience has taught mankind the necessity of auxiliary precautions.

This policy of supplying, by opposite and rival interests, the defect of better motives, might be traced through the whole system of human affairs, private as well as public. We see it particularly displayed in all the subordinate distributions of power, where the constant aim is to divide and arrange the several offices in such a manner as that each may be a check on the other—that the private interest of every individual may be a sentinel over the public rights. These inventions of prudence cannot be less requisite in the distribution of the supreme powers of the State.

But it is not possible to give to each department an equal power of self-defense. In republican government, the legislative authority necessarily predominates. The remedy for this inconveniency is to divide the legislature into different branches; and to render them, by different modes of election and different principles of action, as little connected with each other as the nature of their common functions and their common dependence on the society will admit. It may even be necessary to guard against dangerous encroachments by still further precautions. As the weight of the legislative authority requires that it should be thus divided, the weakness of the executive may require, on the other hand, that it should be fortified. An absolute negative on the legislature appears, at first view, to be the natural defense with which the executive magistrate should be armed. But perhaps it would be neither altogether safe nor alone sufficient. On ordinary occasions it might not be exerted with the requisite firmness, and on extraordinary occasions it might be perfidiously abused. May not this defect of an absolute negative be supplied by some qualified connection between this weaker department and the weaker branch of the stronger department, by which the latter may be led to support the constitutional rights of the former, without being too much detached from the rights of its own department?

If the principles on which these observations are founded be just, as I persuade myself they are, and they be applied as a criterion to the several State constitutions, and to the federal Constitution it will be found that if the latter does not perfectly correspond with them, the former are infinitely less able to bear such a test.

There are, moreover, two considerations particularly applicable to the federal system of America, which place that system in a very interesting point of view.

First. In a single republic, all the power surrendered by the people is submitted to the administration of a single government; and the usurpations are guarded against by a division of the government into distinct and separate departments. In the compound republic of America, the power surrendered by the people is first divided between two distinct governments, and then the portion allotted to each subdivided among distinct and separate departments. Hence a double security arises to the rights of the people. The different governments will control each other, at the same time that each will be controlled by itself.

Second. It is of great importance in a republic not only to guard the society against the oppression of its rulers, but to guard one part of the society against the injustice of the other part. Different interests necessarily exist in different classes of citizens. If a majority be united by a common interest, the rights of the minority will be insecure. There are but two methods of providing against this evil: the one by creating a will in the community independent of the majority—that is, of the society itself; the other, by comprehending in the society so many separate descriptions of citizens as will render an unjust combination of a majority of the whole very improbable, if not impracticable. The first method prevails in all governments possessing an hereditary or self-appointed authority. This, at best, is but a precarious security; because a power independent of the society may as well espouse the unjust views of the major, as the rightful interests of the minor party, and may possibly be turned against both parties. The second method will be exemplified in the federal republic of the United States. Whilst all authority in it will be derived from and dependent on the society, the society itself will be broken into so many parts, interests, and classes of citizens, that the rights of individuals, or of the minority, will be in little danger from interested combinations of the majority. In a free government the security for civil rights must be the same as that for religious rights. It consists in the one case in the multiplicity of interests, and in the other in the multiplicity of sects. The degree of security in both cases will depend on the number of interests and sects; and this may be presumed to depend on the extent of country and number of people comprehended under the same government. This view of the subject must particularly recommend a proper federal system to all the sincere and considerate friends of republican government, since it shows that in exact proportion as the territory of the Union may be formed into more circumscribed Confederacies, or States oppressive combinations of a majority will be facilitated: the best security, under the republican forms, for the rights of every class of citizens, will be diminished: and consequently the stability and independence of some member of the government, the only other security, must be proportionately increased. Justice is the end of government. It is the end of civil society. It ever has been and ever will be pursued until it be obtained, or until liberty be lost in the pursuit. In a society under the forms of which the stronger faction can readily unite and oppress the weaker, anarchy may as truly be said to reign as in a state of nature, where the weaker individual is not secured against the violence of the stronger; and as, in the latter state, even the stronger individuals are prompted, by the uncertainty of their condition, to submit to a government which may protect the weak as well as themselves; so, in the former state, will the more powerful factions or parties be gradually induced, by a like motive, to wish for a government which will protect all parties, the weaker as well as the more powerful. It can be little doubted that if the State of Rhode Island was separated from the Confederacy and left to itself, the insecurity of rights under the popular form of government within such narrow limits would be displayed by such reiterated oppressions of factious majorities that some power altogether independent of the people would soon be called for by the voice of the very factions whose misrule had proved the necessity of it. In the extended republic of the United States, and among the great variety of interests, parties, and sects which it embraces, a coalition of a majority of the whole society could seldom take place on any other principles than those of justice and the general good; whilst there being thus less danger to a minor from the will of a major party, there must be less pretext, also, to provide for the security of the former, by introducing into the government a will not dependent on the latter, or, in other words, a will independent of the society itself. It is no less certain than it is important, notwithstanding the contrary opinions which have been entertained, that the larger the society, provided it lie within a practical sphere, the more duly capable it will be of self-government. And happily for the REPUBLICAN CAUSE, the practicable sphere may be carried to a very great extent, by a judicious modification and mixture of the FEDERAL PRINCIPLE.

PUBLIUS

APPENDIX IV

Presidential Elections, Congressional Control, 1789–2012

KEY: Party abbreviations: Dem = Democrat | **DemRep** = Democratic Republican | **Fed** = Federalist
IndRep = Independent Republican | **NatRep** = National Republican | **Rep** = Republican

Election Year	Presidential Candidates	Political Party	Electoral Vote	Percentage of Popular Vote	Control of Congress House	Control of Congress Senate
1789	**George Washington** John Adams Others	None -- --	69 32 35	No Popular Vote	Fed	Fed
1792	**George Washington** John Adams Others	None -- --	132 77 55	No Popular Vote	DemRep	Fed
1796	John Adams Thomas Jefferson Thomas Pinckney Aaron Burr Others	Fed DemRep Fed DemRep --	71 68 59 30 48	No Popular Vote	Fed	Fed
1800	Thomas Jefferson Aaron Burr John Adams C C Pinkney	DemRep DemRep Fed Fed	73 73 65 64	No Popular Vote	DemRep	DemRep
1804	Thomas Jefferson C. C. Pinkney	DemRep Fed	162 14	No Popular Vote	DemRep	DemRep
1808	James Madison C. C. Pinkney	DemRep Fed	122 47	No Popular Vote	DemRep	DemRep
1812	James Madison De Witt Clinton	DemRep Fed	128 89	No Popular Vote	DemRep	DemRep
1816	James Monroe Rufus King	DemRep Fed	231 34	No Popular Vote	DemRep	DemRep
1820	James Monroe John Q Adams	DemRep IndRep	231 1	No Popular Vote	DemRep	DemRep
1824	John Quincy Adams* Andrew Jackson Henry Clay W Crawford	DemRep DemRep DemRep DemRep	84 99 37 41	30.5 43.1 13.2 13.1	Pro Adams Pro Jackson (at midterm)	Pro Jackson
1828	Andrew Jackson John Q Adams	Dem NatRep	178 83	56.0 44.0	Pro Jackson	Pro Jackson
1832	Andrew Jackson Henry Clay	Dem NatRep	219 49	55.0 42.0	Pro Jackson	Opposition Pro Jackson
1836	Martin Van Buren William H Harrison	Dem Whig	170 73	50.9 36.7	Dem	Dem

* Lost the popular vote, won the Electoral College and became president
** Died in office

Election Year	Presidential Candidates	Political Party	Electoral Vote	Percentage of Popular Vote	Control of Congress — House	Control of Congress — Senate
1840	William H Harrison**	Whig	234	53.1	Whig	Whig
	Martin Van Buren	Dem	60	46.9	Dem (at midterm)	
1844	James K Polk	Dem	170	49.6	Dem	Dem
	Henry Clay	Whig	105	48.1		
	James Birney	Liberty (Abolition)	0	2.3	Whig (at midterm)	
1848	Zachary Taylor**	Whig	163	47.4	Dem	Dem
	Lewis Cass	Dem	127	42.5		
	Martin Van Buren	Free Soil	0	10.0		
1852	Franklin Pierce	Dem	254	50.9	Dem	Dem
	Winfield Scott	Whig	42	44.1	Opposition (at midterm)	
1856	James Buchanan	Dem	174	45.4	Dem	Dem
	John Fremont	Rep	114	33.0		
	Millard Fillmore	American (Know Nothing)	8	21.6	Rep (at midterm)	
1860	Abraham Lincoln	Rep	180	39.8	Rep	Rep
	Stephen Douglas	Dem	12	29.5		
	John Breckinridge	Dem	72	18.1		
	John Bell	Constitutional Union	79	12.6		
1864	Abraham Lincoln**	Rep	212	55.0	Rep	Rep
	George McClellan	Dem	21	45.0		
1868	Ulysses Grant	Rep	214	52.7	Rep	Rep
	Horatio Seymour	Dem	80	47.3		
1872	Ulysses Grant	Rep	286	55.6	Rep	Rep
	Horace Greeley	Dem	66	43.9	Dem (at midterm)	
1876	Rutherford Hayes*	Rep	185	48.0	Rep	Rep
	Samuel Tilden	Dem	184	51.0	Dem	Dem (at midterm)
1880	James Garfield**	Rep	214	48.3	Rep	Rep
	Winfield Hancock	Dem	155	48.2	Dem (at midterm)	
	James Weaver	Greenback-Labor	0	3.4		
1884	Grover Cleveland	Dem	219	48.5	Dem	Rep
	James Blaine	Rep	182	48.2		
	Benjamin Butler	Greenback-labor		11.8		
1888	Benjamin Harrison*	Rep	233	47.8	Rep	Rep
	Grover Cleveland	Dem	168	48.6	Dem (at midterm)	Rep
1892	Grover Cleveland	Dem	277	46.0	Dem	Dem
	Benjamin Harrison	Rep	145	43.0		
	James Weaver	People's (Populist)	22	8.5	Rep (at midterm)	Rep (at midterm)
1896	William McKinley	Rep	271	51.0	Rep	Rep
	William J. Bryan	Dem	176	45.5		
1900	William McKinley**	Rep	292	51.7	Rep	Rep
	William J. Bryan	Dem	155	45.5		
1904	Theodore Roosevelt	Rep	336	56.4	Rep	Rep
	Alton Parker	Dem	140	37.6		

* Lost the popular vote, won the Electoral College and became president

** Died in office

Election Year	Presidential Candidates	Political Party	Electoral Vote	Percentage of Popular Vote	Control of Congress	
					House	Senate
1908	William H Taft	Rep	321	51.6	Rep	Rep
	William J Bryan	Dem	162	43.1		Dem
1912	Woodrow Wilson	Dem	435	41.8	Dem	Dem
	Theodore Roosevelt	Progressive	88	27.4		
	William H Taft	Rep	8	23.2		
	Eugene Debs	Socialist	0	6.0		
1916	Woodrow Wilson	Dem	277	49.2	Rep	Dem
	Charles Hughes	Rep	254	46.1		
1920	Warren Harding	Rep	404	60.0	Rep	Rep
	James Cox	Dem	60	34.6		
1924	Calvin Coolidge	Rep	382	54.1	Rep	Rep
	John Davis	Dem	136	28.8		
	Robert La Follette	Progressive	13	16.6		
1928	Herbert Hoover	Rep	444	58.2	Rep	Rep
	Alfred Smith	Dem	87	40.8	Dem (at midterm)	
1932	Franklin Roosevelt	Dem	472	57.3	Dem	Dem
	Herbert Hoover	Rep	59	39.6		
1936	Franklin Roosevelt	Dem	523	60.8	Dem	Dem
	Alfred Landon	Rep	8	36.4		
1940	Franklin Roosevelt	Dem	449	54.7	Dem	Dem
	Wendell Wilkie	Rep	82	44.8		
1944	Franklin Roosevelt**	Dem	432	52.8	Dem	Dem
	Thomas Dewey	Rep	99	44.5	Rep (at midterm)	Rep (at midterm)
1948	Harry Truman	Dem	303	49.5	Dem	Dem
	Thomas Dewey	Rep	189	45.1		
	Strom Thurmond	States Rights	39	2.4		
1952	Dwight Eisenhower	Rep	442	55.2	Rep	Rep
	Adlai Stevenson	Dem	89	44.5	Dem (at midterm)	Dem (at midterm)
1956	Dwight Eisenhower	Rep	457	57.4	Dem	Dem
	Adlai Stevenson	Dem	73	42.0		
1960	John F Kennedy**	Dem	303	49.9	Dem	Dem
	Richard Nixon	Rep	219	49.6		
1964	Lyndon Johnson	Dem	486	61.1	Dem	Dem
	Barry Goldwater	Rep	52	38.5		
1968	Richard Nixon	Rep	301	43.4	Dem	Dem
	Hubert Humphrey	Dem	191	42.7		
	George Wallace	American	41	13.5		
1972	Richard Nixon	Rep	521	61.3	Dem	Dem
	George McGovern	Dem	17	37.3		
1976	Jimmy Carter	Dem	297	50.1	Dem	Dem
	Gerald Ford	Rep	240	48.0		
1980	Ronald Reagan	Rep	489	51.0	Dem	Rep
	Jimmy Carter	Dem	49	41.0		
	John Anderson			6.6		
1984	Ronald Reagan	Rep	525	58.8	Dem	Rep
	Walter Mondale	Dem	13	41.0		Dem (at midterm)

* Lost the popular vote, won the Electoral College and became president
** Died in office

Election Year	Presidential Candidates	Political Party	Electoral Vote	Percentage of Popular Vote	Control of Congress	
					House	Senate
1988	George H. W. Bush	Rep	426	53.4	Dem	Dem
	Michael Dukakis	Dem	111	46.0		
1992	Bill Clinton	Dem	370	43.0	Dem	Dem
	George H. W. Bush	Rep	168	37.4		
	Ross Perot	--	0	18.9	Rep (at midterm)	Rep (at midterm)
1996	Bill Clinton	Dem	379	49.2	Rep	Rep
	Robert Dole	Rep	159	40.7		
	Ross Perot	Reform	0	8.4		
2000	George W Bush*	Rep	271	47.8	Rep	Rep
	Al Gore	Dem	266	48.4		
	Ralph Nader	Green	0	2.7		
2004	George W Bush	Rep	286	50.7	Rep	Rep
	John Kerry	Dem	251	48.2	Dem (at midterm)	Dem (at midterm)
2008	Barack Obama	Dem	365	52.8	Dem	Dem
	John McCain	Rep	173	45.6	Rep (at midterm)	
2012	Barack Obama	Dem	332	50.5	Rep	Dem
	Mitt Romney	Rep	206	47.9		

* Lost the popular vote, won the Electoral College and became president
** Died in office

Glossary

113th Congress: The Congress elected in 2012. The first Congress met in 1789–1790. Each Congress is elected for a two-year session and numbered consecutively.

527 groups: Organizations governed by Section 527 of the federal tax code; they are allowed to raise and spend unlimited amounts for "issue advocacy"—but are forbidden to coordinate their efforts with any candidate or campaign, and their ads cannot mention a candidate, favorably or unfavorably.

1963 March on Washington: A massive rally for civil rights highlighted by Martin Luther King's "I Have a Dream" speech.

Abolition: A nineteenth-century movement demanding an immediate and unconditional end to slavery.

Affirmative action: Direct, positive steps to recruit members of previously underrepresented groups into schools, colleges, and jobs; sometimes involves setting aside positions (known as quotas).

American exceptionalism: The view that the United States is unique, marked by a distinct set of ideas such as equality, self-rule, and limited government.

Amicus curiae: A legal brief submitted by a person or group that is not a direct party to the case.

Appellate courts: The system of federal justices, organized into district courts and circuit courts, who hear appeals from lower courts, culminating in the Supreme Court.

Approval rating: A measure of public support for a political figure or institution.

Bandwagon effect: Tendency of undecided voters to support the candidate who is leading in the polls.

Base voters: Party members who tend to vote loyally for their party's candidates in most elections.

Bicameral: Having two legislative houses or chambers—like the House and the Senate.

The Bill of Rights: The first ten amendments to the Constitution, listing the rights guaranteed to every citizen.

Block grants: National government funding provided to state and local governments, with relatively few restrictions or requirements on spending.

Boomerang effect: The discrepancy between candidates' high poll ratings and election performance, caused by supporters' assumption that an easy win means they need not turn out.

Brown v. Board of Education: The landmark 1954 Supreme Court case that struck down segregated schools as unconstitutional.

Budget resolution: A joint House-Senate creation that outlines targets for federal spending, revenue levels, and the resultant budget deficit (or surplus) for the coming fiscal year.

Bundling: A form of fundraising in which an individual persuades others to donate large amounts that are then delivered together to a candidate or campaign.

Bureaucratic pathologies: The problems that tend to develop in bureaucratic systems.

Call list: A long list of potential donors whom candidates must phone.

Caucus: A local meeting at which registered members of a political party meet to select delegates representing presidential candidates.

Central clearance: The OMB's authority to review and "clear" (or okay) anything a member of the administration says or does in public.

Central service agencies: The organizations that supply and staff the federal government.

Charter school: A privately run school under town or city supervision; usually free to public school children who qualify for admission.

Checks and balances: The principle that each branch of government has the authority to block the other branches, making it more difficult for anyone to exercise too much power. It makes passing legislation far more difficult in the United States than in most other democracies.

Chicanismo: A defiant movement expressing pride in Latino origins and culture in the face of discrimination.

Chief of Staff: The individual responsible for managing the president's office.

Circle of nonparticipation: Resistance by political parties to mobilizing disengaged Americans to vote—because their lack of involvement makes their allegiances to one or the other party suspect.

Circuit courts (US Court of Appeals): The second stage of federal courts which review the trial record of cases decided in district court to ensure they were settled properly.

Civic voluntarism: Citizen participation in public life without government incentives or coercion (speaking at a town meeting vs. paying taxes, for example).

Civil law: Cases that involve disputes between two parties.

Civil liberties: The limits on government so that people can freely exercise their rights.

Civil rights: The freedom to participate in the full life of the community—to vote, use public facilities, and exercise equal economic opportunity.

Civil Rights Act of 1964: Landmark legislation that forbade discrimination on the basis of race, sex, religion, or national origin.

Civil servants: Members of the permanent executive-branch bureaucracy who are employed on the basis of competitive exams and keep their positions regardless of the presidential administration.

Class action: A lawsuit filed on behalf of an entire category of individuals, such as all people in public housing in a state, or all the female managers of a large company.

Classical republicanism: A democratic ideal, rooted in ancient Greece and Rome, that requires citizens to participate directly in public affairs, seek the public interest, shun private gains, and defer to natural leaders.

Clear and present danger: Court doctrine that permits restrictions of free speech if officials believe that the speech will lead to prohibited action like violence or terrorism.

Clicktivism: Democracy enhanced through the click of a mouse.

Cloture vote: The Senate's only approved method for halting a filibuster or lifting a legislative hold. If sixty senators—three-fifths of the body, changed in 1975 from the original two-thirds—vote for cloture, the measure can proceed to a vote.

Committee hearing: The primary means by which committees collect and analyze information as legislative policy making gets under way. Hearings usually feature witnesses providing oral testimony, along with questioning of the witnesses by members of Congress.

Committee markup session: A gathering of a full committee to draft the final version of a bill before the committee votes on it. Markups open to the public are often standing-room only.

Common law: A system of law developed by judges in deciding cases over the centuries.

Compact: A mutual agreement that provides for joint action to achieve defined goals.

Compromise of 1850: A complicated compromise over slavery that permitted territories to vote on whether they would be slave or free. It also included a fugitive slave law forcing northerners to return black men and women into bondage, and permitted California to enter the Union as a free state.

Concurrent opinion: A statement that agrees with the majority opinion.

Concurrent powers: Governmental authority shared by national and state governments, such as the power to tax residents.

Confederation: A group of independent states or nations that yield some of their powers to a national government, although each state retains a degree of sovereign authority.

Conference committee: A temporary collection of House and Senate members, appointed to work out a compromise version of legislation that passed both chambers in different forms.

Congressional caucus: A group of House or Senate members that convene regularly to discuss common interests; they may share demographic characteristics, geography, or issue concerns.

Conservatives: Americans who believe in reduced government spending, personal responsibility, traditional moral values, and a strong national defense. Also known as *right* or *right-wing*.

Containment: American Cold War strategy designed to stop the spread of Communism.

Cooperative (or marble cake) federalism: Mingled governing authority, with functions overlapping across national and state governments.

Cost-benefit analysis: A more complex study of the projected costs and benefits associated with a proposed policy.

Cost effectiveness: The projected costs of a proposed policy, as revealed by a relatively simple study.

Covenant: A compact invoking religious or moral authority.

Credit claiming: The ability of political figures to generate a belief among their constituents or supporters that they are personally responsible for some government action or achievement.

Criminal law: Cases in which someone is charged with breaking the law.

De facto discrimination: More subtle forms of discrimination that exist without a legal basis.

De jure discrimination: Discrimination established by laws.

Debt ceiling: A congressionally mandated limit on how much the national government can borrow to finance federal spending.

Defendant: The party that is sued in a court case.

Delegate representation: When representatives follow expressed wishes of the voters.

Delegated powers: Powers that Congress passes on to the president.

Democracy: A government in which citizens rule directly and make government decisions for themselves.

Demographic group: People sharing specific factors; for example, age, ethnicity/race, religion, or country of origin.

Demosclerosis: The collective effect of the sheer number of Washington lobbyists in slowing the process of American democratic policymaking.

Devolution: The transfer of authority from national to state or local government level.

Diffusion: The spreading of policy ideas from one city or state to others; a process typical of US federalism.

Digital divide: The gap between those with ready access to the Internet and those without.

Din: Shorthand for the sheer volume of information and noise generated by online sources; can be a disincentive to participate politically.

Dissent: A statement on behalf of the justices who voted in the minority.

District courts: The first level of federal courts, which actually try the cases.

Each decision is based not on a statute but on previous judicial decisions.

Divided government: Periods during which at least one house of Congress is controlled by a party different from the one occupying the White House.

Domestic dependent nation: Special status that grants local sovereignty to tribal nations but does not grant them full sovereignty equivalent to independent nations.

Double jeopardy: The principle that an individual cannot be tried twice for the same offense.

Dred Scott v. Sandford: A landmark 1857 Supreme Court decision holding that black men could not be citizens under the Constitution. It created a national uproar.

Dual (or layer cake) federalism: Clear division of governing authority between national and state governments.

Earmark: A legislative item, usually included in spending (appropriations) bills, that directs Congress to fund a particular item in one House district or senator's state.

Economic equality: A situation where there are only small differences in wealth between citizens.

Electoral activities: Public engagement in the form of voting, running for office, volunteering on a campaign, or otherwise participating in elections.

Electoral bounce: The spike in the polls that follows an event, like a party's national convention.

Electoral College: The system established by the Constitution to elect the president; each state has a number of electors (equal to the size of its congressional delegation in House and Senate); the public in each state votes for electors who then vote for president.

Emancipation Proclamation: An executive order issued by President Abraham Lincoln that declared the slaves in all rebel states free.

Entitlement program: A government benefit program whose recipients are *entitled* by law to receive payments. Social Security, Medicare, and Medicaid are the three largest.

Equal Employment Opportunity Commission (EEOC): Federal law enforcement agency charged with monitoring compliance to the Civil Rights Act.

Equal opportunity: The idea that every American has an equal chance to win economic success.

Equal outcome: The idea that citizens should have roughly equal economic circumstances.

Equal protection of the laws: The landmark phrase in the Fourteenth Amendment that requires equal treatment for all citizens.

Equal Rights Amendment: An amendment, originally drafted by Alice Paul in 1923, passed by Congress in 1972, and ratified by thirty-five states, that declared: "Equality of rights . . . shall not be denied or abridged . . . on account of sex."

Equality: All citizens enjoy the same privileges, status, and rights before the laws.

Establishment clause: In the First Amendment, the principle that government may not establish an official religion.

Exclusionary rule: The ruling that evidence obtained in an illegal search may not be introduced in a trial.

Executive Office of the President (EOP): The agencies that help the president manage daily activities.

Executive order: A presidential declaration, with the force of law, that issues instructions to the executive branch without any requirement for congressional action or approval.

Expressed powers: Powers the Constitution explicitly grants to the president.

Expressive benefits: Values or deeply held beliefs that inspire individuals to join a public interest group.

Fair trade: Trade that includes environmental and labor protections in agreements so nations do not get unfair advantages by exploiting workers or harming the environment.

Fairness doctrine: Regulation that required media outlets to devote equal time to opposite perspectives.

Federal budget deficit: The gap between revenues received by the national government (primarily through individual income and corporate taxes) and spending on all public programs.

Federal poverty line: The annually specified level of income (separately calculated for individuals and families) below which people are considered to live in poverty, becoming eligible for certain federal benefits. In 2013, the poverty line was set at $23,550 for a family of four.

Federal Regulation of Lobbying Act: The initial US statute spelling out requirements on lobbyists active in Congress, passed in 1946.

Federalism: Power divided between national and state government. Each has its own independent authority and its own duties.

Fighting words: Expression inherently likely to provoke violent reaction and not necessarily protected by the First Amendment.

Filibuster: Rule unique to the US Senate that allows any senator to hold the floor indefinitely and thereby delay a vote on a bill to which he or she objects. Ended only when sixty senators vote for cloture.

Final rule: The rule that specifies how a program will actually operate.

First Continental Congress: A convention of delegates, from twelve of the thirteen colonies, that met in 1774.

Fiscal year: In budget calculations, the "new year" beginning October 1 and ending the following September 30. Organized many decades ago, for accounting purposes.

Floor: The full chamber, either in the House of Representatives or Senate. A bill "goes to the floor" for the final debate and vote.

Focusing event: A major happening, often of crisis or disaster proportions, that attracts widespread media attention to an issue.

Framing: The way an issue is defined; every issue has many possible frames, each with a slightly different tilt in describing the problem and highlighting solutions.

Framing effects: The influence, on the respondent, of how a polling question is asked; changes in wording can significantly alter many people's answer.

Free exercise clause: In the First Amendment, the principle that government may not interfere in religious practice.

Free rider problem: A barrier to group or collective action arising because people who do not participate still reap the benefits.

Free trade: Goods and services moving across international boundaries without government interference.

Freedom: The ability to pursue one's own desires without interference from others.

Freedom of Information Act: A 1966 law that facilitates full or partial disclosure of government information and documents.

Freedom Riders: Black and white activists who rode buses together to protest segregation on interstate bus lines.

Full faith and credit clause: The constitutional requirement (in article 4, section 1) that each state recognize and uphold laws passed by any other state.

Gender gap: Patterned differences in political opinions between women and men.

Gerrymander: Redrawing an election district in a way that gives the advantage to one party.

Gift ban: A regulation that eliminates (or sharply reduces the dollar amount of) gifts from interest groups to lawmakers.

Going public: Directly addressing the public in order to win support for oneself or one's ideas.

Grand jury: A jury that does not decide on guilt or innocence but only on whether there is enough evidence for the case to go to trial.

Grand Old Party (GOP): Long-standing nickname for the Republican Party; ironically, bestowed early in the party's history in the 1870s.

Grand strategy: An overarching vision that defines and guides a nation's foreign policy.

Granted powers: National government powers set out explicitly in the Constitution.

Grants-in-aid: National government funding provided to state and local governments, along with specific instructions about how the funds may be used.

Great Migration: The vast movement of African Americans from the rural South to the urban North between 1920 and 1950.

Gridlock: A critical term applied to government's inability to advance policy solutions because of clashes among different branches or between national and state officials.

Gross domestic product: The value of all the goods and services produced in a nation over a year.

Hate crime: Crime stemming from prejudice based on someone's personal characteristics, such as race, ethnicity, religion, or sexual orientation.

Hate speech: Hostile statements based on someone's personal characteristics, such as race, ethnicity, religion, or sexual orientation.

Imperial presidency: A characterization of the American presidency that suggests it is demonstrating imperial traits, and that the republic is morphing into an empire.

Incorporation: The process by which the Supreme Court declares that a right in the Bill of Rights also applies to state governments.

Incumbency advantage: The tendency for members of Congress to win reelection in overwhelming numbers.

Indentured servant: A colonial American settler contracted to work for a fixed period (usually three to seven years) in exchange for food, shelter, and transportation to the New World.

Individualism: The idea that individuals, not the society, are responsible for their own well-being.

Infotainment: The blurred line between news and entertainment.

Inherent powers: National government powers implied by, but not specifically named in, the Constitution.

Inherent powers of the presidency: Powers assumed by presidents, often during a crisis, on the basis of the constitutional phrase "The executive power shall be vested in the president."

Initiative: A process in which citizens propose new laws or amendments to the state constitution.

Institutions: The organizations, norms, and rules that structure government and public actions.

Interest group: An organization whose goal is to influence government.

Intergovernmental lobbying: Attempts by public officials in one part of the government to influence their counterparts elsewhere—in another branch, or at a different (state or local) level.

Internationalism: The belief that national interests are best served by actively engaging and working with other nations around the world.

Iron triangle: The cozy relationship in one issue area between interest group lobbyist, congressional staffer, and executive-branch agency.

Isolationism: The doctrine that a nation should not interfere in other nations' affairs and should avoid all foreign commitments and alliances.

Issue advocacy: Organized effort to advance (or block) a proposed public policy change.

Issue network: Shifting alliances of public and private interest groups, lawmakers, and other stakeholders all focused on the same policy area.

Jim Crow: The system of racial segregation in the US South that lasted from 1890 to 1965.

Judicial activism: A vigorous or active approach to reviewing the other branches of government.

Judicial restraint: Reluctance to interfere with elected branches, only doing so as a last resort.

Judicial review: The Court's authority to strike down acts that violate the Constitution and to interpret what the Constitution means.

K Street: A major street in downtown Washington, DC, that is home to the headquarters for many lobbying firms and advocacy groups—and thus synonymous with interest group lobbying.

King of the Hill rule: A special rule governing floor consideration of a bill. A series of amendments on the same topic may all win majority approval, but only the last amendment receiving a majority vote—the "king of the hill"—is incorporated into the bill.

Laws of coverture: An outmoded legal tradition holding that a woman's rights and duties all operate through her husband.

Legislative hold: An informal way for a senator to object to a bill or other measure reaching the Senate floor. The action effectively halts Senate proceedings on that issue, sometimes for weeks or longer.

Liberals: Americans who value cultural diversity, government programs for the needy, public intervention in the economy, and individuals' right to a lifestyle based on their own social and moral positions. Also known as *left* or *left-wing*.

Libertarians: People who believe in minimal government: public officials' only role should be defending borders, prosecuting crime, and protecting private property.

Likely voters: Persons identified as probable voters in an upcoming election. Often preferred by polling organizations, but difficult to specify with great accuracy.

Literacy test: A requirement that voters be literate; in reality, a way to restrict black suffrage.

Litigation: The conduct of a lawsuit.

Lobbying coalition: A collection of lobbyists working on related topics or a specific legislative proposal.

Lobbyist: A person who contacts government officials on behalf of a particular cause or issue.

Lochner era: A period from 1905 to 1937, when the Supreme Court struck down laws (like worker protection or minimum wage) that were thought to infringe on economic liberty or the right to contract.

Loud signal: Media stories with very broad coverage and an unambiguous message.

Majority opinion: A court's official statement in support of its decision in a case.

Mandate: Political authority claimed by an election winner as reflecting the approval of the people.

Margin of sampling error: The degree of inaccuracy in any poll, arising from the fact that surveys involve a *sample* of respondents from a population, rather than every member.

Mass media: Information and entertainment for broad popular audiences—including newspapers, radio, television.

Material benefits: Items distributed by public interest groups as incentives to sign up or remain a member.

Median: A statistical term for the value in the middle of a series when the items are arranged in numerical order.

Mediation: A way of resolving disputes without going to court, in which a third party (the mediator) helps two or more sides negotiate a settlement.

Membership group: An interest group primarily organized around voluntary members: often a nonprofit or public advocacy organization.

Mercantilism: An economic theory in which government controls foreign trade in order to maintain prosperity and security.

Midterm election: National elections held between presidential elections, involving all seats in the House of Representatives, one third of those in the Senate, 36 governors, and other positions.

Miranda warnings: A set of rights that police officers are required to inform suspects of, including the right to remain silent.

Missouri Compromise: An agreement to open southern territories west of the Mississippi to slavery while closing northern territories to slavery.

Motor voter law: Passed in 1993, this act enables prospective voters to register when they receive their driver's license.

Multilateral organization: International body of three or more nations organized around a common goal.

Name recognition: An advantage possessed by a well-known political figure, a political celebrity.

National Association for the Advancement of Colored People, or NAACP: A civil rights organization formed in 1906 and dedicated to racial equality.

National Organization for Women (NOW): An organization formed in 1966 to take action for women's equality.

Necessary and proper clause: Defines Congress's constitutional authority (in article 1, section 8) to exercise the "necessary and proper" powers to carry out its designated functions.

Negative campaigning: Running for office by attacking the opponent. An unpopular tactic that is, nevertheless, very effective.

Negative liberty: Freedom from constraints or the interference of others.

New Deal: Broad series of economic programs and reforms introduced between 1933 and 1936 and associated with the Franklin Roosevelt administration.

New Federalism: A version of cooperative federalism, but with stronger emphasis on state and local government activity, vs. national government.

The New Jersey Plan: Put forward at the convention by the small states, it left most government authority with the state governments.

New media: On-demand access to information and entertainment on digital devices that also features interactive participation with content. Arose in late twentieth century.

Nonattitudes: The lack of a stable perspective in response to opinion surveys; answers to questions may be self-contradictory or may display no ideological consistency.

Nonpartisan election: An election where candidates run as individuals, without any party affiliation. Many towns and cities feature nonpartisan elections.

Occupy Wall Street: A social movement, originating in New York City, that protests the inequality of wealth and power, targeting the "top 1 percent."

Open seat: A seat in Congress without an incumbent running for reelection.

Originalism: A principle of legal interpretation that relies on the original meaning of those who wrote the Constitution.

Overhead democracy: A system by which the people elect presidents, who, through their appointees, control the bureaucracy from the top.

Override: The process by which Congress can overcome a presidential veto with a two-thirds vote in both chambers.

Paradox of voting: For most individuals, the cost of voting (acquiring necessary information, traveling to polling site, and waiting in line) outweighs the apparent benefits. Economic theory would predict very low voter turnout, given this analysis.

Party boss: The senior figure in a party machine.

Party caucus: A meeting of all House or Senate members of one or the other main party, usually to discuss political and policy strategies.

Party identification: Strong attachment to one political party, often established at an early age.

Party-in-government: The portion of a political party's organization that comprises elected officials and candidates for office.

Party in the electorate: The largest (and least organized) component of a political party, drawn from the public at large: registered members and regular supporters.

Party machine: A hierarchical arrangement of party workers, often organized in an urban area to help integrate immigrants and minority groups into the political system. Most active in the late nineteenth and early twentieth centuries.

Party organization: The portion of a political party that includes activists, state/local leaders, and affiliated professionals like fundraisers and PR experts.

Party platform: The written statement of a party's core convictions and issue priorities. Generally revised every four years, in time for the national party convention.

Party system: The broad organization of US politics, comprising the two main parties, the coalition of supporters backing each, the positions they take on major issues, and each party's electoral achievements.

Path dependence: The tendency of policy makers to follow established routines in thinking about or acting on a specific topic.

Pendleton Civil Service Act: The 1883 law that shifted American government toward a merit-based public service.

Personal presidency: The idea that the president has a personal link to the public. Made possible by twentieth-century media.

Plaintiff: The party that brings the action in a lawsuit.

Plessy v. Ferguson: An 1896 Supreme Court case that permitted racial segregation.

Pluralism: An open, participatory style of government in which many different interests are represented.

Policy agenda: The issues that the media covers, the public considers important, and politicians address. Setting the agenda is the first step in political action.

Political Action Committee (PAC): An organization with at least fifty contributors, affiliated with an interest group, that is permitted to make contributions to candidates for federal office.

Political appointees: Top officials in the executive agencies appointed by the president.

Political culture: The orientation of citizens of a society toward politics.

Political elites: Individuals who control significant wealth, status, power, or visibility and who, consequently, have significant influence over public debates.

Political equality: Every person has the same political rights and opportunities.

Political mobilization: Efforts to encourage people to engage in the public sphere: to vote for a particular candidate (and donate money, work on the campaign, etc.) or to get involved in specific issues.

Political order: The set of institutions, interests, and ideas that shape a political era. Great presidents reconstruct the framework launching a new order.

Political socialization: Education about how the government works and which policies one should support; provided by family, friends, schools, parties, and other national institutions.

Political voice: Exercising one's public rights, often through speaking out in protest or in favor of some policy change.

Positive liberty: The freedom and ability to pursue one's goals.

Power elite theory: The view that a small handful of wealthy, influential Americans exercises extensive control over government decisions.

Pragmatism: A principle of legal interpretation based on the idea that the Constitution evolves and that it must be put in the context of contemporary realities.

Precedent: Judicial decisions that offer a guide to similar cases in the future.

President pro tempore: Majority-party senator with the longest Senate service.

Primary election: an election that determines which candidate will represent a political party.

Priming: Affecting voters' or poll respondents' perception of candidates or public officials by raising issues that are perceived to enhance or diminish the candidates.

Prior restraint: Legal effort to stop speech before it occurs—in effect, censorship.

Private contractors: Private companies that contract to provide goods and services for the government.

Proportional representation: The allocation of votes or delegates on the basis of the percentage of the vote received; contrasts with the winner-take-all system.

Proposed rule: A draft of administrative regulations, published in the *Federal Register* for the purpose of gathering comments from interested parties.

Protectionism: Effort to protect local business from foreign competition.

Public ownership: A situation in which media outlets are run by the government and paid for by tax dollars.

Push poll: A form of negative campaigning that masquerades as a regular opinion survey. Usually conducted by a campaign or allied group; features strongly critical or unflattering information about an opponent.

Quasi-suspect category: A legal category that requires governments to have an important state purpose for any legislation that singles out sex or gender. This is not as strong as the *suspect category*, which requires strict scrutiny.

Rational-choice theory: An approach to political behavior that views individuals as rational, decisive actors who know their political interests and seek to act on them.

Reapportionment: Reorganization of the boundaries of House districts, a process that follows the results of the US census, taken every ten years. District lines are redrawn to ensure rough equality in the number of constituents represented by each House member.

Reconstruction: The failed effort, pursued by Northerners and Southerners, to rebuild the South and establish racial equality after the Civil War.

Referendum: An election in which citizens vote directly on an issue.

Reframe the issue: To redefine the popular perception of an issue; to show it in a new light with a new set of costs or benefits.

Regulatory capture: The theory that industries dominate the agencies that regulate them.

Republic: A system of government that rests ultimate governing power in its people, who may rule directly or via representatives.

Reserved powers: The constitutional guarantee (in the Tenth Amendment) that the states retain government authority not explicitly granted to the national government.

Response bias: The tendency of poll respondents to misstate their views, frequently to avoid "shameful" opinions like sexism or racism.

Reverse lobbying: Attempts by government officials to influence interest groups on behalf of their preferred policies.

Roll-call vote: A congressional vote in which all members' votes are recorded, either by roll call (Senate) or electronically (House).

Rule of four: The requirement that at least four Supreme Court judges must agree to hear a case before it comes before the Court.

Sampling frame: A designated group of people from whom a set of poll respondents is randomly selected.

School voucher: A cash payment that enables children to apply to private schools, sometimes outside their immediate neighborhood.

Second Continental Congress: A convention of delegates from thirteen colonies, which became the acting national government for the duration of the Revolutionary War.

Section 504: An obscure provision in an obscure rehabilitation act that required all institutions that received federal funds to accommodate people with disabilities.

Selective incorporation: Extending protections from the Bill of Rights to the state governments, one right at a time.

Self-rule: The idea that legitimate government flows from the people.

Seneca Falls Convention: A convention dedicated to women's rights held in July 1848.

Signing statements: A president's declarations commenting on the bill that is signed into law.

Social capital: Relations between people that build closer ties of trust and civic engagement, yielding productive benefits for the larger society.

Social democracy: A government whose citizens are responsible for one another's well-being and use government policy to assure that all are comfortably cared for.

Social equality: All individuals enjoy the same status in society.

Solidary benefits: The feeling of shared commitment and purpose experienced by individuals who join a public interest group.

Sound bite: A short clip of speech taken from a longer piece of audio. Often refers to a brief excerpt from a speech by a candidate or politician.

Split-ticket voter: One who votes for at least one candidate from each party, dividing his or her ballot between the two (or more) parties.

Spoils system: Government jobs given out as political favors.

Stare decisis: Deciding cases on the basis of previous rulings or precedents.

Straight-ticket voter: One who votes for the same party for all offices on a ballot.

Street-level bureaucrats: Government officials who deal directly with the public.

Strict scrutiny: The tendency to strike down as unconstitutional any legislation that singles out race or ethnicity unless the government has a compelling interest in such legislation.

Strong nation: Robust spirit of national identity shared by a people.

Sunshine laws: Laws that permit the public to watch policy makers in action or access the records of government proceedings.

Super PACs: Organizations that are permitted to raise and spend unlimited amounts of money to promote a candidate or publicize a cause. However, they may not directly contribute to a candidate or coordinate with a campaign.

Super Tuesday: The date on the primary calendar when multiple states hold primaries and caucuses.

Supermajority: An amount higher than a simple (50% plus one) majority—three-fifths or two-thirds are typical requirements in order for a proposal to be adopted.

Supremacy clause: The constitutional declaration (in article 6, section 2) that the national government's authority prevails over any conflicting state or local government's claims.

Symbolic expression: An act, rather than actual speech, used to demonstrate a point of view.

Taliban: A fundamentalist Islamic sect that took control of Afghanistan in 1996 and gave shelter to the Al Qaeda terrorist network.

Tea Party: A national social movement, primarily attracting fiscal and social conservatives, that seeks to limit government spending and cut taxes.

Telecommunications Act of 1996: The major congressional overhaul of communications law that opened the door to far more competition by permitting companies to compete in multiple media markets—radio, television, magazines, etc.

Time, place, and manner clause: The constitutional clause that delegates control of elections to the state governments.

Trade deficit: The deficit arising when a nation imports (or buys) more goods from foreign nations than it exports (or sells) to them.

Trustee representation: Representatives do what they regard as the best interest of the voters—regardless of what the voters might wish for.

Unanimous consent: A Senate requirement, applied to most of that body's business, that all senators agree before an action can proceed.

Underdog effect: Sympathy for a candidate behind in the polls, contributing to a higher-than-predicted vote total—and sometimes a surprise election victory.

Unfunded mandate: An obligation imposed on state or local government officials by federal legislation, without sufficient federal funding support to cover the costs.

Unicameral: Having a single legislative house or chamber.

Unitary executive theory: The idea that the Constitution puts the president in charge of executing the laws; therefore, no other branch should limit presidential discretion over executive matters.

Unitary government: A national polity governed as a single unit, with the central government exercising all or most political authority.

United Farm Workers: An influential union representing migrant farm workers in the West.

Universalistic politics: Government by universal rules, impartially applied.

USA Patriot Act: Legislation that sought to enhance national security, passed in the aftermath of the September 11, 2001, attacks.

Veto: The constitutional procedure by which a president can prevent enactment of Congress-passed legislation.

Veto power: The presidential power to block an act of Congress by refusing to sign it.

The Virginia Plan: Madison's plan, embraced by Constitutional Convention delegates from larger states; strengthened the national government relative to state governments.

Voice vote: A congressional vote in which the presiding officer asks those for and against to say "yea" or "nay," respectively, and announces the result. No record is kept of House or Senate members voting on each side.

Voter turnout: A measure of what proportion of eligible voters actually cast a legitimate ballot in a given election.

Watergate scandal: A failed effort by Republican operatives to break into Democratic Party headquarters in the Watergate office complex in Washington, DC; tapes revealed that President Nixon attempted to cover up the event—costing him the presidency.

Winner-take-all: The electoral system used in US general presidential as well as many primary and other elections. The candidate receiving a simple majority (or, among multiple candidates, a plurality) receives all electoral votes or primary delegates. Sometimes also called "first-past-the-post."

Notes

Chapter 1 The Ideas That Shape American Politics

1. Russell A. Burgos, "An *N* of One: A Political Scientist in Operation Iraqi Freedom," *Perspectives on Politics* 2, no. 3 (2004): 551–56.
2. Harold D. Lasswell, *Politics: Who Gets What, When, and How*, rev. ed. (New York: Peter Smith Books, 1990).
3. *New York Times*/CBS News poll, October 2011.
4. Simon Schama, *Rough Crossings: Britain, the Slaves, and the American Revolution*, (New York: Harper-Collins, 2006).
5. The classic statement comes from Isaiah Berlin, "Two Concepts of Liberty," inaugural lecture as Chichele Professor of Political and Social Theory at Oxford University (1958), reprinted in Berlin, *Four Essays on Liberty* (Oxford: Oxford University Press, 1969).
6. Samuel Huntington, *American Politics: The Promise of Disharmony* (Cambridge, MA: Harvard University Press, 1983); Rogers Smith, *Civic Ideals: Conflicting Visions of Citizenship in U.S. History* (New Haven, CT: Yale University Press, 1997).
7. Quoted in James A. Morone, *The Democratic Wish: Popular Participation and the Limits of American Government* (New Haven, CT: Yale University Press, 1998), 54.
8. Thomas Jefferson, "Response to the Citizens of Albemarle," February 12, 1790; First Inaugural Address, March 4, 1801. Jefferson's first inaugural is the best summary of what we now call Jeffersonian Democracy.
9. James Madison, Federalist no. 10. The quote is from Roger Sherman recorded in Madison's Notes of Debates, in Winston Solberg, ed., *The Federal Convention and the Formation of the Union* (Indianapolis, IN: Bobbs Merrill, 1958), 84–5.
10. Michael Kammen, *People of Paradox* (New York: Knopf, 1972), 31.
11. John Kingdon, *America the Unusual* (New York: St. Martin's Press, 1999), 1.
12. Michael Dawson, *Behind the Mule* (Princeton, NJ: Princeton University Press, 1995).
13. Milton Friedman, *Capitalism and Freedom* (Chicago: University of Chicago Press, 1962).
14. The original statement of this theory is by Louis Hartz, *The Liberal Tradition in America* (New York: Harcourt, Brace, and World, 1955).
15. Franklin quotes from *Poor Richard's Almanac*; can be found at http://www.ushistory.org/franklin/quotable/.
16. James Truslow Adams, *The Epic of America* (New York: Taylor and Francis, 1938). Available from Google Books at http://books.google.com/books/about/The_Epic_of_America.html?id=-VMVAAAAIAAJ.
17. Quoted in Jennifer Hochschild, *Facing Up to the American Dream* (Princeton, NJ: Princeton University Press, 1995), vi, 18.
18. Gordon Wood, *The Radicalism of the American Revolution* (New York: Knopf, 1992), 369.
19. In Bayard Tuckerman, ed., *The Diary of Philip Hone, 1828–1851* (New York: Dodd, Mead, 1910), 260; Tocqueville, *Democracy in America*, 2:541, 462, 621.
20. Timothy Noah, *The Great Divergence: America's Growing Inequality Crisis and What We Can Do About It* (New York: Bloomsbury Press, 2012).
21. FDR and LBJ quoted in James Morone, *Hellfire Nation* (New Haven, CT: Yale University Press, 2004), 347, 427.
22. Tocqueville, *Democracy in America*, 1:9.
23. Tocqueville, *Democracy in America*, 2:558.
24. See Robert Putnam and David Campbell, *American Grace: How Religion Divides and Unites Us* (New York: Simon & Schuster, 2010).
25. Timothy Beal, *Religion in America* (New York: Oxford University Press, 2008).
26. Putnam and Campbell, in *American Grace*, call the religiously unaffiliated "the nones."
27. Tocqueville, *Democracy in America*, 2:122, 187.
28. Madison, in Federalist no. 10.
29. For a robust institutional perspective, see Sven Steinmo and Jon Watts, "It's the Institutions, Stupid! Why Comprehensive Health Insurance Always Fails in America," *Journal of Health Politics, Policy, and Law* 20, no. 2 (2003): 329–72; Theda Skocpol, *Protecting Soldiers and Mothers: The Political Origins of Social Policy in the United States* (Cambridge, MA: Harvard University Press, 1995), chap. 1; Karen Orren and Stephen Skowronek, *The Search for American Political Development* (New York: Cambridge University Press, 2004).

Chapter 2 The Constitution

1. Taylor Branch, *Parting the Waters: America in the King Years 1954–63* (New York: Simon & Schuster, 1989).
2. Edmund Burke, "Speech to the Bristol Electors," in *Representation*, ed. Hannah Pitkin (New York: Atherton Press, 1969), 175–76.
3. Robert Middlekauff, *The Glorious Cause* (New York: Oxford University Press, 1982), 74.
4. Bernard Bailyn et al., *The Great Republic: A History of the American People*, Vol. 1 (1st ed. Boston: Little, Brown, 1977), 256
5. Middlekauff, *The Glorious Cause*, 223–28, quoted at 226.

6. Richard Beeman, *Plain Honest Men: The Making of the American Constitution* (New York: Random House, 2010), 12.
7. Leonard Richards, *Shays's Rebellion: The American Revolution's Final Battle* (Philadelphia: University of Pennsylvania Press, 2002).
8. Beeman, 84.
9. "Madison's Notes," 81.
10. David Brian Robertson, *The Constitution and America's Destiny* (New York: Cambridge University Press, 2005), 139; "Madison's Notes," 122 [swallowed up].
11. Robertson, *The Constitution and America's Destiny*, 140.
12. Beeman, *Plain, Honest Men*, 333.
13. "Madison's Notes," 344.
14. Beeman, *Plain, Honest Men*, 349.
15. Herbert Storing, *What the Anti-Federalists Were For: The Political Writings of the Opponents of the Constitution* (Chicago: University of Chicago Press, 1981).
16. Gordon Wood, *The Radicalism of the American Revolution*.
17. Robert Dahl, *How Democratic Is the American Constitution?* 2nd ed. (New Haven, CT: Yale University Press, 2003).

Chapter 3 Federalism and Nationalism

1. "Palin Says 'We're All Arizonans Now' in Speech Defending State's Immigration Law," Fox News, May 15, 2010, at http://fxn.ws/aPzMoR.
2. Gallup Surveys, October 2009.
3. David Brian Robertson, *Federalism and the Making of America* (New York: Routledge, 2012).
4. Theda Skocpol, *Protecting Soldiers and Mothers*, 9.
5. James Buchanan and Gordon Tullock, *The Calculus of Consent* (Ann Arbor: University of Michigan Press, 1962), 144.
6. William Berry, Richard Fording, and Russell Hanson, "Reassessing the Race to the Bottom in State Welfare Policy," *Journal of Politics* 65, no. 2 (2003): 327–49.
7. Theodore J. Lowi, "Think Globally, Lose Locally," *Boston Review* (April/May 1998).

8. James Morone, *Hellfire Nation: The Politics of Sin in American History* (New Haven, CT: Yale University Press, 2003), part 3.
9. Dirksen, quoted in Richard P. Nathan, "Updating Theories of American Federalism," in *Intergovernmental Management for the Twenty-First Century.* Timothy Conlan and Paul Posner, eds. (Washington, DC: Brookings Institution Press, 2008), 15.
10. Quoted in Robert Dreyfuss, "Grover Norquist: 'Field Marshal' of the Bush Plan," *The Nation*, May 14, 2001.
11. 17 U.S. 316 (1819).
12. Benedict Anderson, *Imagined Communities: Reflection on the Origin and Spread of Nationalism*, 2nd ed. (New York: Verso, 2006).
13. Suzanne Mettler, *The Submerged State* (Chicago: University of Chicago Press, 2011); Christopher Howard, *The Hidden Welfare State* (Princeton, NJ: Princeton University Press, 1997); Jacob Hacker, *The Divided Welfare State* (New York: Cambridge University Press, 2002).
14. David Blumenthal and James Morone, *The Heart of Power: Health and Politics in the Oval Office* (Berkeley: University of California Press, 2009), chap. 3.

Chapter 4 Civil Liberties

1. A minor controversy broke out about Palin's inventing the word *refudiate*. Her supporters said it simply showed how colorful she was in her use of language.
2. Tom Topousis and Joe Mollica, "New Yorkers Wage Jihad Versus WTC Mosque," *New York Post*, May 26, 2010, http://www.nypost.com/p/news/local/manhattan/nyers_wage_jihad_vs_wtc_mosque_UgJiOBYEhrSOw4Q6hpvbQL N.
3. CNN/Opinion Research, August 11, 2010 (New Yorkers); Time/CNN, August 19, 2010 (all Americans). http://www.foxnews.com/opinion/2010/08/17/kt-mcfarland-ground-zero-mosque-god-september-obama-imam-feisal/.
4. Schenck v. United States, 249 U.S. 47 (1919).

5. "Islamic Center Opens Its Doors Near Ground Zero," Associated Press, September 22, 2011. http://www.usatoday.com/news/nation/story/2011-09-22/new-york-city-mosque/50506728/1
6. The two cases are *Minersville School District v. Gobitis*, 310 U.S. 586 (1940) and *West Virginia State Board of Education v. Barnette*, 319 U.S. 624 (1943). Not only did Walter Gobitas lose the case, a clerk for the court misspelled his name and the case is always referred to by the misspelled name, Gobitis.
7. Barron v. Baltimore, 32 U.S. 243 (1833).
8. The Slaughter-House Cases, 83 U.S. 36 (1873).
9. Palko v. Connecticut, 302 U.S. 319, (1937).
10. If you're interested in reading more on any of the cases we discuss, see Corey Brettschneider, ed., *Constitutional Law and American Democracy: Cases and Readings* (New York: Wolters Kluwer, 2012).
11. The cases were *Stenberg v. Carhart*, 2000, and *Gonzales v. Carhart*, 2007.
12. Thomas Jefferson, Letter to the Danbury Baptist Association, January 1, 1802.
13. Everson v. Board of Education, 330 U.S. 1 (1947).
14. The two cases are *Van Orden v. Perry* (in Texas) 545 U.S 677 (2005) and *McCreary County v. ACLU* 545 U.S. 844 (2005).
15. In *Good News Club v. Milford Central School* 533 U.S. 98 (2001) the Court ruled 6–3 in favor of the club.
16. *Employment Division, Department of Human Resources of Oregon v. Smith*, 494 U.S. 872 (1990).
17. The decision that explicitly adopted a preferred position for free speech was *Brandenburg v. Ohio*, 395 U.S. 444 (1969), discussed later in this section.
18. *Gitlow v. New York*, 268 U.S. 652 (1925). Gitlow, the socialist author of a left-wing manifesto, was convicted, but in the process the courts incorporated free speech.
19. *Brandenburg v. Ohio*, 395 U.S. 444 (1969). For a fine discussion, see Harold Sullivan, *Civil Rights and*

Liberties (Upper Saddle River, NJ: Pearson Prentice Hall, 2005), chap. 2.

20. *Snyder v. Phelps*, 132 U.S. 1207 (2011).

21. *Texas v. Johnson*, 109 S. Ct. 2544 (1989).

22. *Chaplinsky v. New Hampshire*, 315 U.S. 568 (1942).

23. *Tinker v. Des Moines Independent Community School District*, 393 U.S. 503 (1969).

24. *Bethel School District No. 403 v. Fraser*, 478 U.S. 675 (1986), and Hazelwood School District v. Kuhlmeier, 484 U.S 260 (1988).

25. *Morse v. Frederick*, 551 U.S. 393 (2007).

26. *New York Times Company v. United States*, 403 U.S. 713 (1971).

27. Bob Egleko, "S.F. Judge Dissolves his Wikileaks Injunction," *San Franciso Chronicle*, March 1, 2008. http://www.sfgate.com/bayarea/article/S-F-judge-dissolves-his-Wikileaks-injunction-3226168.php

28. *New York Times Company v. Sullivan*, 376 U.S. 254 (1964).

29. Joseph Story, *Commentaries on the Constitution of the United States* vol. III (Boston: Hilliard, Gray, 1833), p. 746; Charlton Heston in Chicago Tribune, "Charlton Heston Rips Media," Sept. 12, 1997.

30. *District of Columbia v. Heller*, 554 U.S. 570 (2008).

31. *Olmstead v. United States*, 277 U.S. 438 (1928).

32. *Herring v. United States*, 555 U.S. 135 (2009).

33. *Olmstead v. United States*, 277 U.S. 438 (1928); *Katz v. United States*, 389 U.S. 347 (1967).

34. Linda Monk, *The Words We Live By: Your Annotated Guide to the Constitution* (New York: Hyperion, 2003), 165.

35. *Illinois v. Perkins*, 496 U.S. 292 (1990); *New York v. Quarles*, 467 U.S. 649 (1984); *Harris v. New York*, 401 U.S. 222 (1970).

36. Anthony Lewis, *Gideon's Trumpet* (New York: Vintage, 1989).

37. *Missouri v. Frye*, 132 U.S. 55 (2012).

38. Frank Baumgartner, Suzanna De Boef, and Amber Boydstun, *The Decline of the Death Penalty and the Discovery of Innocence* (New York: Cambridge University Press, 2008).

39. Editorial, *New York Times*, Sunday, May 22, 2011, 7.

40. The two cases are *Minersville School District v. Gobitis*, 310 U.S. 586 (1940) and *West Virginia State Board of Education v. Barnette*, 319 U.S. 624 (1943).

Chapter 5 The Struggle for Civil Rights

1. *The Autobiography of Malcolm X: As Told to Alex Haley* (New York: Random House, 1964), 43; Richard Wright, *Native Son*. [Playing black]; James Morone, *Hellfire Nation: The Politics of Sin in American History* (New Haven, CT: Yale University Press, 2003), 441 [Airline Pilots].

2. Samuel Huntington, *American Politics: The Promise of Disharmony* (Cambridge, MA: Harvard University Press, 1981).

3. Rogers Smith, *Civic Ideals: Conflicting Visions of Citizenship in U.S. History* (New Haven, CT: Yale University Press, 1999).

4. *Pierce v. Society of Sisters*, 268 U.S. 510 (1925); *Romer v. Evans*, 517 U.S. 620 (1996).

5. W. E. B. DuBois, *The Souls of Black Folk* (New York: New American Library, 1982), 220.

6. Garry Wills, *Lincoln at Gettysburg* (New York: Simon & Schuster, 1992).

7. *The Civil Rights Cases*, 109 U.S. 3 (1883).

8. Richard Valelly, *The Two Reconstructions* (Chicago: University of Chicago Press, 2004), 2.

9. *Plessy v. Ferguson*, 163 U.S. 537 (1896).

10. Peggy Pascoe, *What Comes Naturally: Miscegenation Law and the Making of Race in America* (New York: Oxford University Press, 2008).

11. *Smith v. Allright*, 21 U.S. 649, (1944).

12. *Morgan v. Virginia*, 328 U.S. 373 (1946) [bus lines]; *Sweatt v. Painter* 339 U.S. 629 (1950) [law school]; *McLaurin v. Oklahoma* 339 U.S. 637 (1950).

13. *Sheet Metal Workers v. EEOC*, 478 U.S. 421 (1986).

14. *University of California v. Bakke*, 438 U.S. 265 (1978).

15. Leo Kanowitz, *Women and the Law* (Albuquerque: University of New Mexico Press, 1971), 36.

16. Jennifer Lawless and Richard Fox, *It Takes a Candidate: Why Women Don't Run for Office* (New York: Cambridge University Press, 2005).

17. Sheryl Gay Stolberg, "Obama Signs Equal Pay Legislation," *New York Times*, January 1, 2009.

18. Pew Hispanic Center, reported in Erin Rosa, "Pew: Latino Incarceration Rates Increase, Legal Confidence Wanes," *Colorado Independent*, April 7, 2009.

19. Heather Silber Mohamed, "Immigration, Protests, and the Politics of Latino/a Identity" (PhD diss., Brown University, 2012).

20. Rogers Smith, *Civic Ideals*, 361.

21. Tocqueville, *Democracy in America*, I:323–24.

22. Pekka Hamalainen, *The Comanche Empire* (New Haven, CT: Yale University Press, 2008).

23. *Bowers v. Hardwick*, 478 U.S. 186 (1986); *Lawrence v. Texas*, 539 U.S. 558 (2003).

24. Andrew Gelman, Jeffrey Lax, and Justin Phillips, "Over Time, a Gay Marriage Groundswell," *New York Times*, August 22, 2012.

Chapter 6 Public Opinion and Political Participation

1. CNN/Opinion Research Poll, released June 16, 2010.

2. Cynthia Crossen, *Tainted Truth: The Manipulation of Fact in America* (New York: Touchstone, 1996).

3. Franklin D. Roosevelt, address announcing the second New Deal, Madison Square Garden, New York, October 31, 1936.

4. J. P. Robinson, W. P. Rivers, and Richard D. Brecht, "Demographic and Sociopolitical Predictors of American Attitudes Towards Foreign Language Policy," *Language Policy* 5, no. 4 (2006): 419–40.

5. John Zaller, *The Nature and Origins of Mass Opinion* (New York: Cambridge University Press, 1992).

6. Walter Lippmann, *Public Opinion* (New York: Harcourt, Brace, 1922). On the movement to govern through technical expertise, see James A. Morone, *The Democratic Wish: Popular Participation and the Limits of American Government* (New Haven, CT: Yale University Press, 1998), chap. 3.

7. Benjamin I. Page and Robert Y. Shapiro, *The Rational Public: Fifty Years of Trends in Americans' Policy Preferences* (Chicago: University of Chicago Press, 1992).

8. "Wall Street Reform Bill Nears Floor Vote in Congress," CNN, June 22, 2010.

9. John F. Harris, *The Survivor: Bill Clinton in the White House* (New York: Random House, 2005), 331.

10. Harris, *The Survivor*, 159.

11. Lawrence R. Jacobs and Robert Y. Shapiro, *Politicians Don't Pander: Political Manipulation and the Loss of Democratic Responsiveness* (Chicago: University of Chicago Press, 2000).

12. Tocqueville, *Democracy in America*, 1:189-95.

13. Corporation for National and Community Service, "Volunteer Growth in America: A Review of Trends Since 1974" (2007) and "Volunteering in America 2011" (2011).

14. John H. Aldrich, "Rational Choice and Turnout," *American Journal of Political Science* 37, no. 1 (1993): 246-78.

15. Donald P. Green and Alan S. Gerber, *Get Out the Vote: How to Increase Voter Turnout*, 2nd ed. (Washington, DC: Brookings Institution Press, 2008).

16. Robert D. Putnam, "What Makes Democracy Work?" *National Civic Review* 82, no. 2 (Spring 1993), 106-7.

17. James H. Fowler, Laura A. Baker, and Christopher T. Dawes, "Genetic Variation in Political Participation," *American Political Science Review* 102, no. 2 (2008): 233-48.

18. Suzanne Mettler, *Soldiers to Citizens: The G.I. Bill and the Making of the Greatest Generation* (New York: Oxford University Press, 2005).

19. Doug McAdam, *Political Process and the Development of Black Insurgency, 1930-1970*, 2nd ed. (Chicago: University of Chicago Press, 1999).

20. Larry M. Bartells, *Unequal Democracy: The Political Economy of the New Gilded Age* (Princeton, NJ: Princeton University Press, 2008).

21. Benjamin I. Page, Larry M. Bartels, and Jason Seawright, "Democracy and the Policy Preferences of Wealthy Americans," paper delivered at the annual meeting of the American Political Science Association, 2011.

22. John D. Griffin and Michael Keane, "Descriptive Representation and the Composition of African American Turnout," *American Journal of Political Science* 50, no. 4 (2006): 998-1012.

23. E. J. Dionne, *Why Americans Hate Politics: The Death of the Democratic Process* (New York: Simon & Schuster, 1991).

24. John Kenneth Galbraith, *The Culture of Contentment* (New York: Mariner Books, 1993).

25. Theda Skocpol, "Voice and Inequality: The Transformation of American Civic Democracy," *Perspectives on Politics* 2, no. 1 (2004): 14.

26. Wael Ghonim quoted on CNN, February 11, 2011.

27. Clay Shirky, "The Political Power of Social Media: Technology, the Public Sphere, and Political Change," *Foreign Affairs* 90, no. 1 (January/February 2011).

28. Pew Charitable Trusts, Internet and American Life Project, 2011.

Chapter 7 The Media

1. Albert Ibarguen, John S. and James L. Knight Foundation, Senate Commerce, Science and Transportation Subcommittee on Communications, Technology and the Internet, May 6, 2009.

2. W. Lance Bennett and Shanto Iyengar, "A New Era of Minimal Effects? The Changing Foundations of Political Communication," *Journal of Communication* 58 (2008): 707-31.

3. Pew Research Center for Excellence in Journalism, *The State of the News Media*, 2011: http://pewresearch.org/pubs/1924/state-of-the-news-media-2011

4. Linda A. Jackson et al., "Race, Gender, and Information Technology Use: The New Digital Divide," *CyberPsychology and Behavior* 11, no. 4 (2008): 437-42.

5. See Matthew Hindman, *The Myth of Digital Democracy* (Princeton, NJ: Princeton University Press, 2009).

6. Stuart Elliott, "Milk Campaign Ended Amid Social Media Firestorm," *New York Times*, July 21, 2011.

7. See Saul Levmore and Martha C. Nussbaum, eds., *The Offensive Internet* (Cambridge, MA: Harvard University Press, 2010).

8. Doris Graber, *Mass Media and American Politics*, 8th ed. (Washington, DC: CQ Press, 2010), 203.

9. Eric Alterman, *What Liberal Bias? The Truth about Bias and the News* (New York: Basic, 2003).

10. Graber, *Mass Media and American Politics*, 266.

11. European media are increasingly overseen by the European Union, which creates different rules for three different sectors: public media, run by national governments (often the largest); commercial media; and fledgling community media. See Josef Trappel, Werner A. Meier, Leen d'Haenens, Jeanette Steemers, and Barbara Thomass, eds., *Media in Europe Today* (Chicago: Intellect, 2011).

12. S. Ivengar and D. Kinder, *News that Matters: Television and Public Opinion* (Chicago: University of Chicago Press, 1989).

13. *Late Night with David Letterman*, January 7, 2008.

14. The quotations are from a phrase used by Obama's campaign; Jay Leno on McCain; a bumper sticker criticizing Bush; and Robert Frank, "Romney's Top Ten Wealth Gaffes," *Wall Street Journal*, February 28, 2012.

Chapter 8 Campaigns and Elections

1. David Shribman, "In Canada, the Lean Season," *Boston Globe*, May 23, 1997.

2. Stephen J. Wayne, *The Road to the White House: 2012* (New York: Cengage, 2011).
3. For a thoughtful study of this question, see David P. Redlawsk, Caroline J. Tolbert, and Todd Donovan, *Why Iowa? How Caucuses and Sequenced Primaries Improve the Presidential Nomination Process* (Chicago: University of Chicago Press, 2011).
4. Alan Abramowitz, "Don't Blame Primary Voters for Polarization," *The Forum* 5, no. 4 (2008).
5. John Heilemann and Mark Haplpern, *Game Change* (New York: Harper, 2010), 177–96.
6. Lacey Jackson-Matsushima, "New Jersey's Frelinghuysen Has Politics in His Blood," *FB Magazine*, July 21, 2011, http://www.financialbuzz.com/news/new-jerseys-frelinghuysen-has-politics-in-his-blood----blogger---lacey-jackson-matsushima.
7. Jennifer L. Lawless and Richard L. Fox, *It Takes a Candidate: Why Women Don't Run for Office* (New York: Cambridge University Press, 2005).
8. *Shaw v. Reno*, 509 U.S. 630 (1993).
9. David Beiler, "Jon Corzine and the Power of Money," *Campaigns & Elections* 22:2 (2001), pp. 22–23.
10. Gerald Pomper, *Voters, Elections and Parties: The Practice of Democratic Theory* (Piscataway, New Jersey: Transaction Publishers, 1988), 104. See also Sean J. Miller, "Why Technology Can't Replace Old-Fashioned Politicking," *Campaigns & Elections*, April 19, 2012. http://www.campaignsandelections.com/campaign-insider/316967/why-technology-canand39t-replace-oldfashioned-politicking.thtml
11. Scott M. Noveck, "Campaign Finance Disclosure and the Legislative Process," *Harvard Journal on Legislation* 47, no. 1 (2010): 75–114.

Chapter 9 Interest Groups and Political Parties
1. Jonathan Rauch, *Demosclerosis: The Silent Killer of American Government* (New York: Crown, 1994).
2. Kay Lehman Schlozman, Sidney Verba, and Henry Brady, *The Unevenly Chorus: Unequal Political Voice and the Broken Promise of American Democracy* (Princeton, NJ: Princeton University Press, 2012) Chap. 1; E. E. Schnattschneider, *The Semi-Sovereign People: A Realist View of Democracy in America* (New York: Holt, Rinehart and Wilson, 1960), 35.
3. Jonathan D. Salant and Lizzie O'Leary, "Six Lobbyists per Lawmaker Work on Health Overhaul," *Bloomberg News*, August 14, 2009.
4. See Rogan Kersh, "Health Lobbyists: Ten Myths About Power and Influence," in James Morone and Daniel Ehlke, eds., *Health Politics and Policy*, 5th ed. (Stamford, CT: Cengage, 2013).
5. Mark Peterson, "Congress in the 1990s: From Iron Triangles to Policy Networks," in James Morone and Gary Belkin, eds., *The Politics of Health Care Reform* (Durham, NC: Duke University Press, 1994), 108, 127.
6. Quoted in Jack L. Walker Jr., *Mobilizing Interest Groups in America: Patrons, Professions, and Social Movements* (Ann Arbor: University of Michigan Press, 1991), 157.
7. John H. Aldrich, *Why Parties? The Origin and Transformation of Political Parties in America* (Chicago: University of Chicago Press, 1995).
8. See especially Teresa Amato, *Grand Illusion: The Myth of Voter Choice in a Two-Party Tyranny* (New York: New Press, 2009).
9. J. David Gillespie, *Challengers to Duopoly: Why Third Parties Matter in Two-Party American Politics* (Columbia: University of South Carolina Press, 2012).
10. R. Kent Newmeyer, *Supreme Court Justice Joseph Story: Statesman of the Old Republic* (Chapel Hill: University of North Carolina Press, 1985), 158.
11. Daniel Walker Howe, *What Hath God Wrought: The Transformation of America, 1815–1848* (New York: Oxford University Press, 2007).
12. Mark Losey, "Why I Am a Democrat," *Democratic Underground*, http://bit.ly/oHsB2C (accessed July 24, 2011).

13. Orrin Hatch, "Why I Am a Republican," *Ripon Forum* 41, no. 6 (2008): 8.
14. Alan S. Gerber et al., "Personality and Political Attitudes: Relationships across Issue Domains and Political Contexts," *American Political Science Review* 104, no. 1 (2010): 11–133.
15. William Safire, *Safire's New Political Dictionary* (New York: Random House, 1993), 579.
16. David S. Broder, *The Party's Over: The Failure of Politics in America* (New York: Harper & Row, 1972); Martin P. Wattenberg, *The Decline of American Political Parties, 1952–1980* (Cambridge, MA: Harvard University Press, 1985).
17. John H. Aldrich and Melanie Freeze, "Political Participation, Polarization, and Public Opinion," in Paul M. Sniderman and Benjamin Highton, eds., *Facing the Challenge of Democracy: Explorations in the Analysis of Public Opinion and Political Participation* (Princeton, NJ: Princeton University Press, 2011).
18. Nancy Roman, "Bitter Fruits of Partisanship," *Baltimore Sun*, October 19, 2005.
19. David R. Mayhew, *Divided We Govern: Party Control, Investigations, and Lawmaking, 1946–2002*, 2nd ed. (New Haven, CT: Yale University Press, 2005).
20. On the benefits that PR could bring to the United States, see generally Douglas J. Amy, *Real Choices/New Voices: How Proportional Representation Elections Could Revitalize American Democracy* (New York: Columbia University Press, 2002).

Chapter 10 Congress
1. Katharine Q. Seelye, "7-State Backlash for Nelson's Nebraska Deal," *New York Times*, December 22, 2009, http://nyti.ms/7lonfI (last accessed April 14, 2012).
2. Thomas E. Mann and Norman J. Ornstein, *The Broken Branch: How Congress Is Failing America and How to Get It Back On Track* (New York: Oxford University Press, 2006).

3. Robert A. Caro, *Master of the Senate: The Years of Lyndon Johnson* (New York: Knopf, 2002), 52.
4. For more along this line, see Mark Twain and Charles Dudley Warner, *The Gilded Age* (New York: Oxford University Press, 1996).
5. Barbara Sinclair, "The New World of U.S. Senators," in Lawrence Dodd and Bruce Oppenheimer, eds., *Congress Reconsidered*, 8th ed. (Washington DC: CQ Press, 2009), 8.
6. Caro, *Master of the Senate*, 9.
7. Jane Mansbridge, "Rethinking Representation," *American Political Science Review* 97, no. 4 (2003): 515–528.
8. Lawrence R. Jacobs and Robert Y. Shapiro, *Politicians Don't Pander: Political Manipulation and the Loss of Democratic Responsiveness* (Chicago: University of Chicago Press, 2000).
9. Carl Bernstein, *A Woman in Charge: The Life of Hillary Rodham Clinton* (New York: Knopf, 2007), pp. 546–47.
10. Linda Greenhouse, "David E. Price; Professor in Congress Is Doing Homework On Theory and Reality," *New York Times*, Feb. 11, 1988.
11. Juliet Eilperin, *Fight Club Politics: How Partisanship Is Poisoning the House of Representatives* (Lanham, MD: Rowman & Littlefield, 2007), 13.
12. Barbara Sinclair, *Unorthodox Lawmaking: New Legislative Procedures in the U.S. Congress*, 3rd ed. (Washington, DC: CQ Press, 2007), 71.
13. Eilperin, *Fight Club* (2007); Mann and Ornstein, *The Broken Branch* (2006); Lawrence Lessig, *Republic Lost: How Money Corrupts Congress—And a Plan to Stop It* (New York: Twelve Books, 2011); Thomas E. Mann and Norman J. Ornstein, *It's Even Worse Than it Looks: How the American Constitutional System Collided with the New Politics of Extremism* (New York: Basic Books, 2012).
14. David R. Mayhew, *Divided We Govern: Party Control, Lawmaking, and Investigations, 1946-2002*, 2nd ed. (New Haven, CT: Yale University Press, 2005); Keith Krehbiel, *Pivotal Politics: A Theory of U.S. Lawmaking*

(Chicago: University of Chicago Press, 1998).
15. Sarah Binder, *Stalemate: Causes and Consequences of Legislative Gridlock* (Washington, DC: Brookings Institution Press, 2003); Mann and Ornstein, *It's Even Worse Than It Looks*, 110.

Chapter 11 The Presidency
1. Joseph Ellis, *His Excellency: George Washington* (New York: Random House, 2004), 194–95.
2. Paul Harris, Kamal Ahmed, and Martin Bright, "Seeing Eye to Eye," *The Observer*, November 16, 2003, 1.
3. Steven Calabresi and Christopher Yoo, *The Unitary Executive: Presidential Power from Washington to Bush* (New Haven, CT: Yale University Press, 2011).
4. Bush quoted in the Federal News Service, June 20, 1992.
5. Francis Biddle, *In Brief Authority* (New York: Doubleday, 1962), 219.
6. For a description of this episode, taken from White House telephone tapes, see David Blumenthal and James Morone, *The Heart of Power: Health and Politics in the Oval Office* (Berkeley: University of California Press, 2009), 142.
7. See Kevin Evans, "Challenging Law: Presidential Signing Statements and the Maintenance of Executive Power," *Congress and the Presidency* 38, no. 1 (2011). Electronic copy available at: http://ssrn.com/abstract=1464334.
8. Leonard White, *The Federalists* (New York: Macmillan, 1942).
9. For a description, see James Morone, *The Democratic Wish* (New Haven, CT: Yale University Press, 1998), 131.
10. December 21, 1976, memo from Pat Caddell to "Governor Carter," Carter Library. See Blumenthal and Morone, *The Heart of Power*, 249.
11. Richard Neustadt, *Presidential Power and the Modern Presidents*, rev. ed. (New York: Free Press, 1991).
12. Samuel Kernel, *Going Public* (Washington DC: CQ Press, 2007).
13. Lawrence R. Jacobs and Robert Y. Shapiro, *Politicians Don't Pander:*

Political Manipulation and the Loss of Democratic Responsiveness (Chicago: University of Chicago Press, 2000).
14. Barbara Hinckley, *Follow the Leader: Opinion Polls and the Modern President* (New York: Basic Books, 1992).
15. Stephen Skowronek, *The Politics Presidents Make: Leadership from John Adams to Bill Clinton* (Cambridge, MA: Harvard University Press, 1997).
16. Joseph Califano, *Governing America: An Insider's Report from the White House and the Cabinet* (New York: Simon & Schuster, 1981), 431, and personal interview with the authors, June 15, 2006.
17. For a fine description, see Matthew Dickinson, "The Executive Office of the President: The Paradox of Politicization," in Joel Aberbach and Mark Peterson, eds., *The Executive Branch* (New York: Oxford University Press, 2005).
18. Johnson quoted in Blumenthal and Morone, *Heart of Power*, 8.
19. President Barack Obama, Address to the UN General Assembly, September 23, 2009.

Chapter 12 Bureaucracy
1. Pew Research Center. Accessed at http://www.people-press.org/2000/04/12/other-important-findings-and-analyses-23/
2. William Riordon, *Plunkitt of Tammany Hall: A Series of Very Plain Talks on Very Practical Politics* (New York: Penguin, 1995).
3. James Sparrow, *Warfare State: World War II Americans and the Age of Big Government* (New York: Oxford University Press, 2012).
4. See Daniel Carpenter, *The Forging of Bureaucratic Autonomy: Reputations, Networks, and Policy Innovation in Executive Agencies* (Princeton, NJ: Princeton University Press, 2001); and James Morone, *Hellfire Nation: The Politics of Sin in American History* (New Haven, CT: Yale University Press, 2003).
5. Max Weber, "Bureaucracy," in H. H. Gerth and C. Wright Mills, eds., *From Max Weber: Essays in*

Sociology (New York: Oxford, 1946), 196–98.

6. Truman quoted in Richard Neustadt, *Presidential Power* (New York: Free Press, 1990), 10.

7. *RN: Memoirs of Richard Nixon* (New York: Simon & Schuster, 1990), 352.

8. Michael Lipsky, *Street-Level Bureaucracy: Dilemmas of the Individual in Public Services* (New York: Russell Sage, 1980).

9. Joe Soss, *Unwanted Claims: The Politics of Participation in the U.S. Welfare System* (Ann Arbor: University of Michigan Press, 2000).

10. Al Gore, *Common Sense Government: Works Better and Costs Less* (New York: Random House, 1995).

Chapter 13 The Judicial Branch

1. "Outside Terri Schiavo Hospice, A Crowd Waits," *Orlando Sentinel*, March 27, 2005.

2. Alexander Hamilton, Federalist no. 78.

3. John Murrin, "A Roof without Walls: The Dilemma of American National Identity," in Beeman, Botein, and Carter, eds., *Beyond Confederation: Origins of the Constitution and American Identity* (Chapel Hill: University of North Carolina Press, 1987).

4. Alexis de Tocqueville, *Democracy in America*, 1: 270.

5. John Schwartz, "Effort Begun to End Voting for Judges," *New York Times*, December 23, 2009.

6. Charlie Savage, "A Judge's View of Judging Is on the Record," *New York Times*, May 14, 2009.

7. Thomas Jefferson, Letter to Justice Spencer Roane on the limits of judicial review, in Thomas Jefferson, *Writings* (New York: Library of America, 1984), 1425–1428.

8. Eleventh U.S. Circuit Court of Appeals, Docket No. 05-00530-CV-T-27-TBM (March 25, 2005), 14.

9. Ibid.

10. The case was *Worcester v. Georgia*, 1832.

11. Adam Liptak, "Are Oral Arguments Worth Arguing About?" *New York Times: Sunday Review*, May 6, 2012.

12. Justice John Roberts, Testimony before the Senate Judiciary Committee, September 12, 2005.

13. Lee Epstein, Jeffrey A. Segal, Harold J. Spaeth, and Thomas G. Walker, *Supreme Court Compendium*, 4th ed. (Washington DC: CQ Press, 2006).

14. Frederick Schauer, "Incentives, Reputation, and the Inglorious Determinants of Judicial Behavior," *University of Cincinnati Law Review* 68, no. 3 (2000): 615–36.

15. Thomas Keck, "Party, Policy, or Duty: Why Does the Supreme Court Invalidate Federal Statutes?" *American Political Science Review* 101, no. 2 (May 2007): 321 ff.

16. *McCulloch v. Maryland*, 17 U.S. (4 Wheat.) 316 (1819).

17. *Dred Scott v. Sandford*, 60 U.S. 393 (1857).

18. Chief Justice John Roberts, "2006 Year-End Report on the Federal Judiciary," January 2007.

19. Steven G. Calabresi and James Lindgren, "Term Limits for the Supreme Court: Life Tenure Reconsidered," *Harvard Journal of Law & Public Policy* 29, no. 3 (2009): 769–877.

Chapter 14 Public Policymaking and Budgeting

1. Woodrow Wilson, "The Study of Administration," *Political Science Quarterly* 2, No. 2 (1887): 197–222.

2. Rogan Kersh, "Health Reform: The Politics of Implementation," *Journal of Health Politics, Policy, and Law* 36, no. 3 (2011): 613–23.

3. Paul Pierson, "When Effect Becomes Cause: Policy Feedback and Political Change," *World Politics* 45,

no. 4 (1993): 595–628; for a recent overview of policy feedback and path dependence, see Daniel Béland, "Reconsidering Policy Feedback: How Policies Affect Politics," *Administration and Society* 42, no. 5 (2010): 568–90.

4. Walter I. Trattner, *From Poor Law to Welfare State*, 6th ed. (New York: Free Press, 1998).

5. Theda Skocpol, *Protecting Soldiers and Mothers: The Political Origins of Social Policy in the United States* (Cambridge, MA: Harvard University Press, 1995).

6. Suzanne Mettler, *Soldiers to Citizens: The G.I. Bill and the Making of the Greatest Generation* (New York: Oxford University Press, 2005).

7. American Medical Association, "Goldwater-Johnson: Remarks," *Washington News* 189, no. 3 (July 20, 1964): 3.

8. The most detailed accounting comes from Brown University's "Costs of War" study, at http://costsofwar.org/.

9. See Nancy C. Roberts and Paula J. King, "Policy Entrepreneurs: Their Activity Structure and Function in the Policy Process," *Journal of Public Administration Research and Theory* 1, no. 2 (1991): 147–75.

10. George Washington, Inaugural Address, New York City, April 30, 1789. You can find it here: http://www.bartleby.com/124/pres13.html.

11. President Woodrow Wilson, address to joint session of Congress, April 2, 1917; Jimmy Carter, commencement speech given at Notre Dame University, June 1977.

12. "Ron Paul on Foreign Policy," http://www.thepoliticalguide.com/Profiles/House/Texas/Ron_Paul/Views/Foreign_Policy/

13. Robert Mann, *A Grand Delusion: America's Descent into Vietnam* (New York: Basic Books, 2002), 24.

14. President George W. Bush, Graduation Address, West Point, June 1, 2007.

Credits

Photos

p. 217: 04–07–10 © Pamela Cowart-Rickman Copyright © 2012 iStockphoto LP; p. 220: 03–03–09 © Joel Carillet Copyright © 2012 iStockphoto LP; p. 222: AP Photo/Jacqueline Larma; p. 225: AP Photo/Office of Rep. Gabrielle Giffords; p. 225: © The Gallery Collection/Corbis; p. 227: AP Photo/Files; p. 233: Voting Rights Demonstration in McComb, Mississippi, 1962, Erle Johnston Papers, McCain Library and Archives, The University of Southern Mississippi.; p. 237: AP Photo/Ben Curtis, File; p. 237: AP Photo

Chapter 7
p. 242: AP Photo/Paul Beaty; p. 248: The Granger Collection, NYC — All rights reserved.; p. 249: AP Photo; p.251: AP Photo/Carolyn Kaster; p. 260: Photo by James Keivom/NY Daily News Archive via Getty Images; p. 260: AP Photo/Greg Gibson; p. 265: AP Photo/Pablo Martinez Monsivais; p. 267: polyp.org.uk; p. 269: Photo by NY Daily News Archive via Getty Images

Chapter 8
p. 274: UPI/Kevin Dietsch; p. 277: AFP/Getty Images; p. 284: AP Photo/Chris Carlson, File; p. 287: AP Photo/Elise Amendola; p. 288: © Bettmann/CORBIS; p. 289: Time Life Pictures/National Archives/Time Life Pictures/Getty Images; p. 289: AP photo/Spencer Tirey; p. 293: Photo by Ethan Miller/Getty Images; p. 297: U.S. Senate Collection, Center for Legislative Archives, National Archives; p. 298: © Bettmann/CORBIS

Chapter 9
p. 308: Rob Hill Photo; p. 313: Image courtesy of www.savethefrogs.com; p. 315: Rex Features via AP Images; p. 317: AP Photo/Harry Cabluck; p. 325: AP Photo/Alex Brandon; p. 328: 12–11–11 © Gregbo Watson Copyright © 2012 iStockphoto LP; p. 329: National Archives/MCT/Newscom; p. 330: AP Photo/Koji Sasahara; p. 332: © CORBIS; p. 332: AP Photo/Tom Olmscheid; p. 334: Joe Raedle/Getty Images; p. 334: Scott J. Ferrell/Congressional Quarterly; p. 336: MLADEN ANTONOV/AFP/GettyImages; p. 338: © Bettmann/CORBIS; p. 340: © CORBIS; p. 341: © CORBIS; p. 347: Manny Crisostomo/Sacramento Bee/MCT via Getty Images; p. 352: AP Photo/Evan Vucci

Chapter 10
p. 356: AP Photo/Alex Brandon; p. 358: AP Photo/Elise Amendola, File; p. 363: AP Photo/Pablo Martinez Monsivais; p. 365: FPG/Getty Images; p. 371: AP Photo/J. Scott Applewhite; p. 372: AP Photo/Charles Dharapak; p. 378: AP Photo/Tim

Sloan, Pool; p. 380: AP Photo/Giles Communications, Ron Thomas; p. 382: Chip Somodevilla/Getty Images; p. 383: AP Photo/Bradley C. Bower, File; p. 386: Tom Williams/CQ Roll Call; p. 390: Copyright Bettmann/Corbis / AP Images

Chapter 11
p. 394: AP Photo/The White House, Pete Souza; p. 398: © CORBIS; p. 401: Copyright Bettmann/Corbis/AP Images; p. 403: AP Photo/Ron Edmonds; p. 405: AP Photo/Carolyn Kaster; p. 406: Rex Features via AP Images; p. 410: AP Photo/J. Scott Applewhite; p. 413: © Bettmann/CORBIS; p. 415: LBJ Library photo by Cecil Stoughton; p. 421: AP Photo / Michael Stravato; p. 422: AP Photo/Susan Walsh; p. 427: Robert J. Day / The New Yorker Collection / www.cartoonbank.com

Chapter 12
p. 432: Warner Bros/The Kobal Collection/Art Resource; p. 438: The Granger Collection, NYC — All rights reserved.; p. 441: FRED R. CONRAD/© The New York Times; p. 444: Mario Tama/Getty Images; p. 448: Pete Souza/PSG/Newscom; p. 451: EUGENE GARCIA/AFP/Getty Images; p. 451: DAVID J. PHILLIP/AFP/Getty Images; p. 453: © Wathiq Khuzaie/Pool/epa/Corbis; p. 457: © Debbie Noda/Modesto Bee; p. 459: AP Photo/Kate Brumback

Chapter 13
p. 462: AP Photo/Chris O'Meara; p. 468: Pete Marovich/MCT via Getty Images; p. 471: AP Photo/Andy Manis; p. 480: AP Photo/Pablo Martinez Monsivais, File; p. 481: © Evan Golub/Demotix/Corbis; p. 482: CD1 WENN Photos/Newscom; p. 482: AP Photo/Pablo Martinez Monsivais, Pool; p. 486: Daniel Webster, 1830 & 1848–9 (oil on canvas), Harding, Chester (1792–1866) / © Boston Athenaeum, USA / The Bridgeman Art Library; p. 487: AP Photo/Bill Haber; p. 489: © Chris Stewart/San Francisco Chronicle/Corbis; p. 491: GREG GIBSON/AFP/Getty Images

Chapter 14
p. 498: © Kristoffer Tripplaar/Pool/Corbis; p. 505: STAHLER © 1999 Jeff Stahler. Reprinted by permission of Universal Uclick for UFS. All rights reserved.; p. 507: AP Photo/Reed Saxon; p. 512: Walter P. Reuther Library, Wayne State University.; p. 512: UW-Madison Archives, # CLP-A0406; p. 513: AP Photo; p. 519: Alex Wong/Getty Images; p. 522: Russell Millner/Alamy; p. 525: The Granger Collection, NYC — All rights reserved.; p. 527: "War's First Casualty", America First Committee, propaganda poster from World War I (litho), American

School, (20th century)/Private Collection/Topham Picturepoint/The Bridgeman Art Library; p. 529: © STR/epa/Corbis

Figure Credits

Chapter 1
p. 7: Created by OUP based on data from usgovernmentspending.com; p. 8: Created by OUP based on data from the U.S. Census Bureau; p. 19: Created by OUP based on data from the OECD; p. 25: Created by OUP using data from the Pew Research Center Global Attitudes Project. American Exceptionalism Subsides: The American-Western European Values Gap, November 17, 2011; updated February 29, 2012.; p. 29: Created by OUP based on data from Robert Frank, Falling Behind. University of California Press, 2007.; p. 29: Created by OUP based on data from Elizabeth Sawhill and John Morton, Economic Mobility: Is the American Dream Alive and Well? Economic Mobility Project, Pew Charitable Trusts; Larry Bartells, Unequal Democracy (Princeton, NJ: Princeton University Press/ Russell Sage Foundation, 2008), Chap. 1.; p. 34: Created by OUP based on data from Growing Unequal? Income Distribution and Poverty in OECD Countries. OECD, October 2008.; p. 36: Created by OUP based on data from the Pew Research Center; p. 37: Created by OUP based on data from the Pew Research Center

Chapter 2
p. 53: Helen Hornbeck Tanner, Atlas of Great Lakes Indian History (Norman, University of Oklahoma Press, 1987), p. 54. Copyright © University of Oklahoma Press.

Chapter 3
p. 97: Created by OUP based on data from Gallup; p. 108: Goldwater Institute All Rights Reserved © 2011; p. 116: Created by OUP based on data from the OECD National Account Statistics; p. 118: Cornell Chronicle/Cornell Survey Research Institute

Chapter 4
p. 146: Created by OUP based on data from Computed from Justice Policy Institute and the and U.S. Bureau of Justice; p. 147: Created by OUP based on data from CEPR/ICPS; p. 152: Created by OUP based on data from the Pew Research Center

Chapter 5
p. 180: Created by OUP based on data from the U.S. Census Bureau; p. 188: Created by OUP based on data from the U.S. Census Bureau; p. 190: Created by OUP based on data from the U.S. Census Bureau; p. 191:
Created by OUP based on data from the U.S. Census Bureau; p. 195: Created by OUP based on data from the U.S. Census Bureau and the Pew Research Center

Chapter 6
p. 213: Created by OUP based on data from Edison Research, Associated Press, and CNN; p. 219: Created by OUP based on data from Gallup; p. 223: Created by OUP based on data from the Brookings Institution, 2009 Survey of Millennials; p. 228: Created by OUP based on data from Ruuskanen 2001 and Statistics Finland; p. 235: Created by OUP based on data from the U.S. Census Bureau; p. 236: Created by OUP based on data from the National Conference on Citizenship

Chapter 7
p. 246: Created by OUP based on data from the Pew Research Center; p. 247: Created by OUP based on data from the Pew Research Center; p. 252: Created by OUP based on data from the Pew Research Center; p. 255: Created by OUP based on data from the Pew Research Center's Pew Internet & American Life Project, Project for Excellence in Journalism, and The State of the News Media 2011; p. 258: Created by OUP based on data from the Pew Research Center

Chapter 8
p. 279: Created by OUP based on data from the Federal Election Commission and opensecrets.org; p. 281: Created by OUP based on data from opensecrets.org; p. 301: Created by OUP based on data from the Center for Responsive Politics

Chapter 9
p. 310: Created by OUP based on data from Gallup; p. 319: Created by OUP based on data from the Center for Responsive Politics; p. 324: Created by OUP based on Kiyohara, Shoko, "A Study of Current Telecommunications Policy-Making in the U.S.: The Case of Universal Service, in Comparison with the Japanese Case." Keio Communication Review No. 30, 2008.; p. 346: Created by OUP based on data from the Pew Research Center 2012 Values Survey

Chapter 10
p. 385: Created by OUP based on data from the U.S. Senate; p. 388: Created by OUP based on data from Gallup

Chapter 11
p. 402: Created by OUP based on data from Historical Statistics, Statistical Abstracts; p. 417: Created by OUP based on data from Gallup's Presidential Job

Approval Center; p. 419: Created by OUP based on data from Historian Arthur Schlesinger, Sr., who polled historians in 1948 and polled historians and political scientists in 1996; The Wall Street Journal; Sienna College 2010 poll; The United States Presidency Centre [USPC] at the University of London, 2011

Chapter 12

p. 434: Copyright © 2012 Gallup, Inc. All rights reserved. The content is used with permission; however, Gallup retains all rights of republication.; 335: Created by OUP based on data from the U.S. Census; p. 439: U.S. Department of Energy; p. 443: Created by OUP based on data from the Office of Management and Budget

Chapter 13

p. 467: Created by OUP based on data from the Pew Research Center; p. 472: Created by OUP based on data from the Federal Judicial Center; p. 483: Created by OUP based on data from Gallup; p. 484: Created by OUP based on data from the Kaiser Family Foundation Health Tracking Poll (conducted January 12–17, 2012); p. 493: Created by OUP based on data from Gallup; p. 495: Created by OUP based on data from the Administrative Office of the U.S. Courts/Federal Judiciary

Chapter 14

p. 515: Created by OUP based on data from the Congressional Budget Office; p. 517: Created by OUP based on data from TradingEconomics.com and the U.S. Department of the Treasury; p. 518: Adapted from the House of Representatives Committee on the Budget; p. 524: Created by OUP based on data from The World Bank Group

Index

Note: *t* refers to table and *f* refers to figure. Page numbers in italics refer to photographs or illustrations.